*Aldous Huxley*

# ALDOUS HUXLEY

*A Biography*

# SYBILLE BEDFORD

*Ivan R. Dee*

*Chicago*

Library of Congress Cataloging-in-Publication Data:
Bedford, Sybille, 1911–
    Aldous Huxley : a biography / by Sybille Bedford.– 1st Ivan R. Dee pbk. ed.
    p. cm.
    ISBN 1-56663-454-7 (alk. paper)
    1. Huxley, Aldous, 1894–1963. 2. Authors, English—20th Century—Biography. I. Title.

PR6015.U9 Z562 2002
823'.912–dc21

                                                          2002067691

*To Matthew*

I am not concerned here with Aldous Huxley's literary fame; whether future literary historians will rank him with Thomas Love Peacock or with Dean Swift. My concern is his heritage to those who really care about the future of the human race, and in this respect I hope that he will be remembered. . . .

DENNIS GABOR

. . . with that special sensibility to the contours of the future [he] stood on the edge of, and peered beyond, the present frontiers of our self-knowledge. . . . There is a sense in which he knew that he stood on the frontier of the old astrology that was passing and the new astronomy that was beginning in the science of man. . . .

SIR ISAIAH BERLIN

. . . Biography is to give a man some kind of shape after his death.

VIRGINIA WOOLF

He was scientist and artist in one—standing for all we most need in a fragmented world where each of us carries a distorting splinter out of some great shattered universal mirror. He made it his mission to restore these fragments and, at least in his presence, men were whole again.

YEHUDI MENUHIN

# Contents

# CONTENTS

# CONTENTS

# CONTENTS

# Illustrations

xiii

# ILLUSTRATIONS

PLATE XIX
Aldous in April 1948
North Kings Road circa 1952: Aldous, Ellen, Maria,
Marguerite (Mère) Nys, Trevenan, Matthew

PLATE XX
Aldous and cat circa 1952 in California
Laura and Aldous in Italy, 1958

PLATE XXI
Laura and Aldous circa 1959

PLATE XXII
Quote . . . unquote

PLATE XXIII
Aldous in April 1958

PLATE XXIV
Aldous at Saltwood Castle, August 1963

---

*Grateful acknowledgement is given to the following
for permission to reproduce photographs:*

Sir Cecil Beaton for plate VIII (bottom)
Philippe Halsman for plate XXIII (Copyright by Philippe Halsman)
Mrs Rose de Haulleville for plates IV, VI (top), VII, IX (top right),
XII (top), XV (top and center), XIX (bottom), XXI
The Huxley family for the frontispiece and plates I, II (lower right), III,
V, X, XIV, XVI (lower left), XX (top)
Sir Julian and Lady Huxley for plate II (top left and right)
Mrs Laura Huxley for plates XX (bottom) and XXII
Matthew Huxley for plates VI (bottom), XI, XII (lower right),
XV (bottom), XVI (lower right), XVII, XVIII, XIX (top—photograph by
Ralph Steiner), XXIV
Anita Loos for plate XVI (top)
Mrs Julian Vinogradoff for plates VIII (top), IX (top left and lower right)
Dorothy Wilding and Mrs St John Hutchinson for plate XIII

# Preface

The object of this book is to give a truthful and coherent account of the life of Aldous Huxley and of Aldous Huxley as a man. Although it is no way intended as a work of literary criticism or an evaluation of his thought, such a book must—quite inevitably—contain a good deal of his writing and his thought. Naturally I feel presumptuous in attempting the biography of a man of his moral and intellectual quality. I was persuaded by the nearest members of his family, his widow, his brother, his son; I finally accepted because my own fondness for Aldous made me want to do it. (There was perhaps, as well, some element of personal logic: because when I was young and everything seemed easy, I had lightly thought that one day I might do precisely this.) If the work was a labour of love, it was also work done in a spirit of detachment. I have been entirely candid—to the best of my knowledge and ability—about everything concerning Aldous Huxley's character and actions. And although this principle had to be moderated—very occasionally—when writing about people now living, the rule which, throughout, I set before me was a dictum of the late Desmond MacCarthy's: A biographer is an artist upon oath.

Because of the particular circumstances—the destruction of the Huxley papers by fire—a perhaps unusually large proportion of the sources of this biography is oral. I should like to divide all sources into five categories: published sources, documentary, oral-documentary, oral and personal sources.

*Published Sources:* Of these the main ones are of course the works of Aldous Huxley *in toto* and his *Letters* in the admirable collection edited by Professor Grover Smith. Another major source is Laura Archera Huxley's *This Timeless Moment*. Other works, such as the *Aldous Huxley Memorial Volume* edited by Sir Julian Huxley, Sir Julian's own *Memories*, some letters of D. H. Lawrence, etc, etc, will be acknowledged in their place. (I have—purposely—omitted to read books and theses on A. H.'s work.)

*Documentary Sources:* Some of the most relevant original material is found in the letters of Maria Huxley. The three main (extant) collections of these are (roughly chronologically) her letters to the late Lord Sackville, to her sister Jeanne (Mme Georges Neveux), and the letters to her son.

Much of the material for Maria's own youth and background,

for the Huxley's early married years, travels and some of their California life is derived from a memoir of some 30,000 words written originally for the purpose of this biography by Maria's second sister Suzanne (Mme Joep Nicolas)—a most charming work, in French, which, I hope, will see publication in its own right.

Other documentary sources are the letters of the late Robert Nichols, the poet; the journal of Georges Neveux; the diary of Beth (Mrs Sanford) Wendel; Professor Roy Lamson's working copy of Aldous Huxley's lectures at the Massachusetts Institute of Technology; the letters of Aldous's mother-in-law, the late Marguérite Nys; transcripts of B.B.C. Radio and Television interviews; and a large number of letters and memoirs addressed to me which will be individually acknowledged in the text.

*Oral-Documentary Sources:* Five gramophone records made from the original tape of an interview with Aldous Huxley by John Chandos in London in June 1961 commissioned by Record Supervision Ltd. Some tape-recordings in the possession of the University of California at Los Angeles (UCLA); and some tape-recordings made by Laura Huxley.

*Oral Sources:* The first-hand recollections of friends, relations, acquaintances, colleagues—some of whom knew Aldous long and well, others who had had some brief, incisive glimpse—communicated to me in conversations and interviews.

The fifth and personal source is what I saw, heard, learned—and perhaps learned to understand—in the course of forty years' friendship with Aldous and friendship with some members of his family and his circle. Such insight as I may have come to about Aldous's character and development is very much due to foundations early laid by Maria Huxley.

The book owes a great deal to the generous, intelligent and devoted co-operation of Aldous's family and friends. This has made the research an extraordinary experience for which I find it hard to express anything like adequate gratitude.

I want to thank Laura Archera (Mrs Aldous) Huxley, Sir Julian Huxley and Matthew Huxley for their endless goodwill and help of many kinds as well as for their permission to quote from their own works or letters in their possession.

I want to thank the late Gervas Huxley—Aldous's cousin and exact contemporary—for his first-hand account of Aldous's schoolboy years and his first year at Oxford. I want to thank Juliette (Lady) Huxley who provided much of the material for the young Aldous at Garsington and many touches about other episodes in later years, and has been unfailingly kind and resourceful. I want to thank Jeanne Neveux, whose inside knowledge of the Huxleys' life from the 1920s to 1955 makes her one of the mainstays of the biography, and who, step by step, has given me constant help—

answering questions, verifying facts, undertaking journeys, over the last five years.

I want to thank the following for supplying essential material: Suzanne Nicolas; Rina Rontini (Mme Marcel) Eustration; Aldous's niece Sophie (Mme Willem) Welling; Roy Fenton; Beth (Mrs Sanford) Wendel; Roy Lamson of M.I.T. and Peggy Lamson; Dr Humphrey Osmond.

I want to thank Professor Grover Smith, whose published collection of Aldous Huxley's *Letters* provides of course so much of the basic biographical material, for his great personal courtesy and kindness in answering any question I put to him.

I want to thank the following for help or contributions—often considerable—of various kinds:

Madge (Lady) Ashton, Mrs Barbara Bagenal, Enid Bagnold, Sir Isaiah Berlin, Constance Bessie, Denys Blakelock, The Hon. Dorothy Brett, Dr Barbara B. Brown, Miss Olive Brown, Moura (Baroness) Budberg, Joan Collier (Mrs F. A.) Buzzard, Cass and Mrs Cass Canfield, John Chandos, Sir George Clark, Kenneth Clark (Lord Clark of Saltwood), Sir Laurence Collier, Cyril Connolly, Jeff (Mrs Douglas) Corner, Robert Craft, Dr Max Cutler, Denis D. David, Leonard K. Elmhirst, Eugene Exman, Miss Victoire Fairtlough, The Rev. R. A. L. Fell, Mrs Bernadine Fritz, Professor Dennis Gabor, the late Eileen Garrett, the late Sylvester Gates, Ellen (Mrs Adam) Giffard, Mrs Arthur Goldschmidt, Russell Green, Gillian (Mrs Anthony) Greenwood, Ena (Mrs F. Duglas) Curry Grundy, Major Leonard Handley, Yvonne (Mrs Hamish) Hamilton, Miss Patience Hardcastle, Professor Garrett Hardin, the late Lord Harman, Allanah Harper, L. P. Hartley, Rose de Haulleville, Eva Herrmann, Mrs Faith Hiles, Grace (Mrs Edwin) Hubble, Professor Robert M. Hutchins, Jeremy Hutchinson, Q.C., Mary (Mrs St-John) Hutchinson, David Huxley, Francis Huxley, Judith (Mrs Matthew) Huxley, Miss Margaret Huxley, Rosalind (Mrs Leonard) Huxley, Christopher Isherwood, Miss Margaret Isherwood, Lionel Jardine, C.I.E., Professor and Mrs. Frank Pierce Jones, Paul C. Jones, Peggy (Mrs William) Kiskadden, Franklin Lacey, Nadine (Mrs G. W.) Lambert, Rosamond Lehmann, Peter Leslie, Frances Lindley, Yolanda (Mrs Louis) Loeffler, Anita Loos, Sir Alan Lubbock, Edward Maisel, Dr Felix Mann, Miss M. Marshall, C. E. Menor Jr, Yehudi and Diana Menuhin, Professor Andrew Greer Meyer, Naomi (Lady) Mitchison, Ivan Moffat, Professor Ashley Montagu, Sybil Morrison, Raymond Mortimer, Percy Muir, John Murray, Alan Napier, Georges Neveux, Noele Neveux, Mariana Newton, Vicomte Charles de Noailles, Dr Elmer Noble, Liam O'Gallagher,

Sylvia Nicolas (Mrs Luke) O'Neill, Arthur Ormont, Katherine Peak, Eric Petrie and the late Maria Petrie, the late Virginia Pfeiffer, Lawrence Clark Powell, Swami Prabhavananda, Marie Le Put, Rosalind Rajagopal, Mr and Mrs Harold Raymond, Professor J. B. Rhine, Professor Mason Rose, Henry Walter Rowan, Sir Steven Runciman, Elizabeth Salter, Dr William H. Sheldon, James and Radha Sloss, Professor Houston Smith, Vera (Mrs Igor) Stravinsky, H. G. C. Streatfeild, Professor Dauwe Sturman, Professor J. M. Tanner, Theo Townshend, Francis Thompson, Renée (Mrs Jerrard) Tickell, Miss Jane Turner, Professor Patrick D. Wall, Professor Howard Warshaw, Goodwin Weisberg, Sanford Wendel, Claire Nicolas (Mrs Robert Winthrop) White, Sebastian White, Professor George Wickes, Professor Jack Wilkinson, Miss Helen Witt, Dr Charlotte Wolff, the late Leonard Woolf, Marjorie Worthington, Jacob Israel Zeitlin and Maurice Zuberano.

I want to thank my friends Evelyn Gendel, Eda Lord and Richard Ollard for having sustained me, each from their side of the Atlantic, with their indispensable interest, criticism and advice.

# Author's Notes

*Regarding Quotations and Sources*

A number of quotations in this book are not entirely accurate: none are without full authority. In quoting from Aldous Huxley's books and letters I have freely extracted, eliminated, juxtaposed, conflated as best suited my immediate purpose. I have never put words into his mouth.

I have often supplemented the many printed sources whose help I have gratefully acknowledged (Gervas Huxley, Lady Huxley, Enid Bagnold come immediately to mind) by private correspondence and conversation. Particular passages may thus have been fused or even substantially modified.

*On the Nys Family*

Maria Huxley (*née* Nys) had three sisters, Jeanne, Suzanne and Rose.

Jeanne had two daughters; Sophie, by her first husband, René Moulaert, a theatrical designer, and Noële, by her second husband, the French playwright Georges Neveux.

Suzanne married the Dutch artist Joep Nicolas and had two daughters, Claire and Sylvia. Rose married twice: she had one daughter, Olivia, by her first husband, the French *surréaliste* poet Eric de Haulleville, and, by her second husband, a son, Sigfrid (Wessberg).

# PART ONE

## The Young Boy: 1894-1908

"What are you thinking about,
Aldous dear?"
Aldous, aged four, turning his head
from the window, "*Skin*."

SIR JULIAN HUXLEY

His descent both on his father's and
his mother's side brought down on him
a weight of intellectual authority and
a momentum of moral obligations.

GERALD HEARD

Oh, what fun we had walking over
to Prior's Field. A walk with Aldous
was sheer joy. . . .

GERVAS HUXLEY

# Chapter One

## Laleham, Surrey, England

ALDOUS LEONARD HUXLEY was born on 26th July 1894
at Laleham near Godalming in Surrey, the third son of
Leonard Huxley and Julia Frances Arnold.

Leonard Huxley at the time was an assistant master at Charter-
house, thirty-four years old, the son, we need hardly be reminded,
of Thomas Henry Huxley who was still living and survived
Aldous's birth by a short year. Julia Huxley—granddaughter of
Dr Arnold of Rugby, niece of Matthew Arnold, daughter of the
Rev. Thomas Arnold who twice left the Anglican Church for the
Church of Rome, sister of Mrs Humphry Ward, the novelist—
was thirty-two. She had been educated at Somerville, Oxford (a
first in English in 1882). Aldous's two brothers Julian and
Trevenen were aged seven and five.

Laleham (still standing) is a pleasant, middle-sized, late
Victorian house with about half an acre of garden. Family life
was a very happy one; although standards of behaviour were high,
the atmosphere of Aldous's first home was affectionate and gay.
His mother, described by those who knew her as a remarkable,
an admirable, a formidable woman, is remembered nevertheless
with immense affection rather than with awe—"*How she could
laugh*", and she certainly gave her own affection to her children.
Leonard Huxley enjoyed life, was gentle, even-tempered, "jolly,
kindly, full of jokes." Baby Aldous was looked after by the family
servants and a young girl from Königsberg, Fräulein Ella
Salkowski (whom *he* sent for, in due course, for his infant son);
he was treated with love by his parents; his brothers indulged him.
Occasionally he was teased.

What we know about him as a young child is the usual residue
of anecdote and snapshot. During his first years his head was
proportionally enormous, so that he could not walk till he was
two because he was apt to topple over. "We put father's hat on
him and it fitted." In another country, at a great distance in
time and place, when he lay ill and near his end in Southern
California, a friend, wanting to distract him, said, "Aldous, didn't
you ever have a nickname when you were small?" and Aldous
who hardly ever talked about his childhood or indeed about himself (possibly because one did not ask) said promptly, "They called
me Ogie. Short for Ogre."

The Ogre was a pretty little boy, the photographs—he sprawling in Bubble's costume in an armchair, leaning against his mother, leaning against his Aunt Mary Ward, in a tender stance—show the high forehead, the (then) clear gaze, the tremulous mouth and a sweetness of expression, an alertness beyond that of other angelic little boys looking into a camera. Aldous, his brother Julian tells us, sat quietly a good deal of the time "contemplating the strangeness of things.

He showed some quality,[1] some innate superiority, which called for respect even in the nursery jungle. This recognition dawned when Aldous was five and I a prep school boy of twelve.

"I used to watch him with a pencil," said his cousin and contemporary Gervas Huxley,[2] "you see, he was always drawing . . . My earliest memory of him is sitting—absorbed—to me it was magic, a little boy of my own age drawing so beautifully, drawing such wonderful things." "I was always told," (this comes from a much younger second cousin) "that when he was five or six, *everybody knew that Aldous was different.*"[3]

Different; at the same time a young child. "Not only, but also," as the later Aldous would have said. There are a few glimpses. He was delicate; he had mischievous moods; he could play. He carried his rag doll about with him for company until he was eight. He was fond of grumbling. They gave him a milk mug which bore the inscription,

> *Oh, isn't the world extremely flat*
> *With nothing whatever to grumble at.*

Aldous, they say, was mortified. Coming in from the shrubbery one day, he told them, "I was walking along when I saw a mouse—and I *fled*".[4] Then there was the rocking-horse, the great rocking-horse in the nursery at Laleham with flaring nostrils and with flowing mane, "Such a horse!" says Julian,[5] ". . real swing—we got on the five of us, myself, Trev, Aldous, the two Eckersley[6] boys, holding on to the belly and the mane—and then going—oh boy, oh boy. . . ."

And Aldous aged six being taken with all the Huxleys to the

---

[1] Sir Julian Huxley, *Aldous Huxley*, mainly from *A Memorial Volume.* Chatto & Windus, 1965. (Hereafter cited as *Mem. Vol.*)

[2] The late Gervas Huxley, C.M.G., M.C., son of Dr Henry Huxley (youngest son of T. H. Huxley) and of Sophy Wylde Stobart. Talking to S. B.

[3] Jill (Mrs Anthony) Greenwood. Talking to S. B.

[4] Sir Julian Huxley, *Memories*, Vol. I. George Allen & Unwin, 1970.

[5] Sir Julian Huxley, talking to S. B.

[6] First cousin—the sons of William Alfred Eckersley and Rachel Huxley, third daughter of T. H. Huxley.

3

unveiling of the statue of his grandfather at the Natural History Museum by the Prince of Wales, and his mother trying, in urgent whispers, to persuade Julian, then a young Etonian, to give up his top hat—a very young Etonian and a very new top hat—to Aldous, queasy, overcome, to be sick in.

In 1899 Mrs Huxley's fourth and last child, Margaret, was born. Aldous began his education by going to St Bruno's, a day school nearby for very small children. In 1900 Aldous with his brothers, his parents, aunts and uncles, Huxley and Collier cousins drove in four-wheelers—a stable family in a stable era—to the Christmas Pantomime at Drury Lane. The party occupied the dress circle. Aldous and his cousin Gervas lost in awe sat side by side.

Leonard Huxley's biography of his father, *Life and Letters of Thomas Henry Huxley*, which he had been working on for the last five years, was published in 1900 in London and New York with considerable success. ("Do you know the *Life and Letters* by my father?" Aldous wrote in his maturity. "It's a good book.") Leonard Huxley was able to leave Charterhouse after fifteen years of not entirely congenial school-mastering. Originally, he had planned to read for the Bar, but when the assistant mastership was offered to him in 1885 he accepted it in order to be able to marry. He now joined the publishing firm of Smith, Elder as reader and literary adviser, and at the same time became assistant editor of the *Cornhill*.

In 1901, late in the year in which Queen Victoria died, the family left Laleham. They did, however, not move to London but to another house two miles away called Prior's Field. There, as Aldous wrote sixty years later,[1] "My mother founded a girls' school which became very large and is still flourishing."[1]

---

[1] *Letters of Aldous Huxley*, edited by Professor Grover Smith. Chatto & Windus, 1969. All not otherwise attributed quotation from Aldous Huxley in this volume will be from this published collection. (Hereafter cited as *Letters*.)

# Chapter Two

## Prior's Field

MRS HUXLEY'S school opened on 23rd January 1902. There were seven pupils: one girl boarder who brought her dog, five day girls and Aldous. "The school building," Julia Huxley recorded in the School Magazine,

> consisted only of a moderate sized house [which also served as the family home] we had bought six months before together with all the land . . . We had just begun to build what is now the girls' hall.

The land was twenty-five acres of peaceful rural Surrey—a garden, a field, woods full of violets and bluebells in the spring. The house had been built by Voysey who also designed the school buildings and the book-plate—an owl, an olive tree and a heart encircled by the school motto WE LIVE BY ADMIRATION HOPE & LOVE. The teaching staff consisted of three.

> Miss English and Mademoiselle Bonnet . . . Miss English and I taught everything except French and music! . . . there was only one form, though the ages ranged between seven and sixteen.

As for games,

> We could not very well play hockey with only six girls, so we purchased a foot ball . . .

By next term there were new boarders, making fourteen pupils; Mrs Huxley divided them into two forms, the sixth and fifth. Aldous was in the fifth. "His beating me so easily was a source of humiliation to me," writes one of the older girls, Victoire Fairtlough, who did lessons with him. "I did not realize then that I would not be expected to excel the grandson of the great T. H. Huxley!

I did get my revenge by beating him in the junior high jump at sports day at Lady Jekyll's house. Aldous and I reached the finals and after a great tussle I just managed to beat him which he took in very good part. He was rather a quiet little boy and never seemed at all bumptious in spite of his exceptional ability.[1]

[1] Miss Victoire Fairtlough in a letter to S. B.

Aldous used to go out beetle hunting with another little girl, Barbara Hiles,[1] and once at least he did show temper.

We had made a beating net, a yard of cotton fixed to two long hazel sticks; you shoved it into the hedge, all sorts of caterpillars fell into it. We took turns to keep what fell in. One Sunday morning Julian came with us, looking for wild orchids. At one of my turns I got a fine tussock moth caterpillar; Aldous's turn got nothing exciting. Next beat I got another even finer tussock. For a moment Aldous was upset and was going to punch me, when Julian said, "Aldous, Aldous you can't behave like that to a lady."

After deceptively amateurish beginnings Prior's Field grew quickly. Julia Huxley, helped no doubt at first by the Arnold-Huxley aura, built up an unusual, for those days unconventional school. Art and literature, galleries, Shakespeare matinées in London, concerts at Haslemere; books—with the girls free to choose them; no compulsory church or games. At a time when most schools took their walks in crocodiles, they were allowed to go for walks and bicycle rides and sketching parties on their own.

I want to tell you more about Prior's Field [Barbara Hiles Bagenal wrote to me]. It was a wonderful school—and for those days very modern. For instance, none of the staff lived in the school—they all had little houses round the estate. In non-school hours we were looked after by two matrons and by Mrs Huxley.
To me it was heaven, I met civilized people for the first time; and I could go off into the woods alone and look for flowers and toadstools and birds.

Already in the first two years the number of girls had risen to fifty, then "in a flash there were a hundred".[2] They were able to play hockey, croquet and lacrosse. "We beat Heathfield four times in succession in all three games," Mrs Huxley recorded.
Mrs Huxley had a dogcart which she drove with a coachman sitting at the back in a top hat. She (with little Aldous) accompanied the team on away matches. Many of the Prior's Field girls were daughters of the intelligentsia or future intellectuals in their own right. Gilbert Murray's and Maurice Hewlett's daughters, Conan Doyle's daughter, Marjorie Huxley, Margaret Huxley, Joan Collier, Enid Bagnold, Barbara Hiles. The staff was

[1] The present Mrs Bagenal in a letter to S. B.
[2] Enid Bagnold.

"brilliant—two of them outstanding, Ethel Sidgwick and the half-Greek, Emma Neurotsos".[1]

The food was good; the house well-run, comfortable, well-furnished, "rather unschool-like", in various memories, "good prints on the walls," "chintzy rooms, modern with William Morris"; the Huxley family much in evidence. "I cannot think of the lovely gardens without the figure of Leonard Huxley hard at work looking after his alpines and roses."[2] The girls would help him weed "and get to know all the names—for he like his sons was a hand at imparting knowledge."[2] Julian and Trevenen were about when their Eton and Oxford holidays overlapped with the term. They went bird watching, exploring on their own but also joined in the games, the picnics . . .

Although only a small child [Victoire Fairtlough] I can well remember the atmosphere of goodness and kindness that prevailed throughout the school and the home life of the Huxleys.

On Saturday evenings they danced in the gymnasium; the girls (changed into white silk blouses and white serge skirts), the staff, Leonard, the elder boys, a mistress at the piano. "Mr Huxley loved dancing and was very good. He taught us to waltz and reverse. He was very jolly with us and occasionally joined in our games."[3]

He was very tall [Victoire Fairtlough] and I remember him tearing down the field at lacrosse and crashing into me whom he had not seen from his great height . . . I went over like a shot rabbit . . . How scared poor Mrs Huxley looked.

*Mrs Huxley.* "We all loved Mrs Huxley." "She was quite extraordinary." ".. A slender lady with a beautifully shaped small head, as clear as someone now standing by my side." "She made a lasting impression on all of us who were there." "Kind, yes; but away and above my understanding. Each time before she spoke she seemed to reflect."

Her own children loved her intensely, and Aldous even more passionately than the others.[4] Her early influence went very deep; so did her loss; both are keys to his character and development. He very rarely brought himself to speak of her. This is why I am recording here such living memories of Julia Huxley as are left. They are the memories of women looking back on what they

1 Enid Bagnold.
2 Miss Helen Witt, letter to S. B.
3 Miss Helen Witt.
4 Sir Julian Huxley; he used the word "passionately".

experienced when they were schoolgirls half a century ago. We all reshape our memories; yet at times memory has a quality that separates it from our selves, and what we wish to serve as simply as we can is truth. And Aldous too, for his part, only knew his mother as a schoolboy.

We all loved Mrs Huxley and thought her word was law, none of us were ever in the least afraid of her. I never heard a joke made at her expense, or her authority even questioned let alone disregarded.[1]

One saw her every day. Either she spoke in the morning after breakfast, or she read aloud to us in the evening . . . She read [poetry] without stressing the sense: she let the rhyming wave by itself . . in her silvery even voice the words had their head.[2]

When Victoire Fairtlough lost her grandmother she

was deeply grieved. Mrs Huxley somehow knew this and as I was sitting at my desk scanning an examination paper I felt a comforting arm round my shoulders, "You will do your best, Victoire, won't you?" . . . .

And Barbara Hiles lamed at hockey. "Mrs Huxley sent for me and offered to send me home.

I ran across the room to her and said, "Please, please, don't send me home." She was touched and asked if I was unhappy at home? I said I was very happy at home but I am much happier here.

. . In the little room on the right of the front door as you came in she talked to me—I was twelve. I never knew before that grown-up women *could* speak to children like that—so fair, so reasonable. How grateful one was![3]

What had happened was this: Enid Bagnold in nights of full moon and spring flowers climbed out over the roof down the lavatory pipes to sleep in the woods among the bluebells. Once she was seen by the cook, another time she was caught by Mrs Huxley's sister, Mrs Humphry Ward. In the headmistress's study,

I wasn't scolded, hardly rebuked. Mrs Huxley seems to blush a little before explaining—one had to run a school, one was responsible for all of you to your parents—I didn't argue, though she would have let me . . . I was a child and she was soon to die, but the gap was bridged.[4]

Mrs Huxley tried to transfer to us her great knowledge of literature and the arts, sometimes at the expense of the more basic subjects,

---

[1] Victoire Fairtlough.  [2] Enid Bagnold, *Autobiography.*
[3] Enid Bagnold, talking to S. B.
[4] Enid Bagnold, *Autobiography*, and letter to S. B.

illustrated by the fact that most of us failed in arithmetic in the Lower Certificate exam.

And yet as a headmistress she was outstanding. She did not give the impression of a strong personality but of someone with great inner reserves, integrity & a refreshing lack of sentimentality. There was a strain of austerity & reticence about her which could raise a barrier between herself and a shy schoolgirl. Many would not agree with this. Personally, I felt her rather remote.[1]

"Remote?" in the view of another Prior's Field pupil,[2] "Perhaps a being of another order. She was extraordinary. Not at all the headmistress. Yet how good the school was! Her atmosphere, her influence have *lasted all one's life*. Thinking of her, one did not want to tell a lie." And now to that ever puzzling question of Arnold religiosity in the context of Huxleyan agnosticism. "I feel sure that she had a very deep faith, but perhaps no conventional religion."[2]

All her children had been baptized in the Church of England. Here she and Leonard had followed his father's precept and example.

As to the question whether children should be brought up in entire disregard to the beliefs rejected by himself, but still current among the mass of his fellow-countrymen, he was of the opinion that they ought to know "the mythology of their time and country", otherwise one would at the best tend to make young prigs out of them; but as they grew up, their questions should be answered frankly.[3]

So much for principle. As for practice,

. . My wife will have the youngsters christened, although I am always in a bad temper from the time it is talked about until the ceremony is over. . . .[4]

It was in Surrey, in that home, in that atmosphere, that Aldous spent the first nine years of his life. We know more about his elders—naturally—than we know about the child himself. The handful of letters extant might have been written by any

1 Miss Helen Witt.
2 Nadine Noble, the present Mrs Lambert, talking to S. B.
3 Leonard Huxley, *Life and Letters of Thomas Henry Huxley*, Vol. II. Macmillan & Co., 1900.
4 Thomas Henry Huxley in a letter to Hooker of 3rd January 1861, op. cit. Vol. I.

reasonably well-disposed small boy enjoying a nice country childhood. (Possibly, the punctuation is a bit beyond his years.) Here
is a fair sample.

My dear Julian                                        7th December 1902
    It is very frosty weather: and I can stand on the pond. We have
been giving crumbs to the birds; the pigeons can fly nicely now (we
saw them drinking out of the pond just now). The staircase in the
cottage has been put up. I and Kathleen found a mouse in the pig's
bran and we chased it about till it escaped. One of the pigs has a
cough. We went to Church. . . .
Good by, your loving brother
Aldous

And here he is in another light.[1]

    Aldous sat silent, inscrutable, antagonistic, rather green (all the
Huxley boys looked green—they didn't eat; though Mrs Huxley's
food was excellent), aged about eight. I was a fat girl of twelve?
thirteen? Sitting on Sunday at Mrs Huxley's table—at which we
took turns—knowing that I was supposed to make an effort and
talk.
    Eventually (heavily bumping it out) "What have you been doing
today, Aldous?"
    No answer.
    Rising indignation, and louder, "What have you been doing today,
Aldous?"
    He raised his eyes, leant a little nearer, "I *heard* you the first time."

Aldous's cousin, Laurence Collier,[2] too, found him "aloof and
secretly critical at the early age of nine. When Uncle Leonard
held forth, as he was apt to, on the joys of mountaineering, '*Per
ardua ad astra* . . .' Aldous said nothing, but . . gazed abstracted
into the distance with a fixed and enigmatic smile."
Sir Laurence Collier's sister Joan[3] gives us one *instantané* of the
small boy with his mother. They used to go on vast family holidays
in the summer. In 1903 they were in Switzerland.

    I must tell you the nicest story about Aldous [In Joan Collier's
words]. We were all at Rosenlauie being dragged up mountains &

---

  [1] This story was first told to me by Enid Bagnold in 1968; afterwards she
also put it down in a letter to me; some years later I read it in print in her
*Autobiography*. The wording of the present version is a composite of all three.
  [2] Sir Laurence Collier, K.C.M.G., son of the Hon. John Collier and Ethel
Huxley, youngest daughter of T. H. Huxley; thus a nephew of Leonard
Huxley. From *North House*: A Memoir.
  [3] Joan Collier, the present Mrs F. A. Buzzard, a first cousin of Aldous.

there was at our hotel one Canon Rawnsley, who considered himself an authority on the Lake poets. I & my mother and Aunt Judy [Julia Huxley] were waiting outside the hotel when another visitor came up to Aunt Judy and said, "It is so charming to see your little boy listening with such interest to the conversation between his father & dear Canon Rawnsley." At which moment Aldous came hurtling down the path, flung himself on Aunt Judy & said, "Mother! Do you know how many times Canon Rawnsley has said, 'NO Really!' "

## Chapter Three

## Hillside

IN the autumn of 1903 Aldous was sent away from home. He and his cousin Gervas entered Hillside, a preparatory school near Godalming run by Gidley Robinson. Huxley major (Gervas, the elder by three months) and Huxley minor: they were nine years old when they went, rising fourteen when they left. For five years the two boys lived side by side. Through Gervas Huxley we have a first hand account.

At the beginning of the term I had been deposited forlornly by my mother. Aldous' bed, next to mine in the big dormitory for the smaller fry, was empty. As was so often the case in his prep school days Aldous had been ill, and it was a week or more before he arrived. By that time I had begun to settle in . . and was able to offer what feeble protection I could . . in Hillside's strange, rough and often brutal world.[1]

"You see, it wasn't a good school, not any longer. Headmaster far too old . . . All small boys are nasty, I think; the only thing to do with small boys is to supervise them very closely. We weren't. And a lot of bad bullying went on."[2]
The food was abominable, as well as distressingly inadequate.

My stomach still turns at the thought of the breakfast porridge full of greenish, sour-tasting lumps . . . Between lunch and breakfast next morning, all we had was thick chunks of bread at tea, thinly buttered and with a scrape of jam.[3]

Aldous arrived. A new boy, late, rather homesick, looking delicate, perhaps green. They turned on him—Aldous didn't lose his temper; Aldous wasn't afraid. "Oh no, no."
That's very unusual?
G. H. "Very, very unusual."
They tried to bully him, they tried to rag him: it was no good. Aldous wasn't there. "He put on the cloak of invisibility and simply disappeared." Meanwhile the boys discovered that *they*

---

1 Gervas Huxley, *Mem. Vol.*
2 Gervas Huxley, talking to S. B.
3 Gervas Huxley, *Both Hands, An Autobiography*. Chatto & Windus, 1970.

couldn't lose their tempers with him either. "Quite impossible to." So they let him be. "And that is why Aldous was happier I think than *anyone else* at Hillside.

"There was another thing, which seems to surprise people who knew him later, that Aldous was very very much the schoolboy. With all the liking for jokes and japes and pulling people's legs— he joined in all our nonsense, only it was more imaginative nonsense than anybody else's, I mean Aldous's jokes were better jokes . . . and he was enormous *fun* to be with, and *very popular* for that reason."[1]

Gervas and Aldous, inseparable, acquired a mutual great friend, Lewis Gielgud (Sir John's eldest brother), a bright boy, hopeless at games, rather dandified. "He had a poor time at Hillside and needed a lot of protection; he depended more on Aldous than the other way round . . . Aldous was tremendously loyal to his friends . . ."

They played paper cricket, they played football, they played conkers—*cheesers* at Hillside—and Aldous became a champion; they collected puss moths and went bug hunting. Every Sunday afternoon they walked over to Prior's Field, "the main object of the exercise was getting a tremendous blow-out tea [Aldous did eat]. On the way out we'd sing ditties and discuss what we were going to have."

At that tea-table, Gervas, rather awed, first met Aldous's mother, his Aunt Judy. The awe dissolved:

She had a happy laugh, she understood young people. I soon realized why Aldous was so deeply devoted to her and what a key role she played in his life.

The teaching at Hillside was good:

Thanks to such masters as Mr Aston who took the senior boys in classics, Mr Taylor the mathematics master and [later on] Hugh Parr, an unusual and most inspiring young master (he was killed in the 1914 war) who encouraged in us a lively interest in English literature.[1]

There was also Mr Jacques, Jacko, who was unable to preserve discipline but gave interesting lessons in elementary science. Aldous brilliant at his work? "No, Not then. For one thing, his memory was not nearly as good as it became and being ill so often he missed quite a bit of school in the first two or three years (while less gifted boys bore off the prizes). At any rate, he was not

---

[1] Gervas Huxley, talking to S. B.

the kind of boy who is conventionally good at lessons. Lewis was, very much so; and I was, incidentally, much more so than Aldous who was not considered academically outstanding at Hillside." All the same, he was usually among the first two or three of his age. "He was willing and industrious, and never in trouble for idleness or inattention."[1]

Another Hillside boy (Mr Lionel Jardine) told me about a moment that baffled and impressed the form, still grappling with the conventional symbols of elementary geometry—Aldous standing by the blackboard, chalk in hand, at ease, blithely saying, "Let $D$ $F$ $T$ be a triangle."

If Aldous was untroubled at school, there were hints of pressures at home. "*So* much was expected." [Joan Collier, talking.] "His Aunt Mary . . . His health was delicate—all the boys were delicate—yet at one time when Aldous wasn't supposed to be strong enough to get up for breakfast there was displeasure over low marks."

In the summer of 1905 Aldous and Gervas "enjoyed a very happy holiday together up at the house we had in the Lakes— his and my parents rented the house together, Mirehouse on Bassenthwaite. We travelled up with Uncle Leonard, bringing our bicycles. Julian and Trev were there; Julian was in his last year at Eton and brought a very grand friend called Neville Bland.[2] Aldous and I shared a room together contentedly."[1]

They climbed Saddleback, a long tramp for eleven year old boys. In the evenings they played pen and paper games and those charades called Nebuchadnezzars, organized by Julian and Trev. "Aldous was a formidable player—Uncle Leonard had to win at all cost, he'd invent words which he said were in the dictionary, but which weren't; it would annoy my own father and mother, but Aldous took it lightly. *'Father—cheating* again?'

"Yes, Aldous was fond of him. Yes, in a way he was. But he thought he was silly. He *was* silly. He wasn't the kind of father one looked up to, or went to when one was in trouble; I wouldn't have dreamt of going to Uncle Leonard. I would go to Aunt Judy. On the other hand, he was invariably kind to us and I enjoyed his company, I enjoyed his puns and jokes and talk. But I think it was this lack of respect that troubled Aldous and marred his relationship with his father—in those days grown-ups were supposed to behave like grown-ups and not like fellow schoolboys . . ."

In his later years at Hillside Aldous became physically much

---

[1] Gervas Huxley, talking to S. B.
[2] Who indeed became an Ambassador.

14

stronger. "By 1905 or 6 he was quite as strong as I was. He was never an athlete but enjoyed school games—he was scorer for our cricket eleven and in our last year he and I helped to make up a highly unprofessional halfback line in the soccer team—and he was a tremendous walker and climber, and very keen on it." He explored the Surrey countryside on foot as his brothers used to, and he was fond of bicycling (well into adult life) and rode down Devil's Punch Bowl into Milford at terrific speeds.

In the autumn term of 1905 a new headmaster took over, Jimmy Douglas, a comparatively young man and a first-class cricketer, "very much to the school's good". The bullying ceased, lessons became more interesting, the food improved; the school took to acting. "Lewis Gielgud, as a Terry, came into his own." In 1907 the boys did the *Merchant of Venice* on a platform raised at the end of the dining-hall. Aldous aged thirteen played Antonio and (writes his cousin Joan) "we were moved to tears". Gervas confirms this. "How good Aldous's acting was! He did convey emotion. And he was an extremely good speaker of verse. Then of course he always had this very, very beautiful speaking voice—an unhurried voice—it had got this lovely tone in it. . . ."

In the same year Lewis Gielgud, Gervas and Aldous, encouraged by Hugh Parr, the new young English master, got out a literary magazine, the *Doddite*. Two issues (three dozen copies each) appeared, produced on a jelligraph machine. Aldous's first appearance in print. He contributed a poem and a short story illustrated by himself. The poem, called *Sea Horses*, began with the dashing extravert lines,

> *At a gallop we charge up the shingle*
> *At a gallop we leap the sea-wall*
> *With mad exultation we tingle*
> *For we, we can overcome all.*

That summer, the family holiday was spent in Switzerland at Montana. There Aldous was observed by his Collier cousin, Laurence, then between Bedales and Balliol. He saw Aldous as

a very young schoolboy, a pale and apparently fragile child with a big, high-browed head posed unsteadily on a very long, thin body . . . His brothers called him the Ogre, but they listened with interest to his talk, which was well worth listening to even then . . . He had already begun that flow of conversation, both instructive and amusing. . . .[1]

---

[1] Sir Laurence Collier, op. cit.

By 1907, Gervas was head of the school. He over-exercised authority, he says, and was so unpopular that a rebellion was hatched. He was sent to Coventry, books were hurled at him whenever the masters' backs were turned; Aldous alone among the fifty boys stood by him.

After lights went out that Saturday evening in the cubicles where the seniors slept, Aldous's shout of "You swine and curs" silenced the abuse against me. . . . Next day, on the school outing, Aldous walked with me while the rest of the school kept a hostile distance.

Lionel Jardine speaks of another—unselfconscious—act of courage, Aldous's talking away about Swiss wild flowers to the other boys. "You see, he had this curiosity,"[1] [Gervas once more] "the deeply interested curiosity with which he regarded the behaviour of the world." When he was given his first encyclopaedia, he wrote to Julian, "Thank you for the cyclopaedia. I now know everything from who invented dice to the normal temperature of the sea-cucumber."[2]

Between Gervas and Aldous there had "never even been the breath of a quarrel" during those five years of shared daily life. "This was in no way due to any virtue on my part—he was someone with whom you couldn't quarrel: he didn't give way to violent emotions as most of us did. He met ill-nature or spite with serene integrity and detached unselfishness—there was a shining goodness about Aldous. . . . There was that utter trust one had that he'd never say one nasty thing. He seems to have had a perspective, a sense of proportion, even at that age, and that must have helped him in dealing with the inevitable ups and downs of existence at school." Then Gervas added, "*And* he was such a gay character, *such* a gay character: never forget that."[1]

Lewis Gielgud had already left for Eton; Gervas left at Easter; Aldous succeeded him as head of the school for his own last term. In June 1908 he, too, left.

That summer there was another holiday in the mountains. Mrs Huxley had not been well, but was expected to join the family later on. Aldous wrote one of his happy, hearty letters.

This is the most splendid place . . . . We had a vast walk yesterday up a loathsome mountain called le Buet . . . . The day before we went up the glacier and father pulled me about on a rope and we

---

[1] Gervas speaking.      [2] Unpublished letter of June 1908.

had great fun. This place has a splendid air which makes me sleep and eat enormously. There is also a most beautiful view of MONG BLONG . . . there is also an American Bore! It's a great pity mother can't come out yet but I expect she comes in about 10 days,

Your loving,

Aldous[1]

[1] From a letter to Gervas Huxley, part published in *Mem. Vol.*, dated 12th August 1908 from Hotel du Col des Montets, Chamonix.

## Chapter Four

## The Inheritance

ALDOUS HUXLEY is now fourteen. The future will be shaped —up to a point—in terms of the present and the past. We are able to look at both (in fragments). Let us begin with the present, such as it appears: *Les jeux sont faits?* All is still wide open? We can see a boy, getting on for six foot four, slender-boned, congenitally thin, of delicate constitution, under life sentence, as he became so aware, to his own exposed and linear physique. (No wonder he was fascinated when he was able to recognize himself some thirty-five years later as an extreme example of the Third Sheldonian type, The Cerebrotonic Ectomorph.) We see a boy of equable temperament who does not give way to violent emotions, who may not be prone to violent emotions, who is capable already of detachment, capable also of judging, of not suffering fools gladly, of seeing elders plain. ("Cheating, Father?" "I *heard* you the first time", "NO Really!") A boy who shows courage, immense curiosity, is fond of words, jokes, drawing, learning ("Let *D F T* be a triangle"), who is able to inspire respect in young barbarians, whose talk is listened to by Balliol undergraduates and who can speak verse in a voice that moves adults to tears. An exceptional boy, in the judgement of his elders and contemporaries; exceptional not so much in intelligence— though of course he is intelligent, highly intelligent, but in the context of his brothers and his cousins, he is as yet simply conforming to a standard—the *otherness*, the sense that *Aldous is quite different* emanates from a moral quality, one might say a spiritual quality, they discern in him. *Une âme bien née.*

Now to the past. His ancestors, known and unknown; the genetic lottery. They are English: first heard of in the twelfth century (in Cheshire, at Hodesleia-Huxley). The known ones loom large. Aldous is the grandson (the litany once again) of Thomas Henry Huxley, biologist, man of letters, protagonist of Evolution, one of the most forceful minds England has produced —self-educated, a fighter, a formidable member of public bodies, formidable debater, lucid and light-handed essayist, family man, sufferer from poor health, prey to bouts of depression. Aldous is the grandson, on his mother's side, of that curious character the Rev. Thomas Arnold who kept hopping from one religion to another (who appears in *Robert Elsmere* and again in Rose Macaulay's *Told by an Idiot*); he is the great-grandson of that eminent Victorian, Dr Arnold of Rugby, educational reformer, creator of generations of Christian gentlemen. He is the great-nephew of Matthew Arnold (poet *and* educator); the nephew of the earnest, but oh so competent, novelist Mrs Humphry Ward. His mother, as we have seen, founded a school. All took something upon themselves, assumed duties; Aldous's descent, in the words of his friend Gerald Heard, "brought down on him a weight of intellectual authority and a momentum of moral obligations".[1]

Descent. Also class. Aldous was born into a particular and self-conscious enclave, a class within a class, the governing upper middle—an elite, an intellectual aristocracy made up of a handful of families—Trevelyans, Macaulays, Arnolds, Wedgwoods, Darwins, Huxleys—who had produced a number of extra-ordinarily and diversely gifted individuals whose influence, although they never confused themselves with the actual nobility, upon nineteenth-century England had been tremendous. Their common denominator was an intense desire to acquire, to advance and to disseminate knowledge—all of them, it goes without saying were highly though not necessarily expensively educated men and women—a wish to improve the lot as well as the administration of mankind, an assumption of responsibility—*l'intelligence oblige*—and a passion, no tamer word will do, for truth. It was the values, the habits, the glory, and the limitations, of this aristocracy which informed the spiritual and material background of Aldous's youth.

"They lived in houses in which books were part of existence ... Literature of course was in their bones," says Lord Annan in his admirable essay, "The Intellectual Aristocracy", to which I am greatly indebted.

> Their prose at its worst was lucid and free from scholarly jargon; and time and again they produced work of surpassing literary merit ... they wrote not for a scholarly clique but for the intelligent public at large whom they addressed confident that they would be understood.[2]

In the 1860s and 70s they had worked for franchise reforms, women's education, university entrance irrespective of religious beliefs, a civil service open to the talents. (T. H. Huxley, though he only sat two years on the London School Board, "probably more than any man," the *Britannica* dixit, "left his mark on . . national elementary education".) Great as their influence was in the middle of the century,

[1] Gerald Heard, "The Poignant Prophet", article in *The Kenyon Review*, November 1965.
[2] *Studies in Social History: A Tribute to G. M. Trevelyan*, ed. J. H. Plumb. Longmans, 1955.

it was perhaps even more important at the end. For the restraints of religion and thrift and accepted class distinction started to crumble and English society to rock under the flood of money . . . and a materialism of wealthy snobbery and aggressive philistinism arose far exceeding anything hitherto seen in England. The intellectual aristocracy were one of the few barriers which resisted these forces. They insisted that honesty and courtesy were valuable; and they continued to set before the young unworldly ideals. They suggested that if public life was inseparable from spiritual ignomi\ny, another *life devoted to unravelling the mysteries of mind, matter and heart was to be desired* [My italics].[1]

They could be intimidating to meet. "Intellectuals often are. Perhaps they were a little too severe on inconsequential behaviour fully to understand human nature." And here is a passage about their children which concerns us.

. . As infants they had learnt by listening to their parents to extend their vocabulary and talk in grammatical sentences . . . they developed inner resources for entertaining themselves . . . Competitive examination at the schools and universities sharpened their minds, and if those children who did not inherit their parents' intellectual talents suffered unjustly by the feeling that they had failed, the successful children gained by acquiring the habit of thinking accurately in concepts at an early age. Nor was childhood dull: they were freer to read and play as they liked than most middle-class children.[2]

*The successful children.* Aldous's own childhood was a good one. Given his disposition, given the time (post-Victorian England), the inadequacies, then as now, of any education, it might be called a near perfect one. Intellectually he was fish in water; he had a country childhood with its freedom and resources as well as a discipline of work and purpose; he had encouragement and sympathy at home; he had fun and the stimulating presence of his brilliant elder brothers; he had safety, he had affection, he had love.

Much love. (One of the constants of Aldous's life was that he inspired in the men and women he met affection and protective tenderness.) There *were* pressures. *So* much was expected. Those competitive exams, for a start, had to be knuckled down to, passed, passed well. "Huxleys always get firsts." This may have been irksome but I do not think that it weighed unduly on his

1 N. F. Annan, op. cit.        2 Ibid.

spirit (whether the grind overtaxed his physical constitution is another question)—and the obligations put on him by his descent were felt by this boy not as a burden but as a momentum.

Aldous had left Hillside in June of 1908. In the autumn of the year he went to Eton as a scholar.

# PART TWO

## "Impaired": 1908-1914

"For a boy in his teens it was a liberal
education—but *liberal*."
"In what?"
"In Pure and Applied Pointlessness.
And a few weeks after my private course
in the subject came the grand opening
of the public course. World War."
ALDOUS HUXLEY, *Island*, 1962

# Chapter One

# First Damage

ALDOUS is in his first Half at Eton—separated from Gervas who has gone to Rugby—finding his bearings. With ease it would seem and cheerfully. He lives in College, is in the Lower Fifth, will have to do some fagging, "poor little me", for three Halves. "I look so chic in tailcoats . . . M'tutor is a dear man", there's been the awful event of 400 lines of Vergil. There is a brief view of him at that carefree stage. Aldous went to Oxford on a visit, and met George Clark,[1] Trev's and Julian's undergraduate friend.

> He came to us and talked; easily—a lively and intelligent schoolboy.

In the last week of November he writes to Gervas asking if he has done anything bad lately such as putting his fagmaster's tea in the bath or breaking two dozen eggs. He has only been whipped twice so far, "(1) in a general working off of the whole of college . . (2) for forgetting to take VI form cheese out of Hall". Next Monday is St Andrew's Day, the day of the Wall game—"Julian and Trev are coming I think".

Julian and Trev did not come. Julia Huxley died that Sunday, 29th November. She had not been well for only four months, known to be very ill for two. It was cancer. And almost in no time she was dead. The younger children, Aldous and Margaret, had had no real warning.

> At the end one could really give thanks that she was released— even though on the other hand, one could feel nothing but bewildered rebellion that such a thing could be—such pouring out of a life still young—only 45—and so *wanted*, so ineffably *wanted*. . . .

So wrote Dorothy Ward, Julia Huxley's niece, in a long letter to her friend Miss Jewett.[2]

> I cannot tell you what a nightmare of an autumn it has been . . . since the great doctor's final verdict at the end of September—"no operation possible" . . . and [to] watch her week by week . . .

---

[1] Sir George Clark, the historian.
[2] Dated, Stocks, Tring, Dec.13.08.

Mother [Mrs Humphry Ward] went down to see her, even if she could only be with her 5 minutes—slipping down the path of life and out gradually into the Great Unknown. The *pity* of it!

The day my aunt died . . . Mother brought the 2 youngest children back here—Margaret, the little 9-year-old girl . . and Aldous . . poor little fellow. . .

Leonard Huxley that evening read to the assembled school at Prior's Field a poem on his wife's death which he had written a few hours before.

The 2nd boy, a dear of 19, came the next day from Oxford (his first term at Balliol, where his older brother is—both with scholarships, oh! how proud & justly proud she was of them!)—and we tried our best to love and comfort them, and took them to the funeral from here . . .

We lay . . Julia Huxley to rest in the lovely little hillside cemetery in Surrey, whereof Watts designed and painted the little chapel.

It is the small churchyard at Compton—a few graves on a grassy slope in country peace under trees.

It was a funeral never to be forgotten by those who loved my aunt —for the outward and visible signs it brought us of the love in which our dear one was held. You know she had founded & *created* the great school. . . . All the older girls were there—40 of them—in their simple blue serge frocks & schoolhats, just as she would have liked— their young faces awed and hushed at first, and then all breaking down at the last sentence by the grave. ["It was my first terrible grief," said Enid Bagnold.] All the mistresses were there, and all the servants—and many, *many* friends. And her poor husband and boys! it was piteous to see them—and my mother's drawn face.

Joan Collier held Aldous's hand; he was shaking with sobs.

Afterwards they took the children back to Stocks—"The little Eton boy very sensitive and brooding and white, and feels it deeply—and dumbly." Presently he was sent back to Eton for the last fortnight of the Half; Trev and Margaret stayed on for the time being, as "of course it means the breaking-up of the home for my Uncle and the children and *their* plans are entirely unsettled at present". The break-up was complete indeed. "I lost my mother, my home, my school, living in the country and my governess all at one blow" wrote Aldous's sister Margaret sixty-one years after.[1]

---

[1] Miss Margaret Huxley in a letter to S. B. October 1969.

As for the school, Mrs Huxley two years earlier, finding the sheer practical work unmanageable, had taken on a partner, Mrs Burton-Brown, "a rather well-known classical lecturer", and that lady was going to carry on, so the continuation of Prior's Field at least was assured. "But the wonder," Enid Bagnold said, "went out of the school with Mrs Huxley."

As for Aldous, "There remained with him, latent at ordinary times but always ready to come to the surface, a haunting sense of the vanity, the transience, the hopeless precariousness of all merely human happiness."[1]

---

[1] Aldous Huxley on François Leclerc du Tremblay's losing his father at the age of ten. *Grey Eminence*, 1941.

## Chapter Two

## Aldous at Eton

ALDOUS HUXLEY had gone to Eton as a King's Scholar in September 1908. Eleven new boys entered College at the same time, the beginning of the Michaelmas Half (Halves being what the three Eton terms are called), and five more in the course of the school year. Of these, six were killed in the 1914-18 war. Four or five are living today.

The scholars—seventy boys—live together in College. A fellow Etonian, contemporary of Aldous's, the Rev. R. A. L. Fell, describes the physical conditions of their day,[1]

The fifteen junior Collegers are housed in "Chamber", the remains of the Long Chamber, in which till about the middle of last century all the Scholars lived, and were locked in every night. In Chamber each boy has a "stall" containing a fold-up bed, desk and bookcase and a Windsor chair; also a fixed wash-basin with a cold tap, on a spring so that it cannot be left running, a saucer bath and can, marked with his name. [There were no bathrooms—long baths with taps, that luxurious dream—in College till about 1911, when showers were installed, their use being confined to the upper half of College.] Carrying cans of hot water formed an important part of a fag's duty. (In College a boy is a fag for his first year: I do not think the institution of fagging was resented, and I never heard any abuse of it.)

The stalls reached nearly half way up to the ceiling, the bottom of the windows being about level with the top of the stalls; it is a high room so that you have to climb up (on the wash-stand) to open or shut a window. Every stall has a reading-lamp which has to be turned off some time before the Captain of Chamber calls "Good night all, stop talking"—10 pm, I think, 10.30 on Saturdays. A light in the ceiling stays on all night, but no-one could read by that. [Some boys, certainly Aldous, read under the bed-clothes with an electric torch.]

The headmaster at the time was Edward Lyttelton. The tradition still prevailed that the head should be a clergyman and a classic. Lyttelton had succeeded Dr Warre, who had been head-master for twenty years, in 1905

[1] All, needless to say, changed, in the recent reconstruction of College.

and was expected to be something of a "new broom"; but I fancy that he found it difficult to carry some of the older masters with him. He certainly wished to modify the old dominance of the Classics. The general public regarded Lyttelton as a crank . . . It was not realized in what respect and affection he was regarded by the boys . . . The Master in College was A. W. Whitworth, who was also Aldous's Tutor [m'tutor; and still living in 1973]. Every boy at Eton has a Tutor and is under his care for the whole of his school life.

We have three sources about Aldous at Eton. His letters—a dozen of them, mostly to Julian or Gervas, facetious, conformist, rather hearty, full of doggerel and doodles. The recollections of four of his contemporaries, the Rev. R. A. L. Fell, Lord Justice Harman, H. G. C. Streatfeild and Henry Rowan Walker (Lewis Gielgud, Aldous's greatest friend at Eton, is dead). Aldous's later comments in print and conversation.

Other men who were at Eton in his time and alive today were either a few years older or younger, a gap unmanageable in their circumstances then. Sir Alan Lubbock writes that he remembers Aldous well by sight, "I can see him now sitting with a toasting fork by the fire in College Kitchen, talking to Lewis Gielgud. But I never spoke to him, nor he to me."

Aldous at Eton was "a tall lanky youth with a thick shock of hair" (Lord Harman, who says that he knew Aldous as well as anybody). Again there was no bullying—"No one ever dreamt of bullying Aldous!

From the word go, he was clearly going to be a superior being. He possessed a kind of effortless aristocratic approach to his work.[1]

What Aldous himself recorded[2] is that he did a high jump at 4 foot 3, is messing about the lab, finds cricket pretty boring (he was a dry-bob: cricket in the summer, not rowing). The weather is poor . . the provost has died . . . He is in a room of his own now in passages (the two long corridors in New Building where collegers live after their first spell in stalls) . . . By December he and Gielgud have accomplished forty recruit drills and Aldous is "very nearly a full-fledged territorial". Next Half he is fourth in trials which "hurls me forth from upper tea-room fag to

---

[1] Henry Rowan Walker, letter to S. B.
[2] In letters at the time.

captain of Lower Tea", a change he thinks for the better, "for to wield the fork is a superior pastime to carrying the kettle". He sends Julian two longish poems, one in the style of Noyes, the other of Browning, and thanks him for "a box of lush produce". He is beginning to paint.

As for work. "We did classics," (Lord Harman talking) "Aldous preferring Greek." (He must have been a fairly good classical scholar as the Scholarship Examination was mainly based on classics.) "A little modern history, some French which was taught by a man who had fought in the Franco-Prussian war. I think I was better in French than Aldous was at the time."

"Actually," Aldous said half a century later,[1] "the education at Eton was uncommonly good at that time . . . There were a few *very good teachers* . . . There were funny things about it, I mean it was in many respects still a *renaissance* education. We used to spend the whole of every Tuesday from 7 in the summer and 7.30 in winter till 10.30 at night composing Latin verses—we were given a piece of Tennyson or something and were told to turn it into elegiacs or hexameters or Alcaics or Sapphics, and if you were a little further advanced Greek iambics—[with great wonder and relish in his voice]—which was a sort of *immense* jig-saw puzzle game . . . it was the most *extraordinary* proceeding . . ."

Aldous's English work "struck us as a long way out of the ordinary", says H. G. C. Streatfeild (who became a master at Eton). "His potentialities were obvious to us all."

We often worked together (legitimately) . . . I used to read his essays and Sunday questions (an exercise in religious or semi-religious subjects intended to keep us employed on Sunday). My own efforts [he adds with charming unassumingness] were commonplace, and I envied his facility and maturity.

One day when Aldous, aged fifteen, was in 5B, the Upper Fifth, the boys were up to a master called Macnaghten and were told to spend half an hour writing down what they knew about the Conquistadors. Everybody scribbled away. This is what Aldous produced.

> *It's my settled belief that Pissarro*
> *Must have been educated at Harro*
> *This alone would suffice*
> *To account for his vice*
> *And his morals so scroobious and narro.*

---

[1] In a long interview with John Chandos in July 1961, recorded by Lansdowne Studios, hereafter cited as London interview, 1961.

Lord Harman puts Aldous among the Eton Aesthetes. "These were Aldous, myself, Monroe, a man called Pemberton . . . We read Walter Pater, Oscar Wilde, Later G. B. Shaw, all fashionable authors then . . ." H. G. C. Streatfeild found Aldous "apart from his brilliance, ordinary in the best sense. He enjoyed his games . . I can see him now in a muddy wall-sack, wall-cap and corduroy trousers. . . ."

At any rate Aldous read a vast amount. "You were largely left to your own devices . . . Everybody had a room to themselves, [again the slow relish in his voice] which was an *immense luxury* . . This was a curious school, I think it was a very good school, and if one wanted to learn, one *could* learn, one could learn a *great deal*. It was very civilized in many ways."

His other main interest was science (how naturally Aldous's mind vaulted between the two cultures, but then, "I suppose I always had a passion for knowledge, and a certain gift for co-ordinating different fields.") His master was M. H. Hill, the biologist (who kept a cage of lemurs in his garden), "One of the best masters in the place, and he was *very good*." Through most of 1910 Aldous was taking an intensive course in biology. He was sixteen and had decided—or it had been decided, the way such things *emerge* in families—that he would be a doctor, with a view to going in for medical research.

Aldous's father had moved to London in 1909, to a house in Bayswater (27, Westbourne Square)—a bachelor's establishment, though Sarah, Julia Huxley's old parlourmaid whom everybody relied on, had come with him and was doing her best to make it homelike. Aldous spent his holidays mostly at his Aunt Mary's house Stocks at Tring in the Chilterns, or with Gervas's parents, Dr Henry Huxley and his wife Sophy, round the corner in Porchester Terrace. For Easter 1910 they took him down to Devonshire with them. The Henry Huxleys, the Harries, were "very very devoted to Aldous. [Gervas speaking] I think after Aunt Judy died, my mother meant a great deal to him. . . ."

On the day of Edward VII's funeral—20th May 1910—Aldous stood in the ranks of the Eton C.O.T.C. lining the route of the procession. He could not see very much, he complained, as they kept reversing arms, and the heat was simply dreadful.

That summer he was still learning to paint and did a good deal of sketching out of doors "which is very nice". In July he writes to his Gran'Moo (T. H. Huxley's widow) from O.T.C. Camp at Farnborough by the "fitful radiance of a quarter candlepower candle". They have marched 8 miles on Wednesday and 16 on Thursday, "a rather boring proceeding"; the Corps was to be inspected by the Duke of Connaught and kept waiting while "H.R.H. was considerably unpunctual,

> I calculated that the whole brigade together wasted 333 days, allowing each man to have wasted 2 hours and the brigade to consist of 4000 men.

Aldous will be glad to return to hot baths and other than straw mattresses to sleep on; but his tone is boisterous and he seems pleased with himself rather than put out. His last letter of the year is to Julian. Aldous is thinking of talking to his Tutor about specializing in biology; they have had an enormous beano at Fuller's and he has made up a first-rate riddle about a platypus and a cat.

## Chapter Three

# The Second Impairment

IN the winter of 1911, during the Easter Half at Eton, Aldous
began having trouble with his eyes. One morning they were
swollen and extremely red; Matron, who had no medical training
in those days, believed that it was pink-eye and would clear in
a week or so. Nobody appears to have been alarmed. Aldous
himself was curious about his condition and would peer at his
eyes with interest in the looking-glass.[1] Time passed and the
trouble did not clear. Matron told him to stay in the dark; this
he did most reluctantly, having seldom spent a waking moment
by himself without a book. Charles Harman sat up with him for
one whole night. "Next day he was gone."

He turned up at his Aunt Ethel Collier's house in Swiss Cottage
while the family were at luncheon.[2] "What are you doing, Aldous?
Why aren't you at Eton?" A touch of pink-eye, been sent up to
see a doctor. Next time he came to the house he walked into a
four-poster bed.

Within a number of days or weeks—memories of dates and
sequence are uncertain, no medical records subsist—Aldous could
not see. The diagnosis, ultimately, was *keratitis punctata*, an
inflammation of the cornea, in a particularly violent form, and
hope for recovery at the stage the disease had reached was
regarded as slight. Dr Henry Huxley used to tell his son that by
the time he had got hold of Aldous, well, the damage had been
done.

What exactly had happened? For the second time in Aldous's
life sudden illness struck. What was—whatever is—the cause? Ill-
chance, a chain of circumstances? Gervas always believed from
what he heard that Aldous had been run down or ill, had had a
bout of influenza, then went out with the O.T.C. and got some
infected dust into his eye. "Infected dust—that's what my father
always told me."

A pinch of dust at a moment of low resistance. Aldous—
essentially incommunicado since his mother's death two years ago
—growing too tall too fast. (Now, at sixteen, he was nearly his
full height of 6 foot 4½.) No one at school particularly anxious
about him. He was probably over-worked. ("The boys *were* worked

[1] Told by Lord Harman.
[2] Told by Joan Collier Buzzard.

too hard at Eton," said his step-mother[1] later on—one would not have deduced this from the leisurely chatty letters. "He didn't get enough food, he certainly didn't have enough of the right food. Eton was a curious place then—not very healthy.")

The damage had been done and there he was. The boy with the immense curiosity about the world, the boy who wanted to read all the books, was nearly blind. He could just distinguish light from darkness; he was unable to go about by himself. He could not read.

> We were appalled [Gervas speaking] The shock of it. *I* was shattered, but not Aldous. He faced it with fantastic courage; and a complete absence of self-pity.

In the immediate present, Aldous needed medical help and looking after. His father being a single man spending his days in editorial offices, Aldous stayed in turns with the Henry Huxleys, the Colliers in London, with Mrs Humphry Ward and other Arnold relations. He was treated first by his Uncle Henry in consultation with various oculists, then by an eminent eye surgeon, Ernest Clarke, who is believed to have made the diagnosis of *staphylococcus aureus* as the cause of the infection in December 1911. From then on Aldous was taken once a week to the Institute of Tropical Medicine for injections. (Penicillin or cortisone, of course, were not available at the time.) The actual inflammation subsided gradually, leaving opacities in the corneas which grossly impaired the sight.

There was never any question of Aldous's being able to return to Eton. He had left one morning in the middle of a school week and did not come back. His things—the useless books—were packed up and sent to his father's house. He had been in College for just under two and a half years, not long enough to have attained any distinction in work or games. Let H. G. C. Streatfeild have the last word about Aldous at Eton. His simple memoir, from which I have already quoted, ends:

> His books are known to the world, I will confine myself to my memories of him as an ordinary boy . . . We used to take walks on Sundays, and his conversation was never above my head, and now I realize what a gentle and simple companion he was, ready to share with me ordinary not high-brow subjects . . . In fact I cannot recall a single unattractive characteristic in him. .

I cannot remember any more details, as our ways parted all too

---

[1] Rosalind (Mrs Leonard) Huxley.

soon, but I hope that even these inadequate notes will give some impression of Aldous as a boy, enjoying all our activities as a lovable companion, and without a trace of affectation, conceit, or superiority.

Aldous was now on his own; cut off from his friends, his pursuits, his education, at sixteen and a half. They were as good to him as he let them be—"he was not easy to help"—his father, the Huxley and Collier aunts, Aunt Mary Ward ("she would have done anything for him [Gervas] and she did *a lot, always*; and he was very fond of her"). Julian was tied up at Oxford with a demonstratorship and a lectureship at Balliol; Trevenen, still an undergraduate, came to look after his brother when he could. For any positive survival Aldous had to summon up his own resources.

With tough concentration, he taught himself to read Braille and to type on a small portable. He taught himself to play the piano—first with one hand on the Braille page and the other hand on the piano keys; then the other way round: reading with the right, learning to play with the left, until he knew both parts by heart. He trained himself, alone, in upstairs rooms, filling the hours with slow, tedious, constructive tasks. What he felt, what he feared, what he held on to, was not said; he never talked about it. In print, much later, he stated the facts, once, laconically. "At sixteen, I had a violent attack of *keratitis punctata* . . . eighteen months of near-blindness, during which I had to depend on Braille for my reading and guide for my walking."[1] (There is only one blind character in all of Aldous's fiction, a young man appearing briefly in the third act of *The World of Light*; and he is an embittered extravert sketched conventionally, at arm's length as it were.) A two-line note sent by Aldous at the time to his cousin Joan congratulating her on her engagement, begins,

Dearest Joan,
Scuse bad writing which same I can't see.[2]

For the adult family it was a tale of fortitude, pride, withdrawal; to his sister, a child of twelve, Aldous was disturbing, someone to shy away from when he came to stay with the connections in[3] Surrey she had been living with since her mother's death.

[1] *The Art of Seeing*, 1943.
[2] *Letters*. Dated by the editor July 1911.
[3] They were the Rev. E. Carus Selwyn and his wife, Maud; his first wife had been Aldous's mother's sister Lucy who had died in 1894. The house was Undershaw at Hindhead and belonged to Conan Doyle.

He spent hours playing rather curiously on the piano, or shut in his room, typing, typing; or if not upstairs, concentrating on learning Braille and there were very few points of contact between us. I think I was rather frightened by his attempts at re-adjusting himself.[1]

As soon as Aldous had mastered the new techniques, he went on with his education. He got through the required reading, typed his written work and was taught by a succession of tutors. One was the present Sir George Clark, the seventeenth-century historian, and Aldous used to say he had learnt much from him.

He was a very remarkable man—he was a contemporary of my second brother—he had just come down from Oxford and he tutored me. I certainly got a good deal out of *him*. He was extremely well-read and a highly civilized young man . . .[2]

Aldous read a great amount himself at that period—with his finger-tips slowly, maddeningly slowly, off the thick Braille page. He spoke of the tedium of reading Macaulay, "You can't just glance over the page," of how intolerable the style became when spelt out letter by letter. Reading *anything* more than once must have been intolerable, and it was now that Aldous began to develop that extraordinary memory of his.

Never one to fritter away his time—I don't think that he was ever prone to the adolescent's—and the artist's!—commonplace equation: idleness = boredom = guilt = despair—it was actually during that year that Aldous started to write. He began, and finished, a novel on his little typewriter. A novel of about 80,000 words which, he said,

I never subsequently read. It disappeared. I rather regret that it *has* disappeared—I would be interested to know what it was like now.

It was sort of romantic—no it wasn't romantic—it was a rather *bitter* novel about a young man and his relationship to two different kind of women, as I remember it.[2]

By the spring of 1912, Aldous was able to walk about by himself and had hopes of being able to go to Oxford. His Eton contemporary Charles Harman met him again, after more than a year of separation, when they were both staying at Stocks with Mrs Humphry Ward. Aldous appeared unchanged.

[1] Miss Margaret Huxley, in a letter to S. B.
[2] London interview, 1961.

Mrs Humphry Ward's complete works—a set of them—were in every spare bedroom in the house. Aldous went about muddling them up, managing to put three *Robert Elsmere*'s in a row and so on. He loved mischief.[1]

But his sight and all that it entailed was never mentioned between them. Englishmen did not talk about such things.

For these Easter holidays Aldous went to Cornwall with the Henry Huxleys. Gervas talks of his determination to lead an absolutely normal life.

You did not take in how handicapped he was because he wouldn't let you think of him as handicapped. Incredibly, he insisted on bicycling. Although he really couldn't see—my mother would ride in front of him; but Aldous insisted on bicycling to the station on his own. It was terrific courage, it really was.

One bitter cold morning Gervas came into his room and Aldous said, "You know, Gerry, there's one great advantage in Braille, you can read in bed without getting your hands cold."

If there were moments of appalling discouragement and strain "he never showed it", Gervas said. "He never showed it."

[1] Lord Harman, talking.

## Chapter Four

## Pulling Through

ALDOUS'S sight was beginning to recover (to some extent). There is the fact that he was able to bicycle at all, that he was able to pick out *Robert Elsmere*'s from the shelves. Gervas thinks that it was sometime in the spring of 1912 that he first saw Aldous poring over print through an enormous magnifying glass. There is evidence also in a rather pathetic letter typed that May.

> Dearest Father,
>   Many thanks for your last letter, which, I regret to say was rather too small for me to read with any comfort. In fact I was only able to take the cream off each sentence by picking out one word in every four or so . . .

Leonard Huxley had married again in February 1912. He was only fifty-two and had been on his own for over three years. He married Rosalind Bruce, a young woman of twenty-two: they were very much in love, and their marriage turned out to be an extraordinarily happy one. A man marries according to his choice and instincts; his marriage and its timing are his own affair. But a second marriage, inevitably, also involves his children, and the situation for them, for the new wife, for the man himself, is seldom an entirely easy one. Here, the ground seems not to have been well enough prepared, the intended marriage (in Sir George Clark's words) was "casually announced to the boys"; there were undertones of shock and hurt. The bride was very young, younger, in fact, than Julian and Trev, very young to face those particular four step-children. It was late in the day to re-make a home for them, and Julia Huxley would have been hard to replace by *anyone*. Julian was then a brilliant and not particularly considerate young man in his first intellectual pride, steeped in his own conflicts and concerns; Margaret probably still child enough to show a child's feelings; Aldous enigmatic, docile and aloof; Trevenen alone gave warmth, came forward, tried to build the bridges. The second Mrs Huxley did her best. "Oh Lord, yes," Gervas said, "she was very good to them, she was very good to Aldous and Trev." She faced the formidably intellectual brood, and came to have a great affection for them all.

Meanwhile she looked after Aldous—whose home base was now

Westbourne Square—as much as he would let her. As a matter of fact she did one of the nicest things: giving him the use of the piano, a wedding-present from her grandfather.

In May Aldous went off to Germany for part of the summer. It would seem that he made the railway journey, changes and all, by himself. Whether he went mainly to consult an oculist or to study music or to learn German is not clear. (He once told me that as he never *saw* German his knowledge of the language was purely oral.) He stayed at Marburg, lodging with a university professor of geology called Kayser; his letters home were cheerful.

The Kaysers have the most delightful dog . . Professor K. took them on an all-day geological expedition . . He went to a funeral where everyone was in magnificent uniform and he wished he had brought his Eton C.O.T.C. private's uniform to outshine at least the railway porters . . He has made a new philosophy called Space & Suet which is really immense and will satisfy everything . . He has just polished off Beethoven's Funeral March and is going to start on a Chopin Prelude . . in the German line they are doing Schiller and Charybdis. (He regretfully adds that the pun is not his own.) Once he reported on the state of his eyes.

> About the autumn: it all so very much depends on E Clarke's remarks. I don't know if it would be good to use the one eye for doing anything much. The right does not seem to alter much, but the left is certainly progressing well. [16th June 1912.]

Back in England Aldous was again with his contemporaries, spending the end of the summer holiday with Gervas and Lewis Gielgud in Surrey. For Christmas 1912 they were all in London. "We very much tended to go about in threes then," Gervas said, "and we did a great deal together. Later that winter he and Aldous went to Montana with their uncle John Collier and a party.

> Trev. Not Julian, Julian was too old, he was doing other things[1] . . . There again, Aldous came with us when we all went skiing. He couldn't see very much but he skied as well as I did.

1913 began well. In January Aldous went on a walking tour on the South Downs with Trev; in February he was definitely

[1] Julian Huxley was first in America, then Heidelberg in the autumn.

getting ready for Oxford Matriculation. Once more he struggled with his bugbear.

> My most valuable time [he writes to Julian] is taken up . . by reading MacAulay, and ten chapters of him at that, for matriculatio ad absurdum. Dreadful old man to write in Latin Prose style: still, it must be.

That tough capacity for knuckling down may well have come down to Aldous from his grandfather (himself a man far from robust in health). This is how T. H. Huxley taught himself a language (German at the age of sixteen): ". . go straight to the book you want to read, translate the first ten lines with the aid of a dictionary, and learn all the words. Do this day by day and it will not be long before you only need to use the dictionary now and then."[1]

Spring and early summer Aldous actually spent at Oxford, not as yet a member of the university but staying with Trev in his digs in the Banbury Road, reading, working, being read to and tutored by Trev, going about in the afternoons, punting, walking, seeing their friends. The brothers were devoted to each other and these were happy days.

It is time to say something about Trevenen Huxley. He was twenty-three years old then, in his last term at Balliol, and a brilliant mathematician (which Aldous was not, and lightly regretted). Trev had been educated, like his brothers, at Hillside and Eton, had taken a first in Math Mods in 1911 and was now reading for his final in Greats. He loved mountains and rock-climbing and was outstanding at it, he had a mild stammer, and he is remembered as a human being of rare quality. We can only see him now through the wrong end of the opera glass— an unforgotten figure, remote in time. His contemporaries regarded him as the most out-going and human of the brothers. Number Two, he called himself.

> *One Huxley Brother*
> *Is as good as another;*
> *This is the view*
> *Of Number Two.*

"Never, indeed," writes Sir Laurence Collier, "have I known a man so widely liked."[2]

---

[1] C. Bibby, op. cit.
[2] Sir Laurence Collier, op. cit.

Trev, "most radiant and beloved of his generation",[1] was affectionate, gay—sunny—of limitless kindness and great sweetness of nature; he was unselfish to an extreme degree, agonizingly sensitive, chiefly for others (and very much affected by the shock of Aldous's blindness); self-demanding, self-critical; a gay companion but also a conscientious worrier who drove himself too hard, who over-worked, over-exercised, did not bother about when or what he ate or take care of his own health. He had an ascetic streak, detesting jokes and boys' talk about sex, and an inclination to subdue his instincts by his principles. We have Aldous's re-creation of his brother as Brian Foxe in *Eyeless in Gaza* (perhaps his only fully intentional portrait of an actual person).

At Oxford, that May, Trev, Aldous and Lewis Gielgud were enjoying themselves rehearsing a play. The author was Naomi Haldane,[2] then a very young girl, who professes to have forgotten the title. It was a strawberry and gooseberry summer—the summer of 1913; there is a photograph of Aldous doubled up under a bush, eating gooseberries. He was getting on for nineteen, and all of a sudden one *sees* Aldous—he is no longer a boy, already he has become the ageless adult.

He was long and dreadfully vulnerable looking, his long arms and legs dangling across the back of chairs or sofas.[3]

It is also one's first view of Aldous through the eyes of a pretty girl.

We were always having picnics up the Cherwell, making fires and boiling kettles . . We were always laughing and scrapping . . .

Aldous introduced Naomi to literature. He told her mother that of course she must read *Tom Jones*; Mrs Haldane gave in. He asked her general-personal questions. "Are you in love?" "Describe it to me." While all the time she was admiring his yellow tie and white socks and wished he would kiss her.

Oh yes, she says now, "Aldous was very much sought by the girls".

He did not kiss. But "he threw open a whole world to me. French books . . . made me read French poetry . . . Mallarmé . . .

[1] Leonard Huxley, letter to Gidley Robinson 1915.
[2] Naomi Mitchison (the present Lady Mitchison), the writer; daughter of Professor John Scott Haldane, sister of J. B. S. Haldane, the biologist.
[3] This and the following quotation are by Naomi Mitchison, *Mem. Vol.* and conversation with S.B.

He knew an amazing amount about all the arts and took them
seriously in a way that was tremendously encouraging to me in our
somewhat anti-art Oxford home.

Aldous still drew.

In some extraordinary way he did the most brilliant drawings, using
a thick pencil . . . And he played on our schoolroom piano—was it
Beethoven? was it Chopin? What I remember most is his long hands
on the piano and his half-blind face reaching forward into the music.
I only listened, but he was immersed.

Trev in his Oxford finals that summer got a second in Greats.
It was a disappointment. It was due, the family think, to exhaustion, worry and overwork. Trev had been worked too hard
since Eton (at one point Matron had advised withdrawing him
for a time, but his father and mother decided to keep him on[1]).
At a recent examination session at Oxford he had felt so ill that
he handed in blank pages; and whenever he had a holiday
"Leonard dragged him up a mountain"[2] (which *was* what Trev
enjoyed). Whatever the cause, he took the relative failure as a
blow.

In July Aldous went to Grenoble for two months to work at
his French. He had lessons with an Abbé Lincelon, read Musset
and Taine, "filling it up with the Oxford Book of French Verse,"
translated chunks of E. F. Benson with the aid of a dictionary
$1\frac{1}{2}$ inch by 2, and explored the countryside. Again there are long
filial letters, "Dearest Father," with sketches on the margin. The
slopes of Savoy are full of the homeliest trees, just like the low
valleys in Wales . . . the French at the pension are really much
nicer than he thought . . . He has had four letters for his birthday,
three on the day and one two days late . . . and would they send
on the two shirts which were at the wash when he left . . .
Lewis Gielgud arrived. They went up on mules to the Grande
Chartreuse. The maquis is thicker than anything he has seen before,
"Oak, hazel, maple, wild cherry . . . but the thing is to start early,
today we were off by 6.30 and it was delicious—the butterflies
and flowers . . wonderful Apollos and Camberwell beauties and
fritillaries, brand new and shining like new minted coins." (An
instance of what Aldous could see at times—not always, not

---

[1] Rosalind (Mrs Leonard) Huxley.
[2] Joan Collier Buzzard.

consistently—*managed* to see, long before his Bates training, by his own desire and application.)

The letters often end with an affectionate enquiry about his eldest and peripatetic brother, "How, where, when and why is Julian?" (in Texas, actually, teaching biology). "I hope everyone flourishes, Julian in particular."

In September Aldous and Lewis Gielgud returned to England and joined Gervas in Yorkshire who says that Aldous came back with an extremely good French accent.

## Chapter Five

## "That One Glorious Year at Balliol"

AND in October Aldous was able to enter Balliol. He went, as it worked out, at the same time as Gervas who had not missed a day of school at Rugby. Aldous had done it, the tough concentration, the solitary disciplines had paid off.

His sight had reached a platform; it had recovered to the limited extent he described precisely in *The Art of Seeing:*

> I was left . . . with one eye just capable of light perception, and the other with enough vision to permit of my detecting the two-hundred foot letter on the Snellen chart at ten feet.

In practice this meant that he could read, though not with any ease. The pupil of his better eye had to be kept dilated with an atropine solution so that it might see round a heavy patch of opacity at the centre of the cornea; nor was he allowed the use of spectacles as yet, but had to do his reading through a powerful hand magnifying glass or—when the right books were available —in Braille. His other senses had sharpened: he used his long, tactile hands to sort out objects, crossed roads by hearing. He had come to terms with the slow process of Braille. True, one could not skim, he would say, but it made one absorb, it made one *remember*. Aldous actually had done rather more than catch up by the time he went to Oxford.

> We had just gone on at school [says Gervas], Aldous had read a great deal while he was blind—working on his own, he read a lot of things, like French, which we didn't know.

Aldous slid into his first Oxford term with ease. There was Trev, who had arranged to stay on doing post-graduate work, to be with his brother, there was Gervas, there was Lewis, the Haldanes; and then all at once there was that first full plunge into an adult world, a young man's first year at the university: new friends, ideas, freedoms, and time, time seemingly inexhaustible before him.

"Everybody adored Aldous—he fascinated them. He made a tremendous impression, [Gervas] and became the most popular person of the year." Raymond Mortimer—fellow freshman at

Balliol—called him "formidably sophisticated—he was dazzling, *dazzling* . . . The erudition: he had read everything."

The Dean of Balliol was Neville Talbot. Pre-eminence in scholarship, Gervas writes,

> was as great as ever, but the tone had changed in the last few years; rowdiness and drunkenness were no longer fashionable among the bloods, and the college had become a generally sober and serious place, with such eminent undergraduates as Godfrey Elton, Harold MacMillan and "God" Wedderburn, the rowing blue, setting the tone.
>
> As for the dons, "Sligger" Urquhart still kept open house in his rooms every evening, while distinguished scholars like A. L. Smith and Cyril Bailey were our friends as well as our tutors.

It was pre-wars Oxford, pre-industries, pre-motor cars; there were horse trams going up the High and everybody went on foot or bicycle. Aldous's room in college overlooked the Broad; he had a piano and a bright French poster over the fireplace.

> The room seemed always full of people talking and laughing . . . It was the centre where the elite of the year gathered.

It was Aldous who introduced them to Jazz (which he came to loathe so whole-heartedly ever after). Then he was fascinated by syncopation and he would strum with relish,

> *He'd have to get under, Get out or get under* . . .

"He was always picking up something new [Gervas]—and this was certainly brand new to us."

Aldous's allowance at Oxford was two hundred pounds a year. Gervas had two hundred and fifty.

> Money never seemed to mean very much to him—his wants were never extravagant—he managed all right, but couldn't indulge in the clothes or book buying that I could with my extra fifty a year; but I am sure that it never bothered him.

They were blissfully untroubled. There was as yet no thought of examinations—poor Trev sat for the Civil Service exam and again did not do well—for Aldous and Gervas there were only the ridiculous Divvers, Sacred History (which Aldous failed at his first go). They had time for a lot of acting. Naomi Haldane had written another play, performed in her parents' garden—"We

were immediately made completely free of Mrs Haldane's house"[1]
—and they also did scenes from Aristophanes' *Frogs*. Lewis
Gielgud acted and stage managed, Aldous played Charon. "I
was fierce about my plays," Naomi says, "but couldn't fault his
performance. Yes, he could see enough to get himself on and off
stage. How gay we all were!"

We—Naomi's brother Jack, Dick her fiancé,[2] Gervas, Lewis,
some girls in the cast ("a refreshing change"), Aldous, "always
a little apart .. with a book .. he was somehow brooding, not
unenjoyably, without".

As for work, he enjoyed his tutorials. "I had a very able tutor,
Tiddy, R. J. E. Tiddy, lecturer in classics and English Literature . . ."[3] He went to few lectures. "I never attended more than,
at the outside, two lectures a week." He typed his essays and
wrote a good deal of verse. "Well, things flourish," he reported
to his father,

the only fly in the ointment being P. Mods—infernally stupid exam,
trod out by the feet of weeping boys from the wine-press of boredom.

All in all it was tremendous fun, as Gervas put it: "We had
that one glorious year. One year was wonderful for Aldous, it
really was. We took everything Oxford had to offer. And it was
an awful lot."

They broke off for the long vacation in June 1914.

[1] Cherwell Edge in north Oxford, now Wolfson College.
[2] The late Lord Mitchison.
[3] London interview, 1961.

# Chapter Six

## Trevenen

IN August 1914 Aldous was in Scotland at Connel Ferry with his father and step-mother. Julian, temporarily home from Texas, was with them. Trev was not. Since the beginning of the year he had been in a state of depression. The strain over exams, the anxieties for others, the delicate constitution assaulted by fanatical exercising and underfeeding, the conflict between a young man's ordinary sexual impulses and high ideals—it all had become too much for him.

It was in that condition that he was faced by a crisis in his life. He fell in love, idealistically *and* sensually. He gave way to the sensuality. Fifty years ago, such things went very deep. The girl, who was charming and loving, and very unhappy herself, was a girl whom Trev could not have married in the social circumstances of their time without bringing much unhappiness upon them both. The family knew nothing; Trev wrote about it to at least one friend (abroad in the crucial months). Sarah knew, the Leonard Huxleys' old parlourmaid. (Aldous must have been told something because he made his brother's conflict the theme of his opening poem in *The Defeat of Youth*.) By summer Trev was at the end of his tether and had a severe, medically acknowledged breakdown: depression punctuated by fits of melancholia.

T. H. Huxley had suffered from long bouts of depression in his later life; Julian had had a nervous breakdown, or depression neurosis as we would say now (the first of a series), the year before when he had been treated, successfully as far as it went, by a rest cure in a nursing home. Earlier in the summer of 1914 he had returned, on leave from his American appointment, to that same nursing home for another brief spell of rest, and it was there (in Surrey) that Trev was now confined, on psychiatric advice. At the beginning of August he was said to be improving.

On 15th August, a Saturday, he set out for a walk on the downs by himself. He spoke to the nurse on leaving and had appeared to be cheerful and calm. (It is known that the treating London psychiatrist had given explicit orders that the patient must never be left out of sight.)

He failed to return from his walk. The police were told the same evening. A search began—his father came down from Scotland—there was no trace of Trevenen for seven days. It was thought that he might have gone and enlisted in the war. Then

46

there was news that he had been seen earlier wandering about the neighbourhood.

The following Sunday, 23rd August, Trevenen was found in a wood only a few hundred yards away. He had hanged himself from a tree.

The news came to Julian and Aldous by telegraph.

Trevenen was not yet twenty-five. Aldous was twenty. A brother, a loved companion, had taken his life, returned his entrance ticket to God, in that phrase of Dostoevski's Aldous was to use again; a brother had hanged himself. Where does it leave one? Englishmen did not talk about such things.

To Gervas, Aldous wrote a few days after, a seven-line letter:

There is—apart from the sheer grief of the loss—an added pain in the cynicism of the situation. It is just the highest and best in Trev—his ideals—which have driven him to his death . . . Trev was not strong, but he had the courage to face life with ideals—and his ideals were too much for him.

Some weeks later, in a letter to Jelly d'Aranyi,[1] Aldous let go a little. He spoke of his father—he is better now. "he was most terribly broken for a time". He spoke of his sister—she is still so much of a child in some ways, "and I am glad for her sake, because it has saved her from fully realizing the whole tragedy". (Here Aldous did not know enough. When Julian went to America, Trev, in Margaret Huxley's own words,[2] became "the be-all and end-all of my life, and his death was far more shattering to me than my mother's, strange and even unnatural as that may sound . . . Trev was, I think, the hub of the family wheel . .") Aldous spoke of himself—"I . . am sitting . . here in the room that Trev and I used to share together,

where every book and every picture helps to keep alive the memories —which, though they bring a terrible sadness with them, are always of a past time that has been very happy.

It is of that one ought to think, of the past, and one ought to be grateful and thankful for all the years one has spent with one who was among the noblest and best of men—but Oh God, it's bitter sometimes to sit in this room reading before the fire—alone and to think of all the happy evenings we sat there together and all the hours I hoped to have again, when he was better. It's a selfish grief perhaps, but oh Jelly, you know what he was to me.

[1] The violinist; a great friend of the Huxley family, a girl then in her early twenties.

[2] Margaret Huxley, letter to S. B., 1969.

## Chapter Seven
## Return to Oxford

"WHEN we broke off for the long vacation, none of us took the slightest interest in world politics, none of us took the slightest thought . . imagined a future with a war."[1]

Aldous went back to Oxford in October 1914. *Everybody had gone.* Balliol was deserted. "One enlisted at once. We all did. We just disappeared . . ."[1]

Not only had we physically gone, we were mentally gone—one had to cut out Oxford completely in order to survive . . . start an entirely new life in the war. You had to make yourself forget about your friends, that was one of the awful things; we didn't dare to think, you had to train yourself to live wholly in the day.[1]

And there was Aldous, there he was left, his friends gone, the life gone. He was cut off abruptly, for the second time, became again a stranger to the world of contemporary experience. That second isolation must have been a very bitter thing.

"He told me quite a bit about it," Gervas said, "that day I went to France and he saw me off, December I think it was, December 1914 . . ."

Gervas was passing through London on his way to Grimsby to take a draft of his regiment to France. Unasked, Aldous was waiting for him at Paddington. They spent the day together.

"He was terribly anxious, you know, about practical matters—had I got enough warm clothes? He was thinking much more about me than about himself that day."

They bought a Shetland shawl together at the Army & Navy Stores. Aldous did say how much he missed his friends, how *awful* Balliol was now with *nobody* there. He still hoped, he said, not to get actually into the Army but into some kind of war work that he could do.

No, no, he didn't think of himself as lucky—far from it. I think he was feeling rather envious, in the way you do when all your friends are doing something and you can't.

1 Gervas Huxley, talking.

They said goodbye on the platform at King's Cross. Gervas holding this thought in his mind: if one survived one would never need to bother about one's communications with Aldous—"there was something imperishable there".

And then, presumably, Aldous walked out of the station, crossed London, took another train and went back to Oxford.

I spoke to Sir George Clark, the man who had been Aldous's tutor and his friend, who had seen the gay intelligent schoolboy, as it were before the fall, talking at Oxford to his elders. I asked him if he could imagine an Aldous unmarked by the events of those six years. What had they done to him? Sir George used one word. "He was—impaired."

# PART THREE

## The Hard Years: 1914-1921

". . I must say I am amazed that I did get through as much as I did. It must obviously have been rather tiring, this whole process—but I managed to do it."

ALDOUS HUXLEY

# Chapter One

## "The Quiet Life of Anglo Saxon Lectures"

THROUGHOUT his life we have sudden views, *momentanés* as it were, of Aldous imprinted at points in time on the minds of alert observers. At Oxford that winter a woman undergraduate saw him listening at lectures. He always stood; he took no notes.

> One day the then Prince of Wales was sitting in a row above me, and he did not write notes either; a student near him leant forward and offered him a pencil which was gratefully accepted. But behind me was Mr Huxley standing near a pillar by the doorway against the window just listening to the lecture.

"I have always remembered him standing against that pillar, alone and detached, neatly dressed."[1]


Aldous had not returned to his rooms in college and was living with the Haldanes in their house, Cherwell Edge, in north Oxford. "It is nicer, I think, being here than in an empty Balliol. They are very nice people I am staying with."

The Haldanes looked after him with some anxiety but Aldous, who turns out to have been the least neurotic of men, went his way mildly melancholy, resolutely cheerful, always contained.

He had a large room next to the schoolroom where he played the piano for long hours by himself. Again he was looking after Naomi's literary education. "And while I was learning," she said, "he was picking up science from my father." For the present he was making no new men friends; "The last able-bodied British undergraduates", wrote T. S. Eliot,

> were passing from the O.T.C. to the trenches, and beyond the Rhodes scholars from America and the Commonwealth there were hardly any left except those who like Aldous were wholly unfit for military service.[2]

"Practically speaking [Aldous to Julian] Sligger and myself are the only possibles left alive in Oxford; [Tiddy, his own tutor,

---

1 Miss M. Marshall in a letter to S. B.
2 T. S. Eliot, *Mem. Vol.*; T. S. E. and Aldous did not meet that term at Oxford.

is already in the war and soon to be killed] even the few possibilities of last term have now vanished . . . Meanwhile, the quiet
life of Anglo Saxon lectures amid a crowd of painful young
women."

He tried to enlist himself but was of course rejected by every
recruiting office. Aldous's attitude to the war at that particular
time, that year in Rupert Brooke's England when one's friends
"were going off to war with their noble young heads in the air",
was neither original nor extreme. He easily spoke of Boches and
Huns though never quite without his pinch of detachment.

> It is, of course, axiomatic that the Germans are lying . . but still,
> it is for the historian of 2000 to settle that question, for us to ex-
> tirpate the vipers.

And only a few months later, in April 1915,

> This hustling of aliens is rather damnable—mob-law . . [the
> Government] betrays mere feeble-mindedness to drift on the stream
> of popular passion. We are losing our heads and our sense of humour.

Meanwhile he worked. Now on Milton—his special subject—
now on "the mediaeval creatures—terrible people, who never
wrote anything less than an epic". Oh yes, he writes to his old
headmaster at Hillside, there *is* backbone to what is called the
mere reading of literature.

> "Back bone" here at Oxford is provided by the Anglo Saxon branch
> of the school . . . considerably more difficult than Greek . . . and
> the literature obscure and dull.

How bored poor Aldous was! All the same he persevered with
the "nauseous diet of Anglo Saxon", went through the mass of
excruciatingly dull—and for him painful and laborious—reading.
And at the same time he read a great deal for his own pleasure
and instruction.

> Actually I think that the most exciting people I read as an under-
> graduate were French writers . . . I had my introduction to French
> literature at that time. I read Proust when he first came out in 1914,
> *Du Côté de chez Swann,* and I read the French poets then—Mallarmé
> made an *immense* impression upon me.

One should hear his voice—lingering over the word *immense*, giving
every consonant its value.

And still *does*. I am still very fond of him. And Rimbaud made an *immense* impression on me then.[1]

## How did he manage it?

"Well, every handicap is of course a challenge." In that long recorded interview Aldous gave in London to John Chandos fifty years later on, he spoke about it. Lightly, in that serene, clear voice, he said,

> I mean one is limited to what one can do. I was strictly limited in all kinds of otherwise normal activities; many things that I liked doing, like mountain climbing and so on, became difficult or impossible for me. I couldn't practise any kind of sport requiring a ball, because [and his voice rises in a characteristic curve] because I couldn't *see* the balls.
>
> On the other hand . . if the handicap isn't too great and overwhelming, it can also stimulate one to do things which in other circumstances one wouldn't do . . .
>
> I *did* read a great deal. And I am extremely astonished at how much I was able to read. Because . . for about two years after this thing came upon me . . I couldn't read at all. Well, little by little I was able to read again—but I did all my reading while I was at Oxford with a powerful magnifying glass—I must say I am amazed that I did get through as much as I did. It must obviously have been rather tiring, this whole process: but *I managed to do it*.

[1] London interview, 1961.

## Chapter Two

## A Young Man on His Own

NOT only reading—writing. Typing away, bent over his small portable on his knees: "I discovered that I liked writing, and that I had a certain gift for it."

Aldous wrote mostly verse that second year at Oxford. He wrote and translated French verse and pastiche, he competed for the Newdigate Prize (which he failed to get) with a long Byronic poem on Glastonbury. He also tried his hand at prose, writing his first short stories, among them that curious "Eupompus Gave Splendour to Art by Numbers", and of course he wrote the required essays for his tutor.

I must say [the London interview again] I was interested not long ago in looking over old volumes . . They were on all sorts of literary subjects, I mean from Chaucer down to the present day, and I was interested and surprised to find that well, I mean I was writing quite well at the time—I had a certain feeling for style, there was even a certain elegance in what I was doing at the age of twenty.

Aldous added,

I had obviously some kind of natural gift for writing.

"Home-Sickness—From the Town" was published that year in *Oxford Poetry*. As it is Aldous's first (adult) poem in print and has, to my knowledge, never been re-published, it might be worth quoting here as it is typical of one side of early Aldous and of what he liked to do with words when he was young.

> *Frou-Frouery and faint patchouli smells,*
> *And debile virgins talking Keats,*
> *And the arch widow in accordion pleats,*
> *Artfully fringing with the tales she tells*
> *The giggling prurient.*
> *Life nauseous! Let the whole crowd be sent*
> *To the chosen limbos and appropriate hells*
> *Reserved in memory's blackest stagnancy.*
> *Back, back! No Social Contract! From the teats*
> *Of our old wolfish mother nature drink*
> *Sweet unrestraint and lust and savagery.*

*Feel goat-hair growing thick and redolent*
*On loin and thigh; look back*
*And mark the cloven hoof-marks of the track*
*You leave, then forward eyes again; no wink,*
*Lest for an instant you should miss the sight*
*Of moony floating flanks and haunches white*
*Flashed by your fleeing nymph girl through the leaves.*

Naomi still wanted kisses. Indeed, she wanted Aldous to become her lover and told him so. Aldous refused to do anything of the kind. "I think it was his principles."

What were his principles?

Aldous—according to Gervas, and one can well imagine it— was gaily outspoken as a boy and, unlike poor Trev, without prudishness. They used to rag each other about mythical attachments to smaller pretty boys and to Prior's Field girls; at Oxford Aldous joined in the singing of Jack Haldane's extremely bawdy songs. As to actual behaviour,

> Aldous and I had the same code that while one might cherish a romantic love for somebody (I had one for Naomi in 1914!) it all remained purely platonic—no kissing or necking—one cherished from afar (pleasantly, too) but that one only declared one's love or attempted a closer attachment with a girl of one's own class if one proposed marriage and one only did this if one was in a position to marry.

So much for the temporal and explicit. On other levels there is the post-Victorian childhood (which, however, does not appear to have been troubled by the corrupt governesses of Aldous's fiction—Fräulein Ella was no Fräulein Lili[1]); there is Aldous's temperament and physique: the fastidiousness, the sensitiveness, the intense physiological response, the "almost frantic sensuality" of the extreme Sheldonian ectomorph. There is the effect of Trevenen's death and its immediate cause. There is the latent dichotomy between his indulgent, ironical, consciously *dix-huitième* taking to sensuality and his sense, stressed mostly in his writing, of Swiftian and Baudelairian horror.

On a non-verbal level Aldous was extremely susceptible to pretty women. If the girls sought him, it was not least because principles or no principles he was naturally responsive. ("Happily, as I fall in love with every woman I meet . . at any rate

---

[1] Fräulein Lili, a character in the fragment of an unfinished novel by A. H. published in Laura Archera Huxley's *This Timeless Moment*.

with the better women I meet . . ."[1]) Yet Gervas, who would
be the one man to know, thought that Aldous had no serious
love affair or attachment before the 1914 war. There was one
incident (again, only Gervas knew about it) which should be told
to lay the legend of Aldous Huxley the helpless, hopeless, tentative
young man who got it all out of books. It happened in the summer
of 1913, shortly before Aldous went to Grenoble. For some reason
he was alone in the Westbourne Square house. He went out for
a stroll and he picked up a girl (who was, he thought, an au pair
girl on her evening off) and took her home and made love to her
on the sofa. He told Gervas that what had most impressed,
excited and surprised him was the eagerness of the girl's approach
and embraces. ("You must remember that in those days one
imagined that the eagerness only came from the man.")

Aldous was reading Jacob Boehme then, and Blake. "Well, I
was always interested in the descriptions and philosophies of the
mystical life," he said in the London interview; "I read a fair
amount [about it] at the time—with a mixture of admiration and
hostility."

(John Chandos, his interviewer, then asked him, "Mr Huxley,
at that time you regarded mystical experience, I imagine, with
derision?" And Aldous replied mildly, "Not with *derision* but with
a good deal of scepticism. And with a good deal of fascinated
interest.")

During those war years, Aldous's letters were more outgoing
than they became. He was young, he was alone, he was not as
yet a professional writer who must monger words for his daily
bread. He often wrote to Jelly d'Aranyi, the young violinist,
young but slightly older, to whom he had been able to write
about Trevenen. Oxford that June was hot and damp; it was the
time of the long casualty lists, of bad news every day . . . At the
end of the Trinity term Aldous escaped to his step-mother's house
on the west coast of Scotland . .

> I know nothing more beautiful than this place, with its beautifully
> shaped mountains, its great lochs . . and glimpses of broad seas . . .
> These evenings are so wonderfully peaceful—
> > Les lacs éperdus des longs couchants défunts . . .
> It all helps to mellow the thought that one's friends are being killed,
> into a quiet kind of resigned sadness.

[1] From a letter to Lewis Gielgud 29th September 1916.

It is a curious letter—so different in style and mood from his contemporary verse—with its intimations of his future quest.

> One does feel tremendously that one is part of a larger soul, which embraces everything . . . But then again . . when I get back among all the wretchedness of the town it is impossible to recognize this splendid unity.
>
> It looks as though the amount of good and evil were about the same in the world. I think the good will probably win in the end—though not necessarily, unless the most persistent and tremendous efforts are made . . . I'm not a pessimist, and I think it will be all right. I think we shall ultimately work all the disorder into a single principle, which will be an Absolute—but which at present exists only potentially and at the nature of which we can only very dimly guess.

A few weeks later, in London in his father's house, Aldous came of age. "Well, I'm twenty-one today—grown up." Later on he wrote again to Jelly d'Aranyi:

> . . This war impresses on me more than ever the fact that friendship, love, whatever you like to call it is the only reality . . . You never knew my mother—I wish you had because she was a very wonderful woman: Trev was most like her. I have just been reading again what she wrote to me just before she died. The last words of her letter were "Don't be too critical of other people and 'love much' "—and I have come to see more and more how wise that advice was. It's a warning against a rather conceited and selfish fault of my own and it's a whole philosophy of life.

58

# Chapter Three

## Starting Points

AFTER a family summer spent mostly at Westbourne Square and Prior's Field, Aldous went back to Oxford for his third and last year. Naomi Haldane was having scarlet fever and so he moved back into Balliol; "to a nice room in the new building—airy and light," and finds living in college again "very nice in some ways, but rather sad too".

Yet Oxford was brightening up. "It's a very curious place now," he writes to his father, "there are a good many (relatively) nice people, most of them oddities of one kind or another—aesthetic, exotically religious and the like."

He joined a small club which met once a week to read members' poems, where he met Eric Dodds, later Regius Professor of Greek; Roland Childe, Roy Campbell and above all Tommy Earp,[1] a rich and eccentric young man who like Aldous was fond of French poetry and strange stories about people. They became great friends. And there was Russell Green, another eccentric, the future author of the novel *Prophet Without Honour*. It was he who had won the Newdigate, for which Aldous had competed, with a poem on Venice. From that moment, Green maintains, Aldous developed an affectionate attitude towards him. He was a classical scholar at Queen's and had also won the Chancellor's English Essay prize of 1915. "Thus," he writes, "for a brief space Aldous and I ran neck and neck . . . Alas, how widely our paths diverged." By Green we have another of those *momentanés*.

Aldous was highly sensitive to the faintest hint of feminine allure . . . Once in Oxford we were lunching with Tommy Earp at a seat separated from the waitresses, who were dishing up food, by a screen of some soft material draped from a rail six feet high down to the floor. When, in my insatiable curiosity, I lifted it up with my left hand (what a memory I have!) Aldous sniggered, since it suggested to him the lifting of a skirt.

That term, L. P. Hartley fit for home service and waiting to be called up, had rooms on the same staircase. There he heard Aldous typing away, playing the piano, declaiming to himself

---

[1] The late T. W. Earp; his father was a Liberal M.P. for Newark and member of the firm of maltsters, Gilstrap, Earp & Co.

"To a Coy Mistress." "I loved his voice." Then Aldous asked him to cocoa—"quite a fashionable drink in those diminished days. Aldous talked of T. S. Eliot; the first time I had heard of him.

> I had never known anyone like Aldous. His voice, his rangy height, his elegant clothes, his noble white brow, crowned with a patch of unruly black hair, his mysterious rather glaucous eyes . . peering through the oblong magnifying glass he used when he was reading —these left an ineffable impression. Culture had found a mortal envelope worthy of itself.[1]

"I had an amusing day on Sunday—going out to Garsington for luncheon to the Philip Morrells, who have bought the lovely Elizabethan manor there." So wrote Aldous casually to his father that December. When one is young, any encounter may be a starting, a turning point; we half expect this, yet run into it blindly. Aldous had been brought over to Garsington by Desmond MacCarthy and introduced as the grandson of T. H. Huxley.

> Lady Ottoline, Philip's wife [he went on in that letter], is a quite incredible creature—arty beyond the dreams of avarice and a patroness of literature and the modernities. She is intelligent, but her affectation is overwhelming.

There is another record of that casual Sunday. Juliette Baillot's, as she was then, young and Swiss and living at Garsington as part-time student at Oxford and governess-companion to the Morrells' little girl, Julian. "Then Aldous came. Very silent, very young.

> . . His six foot four seemed even taller because of the slenderness of his body and his slight stoop. Under the thick brown hair, his wide face was pale with full lips and blue eyes which had an inward look . . . He did not talk much at his first visit, but as soon as he was gone, everyone agreed about the deep impression of unique quality, of gentleness and depth.[2]

One of the immediate consequences was Lady Ottoline's writing to D. H. Lawrence to suggest that he should meet Aldous. D. H. L., who was living at Hampstead with Frieda, wrote a note asking Aldous to tea. Aldous went.

---

[1] L. P. Hartley, talking on a B.B.C. broadcast 17th August 1964.
[2] Juliette (Lady) Huxley, in *Mem. Vol.*

The place was London, the time 1915. But Lawrence's passionate talk was of the geographically remote and the personally very near. Of the horrors in the middle distance—war, winter, the town—he would not speak. For he was on the point, or so he imagined, of setting off to Florida—to Florida, where he was going to plant that colony of escape of which to the last he never ceased to dream . . . That wintry afternoon it was Florida. Before tea was over he asked me if I would join the colony, and though I was an intellectually cautious young man, not at all inclined to enthusiasms, though Lawrence had startled and embarrassed me with sincerities of a kind to which my upbringing had not accustomed me, I answered yes.[1]

So Aldous wrote fifteen years after the event. In that actual wintry month of 1915, he described the meeting to Julian with the same blend of recognition and aloofness.

. . One D. H. Lawrence, a novelist . . . whose recent work *The Rainbow* was regrettably burnt by the common hangman for obscenity . . . well, this good man, who impresses me as a good man more than most, proposes . . to go to the deserts of Florida with one Armenian [Michael Arlen], one German wife and, problematically, one young woman called Dorothy Warren . . to await a sort of Pentecostal inspiration of new life, which, whether it will come is another question. But Lawrence is a great man, and as he finds the world too destructive for his taste, he must, I suppose be allowed to get out of it . . .

D. H. L. himself, again in that same December, added a postscript of one line to a letter to Lady Ottoline Morrell.

I liked Huxley *very* much. He will come to Florida.

The scheme fell through. Cities of God, in Aldous's words, have always crumbled.

[1] A. H. in the preface to *The Letters of D. H. Lawrence.* Heinemann, 1932.

## Chapter Four

# "The Artificial Roses of Academic Distinction"

ALDOUS'S last winter and spring at Oxford were full and strenuous. He had decided to compete for the Stanhope Historical Essay prize (theme, The Development of Political Satire in England from the Restoration to the Revolution), and was doing his reading in Bodley which they kept, he said, so hideously stuffy that it was hardly possible to stop going to sleep.

Meanwhile conscription had come in and he had to present himself to get classified. He was declared totally unfit.

He went over to Garsington quite often now and was meeting people. "The strange creature Lytton Strachey," and Barbara Hiles, his friend of the caterpillar hunts at Prior's Field, "delightfully cheerful and irresponsible as ever—with her hair still close-cut and curly and gold, gipsy-like rings in her ears." Juliette Baillot he asked to tea with him at Balliol; she came bringing little Julian Morrell.

> His room was long, rather dark, a curious room, almost like a corridor. He was very gentle with the child and talked more easily to her than he did to Ottoline.

Aldous gave them China tea and crumpets, and recited Carroll and Edward Lear.

Tommy Earp put up the money and he and Aldous were getting out their own literary review, the *Palatine*, and were drumming up subscriptions. (3/6d. a year, six numbers, and already thirty-six paid-up subscribers.) The first issue came out in February 1916 and contained Aldous's poem "Mole" and three other poems.

> *Tunnelled in solid blackness creeps*
> *The old mole-soul, and wakes or sleeps,*
> *He knows not which, but tunnels on*
> *Through ages of oblivion. . . .*

The editor of the *Nation*, H. W. Massingham, wrote to say how much he liked "Mole" and asked Aldous to send some poems to the new quarterly *Form*.

Aldous had mistakenly supposed that the Stanhope essay had to be in by 31st March. On 22nd February, late in the shortest month, he discovered that the date was 1st March—"and not a word written". On top of it he had neuralgia and a cold. "I never spent a more beastly week." He made the dead-line.

That exertion was followed almost at once by terminal exams in early March, "nightmarish collections in Anglo Saxon—that loathsome language is a nuisance beyond all words".

Julian Huxley was considering returning from America to England and the war. Aldous wrote him that he could not help thinking that it would be unwise to come home.

There is very little to be done unless one means to fight—and in these days when one can't get commissions it is impossible to fight with that elegance and efficiency which in the old days, as an officer, were within one's reach. Work in munitions factories is intolerable [because of systematic overworking] . . Government departments are sometimes interesting but of a fearful strenuity.

For his own part he had thought of going into the Foreign Press department of the War Office last winter but had found that 12-14 hours work a day was normal so that it "would have been quite beyond my ocular abilities to stand the strain.

The longer this war goes on, the more one loathes and detests it. At the beginning I should have liked very much to fight; but now if I could (having seen all the results), I think I'd be a conscientious objector, or nearly so.

In May Aldous went into training for his Oxford finals. "Three hours of strenuous writing this afternoon [doing papers under examination conditions] . . . I fear I have not the Bensonian faculty of writing 1500 words an hour—600 is about my exam rate."

And in June Finals are upon him. The papers were bad, he found, bad and stupid. An uninteresting paper on Chaucer, an uninteresting one on Shakespeare, and the history of literature one a disgrace to the University. As for himself:

I am in the middle of Schools—which I find more tiring than any labour I have ever undertaken. Not only is the mental strain great, but the physical strain on the eyes—even using a typewriter . . . I stagger out . . feeling as if I had been bruised all over.

Meanwhile he heard that he had "picked off the Stanhope . . quite unexpectedly . . for it was a shoddy piece of work, my essay".

It was a comfort though, "even if one does badly in Schools". The prize was £20 in books. "Regrettably—one would have preferred the naked cash."

Aldous did not do badly in Schools. He got a first in English. "Well, Oxford is over," he wrote to Julian.

Crowned with the artificial roses of academic distinction, I stagger, magnificently drunk with youthful conceit, into the symposium, not of philosophers, but of apes and wolves and swine . . . No more of the sheltered, the academic life . . the life, which, I believe, when led by a man of high and independent spirit, is the fullest and the best of lives, though one of the most bedraggled and wretched as led by the ordinary crew of bovine intellectuals.

I should like to go on for ever learning. I lust for knowledge, as well theoretic as empirical. Comparing small things with great, I think I am rather like the incomparable John Donne.

# Chapter Five

## Prospects

"WHAT I'm going to do—God knows."

It was expected as a matter of course that Aldous must earn his living. Earn it at once, what's more, as his allowance ceased as soon as he was down from Oxford.

The scientific career he had wanted was out of the question, as he could not have used a microscope or done any of the laboratory work. As for writing, his poems and short stories were seeing the light of print in periodicals such as *Oxford Poetry* and the *Palatine* and he had a book of verse coming out in the autumn; yet writing as a profession, if he did have it in mind, was not an immediate prospect. "The solution of the HEIRESS presents itself," he wrote to Julian. ". . Of the more repulsive solutions two main ones appear. (*a*) To disseminate mendacity in our Great Modern Press. (*b*) To disseminate mendacity in our Great Modern Public Schools." And indeed in July, having hardly left Oxford ("a wrench, so personal has it become"), after only five pleasant days in London, Aldous found himself translated—"I am very much alone and at times depressed"—to Repton. His predecessor, he suspected, had been sacked, and the headmaster, G. F. Fisher,[1] had asked Aldous to fill the post till the end of term.

> I am in quite pleasant digs [he wrote to his father], the job—teaching Latin, history and English to the lower forms—is quite interesting. The boys know nil and so whatever I manage to teach them will be pure gain.

Rather a waste, he felt though, teaching on the strength of Pass Mods when one has a first in English. He must look for a university job. To his young friend Frances Petersen,[2] he admitted that though the boys are very well behaved, "the masters—what a set of Calibans . . . It really is too utterly bloody living alone. To bed, to bed! I have to get up at 6.30!" To Julian he wrote about his need for friends,

> How essential to one. I am utterly stranded and wretched without them.

[1] The future Archbishop of Canterbury.
[2] Frances Petersen, a granddaughter of P. W. Henderson, Warden of Wadham College, then a young girl at Oxford.

Term, however, will be over by the end of the month. And after Repton, *what*? He has quarrelled with Rugby, somewhat to his relief, and he doesn't want any of the other jobs he has been offered. But what to do? "I cannot even play the clarinet outside public houses." Perhaps he will go and hoe the ground somewhere. "I have a belief that it would be very good for one . . better than schoolmastering at any rate."

In August: summer holidays and return to civilization. First a week at Garsington—"hectically talking after the enforced silence of Repton . . . talking with intelligent people." The interlude has been even more amusing than usual; but he will not describe his adventures. "They are always peculiar." At least they make one forget the hollowness of existence, ". . a hollowness I find particularly reverberant when I come to regard my future prospects. Damn them!"

On to Prior's Field, boring but placid, where the days "slide away, as rapid and elusive as macaroni from the corners of an Englishman's mouth," but where he hopes to do some writing.

The *Nation* had published three of Aldous's poems, but by mistake over the signature of Leonard Huxley, who, Aldous says, received a letter from A. C. Benson congratulating him on the extreme beauty of his verse. "And now wherever my father goes showers of felicitations fall upon him." However, it is Aldous who is paid, gratifyingly, a guinea a piece—"I think I shall write an ode to money."

In September he is back in London and has made up his mind about the future. He will hoe the ground "or rather like G. Washington cut down . . trees, for it is, they seem to think, as a forester that I am going to function upon that curious and utterly unknown quantity, THE LAND". But it will be on the farm of his very dear friends the Morrells and the experience should be pleasing.

Aldous's first book came out in September. *The Burning Wheel*, a volume of poetry. "A tomelet of fifty pages and on every page a deceased personality," he wrote to Julian; "one changes, grows with the rapidity of one of those amorphophallic tropical fungi." These are a very young man's protestations, yet Aldous was to prove himself more capable of changing than most men; at the same time there was also a continuous thread and one may find it here already.

> *Wearied of its own turning,*
> *Distressed with its own busy restlessness,*

*Yearning to draw the circumferent pain—*
*The rim that is dizzy with speed—*
*To the motionless centre, there to rest,*
*The wheel must strain through agony*
*On agony contracting, returning*
*Into the core of steel.*
. . . . . . . . . . . . . .
. . . . . . . . . . . . . .
. . . . . . . . *the wheel that yearns—*
*Sick with its speed—for the terrible stillness*
*Of the adamant core* . . . . . . . . . . . [1]

*The Burning Wheel* is the verse of a young man who—after private tragedy—had to begin life in 1914, and is charged with a sense of the moral and physical suicide of the world.

> The West has plucked its flowers and has thrown
> Them fading on the night.[1]

A recurrent theme—as again in *The Defeat of Youth,* the second collection of Aldous's wartime poems—is the defeat of hope. The verse reflects scepticism, revulsion, longings. Much of it is clever, intricate, allusive, much is gruesome, deliberately appalling; there is also another and less well-remembered strain. I am transcribing "The Canal", one of his sonnets, for its lyrical and visual quality.

> No dip and dart of swallows wakes the black
> Slumber of the canal: —a mirror dead
> For lack of loveliness remembered
> From ancient azures and green trees, for lack
> of some white beauty given and flung back,
> Secret, to her that gave: no sun has bled
> To wake an echo here of answering red;
> The surface stirs to no leaf's wind-blown track.
>
> Between unseeing walls the waters rest,
> Lifeless and hushed, till suddenly a swan
> Glides from some broader river blue as day,
> And with the mirrored magic of his breast
> Creates within that barren water-way
> New life, new loveliness, and passes on.[1]

[1] From *The Burning Wheel,* republished in *The Collected Poetry of Aldous Huxley.* Chatto & Windus, 1970.

At the time of publication Aldous wrote to Lewis Gielgud (back from the war and wounded) that he was so nauseated by the sight of his own poems that he had not had the strength to cut a copy.

Reviews appeared in due course. The one in *The Times* "pleasantly offensive", the one in the *Morning Post* quite pleasing. "They make me out very distinguished. Don't they?"

## Chapter Six

## "The Extraordinary Good Fortune"

ALDOUS'S statement that he was off to grapple with that unknown quantity the land was misleading. Garsington, his "dear friends' household", is now part of English social and literary history.

We have heard about and read about the moderate-sized Elizabethan manor house six miles from Oxford, we have read about Lady Ottoline Morrell, we have read about the house parties and the men and women who were the guests: Bertrand Russell, Asquith, Maynard Keynes, Lytton Strachey, D. H. Lawrence, Virginia Woolf, T. S. Eliot, Clive Bell and Roger Fry, Katherine Mansfield and John Middleton Murry, Duncan Grant, Mark Gertler, Siegfried Sassoon, Robert Graves . . . We have read their works and about their works, read their biographies and autobiographies, their diaries and their letters. We know that the severity of the intellectual atmosphere was lightened by the presence of young girls—Brett and Carrington, Mary Hutchinson, Juliette Baillot—and that in the early days there was a heady sense of freedom.

> . . Of nights [Aldous about one of his summer weeks at Garsington] I have been sleeping out on the roof in company with an artistic young woman in short hair and purple pyjamas . . . spending most of the night in conversation or in singing folk-songs and rag-time to the stars . . . while early in the morning we would be wakened by a gorgeous great peacock howling like a damned soul while he stalked about the tiles showing off his plumage to the sunrise.

In his maturity he spoke of Garsington as an education.

> I had the extraordinary fortune to meet a great many of the ablest people of my time. There were the Bloomsbury people . . . There was Virginia and Vanessa, there was Maynard Keynes . . *He* was always facinating—he had this immense range of knowledge, and he would come out with these *curiously* elliptical remarks about things: he was a very fascinating character . . . Russell I met then, and Roger Fry—from whom I learnt a *great deal* about art—well, he remains a very good art critic, I mean he had extraordinary sensibility and great knowledge, and enthusiasms; and he was a genuinely *good* man, as well as immensely charming and interesting.

He was very kind to me. And then Clive Bell—*he* was always extremely stimulating and very kind to me—from them, I learnt a great deal about art which I really didn't know anything about at all before. They introduced me to modern art, to Post-Impressionism, Cubism and so on . . .

The meeting of all these people was of capital importance to me.[1]

Lady Ottoline told him to read *War and Peace*; he met T. S. Eliot (what struck him was the contrast between the works and the man—"just an Europeanized American, overwhelmingly cultured, talking about French literature in the most uninspiring fashion imaginable"[2]).

. . And all this happened at the house of Lady Ottoline Morrell. . . .[1]

Lady Ottoline. How much recognition she has had, and how much abuse. She did a great deal, for the young, the unorthodox, the talented (whose talents she did recognize: on her own, early on); she helped young men who were making a stand against the war; she tried to help Lawrence and Frieda; she took young Aldous under her wing. She inspired some love, less loyalty, little gratitude. Aldous described her (though only at first shock) as affected beyond wildest dreams; she was naturally, congenitally, aristocratic and eccentric to an outrageous degree. Her appearance, and her presentation of it, loomed large. No-one who has known her will forget it, nor the extraordinary voice, the modulated, entirely unselfconscious Boom. The Augustus John portrait reveals her admirably. One must recall that she was immensely tall with an elongated, huge Elizabethan face, Elizabethan with a touch of Aubrey Beardsley, heavily made up, sometimes in haste, topped with a great mass of high coiffure. She exaggerated her height by heels and elevators in her shoes—a towering figure with immense poise. Sometimes grotesque, she could be very beautiful in her strange grand way. Then there were the startling clothes, the enormous pearls, badly strung and kept.

Her dresses were made by her maid.[3] Ottoline went and had a look at fashion shows in London or Paris or Venice and then described what she thought she had seen. She deviated on purpose, she did not follow the fashions. She always wore longer dresses. And there were those wide hats with georgette veils in different colours flowing behind her.

Juliette Baillot had come to Garsington through an agency, meeting the Morrells by appointment in the first-class waiting-

---

[1] London interview, 1961.  [2] *Letters.*
[3] Juliette (Lady) Huxley, talking.

room at Oxford station. (They nearly missed meeting at all, one party having gone to the waiting-room on the Up platform, the other to the Down platform.) Philip Morrell said nothing at all, Lady Ottoline talked of the horrors of war. No one asked for credentials from the future governess. "They just took me on."

She arrived (by pony trap with her trunk)—and there was the perfect stone house and the forecourt flanked by immense yew hedges. She was shown straight into the big drawing-room, the red room:

> Well, it was a fantastic room. It was painted Chinese red—the little square Tudor panellings were all painted red, and the grooves were gilt. There were yellow and flame-coloured curtains framing the tall windows, gold and salmon Samarkand rugs, Chinese lacquer cabinets, black and gold, logs burning in the stone fireplace . . .[1]

The dining gallery and the smaller drawing-room were painted turquoise green; there was a pianola in the hall and an Italian cassone with dressing-up clothes, enormous armchairs in shiny chintz and a vague scent of incense and pot-pourri. The furniture was Philip's and inherited; the paint, the gilt, the colours were Lady Ottoline's. Her taste and most of her appreciations were her own. Many say that she was intelligent; she was generous and often very kind. She also gave a sense of some vicarious avidity —for art, for those who were able to produce it—that made people feel that she was not a happy woman. In the succinct wording of Brett,[2] "Lady Ottoline was a very strange woman with a heart of gold and a yen for men." Brett was evoked by Aldous in *Crome Yellow* in the character of Jenny, the disquietening secretive observer, who "sat apart looking down at the world through piercingly sharp eyes. What did she think of men and women and things?"

What Lady Ottoline's heart prompted was often resented rather than appreciated. For instance she was always crocheting for the Garsington poor—great counterpanes made up of bits of bright wools, which they were given for Christmas and which they hated. One year she made a counterpane for Lawrence. He hated it too; in fact, he was deeply offended, saying that Ottoline treated him like one of the poor. She had thought that he would like the colours.

Aldous guyed her later on in *Those Barren Leaves*. Not consistently: her trappings served as a point de départ and soon deviated into fiction. Nevertheless there was a grain or two of

[1] Juliette Huxley, *Mem. Vol.* and talking.
[2] The Hon. Dorothy Brett, in a letter to S. B., 1969.

truth—Lady Ottoline, like Mrs Aldwinkle, had sometimes bought the stars.

Garsington was anti-war. Philip Morrell, Liberal M.P. for Burnley, was one of the few men in public life who spoke up against it. He and Lady Ottoline made Garsington a refuge for some extremely civilized conscientious objectors. On the home farm—run by Philip with loving care—men like Bertrand Russell, Clive Bell and Gerald Shove, the Cambridge scholars, were able to do the agricultural work they had been sentenced to by the tribunals without too great a break in their mental and physical habits.

So there was "Bertie Russell with his laugh like a crazy horse and his dominating ego [this *is* what Jenny saw] commanding all attention"; there was Clive Bell, "kind-hearted with a noisy voice whom the farmers loved though he never did a lick of work, giving birthday cakes to the farmers' wives"; there were the Bloomsberries who "would sweep down at weekends with their superiority—Duncan Grant nearly cut his foot off dancing the sword dance"; there was Katherine Mansfield "afraid of the Bloomberries, cautious and withdrawn"; Juliette Baillot, "very young, and beyond words charming"; Ottoline's little girl, Julian, "a beautiful child," and Philip, "always admirably dressed, trying to look like Lord Ribblesdale. . . ."[1]

[1] The Hon. Dorothy Brett, in a letter to S. B., 1969.

## Chapter Seven

# Aldous at Garsington

AND there was Aldous. He lived in the house (the C.O.s. lived in cottages on the estate). He had breakfast on the lawn with Ottoline, Juliette and little Julian, and afterwards took up his axe and went off to work.

Inside the week the household was quiet, no Bloomberries, no sword dances, no rag-time on the roof. Philip was in Parliament or at agricultural sales; Lady Ottoline spent the mornings in her tower room keeping up her diary; Julian did lessons with Juliette. At noon they bathed in the pool which was always bitter cold —Ottoline in pink jersey and Greek tunic, stately, ignoring the cold, stepping forth into the water. Aldous, diligently in the woods, did not appear.

> He has dressed himself—fastidiously—according to his new status. He wore corduroy breeches, they were jodhpurs, fawn-coloured, with yellow stockings, brogues and a corduroy jacket. The jacket was dark-brown and he always had a charming coloured tie which he chose himself. Sometimes Ottoline brought him back a tie from London as a present.
>
> He looked absurdly romantic and beautiful.[1]

For a while Aldous enjoyed Bovarizing himself into a successful woodsman:

> I have been doing my usual wood-cutting [letter to his father]— useful for a house which exclusively uses logs for fuel—and have been lopping a big branch from the huge immemorial ilex in front of the house, sawing it into lengths and splitting them with wedges and beetle into suitable billets.

Yes, he cut down branches, Juliette says, "that was what he *could* do. He did his best." At dusk he would come in exhausted, physically exhausted.

> How very tall he was—even in that big room—with his legs wound round chairs. He just sat, saying nothing.

---

[1] Juliette Huxley, *Mem. Vol.* and talking.

He could be tangibly silent. "I think [Brett writes] he enjoyed embarrassing people with his silences. He told me so."

Exhausted, silent, draped over those armchairs: but observant, immensely observant. Brett was not the only one, hers not the only notebook. Sometimes they joined forces. "He and I [Brett] would sit over the fire in the red room and have what we called a gossip *in camera*. He was moody, always a bit ailing, always scribbling. When he did talk he was brilliant—he was ribald and cynical and brilliant. He was penniless and he was full of ambition. When Julian came down [Julian Huxley, back from America that Autumn, not Julian the little girl] he told me that Aldous was the one genius in the family."

(Julian on that visit fell in love with young Juliette; but that went unnoticed at the time. Except by Brett.)

There was much frost early that winter; Aldous was plagued by colds. He still had to do his reading through a magnifying glass. "I hope Clarke [his oculist] will give me goggles, I shall urge him to .. They w'd simplify things so much." Instead he was promoted to an eye-glass for the time being. He wore this on and off for a number of years; it amused him. "My monocle is very grandiose, but gives me a rather Greco-Roman air of rocococity."

Garsington became animated again at Christmas. "[we performed] a superb play invented by Katherine, improvizing as we went along. It was a huge success with Murry as a Dostoevsky character . . ."

The members of the party as put down by Aldous were, "Murry, Katherine Mansfield, Lytton Strachey, Brett, Carrington, Bertrand Russell and Maria Nys".

## Chapter Eight

## The Beginning

MARIA NYS. A name at the end of a list. Our first sight is through Juliette.

That day she first came to Garsington in the summer of 1915 and walked straight into the red drawing-room, there was Maria—

> On the top of a tall ladder with a little pot of gilt in her hand and a brush, she was outlining a panel—and there she was, very young, sixteen, with her bell hair and the large blue eyes, rather plump— she was plump in those days—quite beautiful . . . She came down, very sweet, shook hands and said hello in French.[1]

She may have been there on the December Sunday when Aldous himself came to Garsington for the first time; she was there when he came again, was there—on and off—when he came to live in the house to work on the land.

There remains now only one earlier mention of her by Aldous —a P.S. to Julian of July 1916,

> I have at last discovered a nice Belgian: wonders will never cease.

Who was this *rara avis*, this Belgian child? Who was she and how did she come to be at Garsington?

Maria Nys, the eldest child of Norbert Nys and Marguerite Baltus, was born on 10th September 1898, at Courtrai in the province of Flanders where her parents lived in substantial bourgeois comfort in a house on the Boulevard Peereboom. The Nyses were prosperous tradespeople who with their numerous relations and connections ruled the roost of the town. Old Monsieur Nys, Maria's grandfather, owned a textile business of which her father and his brothers were partners. The Baltuses— in a rather grand way—were artists. Both families were Catholic. The marriage having been childless for some years, Marguerite Nys undertook to make three pilgrimages; Maria was born after the second. She was dedicated to the Virgin and dressed for some years in blue and white exclusively. Madame Nys in due course gave birth to three more girls.

[1] Juliette Huxley, talking to S. B.

She had been in love with another Nys brother. He married someone else; she took Norbert. Mme Nys had looks—beauty in youth, considerable distinction in old age—and a dominating personality. She was energetic, active, bright; she had interests; she was what is called cultivated, read a great deal and was in fact well-read. Courtrai (Kortrijk) is a Flemish town much given to fat good-natured jokes and jollities—"*Le Courtraisien est de nature taquinne*".[1] Mme Nys, who did not come from that part of the country, felt herself superior. Her own brother, George Baltus, painter and professor of fine arts at the University of Glasgow, was very much regarded as the crème de la crème. His wife, Vivi, who had been a playmate of the Princess Elisabeth of Wittelsbach, the future Queen of the Belgians, was the daughter of "the Rodin of Munich", Adolf von Hildebrand, sculptor, Maecenas, classicist, who had *palazzi* in Munich and Florence where he lived like a Medici giving concerts for the King of Bavaria. Mme Nys's husband, Norbert, liked to spend his time over cards and beer with his friends and brothers. Being kind-hearted and weak, he agreed to leave Courtrai, give up his cosy life and flourishing family business and move to Bellem, a village in East Flanders on the canal between Ghent and Bruges. His father gave him a million gold francs to start a business of his own, a wool business, alas, in a cotton-spinning region—"*Affaire*," his daughter Suzanne says gloomily, "*vouée à la ruine,* doomed to fail."[1]

The house by the canal was long, low, white. For the little girls there was a magic garden, barges passing by, Proustian walks . . .

It was a house of delicious smells, of confitures bubbling in copper vats, good things a-simmering, fine linen in high stacks and well-stoked stoves: a warm house where feasts were kept and Saints' days with cakes and presents, *gâteries*, ribbons, frills.

It was a feminine household—except for the odd stable boy they were not supposed to play with—their father, going up and down the country seeing about his business and his boon companions, was not much at home. It was *Mère* (they always called her that, not *maman*, even to Aldous she became *Mère*) who was the fount of so many material refinements (and how very unlike an English middle-class household of the time it was); *Mère* who created the daily life that revolved round the little girls. First there were three of them, in fairly close succession: Maria, Jeanne, Suzanne; six years later, Rose. They were cosseted, they were pampered (at Courtrai each child had a nursemaid of her own who walked her in the park), but they were also taught their

[1] Maria's sister, Suzanne Nicolas, the third of the Nys sisters, in a memoir of her childhood, youth, and life up to the 1960s written originally as a source for this biography.

manners and to brush their hair, and from time to time packed off to convents for their schooling.

Maria, for her part, spent some of her earliest years in her grandparents' house at St Trond. She was an extremely delicate child and had to be treated for some spinal trouble. Emérence Baltus, her grandmother—"very grand, very elegant, formidably capable, high-handed with charm"[1]—nursed her with her own hands, and old lady and grandchild came to love one another very much. Aged seven, Maria was sent to the Sacré Cœur at Liège as a boarder. At nine she returned to live with her own family at Bellem.

> The door opens. [It is Suzanne speaking] Enter my mother and Maria. Already then she was pale, had bones as fragile as a bird's, and those great blue eyes which dominated her face. I was impressed —this was my sister, *ma grande sœur*, whom I had not seen for a long time.

For a while they went on with their education at home (Maria curious, willing, quick). They were taught by a governess and occasionally by a Baltus cousin—"*un beau jeune homme à barbe noire*," who was a professor of anatomy of all things. They spoke a profusion of languages, switching as the day went: French basically, Flemish (when *Mère* became *Moeske*), a Flemish patois to the villagers and servants, English to their governess. Mme Nys read Andersen's *Tales* in German to Maria, her eldest, her favourite. Maria was fascinated by the story of *The Little Red Shoes* and determined to become a dancer. Her mother ended by taking her to Brussels for lessons with the Ballet Master of the Opera. She showed talent and was asked to take part in a Royal Command performance. The family consulted and refused. Maria's other childhood passion was riding. After a bad fall she was forbidden to go out alone; she woke herself at six, saddled a horse and went off for a long ride along the canal. Before breakfast-time she was back in bed, glowing, telling her adventures to Suzanne who adored her and who was discreet.

Maria as a child was high-spirited and wilful, much given to thinking up some gay, fantastic project which she would carry through. Once in her mother's absence, she turned the drawing-room into a greenhouse and the greenhouse into a stage; it looked so ravishing that she wasn't even scolded.

She read voraciously (encouraged by her mother, imitated by Suzanne), the *Bibliothèque Rose*, Jules Verne, *Robinson Crusoe*,

---

[1] As described by Jeanne, the second Nys sister, the present Madame Georges Neveux.

*The Last of the Mohicans*, Jack London, Kipling, Racine, Corneille, Molière, the *Iliad*, the *Odyssey* and *The Life of Helen Keller*.

She showed much loving tenderness for others and a great longing for wider fields. When I am married, she used to say, we shall go round the world—*nous ferons le tour du monde*. She would watch the barges being pulled up the canal, slowly, strenuously by the boatmen and their wives. One day she took her mother's hand and said: *Plus tard, je tirerai ton bateau*—Later I shall pull your boat.

Maria made her first communion (with some intensity) at the age of twelve. At fourteen she went to spend six months at Glasgow with George and Vivi Baltus. There she had more ballet lessons, was allowed to go to tea and dinner-parties meeting the learned and the famous, and to ride about the Scottish countryside—"*La grandiose et romantique campagne d'Ecosse*".

When the war broke out and the Germans invaded Belgium, she was sixteen. Refugees reached Bellem, carrying (Suzanne maintains) dead babies in their arms, telling tales of horror; the German Army was not far behind. Mme Nys packed trunks, managed to procure transport and they reached Ostend. One fine late-summer morning she and the four girls sailed for England. (Their father stayed behind to look after his affairs.)

To begin with they lived in an agreeable boarding-house run by an Irish gentlewoman—"*Une pension de famille dans le quartier chic à* Grosvenor Square"; and Mme Nys became a useful member of the Belgian refugee committee.

They had brought money to last them for two months. They were cut off from their home resources. For a woman on her own with four daughters on her hands, one a child of six and all in need of further education, the situation was a difficult one. For the girls, tearful though they had been on leaving their white house by the canal, it was all more in the nature of a lark—new friends, freedoms, travel. As money ran out, immediate solutions presented themselves: people in England were very willing to look after the Belgians; Mme Nys, moreover, had entrées through her Baltus brother. Invitations came. She and little Rose went to Kent as the guests of the vicar of Malling; Jeanne and Suzanne, after an enjoyable couple of months in a country house with a large park and masses of young people, were given places at Cheltenham College; Maria, as Suzanne puts it, went to live with a gentleman farmer.

Lady Ottoline—by way of her and George Baltus's mutual friend the painter Henry Lamb—had written to Mme Nys offering hospitality for the duration. Mme Nys, installed already in her Kentish rectory, sent Maria to Garsington in her place.

Maria was very young. If she was precocious—in her world of younger sisters, at her uncle and aunt's dinner table—she was so in the bookish, lively manner of a child. Garsington, though it drew some of the very young, was a tough place for children. Maria was bowled over by the whole thing, bowled over by Lady Ottoline. She was fascinated, she was dazzled—she adored. She was not very happy. For Aldous, with his discipline and capacity for detachment, his mental digestion, his family and academic backgrounds, Garsington was a golden windfall, an opening of horizons, intellectual, moral and aesthetic—baroque statuary, cubism and French symbolist poetry not being part of the Huxley-Arnold inheritance any more than was sensual (as opposed to educational) liberty for women. Aldous strolled about at will in the new open spaces and if at times he got a bit tipsy, there was not much danger of his losing his own way. For Maria, head-long, a little spoilt, with her intensity, her untrained mind and loving heart, it was less of an open sesame than a hard school. In later life she spoke of Garsington with affection, reticence and pain. Ottoline blew hot and cold. If the atmosphere of the house-parties was light-hearted, it was above all overwhelmingly sophisticated, always exacting, sometimes heartless. If Katherine Mansfield was scared of the Bloomberries, it does not mean that she did not have her own pretensions. At Garsington, if you weren't very able or very amusing, you had at least to be pretty, and Maria did not think then that she was. She very much disliked being plump, and Ottoline did tease her. (That plumpness, which Aldous and some others found enchanting, was a transitory stage: as a child and again through adult life, Maria had the thinness of an El Greco adolescent.)

Lady Ottoline's maid sewed her dresses; Philip Morrell cut her hair. (The fashion was just beginning at the Slade, and Philip cut off all the Garsington girls' hair.) Lytton Strachey gave her Latin lessons; she brushed the pugs, took walks with Aldous round the pond and had her tea with little Julian and Juliette.

There was another thing, Maria had no money. No pocket money, often no money at all. Juliette, of course, had her salary; Maria was in the demoralizing situation of a refugee. She was bought presents but would have to ask for a postage stamp. For a girl so used to holding up her head in her lavish home, this was awkward and humiliating. Besides she then had that wild longing for things that can possess the young—for a necklace, a motor bicycle, a pair of gloves. Years after, when *she* had a young girl in her charge, she wrote of *"Les désirs foux que j'avais à son âge"*.

It was in those early days that Maria developed her own style of dressing—fastidious elegance with a touch of fantasy. In 1916 it was yellow cotton stockings. Augustus John used to sketch her in an indigo blue pleated skirt, a wine-coloured blouse Ottoline had given her, a broad red belt and the lemon yellow stockings.

Maria had no steady occupation at Garsington; her future was vague. Mme Nys scraped up some money for ballet lessons in London. Talent was confirmed, Nijinsky briefly taught her; but she was still delicate and was told that her health would not stand a professional dancer's career. After a few weeks she had to give it all up. In the spring of 1915, before she ever met Aldous, there had been some kind of crisis. Ottoline was off somewhere without taking Maria, or Ottoline had been talking of sending her away for her own good; whatever it was, Maria in a moment of passionate grief swallowed some chloride. There was commotion, the doctor in the night, she was saved. They were very angry with her. (Later she blamed herself.) The wicked corrosive stuff burnt her insides, possibly affected her health. There exists one reference to this episode in print, a letter from D. H. Lawrence.[1]

My dear Lady Ottoline,

We were shocked about Maria: it really is rather horrible. I'm not sure whether you aren't really more wicked than I had at first thought you. I think you can't help torturing a bit.

But I think it has [shown] something—as if you, with a strong, old-developed *will* had enveloped the girl, in this will, so that she lived under the dominance of your will. . . So that when she says it was because she couldn't bear being left, that she took the poison, it is a great deal true. Also she feels quite bewildered and chaotic . . .

We English, with our old-developed public selves, and the consequent powerful will, and the accompanying rudimentary private or instinctive selves, I think we are very baffling to any other nation. We are apt to assume domination, when we are not really personally implicated. A young foreigner can't understand this—not a girl like Maria.

Why must you always use your *will* so much, why can't you let things be, without always grasping and trying to know and to dominate. I'm too much like this myself.

There, now I'm scolding you, even. But *why* will you use power instead of love, good public control instead of affection. I suppose it is breeding. Don't mind what I say.

[1] Dated 23rd April 1915, *The Collected Letters of D. H. Lawrence*, ed. Harry T. Moore. Heinemann, 1962. (Hereafter cited as *D.H.L. Letters*, 1962.)

Later on there was a hope of Maria getting a place at Cambridge and she went up to Newnham for a term on a trial basis. That too failed.

Maria was not quick to respond to Aldous. Ottoline still loomed very large. Aldous was gently persistent. She was aware of his damaged sight, agonizingly sympathetic. Aldous, Brett says, "needed sympathy, needed help, needed love". One day Maria went to Brett for counsel: Brett said, "Go ahead. But don't tell anyone."

Mme Nys by then—the summer of 1916—had become very tired of her position as a permanent guest. She contrived somehow to take her girls for a few weeks into the wilds of Scotland, where they walked from loch to loch, sleeping in shepherds' huts, living frugally and gaily. The younger girls had an extraordinary time; Maria, temporarily plucked from Garsington, from Aldous, mainly sulked. After Scotland, Mme Nys, listening to the siren song of a Dutch agent who was promising to make funds available to her on the Continent, decided to leave England. The trunks were packed, the girls gathered; Maria refused to go. They left without her and got stuck in Paris. They were lodged in one spacious room at the Grand Hotel Terminus where Mme Nys was known from better days; but there was hardly any cash and for two months Jeanne and Suzanne lived on tap water, French bread and jam. Only Rose got milk. Their mother, being taken out from time to time to some splendid dinner, brought home to her famished brood the only items she could bear away with any decency, cream-puffs and petit-fours. Then money trickled in and they were able to eat occasionally at some cheap restaurant in the Latin quarter. Presently Mme Nys managed to collect visas and fares and they set out by train for Italy.

Aldous proposed on a rug on the lawn at Garsington. They promised to wait for one another. He gave her a scarab ring. Maria wore it until it became too large. Suzanne has it now.

In October Maria left Garsington and went to live in a furnished room in London. Aldous went to see her as often as he could. Maria tried to earn her living—not very successfully—by giving French lessons. It must have been all very precarious and impermanent. Maria was still only just eighteen. It was unlikely that her mother would let matters be. Aldous and Maria could not meet often but when they did it was in freedom. *Carpe noctem* —he willed them not to think beyond their dateless space of hours.

## Chapter Nine

## "Hélas, il faut que l'on vivote"

"THE worst, my dear Lewis, has not lost the opportunity of happening. It rarely does." So Aldous on New Year's Day, 1917. "Poor Maria is being hustled out remorselessly by her ghoulish mother in Florence. One achieves resignation . . incomplete and somewhat rebellious . . but not gaiety. It is altogether painful . . And then for how long? It's the indefiniteness that is so distressing. Six months, a year, three years . . ."

The thing is to get a job. "I missed one in Munitions by twelve hours. Eton won't have me. I dangle for Charterhouse . . . God preserve me!" Meanwhile there is some reviewing for the *Statesman*.

It was a cold winter at Garsington. One day as Aldous was chopping wood, a splinter hit him near his good eye. That was the end of that; they did not allow him to do any more manual work.

> Aldous mooned about the place, silent and bottled up. After a long evening without a word, he would follow Ottoline to her bedroom, as if unable to bear his own loneliness, and just sit by the fire, brooding; finally sent to bed, he oozed away like a ghost.[1]

And one evening Aldous suddenly blurted out his feelings to Juliette—the awfulness of the separation from Maria, the miserable uncertainty of it all. Another night, when they were up on the roof to look at the moon—the gibbous moon of *Crome Yellow*—it all came out. ". . the death of his mother when he was fourteen years old . . . a betrayal by life . . . Two years later blindness. Believed at first to be final . . . living behind a black band, learning to be blind." He talked about his father's marrying again, his brother's suicide. Juliette, shaken but too young, could find no words.

In the spring Aldous advertised for work in the Agony Column of *The Times*; at the same time Lady Violet Bonham-Carter was trying to get him into a Government office. By Easter a clerical job at the Air Board materialized. "It is all settled and I go there next week—screw, they tell me, from £200 to £250."

[1] Juliette Huxley.

In that job, which turned out utterly time-wasting, Aldous stayed until July, living with his father and stepmother in Hampstead, at 16 Bracknell Gardens to which they had recently moved.

> . . . Whether ALH can bear this Dept much longer is another question. [In May, to Julian] Porco di Madonna, the people in this place—suburban businessmen, with absolutely no interest in life but making money and gossiping about their hideous homes. They add to the soul-weariness with which this place overcomes one, as well as with physical fatigue. It is all too too bloody.
>
> . . I have ceased to read now: it's quite impossible as I'm always too tired in the evening—and I take almost no interest in anything but my food, which is a poor subject to be interested in these days.

And to Lewis Gielgud: "There is no particular news—the misery of life proceeds." And the war too is becoming "more ghastly every day . . I think that it is folly and a crime to go on now."

In May, yet another Medical Board, again with the result of complete rejection. "But oh—the process of being rejected.

> I presented myself at 10 at the Oxford recruiting office—and there I waited till 4, herded in a sort of pen with some 80 or so . . . all of whom were additionally horrible by being hospital cases of the most painful kind—halfwits, syphilitics . . goitrous cretins, men with unprecedented combinations of disease, diabetic consumptives suffering from Bright's disease, rheumatic lepers . . . There, as I say, we waited . . [in] sweltering heat . . no place to sit down: men swooned and vomited all about: when anyone tried to repose an instant on the steps of the doctors' motors, soldiers with fixed bayonets drove them away . . .

To Juliette he wrote long letters in office hours. She had sent him some of her poems.

> Try using very simple words and straightforward expressions [he advised] . . use practically only the words of everyday speech . . .

Unexpected counsel rather from one who could hardly have been called the Ernest Hemingway of verse.

> . . Educated speech, of course, not necessarily words of one syllable.

As he is writing they are being "pestered by German aeroplanes —a fiendish banging of bombs . . ." But Aldous goes on copying a French sonnet[1] he has written, a little obscure, he fears, as well as flippant. "But then I rarely write in French—and then only when I want to be *un peu scabreux* . . . the best language for indecency ever invented. . [only the French] can combine grossness with grace." Another day he sent Juliette his *"Hommage* to Jules Laforgue"[2] whose verbal ingenuities he found so irresistible an example in those days.

> *Que je t'aime mon cher Laforgue,—*
> *Frère qui a connu les nostalgies. . . .*

"Hélas", Aldous's last stanza opened, "Hélas, il faut que l'on vivote."

Meanwhile, every day, Aldous wrote to Maria; and she to him. Those letters no longer exist.

---

[1] "Sonnet à L'Ingénue" subsequently published in *Jonah.*
[2] *Jonah.*

# Chapter Ten

# Interludes

AND then it is summer and Aldous is quit of the Air Board (and certain of a job at Eton in the autumn) and he has a "great new friend" and they motor about the country having curious adventures and Aldous suddenly speaks of himself as having the greatest fun. The new friend is "The inimitable Evan Morgan,[1] poet, painter, musician, aristocrat and millionaire . . . the unique fairy prince of modern life," whom Aldous met at Garsington and made to re-appear at Crome. ("Nature and fortune had vied with one another in heaping on Ivor Lombard all their choicest gifts.") In life, Morgan and Aldous encounter a young woman in a forest, "a young woman of eighteen exactly like Nell Gwyn.

. . Immense cherry trees, laden with fruit . . . Nell Gwyn . . ascends ladders and throws cherries at the young men . . . and so it begins. [It is to Carrington that Aldous narrates this story.] In the heart of Nell Gwyn the most dangerous passion is kindled . . not merely for one but for both simultaneously . . .
Scene two. In the forest at evening the mosquitoes bite; so do the young women. Rather disquietingly it begins to occur to us that the creature is perfectly innocent.
Then the strangest scene in our bedroom. We become perfectly convinced that she is completely virginal. Without any shame she caresses both of us with all the fire of her native sensuality. We explain that we cannot take her virginity; we are simply passers by . . . She is in tears about it, begs and implores that we should. We are inexorable; Evan sitting up in bed like a young Sicilian shepherd with no clothes on orders her back to her room with his most imperious manner; he is the descendant of Welsh princes; she obeys and creeps off to a cold and solitary couch. We sink to sleep. At about three I wake up, aware that someone is passionately kissing my neck and shoulders. I hasten to add that it was not Evan. Nell Gwyn has returned. I give her the hospitality of my bed for a few minutes and send her away; it was all a little nerve-racking. The next night she goes to Evan; the fate of virginity hangs in the balance, but escapes intact; this time we lock the door. On Monday we depart, and there are terrible adieus . . . However, in my case the adieu is an au revoir, for making my way from Beaconsfield to Eton on

---

[1] The late Viscount Tredegar.

Wednesday it occurs to me that it would be more amusing to spend the night with Nell Gwyn than with my tutor at Eton . . .

But the half of it can never be told; it was all so peculiar . . like something which must have happened in the Balkans, impossible in England.

Next there was Morgan's birthday party, a tremendous affair with the drink flowing and Aldous "achieving a rapprochement . . a mutual épanchement, in our cups . . sober we have always been rather alarmed of one another," with Marie Beerbohm.[1] Aldous has ceased to feel morose in the company of the gay, the charming, the mercurial Evan Morgan. All in all it was not a bad summer. He stayed at Oxford with the Haldanes and the Petersens, he went to Garsington; he was writing again. His translation of Mallarmé's *L'Après-midi d'un Faune*,[2] begun at Balliol, finished at Garsington, is coming out in *Oxford Poetry* and he is contributing to "the well-known Society Anthology *Wheels*, in company with illustrious young persons like Miss Nancy Cunard, Miss Iris Tree . . . The folk who run it are a family called Sitwell . . ."

*And* the news from Italy is good—"will this bloody war be over in time for me to get out there before Christmas or Easter?"

When Mme Nys the year before had succeeded in leaving Northern Europe with her three younger children, they made straight for Forte dei Marmi, the village by the sea on Shelley's coast between La Spezia and Leghorn. It was still summer and the place was full of good-looking Italians *in villeggiatura*. They put up at the Pensione Tirreno where the food was delicious and plunged into Italian life. Friends of George Baltus, the Fasolas, had a house at Forte on their own beach among vineyards and pines. Signore Fasola was a disciple of Tolstoy and professor at the University of Florence, his wife was German, elderly and rich; they had a daughter, "Costanza, twenty-one years old—A dream: charming and graceful as a young goat [Suzanne speaking], full of caprices, gaiety and games".

They were introduced to other families of beautiful young women, bright adolescents—men were at the front—learned parents. It was Italian life at its most light-hearted and civilized. Mme Nys, appreciated for her charm (she had charm), her vitality, her Flemish stories, found congenial company; for Jeanne

---

[1] Max Beerbohm's niece. One of the sirens of the day.
[2] First republished in *The Defeat of Youth*, 1918.

and Suzanne it was the lightning friendships of the young. They swam, sailed, sketched, talked books with Costanza and some half-dozen other girls and boys, moved about the pine forests, the hills, the marble quarries of the Tuscan countryside—it was Balbec, *la petite bande*, the perennial charmed circle of youth.

In October the Fasolas went back to Florence and the Nys's went too. They found an apartment on the Lungarno Aciaioli with a view of the church of Santa Trinità across the river. (Mme Nys had resolved the problem of getting money out of Belgium, precariously; but for the remainder of the war they were never again reduced to living on jam and water, or on hospitality.)

Suzanne went to a pleasant school, Jeanne studied painting, Rose the piano; Mère took them to see all the churches, all the pictures, they drew in the Uffizi, had dancing classes and Italian lessons given by delightful persons and there was a good deal of that Florentine social life—artists, nobility and foreigners at teas, musical evenings in hillside villas and the vast, draughty, frescoed drawing-rooms of the *palazzi*. It was, Suzanne affirms, *"une existence bien agréable"*.

It was into this that Maria was translated when she arrived from England in January of 1917. She was looking thin and ravishing, and at once she carried all before her. She eclipsed her sisters. Her turn now for the lightning friendship with Costanza Fasola, with Rocca, their young dancing mistress. Once more, she was swept off her feet. By her new friends, and by what she saw —by the sheer beauty of everything about her. Overwhelmed by Italy, seduced by Italian life—for those who have lived it, the two are inseparable—she responded with what was most headlong in her nature and her life became (as Aldous put it somewhat distantly) a mere sequence of sensuous enjoyments.

Costanza called Maria *Coccola*, the Italian diminutive for dear one or my darling (and a word that in its straight sense means pip or berry); it became the name used by her sisters and later by their children. When Aldous used it, he dropped the second c.

The Russian Ballet was in Florence that winter. Maria too danced again; in the Fasola's drawing-room and with Costanza publicly for charity. Off stage she wore a sky-blue cloak, Mme Nys had made for her, cut like the cloaks carried with such swagger by Italian army officers, and on Maria it looked piercingly stylish and romantic.

In June they all returned to Forte for the summer. They took a pleasant house near the Fasolas, their young friends were there, all was as before; only that now Maria was the animator and the favourite.

## Chapter Eleven

## Master at Eton

THE war was *not* over and besides Aldous had to think of a financial future and support himself as well for the time being. Another office job—even if his eyes could have taken the strain of a sixty-hour week of paper work and it was clear that they could not—would have been crushing because of the dead loss of time; teaching was another matter, there being always hope of getting down to one's own work in the holidays. Aldous took up his new post at Eton. It was poorly paid; he did not think he was a born schoolmaster or would be teaching the boys anything very much.

But we get on moderately well, which is all that is needed for a quiet life.

A quiet life! That precisely, as legend has it, is what Aldous did not have at Eton.

I was, I suppose, in my second year in College [writes Sir Steven Runciman] when we were told that we were to be taught by this remarkable young writer. We Collegers were little intellectual snobs and we were much impressed. None of us had read a word that he had so far written . . but the name already had a glamour. The impression was deepened when we actually saw him.
I still have a vivid pictorial recollection of that elongated, stooping, myopic figure, with a face that was far younger than most of our masters' [he was twenty-three] and yet seemed somehow ageless, and usually hidden by an infinite variety of spectacles, eyes that were almost sightless and yet almost uncomfortably observant. He stood there looking something of a martyr but at the same time extraordinarily distinguished.[1]

The boys had been warned of the new master's defective sight and told to behave decently.

Not all of us did behave decently. At the back of the form-room there was always a certain amount of reading of magazines, passing of notes and murmured gossip. But the misbehaviour never went

[1] Sir Steven Runciman, *Mem. Vol.* and from a letter to S. B.

too far, less from the feeling that there is little fun in misbehaving in front of a master who cannot see it than from the certainty that misbehaviour left him completely indifferent and unmoved.

I personally think that the legend of the chaos in Aldous's Eton class-rooms has been a bit exaggerated . . . but [possibly] the slightly older boys were a bit rowdier than we were.[1]

And according to Eddy Sackville-West,[2] who was sixteen and in a different division, they were.

Poor Aldous! He must have been one of the most incompetent schoolmasters who ever faced a class . . . his solution was to read aloud, with occasional comments the poems of Verlaine. This he did in his scholarly, highly modulated voice . . . [it was] impossible to hear more than an occasional word of what he read or said for the general tumult was indescribable. Those in the back row but one turned their backs on the rest of the form and made up a bridge four with boys in the back row. The middle rows played noughts-and-crosses with white chalk on the shoulders of the boys in front of them. The majority simply conversed in loud voices. A very few, of whom I was one, did genuinely want to listen to Aldous; but it was useless in that pandemonium . . . From time to time, Aldous would pause, look up, and say, in an imploring tone, "Oh! Do be quiet!" No one took the slightest notice.[3]

Then there is Aldous's own view. Having spent the morning correcting twenty-eight essays on the League of Nations, he wrote to Lewis Gielgud "with such few exceptions they are all so stupid . . ." But,

They are most of them nice fellows and treat me, all being considered, wonderfully well, though I wish I could see them more penetratingly: I expect the secret of their quietness lies in the fact that they are deeply engaged in something very far removed from the sordid present, poles apart from any claptrap I may be talking about English literature or Molière's plays.

Most of my creatures are immensely grown-up; one division consists almost entirely of members of Pop, for whom it is very difficult not to feel awe and reverence. It is a wonderful tribute to the efficacy of their youthful training that these superb lions refrain from rending me as they so very well might—the most they do is occasionally to shirk my school, taking advantage of the fact that I don't yet know

1 Sir Steven Runciman, ibid.
2 The late Lord Sackville, the writer and music critic.
3 Lord Sackville, from a letter to Professor Gover Smith.

them by sight and getting their names answered by somebody else
. . . but they were regrettably caught.

Aldous was lodging in the Old Christopher, the ancient pub
in Eton High Street, where the senior Eton boys were allowed
to drink mildish beer, sharing his quarters in that strange old
house with another beak, an absurd but good-hearted clergyman
called Cobby Bevan. Aldous found him a placid though not very
bracing companion. "A very good soul ('soul' by definition does
not include mind) and we live very snugly and with no friction,
talking over our meals, which are frequent and large—for the
Reverend Bevan is something of an epicure . . . Then we retire
each to his separate room and all is well, except that sometimes
I feel almost intolerably lonely; these ushers are so nice, but so
remote, so alien."

There was not much chance for escape to London as Aldous
was seldom free before 4 p.m. and full weekends were impossible
as he had to be back for early school on Monday. If only "there
were someone jolly on the staff with whom one could walk and
talk: I say walk and talk, for as things are, all the beaks rush off
to play football or run to Maidenhead or dig potatoes when they
are not working, and the only people who take life quietly are
the antiques . ." With those Aldous took constitutionals round
the golf course, fretting and fuming at having to walk at two
miles an hour and wait minutes at each bunker. As for that
hope of writing, just as he was trying to settle down to it "in
comes another batch of essays to correct, or I have to go and
stand up in face of these sinister young men and try to keep them
amused".

All the same he managed to write a few things, and was
encouraged by hearing that Blackwells would like to publish *The
Defeat of Youth* and there was *Jonah*[1] being printed by the Holywell
Press at Oxford.

In November he has an exceptionally diverting week—luncheon
with Juliette on Wednesday in London; Gervas, on leave, on
Thursday; a tea-party at Eton on Saturday when his bright young
pupil De La Warr had invited George Lansbury to meet him.
(Aldous found Lansbury "extremely interesting, very tolerant, not
bitter like so many of these labour men . . . full of constructive
rather than destructive enthusiasms. He is a great friend, I find,
of Lady Ottoline's brother, Lord Henry Bentinck; their view on
most things appears to be almost identical, despite the fact that
Lord H. is nominally a Tory.")

[1] *Jonah*, that bibliographical rarity, consists of twelve poems printed on a
single folded and sewn sheet of 16 pages; the issue was limited to about fifty
copies most of which Aldous sent out to his friends as a Christmas card.

Aldous now became involved in *The Eton Review* and the founding of an Eton Political Society, the moving spirit of which was his "young friend the Earl, De La Warr, who is a passionate Socialist". Aldous was asked to find out if Asquith and Haldane would come and speak to the boys. "The whole idea amused me very much and should be encouraged, I am sure."

And then there is theosophy, which appears to have excited some of the more serious-minded boys. "I point out Mrs Besant's errors in science and history, which thickly encrust her books, and try to wean them from the merely superstitious side." But except for the bunkum about astral bodies and so forth, "theosophy seems a good enough religion; the main point being that all religion contains some truth and that we ought to be tolerant."

On 1st December Aldous is summoned *again*—such is the shortage of manpower—before the military. For the rest, "the grim solitude of Eton punctuated by brief jaunts to London". He's been seeing the dashing Evan Morgan, he's been seeing Carrington, he's looked in on Katherine Mansfield "in her curious little kennel in Chelsea," and on T. S. Eliot, whom he found haggard and ill-looking as usual. On the 12th Aldous took part in a poetry reading at Sybil Colefax's,[1] a charity affair before a large and expensive audience with Gosse in the chair and Robert Nichols, Aldous, Viola Tree, the Sitwells and Eliot (in that order) reading. Aldous found the whole thing quite appalling. "Eliot and I were the only people who had any dignity: Bob Nichols raved and screamed and hooted and moaned his filthy war poems like a Lyceum villain . . . The Sitwells were respectable, but terribly nervous."

In less than a week now the Eton Half will be over. Aldous is very tired—"this teaching takes it out of one"—and looking forward to Christmas at Garsington. "What amusements we had *last* year, in spite of the somewhat wet blanket of Bloomsbury!"

Too soon this year also becomes last year and, inexorably in January, Aldous is back at the Old Christopher, wintry and bleak. His school work is now mostly tutorial, no more standing up in large forms, but some fifty elder boys coming in for half an hour each a week to have their essays commented upon, and this he found on the whole more interesting. If only there were more leisure to write, he can't even get a batch of reviews finished; all he can do is to get down a line of poetry here and there (". . a most luscious poem about Leda, the lady whom Jupiter visited in the form of a swan . . . it is the most charming story . . .")

Meanwhile the Eton Political Society was functioning and Aldous had discovered "another young aristocrat, Lord David

---

[1] The late Lady Colefax, the hostess, who became a friend of Aldous's.

Cecil, who is in point of sheer brains and imagination beyond De La Warr. . . . He is only sixteen, is the most brilliant conversationalist, has written one or two uncommonly good poems . . . He is one of the people who give one the sense of being enormously thorough-bred; a wonderful character in his way."

And there was Eddy Sackville-West:

> When he saw that I was really interested in French literature he thawed and we became friends. He taught me a lot about such writers as Laforgue and Mallarmé; I never lost touch with him from that time on.[1]

Still Aldous chafed at the attitudes imposed by schoolmastering: the unceasing pretence of knowing better, of being respectable and a good example; he is afraid that it will make him old. "I do my best to make my boys have no respect for me whatever." How far did he succeed?

> At first we thought his voice affected [Sir Steven Runciman], but soon some of us were trying to copy it. Above all it was his use of words that entranced us. Eric Blair—the future George Orwell— who was my exact contemporary—would in particular make us note Aldous's phraseology. "That is a word we must remember," we used to say to each other . . . The taste for words and their accurate and significant use remained. We owe him a great debt for it.[2]

And Sir Steven sums up:

> I cannot say that Aldous was a good teacher in the narrow sense of the word, I have to confess that I cannot now remember a single thing he taught us. But he was an educator in a wider sense. He showed us glimpses of the fascination to be found in an unhampered intellectual approach to things.

[1] Lord Sackville, ibid.
[2] Sir Steven Runciman, from *Mem. Vol.* and a letter to S. B.

## Chapter Twelve
## Strain

JULIAN HUXLEY, who had joined the Army, was being posted to Italy as a lieutenant in the Intelligence Corps and Aldous asked him to see Maria. "I hope you will go, if only to tell me what the rest of the family is like." For Aldous had not set eyes yet on Mme Nys, nor Jeanne, Suzanne or Rose.

His own existence was pretty miserable that spring. A severe attack of intercostal rheumatism; exams; icy winds—and how tired he is of being ridiculously underpaid and the war is looking gloomier every day. "Bertie Russell, did you see? has been sentenced to six months for saying the American troops were to be stationed here to put down strikes—a task to which they were so well used at home. Not a thing I'd choose to be sentenced on—it is so curiously foolish."

In April, Easter holidays and brief liberty. A week in London whizzing around "mixing one's people like discordantly flavoured drinks—Eliot for luncheon, Aunt Mary [Ward] for tea, Sitwells . . for dinner . . or else one sticks to one rich vintage all day long—Marie Beerbohm, at lunch, tea, dinner and half the night long. A very remarkable character, Marie; tremendous vitality to carry her through the arduous frivolousness of a perpetually whirling life; the marvellous niceness common to all Beerbohms, which keeps her charming and unspoiled through episodes in themselves somewhat sordid; a good mind, rather like Max's in its fantastic cleverness, which you won't discover till you know her well."

A weekend in Surrey with Aunt Sophy Huxley; more London, then retreat to Garsington where he contrived to do a little writing and reading. Then back again "to the grind and three more months of Cobby".

In May he is doing proofs of *The Defeat of Youth*, and has read "our secret treaty with Italy". (How? Could it have been by way of Maynard Keynes?)

> It really makes one gasp; [he writes to Julian] one wonders which is the greatest, the stupidity or the wickedness of our rulers. I think their stupidity.

Maria and her family were now living above Florence, across the road from the Fasolas, in Castel a Montici, one of those grand

and spacious villas above Florence, rich in views and gardens and painted drawing-rooms, short of water and innocent of electricity. It was the spring of their second year in Italy—the fourth year of the war—times were no longer easy. The winter if anything had been more icy than the one in England; food shortages had become severe. Mme Nys, who bore the brunt, went about collecting firewood, sugar, flour, olive oil. Cooking was done on a sawdust stove. The girls were left much on their own. Sometimes Maria took a hand in keeping house. Their staple diet seems to have been figs, oranges, chestnuts and Brussels sprouts. Maria, for her own part, lived mainly on lettuce leaves and grapes.

Julian's eventual visit was brief—a man in uniform surrounded by a number of young women. Afterwards he wrote to Aldous what must have been a letter of brotherly concern. Aldous's answer reads a little chilly. "As to what you say of Maria, I think I realize her faults clearly enough." The fundamental thing about her is her very great aesthetic sensibility, and aestheticism, he thinks, is a dangerous thing. He does not believe that anyone who lives wholly on sensation is "safe". He recalls how completely Maria was bowled over when she first went to Italy. Now, judging from her letters, she has settled down a good deal.

> What I have tried to persuade Maria to do is to centre her life on thought rather than sensation, to adopt some fixed intellectual occupation, involving a certain amount of effort and mental concentration, and not merely to live on the aesthetic sensations of the moment. She is educating herself—in a rather desultory way perhaps —but the process gives her a solid foundation for her existence.

He thinks she will grow up all right. " 'Grow up!' for you mustn't forget how absurdly young she is, only nineteen . . . I only wish I was with her, for I think I could be of help to her in growing up—not to mention the fact that she would help me out of the curiosly unpleasant slough of uncertainty in which one seems to wallow so hopelessly these days." At this point Aldous may have become aware of his own dryness.

> I have spared you more lyrical effusions about her, not because I don't feel lyrically, but because it would be so tedious for you. One's aim . . should be to combine the lyrical with the critical . . Shelley and the *Edinburgh Review*. I have only given you my *Edinburgh Review* opinions about Maria—for the others see my Works passim!

Maria who never learnt to have, who never could have had, *Edinburgh Review* opinions about anything, was sustained by

Aldous's letters; and her life during those months and months of separation was, in contrast to his, delicious and indulgent. Yet from her end the uncertainty was as great. On the surface there was an improbability about the whole thing. Some thirty years later she wrote to her son.[1]

Why, why in the world did Aldous choose me out of the many prettier, wittier, richer etc young girls? Why in the world did he come back to fetch me after two long years of running around with more of those pretty and amusing ones of his own world? Knowing all the time by my letters that he could never teach me to write poetry or remember what I read in a book, or spel, [*sic*] or anything he did set value on.

The code at Garsington was what we now call permissive. Sexual freedom of action was a prerequisite of being civilized. Lady Ottoline had the well-known affair with, *entre autres*, Bertrand Russell; Philip Morrell pursued young women; homosexualities were accepted as a matter of course. Constancy and the loyalties of the heart were looked upon as philistine and a bit ridiculous.

And why [so Maria went on] did I who was so horrified by those Garsington men (and women) I who was so squashed by the English and terrified of them, why did I let Aldous approach me, then wait for him though I never thought he would come back to me considering the theories of the world of Ottoline's: just flit round for fun; why tie each other down. Why did I not get for a single moment entranced by the Italian men and easy life and certainly less terrifying intellectual strain of it?

[1] To Matthew Huxley in 1952.

## Chapter Thirteen

## Marking Time

AT Eton Aldous was dragging through another Half. His only bearable hours were passed in writing, talking to the three or four intellectual boys, and escapes to London. The playing fields—"those elm-shadowed expanses of soggy turf",[1] the river, the Fourth of June, colours and summer air, might not have existed; he was too miserable, and temperamentally he had no liking for routine, no feeling for ceremonial or traditional repetition. To him these were distractions from the pursuit of the significant—knowledge and art. Time well spent was spent in learning and creation. "I never really feel I am performing a wholly *moral* action, except when I am writing."

Yet there were many things that he enjoyed doing. Apart from conversation with the instructed and exceptional, he enjoyed the company of his friends, he enjoyed the company of women whom he preferred to be amusing and educatable as well as pretty.

The letters of these years are very detached from events. Julian asks about new books and Aldous answers that he is the last person to apply to "seeing that I almost never read anything under a century old, and then preferably in a foreign language". As to the state of the world, he knows nothing about it except by conversation, "and of conversation I am completely deprived here. The only modern book I have heard of at all is Lytton Strachey's *Eminent Victorians*, which I have not read—except parts in MS—but which everybody says is very good."

He gives a fastidious glance at the Pemberton Billing Trial:

. . the after-swell of the storm in the cess-pool still heaves . . . Such as the letter sent by Robbie Ross to the public prosecutor calling him a bastard . . for not having dealt faithfully with Alfred Douglas:— poor Robbie, it is still the dismal idée fixe of the Wilde case, which everyone is getting so bored with.

(Yet when Robbie Ross died quite suddenly in his sleep a few months later, Aldous wrote, "Poor Robbie, it is very sad. He was the most charming creature.")

[1] *The Olive Tree*, 1936.

96

Aldous attempted to write a play. It turned out "wholly un-dramatic with a plot more suitable for a Henry Jamesian story". All the same, "I shall try and write a farce with a perfectly good machine-made plot—not an easy task, I imagine; but it will be good practice and might, if acted, make money." Here one can see the beginnings of an illusion that was going to cost Aldous a good deal in time and disappointment. He was even thinking of reforming stage convention to overcome some of the crudities of the theatre, "one must be permitted to have hundreds of scenes like Shakespeare—the cinema has already given a very good example in that respect". Anyway, "I am determined to make writing pay."

> . . I have no money whatever . . . This bloody place pays me so atrociously [nothing is left after board and lodging and the haber-dasher's bill] . . . It is all very sordid and irritating.

Holidays once again, spent mainly at Garsington and at Prior's Field where all is very pleasant and the garden blooms and blazes, "and I sit with my faithful typewriter outside, surrounded by gillyflowers and peacock butterflies, and write immortal works in prose—a short story".

He is also contributing more poems to the Sitwells' magazine, *Wheels*, of which he now speaks with some approval. He rather likes "its toreador attitude towards the bloody-bloodies of this world".

He sees Gervas who is on leave and in good form on the whole, confident that the war will be over in a year. But whatever happens, Aldous thinks, we may be sure it will be for the worst. "I dread the inevitable acceleration of American world domina-tion [he wrote to Julian] which will be the ultimate result of it all. It was a thing that had got to come in time, but this will hasten its arrival by a century. We shall all be colonized. Europe will no longer be Europe. . . ."

In September Aldous is at Hampstead in his father's house and in low spirits. What he longs and pines for is domesticity, domes-ticity combined with intelligence, he writes to Juliette who, too, is rather lonely in a large, isolated house in Scotland. (She had left Garsington and become governess to the children of Brett's sister, the Ranee of Sarawak.) The only thing that brightens the general darkness is the Russian Ballet "Which is pure beauty, like a glimpse into another world.

We—Ottoline, Julian, Brett, Gertler and I—had a great evening of it the other day: almost everybody in London was there, and we all went round to the back afterwards to see Lopokova the première danseuse, who is ravishing—finding there no less a person than André Gide, who looks like a baboon with the voice, manners and education of Bloomsbury in French.

# Chapter Fourteen

# Post Armistice

JULIAN had been in England on leave and Aldous heard that he had spent the last days of it going all the way up to Callander in Scotland to see Juliette Baillot. "I knew nothing about it from him," Aldous writes to Lady Ottoline.[1] "Is it a Romance?"

And then, at last! the war is over. Aldous's rejoicings were brief. "We have got over the jollifications of the first days of peace and are beginning to examine the facts."

The facts—well, again Aldous expects the worst. Bolshevism is a serious possibility. There is the repulsive immediate prospect of Lloyd George's triumphant return to power in the elections, and that will mean the substitution for any kind of serious parliamentary government of bureaucracy, big money interests and the press, with a consequent exacerbation of revolutionary elements. "One has to remember that two-thirds of the adult male population is highly skilled in the use of the most complicated weapons." Aldous has no desire to find himself in the middle of a revolution and rather thinks that America will be the only place where it will not break out. "Great events are both terrifying and boring, terrifying because one may be killed and boring because they interfere with the free exercise of the mind." He sent a message to Brett to vote Labour.

If the prospects of the universe were dim and dismal, they were as nothing to his personal prospects which were, Aldous said, what the Russians would call Nevsky prospects, the Nevskyest of prospects. Eton will have its normal and permanent staff back by next Half, and he will soon be out of a job. He has been sounding Oxford and has heard that there will be nothing for him at Balliol as they took on a good man during the war whom they did not want to turn out. "A future of poverty, hunger and dirt looms menacingly." Julian offered to lend some money; Aldous will accept, gratefully, if and when the time comes. At present his situation is obscure and further complicated by the uncertainties of Maria's movements. Mme Nys had gone to Naples in the autumn with the younger girls. Maria is on Capri with

---

[1] Who is supposed to have said, "Have I been running a marriage bureau for Huxleys?"

Costanza. Supposedly they will return to Belgium as soon as they can get passports.

Meanwhile Eton has been thrown out of gear by influenza, two hundred and fifty cases in the school. Aldous has been able to read Flaubert and Stendhal, and to do a little more work on his dual personality story. As for Julian and Juliette, "I am glad," he wrote to Brett, "you are keeping your ears pricked at your end of this strange potential romance.

> I know very little .. except that Brother J, when I wrote to him saying I thought his Scottish journey romantic, did not deny the soft impeachment, but said he had taken on Mlle as his Marraine for the war. Whether the wartime .. arrangement will blossom into any other kind of relationship in the piping days of peace remains to be seen. I know nothing.

December and still no solutions. Aldous does not even know where he will go for Christmas. To Garsington, probably. He would like to try to get to Paris as Maria might be stopping there on the way North. Money again is the problem. "It haunts me sometimes, the horror of it . . . whether it will ever be solved seems to me extremely doubtful."

Mme Nys had wished to stay on in Italy until the spring, not an unreasonable plan seeing the difficulties of travel and shortages of food in Belgium. The house at Bellem and the wool mill was damaged in the last allied offensive. The girls persuaded their mother to return at once. After days of slow travel in icy, crowded trains, delayed by strikes and breakdowns, they reached St Trond and the grandparental house on a day of deep snow before the end of the year.

Yet there was still no question of Aldous being able to see Maria. All he could hope for was to go to Belgium in the Easter holidays. *If* he'll have the money. Only his intentions were clear. "What I want is to marry and settle down to write . . . What I want more than anything really is to get a year with nothing to do except to write."

By February he is still hoping for something at Oxford and at the same time "poking about among editors" trying to get some regular reviewing or other literary work. He is not proposing to marry on nothing at all; in fact, he sums up the position to his father, he would not like to risk it on under £500 a year. "If Maria had a little money of her own, it would be rather a comfort," but he doesn't know how far her people have been ruined by the war and whether they will be able to let her have anything at all.

As for his own people, Leonard had become chief editor of the *Cornhill* a few years before and there also was some money coming in from Prior's Field; on the other hand he now had a second family, two sons, David and Andrew, to look after and educate. Aldous's Aunt Mary, Mrs Humphry Ward, a best-selling author in her day, was facing greatly changed circumstances, her vogue and royalties having abruptly ceased during the war just when she was being faced by considerable financial liabilities in her own family. Aldous finally wrote to his father.

. . It would be a very great help if you could let me have a little—though I feel rather odious in asking you for anything: for I seem already to have claimed—and as a matter of course—so much of your work and of your life. I hope I shall do something not unworthy of all you have given me.

Julian meanwhile got demobilized with an appointment waiting at Oxford. In March he and Juliette Baillot were married. Aldous was best man. He saw them off; looking, Juliette says, lost and wistful standing on the platform.

Then, in a matter of weeks, Aldous's luck turned. He was offered a job in London. The salary was adequate and it was not teaching but a post on the editorial staff of that highly literate weekly—now long merged with the *New Statesman*—the *Athenaeum* under the editorship of John Middleton Murry. Aldous was to start at the end of April; his father lent him a few hundred to start life on. Aldous resigned from Eton. At the end of Easter Half of 1919 he left Cobby and the Old Christopher, dumped his books and clothes at Hampstead and set out for Belgium.

## Chapter Fifteen

## A Family Reunion

THEY met after a separation of two years and three months at St Trond. It was the small town in the province of Limbourg, the Longres of "Uncle Spencer",[1] that leisurely story of gentle ironies, Longres-St Trond of the Grand'Place with the little seventeenth-century Hôtel de Ville, the kermesse and the weekly pig market seething away below Grandpère Baltus's house; St Trond of the aerial music where "at the hours the bells play a minuet and trio, tinkly and formal like the first composition of an infant Boccherini".

They met. Maria was staying at her grandparents, Aldous put up by *Mère* in another house. The young English poet was accepted as a matter of course. If there was anxiety about the future it was not shown; Aldous was very well received. He fitted into "a rather oddly un-English life". At St Trond everybody, who was anybody, was everybody else's relation, and old Monsieur and Madame Baltus were the patriarchs of the town. At a family dinner they easily sat down twenty-five. At the stroke of half past one every day of the year, children, grandchildren, uncles, aunts and cousins arrived *en voisin* at the house on the Grand'Place for after-luncheon coffee in the smoking-room followed by a general armchair siesta. *En voisin* meant without a hat. All relations were rich *commerçants*, "living in large and hideous houses dotted about the town. Some make cloth, some sugar . . . A few are very cultured, the rest not at all."

It was all a very far cry from Garsington or their privacy in the London of 1916. Aldous did not see enough of Maria, but he surveyed the scene with literary detachment. He described the grandparents to his father,

> . . He with the appearance of a retired colonel, deaf, very kindly and human, devoting his old age to reading which he never had time to do in his active days of cloth-manufacturing. The old lady [Maria's beloved Emérence] is a person of rather witchlike appearance, not quite so amiable as he is, I think.

Uncle George Baltus, the Glasgow professor and his wife, he found very cultured and him extremely amusing; and Mère,

---

[1] *Little Mexican*, 1924.

"whom I like very much," intelligent and nice, "tho' rather a creature of moods (some of the moods tiresome)". As for himself, he thought that they were fairly reassured. "They had, I fancy, rather anticipated a roaring lion: they are relieved to find a sheep."

Monsieur Nys's business had indeed been ruined (there was to be no allowance or settlement for Maria), though the grand-parents' was not, thanks to Emérence Baltus who had stood up both to Germans and hard times.

The Belgian visit was brief but everything was settled. Aldous went back to England to take up his job and find a place to live. Maria with her grandmother's assistance was to see about her trousseau.

## Chapter Sixteen

# Adjustments

ALDOUS and Maria were married on 10th July 1919 at the Hôtel de Ville at Bellem. They were married in the simplest fashion. Aldous's father did not come over for the ceremony; nor did any other member of the Huxley family. (Nobody liked the expense and fuss of a big wedding.) Maria's father was laid up in Brussels with the gout. (Both parents, by Belgian law, had to telegraph their consent.) The only relations present were Mère and Jeanne.

Aldous had found a small flat in Hampstead[1] in a house surrounded by grass and trees, quiet as the country, fifteen minutes' walk from his father's house and only twenty-odd minutes by underground or bicycle from Charing Cross. He had furnished it practically with his own hands. He had sawed shelves, painted tables and chairs, hunted for some "nice pink wallpaper"; his step-mother had helped him to shop; his cousin Marjorie[2] had done the paper-hanging. Aldous and Brett painted the woodwork in the sitting-room dove grey; a carpet arrived from Heal's and crates from Belgium with china, silver, linen. Aldous was particularly pleased with "a marvellous instrument for heating water" which he had found and bought himself.

> A little bar which you fasten to the light and dip into your water: it will boil a pint in 5 minutes—very useful . . for simple cooking, such as eggs and tea: much quicker than a spirit lamp.

Here they arrived. Maria twenty, Aldous nearly twenty-five, in the first home of his own. In her trousseau, Maria had brought silk jackets, exquisite gloves, good scent, diffusing an ambience of feminine elegance, a hint of Persian luxury, which Aldous, raw from a decade in digs and college, became quite fond of. The solitary years were over—they were going to have a Siamese cat and a pug from Garsington and live happily ever after.

When Aldous married Maria—and he had never wavered in his determination to do so from the time he spoke on the lawn at Garsington—he was very much in love with her. (In their middle-

---

[1] At 18 Hampstead Hill Gardens.
[2] Marjorie Huxley, Gervas's sister.

age when they had been married thirty-three years to the day
and Aldous unexpectedly remembered, Maria brought it up,
"What made you marry me?" she asked him. Aldous answered
artlessly, "Well, you were rather pretty then." Maria roared with
laughter.) For Maria in the earliest days it had been both less
and more. She was less carried away by the present, what held
her was a sense of doing the right thing in the long view. There
was Aldous: a quality in Aldous, and this she dedicated herself
to serve. If it was not explicit, it was already conscious; one may
call it a sense of vocation. *Je tirerai son bateau.* Meanwhile, she
was young, innocent and quite worldly, full of gaiety, love, good
will; and she was very scared.

She was most frightened of the "brilliant ones", Aldous's intellectual friends and women friends, Tom Eliot, the Sitwells, the
Bloomsberries, Murry, Evan Morgan, Tommy Earp; Marie
Beerbohm, Mary Hutchinson, Iris Tree, Nancy Cunard. There
were also the Huxleys and the Arnolds to be met. Aldous's father
and stepmother were still in Scotland, and besides had written
kind welcoming letters; the immediate ordeal was meeting Mrs
Humphry Ward. "We go to Stocks next weekend," Aldous
wrote to his father on 5th August, "—a prospect which M regards
with certain qualms of terror!"

They went. Maria found "such a nice and charming old lady
that all terror vanished," she wrote to Julian,[1] "except my
momentary astonishment at her being so unlike Vernon Lee."

However, on Sunday by tea time "an immense family party
was spreading itself as far as one could see and for one moment I
really thought I would give way to terror and despair—

> a very snooty cousin and a sporty one—young ladies and old ones
> and an uncle and lady—very thin and stern poor woman suffering
> from rheumatism.[1]

How un-English Maria must have appeared to that world! And
how well she knew that this precisely was original sin.

The family was very much aware that both the Huxley brothers
—Leonard's boys—had married foreigners, and it took the best
part of half a century to live it down. It is now conceded that
they made excellent wives. Aldous's sister, Margaret, trying to
explain the lack of contact between brother and sister ("the
actual amounts of time during which Aldous and I merely lived
in the same place were remarkably small, and we never corresponded") declares,

> When Aldous eventually got married, that didn't help as far as I

---

[1] From a letter published in *The Letters of Aldous Huxley*.

was concerned at all, because to be perfectly frank, I didn't take to Maria, not one bit! I was madly keen on games in those years, and I'm sure I didn't appeal to her at all either.[1]

Aldous, who had a marvellously useful unselfconsciousness, remained largely unaware of such undercurrents. For Maria it was, "Next week it is to your Aunt Sophy we go. She of course terrifies me to extremes though I have seen her twice—always equally energetic and wanting to rule."

To Gervas she took at once—*he* was Aldous's favourite cousin. She enjoyed the return to Ottoline, to Garsington (where they spent many of their weekends). Then there was their own flat, "delightful and comfortable," where seriously, amateurishly, they kept house. Maria was amused to see Aldous pottering about, still painting and sawing—"I never suspected him of being so handy at all." They had a daily maid who did the cleaning; no cook. There was no kitchen. What they had was "a hole with a sink", a spirit lamp and Aldous's prodigious instrument for boiling water. One might possibly manage with these if one were very experienced and very patient. Maria became the latter by sheer effort of will (temperamentally, she was extremely quick) and managed to feed Aldous. On tinned soup, bread and jam, an egg beaten into the top of the milk. She used to tell me how she would boil a potato for him over the pilot light of the geyser in their bathroom. The pilot light sprang from a movable bracket that could be turned clear of the geyser casing, and she would hold up a tiny saucepan over that single flame for as long as it took.

Aldous's Aunt Sophy, wishing to help, was much concerned. "My mother", Gervas says, "was worried about the Hampstead flat. They were very hard up . . . She thought Aldous wasn't getting enough to eat. She had them in for meals, gave them a good meal . . . But Maria did her very best. I was very very fond of her—she was awfully good to Aldous."

Aldous and Maria *were* hard up, but no more so than seems acceptable to many young couples, if anything they were rather pleased and proud of being able to manage, and at first it did not occur to anyone that Aldous might be worked above his strength. "Aldous is working very hard but is well I think and happy," Maria wrote to Julian. His work on the *Athenaeum* consisted mainly of reviewing and doing the mass of shorter notices. At once after his marriage he became "frantically busy with a host of books to review and odds and ends of all sorts to write".

[1] Margaret Huxley, from a letter to S. B., 1969.

At the same time he was doing a fair amount of work for other papers and trying "in the somewhat rare intervals" to do things of his own.

How much he was doing, and how rare the intervals must have been, becomes clear when one counts up the items listed in the bibliography.[1] In 1919, in the course of the eight months-odd he was working for the *Athenaeum*, Aldous contributed 29 signed articles and 171 anonymous notices and reviews to the paper, did 8 articles for the *London Mercury* and some reviews for the *Statesman*, published 7 poems in *Wheels* and one story in *Coterie*. His subjects included Aeschylus, Walter De la Mare, Jacob Boehme, John Galsworthy, John Donne, C. H. B. Kitchin, Lord Alfred Douglas, Flaubert, Maeterlinck, John Masefield, Rose Macaulay, Vita Sackville-West, Blaise Cendrars, Paul Claudel, Ronald Firbank, Leonardo da Vinci, Laurence Housman, Latin poems of the Renaissance, a handbook of Greek vase painting, Charles Maurras, André Gide, Mark Twain and Marcel Proust.

It is a crowded sort of life [he wrote four weeks after his wedding to Gidley Robinson, his old headmaster who had sent a present] but I enjoy the work, and the whole atmosphere of the *Athenaeum* is so delightfully remote, in its purely literary preoccupations, from the horrors of the present that it is in a way restful work.

What Aldous needed at that stage of his life was a breathing space; time to sit back and recover, a measure of security, manageable, not crushing, responsibilities. Sadly, for him, for the child, who simply came too soon, he did not get this breathing space; in August already an ominous sentence appears in one of Maria's letters. She is speaking of their flat and how much she loves it, "I [am] already studying how one might find one more room so as to enable us to remain here all our life."

To that letter (to Julian) Aldous added the postscript: "I wish one could do without sleep, that the days were twice as long and that my strength were the strength of ten so that I could do all I want to do."

Now he had to snap up whatever might be going. He signed an agreement with Constable's to do a book on Balzac, fifty pounds on receipt of the MS and the book to be finished by the end of 1920. It will be a big task, he thought, but interesting— "I am rather appalled at the prospect of having to read *all* Balzac!"

[1] *Aldous Huxley, A Bibliography 1916-1959*, by Claire Eschelbach and Joyce Lee Shober, University of California Press, 1961.

## Chapter Seventeen

## "My Two Children—*Limbo* and *Leda*"

ALDOUS had finished his first long story, "The Farcical History of Richard Greenow", earlier in the year; by the autumn he thought that he had enough short stories—five more and a little play—to make a book, and took the MS to Chatto & Windus where Frank Swinnerton read it and approved. The book was accepted. Chatto's were the first publishers Aldous had approached; he remained with them for life.

Maria, pregnant and none too well, stayed much at home; Aldous went his round, from the *Athenaeum* offices to the London Library, to Soho luncheons with a friend, to evenings at the Eiffel Tower restaurant in Charlotte Street or Osbert Sitwell's house in Swan Walk or the Café Royal. In January he managed a week in Paris, staying with a new friend, Drieu La Rochelle, the young writer, "a charming and interesting creature," and meeting "the cubists of literature," Aragon, Tzara, Picabia, Soupault, André Breton.

Aldous's book of short stories, *Limbo*, was published on 29th January (these things were ordered more quickly in those days). The actual sales were only about 1,600 copies but the book was pounced upon by the high-brows and the literate young who were carried away by the cool bugle call of that new astringent voice expressing so essentially the coming post-war mood. Anticipating a roaring lion, the Belgian family had been relieved to find a sheep; Aldous in life was one thing then, Aldous on paper another. There was nothing sheeplike in the sentiments of Richard Greenow.

Mrs Humphry Ward died on 24th March at the age of sixty-nine. Aldous was much affected. Juliette went with him to the funeral. Aldous, tears streaming down his face, wept openly.

The baby was expected any day. Aldous took on another job, a night job as it were, he became second-string dramatic critic on the weekly *Westminster Gazette*. The main critic was the late Naomi Royde-Smith, the novelist (who was also poetry editor and problems editor), an influential figure in the literary world of the time (she published two first poems, Rupert Brooke's and Graham Greene's). Later she married the actor Ernest Milton. She was an extremely nice woman who became an intimate friend of Aldous and Maria.

## "Limbo *and* Leda" | *1920*

On 19th April Matthew Huxley was born. The delivery was an extremely difficult one; Maria had a haemorrhage and nearly died. By her contrivance these facts were largely kept from Aldous. She was told—and this he knew—that it would not be wise for her to have another child.

On 20th April, the very next day, Aldous started his stint as theatre critic (to which he stuck for some eight months). Always reluctant to look too hard at disaster which might after all not occur, and which in this case had *not* occurred, he wrote to Arnold Bennett:

> My wife has just had a son and has, I am thankful to say, weathered the tempest safely and auspiciously. These works of nature really do put works of art in the shade.

Maria and the baby went to Garsington for a longish convalescence. Aldous took on a third job. Part-time work at the Chelsea Book Club, a high-brow book shop cum small art gallery in Cheyne Walk run by a painter called Arundel del Re. Aldous's role was to be knowledgeable and to sign the cheques. The enterprise soon ran into financial trouble and he was not paid. All the same he carried on, putting in a few hours a day. This meant travelling between Hampstead, Chelsea and the Strand: "I have bought a bicycle on which I now do my voyages. Very good exercise . . quite ten miles, I imagine, the double journey, which I take through two parks, so that it is very pleasant. Also from Chelsea to the *Adelphi* and the *Athenaeum* which I do by the long embankments."

What he detested most in his existence was the theatre going. Then, and later, he never ceased to complain about "the quite extraordinary badness of the ordinary play", and became more and more convinced that it ought not to be too difficult to beat the playwrights at their own game. "I shall go on producing plays", he wrote to his father, "till I can get one staged and successful.

> It is the only thing to do . . . There is nothing but a commercial success that can free one from this deadly hustle.

That May Chatto's published *Leda*, Aldous's third collection of poems. "My two children," Aldous said, "*Limbo* and *Leda*."

> *Brown and bright as an agate, mountain-cool,*
> *Eurotas singing slips from pool to pool;*
> *Down rocky gullies; through the cavernous pines*
> *And chestnut groves; down where the terraced vines*

*And gardens overhang; through valleys grey*
*With olive trees, into a soundless bay*
*Of the Aegean. . . .*

So opens the title poem, some five-hundred lines in rhymed couplets, on which Aldous had laboured in the darkness of the Old Christopher at Eton.

*Couched on the flowery ground*
*Young Leda lay, and to her side did press*
*The swan's proud-arching opulent loveliness,*
*Stroking the snow-soft plumage of his breast*
*With fingers slowly drawn, themselves caressed*
*By the warm softness where they lingered, loth*
*To break away. . . .*

Among the shorter poems were the then notorious *Philosopher's Songs*, the fifth being possibly the most quoted of Aldous's verse:

*A million million spermatozoa,*
  *All of them alive:*
*Out of their cataclysm but one poor Noah*
  *Dare hope to survive.*

*And among that billion minus one*
  *Might have chanced to be*
*Shakespeare, another Newton, a new Donne—*
  *But the One was Me.*

The volume ends with another long poem, "*Soles Occidere Et Redire Possunt*," a poem as anguished, contemporary and fragmented as *Leda* is homophonous and serene, an illustration indeed of what Aldous called the multiplicity of man. "*Soles Occidere*" is a curious work and it is prefaced by an equally curious introduction.

John Ridley, the subject of this poem, was killed in February 1918. "If I should perish," he wrote to me only five weeks before his death, "if I should perish—and one isn't exactly a 'good life' at the moment—I wish you'd write something about me. It isn't vanity (for I know you'll do me, if anything, rather less than justice!), not vanity, I repeat; but that queer irrational desire one has for immortality of any kind, however short and precarious—for frankly, my dear, I doubt whether your verses will be so very much more perennial than brass. Still, they'll be something. One can't, of course, believe in any *au-delà* for one's personal self . . . No, my only hope is you—and a damned poor guarantee for eternity. Don't make of me a khaki image . . . I sincerely hope, of course, that you won't have to write the thing at all—hope not, but have very little doubt you will. Good-bye."

The following poem is a tentative and provisional attempt to comply with his request. Ridley was an adolescent, and suffered from that . . . characteristic instability of mind which makes adolescence so feebly sceptical, so inefficient, so profoundly unhappy. I have fished up a single day from Ridley's forgotten existence. It has a bedraggled air in the sunlight, this poor wisp of Lethean weed. Fortunately, however, it will soon be allowed to drop back into the water, where we shall all, in due course, join it. "The greater part must be content to be as though they had not been."

It is strange to think of Aldous fifty years ago taking up that grudging challenge. And when did he find time to write that elaborate poem of nearly five hundred lines? Nobody remembers him referring to the dead friend and his weird legacy. Did Aldous work at "*Soles Occidere*" in spare moments at Eton, in holidays at Prior's Field or Garsington in the intervals of writing *Leda* and "The Farcical History of Richard Greenow"? Or in London during the first year of his marriage, in the year of the great journalistic grind? Well, he wrote it, and there survives now of John Ridley his own letter and Aldous's poem, in print both after some fifty years—a far cry from immortality though, as Ridley might have said, it's something.

*Leda* in a sense was the last of Aldous as a poet. Although he went on writing and publishing verse for another ten years (in fact never entirely ceased to), his main creative impulse after his mid-twenties flowed no longer into poetry. His quantitative output, the sheer fact of writing so much to earn a living had something to do with it doubtlessly, though the demands on his time and energy were heavier if anything during the decade of *The Burning Wheel*, *The Defeat of Youth* and the Mallarmé translation; but then fatigue can be cumulative and surreptitious. The partial silting of one channel was an unconscious, unwilled process and not, I think, the result of any deliberate, practical or critical, decision on his part. Aldous did not give up poetry and "confine himself" to prose in the way described by T. S. Eliot.

. . My prestige [in 1919] was such that Aldous submitted for my opinion his own book of Verse, *Leda and Other Poems:* I am afraid that I was unable to show any enthusiasm for his verse. After this attempt he wisely confined himself to the essay and that variety of fiction which he came to make his own.[1]

"Luckily," Aldous wrote in another context, "people don't leave much trace on me. They make an impression easily, like a ship on water. But the water closes up again."[2]

In June Maria and the baby returned from Garsington to the flat which had meanwhile been improved with some ingenuity. "Our little hole with the sink," Aldous wrote, "has been given gas and lined with shelves, so that it makes a really excellent little kitchen. M's room has been distempered and serves pretty comfortably as a nursery."

They had a nurse-maid for the infant, but decisions were up to Aldous and Maria. "Shall we boil the teat?" they asked Juliette. "Oh, I think so."

In August Aldous decided to give up the job with the Chelsea Book Club; he could not afford to spend his time for nothing. As it was, he felt "excessively busy and overworked" and never had a holiday. However, there was now a good job in prospect: "Sordid journalism but a screw of £400 which, at the moment and in the circs, I can't refuse. Journalism is paying in the inverse ratio of the goodness of the paper, which is rather melancholy." He added, "I should like to be rid of the whole damn thing, but there's no chance yet."

So in October Aldous left the *Athenaeum* (though he went on contributing to the paper) and went to work for Condé Nast. At first he would seem to have been caught by some enthusiasm.

> I have just helped to float [he wrote to Naomi Mitchison] a marvellous paper belonging to the *Vogue* people,—*House and Garden* (run by a "staff of experts" . . otherwise by me and a young girl). It is a huge success: more than £1000 worth of advertisements in the first number . . . I wish I reaped more of the profits than I do; but I won't do too badly . . .

Aldous and Maria were better off now and Aldous's work was less dispersed, though he had kept on the theatre job for the time being. Yet Maria was still far from well and, as might have been obvious from the first, existence with baby and nurse-maid in that flat for two was not really possible. The baby yelled when Aldous had to write or sleep. In spite of the recent alterations, they decided to give up the place. A very typical thing for them

---

[1] In *Mem. Vol.*     [2] Philip Quarles in *Point Counter Point.*

to do as it turned out. Again and again it was to be—convert, furnish, buy or build—Maria proclaiming that it was for the rest of their natural days—then in no time move out lock, stock and barrel. Now they suspended home life altogether. Maria and the child were to go to her family in Belgium for the winter, while Aldous was to toil on in London, put up by friends. Though gloomy enough in the short run, this was a constructive plan: Maria was to get well and Aldous to make enough money to get away from journalism for a time. Their aim was Italy by the spring with something like four or five clear months in hand.

They packed up before the New Year. Maria took Matthew to Mère at St Trond; and Aldous, after a solitary Christmas doing two or three theatres a day, was able to see Maria again in Paris, "snatching a brief and restless holiday". They stayed with Lewis Gielgud and his French wife, Mimi, Aldous and Lewis trying "to write up a new play in frantic haste". (The play came to nothing.)

Aldous now spent the rest of the winter in a flat in Bloomsbury belonging to Tommy Earp. Russell Green, their mutual Oxford friend explains the amiable, haphazard set-up. Earp, Russell claims, had just inherited forty thousand pounds and proposed to take an extra flat at 36 Regent Square.

"I like having several places, don't you know. Why not furnish it and we will live there." Tommy Earp handed me the cash to furnish the flat, and we resided there until 1924. (I must say the constant hot water was a great boon.)
It was there that dear Aldous joined us.[1]

Russell Green of the photographic memory goes on:

I can still see him, sitting back on the Minty basket chair [this would be after Aldous's office day at *House and Garden*] typewriter on knees, producing reports on (I fancy) orchestral concerts for the old green *Westminster Gazette*.

(Aldous had gone on to doing the infinitely more congenial concert notices; he was succeeded as dramatic critic by A. P. Herbert.)

Before this effort Aldous would brace himself with a cup of tea, using what he termed "my silver egg", which he lowered into a cup,

---

[1] Russell Green, in letters to S. B.

poured on boiling water till infusion was complete. I noticed how pallid and strained he seemed. But it all helped to accumulate enough cash to enable him to travel, with pretty wife Maria, to write a new book.

Green was struck—as we all so often were—by the inconsistencies in Aldous's seeing.

Though I have seen him, in that basket chair, reading Braille, he was quite capable of riding his bicycle about London . . .

One day Green plucked up courage to read Aldous passages from his own first novel. "At a pause, his silvery voice emitted the damning question, 'But, my dear Russell, do you suppose that anyone will ever *read* it?' . . He was quite right—nobody ever did."

By the end of March Aldous had saved enough money. Maria was already in Italy; the Fasolas had found them a place to live. Aldous packed his books, watched by Russell Green.

I can see them now before me piled on the carpet. He took with him the new *Handy Volume* of the Encyclopaedia Britannica.

But Aldous was tired out. The London Life Association refused to insure him in his present condition. "It is absurd and rather humiliating to be a Bad Life," he wrote to his father the day before he left England, "and I am resolved [to become] definitely a Good Life . . by leading a decent existence for a few months. I shall try and get really well while I am in Italy."

# PART FOUR

## European Decade: 1921-1930

La bêtise n'est pas mon fort.
PAUL VALÉRY

The performance took place against
a background of relatively few, simple,
moral convictions; they were disguised
by the brilliance of the technical accomplishment, but they were there . . .
like the monotonous, insistent, continuous ground bass slowly pounding
away through the elaborate intellectual
display.

SIR ISAIAH BERLIN

# Chapter One

## Tuscan Summer

THEY were in Florence on their son's first birthday. "Darling," Maria wrote to him twenty-seven years later from California in another April,

> This is a little letter full of sentimental affections because we have just returned from a birthday party for little Bill.[1] And it reminds me so much of your birthday party; there is nothing again like the first one.
>
> We were in the Villa Minucci, which you cannot remember, it was cloudy and sunny as always when the lilac bloom and they were blooming all around the house and scenting through the open windows. You were as blonde and pink as little Bill and you said your first word and had your first tooth on that day. The Sitwells and Willy Walton the composer came to tea and you were as unconcerned as little Bill about the whole thing.

The Villa Minucci. It stood on the Via Santa Margherita a Montici, country then, above a valley planted with olives and vines. The Huxleys lived in a wing of it; on one side the whole of Florence lay before them in the plain below, on the other there was an exquisite Tuscan view of hills and San Miniato. They lived in two rooms, one of them large and long, a kitchen and a garden, and paid 150 lire a month, two pounds in terms of the exchange. They had divided the long room with a screen, Aldous and Maria slept in one half and sat in the other, nurse and baby had the second room and all ate in the kitchen. Maria was well again, Matthew had grown healthy and big, and there was a nanny now, Julian and Aldous's old Fräulein (Bella to Matthew) back from out of the past with "her round red face a little wrinkled, like a ripening apple".

At first Aldous did little but eat and sleep. (For much of his life he had the gift of flawless sleep, nine hours easily, ten given the time.) It was his first view of Italian Italy (he had been as far as Lake Como one Easter holiday as a boy). He kept his head about Florence. Too tre- and quattrocento for his taste—too much Gothic in the architecture and too much primitive art in

---

[1] Bill Kiskadden, godson of Aldous and Maria, a child of their friends Dr William and Peggy Kiskadden.

the galleries. "I am an enthusiastic *post*-Raphaelite. Sixteenth and seventeenth century . . is what I enjoy . . ."

One must go to Rome for the architecture and to Venice for the painting and of course to the masses of little towns where you find "the most fabulous outflowings of baroque buildings". He had not yet been to any of these places but hoped to get to them in time. As for people. The English colony is "a queer collection; a sort of decayed provincial intelligentsia". Among the permanent inhabitants he liked Vernon Lee, and Geoffrey and Lady Sybil Scott. From "the number of awful people of one's acquaintance, or wanting to make one's acquaintance, who pass through the town, we escape by chance and cunning".

Quite soon Aldous was well enough to be thinking about work. They had an idea that the sea might suit him and Forte dei Marmi was the obvious choice: the Fasolas were going, Aldous *liked* Costanza. In May they went and took "a minute little house [Aldous to his father] with four rooms, very clean . . and well-furnished with comfortable beds and a good batterie de cuisine, with a garden . . ." Aldous hopes that now all will be perfect. It is the perennial wish expressed by those who have resolved to produce work in a new place and a given span of time. How many writers, before Aldous and after, surfacing from some lucrative, exhausting stint, have been first daunted then defeated by the daily imperative of their hard-earned and counted mornings. At Forte Aldous knuckled down point-blank to write a novel, pledging himself to finish it within two months. And writing *Crome Yellow*—such can be the reward of virtue—turned out to be not the least like reading Macaulay in Braille; it was like being in a state of grace. Happy countries, he wrote to his father, have no history.

The life of the household was even and revolved around Aldous's needs. His days fell into a pattern which he was to reproduce, *mutatis mutandis*, for much of his life. Work in the morning; a bathe in a warm sea, luncheon, walking or reading till tea; more work; a latish dinner, often with friends, and after dinner music or reading.

At Forte they ate out of doors in the shade and wore the light, free clothes of the Mediterranean summer. Aldous was thriving; born into the rain, he said, he had always had a craving for sunlight and heat.

At the hour before dinner, alone in their room Aldous and Maria talked. This became their habit. Aldous pacing perhaps, Maria sitting at her looking glass told him about the day, told him what she had seen; the early light on the hills, the first cicada, the neighbours' ménage à trois. Maria was Mercury, was the messenger, bringing the news of her world. Aldous asked, Maria told. Too *curious*, he said, too *extraordinary*; then used it, changed it, made it his own.

He *was* working well. For so many years circumstances had forced him to hold back sustained writing; in the meantime he acquired experience by the incessant practice of literary journalism. (Of a high standard of excellence. Bruce Richmond, the editor of the *Times Literary Supplement*, whose taste was a hundred per cent classical, said of Aldous's prose, using the colloquial English of the late Victorians, "He is a real swell."[1]) Now, the Peacockian novel—the form so deliberately chosen—flowed. An entertainment he called it, though not on the title page, and he was delighted by what he found was there to shape and say—the fireworks of ideas, the erudite digressions, the mild (from today's view) human ironies—and some of this joy, this freshness of a young writer's easy dip into his treasures, still comes through.

In their first Hampstead days Maria had been amused to find Aldous capable of being handy about the house. She soon decided that this would not do. Aldous's gaiety—he was a far gayer man, a more light-hearted companion, than one might deduce from the letters—his zest when stimulated, his unassuming attempts to ride bicycles and buses like everybody else, made people forget or underestimate both the extra strain imposed by his sight and the great need he had to recuperate from the events of his early years. Maria did not forget; on the immediate level she was resolved that all should be done to make his daily life peaceful, effortless and agreeable, that he should be spared concerns extraneous to his work and thoughts, should be free, above all should feel free, of any domestic and practical demands. This she carried out in sickness and in health for thirty-six years. All who knew them saw this and how she went about it, and there are revealing passages in her own letters. In the 1940s, for instance, she advised her young, and slightly rebellious niece, Claire Nicolas,

> As-tu jamais pensé qu'il fallait se préparer pour la vie intime avec un amant dans la vie intime de la famille? Une chose aussi délicate que l'amour, l'affection, l'admiration ne doit pas être dérangée par des détails dangereux, petits mais continues, de la vie journalière ...
>
> Par le plus grands des hazards j'ai découvert, étant de ton age, que ce sont les efforts incessants, invisibles et inconnus du passant, qui nous donnent le plus de sécurité et de joie ...
>
> .. Ton mari, ton amant, sans savoir pourquoi sera toujours heureux et calme avec toi—parceque tu fera des choses dont il ne doit pas se fatiguer à te remercier.[2]

[1] As told by Sir George Clark.
[2] See footnote, page 400.

For all this concentration on the novel, Aldous had some leisure to look at Italy. There were jaunts into Lucca, Pisa, a day or two at Siena. (". . English strangers wandering about the streets," seen by their future friend Yvonne Franchetti,[1] "tall, tall Aldous peering at the façades, beside him tiny Maria, trailing behind them a baby and a nanny . . .") English strangers—not entirely absorbed by the façades: The fascisti [Aldous to his father] ". . One cannot imagine how the Italian population suffers an entirely irresponsible private organization [which in fact it still was in 1921] to act as the fascio does—sometimes usurping powers that should belong to the state, sometimes resorting to incredible acts of violence and brutality. People look on with a sort of resignation.

"It is the same attitude as one sees over the whole world— blank fatalistic resignation to stupid and wicked governments, to anything or any person with power."

Aldous finished *Crome Yellow* in the second week of August, and the MS, re-typed by Maria, was sent off to Chatto & Windus. "Practically, I have written the whole thing, some 60,000 words, in the 2 months I have been here: which is pretty good going."

He hopes that the book will amuse, "It is pleasingly baroque." The last weeks *have* been a strain and he is looking forward to a rest, though he is already thinking of doing another Peacock, "a gigantic one in an Italian scene". Meanwhile he and Maria went to Rome; they had been lent a flat for a week. Now Aldous *was* swept off his feet. "What a place! It inspires one at once with a kind of passion to know it utterly and inside out . . . It is certainly the place where I shall come to spend my old age and if possible, large portions of my existence . . ."

He discovered that architecture, sculpture and painting gave him as much pleasure as music. When he could indulge his post-Raphaelite tastes that was—"Rome being practically invented by Bernini.

I feel sorry for people who come to Rome with the preconceived certitude of the badness of Bernini and the seventeenth century. They are left nothing but Michelangelo and Raphael, the Colisseum, the columns and arches and the insupportably dreary spectacle of the rubbish in the forums.

When Aldous's grandfather T. H. H. visited Rome in 1885 he expressed dissimilar if equally forthright views. He railed

---

[1] The present Mrs Hamish Hamilton.

against "the ill-proportioned, worse decorated tawdry stone mountain on the vatican," and described some of the rites performed in St Peter's as "elaborate tomfooleries . . . devised, one would think, by a college of ecclesiastical man-milliners for the delectation of school-girls.

> The best thing, from an aesthetic point of view, that could be done with Rome would be to destroy everything except St Paolo fuor le Mure, of later than the fourth century.[1]

Aldous left Rome inspired with an intense desire to live. "What I should like now more than anything [he wrote from Forte] is a year or two of quiet devoted simply to seeing places and things and people: to living, in fact. When one hasn't much vitality or physical energy, it is almost impossible to live and work at the same time . . . Circumstances demand that I should work almost continuously, and I can't squeeze in enough living."

Aldous had to make up his mind about the immediate future, whether to go on living in Italy or to return to England. In Italy they could live comfortably on less than 2,000 lire a month, £300 a year, and live more comfortably at that than on £800 in England. The question was could he be certain of making that £300? "I hope to have from £70 to £100 in hand in the autumn. My book, if it does as well as the last, should bring me another £100." What with getting some short stories into magazines and writing enough of them for another volume in the spring, he ought to be able to make up the rest. Then there were the drawbacks of Italy: the absence of libraries and the lack of informed and intelligent society; on the other hand the thought of plunging back into journalism appalled him. "I have been living for two years in a perpetual state of fatigue and I don't want to go back to it if I can help it . . ."

In September Aldous still does not quite know what will become of them. Condé Nast has offered £750 a year; if he accepts, they will be "pretty comfortable" in London. If only one could spend half one's time in each country—"but that, alas, seems impossible."

---

[1] T. H. Huxley to his son Leonard, Rome, Jan. 20th 1885. (From *Life and Letters of Thomas Henry Huxley*, by Leonard Huxley. Macmillan & Co., 1900.)

## Chapter Two

## Life in London: Westbourne Terrace

IN October they were back in London. Aldous had accepted the Condé Nast job and they were about to set up house again. They took a ground floor and basement near Paddington in one of those family houses that were being cut up into maisonettes. Hampstead Hill Gardens had been cramped, 155 Westbourne Terrace was all echoing space. The rooms were vast, and two of Maria's sisters came over to help paint them. Jeanne brought her fiancé, René Moulaert, a young theatrical decorator, and he chose the colours. The ground floor consisted of a lofty front room occupied by Bella and the baby, Maria's room opening on a small inner court and, separated by a bathroom, a rather sad back room in which Aldous slept. Below was a kitchen, an immense dining-room and another sizeable back room looking out on dustbins, Aldous's study. This they painted lemon yellow to make it look more cheerful. The basement was infested with black-beetles, and there was a poor, thin local cat who chased and ate them.

*Crome Yellow* was published in November. For Aldous as a writer this was the end of the beginning. People were dazzled; he had made a name. Or perhaps he had only caught up with his own curiously precursory fame. Since early Oxford, with little published and less read, the literary aura had been about Aldous. Proust. conjured him up on the margin of the soirée at the Princesse de Guermantes' in the guise of the nephew of the "illustrious Huxley", who himself appears in the guise of an eminent physician.

L'illustre Huxley (celui dont le neveu occupe actuellement une place prépondérante dans le monde de la littérature anglaise) . . .[1]

*Actuellement*—yet that passage of *Sodome et Gomorrhe* must have been written before the appearance of Aldous's first novel. (Forty years later Aldous made one comment, "I never met Proust and have no idea how he came to know about me—as it was far from being true that . . I occupied a preponderant position in English literature at that time.") When his first novel did appear in 1921

[1] *A La Recherche du Temps Perdu: Sodome et Gomorrhe.*

the literary world was captivated; at the same time—such are the changes in moral fashions—a good many people were shocked as well. While the young were exhilarated, their parents and schoolmasters disapproved; so did Aldous's own family.

> When he produced *Crome Yellow* and the other novels [writes his sister Margaret] I couldn't see any of the Aldous I knew in them and was bitterly upset by their unkindness of attitude (as I saw it).

Aldous saw it too, and put his finger on it in his next book. The American heiress meets Dolphin, the poet, in the Italian moonlight. She asks, "Will you show me your books?" Dolphin replies:[1]

> "Certainly not, Miss Toomis. That would ruin our friendship. I am insufferable in my writings. In them I give vent to all the horrible thoughts and impulses which I am too timid to express or put into practice in real life. Take me as you find me here, a decent specimen of a man, shy but able to talk intelligently when the layers of ice are broken, aimless, ineffective, but on the whole quite a good sort."

Margaret called it unkindness of attitude, the general public had another word for it—the name Aldous Huxley became equated with cynicism. Aldous (again in his next book) permitted himself a retaliation.

> "Oh, you're cynical."
> Mr Hutton always had a desire to say "Bow-wow-wow" whenever that last word was spoken. It irritated him more than any other word in the language.[2]

Mr Hutton goes on to explain that he is *not* cynical.

> I'm only speaking a melancholy truth. Reality doesn't always come up to the ideal, you know. But that doesn't make me believe any the less in the ideal.

That brings us to another matter, one which also irritated Aldous, the game so dear to acquaintances and scholars of pinning down who might be who. It irritated him because he found it trivial and beside the point. He felt that this whole process of writing, this process of transposing life and fiction is far from wholly conscious and a good deal more obscure and complex

[1] "Permutations Among the Nightingales", *Mortal Coils*, 1922.
[2] "The Gioconda Smile", ibid.

than putting Jack Robinson or D. H. Lawrence into a book. It might be true to say that Aldous himself did not so much put "real characters" into his books as use two or three striking aspects of one as a starting point. A novelist may be propelled originally by a face, a voice, a mannerism, a psychological situation or a place, but as he goes on something else takes over, call it inspiration or the exigencies of art, he will leave out, add, develop, change. When he is done there may be little left in Mary Fortinbras's character or story resembling that of Jenny Y, the author's friend. Mrs Fortinbras has turned out quite an elaborate monster whereas Mrs Y for all her affectations is an uncomplicated soul, though both happen to scream like peacocks, dread getting old and have a house in Rome. The great public is unaware of Mrs Y's existence; for the author, his own creation has very likely blotted out her very memory; but in her circle the fat is in the fire.

Aldous often found himself accused. He had a habit of mixing up his starting points—one man's philosophy, another's sexual tastes, one trait from a member of his family, another from a character in history—and as he did not like to stop and think that any particular person might recognize fragments of himself in an otherwise outrageous context, he took little trouble to cover up his traces.

Lady Ottoline was offended by *Crome Yellow* and a breach ensued that lasted many years. Aldous and Maria were distressed, and Aldous genuinely surprised. If the setting of the novel, the country house party, was very much based on Garsington, was not this if anything a rather elegant homage to his hosts? (The actual fictional house, Crome with its privies in the turrets, did not look like Garsington but—mixed starting points indeed—like a very old house in remote Oxfordshire.[1]) And if people, a handful of people, saw Henry Wimbush as Philip Morrell, was this not again a compliment as he is made the author of that moving pastiche, the Dwarfs' Story? And if they thought they recognized a bit of Bertie Russell in Mr Scogan, a bit of Mark Gertler in the painter, and Evan Morgan (or was it Koteliansky?) in the pianist, if they said that Anne made them think of Carrington (or Maria Nys), Jenny of Brett, and Mary of Maria (or of Carrington), surely then people must also see that all these were conceived in a spirit of light-hearted comedy and that their absurdities did not belong to life and dreary *Realismus*, but to a summer's masque? Aldous was puzzled and tried to explain in letters. The Morrells remained offended.

[1] Then belonging to Clothilde Fielding, the daughter of Brewster, Henry James's dentist in Rome.

Meanwhile Max Beerbohm wrote to him about *Crome Yellow*, a very precious letter Aldous called it. Cool though he became to praise or blame, praise from that quarter then delighted him. Thanking the master, he used the identical Victorianism Bruce Richmond had used about himself: "Such a charming and all too generous letter from such a tremendous swell is an honour . . .

. . It also gave me a great deal of pleasure and encouragement, your letter. Thank you very much indeed.

Aldous was even moved to refer to his own circumstances.

Quant à moi, I am very securely wedded and possess a son of two years old, whom I shall train up to be an engineer or a capitalist— none of this literary business—with a view to being supported, during my declining years, in a state of cultured ease.

That year Aldous was elected a member of the Athenaeum Club, proposed by his father and seconded by Professor Raleigh whose lectures on Elizabethan literature he used to attend at Oxford.

Aldous very rarely discussed work in progress so that when we find him sending a draft MS to his father inviting comment, we can surely take it as an indication that their adult relationship (always affectionate) was a good deal more positive than has sometimes been said.

Dearest Father,
I enclose the story about the nun I told you about. ["Nuns at Luncheon", one of the stories Aldous was writing to fill up that volume for the spring.] My impression is that the . . . sexo-religious psychology of the beginning is too long and that the story wd be better remodelled so as to give only the anecdote itself, very quickly and sharply.

Leonard Huxley, it must be remembered, was a most able— possibly underrated—literary man; and certainly in that domain was taken au sérieux by his son. "He was the perfect editor," writes John Murray who worked as his assistant on the *Cornhill Magazine* as a young man.

So firm was his basis of literary scholarship that he could afford to be gentle and humble in dealing with authors of every age or degree of experience or conceit. The gentleness caused me continual problems because, when dealing with his letters, I often did not know if the author's contribution had to be sent to the printer for proofing or returned as a rejection. So gentle and firmly helpful was he that many years later a contributor to the *Cornhill* told me that he preferred a letter of rejection from Leonard Huxley to one of acceptance from any other editor. It was L. H.'s humility and the self-effacing quality of his editorial handling of, for example, the work of Elizabeth and Robert Browning, Jane Welsh Carlyle and Captain Scott of the Antarctic that denied him the public recognition that was his due.[1]

At 50 Albemarle Street, where then as now the *Cornhill* was edited, "business and pleasure were indistinguishably blended". Aldous occasionally called. "It always seemed to me surprising that they were father and son. Perhaps it was Leonard's litheness of body and mind and Aldous's short-sightedness that were partly responsible for an apparent levelling of age, but it was the way in which they conversed, and disagreed, that strengthened the illusion. And when, on visits to the Leonard Huxleys' home in Hampstead on pleasure, or on *Cornhill* business, Julian and his step-mother were also present, the illusion of a single generation was complete."[1]

Aldous and Maria lived in the Paddington flat for a whole year, black-beetles, journalism and all, a very pleasant one. Aldous kept loose office hours at Rolls House, E.C.4 and was pretty busy writing articles on heterogeneous subjects, drumming up ideas and contributors (he solicited Norman Douglas, Lytton Strachey), even sketching covers; but he was not hounded any longer, there was some leisure and a bit of time for odds and ends of his own; his health, and Maria's, was not radiant, it seldom was—and Matthew too was often ill or believed to be ill as a child—but for London they were all fairly well. They had stimulating and attractive friends. ("We kept *table ouverte* in those early days," Maria used to say, wondering how they did it.) Theirs was still rather a hand-to-mouth existence. When Jeanne got married that April, they were unable to send their small wedding present till the week after. Then, Maria wrote, they would send three English notes, three pound notes, which Jeanne should be able to change—those were the years of the monster inflations in Europe—at a good rate. And they must come and stay, Jeanne and Moulaert, any time they please, *avec joie*, there will always be beds for them and rice *à discretion*—"*Que faut-il de plus?*"

[1] From a letter of John Murray to S. B., 1971.

They were young. Domestic life at Westbourne Terrace was gay. From Suzanne, who came to live with them for some months, we get a memory of it as fresh as paint. Suzanne, nineteen then, had a yet undirected talent (she became of course a sculptress) and Aldous and Maria wanted to assist her training. (Moreover, the poor girl needed a change of scene having lately been involved in a rather macabre incident, a piece of family lore treasured by Aldous. A rejected suitor—Suzanne was of angelic beauty—upon hearing the final No, shot himself in the Nys's drawing-room. Her father, on hearing a pistol shot, came out of his study to find a young man, smoking weapon by his side, lying on the carpet in his blood. "This is inconceivable!" Monsieur Nys exclaimed. The expiring young man opened his lips: "Monsieur it *is* conceivable.") In London, Suzanne was given a bed in Aldous's room, separated from his by a screen. Aldous produced ideas and sketches for magazine covers, she was to turn them into commercial copy. There were elliptic Boromini staircases, façades of the Acropolis adorned by *jeunes filles en fleurs*, and there was the black and white cover, over which she laboured long and hard and which was finally accepted by Naomi Royde-Smith (who paid £10)—a piece of Negro sculpture set next to a white plaster statuette of Queen Victoria. As for Maria, "Coccola was adorable. She did everything to encourage me . . ." Suzanne helped with the housework, moth-balling winter clothes, getting the evening meal (breakfast and luncheon were produced by Matthew's Bella and there was a Mrs Jones to do the cleaning). Things that Suzanne would have shirked at home became a pleasure with Maria,

. . devenaient une fête et aussi m'ont rendue un peu plus pratique plus tard, dans mon ménage.

She was not allowed, however, to wash up having once been caught out not plunging soapy plates into pure water. Always wonderfully soignée, Maria had now become competent as well. She sewed beautifully—as many people do who were taught by nuns—and was making her own hats and dresses. Even the food had become sensible (for the time being): they did not live on rice alone nor on the grapes and lettuce leaves of wartime Florence; Aldous had a proper breakfast every morning, porridge with fresh cream, tea, bacon and eggs.

On Thursdays Naomi Royde-Smith, Osbert, Sacheverell and Edith Sitwell came to dinner and afterwards they all went to the cinema. On other evenings they had Jack[1] and Mary Hutchinson,

---

[1] The late St John Hutchinson, K.C.

Sullivan,[1] Mark Gertler, Tommy Earp. When they were by themselves Aldous and Maria would dance to the gramophone after
dinner, foxtrots, tangoes, with Matthew following in their steps
clinging on to one of Aldous's trouser legs. (When Joan Collier
Buzzard came to see them, Matthew would meet her in the hall,
take her hand and say, "Come, I will show you Daddy.")

Aldous took a certain pleasure in his clothes, which he wore
with casual elegance. He was then and always mildly, idio-
syncratically dandified. His suits were made by a good London
tailor (Studd and Millington for a long time); they were never
blue or pin-striped or a solid colour, they were speckled, softly
patterned, snuff coloured, cinnamon coloured or what Maria
called a nice brownsy grey. (Incidentally he looked very well in
dark and plain, and irresistible in tails—Aldous would have made
the most distinguished-looking conductor who ever stood on
platform.) He wore a waistcoat and a watch-and-chain. His
shirts, soft collars, were usually white and his socks always white.
His ties often verged on the cubist or the floral. Sometimes he
wore a snake-skin tie, or was it a lizard tie? and I don't think
that he as much as owned an Eton one. In later years he wore
no hat—except occasionally a French beret—but then he still
sported a black hat with a very large brim indeed, to all effects
a sombrero. "Here", the St John Hutchinson's young children
would cry when they saw his long form ambling up their garden
path, "Here comes the Quangle-Wangle!"

Their poor alley cat died. (Aldous evoked her in *Those Barren
Leaves*: Mr Cardan is alone in church at Montefiascone with the
body of Grace Elver, the moron who has died of fish poisoning,
on a bier.

> Once, years ago, he had a . . . cat. She ate too many black-beetles
> in the kitchen and died vomiting shreds of her shard-torn stomach.
> He had often thought of that cat. One might die like that oneself,
> coughing up one's vitals.)

Now, Aldous acquired one of his perennial loves, a Siamese,
who did not live in the kitchen but attached itself to him. They
played together and when Aldous went back to writing the
creature would settle itself snugly on his neck.

Mark Gertler asked Suzanne to sit for him in the house on
Hampstead Heath that he shared with Dorothy Brett. (There
she saw Brett—listening to them through a great copper ear-
trumpet.) Pocket money having run out, Maria allowed Suzanne

---

[1] The late J. N. W. Sullivan (mathematician, music critic and scientific
journalist).

2/6d. a week out of the house-keeping for the bus fare but had warned her of Gertler:

"Méfie toi car il embrasse les filles derrière les portes." Doubtlessly, Suzanne adds, "a memory of the time she was at Lady Ottoline's." She found Gertler charming. He did not kiss behind doors—"tout beau comme il était, pareil à un personnage de Carpaccio," and she soon met the young woman he was head over heels in love with, Carrington. Gertler did two portraits of Suzanne; between sittings they walked on the Heath, lay on the grass, he talking to her about Chekov, about life at Garsington, telling her not to go there (someone had suggested her as young Julian Morrell's companion).

Aldous was still doing concert notices for the *Westminster Gazette:* Suzanne usually went with him. On the bus he would talk to her, on his own level, about music, literature and art.

> Aldous prenait à cœur de m'éduquer, de me donner des conseils, souvent par l'intermédiaire de Coccola . . . Aldous avait la courtoisie et la politesse de son éducation d'origine victorienne, malgré l'influence de la révolution dans les mœurs à Garsington . . . Quoique Aldous était cérébralement agnostique, libertin et sceptique, de nature il était timide, donc peu entreprenant, un peu hypocrite et très critique, tout en étant plein d'égards pour les gens les plus simples telle la femme à journée, Mrs Jones.

After a concert Aldous and Suzanne would find Maria waiting up in her large divan bed, where "on s'installait tous les trois," and the sisters would take turns in reading aloud to Aldous *Les Voyages du Père Huc au Tibet*, after which Suzanne went off to sleep behind the screen in Aldous's room. Sometimes she would perceive Aldous late at night creeping about the dark, get a bottle out of a cupboard and take a swig. "Je croyais que c'était un 'night cap'. Ma mère prétendait toujours que les anglais buvaient dans leur chambre à coucher, surtout les femmes, même de l'eau-de Cologne . . ."

She was much relieved when she discovered that the bottle in the cupboard was a cough mixture. Often Aldous and Suzanne, each on their side of the screen, had nocturnal conversations. He told her stories from the Bible and one night when the flat was cold he told the story of King David and Bathsheba. "Je lui disait que c'était dommage qu'il n'était pas David et on finissait par s'endormir chacun de son côté du paravent avec regret."

Suzanne summed up those months with Aldous and Maria— "in their atmosphere of perfect lovingness"—as one of the most harmonious of her life. There was one anxiety, Maria's when Aldous was abroad in the London traffic on his own. (His bicycling terrified her, yet she never stopped him.) When friends left after dinner he liked to walk them home; one night when he was late returning, Suzanne saw Maria stand in tears by the front door.

In May, only six months after *Crome Yellow*, *Mortal Coils*, Aldous's second book of fiction, appeared. It contained what has become one of his best known stories, "The Gioconda Smile", the story he re-wrote—with such changes of emphasis and range —twenty-five years later as a play. It also contained a good deal of 1922 Aldous. To quote once more from *son semblable*, *son frère*, Sidney Dolphin the poet:

> His two volumes of verse, "Zoetrope" and "Trembling Ears", have been recognized by intelligent critics as remarkable. How far they are poetry nobody, least of all Dolphin himself, is certain. They may be merely the ingenious products of a very cultured and elaborate brain. Mere curiosities; who knows? His age is twenty-seven.

And here another character compliments Dolphin on his philosophical detachment, " 'Brooding on the universe as usual?'

> "My philosophical detachment? But it's only a mask to hide the ineffectual longings I have to achieve contact with the world."

*Crome Yellow*, meanwhile, had been earning its advance, and Aldous was being paid royalties. The book sold 2,500 copies in the first year and 86 the year after. (*This Side of Paradise*, Scott Fitzgerald's first novel published the year before, sold forty-five thousand.) Cash in hand, Aldous enrolled Suzanne in an art course he had seen advertised in *Vogue*.

All good things come to an end. First Matthew left with Bella to visit her family in what was now Poland. Then Maria went off, bound for Paris and Forte. For a while Suzanne kept house for Aldous and made the Siamese cat's nauseous dinner of boiled cods' heads as instructed. Then Aldous, too, went to join Maria, and Suzanne alone remained behind to finish her art course after seeing Aldous off one fine morning, cat in basket, from Victoria station.

## Chapter Three

## Proboque, Deteriora Sequor

THE publishing agreement with Chatto & Windus which was to have such an effect upon Aldous's literary and material life was not signed until January 1923. However, the main principle—a regular income enabling him to give up jobs and journalism and devote all his energies to his own writing—must have been under discussion, and very likely settled in rough detail, several months before. This seems to be borne out by Aldous's and Maria's moves.

Another stretch of summer at Forte, another villa, reunited with Baby "splendidly well" after his travels, preceded by a little travelling on their own: Salzburg Mozart festival, expenses footed by the *Westminster*; a day or two in Vienna where they were so appalled by what they saw of post-war misery that the memory of it still beclouded their views on European revival in the 1940s; their first sight of Venice. In the autumn they returned to London, having made up their minds to settle down in England. First, half-heartedly, it was to be the country, then became London after all. By the new year they had moved house, to Kensington this time, to 44 Princess Gardens, the first of their more conventional abodes. Aldous was able to invite Suzanne in these positive terms, ". . . When are you coming to stay with us again? We can offer you le confort moderne in this house: no horrors of the kind which abounded at Westbourne Terrace. Do come."

The "MEMORANDUM of AGREEMENT Made this Eighth Day of January Nineteen Twenty-Three between Aldous Huxley of the one part and Messrs Chatto & Windus of 97 & 99 St. Martin's Lane, London W.C.2 . . ." was clear, uncomplicated and, by today's standards, brief. The substance was contained in two clauses, numbers One and Six.

1) The Author agrees to supply the Publishers with two new works of fiction per annum (one of which two works shall be a full-length novel) written by himself during the next three years.

6) The Publishers agree to pay the Author for the period of three years . . . . the sum of Five Hundred Pounds per annum . . . such sum to be considered an advance on account of royalties upon the earnings of the Author's books.

Financially, the arrangement was almost perfect. Five hundred certain was a reasonable basic income; three years were a reasonably solid chunk of time. And this was only the foundation: Aldous was retaining his American rights—*Limbo*, *Crome Yellow*, *Mortal Coils* and *Leda* were already published in the United States[1] —and there was a reassuring and flexible option clause:

7) On the termination of the period of the three years aforesaid, the Publishers shall have the option of making another contract with the Author for a further period of three years on similar lines or as may be otherwise mutually agreed.

The arrangement was also realistic. Aldous was not paid so much that he need fear accumulating debt; no-one was doing a Mr Micawber in expecting the advance to be safely overtaken by the sales. The royalty scale was excellent: starting on works of fiction with 15%; rising to 20% after the first two thousand copies sold; and to 25% after eight thousand.[2]

So far, so good. There was the other side to the arrangement, the obligation to produce two books a year. Two books of fiction, what is more, and one of them a full-length novel; two books a year for three years running, six books in fact in a row, commonplace enough to the Victorians, but what writer of today—of similar talent and literary conscience—would, *could*, take on such an engagement? Yet that kind of contract in those post-war years was by no means rare.

Aldous did not quake. He had formed the habit of meeting date-lines under the most trying conditions; he had written a novel in two months (a daily average of a thousand words); even if he were to write the next ones at, say, half that rate he would still have more time on hand for living than he had had since he left Oxford. As for subjects—he was beginning to spread his wings and what he wanted to explore must have seemed inexhaustible at that point. Novels do not feel so difficult to write when one is young.

The books were supposed to be delivered in January and July each year "commencing July 1923". (Quarterly payments had begun that April.) During the course of the winter Aldous still had some decks to clear, finish off his journalistic commitments and wind up at Condé Nast's. "But I can see an end to it," he wrote to Suzanne in February. "After April I shall be able to write what I want."

[1] By Doran.
[2] Royalties on non-fiction—essays, poetry, drama—were rather lower: 10% on the first 1,000; 15% on the next 2,000 copies; 20% thereafter.

*To write what I want.* The wish that had been echoing through the years of lonely schoolmastering without prospects, the years of treading time. "*. . I want to marry and settle down to write . . . What I want more than anything really is to get a year with nothing to do except to write.*" And now at last Aldous might say that he had his wish (*quant à moi, I am very securely wedded . . .*) He was nearly twenty-nine; he had come a long way since the days he mooned in digs shared with a chatty old clergyman.

Yet it is doubtful that Aldous drew much solace from that reflection. The thought of our past sufferings does little more to alleviate our present ones than does the thought of earthquake in Peru. It is doubtful that Aldous during that winter and spring of 1923 gave any thought to his former condition. There is no end, it would seem, to the tricks the gods may play. Nor does the bolt from the blue come always in the form of tragedy: "There are confessable agonies," Aldous wrote five years later on, "sufferings of which one can positively be proud. Of bereavement, of parting, of the sense of sin and the fear of death the poets have eloquently spoken. They command the world's sympathy. But there are also discreditable anguishes, no less excruciating than the others, but of which the sufferer dare not, cannot speak."

It was May and of the novel to be delivered to Chatto & Windus in July not a word was down. What had happened was that Aldous had fallen in love with Nancy Cunard. Madly in love, "Against reason, against all his ideals and principles, madly, against his own wishes, even against his own feelings . . ."[1]

Nancy Cunard. It is difficult not to say either too much about her or too little. There are many—they will become more numerous—who have never heard of her; there are those who know of her as a valiant, or a strident figure on the margin of our recent history, know about her anthology *Negroe* and her early and passionate championship of that cause, of the Hours Press, the association with the French surréalist movement, the public brawl with her mother (her White Ladyship), the involvement with the Spanish Civil War; remember perhaps the great friendships with George Moore and Norman Douglas, have read her poetry and her books on those two men. There are those who knew her. To us she was the friend one loved, whose arrival one often dreaded. She always astonished: never for a second was it possible not to be aware of Nancy. Now that she is no more, she is still loved: better perhaps, more safely, than when our existences could be swept by her actual turbulent presence. Nancy, impeccably outrageously extravagantly courageous, generous, violent, self-destructive, fanatically wrong-headed, waywardly elegant,

[1] *Point Counter Point*, 1928.

incarnately alluring, was unique. What struck first was her appearance, and her appearance was itself a condensation of her temperament, her comportment, her ideals.

> Nancy Cunard was a fiery and furious angel, like the angel in Mathias Grünewald's triptique or the angel in Rainer Maria Rilke's *Elegies*—a terrible messenger descending with a fiery sword upon bourgeois hypocrisy and those ignorant persons who discriminate between race or colour of skin . . . If as Dante wrote, "Heaven and hell reject the lukewarm", Nancy will certainly come into her own.[1]

What did she actually look like?

> Miss Nancy Cunard is wonderful, made of alabaster and gold and scarlet, with a face like Donatello's Saint George . . . [Mary Hutchinson in a letter of 1919. And in 1924:[2]] . . Behind [her façade] one seems to see a shadow moving—an independent, romantic and melancholy shadow which one can never approach; the façade is exquisite, made of gold leaf, lacquer, verdigris and ivory.

She was often painted (not very well); there are many telling photographs; the most quintessential remains Cecil Beaton's taken when Nancy was thirty-four. There she is with her extraordinary eyes—arctic blue, tiger's eyes, triangular eyes shaped like arrowheads, with their *"regard* (there is no English word meaning not only the eyes . . . but the way in which they confront the visible world)"[3] with her thinness—"she was dangerously thin," and her carapace of African bracelets. What the portrait cannot give are Nancy's walk and Nancy's voice.

> First and instant impression—tigress-dragonfly. No: cheetah . . . Then, seated, one *heard* her . . . Nancy's voice was a miracle. And so was the way she walked . . . she flowed swiftly forward, as I have said like a cheetah, and also like a slim and splendid fish.[4]

> The mixture of delicacy and steel in her build, hips, legs, ankles all of the slenderest, weighed with massive ivory bracelets . . . that they seemed too fragile to support . . . the head held high with its short fair hair, and one foot placed exactly in front of the other, not with mannequin languor, but spontaneously, briskly, boldly, skimming the pavement.[3]

[1] Allanah Harper in *Nancy Cunard: Brave Poet, Indomitable Rebel*, edited by Hugh Ford. Chilton Book Company, 1968.
[2] Mary Hutchinson in op. cit.
[3] Raymond Mortimer in op. cit.
[4] Kenneth Macpherson in op. cit.

Whatever she did, however violent she was, Nancy always looked more distinguished than other people.[1]

Nancy Cunard was born in 1896. She was thus two years younger than Aldous, whom she survived again for two years. Her father was Sir Bache Cunard (of the shipping line), though it is likely that her natural father was in fact George Moore; her mother, a legend in her own right, was Maud (later Emerald) Lady Cunard, born and raised in the American West. Nancy was brought up as a member of the ultra rich but soon managed to put an end to that. She wrote and published a foolish and insulting pamphlet about her mother, *Black Man and White Ladyship*, resulting in a life-long breach and her cutting herself off from the family money. It was generally assumed that Lady Cunard had stopped Nancy's allowance, in fact she never ceased to provide her daughter with an income: it accumulated in a bank in Nancy's name, untouched, unacknowledged, over the decades. Nancy, in her integrity or intransigence, lived in poverty, often squalid poverty. It hardly seemed to affect her. What little money came her way she gave to her friends, to artists, to refugees. She lived in rudimentary cottages in France, in cheap hotel bedrooms all over the world; her clothes often came from thriftshops and street markets; she had no possessions besides a few paintings, books and her collection of African bracelets. She hardly ate. Like Maria, she had that partly moral loathing of food; her only material wants were drink (cheap red wine) and cigarettes; her true mainstay was her own emotions and these went into causes, friends and lovers. The causes sometimes suffered. "Nancy's back: We're in trouble!" the cry would go up in Harlem. "Hold on to your hats, kids, Nancy's back."

There was no middle way for Nancy. She was *entière*, as the French would say. She had an innocent, an almost naïve belief in the causes she so strongly upheld. She seemed incapable of abstract reflection; or of separating political reality from her own emotional conception.[2]

Nancy became *persona non grata* in the United States; the Loyalists' defeat in Spain affected her as a personal grief; during the Second World War her little house in Normandy was vandalized by occupying Germans and, more bitter to her, by local French collaborationists. As time went on, her gallant wanderings —in cargo boats, in third-class railway carriages—seemed to become more desperate; the man or two she always had in tow were still young, but her hold over men was diminishing and her

[1] Allanah Harper in op. cit.      [2] Ibid.

need for their company was not, and sometimes they were not very nice to her. She believed herself persecuted—by the ever-present bogies, the bourgeois and the police—and indeed she got into bad trouble, in England of all places, with the law (a breach, "how not!" of the peace). She looked emaciated; she was beginning to be very ill (emphysema, a broken hip that would not mend), and defied it all, would not keep still, it was not Nancy who would go gently into that good night. And yet in those last years there were moments when she could be ruefully mild, strangely tolerant, defeated and undefeated at the same time. Ultimately, Nancy Cunard was a tragic figure. With exquisite aptness, Allanah Harper quotes these lines from Léon Paul Fargue, a poet loved by Nancy.

> *Gare de la douleur, j'ai fait toutes tes routes.*
> *Je ne peux plus aller, je ne peux plus partir.*
> *J'ai traîné sous tes ciels, j'ai crié sous tes voûtes.*

All that was still a long way into the future in 1923 when Aldous hung about Nancy Cunard and her entourage through the London nights. She was in her gilded youth, a divorcée, independent, madly attractive to men, spoilt. ("You are late, Nancy." "But *of course*, darling.") Her energies in those days went into poetry—her own much influenced by T. S. Eliot's—not politics, her rebellion against her upbringing, against the luxury of her mother's house, against chaperones and chastity and the conventional morality of the time. Nancy and her bright friends were part of the vanguard of the post-war Twenties. Her daily existence was hectic; pleasure, the pursuit. There was already the shadow. The 1914 War had bitten very deep into the world of Nancy's generation, she was shaken early in her personal life. A charming and handsome young man called Peter Broughton-Adderley, whom she had been in love with, was killed in the last months of the war; Nancy got married, briefly, disastrously, to a man of her mother's choice.

One cannot say exactly when Aldous fell for Nancy. No records of this episode have emerged. Aldous did not speak of it; on Nancy it left small mark. What remains are his own transparent generalizations scattered through the novels, wisps of the gossip of the time, and what Maria told to a few friends. Jeanne knew, and Mimi Gielgud and Costanza; Maria talked to Juliette and to Moura Budberg[1] and later on to me. Aldous, then, fell in love with Nancy sometime in 1922; possibly in the autumn after

---

[1] Baroness Budberg, an intimate friend.

his return from Italy. It almost certainly lasted less than a year and longer than six months. They had known each other since 1917; one recalls Aldous's rather *de haut en bas* reference when he was first contributing to the Sitwells' *Wheels* ". . in company with such illustrious young persons like Miss Nancy Cunard," and though Nancy was in Paris a good deal they must have met often enough with their mutual friends on their mutual round, the Sitwells, Eliot, Earp, the Hutchinsons, the Trees at the Café Royal, the Eiffel Tower. It was not a passion, then, at first sight; nor was it mutual. Aldous's feelings were unrequited—the unconfessable agony, the discreditable anguish he speaks about in *Point Counter Point* was the anguish of thwarted desire.

Nancy went through a good many lovers; she had the kind of bad reputation, that aura of casual lasciviousness, that can be an added bait. To Aldous it was the ultimate of the pendulum swing of his flight from puritanism, beyond the liberations of Garsington, beyond Maria's serene Latin sensuality. But if Nancy was promiscuous she was also capricious, and she was choosy. What she wanted were men who were more than a match for her, strong men, brutes. Aldous simply was not her type. He was far too gentle, too unexcessive and, with her, too hang-dog, too love-sick. Unfortunately for him she happened to like him and enjoy his company. If she did not strictly lead him on, she did not let him go.

> Tiresome as he was, his love-sickness did at least make him faithful. That, for Lucy, was important. She was afraid of loneliness and needed her cavalier servants in constant attendance. Walter attended with dog-like fidelity. But why was he so like a *whipped* dog sometimes? So abject. What a fool![1]

He was obsessed, and remained lucid. He observed as an intelligent, disapproving helpless parent might observe the aberrations of a son without being able to deflect the son's pursuits. He went on wanting Nancy, as he had said, against his principles, ideals and reason, even against his own feelings. "For he did not like Lucy, he really hated her."[1]

Aldous had little interest in Nancy, the individual. What engaged him was a distillation of her sexual power, the erotic and exquisite façade: the voice, the look, the walk.

> The strong gardenia perfume was in his nostrils; he was breathing what was for him the very essence of her being, the symbol of her power, of his own insane desires. He looked at her with a kind of terror.[1]

[1] *Point Counter Point.*

*He looked at her with a kind of terror*. It was thus that Aldous nightly sat at Nancy's crowded table in a public place. After dawn he walked home to Maria awake and waiting.

Life at Princess Gardens was at a standstill. Days were dominated by whether Nancy had telephoned or not. Maria not only suffered from the conventional reaction—though already then she was lightly, wisely tolerant of "infidelities"—she was disoriented: Aldous was behaving so unlike himself, and he was so unhappy. She saw little of him (he was still at Condé Nast's) and when he was at home he was dumbly miserable. Maria was sorry for him but he also infuriated her. Nancy represented all she most feared in English life, the attitudes and morals of a certain world; and to this one has to add her invincible anxiety for Aldous's safety when he was out and late. At one time she went abroad waiting for events to take shape. At another, Nancy and Aldous had a brief affair. Nancy gave in, out of affection, exasperation; after a few days discarded him. Once, for a whole night, he paced the street below her window.

There were intermissions. Nancy was out of England for some of that winter; Aldous made an attempt to follow her but she put him off. In April he joined Maria for a few weeks in Florence. But when he got back to London, there was Nancy. On top of it all he was feeling more and more ill. Nightlife was constitutionally poisonous to him; he could never stand hot crowded places, stale air and the smells of food and whisky (nor could or ever did he drink himself; anything beyond a glass or two of wine would make him queasy). Then one day there came a stop to the whole thing. Maria told the story to me some ten or twelve years after the event. She told it in a spirit of reminiscence and also with a view to educating me. I listened, I was at an impressionable age, I was learning something about Aldous, I listened with all my ears. Maria may have been telling the literal sequence of events, she may have been giving a revised memory. This is what she told me. One evening—she gave no month or date, that was not her way, but the impression was one of a long light evening in late spring—Aldous came home to Princess Gardens looking miserable and ill. Maria was seized by sudden resolution. She put an ultimatum then and there. She would leave England the next morning with him or without; for him to make up his mind, but he must make up his mind *now*. They packed all night. That is, Maria packed; Aldous hovered, sat on the lids of trunks, tried to read, scribbled in a little book; when allowed gave a hand. Maria was getting more and more exhausted and there seemed to be no end of objects to be packed. At first light she opened a window and threw out every article that was still about. Whether they fell into the street or a front garden was not clear; one does not interrupt such tales. Nor can I say what happened to the furniture or the keys, or whether the trunks went with them in the cab or were picked up later on by Thomas Cook's. All I was told is that in the morning, unslept, unbreakfasted, in the clothes they stood in, Aldous and Maria left the house, drove to Victoria and caught the first train out of England.

They went straight to Italy. There, in two months, Aldous wrote *Antic Hay*. He wrote it all down, Maria said, he wrote it all out; it was over. He never looked back. The possession—that one descent of Até—left a mark on his novels; not his marriage.

## Chapter Four

## The Second Novel—*Antic Hay*

ALDOUS wrote practically no letters between October 1922 and July 1923, or at least few have come to light. Only six appear in the published edition: one to Suzanne, one to E. S. P. Haynes, neither of them long, the other four mere notes. The next full-fledged letter is dated 2nd July. It is to Robert Nichols and contains this opening paragraph:

> I am ashamed at my remissness in not having written to you before . . . I was leaving England in rather a hurry—Maria not having been at all well, and we deciding all of a sudden to get away out of the piercing English spring and the odious tumult of London into warmth and peace . . . and ever since I have been in Italy I have been so wildly busy tapping on this machine for my living—a book to be finished by the beginning of August and hardly ten words on paper before I started.

Aldous and Maria were at Forte staying with the Fasolas and the book was going well enough to be thinking about plans, they were arranging to take a villa outside Florence on a long lease from September. "We are proposing to settle, more or less permanently—as far as any arrangement with us is ever permanent —in Italy . . ."

It is a choice of sunshine, dust, grapes and scirocco—not to mention icy winters in imperfectly warmed houses—as against grey days and mud. The house itself was presented by circumstances; Castel a Montici, the house Maria had lived in during the war with her mother and sisters was for rent again; the view was incomparable, disadvantages known. So "There I shall settle down to grind out two yearly books of fiction for Chatto's and any other thing I can manage. The life, I think, ought to be agreeable and one's money goes nearly twice as far as in London. I shall come back to civilization a few months each year to find out what is going on."

By August the novel was finished and the MS posted off. Once more Aldous had written the best part of a hundred thousand words in two months. He and Maria were able to go to Belgium where they were expected for her grandparents' Golden Wedding at St Trond. They found the family assembled in strength: Maria's father, Mère, the George Baltuses and the Raymond Baltuses,

Jeanne with her husband and little girl, Matthew and his cousin Ado Baltus, Suzanne and Rose. Suzanne had just become engaged and brought her fiancé, a charming looking young Dutchman, trained as a lawyer who had chosen to be a painter: Joep Nicolas. They were photographed, jubilants to baby-in-arms, in a group on the lawn, and there was of course a Gargantuan repast. There was also music. It was the unexpected produced so often by that family ("some make cloth, some make sugar . . . a few are very cultivated, the rest not at all"). George Baltus had arranged for the Pro Arte Quartet from Brussels and they played music very rarely heard yet at that time, Vivaldi, Pergolesi, Josquin des Près, Pierre de la Rue. "It was a revelation," Suzanne writes, "even for Aldous." There were long afternoon walks across country through the Flemish fields and orchards; the two future brothers-in-law took their first liking to one another, Joep discovering Aldous's conversation, Aldous Joep's painting, "Suzanne," he said, "has chosen well." But it was too hot and Aldous who was still tired developed a "sort of suppressed jaundice". Feeling pretty wretched, he travelled back to Italy with Maria, Matthew and Bella "in a heat wave of the first magnitude". In the train young Matthew kept howling for water.

. . You used the word *wasser* [Maria recalled that journey in a letter to him twenty-five years later] . . . to our despair . . when there was none to give you. I even got so despaired that I ran out to fill the thermos to find out that it was the tap of the "eau non potable" so Bella would not give it to you. I might have to keep you quiet . . You were so loud. So I can never forget it.

At Milan, they escaped from that train, and next morning picked up the motor car they had ordered. It was their first. Aldous had deliberately saved the money to buy it, Maria had just learnt to drive. (She had passed the test, the first woman in Italy to obtain a driving licence.) The car was a 10 h.p. four-seater Citroën. They set out, the first of a thousand such journeys, in the cool of the evening, rested at Forte (Aldous still gloomy and nursing his jaundice), left child and Bella with the Fasolas, and went on to Florence and their new home on Montici.

It was still frightfully hot and there was a bad drought and trouble with the electric water pump; they had to do everything themselves and their trunks were slow in turning up. But the inside of the house was cool and certainly spacious: four rooms downstairs, one of them a *salone* twenty-five feet square, six bedrooms, several waterless baths, a study in the tower, a balcony-terrace running the breadth of the house. And the prodigious view from five hundred feet above the town—the view of Florence and the Arno valley up to the Apennines.

In a matter of weeks they are straightened out, have servants; Matthew is with them, Aldous recovered and Maria too getting reasonably well. "We are firmly settled here once more and very busy." Writing and reading; writing regularly, but at an agreeable pace (six months to go before the next book is due, and it is going to be short stories). Aldous is in fact at work on "Uncle Spencer" and "Young Archimedes".[1]

Summer "still lingers deliciously". Occasionally, they descend into Florence to see Norman Douglas or Geoffrey Scott.

It is so pleasant up on our hill, that one rarely feels tempted to venture into the town, even for the sake of seeing pleasant people . . .

And there was the stupendous discovery of Italy. They drove to Rome.

We went by Arezzo and Cortona—grim Etruscan town on an immense mountain with a view over Trasimene—stopping the first night at Chiusi . . . Orvieto . . Montefiascone . . . what a town! Two thousand feet up, a hill crowned by an immense Renaissance cupola looking over the perfectly circular bright blue lake of Bolsena . . to Viterbo over the volcanic hills past the incredible Lago di Vico and then on, through the Campagna, . . to Rome.

Tivoli, Frascati, Albano, Neni, Ostia . . . They went back along the Tiber valley "over a range of perfectly enormous mountains —hugely high and quite barren . . .

apparently a way which no knowing motorist ever takes, owing to the terrible climbing . . . and the complete absence of any assistance if you break down.

Fortunately, "our little Citroën did the whole thing without turning a hair". On over the Somma pass to Spoleto, through the plains of Clitumnus, past Trevi, past Assisi ("Saw the Giottos —and my word . . .") to Perugia and by Trasimene back to Florence. It was the journey, almost exactly the Italian journey, of *Those Barren Leaves*.

These were good days; a stretch of time in mid-life when the present is satisfying and the ultimate threats still far off. There were reminders: Costanza's mother incurably ill, a question of

[1] *Little Mexican*, 1924.

months. And there was the world, the post-war world of unemployment, inflation, revolution, led or handled by Poincaré, Baldwin, Lenin, Mussolini, President Harding. "I try to disinterest myself from politics [Aldous to Julian] but really, when things are in the state they are, one can't help feeling a little concerned . . . Society can less and less afford to be governed by imbeciles or even by charlatans of genius . . . These monsters will end up by making such a mess that we shall all suffer."

*Antic Hay* was published that November. Aldous's second novel came very near the knuckle. It reflected, perhaps crystallized, attitudes of the time, and many young people began to see and judge in Huxleyan terms. Sir Isaiah Berlin[1] speaks of Aldous as one of the great culture heroes of his youth, and the transforming power of the early Huxley, "the 'cynical', God-denying Huxley, the object of fear and disapproval . . . the wicked nihilist . . . [the delight of] those young readers who supposed themselves to be indulging in one of the most dangerous and exotic vices of those iconoclastic post-war times . . ."

Friends and strangers wrote to Aldous; the novel sold well (5,000 copies within a year of publication). Again Aldous's own family shared the disapproval. "I am sorry [he wrote to his father from Florence] you should have found my book so distasteful." He had no desire, he went on, to enter into argument as they would be starting from entirely different premises. *Antic Hay*

. . is a book written by a member of what I may call the war-generation for others of his kind; and . . it is intended to reflect—fantastically, of course, but none the less faithfully—the life and opinions of an age which has seen the violent disruption of almost all the standards, conventions and values current in the previous epoch.

The book is, I may say without fatuity, a good book. It is also a very serious book. Artistically, too, is has a certain novelty . . all the ordinarily separated categories—tragic, comic, fantastic, realistic—are combined . . into a single entity, whose unfamiliar character makes it appear at first sight rather repulsive.

I can't say that I expected you would enjoy the book . . . I expected that my contemporaries would; and so far as I know by what people have written to me, they have.

And there, I think, I had better leave it, only pausing long enough to express my surprise that you should accuse me, when I speak of a young man's tender recollections of his dead mother, of botanizing on my mother's grave.

1 *Mem. Vol.*

The young man is of course Theodore Gumbril Jr., he of the Patent Small-Clothes and the artificial beard, the protagonist of *Antic Hay,* not Aldous's *alter ego* to be sure, but a young man with a good infusion of Aldous all the same. There he is meditating in the School Chapel while the Reverend Pelvey, M.A., is fog-horning away at the lesson. "Could it be that he had an answer and a clue? That was hardly believable. Particularly if one knew Mr Pelvey personally. And Gumbril did." Diligently unto thy children, the reverend intones and Gumbril remembers his own childhood, his mother. Her diligence had not been dogmatic. "She had just been . . good, that was all.

> Good; good? It was a word people only used nowadays with a kind of deprecating humorousness. . . . But good in any case, there was no getting out of that, good she had been . . . good. You felt the active radiance of her goodness when you were near her. And that feeling, was that less real and valid than two plus two?
>
> The Reverend Pelvey had nothing to reply. He was reading with holy gusto . . .
>
> She had been good and she had died when he was still a boy; died—but he hadn't been told that till much later—of creeping and devouring pain. Malignant disease—oh, *caro nome*!
>
> 'Thou shalt fear the Lord thy God,' said Mr Pelvey.[1]

It is curious to recall here Maria's assertion about *Antic Hay* as a means of exorcism. She was referring, of course, only to one, then all too recent, episode. "He wrote it all down. He wrote it all out." *Did he?* Nancy Cunard, a member of that war-generation *par excellence,* fitted into his theme. Aldous had to put in someone like her. But *is* the fictional Myra Viveash really in the least like Nancy? Both are wilful, dangerous, alluring and have lost the one young man they cared for in the war. Mrs Viveash has been given Nancy's voice and Nancy's walk.

> He watched her as she crossed the dirty street, placing her feet with a meticulous precision one after the other in the same straight line, as though she were treading a knife edge between goodness only knew what invisible gulfs. Floating she seemed to go, with a little spring at every step . . .[2]

There is also a version of the famous *regard*:

> Mrs Viveash . . turned on him . . her pale unwavering glance. Her eyes had a formidable capacity for looking and expressing nothing;

---

[1] *Antic Hay*, Chatto & Windus, 1923.        [2] Ibid.

they were like the pale blue eyes which peer out of the Siamese cat's black-velvet mask.[1]

And yet Mrs Viveash is not so much Nancy Cunard disguised, as Nancy dis-individualized, turned into a type, a type, what is more, representing but a fragment of her personality. There is no trace of Nancy's fire and crazy idealism in that poised and sophisticated figure, none of her partisanships and her violence, no hint of any passionate involvement outside a personal universe of *ennui*, disillusion, lust and a little art. It is rather remarkable that Aldous did not even attempt to explore the character of the actual Nancy, that he showed no literary interest in anything that did not lend itself to a generalization. (Perhaps this was the way Aldous preferred, or was temperamentally compelled, to handle his raw material.) As for the personal episode, he wrote about it at arm's length as it were, in one passage firmly situated in the past—exorcism by way of the wrong end of the telescope. Another character, Shearwater, is about to fall for Mrs Viveash and Gumbril suddenly feels the need to speak. " 'There was a time,' he said in a tone that was quite unreally airy, off-hand and disengaged, 'years ago, when I totally lost my head about her. Totally.'

> Those tear-wet patches on his pillow . . . and oh, the horrible pain of weeping, vainly, for something that was nothing, that was everything in the world! 'Towards the end of the war it was. I remember walking up this dismal street one night, in the pitch darkness, writhing with jealousy.' He was silent. Spectrally, like a dim, haunting ghost, he had hung about her; dumbly, dumbly imploring, appealing. 'The weak, silent man', she used to call him. And once for two or three days, out of pity, out of affection, out of a mere desire, perhaps, to lay the tiresome ghost, she had given him what his mournful silence implored—only to take it back, almost as soon as accorded. That other night, when he had walked up this street before, desire had eaten out his vitals . . . That was a long time ago.

It was Aldous's ferocious sincerities, his iconoclasm, his scepticism that struck the readers of the time; few of them when they recall the early Huxley so much as remember that there were other trends. Yet even then, Aldous wrote this passage:

> . . . Gumbril took off his hat, breathed the soft air that smelt of the greenness of the garden.
> 'There are quiet places also in the mind', he said meditatively.

[1] *Antic Hay.*

'But we build bandstands and factories on them. Deliberately—to put a stop to the quietness . . . All the thoughts, all the preoccupations in my head—round and round, continually . . . What's it for? What's it all for? To put an end to the quiet, to break it up and disperse it, to pretend at any cost that it isn't there. Ah, but it is; it is there, in spite of everything, at the back of everything. Lying awake at night—not restlessly, but serenely, waiting for sleep—the quiet re-establishes itself, piece by piece; all the broken bits . . . we've been so busily dispersing all day long. It re-establishes itself, an inward quiet, like the outward quiet of grass and trees. It fills one, it grows—a crystal quiet, a growing, expanding crystal. It grows, it becomes more perfect; it is beautiful and terrifying . . . For one's alone in the crystal, and there's no support from outside, there's nothing external and important, nothing external and trivial to pull oneself up by or stand on . . . There's nothing to laugh at or feel enthusiastic about. But the quiet grows and grows. Beautifully and unbearably. And at last you are conscious of something approaching; it is almost a faint sound of footsteps. Something inexpressively lovely and wonderful advances through the crystal, nearer, nearer. And, oh, inexpressively terrifying. For if it were to touch you, if it were to seize and engulf you, you'd die; all the regular, habitual daily part of you would die . . . one would have to begin living arduously in the quiet, arduously in some strange, unheard of manner. Nearer, nearer come the steps; but one can't face the advancing thing. One daren't. . . .[1]

The passage has affinity with the opening lines of Paul Valéry's poem "*Les Pas*":

> *Tes pas, enfants de mon silence,*
> *Saintement, lentement placés,*
> *Vers le lit de ma vigilance*
> *Procèdent, muets et glacés.*

[1] *Antic Hay.*

## Chapter Five

## Santa Maria a Montici

THE Huxleys lived in Italy for rather more than four years.
Seen as a whole those years were perhaps the most easy of
their lives. They were also immensely enriching; Oxford, Garsington, London, followed by another education—in the Italian years
the beloved pastime was travel, doors opened to the visual worlds
of countryside and art. "C'est probablement l'Italie qui est le
plus empreint dans ma visualité," Maria wrote in later life. What
had so captivated her in 1917, the aesthetic sensations she had
tried to present in her letters during their engagement, now came
to Aldous and they were able to share a kind of impassioned
sightseeing.

They always went by car. Aldous had found another interest:
"If I had any strength of mind, I should stop talking about
Citroëns and return to higher themes. But the temptation of
talking about cars, when one has a car, is quite irresistible. Before
I bought a Citroën no subject had less interest for me; none, now,
has more."[1]

He read the motoring papers, technical brochures, reports of
Grand Prix racing. He sat in the car, as he sat in all their subsequent ones, in the passenger seat, riveted as far back as it would
go so that he might unfold his grasshopper's legs, peering through
an assortment of optical glass at the landscapes whizzing by. At
his side, Maria, slight as a jockey, drove. She drove very well.
She brought to it the style and the control that might have gone
into her dancing. She would get up at first light to wash and
tend the car just as at Bellem as a girl she had got up to look
after her horse. Maria became an outstanding driver, well up
to professional standards, very precise, very safe, very fast. The
speed was for Aldous's pleasure, the only new one, he used to
say, mankind had invented since the palaeolithic age. Maria
never drove in a race though this would have been tempting to
a side of her; duty to Aldous and to Matthew made it inconceivable. She was always conscious that she was "driving Aldous"
(and, when out alone, of her duty to come safely home); in some
thirty years and what perhaps amounted to a million miles,
Maria never had anything that could be called an accident.

1924 turned out a stable year. Aldous was quietly working away

1 *Along the Road*. Chatto & Windus, 1925.

on their Florentine hill with a short journey now and then. There was no house move (though they were already thinking about one).

In January he had been relieved of a nagging worry. As he was finishing *Little Mexican*, his next lot of short stories, and turning up ideas for a novel, "that bloody book on Balzac, which in an insane moment years ago I pledged myself to write", came home to roost. Constable's seemed to take the contract seriously. They had written to say that the MS was three years overdue. "I don't blame them." Aldous feared that he would have to write the book. The thought filled him with horror. He was bored stiff with Balzac; the more familiar he became with him, he told his father, the less he thought of him. He found him marvellous in his energy, his power of rapidly and effectively creating, "but so astonishingly remote from life—at any rate from interior life . . I always enjoy his books; but there are very few of them I think particularly good. What an immense difference between him and a really great novelist like Dostoevsky or Tolstoy. And what a difference, in his own sphere of fantastic creation, between him and the incredibly much more fertile and juicy Dickens."

Aldous turned to Eric Pinker, then his agent, asking if there were a way of getting out of the agreement he had made "being at the time very young, very foolish and poor". Pinker persuaded Constable's to take a book on some other subject in lieu of the impossible Balzac; but now Chatto's, understandably, objected. Fortunately no money had passed, and Pinker was finally able to cancel the whole thing.

That winter in Florence was particularly icy, though there were the single miraculous days of sitting out in a morning sun. Aldous's friend J. N. W. Sullivan stayed with them. "He has a very clear, hard, acute intelligence," Aldous wrote to his father— Sullivan had contributed articles on the Einstein theory to the *Cornhill*, "and a very considerable knowledge, not merely on his own subjects—mathematics, physics and astronomy—but on literature and music. A stimulating companion." Aldous often worked the better for having a man to talk to on his walks and in the evening. The finished MS of *Little Mexican* was sent off in the last days of February. "Six short stories, the first of considerable length, about thirty thousand words . . . some quite good stuff in it, I think." Aldous and Maria went off on a trip. They got stuck in the snow trying to cross the Apennines but eventually got down to Bologna, Parma—Aldous had a *faible* for Correggio —Mantua, Padua, Venice and home again by Ferrara and Ravenna. Home meant buckling down to the next book. There were some false starts. "It is horribly difficult to find the right way of saying what one wants to say. What I am working on now . . is to be . . a discussion and fictional illustration of different views of life. *The mere business of telling a story interests me less and less*" [my italics].

How difficult to understand the mentality of a man like Bennett who could sit down and spin out an immense realistic affair about life in Clerkenwell. "When it was first done that sort of thing had a certain interest . . . But it is a purely factitious interest. The only really and permanently absorbing things are attitudes towards life and the relation of man to the world."

In April Suzanne was married to Joep Nicolas. While Aldous was getting on with his novel—*Those Barren Leaves*—Maria went to St Trond for the wedding (a proper white one with the family assembled in strength). Suzanne found her sister's presence a great comfort, and the night before they slept together in their Uncle Julien's room. Maria had sent advice already during the engagement: Suzanne must learn to spell. Spelling was Maria's own bugbear, but if her own was eccentric, Suzanne's was a family byword; neither grappled well with dates and figures. (Suzanne first chose 30th February for her wedding day.) Now Maria, five years married, gave some more advice. Suzanne listened.

I think it is thanks to her that I have not made myself unhappy in my marriage . . . [Suzanne writing].

"Un homme à femme," Maria said of Joep, "il me plairait." Suzanne took it as a compliment. In essence Maria's advice was to create an emotional and domestic atmosphere in which a man could do his work in peace: artists and writers needed experience, needed variety. How much nicer—and wiser—not to make a fuss, to consent, not hinder; not to break one's heart.

Joep and Suzanne went to Italy for their honeymoon, staying with the Huxleys well into the summer. Everybody got on beautifully; life was agreeable, so were friends and neighbours, Robert Nicolson, Sullivan (humanly a very odd fish), Costanza of course. There was an excellent cook. One of Aldous's young second cousins, Renée Haynes,[1] a girl about to go to Oxford, was also in the house.

. . It was an extraordinary kind of time [Renée Tickell talking]— because there he was—and he knew so much about everything. It was always a bit daunting, not because you felt stupid, he wouldn't

1 The present Mrs Jerrard Tickell.

have let you feel stupid . . . he talked about Florence and painting and Italian gardens and what Italians were like. When he was talking one saw things through his lens, through his mind, they became alive. There were times though—one was much less grown up than as seventeen now—when I wished I could have gone swimming.

Matthew, four and very large and lively, ate at table. There were fearful scenes. He was difficult about his food and refused to eat meat or fish. Aldous put it down to his extreme sensitiveness to smells and to sentimental reasons, "he realizes that meat is dead animals". Perhaps a course of mild hypnotism? And the boy was too lazy to read although he knew his letters. "We don't worry him," Aldous told his own father, "too early a passion for reading distracts from the powers of observation."

In June the Huxleys took Joep and Suzanne on a slow tour to Rome. One looks upon the 1920s as the brief golden age of motoring. Comic breakdowns were past, self-starters and balloon tyres in; cars had become reliable and there weren't too many of them—the road was for the few. But in Italy roads were narrow, winding, rough; there still obtained the dangerous habit of keeping to the right in towns and to the left in open country. Dust and pebbles flew in one's face, donkeys zigzagged, peasants dozed upon their carts. It could be broiling hot. Aldous liked to have the hood down and they had to wrap in dust-coats, veils and goggles. We looked like brigands, says Suzanne. They ploughed on, Maria at the wheel, the two men sight-seeing untiringly. They explored places little visited at the time, Etruscan tombs, abandoned Byzantine churches. There was much gaiety. One evening at a small hotel in Viterbo with the dining-room full of elderly English ladies, Joep ordered a young bubbly wine; it had been a long day, soon they were in very high spirits: Maria, Suzanne and Joep were taken by the giggles. Aldous remained impassive. He tried to hush Maria. "But why not, darling?" she said to him. "Why not?"

"Because it isn't dignified, darling."

Whereupon they only laughed the harder.[1]

For Aldous the impressions of the day were not washed off by a glass of *spumante*. He was enmeshed in the aesthetic round. Italy —"The real place. The more one goes into it, the more one is astonished by its richness." At the same time he was puzzled, not entirely satisfied, seeking. "All that these creatures poured out in

---

[1] Suzanne Nicolas, memoir; see p. 76.

the past—and *cui bono?* What has become of all their thought and passion? It seems to have had no particular effect on anything. The fossilized remains are still here—miraculous: the tourists look at them—and that's all."

In July Aldous and Maria went again to Forte. Villa Fasola: Aldous wrote, bathed. *Those Barren Leaves* was near the end, Maria was typing fair copy. The house was full of young children, and Matthew at last was beginning to eat properly. "He now puts away beefsteak and fish like a hero," Aldous reported. In mid-August his parents set out for England in the Citroën. Aldous planned to stop somewhere on their way across the Alps to finish his last chapters, but when they got to the top of Mont Cenis the rain came down in torrents and the summer temperature dropped to near freezing point. They were driven back into the plain, the hotels were full up; after a night of sleeping in a kitchen they found rooms at "an absurd little place called Ambérieu, where we stayed ten days. When I got my work done, we drove on . . ."

Paris: a few days at the Lewis Gielguds'—galleries, bookshops, the Louvre—September in London, Aldous's first return since his flight in the spring of 1923. They lodged in rooms in the King's Road, Chelsea. Aldous saw his family, attended to business with his publishers, doctors, tailor. For the moment he was feeling quite satisfied with the finished novel. "It comes off fairly well," he wrote to Bob Nichols. And a few weeks later to his American editor, Eugene Saxton,[1] ". . . It cuts more ice . . than the others and is more explicit and to the point. The characters, too, are better, I think."

After London, Holland. They stayed with Joep and Suzanne in their first home, an old farmhouse by the sea at Groet; then, inevitably, the four of them went on another trip. ". . entirely successful. Holland was a revelation, especially the country . . . But my word, how cold!" Aldous was spell-bound by the number and virtuosity of the cyclists on the road. "Il s'attendait même à ce qu'ils fassent l'amour en bicyclette" [Suzanne].

They continued into Belgium, driving down the Meuse valley in the rain. But it was "marvellously lovely," (Aldous to his father) "exactly like those strangely improbable little landscapes of Patinir . . . which I always thought mere fancies . . ."

The Huxleys returned to Italy in still, settled autumn weather by the long route south through France. Reims, Chartres, Orléans,

---

[1] Eugene Saxton, who later became a great friend of Aldous's, former editor of *The Bookman*, later editor in chief of Harper & Brothers, was then on the staff of Aldous's first American publishers, George H. Doran.

Bourges—"Chartres fine, but Bourges unbelievably magnificent" (ever after Aldous preferred Bourges to Chartres), Moulins, Lyons, Provence; Marseilles, the Esterel, Nice, the Ligurian coast. Some of the roads were atrocious. The car, Aldous could not forbear to tell, "went through its ordeal in a marvellous fashion, the only weakness being . . a leak of oil into the clutch". All the same he envied his father for having a new Morris.

> If we get a new car, which won't be yet awhile, it will be Italian and more powerful than the Citroën . . Possibly the new Lancia, or even, if it's not too dear, the new 6 cylinder Itala which is said to have all the qualities of the Alfa Romeo . . .

They were back in Florence in late October. Aldous, stimulated and refreshed, began work on a book of travel essays—breathing space before his next go at fiction—hoping to have the MS ready by Christmas. For the next few months they remained settled in a quiet and pleasant existence. Aldous had put on some needed weight, so had Matthew and Maria ("I think we should all have been in the grave by this time if we had stayed in London"). Italy was serving them well; only Florence was beginning to pall. "Too much fog in the valleys and too little water in the hills, too many bores to be avoided . . ." They had a look at a house on the coast south of Rome at Monte Circeo on the edge of the Pontine marshes—sea air for Matthew, the advantages of Capri without its intolerable disadvantages (an island and inhabited by sodomites)—they will move there probably in the spring. One thing is sure: "I shall certainly stay in Italy . . . I shall stay here for the next few years . . . until it is time for Matthew to be educated. Then, I suppose, London or Oxford. Qui sa? . . But it is still fairly remote."

## Chapter Six

## Those Barren Leaves

THROUGH the winter the quiet productive life continued. "The greatest luxury of this existence," Aldous wrote to Julian, "is the feeling and being well." The book of travel essays, having taken only a little longer than Aldous had bargained for, was finished in January: a few days' relaxation—catching up with letters, buying a tie—and start on a long story for the next book due.

*Those Barren Leaves* was published on 21st January 1925. It was well received (eight thousand copies sold in the first year). But Aldous, for his part, was no longer certain that it had come off. He was at the beginning of his dissatisfaction with his writing.

I'm glad you liked the *Leaves* [he wrote to Naomi Mitchison that winter]. They are all right, certainly; tremendously accomplished, but in a queer way, I now feel, jejune and shallow and off the point. All I've written so far has been off the point. And I've taken such enormous pains to get off it; that's the stupidity. All this fuss in the intellectual void; and meanwhile the other things go on in a quiet domestic way, quite undisturbed.

Some of this was bound up with Maria. There was Aldous's cognizance that Maria—who did not formulate, who did not, in his sense, think—was *on the point*, by intuition, by straight experience. Aldous was becoming able to use that faculty of hers. He often called her his dragoman. It was closer than that, more organic: at times he saw in an almost physical way through her. (After her death he would speak consistently of amputation.)

That letter to Naomi ended with a new version of Aldous's old *cri de cœur*: I wish I had time to do nothing but write. Now it was: "I wish I could afford to *stop* writing for a bit." The essence of the plea remained the same: he had realized that there is a price to pay for writing two books a year.

The main theme of *Those Barren Leaves*, Aldous wrote, "the main theme is the undercutting of everything by a sort of despairing scepticism and then the undercutting of that by mysticism." Again he had deliberately mixed the unities. There is comedy (poor impossible Mrs Aldwinkle), melodrama, farce, young love, there are the Tuscan and Umbrian landscapes of the Italian journey with Irene and young Lord Hovenden driving round and round Lake Trasimene for ever. There is much about death. Death and the thought of death, the undercutting of everything by death.

Aldous happened to write this book during one of the most serene periods of his existence. "The wise man does not think of death lest it should spoil his pleasures."[1] If Aldous was a wise man, he was one marked by the experiences of his past. The pleasant life on the hill, the journeys with Maria by his side, the lively little boy, his son, the splendours of art and learning were undercut by memories of *staphylococcus aureus*, of his mother's painful senseless death. Was there a way of side-tracking lurking horror, a hope short of literal belief in a compensatory heaven? Mr Cardan, the ageing hedonist (a one-dimensional Norman Douglas figure) snorts that there is not; but Calamy, ex-guardee, big-game hunter, accomplished lover ("my greatest talent"), the man turned thirty who has come to a dead end, is willing to suspend his ways in order to find out. He goes off into the mountains to be alone to think ("to get to the bottom of the universe, eh?" says Mr Cardan).

*Those Barren Leaves* was a signpost in Aldous's development. It is for this reason that I am proposing to quote from it at length. All but the first passage (chosen for a visual quality) are taken from the fifty concluding pages of the novel. The house-party have arrived at Perugia; Irene and Lord Hovenden are as good as engaged and go for a stroll at dusk. "I like vis place," says Hovenden who has trouble with his th's.

. . Leaving the stately part of the town, they plunged into the labyrinth of steep alleys, of winding passageways and staircases behind the cathedral. Built confusedly on the hillside, the tall houses seemed to grow into one another, as though they were the component parts of one immense and fantastical building, in which the alleys served as corridors. The road would burrow through the houses in a long dark tunnel, to widen into a little well-like court-yard, open to the sky. Through open doors . . one saw in the bright electric light a family sitting round the soup tureen. The road turned into a flight of stairs, dipped into another tunnel, made cheerful by the lights of a subterranean wine shop opening into it. From the mouth of the bright cavern came up the smell of liquor, the sound of loud voices and reverberated laughter.

And then, suddenly emerging from the high houses, they found themselves standing on the edge of an escarped slope, looking out on to a huge expanse of pale evening sky, scalloped at its fringes by the blue shapes of mountains, with the round moon, already bright,

[1] *Those Barren Leaves*, 1925.

hanging serene and solemn in the midst. Leaning over the parapet, they looked down on the roofs of another quarter of the city, a hundred feet below. The colours of the world still struggled against the encroaching darkness; but a lavish municipality had already beaded the streets with yellow lights. A faint smell of wood-smoke and frying came up through the thin pure air. The silence of the sky was so capacious, so high and wide, that the noises of the town —like so many small, distinctly seen objects in the midst of an immense blank prairie—served to intensify the quiet, to make the listener more conscious of its immensity in comparison with the trivial clatter at its heart.

"I like vis place," Lord Hovenden repeated.

They stood for a long time, leaning their elbows on the parapet, saying nothing.

A few days later Grace Elver, the moronic girl, has died and there is Mr Cardan, who had been about to marry her to provide for his declining years, is meditating in the empty church before her funeral.

The tragedy of bodily suffering and extinction has no catharsis. Punctually it runs its dull, degrading course, act by act to the conclusion. It ennobles neither the sufferer nor the contemplator. Only the tragedy of the spirit can liberate and uplift. But the greatest tragedy of the spirit is that sooner or later it succumbs to the flesh. Sooner or later every soul is stifled by the sick body; sooner or later there are no more thoughts, but only pain and vomiting and stupor. The tragedies of the spirit are mere struttings and posturings on the margin of life, and the spirit itself is only an accidental exuberance .. like the feathers on the head of a hoopoe ... The spirit has no significance; there is only the body. When it is young, the body is beautiful and strong. It grows old, its joints creak, it becomes dry and smelly; it breaks down, the life goes out of it and it rots away. However lovely the feathers on a bird's head, they perish with it; and the spirit, which is a lovelier ornament than any, perishes too ... the body, the doomed, decaying body, is the one, appalling fact.

.. Mr Cardan wondered how he would die. Slowly or suddenly? After long pain? Intelligent, still human? Or an idiot, a moaning animal?

A few pages later comes the passage about the human hand— Calamy's discourse, in bed with Mary Thriplow. He holds up his hand. "Look .. it's just a shape that interrupts the light:

To a child who has not yet learned to interpret what he sees, that's all it would be, just a shaped blotch of colour ... But now, suppose I try to consider the thing as a physicist ...

Calamy, in fact, is talking about the extraordinariness of existence.

"And the more you think, the more obscure and mysterious it becomes."

He speaks of atoms . . of units of negative electricity whirling several million times a minute round a nucleus of positive electricity. He speaks (Calamy is one of nature's guardsmen, but what we hear is Aldous's voice) of the structure of molecules, of electromagnetic radiations, of electrons moving from one orbit to another without taking any time . . covering any space . . .

Mary Thriplow (a bright lady novelist) observes that he is making her feel dizzy. Calamy remarks in passing that the behaviour of light is satisfactorily explained by one theory of electro-dynamics, while the behaviour of electrons in the atom can only be explained on a theory that is entirely inconsistent with it. He goes on:

"Well, here are two ways already in which my hand exists . . . then there is the chemical way . . . it is enough to think of it for five minutes to perceive that [my hand] exists simultaneously in a dozen parallel worlds."

*Simultaneous existence in a dozen parallel worlds*—this is what always exercised Aldous's mind. What most of us most of the time choose to ignore because it is too complicated, too out of stride with our daily requirements and habitual sense perceptions, too dizzy-making in fact, was for Aldous evident philosophical and literary raw material. He would think, and what had appeared comprehensible on the routine surface became utterly mysterious. This fascinated him—how he adored the *extraordinary*—it gave him a sense of adventure, of getting off the map, allowing him to believe that *anything* might be possible. It informed his writing. "This is what *interests me*," he would say. So over and over again he attempted to put across simultaneous existence, to co-ordinate disparate fields; to bring off, in literary terms, the grand composition. (Unifying, as he might have put it, the subject matters of Piero della Francesca, Blake, El Greco, Chardin, Rubens and the Elder Breughel.) He doubted whether it *could* be done in words; spoke of it having been done in music; kept on trying. It enriched his writing but at times overloaded and distorted it. Those whizzing electrons, those anatomical analyses of love-making, do we see them as lapses now or as an enhancement of reality? In *Those Barren Leaves* Calamy went on about the human hand.

"Now if, like Cranmer, I were to put my right hand in the fire . . these molecules would uncombine themselves into their constituent atoms . . . But this leads me on at once to a set of entirely different realities. For if I were to put my hand into the fire, I should feel pain . . . For I am alive, and this hand is part of a living being, the first law of whose existence is to preserve its life . . .

". . . The hand is part, not merely of a living being, but of a being that knows good and evil. This hand of mine can do good things and bad things . . . it has written all manner of words; it has helped a man who was hurt; it has touched your body." He laid his hand on her breast ". . and when it touches your body . . it also touches your mind. My hand moves like this, and it moves through your consciousness as well as here, across your skin. And it's my mind that orders it to move; it brings your body into my mind. It exists in mind; it has reality as a part of my soul and a part of yours . . .

". . these are some of the ways in which my hand exists . . . And from this one goes on to ask, inevitably, what relationship exists between these different modes of being."

What is there in common, he asks, between life and chemistry, between a collection of cells and the consciousness of a caress?

"It's there that the gulfs begin to open. For there isn't any connection—that one can see, at any rate. Universe lies on top of universe, layer after layer, distinct and separate . . ."

"Like a Neapolitan ice," says Miss Thriplow.

". . . The only hope . . is that perhaps, if you went on thinking long enough and hard enough, you might somehow get through, get out on the other side of obscurity . . . But into what precisely, into what?"

And now we are in the last chapter. Calamy has gone to live in a hut by himself in the mountains—for a week, for a year?— to think, as he had said, in freedom.

*In freedom.* And here Aldous returns to something that he already knew when he was writing *Antic Hay.*

"The mind must be open, unperturbed, empty of irrelevant things, quiet. There's no room for thoughts in a half-shut, cluttered mind. . . ."

Most of us pass through life without knowing that the thoughts are there at all, "If one wants to lure them out, one must clear a space for them:

One must open the mind wide and wait. And there must be no irrelevant preoccupations prowling around the doors. One must free oneself of those."

Calamy is interrupted by Mr Cardan and Francis Chelifer who have come to see what he is up to. The final fifteen pages consist of their argument. Again Calamy speaks of his wish of "getting through"—how many days did Gotama spend under the bo-tree?—the undercutting by mysticism is out now in the open. If you try long enough and if your mind is the right sort of mind,

"Perhaps you really do get, in some queer sort of way, beyond the limitations or ordinary existence. And you may see that everything that seems real is in fact entirely illusory—*maya*, in fact, the cosmic illusion. Behind it you catch a glimpse of reality."

Mr Cardan won't have any. What bosh your mystics talk about, he says, lights and darknesses, sweets and bitters, wheels, mercury, salt and sulphur—it's a rigmarole. Chelifer concurs. Only soft-heads and sentimentalists engage in that kind of activities.

On the contrary, Calamy replies, mystics, in point of historical fact, have generally been men of the highest intelligence. Buddha, Jesus, Lao-Tze, Boehme, Swedenborg. And what about Sir Isaac Newton, who practically abandoned mathematics for mysticism after he was thirty?

"Not that he was a particularly good mystic; he wasn't. But he tried to be; and it can't be said that he was remarkable for the softness of his head. No, it's not fools who turn mystics."

And again we seem to hear the voice of Aldous:

"It takes a certain amount of intelligence and imagination to realize the extraordinary queerness and mysteriousness of the world in which we live."

Mr Cardan has to come back to the fact of death—you cannot get over that. When the flesh dies, there's an end to mysticism with all its by-products, God, justice, salvation . . .

Perhaps it is, says Calamy. Let's admit it as certain even. Does it make the slightest difference?

"Salvation is not in the next world; it's in this . . . here and now. The kingdom of God is within you—if you'll excuse the quotation . . ."

Mr Cardan shakes his head. "All this, my young friend, doesn't in any way mitigate the disagreeableness of slowly becoming *gaga*, dying and being eaten by worms . . . When my soul is at the mercy of my slowly rotting body, what will be the use of salvation then?"

"It will have profited during the fifty years of healthy life," said Calamy.

## Chapter Seven

## "Lève l'ancre pour une exotique nature!"

THE house at Monte Circeo fell through, the Florentine lease was up at the end of June, they thought of moving to Rome in the autumn. "After a third-rate provincial town, colonized by English sodomites and middle-aged lesbians," Aldous wrote to Julian, "a genuine metropolis will be lively. Not to mention the fact that Rome is incomparably the most lovely place in the world."

In March they went over to North Africa for a brief journey into Tunisia. Aldous had been working on the title story of *Two or Three Graces* since February; it was the sort of thing he could do easily enough but did he want to go on doing it? "For me," he said in a long letter to Robert Nichols, "the vital problem is not the mental so much as the ethical and the emotional. The fundamental problem is love and humility, which are the same thing. The enormous difficulty of love and humility—

> a difficulty greater now, I feel, than ever; because men are more solitary now than they were; all authority has gone; the tribe has disappeared and every at all conscious man stands alone, surrounded by other solitary individuals and fragments of the old tribe, for which he feels no respect. Obviously, the only thing to be done is to go right through with the process; to realize individuality to the full, the real individuality, Lao-Tze's individuality, the Yogis' individuality, and with it the oneness of everything. Obviously! But the difficulty is huge.
> . . And meanwhile the world is peopled with miserable beings who are neither one thing nor the other; who are solitary and yet not complete individuals . . .
> . . What's to be done about it? That's the great question. Some day I may find some sort of an answer. And then I may write a good book, or at any rate a mature book, not a queer sophisticatedly jejune book, like this last affair, like all the blooming lot, in fact.

One fine morning it was brought home to Aldous and Maria that they were living in Fascist Italy. Four ruffians in uniform forced their way into Castel a Montici and demanded to search the place. Now Aldous did not like the regime. He deplored its acts of brutality; he found it wicked. Wicked, stupid and fantastically incompetent—"curious country! [it] would be comic if it weren't tragic." In fact, he was "against it" as a rational matter of course. He did not, as so many contemporary writers, feel passionate about it. Temperamentally Aldous inclined to the wide-range view; he would not be doctrinaire, would not be a labelled anti-anything. Musso and the Fascisti, he would have said if pressed, were worse, yes a good deal worse, than a democracy, say, such as France or England (with their bitter inequalities and hypocrisies); but they were part of the general inhumanity and folly, the Human Vomedy as his typewriter once slipped into naming it. As for living in Fascist Italy (as people may well ask today), there was fortunately something hit or miss about the regime, horrible though it was; it did not succeed in becoming as efficiently totalitarian as other dictatorial regimes right or left, and it did not crush out the humanity of the Italian people. It was possible for a man of conscience to live in Italy (I am speaking as one who remembers the time and was passionately and emotionally "anti"), while it would have been unthinkable for such a man to have lived in Nazi Germany.

The four ruffians on that June morning of 1925 were members of the political police and looking for an Italian professor, for Gaetano Salvemini, in fact, the historian, who had written against the regime and whom they believed to be in hiding at the Huxleys (who had never even met him as it happened). Aldous stood up to the louts and invoked his ambassador, demanding to see their warrant (they didn't have one). They searched all the same. When they found no trace of either Salvemini (who was arrested elsewhere shortly after) or incriminating documents, they ended up rather ashamed of themselves. "But it was a tiresome and unpleasant business."

It was the Huxleys' last month at Castel a Montici; they were already crating books with no very clear idea of where they'd be living next. ("Plans a bit vague," Aldous wrote to Norman Douglas, "but I prefer them so.") His glimpse of the African oases had stimulated his desire for remoter travelling. He and Maria were beginning to talk about going to India in the autumn "to take a look round". And after that, who knows? Meanwhile they made the most of family life. Maria's sister Jeanne was staying with them with her husband and child, so that there were now two small children living in the house; Sophie two years old against Matthew's five. Aldous and Maria were no longer the babes in the wood they had been in that Hampstead flat when they were barely married and did not know whether to boil the teat or how to stop Matthew from howling; they no longer had to cope with cramped quarters and overwork. The shades of having to write Balzac's life were laid. There was space now for young children. Aldous read to Matthew, took a mild interest in

Sophie, playing tricks on her dolls; Maria loved her. "Je me suis attachée d'une manière toute nouvelle et si profonde," she wrote to Suzanne . . . D'ailleurs elle m'aime aussi . . . car elle sent que je l'adore; une petite créature déjà si vivante et alerte et surtout si bonne . . ."

Suzanne herself had just had her first child, also a girl, Claire. (The Huxleys sent her Matthew's old pram, a vast and splendid English affair.) Aldous became greatly attached to his nieces (there were to be five in all) but it was Sophie who lived with the Huxleys during most of her childhood and adolescence, and became almost their second child.

The Huxleys left Castel a Montici for good at the end of June. They went by car to England, leaving Matthew with his grand-mother at St Trond. It was not an easy parting for Maria—the Indian idea was expanding into one of a much longer journey. In London the thing took on concrete shape as Aldous was able to arrange for a series of travel articles to cover the worst of the expense. "Seeing that one practises a profession that does not tie one down, I feel that one ought to see as much of this planet as one can."

It was *le tour du monde,* the journey round the world Maria had talked of as a girl. She still longed to go; Aldous needed no urging; they were leaving the small boy in responsible and loving hands, but the separation in terms of distance and time—with no return except by sea—was a serious one. As usual, Maria made her choice; as often, she was divided. She and Aldous spent the rest of the summer in London, seeing to passages and equipment. Invitations accumulated; the last story for *Two or Three Graces* was all but finished. On 15th September they sailed from Genoa bound for Suez.

## Chapter Eight

## The Journey Round the World—India

THEY landed at Bombay "hot, muggy and expensive" on 2nd October; met "the local intelligentsia, journalists, politicians, etc., frail little men, very gentle and underfed-looking . . . no wonder the British rule"; went on to Lahore by train—two nights and a day, tolerable in spite of heat and dust—stayed with a young Indian barrister Aldous knew at Oxford, looked at some Mogul monuments "in a style of architecture I really don't like at all"; then up to Kashmir by way of Rawalpindi, "a desolate beastly sort of place", reaching Srinagar by October twelfth. During their first ten days in India, Aldous wrote home, they had lived strenuously, seen many people and things and travelled sixteen hundred miles.

People called at their hotel, bore them off to look at sights. They met Provincial Governors, English Residents, Chief Justices, heads of customs, medical officers, missionaries, Maharajas. "Once one has a little start in this part of the world, one goes automatically a long way."

At Srinagar they were lent a bungalow and stayed for a month. Their windows looked out across a valley to blue foothills and snowy peaks, the days were brilliantly clear, the air bracing, the nights deeply cold. They continued to live strenuously. They saw temples and gardens, were taken on day-long drives, visited the gaol and lunatic asylum. They saw the Tartar traders from Yarkhand come down the mountainside and bought two fur coats for a few pounds, a sheep-skin for Aldous and a beautiful Russian arctic hare. From Srinagar they set out for nearly three months of continuous land travel. Taxila, Peshawar, down again to Lahore, Amritsar; a tour through Rajputana: Agra, Ajmer, Chitor, Bikaner, Jodpur, Udaipur; Indore, Bhopal, Cawnpore for the All India Congress in December, Lucknow, Delhi, Benares, Calcutta . . .

Aldous went down well with Indians and more improbably with all types of English. (Once he dined as a guest in the mess of a rather stolid infantry regiment; one of the officers later told Gervas that Aldous asked innumerable questions, taking an intense interest in what daily military life was like.)

Maria did their packing and unpacking; Aldous went to Thomas Cook's to collect post and tickets, and wrote letters; together they counted their money which seemed to be slipping rapidly between their fingers. "Great wads of it have to be handed out every time one gets into the train; for fares are high and distances enormous."[1]

Once or twice they became extremely worried. (Neither of them was ever good at working out sums in perspective, a workable budget was beyond Maria's arithmetic and Aldous's patience; what they did was fall into a money panic now and then.) Now they decided to travel second-class. The compartment filled to overflowing by a holy man in yellow robes and his followers; at stations more followers crowded in to kiss his feet. The holy man hoicked and spat all over the compartment, he and his admirers exhaled the sour stink of garments long unwashed. The day was very hot. Aldous sat reflecting on the fact of cleanliness dividing man from man. After seven hours of it, they paid out twenty-two rupees and had their luggage transferred into a first-class carriage.

They carried phials of disinfectant to drop into their drinking water; Maria shrank from the insects and small squashy animals and was often disgusted by the food that politeness bade them swallow. At a political party they were offered a meal of ice cream, hot dumplings stuffed with curried mice, chocolates and spice-flavoured mineral water. Aldous, stoical by principle and schooling (few things in adult life could equal the breakfast porridge at Hillside), described it as "altogether most curious and amusing," Maria on such occasions would look imploringly at her husband. Aldous avoided catching her eye or returned a glance of disapproval.

What were Aldous's impressions at this first meeting with the East, with India? Most of them can be found in *Jesting Pilate*, the diary of the journey which he began at sea and wrote as he went along, and in half a dozen letters home. Later he often talked about it with or without second thoughts. At the time his main emotion was one of horror. At Srinagar there had been the blue foothills and white mountains in the distance, in the streets, on the doorsteps wretchedness and dirt . . . "Srinagar fairly festers. The people are dressed in ancient rags and suffer agonies from cold . . ."

After a century and a half of Western domination, peace and settled government, the country was still as poor as in the days of anarchy. "Millions are still without enough to eat, all their lives . . . Custom and ancient superstitions still as strong . . .

. . Nine Indians out of ten cannot read or write, and the tenth, who can, detests the Europeans who taught him. The educated . .

[1] *Jesting Pilate*. Chatto & Windus, 1926. All quotations in this chapter unless otherwise indicated are from *Jesting Pilate*.

profess democratic principles; but their instincts are profoundly and almost ineradically aristocratic . . . Meanwhile the mountains of evitable hardship and superfluous suffering are piled up. . . .

At Jaipur one of the great landowners lent his elephant to the Huxleys, "a superb and particularly lofty specimen". One morning emerging from the palace precincts,

Our monster halted and, with its usual deliberation, relieved nature, portentously. Hardly . . had it resumed its march when an old woman . . darted forward and fairly threw herself on the mound of steaming excrement. There was fuel . . I suppose, for a week's cooking . . . Our passage had been to her like a sudden and unexpected fall of manna. She thanked us, she blessed the great and charitable Jumbo for its Gargantuan bounty.

The elephant lurched on. Aldous's thoughts were moved to mournful eloquence:

Why are we here, men and women, eighteen hundred millions of us, on this remarkable and perhaps unique planet? . . immortal souls, first cousins to the angels, own brothers of Buddha, Mozart and Sir Isaac Newton . . . is it to go about looking for dung?

Hard enough to find a reason anywhere, West or East, but in India Aldous saw no conceivable answer. "India is depressing as no other country I have ever known. One breathes in it, not air, but dust and hopelessness."

Aldous's secondary reaction to the East was exasperation.

> There was an old man of Thermopylae,
> Who never did anything properly.

"To the Westerner all Indians seem old men of Thermopylae. In the ordinary affairs of life I am a bit of a Thermopylean myself. But even I am puzzled, disquieted and rather exasperated by the Indians." He was struck by the extraordinary sloppiness of the ceremonies, the casual mixture of the magnificent with the cheap in the abodes of the potentates—ante-rooms filthy with pigeon droppings, marble halls furnished with bamboo chairs, the brass bedstead standing in the throne room . . . And those cows!

To the eye of pure reason there is something singularly illogical about the way in which the Hindus shrink from killing cows . . but have no scruples about making the life of the sacred beasts . . a hell on earth. So strict is the orthodoxy of Kashmir, that Bovril is confiscated at the frontier . . . And yet nothing is done to protect these god-like animals from any cruelty that does not actually result in death . . . To the eye of reason, I repeat, it certainly seems strange. But then the majority of human actions are not meant to be looked at by the eye of reason.

And as for Hindu spirituality, it is interesting to recall some of Aldous's remarks then.

To my mind "spirituality" (ultimately, I suppose, the product of the climate) is the primal curse of India and the cause of all her misfortunes. It is the preoccupation with "spiritual" realities, different from the actual historical realities of common life, that has kept millions upon millions of men and women content, through centuries, with a lot unworthy of human beings. A little less spirituality, and the Indians would now be free—free from foreign dominion and from the tyranny of their own prejudices and traditions. There would be less dirt and more food. There would be fewer Maharajas with Rolls Royces and more schools . . .

It is for its "materialism" that our Western world is usually blamed. Wrongly, Aldous thought. For materialism—"if [it] means a preoccupation with the actual world in which we live —is something wholly admirable". If Western civilization is unsatisfactory, that is not because we are interested in the actual world, but "because most of us are interested in such an absurdly small part of it".

And what about English rule in India? On the whole Aldous seems to have been in no doubt about this issue, though at times he wrote himself into his long-range view. He is quite unequivocal, for instance, in a letter to Lewis Gielgud from Lahore.

The sort of Englishman one meets here in trains, stations, restaurants and Dak bungalows is beyond words repulsive. Stupid, uncultured, underbred, the complete and perfect cad. In their company, one understands the Indian nationalistic aspirations. As a matter of fact, I understand them even when I am in the presence of the nice Englishmen. We really have no business here. And there is no doubt whatever that we are steadily making the country poorer and poorer . . .

In the published diary he qualifies. Are the Indians in a position to govern themselves at once? Would they do the job as well as the English, or better or worse? Nobody is able to say. Politics are not a science. His own prejudices "happen to be in favour of democracy and self-determination, and all the rest of it. Yet if

I had been brought up a little differently..." Nor does he see that the mere fact of his liberal prejudices on the one hand, and his being an Englishman on the other, "makes me .. responsible for either the integrity of the British Empire or the liberation of the Indian people.

When I am honest with myself, I have to admit that I don't care two pins about political principles. Provided that it guaranteed my safety and left me in peace to do my work, I should live just as happily under an alien despotism as under the British constitution.

Yet on the very page before (the diary entry of another day?) he sounds a different note. Easy enough, he says, to suspend judgement on the Indians' ability to govern themselves, but "if I were an educated Indian, I should almost certainly have gone to gaol for acting on my belief—"the belief that even if it could somehow be proved that [self-government] would bring, as its immediate consequences, communal discord, religious and political wars .. inefficiency and corruption—even if this could be proved, I think I should still go on trying to obtain Swaraj. There are certain things about which it is not possible, it is not right to take the reasonable, the utilitarian view."

The high point of the journey was probably the visit to the Bose Institute at Calcutta. Their guide was Sir J. C. Bose himself, the famous researcher who had worked earlier on the effects of stimuli on metal and then on vegetable organisms, the man who had proved the "sensitivity" of plants. Aldous and Maria were shown round for three hours and saw the experiments in full blast. Here indeed was grist to Aldous's mind: Bose had devised instruments that made visible things that had so far been impossible to see even with the aid of the most powerful microscope. They watched the " 'heart beat' of a plant .. recording itself point by point on a moving plate", they watched a plant feed in the sun and stop feeding when the sun was shaded, watched it exhale minute quantities of oxygen; they saw "its sudden shuddering reaction" to an electric shock, and saw its 'heart' becoming more rapid when a grain of caffeine was added to its water.

Aldous had been sceptical—"But when you *see* the plants making records of their own sensations—well, you've got to believe."

Through the afternoon, they followed Bose "from marvel to marvel". He showed them the full-grown tree that had been brought from a great distance under an anaesthetic, and transplanted; the tree had taken root immediately in its new place and flourished. They saw a plant die. "We administered poison. A mortal dose of chloroform was dropped into the water. The graph became the record of a death agony.

> . . The poisoned flower manifestly writhed before us . . . As the poison paralysed the "heart", the ups and downs of the graph flattened out into a horizontal line . . . But so long as any life remained in the plant, this medial line did not run level, but was jagged with sharp irregular ups and downs that represented in a visible symbol the spasms of the murdered creature desperately struggling for life. After a little while, there were no more ups and downs. The line of dots was quite straight. The plant was dead.

Its last moments were so distressingly like those of a man that Aldous was shocked into feeling a new sympathy. Fascinating, that afternoon in Calcutta; also immensely disturbing in its implications. The aliveness of matter "may seem absurd and impossible . . But a little thought is enough to show that it is . . . *a priori* probable.

> Life exists. Even the most strict and puritanical physicists are compelled, albeit grudgingly, to admit the horribly disquieting fact.

> I am always a little uncomfortable when I find myself unable to admire something which all the rest of the world admires—or at least is reputed to admire. Am I, or is the world the fool?

Some of Aldous's readers were disappointed by his attitude to India as expressed in *Jesting Pilate*; nothing in the book, however, has given so much offence, has rankled so long in East and West as Aldous's lack of reverence for the Taj Mahal. He failed to admire it. "The Taj Mahal is one of the seven wonders. My guide assures me that it is 'perhaps the most beautiful building in the world.'" Aldous and Maria drove out for their first sight by the light of the setting sun.

> Nature did its best for the Taj. The west was duly red, and orange and yellow, and, finally, emerald green, grading into pale and flawless blue towards the zenith . . The sacred Jumna was like a sheet of glass between its banks . . The gardens were rich with turf, with cypresses, palms, and peepul trees, with long shadows and rosy lights . . . Nature, I repeat, did its best. But though it adorned, it could not improve the works of man. The Taj, even at sunset, even reverberated upside down from banks and river, even in conjunction with melancholy cypresses—the Taj was a disappointment.

Worse. "Milk-white amongst its dark cypresses, flawlessly mirrored, it is positively the *Toteninsel* of Arnold Boecklin come true." Aldous goes on with evident relish about the interest (which he does not share) in the expensive and the picturesque as such. It is the "inordinate costliness" that most people seem to like about the Taj. "The average tourist is moved to greater raptures by St Peter's than by his own St Paul's. The interior of the Roman basilica is all of marble . . and marble covers a multitude of sins. St Paul's is only Portland stone." Back to the Taj. The minarets, "these four thin tapering towers . . . are among the ugliest structures ever erected by human hands". And the classicism is the product not of intellectual restraint imposed on exuberant fancy, but on an actual deficiency of fancy. The Temples at Chitor, by contrast, "are specimens of true classicism. They are the products of prodigious, an almost excessive, fancy, held in check and directed by the most judicious intelligence . . . And when you compare the Taj with more or less contemporary European buildings in the neo-classical style . . . take Palladio's Rotonda at Vicenza for example . . . [how] much richer, more subtle and various than the poor, dry, negative elegance of the Indian building."

## Chapter Nine

## "The Range, the Confluence of Associations"

*TAKE Palladio's Rotonda at Vicenza* . . . Aldous's measure was still Italy. At Taxila, the ancient city in North India where Alexander rested, the landscape merged into the Roman Campagna.

> The outworks of the Himalayas play the part of the Alban and Sabina mountains. Ranges of woodless Frascatis and desiccated Tivolis subside into a grey and rolling plain. On sudden and unexpected eminences . . stand the Indian equivalents of Neni and Civita Castellana . . .[1]

In the week Aldous had sailed, his latest book came out in England. *Along the Road,* his second collection of essays. His first, *On the Margin,* published two years earlier, had been recognized for the particular combination of lightness and learning. (And point: what he had to say in the early 1920s on re-reading *Candide,* for instance, is only too acutely relevant today.) Most of the essays of the first volume, though, had been originally written for the *Athenaeum* and other journals; they were the products of Aldous's most hard-worked years and much of what he wrote was what he had been asked to, rather than what he might have wished to write. A Wordsworth centenary comes along, there is a Flemish exhibition, someone has written another damn thick book about someone else—the subject has got to be mugged up and, as every literary journalist well knows, he has also got to rev up ideas and emotions; this, useful training though it may be, in the long run tends to exploit rather than develop what original talent he may have. When Aldous came to write *Along the Road,* his working conditions had changed: he was free to choose his subject and his length; he was able to let himself rip in a form that suited him—a form which he refreshed and of which he became a master. Tracts of his novels read like essays; conversely he often attacked an essay with a novelist's latitude. *Along the Road* was written *con amore,* with exuberance. The book is about travel, works of art and places, and most of the art and places are in Italy. Yet Italy is but the home-base, the playground of what Kenneth Clark has so well called "the range, the confluence of

---

[1] *Jesting Pilate.*

associations, the power of speedy cross-classification,"[1] that was so characteristic of Aldous's mind, works and conversation. He is snowed up in his Citroën among the Apennines in a howling wind, and he is off to the sands of Yarmouth in a Beerbohm Tree production of David Copperfield, in another flash it is Hilaire Belloc's rhyme on the Polar bear and the Great Wall of China, in the next the second volume of the *Encyclopaedia Britannica*. Obliged in the flesh to spend the night at the inn at Pietramala, his mind moves to 1813 when men could travel in spite of the Napoleonic wars and make experiments on iodine at Mount Vesuvius, and English scientists were presented with medals by the Emperor. And now he is getting down to Sir Humphry Davy, young Michael Faraday and James Clerk Maxwell. "A Night at Pietramala" is a serene essay, postulating a serene view of the continuity of science. How satisfactory, Aldous exclaims, "these lives of born men of science always are!

> There is an integrity about these men, a unity of purpose that to the rest of us distracted mortals seems wonderfully enviable and wonderfully beautiful.[2]

If *he* could choose his next existence he would like to be a man of science—"by nature, inevitably . . . The only thing that might make me hesitate would be an offer by fate of artistic genius. But even if I could be Shakespeare, I think I should still choose to be Faraday."[2]

Men of science ought to be happier than other men. "And when one reads their lives one finds that in point of fact they generally were happy. [Whereas the artist] must fatally pass much of his life in the emotional world of human contacts . . . these form the subject matter of his art . . . I personally would rather be subdued to intellectual contemplation than to emotion, would rather use my soul professionally for knowing than for feeling."[2]

*Along the Road* contains the essays on Leon Battista Alberti, on Breughel and on Piero della Francesca which much influenced contemporary taste. Aldous's physical sight, as we know, was defective; when he looked at a picture he would put a squat little telescopic instrument to his good eye and peer at the canvas from a distance of a few inches. Yet the fact remains—I am quoting once more Kenneth Clark, and who should know better?—that what Aldous "wrote about painting proves him to have been one of the most discerning lookers of our time.

> . . Aldous had an astonishing faculty for seeing what an artist really meant. This allowed him to follow what I believe is one of

---

[1] *Mem. Vol.*          [2] *Along the Road.* Chatto & Windus, 1925.

the most enlightening of all forms of criticism—the description of the subject of a picture in the artist's own terms . . .

Should we say that Aldous's gift of perception was not so much a matter of eye, as a part of a general sensibility to all forms of orderly or impassioned communication . . . It is true that Aldous responded with equal intensity to all the arts . . .[1]

And with so much pleasure. One of the most endearing experiences was to follow Aldous round a gallery or a museum: he was so pleased, so eager, so oblivious of his own exertions.

The river [Patinir's] flows in a narrow valley between hills. A broad, a brimming and a shining river. The hills are steep and all of a height . . The sky is pale above this strip of fantastically carved and scalloped earth. A pale sky from which it must sometimes rain in Chinese white . . . and the green of the grass and the trees is tinged with white till it has taken on the colour of the "Emerald Green" of children's paint-boxes.

. . Peering into the little pictures, each painted with a million tiny strokes of a four-haired sable brush, I laughed with pleasure at the beauty of the charming invention. This Joachim Patinir, I thought, imagines delicately . . .[2]

It is in the essay on Piero della Francesca that Aldous declares his values. The essay is called "The Best Picture". "You smile . . . the expression is ludicrous . . ." There are a great many kinds of merit and classifications are futile. "But there does exist, none the less, an absolute standard of artistic merit. And it is a standard which is in the last resort a moral one."[2]

Whether a work of art is good or bad depends on the quality of the character which expresses itself in the work. Not that all artists are conventionally virtuous. "Longfellow was a bad poet, while Beethoven's dealings with his publishers were frankly dishonourable." The virtue that is necessary to a good artist is "the virtue of integrity, of honesty towards oneself". Bad art can be negatively bad, that is merely incompetent or dull; it can be positively bad, that is "a lie and a sham". When the lie is well told one is taken in—for a time. In the end the lie is always found out. "Sometimes the charlatan is also a first-rate man of genius and then you have such strange artists as Wagner and Bernini, who can turn what is false and theatrical into something almost sublime."[2]

The best picture is Piero della Francesca's "stupendous"

---

[1] Lord Clark of Saltwood, *Mem. Vol.*
[2] *Along the Road.*

Resurrection at Borgo San Sepolcro. Christ is standing, "a banner in his right hand, his left foot already raised and planted on the rim of the sepulchre, preparing to set out into the world.

. . But the being who rises before our eyes from the tomb is more like a Plutarchian hero than the Christ of conventional religion. The body is . . like that of a Greek athlete; formidably strong . . . The face is stern and pensive, the eyes cold. The whole figure is expressive of physical and intellectual power. It is the resurrection of the classical ideal, incredibly much grander and more beautiful than the classical reality. . . .

The picture is great, "absolutely great, because the man who painted it was genuinely noble as well as talented.

And to me personally the most moving of pictures, because its author possessed . . those qualities of character which I most admire . . A natural, spontaneous, and unpretentious grandeur—this is the leading quality of all Piero's work. He is majestic without being at all strained, theatrical or hysterical—as Handel is majestic, not as Wagner . . . Piero seems to have been inspired by what I may call the religion of Plutarch's *Lives*—which is not Christianity, but a worship of what is admirable in man.[1]

[1] *Along the Road.*

## Chapter Ten

# The Journey Round the World—Malaya, The Pacific, Japan, The United States

THE Huxleys left India—"rather glad to escape"—early in February, sailing from Calcutta for Burma. There were still another four full months of travelling before them; much of it by sea and more leisurely; they had reached a saturation point and were taking their impressions with detachment. They spent some weeks looking at Burma and Malaya, ending up at Government House in Singapore. From there they went to Java, cruised among the islands, changed to a ship that went along the coast of Borneo to Zamboanga in the Southern Philippines, where "(with luck) we shall get another ship to take us to Manila in time to catch the liner leaving for Frisco on April 7th. It ought to be very pleasant."

It was. The ships were Dutch and comfortable; Aldous read what he could find and wrote up his travel diary. He would not allow Maria to help herself more than very sparingly to the caviare that was profusely offered (one of the few things she liked to eat); taking advantage, he explained to her, was vulgar. Off North Borneo they were faced with violence. A member of the crew entrenched with a dagger threatening to run amok. Only a week before another determined sailor had stabbed to death the captain in his own ship and twelve others within five miles of Singapore. While the ship's officers conferred and the passengers stood huddled, Aldous reflected on "the precarious artificiality of all that seemed most solid and fundamental in our civilization, of all that we take for granted.

> An individual has only to refuse to play the game of existence according to the current rules to throw the rule-observing players into bewildered consternation . . .
> They are appalled, they are at a loss, they are helpless.

The sailor, fortunately, lost his nerve.

In Japan they only spent a few days, landing at Kobe, going on to Kyoto by rail, joining ship again at Yokohama. It rained incessantly, the streets were deep in mud and the light as grey as a Scotch November. From the train they saw dim country bristling with factory chimneys. Kyoto looked like a mining camp. Yokohama like a camp that had not yet been finished. In Kyoto they walked through the city and it was like walking through an enormous Woolworth bazaar. "Such a collection of the cheap and shoddy, of the quasi-genuine and the imitation solid, of the vulgar and the tawdry . . ."

The news from home had not been reassuring. Matthew was not well and the doctors advised sending him to Switzerland to improve his lungs. Madame Nys was against this, and Aldous and Maria had to accept her judgement. Although they heard soon after that the little boy was better and Switzerland no longer urgent, they realized that they would have to give up their plan of moving to Rome on their return; instead, it would have to be some suitable mountain place. From Udaipur they had cabled Mme Nys, "Belgium for the moment—the mountains with us when we come back."

In April they were crossing the North Pacific and what Aldous called the somewhat Extreme Orient was behind them. The shock of re-entry into the West was near. One morning Aldous was handed the ship's bulletin of daily news. "Mrs X of Los Angeles," he read, "girl-wife of Dr X, aged 79, has been arrested for driving her automobile along the railroad track, whistling like a locomotive."

This piece of information had been transmitted through the ethereal holes between the molecules of air. From a broadcasting station more than five thousand miles away it had come to our ship . . . The labours of half a dozen men of genius, of hundreds of patient and talented investigators, had gone to creating and perfecting the means for achieving this miracle . . The ether reverberated with the name of Mrs X . . . The wave that bore it broke against the moon and the planets, and rippled on towards the stars and the ultimate void . . . Ah, the fire of Prometheus is put to the strangest uses . . .[1]

Meanwhile Aldous and Maria admitted interest in the exploits of Mrs X. She was bailed out, they presently heard, by her ancient husband, went home and began to smash the furniture . . . "What ultimately happened we never learned. The anonymous powers

[1] *Jesting Pilate.*

which purvey wireless news are strangely capricious. [One morning] the name of Mrs X no longer rippled out towards Aldebaran and the spiral nebulae. The bulletin announced that Bebe Daniels had fallen off her horse."

The last weeks of the voyage were spent in the United States. They landed at San Francisco and took the Daylight Limited to Los Angeles. It was the America of the boom years, the jazz age, prohibition America; the Huxleys were at the end of a long and wearing journey. Aldous's comments on bootlegged cocktails and *Yes, Sir, That's My Baby* were predictable. California fascinated him there and then, though he found Hollywood "altogether too Antipodean to be lived in".

They crossed the continent by train, spent a few days in Chicago, went on to New York. If there was one person Aldous wanted to meet, it was Miss Anita Loos. He adored *Gentlemen Prefer Blondes*. He wrote her a fan letter.

. . I was enraptured by the book, have just hugely enjoyed the play, and am to be in America so short a time that I have no leisure to do things in the polite and tortuous way . . .

They met. Anita Loos was in her twenties; Aldous found her ravishing. "One would like to keep her as a pet," he wrote to brother Julian.

Of course the Huxleys were rushed and fêted. Aldous became interested in the phenomenon of American vitality, a psychological by-product of prosperity, he concluded. "In less fortunate countries the precariousness of existence keeps large classes of the population in a state of chronic fear. Unemployment is a haunting apprehension . . . so little is needed in Europe to precipitate a man . . . Fear is the enemy of life." In the America of 1926 that fear did not exist.

. . Americans live with confidence, and therefore with enhanced vitality. A generous extravagance, undreamed of in other parts of the world, is the American rule.[1]

But this vitality is externalized "in places of public amusement, in dancing and motoring . . . What is known as 'night life' flourishes . . . And nowhere, perhaps, is there so little conversation . . Hence there appears to be even more vitality in the Americans than there really is.

[1] *Jesting Pilate.*

. . It is all movement and noise, like the water gurgling out of a bath—down the waste. Yes, down the waste.[1]

Presently the voyage was over. In *Jesting Pilate* Aldous summed up on a note of human unity. All values everywhere are broadly the same, "Goodness, beauty, wisdom and knowledge. . . ." In a letter a little later on he almost reversed it,

The more I see of human beings, the more I am convinced of the specific, almost generic, differences between them. One species can hardly communicate with the other. It is, perhaps, unfortunate that they can breed together. No, on second thoughts, it is probably a good thing.

At the end of May, willingly, they sailed for England.

[1] *Jesting Pilate.*

## Chapter Eleven

# Taking Up—New Starting Points

AFTER their return Aldous spent an agreeable June and July in London. Maria went to St Trond. He saw his family, dined with friends, strolled about the summer streets; he was staying with his Collier aunt, Aunt Ethel, in Hampstead, using the Athenaeum during the day. There was time to sit at last for his Uncle Jack. The Hon. John Collier had done a portrait of Maria in 1919, a large canvas, three-quarter length, Maria sitting, hands folded, in a décolleté dress. It was shown in the Royal Academy of 1920. Curiously, the portrait John Collier painted now, seven years later, turned out a companion piece—Aldous, rising thirty-two, looks as absurdly young as did Maria. It is a charming portrait, to my mind, academic or not, even a rather moving one. There he sits, young Aldous, in his nice brownsy suit and his floppy sofa-cushion tie drawn through a ring in the fashion of today, contriving to look at the same time romantic, casual and noble. John Collier's granddaughter, Jill,[1] aged sixteen, watched the painting's progress in the studio.

. . It was one of him sitting, sort of gazing into the distance . . . It was the first time I ever knew anything about Aldous—and I thought how fascinating he was. I fell in love with him, literally, as a portrait before I had actually met him.

The portrait was exhibited in the Academy of 1927.[2]

The three-years' contract with Chatto's had run out in January. Aldous had fulfilled it in so far as he had written and delivered two books per annum thrice running, though only two of them, instead of the agreed three, were novels, *Antic Hay* and *Those Barren Leaves*. Two volumes of short stories, *Little Mexican* and *Two or Three Graces* (just out), two of non-fiction, *Along the Road* and *Jesting Pilate* (about to be delivered), and *The Discovery*, an adaptation of the play by Sheridan thrown in, made up the bag. (Chatto's were preparing also a collection titled *Essays New and*

---

1 The present Mrs Anthony Greenwood, née Gillian Crawshay Williams.
2 Both portraits are in the possession of Rina (Madame Marcel) Eustration, who lives at present in Marseilles.

*Old*, containing exactly that.) There was a small over-all deficit in royalties against the annual advances, amounting to £76.9.5d. Chattos now proposed a new agreement on the same lines and Aldous signed it on 7th June. It was again for three years and two books per annum "one of which at least a full-length novel", and "possibly three other books during the said three years". Royalties on fiction were increased to an initial 20% up to 8,000 copies, and remained at 25% thereafter. The advance, Aldous's main fixed income, was increased from £500 a year to £650.

In August Aldous went to join his family at St Trond. He found Matthew "very well and in uproarious spirits", eating copiously; yet a longish stay in a high, dry climate was still indicated. They decided to try Cortina d'Ampezzo in the Dolomites, a resort at seven thousand feet with a reputation for winter sun. By September the Huxleys were installed in a nice warm house with long balconies and the right exposures, a small house simply and comfortably furnished (the rent, Aldous noted with satisfaction, was under £9 per month). Maria loathed the mountains and the cold however dry and sunny, and the lack of friends. Aldous chiefly looked at it as a good place to work in, and Matthew, the object of the exercise, was getting more robust. Old Bella had been replaced by a highly trained young governess, Mademoiselle La Porte, whom Aldous and Maria found a charming person, intelligent and a treasure. Fortunately, Matthew also liked her and was learning quickly.

They "existed in tolerable contentment". Julian and Juliette briefly appeared on their way from a journey in the Balkans (Aldous regretting not having had the time to go with them); *Jesting Pilate* came out in England (". . an elegant chaos"); Aldous was immersed in "the first bits and pieces of an ambitious novel".

In October, brief escape to Florence. Aldous got a tiresome tooth infection and had to see his dentist. It was there that Aldous and D. H. Lawrence met again, eleven years after their first, single meeting during the war in Hampstead.[1]

Lawrence and Frieda had returned to Europe the autumn before from their years of wandering, from Ceylon, Australia, Mexico and the ranch at Taos, from his long experience of search and flight. He was already a very ill man, struggling to keep alive. "Last year I nearly fell into the Styx," he had written to

---

[1] In point of fact, they had met once again very briefly in the intervening years, at a London party probably in the winter of 1923-24.

Middleton Murry, ". . all I want is to live and be well alive, not constrainedly half dead."[1] *The Plumed Serpent* had come out nine months before, Lawrence was writing *Lady Chatterley's Lover*; he and Frieda were wintering at the Villa Mirenda at Scandicci. The Florentine encounter was the starting point of the friendship between Lawrence, Aldous and Maria; it flowered almost at once. (It had only three and a half years to run.)

What got Aldous was Lawrence's *extraordinariness*, his difference in kind; a quality he looked for and accepted with humility and joy. ("I like him so much.") Lawrence confronted with Aldous on his own might have bristled. At Aldous's reticences, his good manners, his incisiveness of word—though that was undercut by gentleness of being—by Aldous's intellect and all that it entailed. As it turned out, the Huxleys were among the very few people with whom Lawrence did not at one time or another have a quarrel. Between him and Maria there was a straight intuitive affinity: they got on right away. Maria loved him; Lawrence, in Aldous's words, "was very fond of her". As well they had much fun. The four of them; as there was of course Frieda. She could irritate Aldous (" . . . being with her makes me believe that Buddha was right when he numbered stupidity among the deadly sins.") Much later, when Frieda was all that was left, they became very fond of her. This and much else was in the future: in point of time the meeting in Florence was short; a couple of walks, a picnic (at Vernon Lee's whose conversation Aldous admired), a meal or two at a trattoria. Traces are in letters.

. . Aldous Huxley just telegraphed, asking us to lunch Friday . . . Aldous Huxley, a writer and his wife came for the day, in their fine new car . . . Maria driving.[2]

. . Aldous Huxley was here on Friday; how he loathed India! I think it frightened him with a sense of squalor.[3]

. . I have started painting, quite seriously, on my own. Maria Huxley . . . brought me some canvases that her brother [*sic*] had daubed on . . . Maria looks like a *very* small edition of Ottoline: like Ottoline's Cinderella daughter—same peculiar long cheeks, and rather nice eyes. I liked her, too. . . .

The Huxleys seemed very bored. They are living pro-tem up in Cortina, North of Venice, in the higher mountains, because their child is supposed to have a lung. And they are very lonely—nobody

---

[1] D. H. L.'s Letters, 1932 edition.
[2] D. H. L. to Dorothy Brett, 18th October 1926, from *D. H. L. Letters*, 1962.
[3] D. H. L. to Earl and Achsah Brewster, 25th October 1926, from *D. H. Lawrence Reminiscences and Correspondence*, by Earl and Achsah Brewster. Martin Secker, 1934.

there . . . I wish they lived a bit nearer so that I could walk over and see them . . .[1]

Some snapshots were taken; the Huxleys returned to their mountains.

[1] D. H. L. to Dorothy Brett, 24th November 1926, from *D. H. L. Letters*, 1962.

## Chapter Twelve

## One Year

MOUNTAINS and November rains and the "inordinately large and complicated novel". Aldous was attempting to give plot and action to the hand theme in *Those Barren Leaves*. "I want to make a picture of life in its different aspects, the synchronous portrait of the different things an individual simultaneously is . . . Very difficult, and I doubt if I shall succeed . . but . . interesting."

He had been reading Gide's latest novel, *Les Faux Monnayeurs*. He usually found him disappointing—too elegant, too literary. Now he was interested, "The only good book he has written . . . in its way very good.

It is good, I think, because it is the first book in which Gide has ventured to talk about the one thing in the world that really interests him—sentimental sodomy.

It was also, it might be said in passing, one of the things that *least* interested Aldous, he was rather hoity-toity about sodomites sentimental or otherwise; whereas Maria got on extremely well with what she loudly and to their faces called our bugger friends, Aldous was made rather uncomfortable by evident male homosexuality. About lesbians he was tolerant, even had a *faible*—after all he shared their taste—as long as they were feminine and not too orthodox.

Aldous and Maria persevered for another long three months. "We sit perched on an icy solitude," Aldous wrote on Christmas Day, "which would be intolerable if it didn't do us all so much good." They had young visitors, Maria's sister Rose—now old enough to enter the picture—came out with another girl and a little Belgian boy as company for Matthew. On New Year's Eve Aldous and Maria took the girls to a dance, their first, "at the smart hotel.

It was very funny to be and feel a chaperon looking after those two ravishing creatures . . straight from the convent . . in white frills . . who missed not a single dance and got very gay on almost no champagne. Aldous and I looked pompous and spent most of our time playing at games and though winning many silly prizes losing much money . . .

"Perhaps it'll bring us luck in the New Year . . . It's already started: We shall go away soon . . . to London . . . Aldous's work be praised for that necessity . . . London for a long time . . . Cortina I have hated for so long so intensely that now I quite like it."[1]

The event of the winter was a new car. "A really rather tremendous car," Aldous called it. He had sold two articles in America "for a thousand dollars apiece! Crazy—and it probably won't be repeated." So they parted from their faithful Citroën that had cost so little and behaved so well and whose "habits had been as regular as those of Emanuel Kant", and bought the new Itala six cylinder two litre, the car with all the qualities of the Alfa Romeo. "What a machine . . ."

In February Arnold Bennett spent some weeks at Cortina, "in excellent form . . . My word,

> what sums these literary nabobs can command . . . [Bennett] revealed a few of the secrets. He himself never writes for less than two shillings per word, like an Atlantic cable!

Aldous ran into trouble with his novel—"The thing is simply getting too formidable for me." (The thing became *Point Counter Point*.) *Antic Hay* had taken under three months, *Those Barren Leaves* six; Aldous was used to going on with a book till it was finished. Now, with some fifty thousand words down, he felt that he needed time for "further thinking and ruminative living", and decided to stop altogether. Meanwhile there was nothing to send to Chattos for spring publication. From the money point of view this was not so worrying; *Jesting Pilate* had sold 3,000 copies, *Two or Three Graces* 2,000 in the regular and another 3,500 in the cheap edition, and an extra £200 had been made by the limited edition of reprinted essays. These were not large sales but good enough to wipe out the deficit and put Aldous a couple of hundred pounds ahead. He began to write some essays for autumn publication, something he could count on doing with reasonable certainty and speed.

All the same he was worried about the novel. A standstill in work is often outside the writer's conscious control and accompanied by a sense of having somehow made *fausse route*. *What* if the thing will never move again? There is nothing to do but wait (and meanwhile try to handle the waiting time in some constructive fashion). Perhaps it was a good thing to go on writing hard at something else; perhaps it would have served Aldous

---

[1] Maria Huxley in a letter to Eugene Saxton, published in *The Letters of Aldous Huxley*.

better to be idle. There was no choice, he had to earn his living; he could not afford to follow his own instincts as Lawrence, who could afford it even less, would certainly have done; but then Lawrence, as Aldous said, obeyed his daemon, was possessed in a real sense by his creative genius,[1] whereas Aldous, in humility and honest doubt, did not believe in his. (And how he often longed to be possessed, longed for the overriding impulse, whether it would have driven him into being Faraday or a great musician or a mystic or into seizing for himself a richer slice of life.) When the book stopped he went about the house morose and silent.

They left Cortina in late February (Matthew glowing with health), meaning to stop in Florence for a little motoring in the Tuscan spring. Instead Aldous went down with influenza. They saw Lawrence,

> Aldous still absolutely gone in the grouches—is writing a political novel [*sic*], heaven save him. [D. H. L. to Brett] I feel myself in another world altogether. They seem to me like people from a dead planet ... It's no good, for me the human world becomes more and more unreal, more and more wearisome.

The Huxleys drove on to England, and remained in London until May when they were suddenly called to Belgium. Maria's grandfather was dying, Monsieur Baltus, the old gentleman, now really old, who looked like a retired colonel and had spent his active days manufacturing cloth and his declining ones in reading, who had given Aldous his first welcome at St Trond. It was a formal death-bed.

> We were all there—kneeling around his bed. [Suzanne in her memoir] . . The Monk, Père Auguste, a family friend, an intellectual from the neighbouring Capuchin monastery, read the prayers. My grandmother was kneeling with us. Grandfather's last words were, "Emérence," his wife's name; she rose and gave him her hand—*et tranquillement il a poussé son dernier soupir.*

The recollection of that first death-bed remained potent with Maria. When in California, decades later, a dying woman asked for her help, she wrote to her great friend Rosalind Rajagopal, trying to clarify her feelings. ". . We all knelt around my grand-father's bed and prayed with the monks and the nuns and the older servants . . . But I could not tell—brought up as Catholics, heaven and hell clutter up all one's reactions and that personal God too . . . Perhaps I was too young. I think I mean not

[1] Introduction to *The Letters of D. H. L.*, 1932.

interested, only impressed."[1] Her active pity went to her grandmother who, very frail, took a dose of valerian in the night and
nearly died herself.

I can still see Coccola [we are back with Suzanne] a very tender
nurse by her side, holding her hand, renewing the ether compresses
although the smell of ether made her ill . . .

Aldous tried to keep aloof. "It will be impossible [he wrote to
Lewis Gielgud] to get out of staying several days [after the
funeral] as M's grandmother finds her presence particularly comforting. In the circumstances we cannot refuse to stay.

All this is . . at once lugubrious and farcical—the real Balzacian
comedy of a funeral in a little town; friends and relations in crêpe;
lettres de faire part; prodigal sons turning up to be reconciled and
pinching the cigars and a thousand francs for a black overcoat; the
poor old man's body in full evening dress; monks and sisters of
charity padding about; preparations for a colossal funeral banquet
—all very fantastic and everything happening to the strains of the
steam organs and electric pianos of the inevitable Flemish kermesse
just round the corner. . . .

That year they had another long summer by the Mediterranean.
They had missed Forte two years running; now they came back
with relief. Forte was the hub of their Italian life, here Aldous
felt in health, had a sense of basking however hard he worked;
there were sea, olive trees, cicada sounds in soft nights; they had
attractive, gay, affectionate friends at hand. For Maria the
mechanics of living were easy. They were in a new house, the
Majetta; basically all were much the same, smallish, clean, quiet
and equipped with the necessities of outdoor life—a garden and
a vine-wreathed pergola. Aldous was working away at his essays
(despatched in July). The Léner string quartet was staying practically next door, there was live music at night: Beethoven trios.
Rose was expected again, George and Vivi Baltus were in their
castello above Carrara; the Gielguds, Lewis and Mimi, were
coming to stay in August; as usual their closest, their permanent
Italian friends were more or less in residence. Yvonne Franchetti
—adorably pretty, a joy to Aldous and already to young Matthew
—and her husband Luigino, the pianist. And of course Costanza.
She would come swinging into the house early of a morning, sit
down on Aldous's bed and tell him—all ears—about everybody's

[1] Letter dated Llano, 27th February 1943.

love affairs including her own. The name of her first and brief lover was, to Aldous's utter joy, Dottore Cherubini. Costanza was now married, after some experiments and romantic attachments, and beginning to have daughters. She had finally accepted one of the boys of the *petite bande* of their youth, his name was Ecki Petterich and he was a German intellectual, very German, in a sugary artistic way, with Greek ideals. (The marriage fizzled out after some years.) The Huxleys did not like him much. In a certain way—says Jeanne, who knew it all so well—Costanza belonged to them.

Aldous and Maria had a way of drawing people into their life. Costanza was the first; she set the pattern. There were variations, it could be a woman on her own, a single man, or a man and wife, but wherever they were they gathered an eclectic family about them. It was a matter of sharing daily things, hearing confidences (entirely one-sided on Aldous's part), sharing the friends' troubles. These relationships might wane with time and geographical separation; they never ended in a quarrel.

It was the summer Rina came to them, Rina Rontini. She was the child of Italian peasants, one of nine; at the age of eight— after one and a half year's schooling in all—she was sent away from home into the mountains to mind sheep. Not for wages— for her daily food. "My mother didn't have to feed me any more."[1] In that manner she lived till she was fifteen, then, through an elder sister in service with the Fasolas, she was sent to Forte to the Huxleys. "I knew nothing—the *patience* Signora Maria had with me. She taught me. When I think of it, the things I couldn't do ... Luckily there was a cook ... The *patience* ..." Rina loved Baby (as Matthew was called well into boyhood), Maria she worshipped, for Aldous at first there was awe. "I was shy as a girl, I was shy being in the house with him. But he was kind— *era sempre gentile*—oh yes, he talked, he talked to everyone, but not *like* everyone." (And Rina is laughing—she is dark-eyed with the bone structure showing now in the fine Tuscan face—makes a gesture that includes the street, the city she now lives in.) "You see, he didn't talk like a *Marseillais*."

Her own trouble was sweets. "I hadn't ever had even sugar to eat, so I had this craving ... I took cakes, I stole chocolates. I couldn't help myself. Signora Maria would hide the chocolates, lock them up; I could always get at them. I knew it was wrong— it made her sad. But it was *plus fort que moi*. And you know what she did the first thing after the war, in 1945, Signora Maria? She sent me a parcel with chocolates from America."[1]

Rina remembers her youth and ignorance; what Aldous and

---

[1] Rina Rontini, the present Madame Marcel Eustration, talking to S. B.

Maria spoke of was her goodness and intelligence. And she was observant. Aldous liked to hear about what was going on, to hear, she says, about the funny things. She told him to come out to see the Contessa della Gherardesca next door give sugar to her horse from a gloved hand, the groom standing by with napkin and the lump of sugar on a silver salver. Aldous was enchanted and Rina had to call him every morning for the Contessa's *zucchero*.

Into that Forte life Lawrence arrived: in June, by himself, for a couple of weeks, not in an easy mood. "Stimulating," Aldous wrote, "but difficult to get on with, passionate, queer, violent." Rina found him gentle and expansive—"*He* really talked to everyone."

Gentle to Rina; less so about the Huxleys' friends. Wretchedly unwell, he was apt to lash out. ". . He is a Jew, Barone Luigi [Franchetti]—and as rich as Croesus. He plays the piano very well, and is quite nice . . . but I have absolutely no basic sympathy with people of assured incomes. All words become a lie, in their mouths, in their ears also. I loathe rich people."[1] Nor did he share the Huxleys' love for Forte, ". . beastly as a place: flat, dead sea, jellyfish and millions of villas." And the sun and bathing were bad for him; within days of his return to Florence he went down with a bronchial haemorrhage. Aldous and Maria rushed to him. They found him in bed, "touchingly gentle now and very ill.

. . And the poor wretch is not strong enough . . to move into the cool of the mountains . . . I hope profoundly he'll get over this business. The doctor seemed to think he'd be all right; but with these haemorrhages . . the end can be quite sudden and unexpected.

As we know, Lawrence pulled through. He managed to get away to Austria. "It is such a mercy to be able to breathe and move. I take little walks in the country," he wrote to the Huxleys, and in the autumn they had a letter full of new plans which ends with this spirited passage:

I'm glad Maria has met Mrs Beeton . . . Right-o! Maria! You wait a bit, and I'll be eating your puddings for you. God gives us a good meeting, as the Methodists 'd say.—Though I'm sorry Rose has gone. The boy must miss her terribly, lessons or not!—Maria, have you greased the car?—I feel I don't want to do a thing, except curse *almost* everybody. Never mind! *Hasta la Vista!*

D. H. L.[2]

---

[1] *D. H. L. Letters*, 1962. (To Koteliansky, 13.6.27.)
[2] Ibid., 1932.

Aldous had gone back to the novel. It grew but he was "getting more and more involved in its difficulties". He wished that he could afford, he wrote to Julian, to spend four or five years over a book like Flaubert. "There might be a chance then of making it rather good." Instead he was still aiming at spring publication, and they stayed put in the "balmy warmth" of autumnal Forte, "I sit working on the beach with nothing but a pair of bathing drawers." Yet Italy *per se* was getting more irritating daily—petty regulations, police persecutions. At the moment the Italian press was fulminating against birth control. "I see that Musso wants twenty million Italians in twenty-five years. Presumably to fight France with . . ." As for the rest of the world, he'd been reading *The Mind and Face of Bolshevism*

> It's really humiliating that human beings can be so stupid as the Russians seem to be. They really are the devil. Europeans must join together to resist all the enemies of our civilization—Russians, Americans, orientals—each in their own way a hideous menace . . .

*Proper Studies*, the new book of essays, was published in November. The book can be read as an exposition of Aldous's current views on the social fabric—democracy, education, equality, eugenics . . . Much of the inspiration came from the Italian sociologist Vilfredo Pareto.[1] "He really does take the lid off and shows you the works [Aldous to Robert Nichols] at some length unfortunately . . . three thick volumes in Italian [and the writing] slow, subfusc and grim . . ." Aldous's regard for Pareto (who has three faintly dismissive lines in the *Britannica*[2]) was lasting. In 1934 he wrote,

> About old Pareto—I . . . feel he is one of the very few people who have approached sociology in a genuinely scientific spirit, without any metaphysical axe to grind, without violent political prejudices (beyond that conservatism and disbelief in progress which seems always to come to people who spend a lot of time studying the facts of human activity) and without, above all, any propagandist zeal for any *one*, or all explanatory hypotheses. This last is what makes most sociologies such rubbish. The mania to explain everything in terms of one set of causes—economic, climatic, psychological, religious and so forth. Pareto is prepared to admit that there are a great many causal factors always at work . . .[3]

[1] Vilfredo Pareto (1848-1923). Author of the monumental *Trattato di Sociologia Generale*, 1916. English translation, *Mind and Society*, 1935. Reviewed by A. H. in *N.Y. Herald Tribune Books*, 9th June 1935.
[2] Expanded to full article in recent editions.
[3] In a letter to Marjorie Seabrook.

In *Proper Studies* Aldous, too, attempted to approach sociology in a scientific spirit. The result is a very intelligent and arid book, perhaps his most arid. It has the aloofness of *Jesting Pilate* without the lightness, and in spite of many nails hit on the head, I cannot find it a sympathetic book. But let D. H. Lawrence have the word.

Dear Aldous,—

Many thanks for *Proper Studies*. I have read 70 pages, with a little astonishment that you are so serious and professorial. You are not your grandfather's *Enkel* for nothing—that funny dry-mindedness and underneath social morality. But you'll say I'm an introvert, and no fit judge. Though I think to make people introverts and extraverts is bunk . . . You are an extravert by inheritance far more than in *esse*. You'd have made a much better introvert, had you been allowed. "Did she fall or was she pushed" . . . But, my dear, don't be dry and formal and exposition all that—What's the odds! I just read Darwin's *Beagle* again—he dried himself—and *tant de bruit pour des insectes!*—But I like the book.

There is a P.S. to this letter:

I don't mean I didn't find the 70 pages good—they're very sane and sound and good—only I myself am in a state of despair about the Word either written or spoken seriously. That's why, I suppose, I wrote this, when I wasn't asked . . .[1]

The Huxleys had been without anything like a permanent home since they left Florence over two years ago. Soon Matthew would have to go to school. Once more they thought of settling in England. It was to be the country—in easy reach of London, and Aldous is looking forward to it rather, looking forward, he wrote to Julian, to being more in England. "If only the sun shone!"

Their immediate plans were for another Alpine winter, joined this year by Julian and his family. (Julian was working at his share of the encyclopaedic work on biology, *Science of Life*, in collaboration with H. G. Wells, and was geographically his own master.) One gloomy day Aldous nearly called it off.

I have realized [he wrote to his brother] with increasing certainty that my novel can't be finished, as I hoped, by the beginning of January and that I shall need at least an extra month's work to get it done . . I shall have to go on working at it all through January

---

[1] *Letters of D. H. L.*, 1932.

—seven or eight hours a day, which would make rather nonsense of a joint holiday. So that I think . . it would be wisest if I . . . dug myself in somewhere with Maria . . . I really must get this bloody book off my hands and I know that I should find the task almost impossibly difficult in the midst of a friendly party . . .

Matthew and Mademoiselle could go if Juliette was able to take them on, and Aldous would lend Julian his own skis . . . By next morning Aldous had changed his mind. He sent a note,

My Dear J,
    Thinking it over again—after all I could get my work done all right, particularly if we were in a house; and it would be very nice to be together.

And so Juliette took a house for all of them, the Chalet des Aroles, at Les Diablerets in Switzerland.

Presently, late in the year, Aldous and Maria left Forte. They spent Christmas in Florence. On Christmas Day they drove out to Scandicci and picked up Frieda and Lawrence who had written that he wanted to go where they could "eat turkey and be silly—not sit solitary . . ."

## Chapter Thirteen

# A Family Holiday—Involvements with D. H. Lawrence

THEY were a large party, in their capacious chalet at Les Diablerets, the two brothers, Juliette and Maria, their three children, Anthony, Francis and Matthew; Mademoiselle, visiting relations. The men wrote in the morning, then came outdoor exercise, picnics, teatime talk, reading aloud in the evenings—Julian and Aldous had regained the family holidays of their youth; taking turns, they got through the whole of *The Pickwick Papers*. Everybody felt well. In his memories,[1] Julian speaks of it as a cheerful, a happy time. As a mountain resort, a ghastly species, Aldous complained, Les Diablerets was a poor specimen. But the sun was marvellous. He very much wanted Lawrence to join them ("I'm waiting to hear . . what it's really like and how dear it is,"[2] Lawrence wrote). Presently he and Frieda arrived and settled "two minutes away across the snow in another wooden hut".

The men laboured. To Aldous it soon became clear that he could not get the novel done in time. Even in those days of quick production a book for spring publication had to be in by February. For the second year Aldous was about to fail his contract. Maria restored his peace of mind by firm advice. "Darling—tell them." On 23rd January Aldous sat down and wrote to C. H. C. Prentice of Chatto's, a letter typical of his attitude to his publishers and his money dealings.

> I feel very apologetic; but this wretched book refuses, in spite of incessant labours, to get finished. I might perhaps contrive to scramble through the final additions and alterations in the course of another month; but I'd much prefer to take more time and produce for the autumn something which I hope would be better. I hope this won't be a great inconvenience; but I do want to get this thing thoroughly ship-shape.
>
> Meanwhile I am bothered by the thought that this delay of mine may involve you in financial loss; and since I haven't fulfilled my side of the contract, I think it would be only fair if the next two quarters' instalments were at least reduced. . . .

[1] Sir Julian Huxley, *Memories*, Vol. I. Allen & Unwin, 1970.
[2] This and all subsequent quotations from Lawrence are from *The Letters of D. H. L.*, 1932, unless otherwise stated.

Prentice's answer arrived a few days later.

Dear Huxley,
It is a pity about the novel, but to push it through, simply in order that it should come out quickly, would be a great mistake. Please do take your own time over it. Autumn will be quite all right . . . *Point Counter Point* is rather a critical book; so it would be madness to prevent you from doing all to it that you wanted . . . Do you think the MS will be ready for us by April? . . . [Harold] Raymond and I are both in the highest fizzle of curiosity.
It is charming of you to suggest that the next two quarterly instalments should be reduced. There may not be a necessity for this, but it does just look possible that the current year will show a deficit. *Proper Studies*, being not quite the kind of book that many people expected, has not started off so briskly . . . There is, however, the possibility that the royalties from the other books . . will have completed the annual sum . . . Perhaps it would be the easiest thing to go on paying your quarterly cheques as usual, and to carry on any deficit from this year to the next . . . It is really awfully good of you making the suggestion, but we do not wish to incommode you in any way.

There had been hope that sun and altitude might do something for Lawrence. At first all he could say was, "I'm no worse". Later he wrote to Orioli,

I think the place is really doing me good, I do feel stronger. I don't love snow, exactly—it's so beastly white, and makes one's feet so cold. But sometimes it's beautiful. Yesterday we drove in a sledge to the top of the pass and picnicked there, with Aldous and Maria and Rose, and Julian Huxley, Aldous's brother, and his wife Juliette. I really liked it. It does put life into one.[1]

He had brought the MS of *Lady Chatterley's Lover* and Maria was typing it for him. Maria, Aldous and Juliette were the first people to read it. "Aldous and Maria liked it very much—so they said." Juliette, apparently, was "*very* cross, morally so . . ." Nor did Lawrence and Julian see always eye to eye. When the Huxley brothers talked science to one another, Lawrence "exploded with a snort of impotent rage".[2] What infuriated him particularly were evolutionary and physiological ideas; he believed of course, writes Julian, that

[1] *D. H. L. Letters*, 1962.   [2] Sir Julian Huxley, op. cit.

More power exercised by the "dark loins of man", greater freedom for our instincts and our intuitions, would solve the world's troubles. His anger was particularly directed against myself, as a professional scientist. I learnt to disregard his outbursts of fury, but we had many stormy passages.[1]

And "Well, of course," said Aldous, "I never understood his anti-intellectualism . . . His dislike of science was passionate and expressed itself in the most fantastically unreasonable terms. 'All scientists are liars,' he would say, when I brought up some experimentally established fact, which he happened to dislike. 'Liars, liars!' It was a most convenient theory.

I remember in particular one long and violent argument on evolution, in the reality of which Lawrence always passionately disbelieved. "But look at the evidence, Lawrence," I insisted, "look at all the evidence." His answer was characteristic. "But I don't care about evidence. Evidence doesn't mean anything to me. I don't feel it *here*." And he pressed his two hands on his solar plexus.[2]

But then Lawrence could give so much, and what he gave was so valuable (as Aldous said in the London interview) that it was absurd and profitless to spend one's time with him disputing about a matter in which he absolutely refused to take a rational interest. This anti-intellectualism was all the more curious,

as he was an intellectual . . . I mean as a young man he was a great passer of examinations. [Chuckle in Aldous's voice] I mean he had a large store of knowledge, he didn't like to say so, but *he did*. He was very well read. . . .

By mid-February Julian had had to return to England, Frieda had gone to Germany, Maria was in Florence. *Gli autori* and the children stayed on, Juliette and Mademoiselle looking after them "like angels". Aldous was still glued to his "bloody novel . . . Such are the difficulties of fiction," he wrote to Lewis Gielgud, "especially to one who, like myself, isn't really a born novelist but has large aspirations."

Plans were vague again; he was tempted to fall in with Lawrence's idea and go out to live for six months on his ranch in New Mexico. In the meantime he and Maria went to London (in the Itala) to look at schools. Leaving Matthew in Belgium, they took a furnished flat in Onslow Mews for three months.

---

[1] Sir Julian Huxley, op. cit.
[2] Intro. to *Letters of D. H. L.*, 1932.

Your letter and Maria's today—[Lawrence wrote from Florence] and first sound you've made since leaving Diablerets—those 2 post-cards were ghosts . . . The printer is printing my novel. [The miserable trouble over *Lady Chatterley* had just begun. Lawrence had decided to print the unexpurgated version in Florence—a thousand copies to be sold by mail order one by one.] Secker won't do it—*meno male*—but what about the copyright . . . you must help me. I'll send you a little batch of order-forms, and I'm sure you and Maria will make a few folks buy. That novel must be put down their throats. Mind you stand up for it, when the pigs begin to grunt. . . .

The letter ends with a litany:

> Let's go to New Mexico in autumn. Let's be amused.
> I've said May fifteenth for my novel.
> Damn everybody!
> What is Julian's address?
> We *must* put salt on the hypocritical and snaily tails, the good public.
> Dear Maria, don't be downhearted.

And a few days later,

> My dear Maria,
> Your letter yesterday. Glad you are happy in London. You wouldn't be happy in Italy—it only rains . . .
> . . Secker wrote that he didn't see how the novel could possibly be expurgated for public sale—so I'll just go on with my private one . . . Did you get some of the little order-forms? . . And I've made my design of a phoenix rising from the nest in flames for the cover . . . Shall send you a specimen.

It is a long letter and in it Lawrence touches on what he and Maria seem to have understood so well about one another.

> I think myself it's rather nice to be busy and practical on the out-side—and day-dreams, as you call it, inside. The things one cares about are all inside, like seeds in the ground in winter. But one has to attend to the things one only half cares about. And so life passes away . . . Luckily the inside thing corresponds with the inside thing in just a few people. I think it is so with us. We don't fit in very well outside—but the inside corresponds, which is most important.

The sale of *Lady Chatterley's Lover* is already forbidden in Italy. Now Lawrence decides that no more English publishers are to be shown the novel. Aldous went to Curtis Brown's on his behalf. "They are furious in that office," Lawrence writes him, "that I publish my novel: daren't say much . . . I shall ask [them] to send the MS to you—do you mind? Perhaps Maria will deposit it somewhere for me. . . ." And in the P.S.: "Dear Maria—if you're passing Curtis Brown's office with the car, will you call and demand the MS of *John Thomas*, and carry it away from them. I don't want them to have it any more. And you can do what you like with it."

Lawrence had been correcting Orioli's page-proofs, "and it was *almost* Maria's typing over again. Dear Maria, all those little mistakes you made, and I followed like Wenceslas's page so patiently in your footsteps: now it's a Florentine printer. He writes dind't, did'nt, dnid't, dind't, din'dt, didn't like a Bach fugue. . . ."

Aldous and Maria and other friends were getting orders for *Lady C.* Maynard Keynes, the St John Hutchinsons, Lady Colefax subscribed; cheques were coming in. The price was £2 and $10 respectively. Lawrence was already thinking of a sea voyage with Frieda. "Believe me," he advised Aldous, "that's the thing to do: publish for oneself at £2. It's the solution for us small-selling authors."

Matthew's first school had been chosen, Frensham Heights, near Godalming, near Prior's Field, in Huxley country. He arrived from Belgium to be fitted out. "There are moments," Aldous groaned, "when parenthood really is a whole time job." What with shopping, zoo-visiting, calling on relations. . . . Presently the boy went off to school and Aldous did his last revisions. In the second week of May the T/S was sent in. *Point Counter Point* was off his hands. He was a free man once more. He and Maria left London for a stay in Paris before going on to Forte.

## Chapter Fourteen

# Cottage on the Seine

IT was not going to be Rome after all; nor as yet New Mexico, nor the house in the Home Counties. Aldous and Maria saw a house just outside Paris and took it then and there on a long lease: 3 rue du Bac, Suresnes, beyond the Porte Maillot. It was a compromise solution, and for such one usually finds a number of good reasons. None of them were climate. The sun was not likely to shine much more on that part of the Seine valley than it would on Surrey. If Aldous shied again from settling down in England it was perhaps because of an instinct that he functioned better where he was not actually belonging; the freedom of the outsider *in perpetuum* did suit him; like so many idiosyncratic and distinguished Englishmen and women before him he chose to live in foreign parts without losing an essential Englishness. Italian plans had to be shelved because the political nonsense had become too intrusively obnoxious. Suresnes was near a civilized metropolis and at the same time quiet; it was a handy distance for Matthew's holidays (Aldous and Maria's bright idea of the best way for an unaccompanied boy of eight to travel was to fly and many of Matthew's childhood journeys began by his being put on one of those small aeroplanes at Croydon); Lewis Gielgud lived in nearby Passy; the literary world of Paris might prove pleasant it was hoped; and Maria would be with her sister. Indeed it was planned that the Moulaerts, René, Jeanne, Sophie, should have a permanent apartment in the house. Moulaert, who had mixed the colours for the flat in Paddington, was to do a professional decorating job.

The landlord agreed to put in central heating; Maria found materials designed by Dufy for sofas and cushions; armchairs made to Aldous's measure were ordered from Maple's in London. (Most of this furniture has endured.) Aldous, for his part, was pleased.

I look forward to getting into the "Cottage" at Suresnes . . . The surroundings are really delightful—a tiny provincial town enlivened by Sunday boating, with the river at the door and the Bois—where one can walk on weekdays for an hour and hardly see a soul—3 minutes away; and the whole a quarter of an hour from the Rue de la Paix.

(Though I wonder if we shall ever be there. We have already

planned to visit Germany, Spain and Khartoum in the course of the next year! But then, what are plans for unless to be unmade?)

They left Paris for their summer at Forte, seeing Lawrence in Switzerland on the way (three days at Chexbres above the Lake of Geneva—Lawrence surprisingly well, all things considered). Thence over the Simplon into Italy, Aldous's first experience of a modern motorway—"40 miles . . where you . . are guaranteed a perfect surface, no crossroads . . no towns and no traffic except fast moving cars". Rina and yet another Forte house were waiting for them, Il Canneto, minute, in the pinewoods, very green, neither noisy nor dusty.

The weather—it always seems to have been—was perfect. Aldous had acquired an electric fan and so could work in the hottest hours after luncheon; "the difference between still and moving air," he remarked to his father, "is really incredible." What he was working on were "beastly proofs" and notes for some biographical essays on Pascal, Burns, Baudelaire . . .

*Point Counter Point* was to be published in the autumn, meanwhile Aldous learnt that it had been selected in advance "by a thing called the Literary Guild of the USA as their book of the month, which means a considerable sale over and above the ordinary figures and a corresponding quantity of filthy lucre. Which is very agreeable."

They returned to Paris in October, staying with the Gielguds as their house was still full of workmen. Suddenly, once again, Maria was called to St Trond. Emérence Baltus was dying. Maria was in time. Aldous and Jeanne followed for the funeral.

In late October they moved into the new house which was hideous. A narrow red-brick and stone frontage with gabled windows, a strip of back garden, the whole too small and not very convenient. A living-dining-room took up the main floor, the first held two bedrooms (Aldous worked in his), a bath and a tiny sitting-room for Maria. A crooked little staircase led to an attic floor with two rooms for the Moulaerts and a minute one for Matthew. As it turned out, Moulaert never came to live there; he had met another young woman in the summer and gone off with her. (He finished the decorations.) The house was well run, with "Rina adorable and perfect," Jeanne describes their new life; Maria had her dresses made at Nicole Groult (*haute couture* thought more individualistic and approachable than the classic establishments) and looked ravishing in the evening. They were very social, with people for luncheon nearly every day (after nightfall, they found out, Suresnes became inaccessible by public transport), Drieu La Rochelle, Gabriel Marcel, James Joyce—"*he* was a very strange man," Aldous would say. Their dining-table, by Moulaert, had a looking-glass surface that allowed a weird view of faces chewing, disconcerting to new guests.

The houses were very close, the Huxleys' next-door neighbour happened to be a middle-aged French writer, "not a great writer". Rina whose story this is explains, "comme Monsieur, mais un écrivain de livres de poche à frs. 1.50". *Contrepoint* was being written up in *Les Nouvelles Littéraires* and the poor man was jealous. When Aldous stepped into his garden the *homme de lettres*, lying in wait, would turn the garden hose on him. Aldous got wet and Maria very angry. After the third time, she went to the police who came to remonstrate with this unamiable character. He told them, "Cet Anglais n'a qu'à rentrer chez lui."

When Aldous took a day off, they would all set out in the car to Fontainebleau or Chartres . . . Yvonne Franchetti came to stay, and Mary Hutchinson's young daughter Barbara.[1] There were money panics. One evening as Aldous was talking about the bills and the need for cutting down, Maria, after a moment's reflection, called in Rina, "*Domani niente uovo bollito*—no boiled egg tomorrow". Thereafter Aldous asked Jeanne's advice on money matters. "Il trouvait que j'avais du bon sens. Il est évident que je connaissais mieux la valeur de l'argent que Coccola."

Suzanne, living with her sister and brother-in-law in London six years earlier, had been a young girl, a learner of the adult world. Jeanne, at Suresnes, was a married woman with a child of her own whose life had just gone to pieces. She was unhappy, and not particularly sociable. She was setting out to earn her own and Sophie's living. France, the year before the Wall Street crash, was already in a state of financial instability; it was a hard time for an untrained young woman who had wanted to be an artist. She turned to hand-painting scarves and dress materials which for a while sold well. Aldous was affectionate and did much to make a cheerful home for her and the little girl; Maria was terribly concerned and beset by guilt about her own happy and so much easier existence. Their life *à trois*, in Jeanne's words, was both cozy—with long late-night and morning chats across the landing—and difficult. There was a profound—a very profound—attachment between these two sisters; yet they were, and remained, so different in many ways. Jeanne very straight, blunt at times; Maria, "toute souplesse, charme et savoir faire (avec un côté bourgeois si on veut). Je n'aimais pas les formes extérieures," Jeanne says of herself. "J'ai dû leur rendre la vie peu agréable."

Maria also tried to look after Rina's future and sent her to

---

[1] Barbara Hutchinson, the present Mrs Nico Ghika.

evening classes to improve her R's. Rina admits to going to the
cinema instead.

Everything was going wrong for Lawrence. Now the pirating
of *Lady Chatterley* had begun. In December he wrote from Bandol:

> Would you or Aldous do a little thing for me when you are in
> Paris? There have come out *two* pirated editions of *Lady C.* in America;
> they are being sold in London at £3 . . . I believe they are being
> sold in Paris too, in Galignani's and other shops . . . I do wish when
> you are in town you would ask these shops if they have copies of
> the book, and how much, and ask to see one . . and tell me if it's
> the pirated edition—and tell them, the brutes. The pirated editions
> were *photographed* from my edition, so they may look superficially
> the same. . . .

They were indeed selling the stolen edition, asking 5,000 frs a
copy, more than £60 or $250! Aldous advised offering the
legitimate Florence edition to the Paris book-sellers "at some
reasonable rate between the original 2 guineas and the 5,000 frs
asked by the pirates . . . [to] undersell the devils and at the same
time turn an honest penny". In the same letter Aldous reported
about himself: the house, the weather, reading. The house is
beginning to look like one . . . The weather is a damp cold hell
. . . His reading, "a tiresome book by Virginia Woolf—*Orlando*—
which is terribly literary and *fantaisiste* that nothing is left in it
at all . . ."

Unfortunately Lawrence did not have sufficient stock in hand
to undersell the pirates (so many copies had been confiscated by
the US customs). "If only I had 2,000 I could kill the pirates,"
he wrote. Aldous went to Sylvia Beach to see if she could be
interested in re-publishing *Lady C.* We know that she was not.
So Aldous went into the possibility of photographing the Florence
edition, and wrote at length to Chatto's to get the facts about
this new process. Did it cost less than ordinary setting? How many
copies from the plate? Do most printers undertake the job? "I'm
sorry to bother you . . . but I am anxious to get all the information
I can to help Lawrence in his campaign against the pirates . . ."

At this time Aldous's own novel was being bought at a great
rate. Before the year was out the sales of *Counterpane*, as Lawrence
called it, had passed the 10,000 mark. Aldous had ceased to be a
small-selling author.

## Chapter Fifteen

## Point Counter Point

ALDOUS had a correspondent whom apparently he never met. Mrs Flora Strousse who lived in Philadelphia and published under the pseudonym of Floyd Starkey. She wrote first and he occasionally answered with a frankness both unusual and detached. The situation has been irresistible to other writers. Aldous began with Dear Mr or Miss Floyd Starkey, soon went on to My dear Starkey, and this is the kind of thing he wrote, "I have almost no ideas about myself and don't like having them—avoid having them—on principle even—and only improvise them, when somebody like you asks to know them . . . 'know thyself' was probably one of the stupidest pieces of advice ever given . . . introspection which distracts one from the outside world is a kind of suicide. . . ." When *Point Counter Point* came out, he wrote to her, "I have at last written a rather good, but also a rather frightful, novel."

Meanwhile D. H. Lawrence wrote to Aldous. "I have read *Point Counter Point* with a heart sinking through my boot-soles and a rising admiration.

I do think you've shown the truth, perhaps the last truth, about you and your generation, with really fine courage. It seems to me it would take ten times the courage to write *P. Counter P.* than it took to write *Lady C.*: and if the public knew *what* it was reading, it would throw a hundred stones at you, to one at me.

Lawrence admired, he did not like the book. "I do think that art has to reveal the palpitating moment or the state of man as it is. And I think you do that, terribly. But what a moment! and what a state!" And Lawrence went into a rave about Aldous's thrilling only to "murder, suicide and rape.

All I want to do to your Lucy is to smack her across the mouth, your Rampion is the most boring character in the book—a gas-bag. Your attempt at intellectual sympathy! It's all rather disgusting, and I feel like a badger that has his hole on Wimbledon Common and trying not to be caught. Well, *caro*, I feel like saying good-bye to you—but one will have to go on saying good-bye for years.

D. H. L.

*Point Counter Point* was published in October 1928 and became a best-seller on both sides of the Atlantic. It was translated into every conceivable language, European and Asiatic, enjoyed a huge vogue in France and Germany, broadened Aldous's English public and became one of the cornerstones of his international reputation, not to say his fame.

Since then—the best part of a half century—a good deal of printer's ink has flowed. Aldous's ambitious novel has been weathering eclipses as well as heights of fashion. It has been acclaimed as a great novel, debunked, disserted upon, fitted to many a Procrustean bed; it has been regarded as a work of stark realism, cynical despair, universal range, excessive intellectualism, eroticism, defeatism, a rogue's gallery of satanic creations, and a major portrait of English society of the time. Cyril Connolly has pointed out that the opening reads like a story in a woman's magazine—" 'You won't be late?' There was anxiety in Marjorie Carling's voice, there was something like entreaty." The book has been called vulgar and it has been called sublime; and of all the scoldings, Lawrence's is perhaps the oddest. "*Murder [etc.]* is what you thrill to . . .*" The murder in *Point Counter Point* appears to be dragged in, much like the death of Leonard Bast in *Howard's End*, with a visible effort on the author's part.

It is Lawrence's famous subjectivity that comes out in his splenetic complaint. The narrowness of scope he was capable of indulging in is pointed up by a passage of Sir Isaiah Berlin's.[1] Sir Isaiah places Aldous with Ezra Pound and J. B. S. Haldane among the major intellectual emancipators of his generation:

As men of letters—led by Voltaire, the head of the profession—rescued many oppressed human beings in the eighteenth century; as Byron or George Sand, Ibsen, Baudelaire, Nietzsche, Wilde and Gide and perhaps even Wells or Russell have done since, so members of my generation were assisted to find themselves by novelists, poets and critics concerned with the central problems of their day. Social and moral courage can, on occasion, exercise a more decisive influence than sensibility or original gifts. One of my own contemporaries, a man of exceptional honesty, intellectual power and moral responsiveness, inhibited and twisted by an uncertain social position and bitter puritanism on the part of his father, was morally freed (as others have been by psycho-analysis, or Anatole France, or living among Arabs) by reading Aldous Huxley: in particular *Point Counter Point* and one or two short stories. Light had been thrown for him on dark places, the forbidden was articulated,

[1] Sir Isaiah Berlin, *Mem. Vol.*

intimate physical experience, the faintest reference to which used to upset him profoundly and affect him with a feeling of violent guilt, had been minutely and fully described. From that moment my friend advanced intellectually, and has become one of the most admired and productive men of learning of our day. It is not this therapeutic effect, however, that appealed to the young men of my generation so much as the fact that Huxley was among the few writers who, with all his constantly commented upon inability to create character, played with ideas so freely, so gaily, with such virtuosity. . . .

And now follows what is, to my mind, the most acute analysis of a constant element in Aldous's writing:

The performance took place against a background of relatively few, simple, *moral convictions; they were disguised by the brilliance of the technical accomplishment, but they were there, they were easily intelligible, and like a monotonous, insistent, continuous ground bass slowly pounding away through the elaborate intellectual display,* [my italics] they imposed themselves on the minds of boys of seventeen and eighteen—still, for the most part, eager and morally impressionable, no matter how complex or decadent they may in their naiveté have conceived themselves to be.

Aldous's intentions in *Point Counter Point* are largely expressed by the stanza from Fulke Greville on the title page.

> *Oh, wearisome condition of humanity,*
> *Born under one law to another bound,*
> *Vainly begot and yet forbidden vanity,*
> *Created sick, commanded to be sound.*
> *What meaneth nature by these diverse laws,*
> *Passion and reason, self-division's cause?*

*Diverse Laws*—"Just what I want." This was what he tried to put across (contemporary English society being but the raw material to hand), this, and again the queerness of reality, the *extraordinariness* of everything. "That's what I want to get into this book—the astonishingness of the most obvious things," says Philip Quarles, the novelist inside the novel. And for that any plot or situation would do. "The whole book could be written about a walk from Piccadilly Circus to Charing Cross." But it was not. Aldous was aware of the limitations of the discursive novel, the novel of ideas. "Not only must you write about people who have ideas to express—.01 per cent of the human race. Hence the real, the congenital novelists don't write such books. But then I never pretended to be a congenital novelist."[1]

In *Point Counter Point* Aldous tried to balance talk with action; ideas are translated into the lives of men and women, into case histories if you like. The characters act as well as talk; things happen to them. Was Aldous really as reluctant or defective a novelist as he made himself out to be? When it comes to his major characters, one can see what he (and his critics) meant—his talent for generalizing is allowed to get the better of his talent for exploring the particular. And he over-insists. To what extent are Rampion, Spandrell, Illidge, Burlap credible in the round? The question raises questions within questions and one of them is that of genesis —like *Crome Yellow, Antic Hay*, like in fact the lot, *Point Counter Point* has been regarded as a roman à clef. Let's take Mark Rampion now. We know what Lawrence himself thought about him—a gasbag and a bore. Floyd Starkey, Aldous's unseen correspondent, asked him straight. Aldous answered, "Have I 'done' Lawrence? No. Kingham [another Lawrentian character, in *Two or Three Graces*] was concocted before I knew him—at least I'd only seen him once . . . Rampion is just some of Lawrence's notions on legs. The actual character of the man was incomparably queerer and more complex than that."

Aldous "did" Baudelaire in so far as Spandrell's disastrous adolescent history was Baudelaire's; he did John Middleton Murry in *some* aspects of the revolting Burlap; he did Maria in Elinor, Philip's wife; Matthew in their child; he put something of himself into Walter Bidlake and a good deal into Philip Quarles. And there again are the shades of Nancy Cunard whom this time he did not attempt to do at all, Lucy Tantamount is any stylized siren of the 1920s; what he did was the tale (recollected in tranquility) of a young man's unrequited physical passion for a woman he dislikes.

*The actual character was incomparably more complex*—Mark Rampion *v*. D. H. Lawrence; Philip Quarles *v*. Aldous Huxley. All the same, there is very much of Aldous in *Point Counter Point*—Aldous on himself, though selective and with little regard for fairness, is biography at first hand and as such must have its place here.

Was Aldous ever really influenced by D. H. L.? If so, did it last? How serious, later on, was the influence of his friend Gerald Heard?

. . In point of fact [Philip Quarles says of himself] . . he had never deeply and whole-heartedly admired anyone. Theoretically, yes; but never in practice, *never to the point of wanting to make himself a disciple*,

---

[1] From Philip Quarles' notebook in *Point Counter Point*. Chatto & Windus, 1928. All quotations in this chapter, unless otherwise stated, are from this book.

*a follower.* [My italics.] He had adopted other people's opinions, even their modes of life—but always with the underlying conviction that they weren't really his, that he could and certainly would abandon them as easily as he had taken them up . . .

. . At different times in his life . . he had filled the most various moulds. He had been a cynic and also a mystic, a humanitarian and also a contemptuous misanthrope; he had tried to live the life of detached and stoical reason and another time had aspired to the unreasonableness of natural and uncivilized existence. The choice of moulds depended at any given moment on the books he was reading, the people he was associating with. Burlap, for example, had redirected the flow of his mind into those mystical channels which it had not filled since he discovered Boehme in his under-graduate days. Then he had seen through Burlap and flowed out again . . . After a few hours in Mark Rampion's company he really believed in noble savagery; he felt convinced that the proudly conscious intellect ought to humble itself a little and admit the claims of the heart, aye and the bowels, the loins . . . The moulds were emptied as easily as they had been filled . . . But the essential liquidness that flowed where it would, *the cool indifferent flux of intellectual curiosity* [my italics]—that persisted and to that his loyalty was due.

If there was any single way of life he could everlastingly believe in, it was that mixture of pyrrhonism and stoicism which had struck him, an enquiring schoolboy among the philosophers, as the height of human wisdom and into whose moulds of sceptical in-difference he had poured his unimpassioned adolescence. . . .

And here is Aldous speaking of his indifference to possessions. He calls it his under-acquisitiveness and regards it as hereditary as well as developed. "The instinct of acquisitiveness has more per-verts, I believe, than the instincts of sex. At any rate, people seem to me odder about money than about even their amours . . ."

In any case I find myself uninterested in possessions and rather unsympathetic with, and without understanding of, those who are. No predominantly acquisitive character has appeared in any of my stories . . .[1]

And here on his dislike of human contacts,

. . From those who served him Philip demanded little, for the good reason that he wanted to have as little as possible to do with them. Their presence disturbed him. He did not like to have his privacy

---

[1] From Philip Quarles' notebook, op. cit.

intruded upon by alien personalities. To be compelled to speak with them, to have to establish a direct contact—not of intelligences, but of wills, feelings, intuitions—was always disagreeable to him. He avoided it as much as he could; and when contact was necessary, he did his best to dehumanize the relation.

The exception was of course Maria. Elinor Quarles, if no portrait, is a tender evocation.

"What I want to do is to look with all those eyes at once. [Philip is off on the different levels of reality.] With religious eyes, scientific eyes, economic eyes . . ."
"Loving eyes too."
He smiled at her and stroked her hand.

And now they are in India, in a garden under a full moon. To Elinor the night evokes "Gattenden" and their first summer. "Do you remember those evenings, Phil?" she asks. "Which evenings?" he answers. She begins to cry, but after a while is laughing at him and herself. "You do your best to be nice to me," she says. "You make such efforts. It's sweet of you." He protests,

"You know I love you."
"Yes, I know you do." She smiled and stroked his cheek. "When you have time and then by wireless across the Atlantic."

Presently the Quarleses are back in England. A month ago, says Elinor, as their taxi drives out of Liverpool Street station, "we were in Udaipur". Philip agrees, it certainly seems improbable. These ten months of travel have been like an hour in the cinema, she says. She begins to doubt whether she's ever been away. "It's rather a dreadful feeling." "Is it?" says Philip. "I suppose I'm used to it. I never do feel that anything has really happened before this morning." They pass St Paul's, he brings up the Taj Mahal, then goes on, "I often doubt whether I ever had a childhood".
"That's because you never think of it. Lots of my childhood is more real to me than Ludgate Hill here. But then I constantly think of it." (Now this was entirely Maria—St Trond, Bellem *were* her present.) Philip says, "I don't often try to remember. Hardly ever in fact. I always seem to have too much to do and think about."
"You have no natural piety," says Elinor. "I wish you had."
At one point Elinor is stung into asking Philip where he would be if she left him. "Where would you be?"

. . Where *would* he be? . . . in the ordinary daily world of human contacts he was curiously like a foreigner . . finding it difficult or impossible to enter into communication with any but those who could speak his native intellectual language of ideas. Emotionally, he was a foreigner. Elinor was his interpreter, his dragoman . . Elinor had been born with a gift of intuitive understanding and social ease. She was quickly at home with anybody. She knew, instinctively . . just what to say to every type of person.

He tries to see their marriage from her side, make her reflect on his emotional poverty.

. . After an outburst, she would settle down and try to love him as reasonably as she could, making the best of his kindness, his rather detached and separate passion, his occasional and laborious essays at emotional intimacy, and finally his intelligence . . that could understand everything, including the emotions it could not feel and the instincts it took care not to be moved by.

. . All that the intelligence could seize upon he seized. She reported her intercourse with the natives of the realm of emotion, and he understood at once, he generalized her experience for her . . he classified it, found analogies and parallels. From single and individual it became in his hands part of a system. She was astonished to find that she and her friends had been, all unconsciously, substantiating a theory, or exemplifying some interesting generalization. Her functions . . were not confined to mere scouting and reporting. She acted also directly as personal interpreter between Philip and any third party he might wish to get in touch with, creating the atmosphere in which alone the interchange of personalities is possible . . . Left to himself Philip would never have been able to establish personal contact.

. . Elinor . . acted as go-between . . . not only for her own sake, but for the sake of the novelist he might be . . . Heroically, she had even encouraged him in his velleities of passion for other women. It might do him good to have a few affairs. So anxious was she to do him good as a novelist, that on more than one occasion seeing him look admiringly at some young woman or other, she had gone out of her way to establish for him the personal contact . . . Elinor took the risk, partly because she thought that his writing ought to come before anything else, even her own happiness, and partly because she was secretly convinced that there was in reality no risk at all . . . The cure by affairs, if it worked at all, would be gentle in its action . . . Philip's infidelities amounted to very little and had had no appreciable effect on him. . . .

Elinor discusses him with her mother-in-law who says, "Even as a little boy he always shut doors." "And now," says Elinor, "he has his work, which makes it worse . . It's like a castle on the top of a mountain, his work. He shuts himself up and he's impregnable."

Old Mrs Quarles smiles sadly. "Impregnable . . . Perhaps in the end he'll surrender of his own accord."

And now a domestic scene: Philip as a father. The little boy is trying to read from a magazine. The big word begins with a D, it is a dentifrice advertisement but the picture shows a fox-trotting young couple. Little Phil unhesitatingly reads, "Dancing". "You old humbug," says his father. "I thought you said you could read." "But they *are* dancing," says the child. He is told to try again. He takes a long look at the picture. "Dynamo." Now his father starts to tease him, "Or why not dinosaurus, while you're about it? . . Or dolicocephalous? Or dicotyledon?" Little Phil is deeply offended.

"Try again. Try to *read* it this time. Don't guess."

The boy turns his head away. "It bores me . . . But would you like me to make you a drawing?" He turns back with a captivating smile.

"I'd like you to read," says Philip.

"But it bores me."

"Never mind. You must try."

"But I don't want to try."

"But *I* want you to. Try."

Little Phil bursts into tears. Elinor intervenes. Philip says, "If you imagine that's the way to educate a child . . . seeing that he has the misfortune to be an only child, one really ought to make an effort not to spoil him". Elinor presses her cheek against the boy's hair. "Seeing that he is an only child, I don't see why he shouldn't be treated as one." Philip retorts that it's high time for them to settle down so that the boy can have a chance of being brought up rationally.

"And who is going to do the rational upbringing?" asks Elinor. "You? . . At the end of a week you'd be so bored that you'd either commit suicide or take the first aeroplane to Paris."

"Naughty father!" says the child.

Aldous and Maria were here [Lawrence wrote to Lady Ottoline from Bandol in the winter after the novel]

> . . . neither of them very well, run down . . . and Maria going very thin and not eating enough. I think the *Counter Point* book sort of got between them—she found it hard to forgive the death of the child—which one can well understand.

And at the same time to the Brewsters,

> . . The Huxleys left a week ago . . . I'm a bit worried, as they are neither of them well. He was run down and livery, and if she doesn't

watch out, her lungs are going to give her trouble again. People
live the wrong way of their nerves, and of course it destroys them.
She minded *Point Counter Point*—his killing the child—it was all too
lifelike and horrible—and the love affair with Lucy was A's affair
with N C.[1] I think Maria hardly forgives it. And perhaps now he's
sorry he did it. But it has made them money. And Maria wants
money—says so. Yes, she wants to buy a new car in Paris. But I
say there are many men in a man, and the Aldous that wrote the
*Point Counter Point* and killed the child is only one of the Aldouses,
and perhaps by no means the best or most important. I think he's
really nicer—realizing the things one mustn't do, if one is to live.[2]

The child in the book has Matthew's ways as a small boy. Like
Matthew, he muddles up his longer words to his governess's distress
and everybody else's joy. The gardener pulls the mow-lawner,
there are hop-grassers and crack-nutters. In life, Matthew once
came back to their Swiss hotel saying he'd been playing a nice
game with some Seraphic Jews. *Like* Matthew; not *Matthew*. So
have painters used their wives and mistresses to stand in for Salome
or Joan of Arc, used the models that came handy. The child in the
novel dies of meningitis (a death probably suggested by that of the
Mitchisons' eldest boy the year before). For a writer with the bit
between his teeth such an end is the inevitable conclusion to a
theme (pointless horror, the irony of fate); Thomas Mann in much
this way "killed" his favourite grandson in *Dr Faustus*; little Phil in
Aldous's novel—whatever the resemblances and starting points—
is a character in fiction, on paper, a creation with its own compulsive reality and no reality in life. And like Philip Quarles,
Aldous had no natural piety; superstitious dread was among the
emotions he was unable to feel. For him there was no reasonable
connection. (And indeed Matthew, the heavens be praised, continued to flourish.) For others, as inevitably, the connection was
there. Women on the whole are more superstitious, or more sensitive. Lawrence, more feminine in his perceptions, guessed or knew
Maria's feelings.

*Point Counter Point* as a whole is not easy to pin down. I should
like to end by condensing some evocative lines. There is the passage
of Everard Webley's slow drive through Hyde Park on a summer
evening, in love with Elinor, on his way to Elinor, seeing the world
transfigured—a psychedelic passage before the word. Unfortunately it does not lend itself to quotation without context. Instead

---

[1] Both names were replaced by asterisks in the 1938 edition of the letter.
[2] *D. H. Lawrence Reminiscences and Correspondence*, op. cit.

here is an extract from the opening set-piece, the evening at Tantamount House in Pall Mall. The concert has begun. In *Barren Leaves* Calamy held up his hand against the light and talked; now Aldous tried to give the sense of synchronous existence in action.

Meanwhile the music played on—Bach's Suite in B minor, for flute and strings. Young Tolley conducted with his usual inimitable grace . . . as though he were dancing to the music. A dozen anonymous fiddlers and 'cellists scraped at his bidding. And the great Pongileoni glueily kissed his flute. He blew across the mouth hole and a cylindrical air column vibrated; Bach's meditations filled the Roman quadrangle. In the opening *largo* John Sebastian had, with the help of Pongileoni's snout and the air column, made a statement: there are grand things in the world, noble things; there are men born kingly . . . But of an earth that is, oh! complex and multitudinous, he has gone on to reflect in the fugal allegro. You seem to have found the truth; clear, definite, unmistakable, it is announced by the violins; but it slips out of your grasp to present itself in a new aspect among the 'cellos . . . The parts live their separate lives; they touch, their paths cross, they combine for a moment to create a seemingly final and perfected harmony, only to break apart again. "I am I," asserts the violin, "the world revolves around me." "Round me," calls the 'cello. "Round me," the flute insists. And all are equally right and wrong; and none of them will listen to the other.

In the human fugue there are eighteen hundred million parts. The resultant noise means something perhaps to the statistician, nothing to the artist. It is only by considering one or two parts at a time that the artist can understand anything. Here . . is one particular part; and John Sebastian puts the case. The Rondeau begins, exquisitely and simply melodious . . It is a young girl singing to herself of love . . singing among the hills, with the clouds drifting overhead . . solitary as one of the floating clouds, a poet has been listening to her song. The thoughts that it provoked in him are the Sarabande that follows the Rondeau. His is a slow and lovely meditation on the beauty (in spite of squalor), the oneness (in spite of such bewildering diversity) of the world. It is a beauty, a goodness, a unity that no intellectual research can discover, that analysis dispels, but of whose reality the spirit is from time to time suddenly and overwhelmingly convinced. A girl singing to herself under the clouds suffices to create the certitude. Even a fine morning is enough. Is it illusion or the revelation of profoundest truth? Who knows? Pongileoni blew, the fiddlers drew their rosined horse-hair across the stretched intestines of lambs; through the long Sarabande the poet slowly meditated his lovely and consoling certitude.

## Chapter Sixteen

## And Another Year

ALDOUS was in London briefly in January 1929. There he signed his third agreement with Chatto & Windus. Three years go quickly. He had delivered three books instead of six to nine, one novel instead of three. The new agreement was more realistic; two novels in three years, three further books "if possible". The annual advance was raised to a thousand pounds. Beaverbrook made a handsome offer for a weekly book review which Aldous ruminated and presently declined. The most enduring consequence of that London visit flowed from Aldous's first meeting with Gerald Heard. Raymond Mortimer introduced them, Gerald being one of his greatest friends.

> On a typical London January evening thirty-five years ago [Gerald Heard's description of the first encounter[1]] Aldous Huxley sailed into my view . . . his approach, his "port", had about it something of a galleon's. He came in, as it were, under full sail, a long coat billowing around him. The voice, however, was as neat as a seamstress's stitching. And, indeed, the long fingers made the precise movements of a needlewoman handling thread and seam . . .
> . . the discourse . . was not only ironic and entertaining, but fantastically informed.

Now Gerald Heard himself was a tremendous talker who would shoot off ideas and information from the split second he entered a room. He was as extraordinary to listen to as Aldous if a good deal less lucid.

> Our host . . [Raymond] had asked no other guest. We stayed talking till past 1 a.m., when all buses had finished their routes, all taxis ceased their cruising. Consequently each of us had before him a more than three-mile walk. To my surprise, for our directions were divergent, Huxley accompanied me all the way to my block of flats and then, changing tack, sailed off for another couple of miles of solitary striding to his own rooms. But not before he had invited me to another session the following week. . . .

Hardly returned to Suresnes, Aldous, with Maria, left again. For the South of France to see Lawrence who was wintering in Bandol

---

[1] Gerald Heard, "The Poignant Prophet", *The Kenyon Review*, 1965.

at the Hôtel Beau-Rivage. "I would like to see you both," he had written. "But these little *en passant* glimpses like Lavandou and Chexbres don't amount to much, do they?"

Or did they? Florence, Forte, Les Diablerets—"We saw a great deal of him," Aldous said thirty years after, in the London interview. John Chandos led him off: "You said something very strong, you said—in your preface to *The Letters*—'He is one of the very few people I feel real respect and admiration for. He is something superior and different in kind.' "

"Of course, you are quite right," said Aldous. "He was perfectly extraordinary as a human being. He was extremely fascinating, and he was always stimulating. A little alarming to be with . . ."

Chandos put in: "Why did he quarrel with people?" Aldous, chuckling: "He somehow did it on principle, I believe. Or perhaps that's wrong—it was a very strange thing, he would burst out in that *curious* way against people. But it was always a pleasure to be with him, and hear his comments on things; his reactions to nature were always very very fascinating. I mean it was a great pleasure to go for a walk with Lawrence. The way he perceived the world— so intense, and exciting."

Chandos says, "But he was always hectoring people—he must have had atrocious manners?" "Well, no," says Aldous mildly, "he was very charming generally. Sometimes he would get sort of cross. But he could be very amusing. Entertaining. I mean he was happy; Happiness is the greatest virtue, he would say. And he *was* happy. He was happy sort of sitting on a grey stone—very like Words-worth's Expostulation and Reply . . . and of course a lot of his life was spent in this way. And then he would get the urge to write: and then write for eighteen hours a day. It was very extraordinary to see him work, it was a sort of *possession*; he would rush on with it, his hand moving at a tremendous rate. And he never corrected anything; because if he was dissatisfied with anything he would start again at the beginning.

". . of course one of the things I often speculate about is what would have happened to him if he had lived on to a reasonable age. It is absolutely extraordinary to think that this man who died at the age of forty-four produced this *immense* volume of stuff which he did—some of it is very fine. I do think the short stories and some of the very long novelettes are most remarkable. And some of the longer novels. I don't think all of them are successful, by any means. And some of the later poems, I think, are very beautiful. But it's amazing to think that all this was produced by a man who died at forty-four and who was *sick* for a great deal of the time . . .

"But *where* would he have gone from the point he was at when he died? This is a very interesting speculation. I don't think he could have *remained* where he was, because I mean there was a certain ambivalence even in a book like *The Plumed Serpent* where he is inviting us to go back to the dark gods and the dark blood and so on; but in the next breath he's saying how awful the Mexicans are because they are so slow and unintelligent and so on. It's a *very* odd book. You get these tirades against the Mexicans, almost in the terms of an English colonel talking about the natives; in the next breath you get these tremendous invitations to sink yourself in the dark blood. So there was even then a kind of ambivalence. I think he would even then have come round to what seems to me a more balanced view—I mean this *whole* thing that we have to make the *best* of both worlds . . .

"The point is that you *must have both*. The blood and the flesh are there—and in certain respects they are wiser than the intellect. I mean if we interfere with the blood and the flesh with our conscious minds we get psychosomatic trouble. But on the other hand, we have to do a lot of things with the conscious mind. I mean why *can't* we do *both*—we *have* to do both. This is the whole art of life: making the best of all the worlds. Here again is one of those fatal examples of trying to make everything conform to the standard of only *one* world. Seeing that we are amphibians—it's *no good*."

Aldous and Lawrence's meeting in the winter of 1929 lasted for some ten days. It was the meeting referred to in Lawrence's letters. to Ottoline and the Brewsters. "Neither of them well . . . the *Counter Point* book . . ." The Huxleys had arrived in late January; the time has some significance because of the ensuing weather. In the night of the 28th there was a sudden severe frost in Southern Europe, followed the next morning by an icy wind that lasted through several days, one of the worst cold spells in memory. Palm trees froze on the promenades, thousands of cars were stranded. At that time houses and hotels had little heating and people were huddling in the doorways of department stores and in the cinemas of Toulon and Marseilles. It had begun before the weekend on the French coast and gradually spread into Italy, but at Bandol it was all over on the Monday morning—the sun shone on a wind-still day and a limp and blackened vegetation, "one sat out again," as Lawrence wrote, "and felt the brightness." But the intense cold had given Aldous one of his liver attacks, a bad one verging on jaundice. Unwisely he and Maria had left by car for Italy on that bitter Sunday. (Their car, Italian registered, had to be repatriated unless they paid a huge duty to the French and went through a morass of paperwork, the bureaucratic pettifoggery being even worse than it is today.) They had a frightful journey. The cold wave followed them; Aldous was getting worse. On the Italian Riviera their magneto gave out which meant spending forty-eight hours in an inn at Albenga where "the only mode of heating was by hot bricks". Later at Chiavari they found the road wiped out by a landslide and had to wait some hours in a cutting *tramontana* for a train to put the car on. They reached Florence with the roads deep in snow and the Arno frozen solid. At last their hotel was warm; a modest hotel, Il Moderno, to which they returned in gratitude for years.

. . The miserable population, quite without proper clothes or houses for such a season, [is] dying in thousands. Out of 250,000 inhabitants 65,000 were ill. And Florence was balmy compared with Trieste and the Adriatic ports, where the sea froze and the trains were blown off the rails by the wind.

They left their car in a garage waiting for a buyer (it was not the best moment for selling the Alfa Romeo-like machine) and crept back by train to Paris.

There Aldous went back to work on the essays, "I'm busy, but not exuberantly well," he wrote to his father, "this quasi-jaundice has left me a little dubious physically." And the journey had taken it out of Maria. Lawrence wrote to her

. . I'm a bit worried about your health, so please be a good child and *really* take care for a while—don't bother about *anything* else. Now do as you're bidden, and don't go squiffing about any more, but keep still and warm and well fed: and don't buy a car just yet. Just be without one for six weeks, really. You need a rest from driving.

. . . Well, let us know you are safely arrived, and safely in bed, and warm and well fed. I shall fidget till I know.

D. H. L.

Could you get me Nancy Cunard's address? I'll ask her if *she* will do *Lady C.*

But they had every intention of getting a new car. "After much trying and testing and on the recommendation of the A.A. engineers in London we have fixed on the new touring model of the Bugatti which has a most extraordinary performance and is a very sound piece of engineering and building." It was ordered from the works at Turin and the body was to be custom-made.

In March Lawrence arrived to see about a new edition of *Lady Chatterley*. He stayed at the Hôtel de Versailles on the Boulevard Montparnasse, felt ill and was borne off to Suresnes for a few days and put to bed in one of Jeanne's attics.

I arrived here [he wrote to Rhys Davies] with a bit of 'flu or something—felt very cheap—but they are really very nice and kind to
me, and look after me so nicely.

Joep Nicolas was in the house and it was here that Lawrence sat
to him for his portrait. Looking after Lawrence was not simple.

. . We actually got him to agree to undertake a treatment [Aldous
to Julian], alone, minus Frieda, and we also actually got him to go
to a doctor in Paris. He was to go back to the Dr. to be X-rayed.
(Meanwhile, however, the Dr. told M that . . he could hear that
one lung was practically gone and the other affected . . .) Then
Frieda, who had been in London, returned. L. felt himself reinforced. He refused to go back to the Dr., refused to think of the treatment and set off with Frieda (of whom he had bitterly complained
when he was alone with us) to Majorca. So that's that. It's no good.
He doesn't *want* to know how ill he is: that, I believe, is the fundamental reason why he won't go to Doctors and homes. He only
went in Paris because he was feeling iller than usual and was even
more frightened of dying at once than of hearing how ill he was . . .
and meanwhile he just wanders about, very tired and at bottom
wretched, from one place to another, imagining that the next
place will make him feel better and, when he gets [to] the next
place, regretting the one before and looking back on it as a
paradise. . . .

The coach-builders were late and the Bugatti only ready by
Easter. Maria and Rina went to Turin to fetch it, and drove it
back across Mont Cenis. The Bugatti was Aldous and Maria's high
point in cars, and their one great personal extravagance (paid for
by *Point Counter Point*). It was a slim, powerful two-seater, scarlet,
with the upholstery in dove-grey leather. Maria sat close under the
large sports car wheel; Aldous's seat had been built to measure for
his outstretched legs. (There was a kind of third perch in the back,
a sort of side-saddle on which one balanced with one's knees up to
one's chin. The boot held their two or three Revelation suitcases
and a portable typewriter.) Ettore Bugatti, the constructor, was
amazed to hear that a woman was going to drive one of his
monsters, and asked to meet her.

The engine needed serious driving in, and Aldous and Maria
did this on a forced journey through France into Spain as far as
Madrid and back again (after one first look at the Prado). Afterwards they went to London.

During the time he nominally lived in Paris, much of Aldous's
work was done in hotel bedrooms elsewhere. (He could set up his
workshop with a minimum of paraphernalia.) In London, Jill, the

cousin who fell in love with his portrait in 1926, now actually met him. He was thirty-five.

I was invited to dinner at my grandmother's house—the Dragon [Aldous's Aunt Ethel]. I must just describe the Dragon to you— she was known as Grand-Dragon to the grandchildren, and I think she originally got the name because she was the chaperone on the trips to Switzerland when there were a whole lot of relations there and she was always put to make sure that everybody behaved themselves. She wasn't really a dragon, only in some ways: the kindest dragon you've ever known. And a lovely person. She had these Sunday night supper parties, which were always cold chicken and then some sort of a mousse—always the same—and she had these two cats who would sit on each side on the chairs waiting . . . And there I met Aldous. And he was sitting, not quite opposite, but nearly opposite me to the right, and I couldn't take my eyes off him. And I wasn't sure whether he was looking at me or not, because he wore these tremendous pebble glasses . . . But afterwards, Maria told me that *he* couldn't take his eyes off *me*. But I didn't know this until many years later.

At the time it was my brother's twenty-first birthday. And when we were all waiting in the drawing room for ten o'clock which was the exact hour at which we all had to leave the Dragon—this was an understood thing—we still felt keen to carry on the evening: I turned to Aldous and said, "Aldous, will you come to the Gargoyle night club where my brother is having a twenty-first birthday, because he would love to meet you?" And Aldous said, "*Yes*". And Maria grasped my arm and said, "*Jill—but how did you do it? We have never been to a night club before. We never go to a night club.*"

Anyway he came with us, and we went to the Gargoyle. As we came down the steps, past the huge Matisse painting, my brother was sitting at the bottom of the stair with a whole group of friends and he leapt up: "How-did-you-do-it!? HOW-DID-YOU-DO-IT!?" He was so excited that I brought him. And he sat down at the table with us. And instead of everybody dancing and the music playing, the band stopped, people stopped dancing, they all came and sat round Aldous to listen to him. He didn't *hold forth*—he *conversed*. I can't tell you at all what he talked about; but he was just fascinating, and even the waiters came and listened, and the place was silent except for Aldous talking.[1]

They did not live much in the house by the Seine. Barely returned from London, they left for their Italian summer. They had turned

[1] Gillian (Mrs Anthony) Greenwood, talking to S. B. in 1968.

against Suresnes—hating it mortally, Lawrence put it—and Aldous realized how little suited he was to life in the north.

> I have reached a point [to Starkey] where I value sunshine more than people, culture, arts, conversation. So I'm off to Italy . . . (Incidentally, it's full of people, culture, etc. as well as sunlight.) I believe and rather hope that the days of the Nordics and their beastly northern countries is nearly over. Civilization will return to the warm and luminous places where it was born.

They spent ten days in Rome, made a tour of the Etruscan towns, then settled down in their little house. It was their last summer at Forte, the last of their living in Italy. There were wind and clouds and Aldous felt melancholy; then once more the weather became "incredibly serene". Their newest acquisition was an inflatable rubber boat. Aldous had begun some short stories. Matthew presently arrived with Rose; he had learnt to swim quite well; "we are also improving his French reading . . by means of the excellent Jules Verne . . ." Lawrence had appeared for a few days in June, even worse in health than he had been in Paris in the spring.

> . . no energy . . . [Aldous to Julian] It's pathetic to see the way he just sits and does nothing. He hasn't written a line or painted a stroke for the last 3 months. Just lack of vital strength. He still talks a good deal and can get amused and excited into a semblance of health for an hour or two at the time. But it is only a semblance . . . He has gone to Germany now—or is just going: for he has been in Florence these last days—of all places in this weather! We have given up trying to persuade him to be reasonable. He doesn't want to be and nobody can persuade him to be—except possibly Frieda. But Frieda is worse than he is. We've told her that she's a fool and a criminal; but it has no more effect than telling an elephant.

Aldous appears to have been convinced then that Lawrence's illness was "unnecessary, the result simply of the man's strange obstinacy against professional medicine". Yet some thirty years later he made a curious remark to Sidney Nolan and his wife; he said that Lawrence had died of chagrin, that T.B. was a disease of chagrin. Was it a new conclusion, was it an echo? In that mellow letter Lawrence wrote to Ottoline in 1928, there is this passage:

> You ask me, do I feel things very much?—and I do. And that's why I too am ill. The hurts, and the bitterness sink in, however much one may reject them with one's spirit. They sink in, and there they lie, inside one, wasting one. What is the matter with us is primarily chagrin. Then the microbes pounce. . . .

In July Aldous took the cure at Montecatini for a week to get over the after effects of his liver attack. A curious experience . . the Carlsbad of Italy. "Have you ever been to a spa?" he wrote to Robert Nichols. "If not, go. It's the most grotesque vision imaginable . . ." Soon after he made good use of it in "After the Fireworks". The Huxleys returned to Suresnes in late September and stayed put for a few weeks. But Paris seemed really rather frightful and the traffic must have doubled in the last year—on the whole Aldous had not found much of what he wanted; "French literary society is really a bit too literary . . ." He bore away some anecdotes which he told in later years with anthropological benevolence. Here is one about James Joyce that survives in his own voice.[1]

Well, *Ulysses* is obviously a very extraordinary book. I don't know exactly why he wrote it. Because a great deal of *Ulysses* seems to me to be taken up with showing a large number of methods in which novels *cannot* be written. I suppose it's a great book—to me it remains a little bit too static. The character of Bloom—But I think there are splendid passages. I don't think it's a success as a whole.

He was a *very* strange man. I used to see him sometimes in Paris. His—what one might call—magic view of words—I shall never forget sitting next to him once at dinner and mentioning to him, which I thought would give him pleasure—and it *did*—that I'd just been re-reading the *Odyssey*. And his immediate response was—he said to me, "Now do you realize what the derivation of Odysseus, the name Odysseus is?" I said [sotto voce] "No, I don't." And he said, "Well, it really comes from the words Udyce, meaning nobody, and Zeus, meaning God, the Odysseus is really a symbol of creation of God out of nothing." Well, I mean this is exactly the sort of etymology which would have been made by Albertus Magnus in the 13th century—with no relation of course to anything we would regard as realistic. But this completely *satisfied* Joyce's mind.

Chandos: But he was enormously a man of words.

Aldous: Absolutely a man of words.

Chandos: This was the lovable thing about him—I love words in my own way . . .

Aldous [with much determination]: Yes, but I mean, surely one has to realize the limitations of words. Joyce—seemed to think that words were omnipotent. They are *not* omnipotent.

Where to go next? Now there was money for a house of their own. Maria's idea was a cool stone house in the depth of a garden. They did not feel that they could return to live in Italy; political

[1] London interview, 1961.

facts apart, it seemed time to move on. The South of France? They
had rather liked the coast round Bandol . . . Meanwhile they went
off in the Bugatti on a tour of Spain. Jeanne stayed behind and
put up jam. Suresnes was isolated at night, Sophie was away at
boarding school, sometimes she felt afraid. Like Maria, Lawrence
was concerned about her situation. "Yes, I have often thought of
you," he said to her in the course of a long letter of advice,

> and of our talks. I like you because you seem to me quite honest,
> you say what you mean, and nearly all people equivocate when a
> subject really touches them, so I think that in the end you will
> come out all right, after this horrible period of frustration. . . .

The second Spanish journey (described as usual by Aldous to
his father) began with a week in Barcelona, then Tarragona,
Valencia (Lawrence had a post card from Maria saying they were
happy; he was fretting about them, "Spain is *hard*"), Alicante,
Murcia, Almeria; across the Sierra Nevada to Granada losing their
way and wandering for some time in the mountain byways of
Andalusia. Then Ronda in its staggering position, Jerez, Cadiz on
its strange promontory, Seville, Cordoba (a letter *from* Lawrence,
"I'm so anxious when I think of that *enormous* way from S. of Spain
by Biarritz to Paris. Too much, too much . . . When we've motored
for one morning, I'm so thankful to have done"). To Madrid
through the desert plateau of La Mancha and Castile, "one isn't
surprised at Don Quixote going mad in a country like that". To
Burgos "with such a wind that the mud was lifted in sheets from
the road and hurled against our windscreen . . . It was a comfort
to get down to Atlantic softness at S. Sebastian . . ." To Starkey
Aldous summed it up,

> Really, the strangest country in Europe . . . one of the oddest in
> the world even. Half very sympathetic, half very repulsive. But
> always very odd and full of the most extraordinary things, natural
> and artificial. The El Grecos, for example, which I admire much
> more (tho' hating them in a way) than when I saw them last . . .

They got back to Suresnes in late November. "So you are safely
back," Lawrence wrote, "that's one mercy, anyhow, and we needn't
think of you on rainy, windy days and imagine the little red car
ploughing on, ploughing on."

With the death of Maria's grandparents, St Trond as a home
base was no more. For that one Christmas the house at Suresnes
served for a family gathering: the three Huxleys, Jeanne and Sophie,
Madame Nys and Rose.

## Chapter Seventeen

## Do What You Will

IN the course of a letter to another impersonal correspondent (Scudder Klyce, who had sent him his recent book, *Dewey's Suppressed Psychology*) Aldous discussed his own viewpoint in *Do What You Will*. He began by saying that he had never managed to make his statements logically watertight, "a feat . . which the literary quality of what I write (such as it is—that quality!) renders less vitally necessary. For after all the most perfect statements and human solutions of the great metaphysical problems are all artistic, especially, it seems to me, musical. Beethoven's 'Missa Solemnis' for example, and his posthumous quartets, Bach's 'Art of the Fugue' have always struck me as the subtlest, profoundest and completest metaphysical works ever composed . . . Such pieces of music, and certain passages in Dante and Shakespeare, certain paintings, certain architectural monuments get closer to the essential fact than any professional philosopher's discourse . . . I do not delude myself with the belief that I am a great artist; but at least I possess a certain literary talent, the use of which serves in some measure to take the place of a sadly deficient logic!

. . . Being an unmetaphysically-minded person preoccupied with phenomenal appearances, not ultimate reality, I think mostly of the diverse Many and not much of the final One. My essay . . ["One and Many"] in . . *Do What You Will* is a statement of the observable facts of diversity so stupidly overlooked by contemporary science and contemporary religion. Any tentative solutions of the problems raised are never . . . metaphysical solutions, only practical, ethical, sociological and psychological solutions.

*Do What You Will* (finished in May 1929, published in October) consists of twelve essays. The essays on Baudelaire, Swift, Spinoza's Worm, Wordsworth in the Tropics, the brief and savage account —"Silence Is Golden"—of the first talking film. The main argument is developed in the opening essay, "One and Many", and in the equally long one on Pascal, and could be summed up as, "The final mystery is unknowable.

Men's confused perceptions of it are diverse and contradictory. The truth—the inward truth, I mean, since that is the only truth we

can know—is that God is different for different men, and for the
same man on different occasions. The testimony of the mystics
cannot be made to prove more than this.

. . A rational absolute is a contradiction in terms. The only absolute
which a man of intelligence can believe in is an irrational one.[1]

God is different . . . So are men. A sense of planetary unity? "To
me it seems in the highest degree unlikely that mankind will ever
feel itself intimately and lovingly one. The differences of race and
place are too enormous.

A Northerner can never feel as a man of the tropic feels; America
imposes a mode of being that is radically unlike the modes of being
possible in the Old World. There is such a thing as absolute alienness. An absolute alienness which no amount of . . movies and
thousand-mile-an-hour aeroplanes . . will ever, it seems to me, completely abolish.[1]

And as for government. There can never be an absolutely right
kind of government. "For the simple reason that societies change
and that the forms of government must change with them."
Aldous's tentative solutions for our various dilemmas were psychological solutions chiefly, and addressed to the fairly exceptional
individual, to *l'âme bien née*, in fact. "If one is well-born and
well-bred one does not behave like a pig; one behaves like a human
being."

To those, *Do What You Will* offered, in distinction to Pascal's
worship of death, a creed of "life-worship" the fundamental
assumption of which is that "life on this planet is valuable in itself,
without any reference to hypothetical higher worlds, eternities,
future existences". (Aldous quoted Blake, "It is not better, then,
to be alone and love Earth only for its earthly sake?") The end of
life "is more life . . the purpose of living is to live . . . The life-
worshipper's philosophy is comprehensive. As a manifold and dis-
continuous being . . he is at one moment a positivist and at another
a mystic: now haunted by the thought of death . . and now a
Dionysian child of nature . . . His aim is the full realization of all
his potentialities—to balance excess of intelligence by an excess of
intuition, of instinctive and visceral living . . ." (Much of *Do What
You Will* was a continuation of ideas turned up in *Point Counter Point*.
Mark Rampion is talking on. The impression of the Lawrentian
ship was still upon the water.) "The life-worshipper will be in turn . .
excessively passionate and excessively chaste." However, the most

[1] *Do What You Will*. Chatto & Windus, 1929. All quotations in this chapter,
unless otherwise stated, are from this book.

suitable postulants for this creed, Aldous branched out, "are probably those who have been strictly educated in Christian or bourgeois morality, in the philosophy of commonsense tempered by religion, and have afterwards revolted against their upbringing". Yet the ideal of completeness was mostly realized "by such men as Burns . . as Mozart, as Blake, as Rubens, as Shakespeare, as Tolstoy before he deliberately perverted himself to death-worshipping consistency, as the adorable Chaucer, as Rabelais, as Montaigne . . ." By artists, in fact, And one thing all life-worshippers have in common is a hatred of the empty fooleries and sordidness of average human existence.

Incidentally the progress of science and industry has enormously increased the element of foolery and sordidness in human life.

The great new menace. How clearly Aldous saw the trends in 1929! The machine—dangerous because it also is a creation-saver.

Creative work, of however humble a kind, is the source of man's most solid, least transitory happiness. Leisure has now been almost as completely mechanized as labour. Men . . . sit and are passively amused by mechanical devices. Machinery condemns one of the most vital needs of humanity to frustration which the progress of invention can only render more and more complete.

Already then there was no workable answer. Machinery had increased production, and production had doubled population in one hundred years. Scrap the machinery . . and you will kill about half the population . . . The machinery must stay; it is obvious. It must stay, even though, used as it is now . . it inflicts on humanity an enormous psychological injury that must, if uncared for, prove mortal. . . .

The real trouble with the present social and industrial system is not that it makes some people much richer than others, but that it makes life fundamentally unlivable for all.

In that same year Aldous published *Arabia Infelix*, a limited edition of poems written at intervals during the last decade. It contained what is perhaps his finest poem, an acceptance of life as it is given, the serene and luminous *Cicadas*.

## Chapter Eighteen

# Endings

I am suffering agonies at the moment over the rehearsals of a stage version of *Point Counter Point* which has been concocted by an ingenious young man and which is to be produced the day after tomorrow—God help us!

THE young man was Campbell Dixon, the producer Leon M. Lion, and the play, *This Way to Paradise*, opened in London on 30th January at Daly's, a very large theatre far from full. On the first night the actors were so nervous that they forgot their lines. It was Aldous's first personal experience with the theatre and though repelled he was attracted as well. ". . Rather awful, very instructive." He described it all in letters to Lawrence and Robert Nichols. The play was a kind of patchwork made up from scenes of the novel; Aldous had had no hand in it. "Lots of things in it made me rather shudder." At the dress rehearsal though, "the whole performance miraculously [came] to life"; and again, after the horrors of the first night, everything got much better. "Some of the scenes turned out finally very well indeed, particularly the last where they play the Beethoven A minor quartet while the audience waits in a long-drawn anticipation for the man to be killed. The effect was exceedingly good, theatrically, and the music created an extraordinary atmosphere . . The scene absolutely held the audience. It showed me what very astonishing things can be done on the stage with a little imagination and the necessary minimum of technique."

Through February the play did quite well. Aldous returned to Suresnes after the first week and then and there began to write a play of his own. "The only thing that deters one from experimenting much with the theatre is the theatrical world . . . God! what a horror to have to depend on other people for your creation—not to be personally responsible for the whole, but be compelled to use instruments . . . Have you ever had anything to do with actors and producers?" Nevertheless Aldous was bitten. When he was young and poor he had flirted with the idea of the successful commercial play; now he was after something else. "There are a few good producers in the world and . . if one could see one's own dramatic ideas well realized by one of them the thrill would be enormous."

*This Way to Paradise* closed on 1st March.

Aldous has made great literary use of the sense of horror which in his life, however, was mitigated by an uncommon equability of temperament. Sufficient unto the day—he was not a man to torment himself (nor others) neurotically without present cause. When he was reasonably in health, when work was going and the immediate sky was clear, he was—one can say this—happy. In a letter to Starkey of that winter he tried to clarify the contradiction. He writes about solitude, about the hopelessness of communication:

> Still, one can be very happy all the same. And in spite of the appalling possibilities of unhappiness and the appalling frequency with which the possibilities are realized, I think on the whole it's most decidedly worthwhile—not for any good reason, of course; but for some mysterious good unreason . . .

He ended this letter with, "I wish you very well, dear Starkey."

Aldous was never much of a reader of modern fiction, and when he did read he remained aloof to much that was moving or exciting to his contemporaries. He was apt to be impatient, for instance, with Virginia Woolf (of whom he *was* fond); she did not provide what he was looking for. "Have you read a novel called *The Man Within* by Graham Greene?" he asked Robert Nichols.

> I think it's most remarkable . . . Much better (between ourselves, for it's a frightful heresy!) than Virginia's *To the Lighthouse* which I'm now rather belatedly reading. It's the difference between something full and something empty; between a writer who has a close physical contact with reality and one who is a thousand miles away and only has a telescope to look, remotely, at the world.

Aldous and Maria were now at Suresnes for their last weeks. They had done with the place. Jeanne had already moved out. (Into a flat of her own and a job on the editorial staff of *Le Jardin des Modes* Aldous had got for her by writing, on Maria's initiative, to his old boss Condé Nast.) The last action of Aldous's Paris life was concerned with Lawrence. "The latest is that *Lady C* is being proceeded against by the French police! [he wrote to Julian] Don't mention it to L. if you're writing . . . If the affair can be arranged —I've been ringing up all the influential literary men I know—he need never know."

In such matters it was Maria who suggested ways and names. They would talk it over, make the decisions together; then Aldous acted. He did not like using the telephone; asking favours he liked even less. He got on to Paul Valéry whom he knew quite well; to Gabriel Marcel; to his friend Drieu La Rochelle who though young was well-known in the *monde*. Possibly he also spoke to André Maurois who had written the preface for the French edition of *Counter Point*. He did not ask Gide. Literary men *have* influence in France and the nasty business was allowed to peter out.

Lawrence was sinking. On 7th February he had written a postcard from Vence to Maria.

> I have submitted and come here to a sanatorium—sort of sanatorium—and Frieda is in the hotel—I came yesterday. It doesn't seem very different from an ordinary hotel—but the doctors are there to look after one—I'll tell you the results . . .

Five days later he wrote to her again.

> . . Here I came at last, as I was getting so feeble and so thin. It isn't a sanatorium, really—an hotel where a nurse takes your temperature and two doctors look after you once a week—for the rest, just an hotel. They examined me with X-rays and all that. It is as I say—the lung has moved very little since Mexico, in five years. But the broncs are awful, and they have inflamed my lower man, the *ventre* and the liver. I suppose that's why I've gone so thin —I daren't tell you my weight . . . I've got a good balcony and lovely view—and the air is much better than Bandol . . . It's dull here—only French people convalescing and nothing in my line. But I'm feeling more chirpy, and shall try to get *on my legs*. It would be fun to see you, end of this month. When I hope I can walk a bit. I wish we could have been somewhere to have a good time like Diablerets. Or I wish I could sail away to somewhere really thrilling —perhaps we shall go to the ranch . . .
>
> Perhaps we might have a few jolly days, if you came down—just jolly, like Diableret.

But on 21st February:

> Dear Maria,—
> . . I am rather worse here—such bad nights, and cough, and heart, and pain decidedly worse here—and miserable. Seems to me like *grippe*, but they say not. It's not a good place—shan't stay long —I'm better in a house—I'm miserable.
> Frieda has Barbey with her—and Ida Rauh. When do you think of coming?
>
> D. H. L.

This was the last letter but one Lawrence wrote. The postscript said, "This place no good."

Aldous and Maria arrived in Vence on 24th or 25th February. They found Lawrence even worse than they had feared. "Terribly changed," Aldous wrote. "He gave one the impression that he was living by sheer force of will and by nothing else. But the dissolution of the body was breaking down the will."

Rina was with them and allowed to see Lawrence once or twice, bringing him flowers. On the afternoon of the 27th, a Thursday, the Huxleys drove over to Villefranche to see the Robert Nicholses.

Aldous and Maria are as sweet as ever [Robert Nichols wrote the next day to Dr Henry Head[1]] . . . Little Maria is much upset over Lawrence. She loves him very much. I am very sorry for her. Her face is worn and peaked over D. H. L. I'm going to see if I can be any use to her. She drives an awful pace in her Bugatti, but I think we rag her too much about it.

*The place was no good*—once more Lawrence insisted on change. So Frieda rented a villa[2] and on that Saturday, the 1st of March, took him over in a shaking taxi. Lawrence lay down on the new bed, exhausted. Frieda slept on a couch where he could see her.[3] Aldous and Maria had gone to Villefranche again for the day and night. When they came back the next afternoon, on the Sunday, they found Lawrence very weak and suffering much pain "and strangely égaré, feeling that he wasn't there—that he was two people at once".[4] He kept saying to Maria, "Look at *him* there in the bed!" It was as though Lawrence were up in a corner of the ceiling looking down on the body in the bed.[5]

Frieda went out for a few minutes.

"Lawrence grasped my two wrists with his hands and said, 'Maria, Maria, don't let me die.' But he was more peaceful a little later; he was interested in the material phenomenon, I think. He told me he saw himself, his head, just there, next to me, and that he knew he would die."[6] Maria held him in her arms. Frieda, and her daughter Barbara, came back. At 9 p.m. Aldous went to find the doctor, who came and gave some morphine. Lawrence became less distressed. He said, "I am better now." Frieda was holding his ankle. "It felt so full of life, all my days I shall hold his ankle in my hand."[7]

[1] The late neurologist.
[2] The Villa Robermond, now Villa Aurella, at Vence.
[3] From Frieda Lawrence's own account as given in *The Intelligent Heart: The Story of D. H. Lawrence*, by Harry T. Moore. Heinemann, 1955.
[4] Aldous in a letter to Julian of 3rd March 1930 from Vence.
[5] Told to Christopher Isherwood by Maria.
[6] Maria in a letter to Rosalind Rajagopal of 27th February 1943; a letter part quoted on page 183.
[7] Frieda Lawrence, op. cit.

" . . and he settled off to sleep—to die quietly at 10.15 . . . He went so quietly at the last."[1]

There is a close account of the next day but one in a letter by Robert Nichols written on 8th March 1930 to Dr Henry Head and his wife. Nichols drove over to Vence on the Tuesday morning and knocked at the door of the Villa Robermond.

[I] was greeted by a tall young woman—Barbara—Frieda's daughter by her first husband. Aldous was seated in a smallish tiled room with Thys, the Paris publisher of *Lady Chatterley's Lover*. Almost immediately Frieda came in and grasped me by both hands. She said: "I'm so glad you've come. He would have been so pleased." And then as I found myself unable to speak, "Don't make me cry again." We sat down. She appeared somewhat exalted. "He was so brave, such a fighter; such a MAN."

We sat down and chatted, smoking innumerable cigarettes. For some time I did not gather that Lawrence was in the next room. Mrs Lawrence opened letters and telegrams. A huge wreath of dark crimson carnations arrived from two or three American painters who did not know Lawrence personally but much admired his work. F. was much touched (she was by turns voluble and silent and when she was silent she stared in an odd manner, the pupils of her all but hazel eyes like pin-points). Barbara opened the door to take the flowers in and I saw Lawrence's nose "sharp as a pen" and his little Greek satyr's beard sticking up (his feet covered by a sheet were towards me). Any time Barbara went in . . she came out crying . . .

. . Little Maria appeared. She looked ghastly—her face was greyish and one could see the blue veins at her temples. From time to time she shivered and enormous tears gathered in her blue eyes. They are a peculiar colour—clear as sapphires, one sees through the lens to the iris and their blue is not the blue of the sky but the blue of water in a white-tiled swimming bath—absolutely translucent and to me very beautiful. They seemed the bluer because the lids were rather red. I must admit that almost my first thought was "This woman is a lot worthier of Lawrence than Frieda" but I doubt whether Lawrence ever really appreciated her. Indeed Barbara told me later that when Aldous and Maria left to come down to me, Lawrence said: "I like them but don't love them anymore." "Because they are intellectuals?" I asked. "I suppose so. I suppose at the last, he felt they weren't his sort." "He felt they were lacking in human warmth?" "Yes." I can understand that. I take it he went back to his miner's world. Probably his pronounced mother-complex worked. But of course A. and M. have plenty of human warmth only it is

[1] Aldous in a letter to Julian of 3rd March 1930 from Vence.

very civilized warmth. I dare say poor little Lawrence wanted somebody to take him in their arms and probably would have recoiled
from it at the same time. [How contradictory this is to what had
actually happened; and yet in another sense perhaps not . . .] Aldous
and Maria will I hope never find out that he said this. Frieda is so
*stupid* (not malicious) that she might let it out.

A. and M. were magnificent throughout. Frieda would have been
lost without them.

Lawrence went very quickly. He refused oxygen saying it made
the pain worse. I fear he suffered frightfully. Just before they gave
him morphia ("I think I'll have a little morphia now!"—he had
refused it for a long while) he ordered Frieda's bed to be moved to
across the foot of his own. Barbara said he smiled as he watched
the long-armed Aldous working it. But I like Aldous working it
better than that smile.

Though they had not been at the villa long (a day?) Frieda had
contrived to get the kitchen into a hell of an unwholesome mess.
Little Maria, though nearly a wreck, spent the morning scrubbing
it out. Aldous and she had the greatest difficulty in persuading Frieda
to take the most ordinary precautions such as burning clothes etc.
When D. H. L. was very ill they were hard put to make her keep
a special cup for him. She is one of life's natural "squatters", a gypsy
and totally unpractical.

Aldous has been at great pains over money affairs etc. If she
follows his advice all should be well, but she is so stupid and such
a fool that she is quite likely to do the wrong thing.

All the while that we talked in the front room I could feel the
presence of Lawrence next door. What I principally felt was the
fighter. And I stuck to this with Frieda.

Aldous took Barbara and Frieda and myself down to lunch at the
hotel . . . We went back to the villa and Maria and Thys went
down to lunch. It seemed hours till four o'clock. We sat in the
kitchen, which smelled of ether, and I talked my head off. Maria
said it was the only thing to do as I was the least hit of those
present . . .

At length I went out for a stroll and saw the hearse approaching.
It was a rickety old thing drawn by one horse and accompanied
by a sort of chorus of grave-diggers—old characters in workaday
darkish clothes with waistcoats half-buttoned up . . but I liked
them. They were respectful. A dreadful silence fell on the house
and they could be heard knocking their boots on the steps to take
the mud off.

Lawrence had been coffined while we were at lunch. The doors
to the bedroom were thrown open and the old Jobbernols set about
lifting the oak coffin. It appeared—though Lawrence was frail and
smallish—perfectly enormous, and I feared they'd drop it. While

this was going on the silence seemed to stretch itself tight from horizon to horizon . . . Aldous was standing absolutely impassive, rather straighter than usual and very pale. His face was beautiful —and there was so to speak a marvellous pianissimo in it. Maria seemed in a dream and the big tears rolled two at a time down towards her nostrils.

We got hold of all the flowers and followed. Aldous had something to arrange and Maria was alone. She looked terribly forlorn and greyer in the face than ever. Aldous came back and took charge of her and I took charge of Frieda. She was quite wonderful. "It's how he would like it," she said, "just friends. And see, the sun's come out!" And so it had and the landscape was beautiful—it's lovely up at Vence and the birds were singing and the huge mass of rocks above the villa towered in a perfect sky . . .

Frieda didn't want the car to follow the hearse but it had to. The crawl to the cemetery was rather a nightmare. But then I suppose it always is! There is something of going to execution in it. But it had redeeming features. Every man took off his hat on the way— though one (Englishman of course) only did it at the last minute after I had stared him out of countenance and even then he kept his pipe in his mouth. I stared at him because a moment before Frieda made her only remark on the ride (Aldous and Maria, Frieda and I stuffed in one tiny taxi, my car was ahead carrying other people), "See how they take off their hats to Lawrence—isn't it nice!" Yes, they took off their hats. More people took off their hats to him on that ride than had ever done in his life. These Southerners respect death. And they are right: death should be respected. There's mystery in it, and when one is convoying a fighter like Lawrence one feels it more than ever. Women crossed themselves. The sky became more and more beautiful for it was just after four and the drama of nature was just beginning to move again after the stillness of a day made more still by descent of rain in short spells from a moveless [*sic*] grey sky. I led the way with Frieda. She said: "It's like being all old soldiers together." And so it was.

We came out on the lowest terrace of the cemetery: a beautiful position. Below the rampart of the cemetery the ground falls away through an orange orchard. A wonderful valley opens out and far away the sea glitters among haze. We all paused. "How beautiful it is," said Frieda. The coffin had gone on to under a further wall, beyond a solitary cypress. Here we sort of broke up into separate units. Not a word was said. The coffin was lowered into the grave. There was a little pause. The Jobbernols looked at us. Perhaps they expected a speech. Mrs Lawrence advanced and dropped some flowers on the coffin. Two or three of us did that and I said "Goodbye, dear Lawrence," because I couldn't bear to let him go absolutely without a word. At that I heard Maria begin to cry softly behind me. Then the Jobbernols began to fill the grave, pitching the stones in the earth to one side before they pushed in a shovel—curious long shovels they used, the oval shape perhaps as that used by the Romans. By God, my dears, it was grand. Why make speeches in the face of death? We don't know enough to say anything. The work was soon done . . .

. . One of the Jobbernols made to put the flowers on the grave. But Frieda said, "Let us put the flowers on ourselves." So I went over to the pile of flowers and handed them over. But Maria wouldn't put any on. She stood like one about whom the heavens had fallen. I stayed a little after most had moved away and put up a prayer to whosoever rules the remains that I might be—that we all might be . . . Then I went back to Frieda and she was quite calm . . . as we went up the path she suddenly stopped. The hearse was there. "It's empty now," she said in all but a whisper.

On their way back from the funeral, Aldous, Maria and Robert Nichols stopped exhausted in a wayside café and drank tea. They talked about the fortuitous nature of Lawrence's illness, how little care he had taken of himself; and Nichols, in the course of that very long letter, also says this: "I am bound to add as a statement of mere fact that I am afraid Frieda Lawrence was worse than useless as regards D. H. L.'s health.

On the Friday (I think, but it may have been the Thursday) before he died, D. H. L. said to her, "Frieda, you have killed me." Aldous told me this . . Aldous would not repeat such a terrible saying unless he felt it to be true. And he said, "I like Frieda in many ways but she is incurably and incredibly stupid—the most maddening woman I think I ever came across. Nevertheless she was the only sort of woman with whom D. H. L. could live." Poor Maria felt the whole thing frightfully. She was devoted to D. H. L. I think perhaps she loved him better than she loved anybody except Aldous among the few people she knew well. I felt more sorry for her than for anybody. The only good that has come out of the episode is that I am now nearer these two, Aldous and Maria . . . I feel profound affection for her. She agrees with Aldous about Frieda but she spoke without an atom of resentment and with great compassion. . . .

A day or two later, Aldous, Maria and Rina drove away to look for their next house up the coast. Mme Douillet, the owner of the Hôtel Beau-Rivage who had befriended Lawrence, gave them advice and help and before the week was out they had found one on a bay at Sanary near Toulon.

# PART FIVE

## The Apparent Stability: 1930-1935

"Meanwhile, one must be content to
go on piping up for reason and realism
and a certain decency."

ALDOUS HUXLEY, *Texts and Pretexts*

# Chapter One

## Villa Huley

VILLA HULEY—the mason had painted on the gateposts in huge, bright, green letters meaning to give them a surprise. Aldous and Maria thought it unkind to wipe out or correct this blaring advertisement of their presence and let it stand for the time being. Soon they ceased to see it. The letters remained, scarcely faded by the sun, in the long years after when the house stood empty.

Then the country round Bandol and Sanary was unspoilt, a classical landscape of hills, olives, vine. The new house though was on a slightly scruffy promontory between the two villages, called La Gorguette, where the dominant vegetation was thin pines and the land already destined to advancing development. (Aldous and Maria were apt to acquire their houses as quickly as they got rid of them.) There were advantages: the sea and a small beach at less than three hundred yards, main water and electricity and a short if bumpy drive to the good road. The original Villa Huley was a cramped little house built by a retired French *fonctionnaire* around 1910. By knocking down walls, cutting windows and enlarging here and there, the Huxleys changed it beyond recognition. The house was re-made, hand-made to their needs by the local builder. This turned out expensive; Aldous worried, but the new play was like a lottery ticket in his pocket ("I hope and pray that someone will take it . . .")

The outside became white-washed and green-shuttered. There was no entrance hall—one walked in, sandy feet, rain or shine, right into the living room. This was a large, well-proportioned L-shaped room, the walls terracotta wash, the floor red-tiled. At once one became aware of a fresh light scent of rosemary, geranium, lime and rose: Maria's pot-pourri in a deep urn by the door. To the right, shut off by long pale greenish oil-cloth curtains, another legacy of René Moulaert's, was the looking-glass dinner-table and a row of squat green oil-cloth covered chairs; to the left the living-room proper—Mexican rugs, the vast Dufy sofa and chairs from Suresnes before a fireplace; beyond in the sleeve of the L, Maria's desk and sewing box and a settee for two. Here she typed Aldous's books; and here they came, one by one, Matthew, Sophie, Raymond Mortimer and Eddy Sackville-West, Gerald Heard, Rina, myself, offering gossip, pouring out our troubles, our stories, answering anything she might ask (and my goodness, she did ask, out of her own quick interest *and* to pass on to Aldous), to be scolded, comforted and teased.

The living-room led into a hall—coat-stand, piles of straw hats—and to the stair-well in the centre of the house: one broad flight up, one narrow down to the kitchen which was on a lower level. Off this hall was a pantry with a food lift and the telephone, a solid wooden instrument with a crank. One was able to make and receive calls from, I think, 7.30 in the morning until 9 o'clock at night. Across the hall was Aldous's room, the room he worked in, his library. It was a good-sized room, almost square, with tiled floor and bookcases to the ceiling. There was a roll-top desk, a swivel chair, his very long chaise-longue and the armchair made to measure. French windows, well-shuttered, gave on to the large East terrace they had built but did not use as nobody except Maria and the Siamese cats went into that room unasked. Messages and crises were not relayed to Aldous during working hours. Sometimes, when he was not actually writing, the door might be open and one could see him standing up with his nose inside a book. When the heat of the day was waning, the shutters were flung open to a pleasant enough view of the garden. There was as yet no other roof in sight. (Quite soon, though, a monstrosity began to rise brick by brick across the fence; shoddy, gabled and pretentious it attained a spindly height. It housed at first a summer-school and when that failed a *pension de famille*, the Huxley household referred to it as Nuremberg.)

There were five bedrooms and one bath upstairs (the spare rooms had modest *cabinets de toilette*). Maria's room was large and light, an East room with a balcony to step out on, light modern furniture in pearly and coral tints. The looking-glass on her dressing-table was framed by sea-shells. The key-note—the key-note of the house —was order and quietness, and the luxury of this. Aldous's bedroom narrow as a passage, led out of Maria's and contained little beside a row of wall-cupboards, a chest of drawers and his extra-long bed (with extra-long sheets from England and an extra-long red quilt). The other bedrooms faced West. Matthew's, the largest and nicest, with toy- and book-shelves; the other two for guests. Rina lived in a cottage in the garden.

Aldous had insisted on adequate central heating, and they installed a water filter for their tea (always Jackson's Earl Grey) and an electric refrigerator, a rare luxury at the time. The kitchen range was coal; bathwater was heated by a stove that had to be hand-fed with small sticks. The Siamese (the protagonists of "Sermons in Cats") were three, Matou, Pussy and their off-spring Matelot.

It was a very pleasant house, the house at Sanary, and it had dignity. It was not beautiful; none of their houses ever was, nor really intended to be, and some of their friends sniffed and shuddered. There were few objects, no good pieces; such bric-à-brac as they collected on their journeys was not fashionable. Maria had one of D. H. Lawrence's paintings in her bedroom and a Marie Laurencin print; downstairs there were a very fine landscape by Joep Nicolas and his portrait of Maria, the rest of their pictures were by Aldous.

I have described the house as it was in its heyday. At first there were neither telephone nor Nuremberg; Mexican rugs, Joep's and Aldous's paintings, all came later. At first, the spring of 1930, there was chiefly brick-dust, hammering, gaping holes and crates. It was in this setting that I, in turn, had my first glimpse of Aldous. It was in the early afternoon of a warm day in spring; I was living at my mother's[1] and step-father's, and the Roy Campbells were staying with us for a few days. After luncheon Roy demanded to be taken to say hello to Aldous who, he had been told, was building in the neighbourhood and whom he had not seen since the days of Tommy Earp and Russell Green's Bloomsbury flat which he had sometimes shared. To me this was a shock. I had read *Antic Hay* (I was an adolescent with passionate intellectual longings), I had read the stories, I had read and re-read *Point Counter Point*. Aldous Huxley's writings were the overwhelming revelation. I was not prepared, I did not think of, an encounter with the writer in the flesh. (Oh perhaps in some dim adult future, when I should have proved myself, become a visible writer . . .) I thought about the books—constantly—of the man who wrote them I knew next to nothing (except rumours about his sight). Publishing being rather more impersonal then, I had not even seen a photograph. Had I been asked to place him—say, in one of those pen-and-paper games my family too indulged in—I might have visualized a disembodied existence in a tower at Balliol. An actual house in this fishing port, on our doorstep practically, if one were to believe Roy, was not credible. At any rate it came too sudden and too soon. My mother, also, was not enthusiastic. She admired Aldous's essays, taking a cooler view about the novels (we used to argue about this); writers, she told Roy, should be read not seen; and besides she did not hold with a pack of strangers dropping in on the poor man. Roy became aggressive. One needn't stand on ceremony with old Aldous, he declared, many was the night at Oxford when he'd carried him home and into his bed dead-drunk. This I refused to believe. (It was indeed a complete fabrication, made up, not in malice—Roy in many ways was a very sweet character—but in one of his spurts of obstinate mythomania.) Roy in those days drank red wine almost continuously, continuously from breakfast. He insisted; somebody

---

[1] The late Lisa Marchesani.

Aldous aged about five

Thomas Henry Huxley with his
grandson Julian Sorell Huxley

Julia Arnold Huxley, Aldous's mother,
at Prior's Field

*Right:* Aldous with his father

### THE HUXLEY FAMILY
*Back row (standing):* Miss Churcher
(secretary to Mrs Humphry Ward), Dorothy
Ward (daughter of Mrs Humphry Ward),
Janet Ward (daughter of Mrs Humphry
Ward, later married to G. M. Trevelyan)
*Centre row:* Miss Ella Salkowski (governess
to Aldous, later to Matthew), Julia Arnold
Huxley (Aldous's mother), Arnold Ward
(son of Mrs Humphry Ward), Mrs
Humphry Ward (Aldous's aunt), Josephine
Benison Arnold (second wife of Thomas
Arnold), Reverend Thomas Arnold
(1823–1900—Aldous's grandfather)
*Front row:* Aldous, Trevenan, Julian

Aldous with his aunt Mrs Humphry Ward

The Nys sisters in 1908: *from left*, Suzanne, Rose, Maria, Jeanne

The Huxley children circa 1903: *from top*, Julian, Trevenan, Aldous, Margaret

THE BALTUS FAMILY, BELLEM, BELGIUM, 1914
*Back row (standing)*: Georges Baltus (Maria's uncle), Grace Baltus (wife of
Raymond Baltus), Raymond Baltus (Maria's uncle), Norbert Nys (Maria's father)
*Centre row*: Rose Nys (Maria's sister, aged four years), Marguerite Baltus Nys
(Maria's mother), Richard Baltus (Maria's grandfather), Emérence Baltus
(Maria's grandmother)
*Front row*: Jeanne Nys (Maria's sister, aged twelve), Peter Baltus (son of Raymond
and Grace Baltus, aged two), Suzanne Nys (Maria's sister, aged ten), Maria
(aged fourteen)

OPPOSITE: Marguerite Baltus Nys with Maria, aged four months, January 1899

Twenty-one years later: Maria Nys Huxley with Matthew, aged about three
months, 1920

Lady Ottoline Morrell circa 1905

Nancy Cunard in 1930 ( Photograph
by Cecil Beaton)

*Left:* Aldous in the fields at Garsington circa 1916
*Right:* Maria, aged eighteen, on summer holiday in Killen, Scotland

Maria at Garsington circa 1916

Maria in the 1920s

Aldous with a goose

Aldous and Matthew, spring 1928, taken just before
Matthew was sent to his first school

*Top:* Les Diablerets, Vaud, Switzerland, January 1928. *From left*, D. H. Lawrence,
Aldous, Maria, Juliette Baillot Huxley, Frieda Lawrence, Julian Huxley
(Photograph by Rose de Haulleville)

Aldous and D. H. Lawrence at Bandol, France, January 1929

had to drive him. Nori Marchesani, my young step-father, volunteered. We set off on what had the hallmark of a wild-goose chase, Roy having no idea of the direction we were to take. Mary Campbell sat in front, Roy and I in the back. He was holding on to a shopping net with two full bottles. We stopped whomever we saw to make enquiries (it was the siesta hour) and quite soon struck lucky. Yes, an *homme de lettres anglais* was building on La Gorguette, about a mile from our house! We drew up in front of the Green Letters. These were the gateposts, there was no gate as yet. We stepped across some planks and approached a hole in the façade. Inside, sitting on the floor beside a large revolving book-cage, sorting books, was Aldous.

He was dressed in khaki shorts, sandals without socks and a light shirt; he looked up and one saw the large round spectacles. Roy spoke, "Aldous—this is Roy." "Roy," Aldous said in a high silvery tone. He got to his feet, uncoiling length. "Dear Roy—how are you?" He shook hands with a little smile, very friendly. Roy introduced his wife.

He struck me—he was looking absurdly young that moment on the floor—as he must have struck Juliette the first day at Garsington, and L. P. Hartley from across the stairs and that young woman who saw him at Oxford lectures standing by a pillar. It is more than forty years ago; the snapshot in the mind is static, clear. I can look at it at will, interpret now, feel; use the words of today, note his absorption—we came upon him when he thought himself alone— the apartness, the vulnerability, the curious young bird's unprotectedness that has caught so many women. Can it be transmitted, that snapshot? Of Aldous by the book-cage, head bent gracefully, thick dark hair dishevelled, long tapering hands moving about books . . .

The next one—Aldous standing head forward, stooping from the shoulders, swaying to one side—is blurred by the overlay of so many later ones. He began to talk—now it was the voice that drew attention—almost the first thing he said was that someone ought to paint a horror picture of The First Day in the New Home. Not that it was the first day, he had been camping in the house since April and had just come back from a brief escape to England on poor Lawrence's business. My step-father, who was on alien territory but had his own perceptiveness, caught my eye: "I must get her," and was gone. At that stage Maria appeared (much intrigued, she told us later, to see the back of a car shooting out of the drive and wondering who was fleeing from their premises and why). Maria, as I said, appeared. This was another turn, as I had no idea that Aldous might be married. Roy—they hadn't met—had probably forgotten. She moved forward swiftly, an ephesian figure in full white sailor trousers and a linen shirt, the face all eyes and profile, auburn hair held by a ribbon and a flower, falling to the shoulders. An Angel of the Annunciation by El Greco with a touch of Degas (in my mother's words). *She*, meanwhile had arrived. The car had come back, there were two more of us, Maria took it in her stride. My mother, though still young, was already very ill then and often rather wayward and eccentric; there were still some traces of a beauty that had been considerable. She was a great talker, as well as a good listener, when there was something worth listening to, and a most amusing story-teller; she also had much charm. Aldous responded. Maria asked us to stay for tea. We settled round a table in an arbour; the ensuing talk was a dialogue between Aldous and my mother. They talked about life in Paris, they talked about local history. Aldous declared himself to be fascinated by a character called General Rose, after whom the main street of Sanary was named, who had built a folly for his mistresses at the age of ninety. The rest of us listened. Roy was meek and mild. (I longed for answers to so many questions but knew that it was not the time.) They talked about French novelists, made jokes about the Goncourts, Maupassant. *Une Vie*, Aldous said, was a much longer and much less effective version of what Wilhelm Busch had so admirably done in his life of *Die Fromme Helene*. While they were talking, there went on a mimed obligato to which most of us paid little attention but which mesmerized Maria. (She told the story later.) Rina came in with a large full tea-pot and placed it in front of Maria. My mother, going on with what she had been saying and without taking her eyes off Aldous, reached across the table, seized the pot and drew it to herself. She was notoriously absent-minded and had no doubt forgotten that she was not in her own house. However, she did not pour out. For some time nothing happened. My mother, hand on tea-pot, went on talking. Maria now made a discreet move to regain possession. My mother grasped the pot more firmly, drew it closer to herself and, still without losing the thread of her conversation, opened the lid, peered inside and quickly dropped the lid again.

Maria was filled with admiration. She had recognized a peer in savoir faire. What presence of mind, what tact! For she was convinced that what my mother had seen and somehow *known* to be inside that tea-pot must be a dead dormouse at the very least. The party took its course. Our cups stayed empty (according to Maria; I have a notion that Rina was signalled for a fresh supply). Roy, by the way, had not dared to bring in his provisions. My mother went on sitting with the tea-pot practically in her arms, only relinquishing her grasp to help herself to the excellent thin brown bread-and-butter. Brown bread was rare in France, and she finished off the platter.

We had been back at our house for an hour that evening when

we heard the snort of a powerful car outside. The red Bugatti stopped, tore off again: Maria had left some tuberoses and a small brown loaf for my mama.

Aldous was not D. H. Lawrence's literary executor. Lawrence died intestate. Frieda and his brother George, who became joint administrators of the estate, asked Aldous and some others to advise on literary decisions. There was, for instance, the question of a biography. Frieda and Aldous felt that it was still too early for a truthful life of D. H. L. Aldous suggested a memorial volume instead, reminiscences by various people interspersed with Lawrence's own letters.

> e.g. an account of his childhood by his sister; early manhood by a schoolmaster friend, and, for a later period, by Ezra Pound; shortly after his marriage an account by David Garnett . . . war-time by Middleton Murry (perhaps) and also Lady Cynthia Asquith and Lady Ottoline Morrell; perhaps a page by Bertrand Russell . . . also Richard Aldington; and Norman Douglas; for the Australian time his collaborator in *The Boy in the Bush*, Miss Skinner; for the American period, Mabel Dodge; for the last 2 or 3 years in Italy and France, perhaps myself.

The recollections to be printed as nearly as possible in chronological order, adding when necessary a bald statement of dates and doings. Aldous offered ("this goes without saying") to do whatever work for nothing. That rather good idea petered out.

During the three months following Lawrence's death, Aldous kept moving between Bandol, Sanary, London and Paris. "I'm hunting up Lawrence letters," he wrote to Robert Nichols,

> What a queer devil he was! The queerer, the more I think and know about him. So many charming and beautiful things in him, such a lot that wasn't sympathetic. I gather . . that you got Frieda a bit on the nerves. Well, I'm not surprised . . .

The idea was to get hold of and copy as many of D. H. L.'s letters as possible at once so that they should not be dispersed or lost. As to what to publish, Aldous's own view was clear. ". . The selection should be as far as possible impersonal. I don't like the body-snatching business."[1] "The rather indecent display of personalities which has become so unpleasantly common now is

---

[1] To Richard Aldington, 1st June 1930.

something which, if I have any say, shall be avoided."[1] "What may happen many years hence is the affair of posterity."[2]

"Here all is exquisitely lovely," Aldous wrote to Juliette from Sanary in May. "Sun, roses, fruit, warmth. We bathe and bask. Best love to all."

Aldous and Maria's first Sanary summer lasted well into September. The house got into shape, daily life reassumed its even pattern. It was still very much as it had been in Italy. Maria got up early. She loved the light and solitude of dawn. Unhurried, day-dreaming, she would garden. Asked what she was doing in those morning hours, she would say, "I paint my artichokes." (To keep off insects.) Family breakfast was at about ten. Aldous would look sleepy and be comfortably silent. There was no post as yet or newspapers. Quite soon he would get up, still silent, and go into his room. The door shut behind him.

He was working during that summer on essays and on the play he started at Suresnes, *The World of Light*, and he was also trying his hand again at poetry. By one o'clock he would emerge—a little sun-bathing on the roof, then everybody in their bathing dress walked down to the sea. Aldous carried the inflated rubber boat. He and Maria wore large hats against the sun which they kept on in the water. Out they swam, the two of them, rather slowly, farther and farther, talking all the while—"swimming together conscientiously," as little Sophie saw it, "with straw hats on, discussing important subjects." On land again, Maria inveterately took photographs—the French had gone to eat, the pebbly beach was theirs—Matthew, looking pensive, holding up a toy ship; Eddy Sackville-West, as thin as a fakir, emerging from the waves; Raymond Mortimer laughing in the spray; Rina, also laughing, in a bathing cap; and of course Aldous. "Aldous was usually cheerful, anchored still, one felt, in his morning's work, but ready for the break, willing to join the talk," I wrote, I find, in the *Memorial Volume*; now, having thought about it so much more, I still believe that this was so. He *was* cheerful and present on one level; he often teased the children. Back in the house, one washed off sand and put on clothes. Few clothes, shorts, espadrilles, and those magically cool Egyptian cotton shirts Aldous and Maria wore interchangeably. Rina banged a gong. Luncheon was indoors. The dining cubicle with the green shiny curtain, the glassy surface and the filtered light coming through the shutters, had an under-water quality. Rina handed round the dishes. (The house ran simply but with smoothness—

[1] To Helen Corke, 7th May 1930.
[2] To Brett, 23rd June 1930.

one did not interrupt conversation proffering things.) Food was risotto or pasta, a green vegetable, some mild cheese, always fruit. Plates and bowls, Italian mostly, were pretty, the Tuscan glass green-tinged. There were carafes of cooled white and red wine and plain water on the table, local wine at noon; at dinner it was claret. Everybody talked. Maria exchanged words with Rina in Italian. Maria's Italian was delightful to listen to; it was the one language, and like Aldous she did know a good many, she spoke without a foreign accent. Her French passed as French, not Belgian, but had alien undertones to acute French ears; her English had a cadence of its own. Luncheon was not long, though unhurried (time was not allowed to be talked away, there was an invisible bar of discipline). Not that Aldous went back to work at once; now he often painted during the dog hours, setting up his easel to do a view from Maria's window or Maria or a child on a chaise-longue.

The post would have arrived while everyone was bathing and been left on a sofa. Book parcels, unsolicited manuscripts and all. Nobody ever seemed to wish to look at it at once. For a writer in working spate this matter of answering letters—keeping on indoors, solitary and cramped, after the day's work—can be a cruel business. For Aldous the problem was perennial. No wonder so many of his letters begin with "Time has been sliding away . . ." Somehow bills got paid and letters opened. Maria did what she could, which had its limitations. Accounts, forms, bank statements, made little sense to her; she typed fast but with all the mistakes Lawrence had found in her script of *Lady C*; she did not often date her letters and the hand-written ones were hard to read. Yet to her friends and sisters she wrote those long, descriptive letters, typed late at night when Aldous was asleep.

The Huxleys did not subscribe to an English newspaper. (No *Times*, no *New Statesman*.) They took in a French daily which generally remained folded in its wrapper, as did the polyglot reviews that were sent from all over the world. Aldous subscribed to *Nature*.

After painting, tea. China tea and a plate of ginger nuts, in Aldous's room, in the garden, anywhere. Then another stint of work.

Before dinner there might be a quick dip in the sea or, if it was cool enough, a stroll. Then Aldous and Maria went upstairs to have their baths and change—the hour of their private talk. Presently they came down (dinner in summer was round nine o'clock): Aldous in a gleaming shirt and endless white cotton trousers (beautifully laundered by the Italian maids); Maria in a cloud of scent, a fresh flower in her hair, often also in white ducks (hers were made at the cost of about fifteen shillings at the naval bazaar on the quai of Toulon). There was a sense of release about these evenings, something of what Aldous had spoken of as the "profoundly satisfying consciousness of being 'in order'."[1] Dinner was lightly *en fête*. And afterwards they went out into the summer night, the garden where hammocks used to swing under the eucalyptus and the lime. Aldous brought his black box, the hand-wound gramophone. There was music. There was silence.

Such was the tip of the iceberg, the manifest part of their daily round. People who were brought up at Prior's Field speak of the atmosphere of goodness and kindness in the home life of another generation of Huxleys. Time and place had changed and Aldous and Maria's home life was in some ways eccentric, yet again the atmosphere was a compound of seriousness and gaiety, of gentleness, niceness, grace. Like his mother Aldous possessed invisible moral authority. There were things one did not do, did not wish to do, in his house, his presence. (There was also of course that dread he had, and communicated, of coming close to uncovered emotion.) Aldous's entourage adopted a certain standard; even strangers did, such as porters and waiters in the more excitable countries. Perhaps Aldous never realized what a good influence he was. (I once said rather naively to a mutual friend, "But *you* don't do such things."—it was something fairly harmless—and he answered, "My dear, you mustn't think of me only as you see me at the Huxleys'.") Much of it was a matter of tone. There never was a harsh word between Aldous and Maria. Nor between them and others. Which does not mean that Maria did not speak up or criticize; she was *very* outspoken, she was *very* critical; in fact she could be quite didactic, particularly with her sisters and the children. One was not allowed to get away with things. And that went for Aldous too. He wasn't let off doing what Maria thought he ought to do; she kept down his sins of omission. And how she could puncture pretension. By teasing or laughing. How often one heard her say, "Matthew, don't be pompous." and to Aldous, the least pompous of men, "Darling, don't be pompous!" (What she was up against was the irreducible masculine pomposity about accurate facts and not making oneself conspicuous in public.) When Maria had to scold in earnest, it was done in sorrow and concern. Once when Rina had again succumbed to the lure of sweets, I came upon them crying in each other's arms. Whereas if Aldous girded himself to rebuke or educate, he generally did it by letter; which of course was so much worse for the recipient.

---

[1] In "On Grace", *Music at Night*. Chatto & Windus, 1931.

## Villa Huley | *1930*

We have left them in the Mediterranean darkness, under leaves and sky.

Moonless, this June night is all the more alive with stars. Its darkness is perfumed with faint gusts from the blossoming lime trees, with the smell of wetted earth and the invisible greenness of the vines. There is silence; but a silence that breathes with the soft breathing of the sea and, in the thin shrill noise of a cricket . . . Far away, the passage of a train. . . .

Music, you say; it would be a good night for music. But I have music here in a box, shut up, like one of those bottled djinns in the *Arabian Nights*, and ready at a touch to break out of its prison. I make the necessary mechanical magic, and suddenly, by some miraculously appropriate coincidence (for I had selected the record in the dark . .), suddenly the introduction to the *Benedictus* in Beethoven's *Missa Solemnis* begins to trace its pattern on the moonless sky.

The *Benedictus*. Blessed and blessing, this music is in some sort the equivalent of the night, of the deep and living darkness . . .

There is, at least there sometimes seems to be, a certain blessedness lying at the heart of things, a mysterious blessedness, of whose existence occasional accidents or providences (for me, this night is one of them) make us obscurely, or it may be intensely, but always fleetingly, alas, always only for a few brief moments aware.[1]

[1] *Music at Night*, written in 1930.

239

## Chapter Two
## The Bad Utopia

IN the three years after *Point Counter Point* Aldous did not attempt any major work. *Do What You Will* was followed by *Brief Candles*, a collection of stories; the longest, "After the Fireworks", was perhaps his last go at story-telling *per se*. It is an accomplished tale, very literary, with a characteristically hybrid genesis—"an elaboration and emendation of an incident recorded in the letters of Chateaubriand. When he was sixty, a very young girl at a watering place came and threw herself at his head. He wrote her a most exquisite letter, which is extant. And there", Aldous explained to Starkey, "the matter ended, even though she did invade his house one evening . . . I thought it would be amusing to give it the cruel ending [the man giving in: the girl getting tired of him in a matter of months]. As one couldn't use Chateaubriand himself—that monstruous pride and loneliness and, underneath the burning imagination, that emotional aridity would have been impracticable to handle—I made the hero one of those people . . [whose identity would be guesswork] who know how to shirk natural consequences and get something for nothing . . ." Aldous's third working year—from the death of Lawrence to May 1931—was ragged. "Time, like an Indian thief [once more to Starkey], has got away with weeks and months of booty, leaving how little, so far as I'm concerned, in return—some essays, a few poems, some on the whole rather melancholy reflections."

Actually Aldous had got through a fair amount of work. He had been tinkering with the idea of a new novel: "a kind of picaresque novel of the intellect and the emotions, [to Robert Nichols] a mixture between *Gil Blas*, *Bouvard et Pécuchet* and *Le Rouge et le Noir* . . quite impossible to do—but will be fun to try". Nothing apparently came of this, but he had finished his play; he had written some of his best or his best-remembered shorter essays, "Tragedy and the Whole Truth", "Meditation on El Greco", "Sermons in Cats", "Music at Night"; he had written a dozen or so new poems. In publishing terms, this meant four titles in ten months. In November 1930 *Vulgarity in Literature*, a somewhat drawn-out essay in a limited edition; in April 1931 the play *The World of Light*; in May, *The Cicadas*, plumped out with some earlier poems; and in September, *Music at Night*. Meanwhile Aldous had also been painting, and coping with a flow of D. H. Lawrence letters as it had been decided to publish a substantial collection of these presently.

As for travel, the Huxleys had been staying relatively put. They had left Sanary in September for England from where Aldous had gone on to Berlin and Paris, accompanying his friend Sullivan on "a tour of great men [Sullivan was interviewing eminent scientists] . . a most entertaining piece of sightseeing". (Later he gave Robert Nichols an account of a night he and Sullivan spent at a homosexual dance-hall in Berlin which Nichols related in one of his letters to the Henry Heads.

. . Incidentally he [Aldous] danced with one of the male prostitutes rather than hurt the fellow's feelings. This last slipped out. He didn't mean to tell it. But I asked him how [they] . . dealt with the men who came to their table. He added, 'I was just a little tipsy when I did it. But I can assure you, my dear Bob, a couple of times round that hall and I was sobriety itself. Horror is a wonderful disintoxicant.')

In October Aldous came back to England and, with Maria, went to Nottingham to see D. H. L.'s relations and then up into the Northern Midlands for some articles he had been asked to do on conditions in the mining villages. It was a bleak time; Aldous was appalled. "What a world we live in. I was staying in the Durham coalfield this autumn, in the heart of English unemployment, and it was awful.

If only one cd believe that the remedies . . (Communism etc.) proposed for the awfulness weren't even worse than the disease . . . The sad and humiliating conclusion is forced on one that the only thing to do is to flee and hide . . .

They went back to Sanary and did not move again until well into the new year when they went to London for the last two winter months. They stayed in rooms in Dalmeny Court, Duke Street, St James's, rooms which never saw daylight but were well heated and comfortable enough and provided with a pantry where they could boil their own kettles and need not go out for every bite. The situation was perfect for Aldous's routine—two steps from the London Library and the Athenaeum.

Some of Aldous's recent verse, we just noted, was to be published in late spring. He asked Robert Nichols for an opinion. "If you have time," he wrote to him, "will you glance at these and tell me what you think of them when we meet. Some, I think, are all right. But I don't really know and rely on your judgement."

Now Robert Nichols was devoted to Aldous; he was also a very emotional young man, a man of feeling, as another age might have called him, and he showed his feelings. (He had an extraordinary harrowing way, a marrow-piercing way, of reading poetry.) One can imagine how he affected Aldous; Nichols, for his part, gave an analysis of their relation (in that letter to the Henry Heads of 1930).

> . . . Aldous and Maria were as sweet as ever. I adore them. I fear Aldous finds me rather a bore—I'm so naïve beside him, so much the "life is real, life is earnest" young man and also so disconcertingly emotional—for when I see him my india-rubber face will give away how I wear him in my heart of hearts. But he's really fond of me and that's one of the reasons he feels shy. I think he's scared that I shall close his ship and set about boarding him emotionally. Nature has erected on the edge of his emotional garden a board "trespassers —against the will of the owner—are apt to be prosecuted". Sometimes I note him rein himself in from emptying a cold douche on my head. He really is a saint. He would like me to steal aboard and somehow arrive without his notice. That I try to do though I feel terribly inclined to rush on board with a loud "O Aldous!" and when I get there I keep one eye on the clock. He is a great man, a great human being and not at all cold really. He also has tremendous pluck.

And now, in his house at Winchelsea, Nichols was expecting the Huxleys once more.

> My beloved Aldous and Maria are coming this weekend . . . [to the Heads, 30th January 1931] He desires me to advise him on some poems to be added to those in *Arabia Infelix* . . which contains the superb *Cicadas*—and published in an ordinary edition. It is very difficult. There is not one of those poems without a good idea, but Aldous hasn't always the power of melting the thought with music —for poetry must have music; if possible various music or it isn't poetry. There is one largish splendid poem called *ORION* among those he sent me. A. H. hasn't the technical resources of T. S. E.— but he's *game* which T. S. E. isn't. He wrestles with his despair. The following comparison is absurd as far as class goes, but as to character one might say that at the present moment, in the prevailing atmosphere of profound discouragement, Aldous is a sort of Beethoven trying to fight his way through, and T. S. E. is a sort of Chopin (recollect I am not speaking of class: I am speaking of character, of spirit). The spirit—and the will to pay—in Aldous is making a desperate battle . . . He has terrific courage and formidable mental integrity—he is a hero: one of the few heroes among the writers of our time . . . In fact, now Romer [Wilson]'s dead—and D. H. L.— I hardly see another.

*The World of Light*, Aldous's first play, had been accepted, by Leon M. Lion, and was being produced at the Royalty in March.

Aldous watched the rehearsals. "He sat there in the darkness of the stalls," wrote Denys Blakelock[1] who played Hugo, the principal part, "silent and as I thought disapproving." And yet after the opening Aldous wrote him a most complimentary letter.

> I wish he could have said a few of [the things he wrote] during the rehearsal period . . . But he was a shy remote man and I think he would have found it impossible to make contact with a company of actors.[1]

Mr Blakelock speaks of the play as "one of the most distinguished and provocative pieces of writing for the theatre of that decade". . . . Yet it was far from a success. It made less money, Aldous said, than any play since the *Agamemnon* of Aeschylus. *The World of Light* is the world of spirits. In Act Two the stage is plunged in darkness and the audience stares at a realistic seance—floating objects, musical box, luminous trumpet. This seance is smashed— seconds before curtain— by the arrival of the spirit in persona and alive. The medium (one thinks) has been unmasked. And yet the messages he transmitted—the thoughts of the living man—turn out to have been minutely accurate. The extra-sensory communication was genuine, only the seeker's premises were at fault. But this is not quite cut and dried; Aldous did not commit himself. It is even difficult to make out whether he was using the spiritualist theme as a trimming and a dramatic bait, or whether he regarded it as parallel or as subordinate to the play's other theme, escape. (Escape from emotional aridity, an undesired marriage, conventional duties, escape into gratuitous action.) Aldous rather side-tracked a critic's demand (Desmond MacCarthy's) for a more definite solution.

> [It seems] justified . . even tho' there would not in fact have been such a solution in life, it is perhaps one of the functions of art to provide definite solutions—to consummate wish-fulfilments . . . The difficulty was (a) finding any plausible solution at all and (b) finding one that could be got into the terribly limited space at a playwright's disposal. A difficulty so great that, after many attempts, I stuck to the mere verisimilitude and left the situation hanging in the void.

In Sanary, in April, Aldous began to write his Bad Utopia. He wrote it in four months. It all began light-heartedly enough. It was time to produce some full-length fiction—he still felt like holding back from another straight novel—juggling in fiction form with the

---

[1] Denys Blakelock, *Round the Next Corner*. Victor Gollancz, 1967.

scientific possibilities of the future might be a new line. Twenty-five years after, an American acquaintance asked Aldous whether he had any idea that *Brave New World* would be considered prophetic, that it would be regarded as an influential philosophical work. "He replied with a kind of tender but self-deprecating affection for his own past that he had been having a little fun pulling the leg of H. G. Wells. At least it had started out that way until he got caught up in the excitement of his own ideas."[1]

Wells' views on the effects of applied science were rosy; Aldous had his doubts. Take eugenics for instance—the increase, by deliberate breeding, of some of the inheritable qualities such as intelligence and ability. An intrinsically desirable change, you might say, but would it have desirable results? What would happen to a society compelled by law to breed exclusively from its most gifted and successful members? Four years earlier already, Aldous had had this to say on the subject.

> . . It is obvious that all the superior individuals of the eugenic states will not be permitted to make full use of their powers, for the good reason that no society provides openings for more than a limited number of superior people. No more than a few can govern, do scientific research, practise the arts . . or lead their fellows. But if . . every individual is capable of playing the superior part, who will consent to do the dirty work and obey? The inhabitants of one of Mr Wells's numerous Utopias solve the problem by ruling and being ruled, doing high-brow and low-brow work in turns. While Jones plays the piano, Smith spreads the manure. At the end of the shift, they change places; Jones trudges out to the dung-heap and Smith practises the A minor Etude of Chopin. An admirable state of affairs if it could be arranged . . .[2]

"Personally," Aldous went on, "I find my faith too weak . . . The intellectually gifted are notorious for the ruthless way in which they cultivate their gifts."

In Aldous's counter Utopia, then, human beings are deliberately bred inferior as well as superior; Gammas and Identical Epsilon Semi-Morons as well as Alpha-Pluses. The principle of mass production, as one of the World Managers explains, is at last applied to biology. The theme, the well-known theme of *Brave New World*, is the effect of science applied to human beings by their rulers at some approaching future point. (The theme was not the progress of science as *such*; Aldous's intention was not scientific prophecy, no foretelling of any probable specific technological development,

[1] Mrs Arthur Goldschmidt of New York, in a letter to S. B. 1968.
[2] "A Note on Eugenics", *Proper Studies*. Chatto & Windus, 1927.

such as if and when we might split the atom—bottled babies were just a serviceable extravagance—it was psychological prophecy.) The theme was that you could dominate people by social, educational and pharmaceutical arrangements:

> iron them into a kind of uniformity, if you were able to manipulate their genetic background . . . if you had a government sufficiently unscrupulous you could do these things without any doubt . . .

And this, Aldous said in the London interview in 1961, "This *was* the whole idea of *Brave New World.*"

*These things*—projected forty years ago for the year 600 After Ford—were Pavlovian conditioning of children before and after birth, hypnopaedia, mind-changing drugs and pleasure-giving drugs, planned sexual promiscuity (". . as political and economic freedom diminishes, sexual freedom tends compensatingly to increase"), compulsory contraceptives, the prolongation of youth, euthanasia, total centralization of power, total government control and above all a foolproof system to standardize the human product. Today, we are still a longish cry from globally controlled production of human beings. Yet (as Aldous pointed out in 1961) "We are getting more and more into a position where these things *can* be achieved.

> And it's extremely important to realize this, and to take every possible precaution to see that they shall *not* be achieved. This, I take it was the message of the book—*This is possible: for heaven's sake be careful about it.*[1]

One can see how Aldous became caught up in his idea in that summer of 1931, writing away in his cool room by the Mediterranean. An artist starting on a piece of work does not know what it will be until he has made it. Nor where it may lead him. The new line led Aldous into some extremely fruitful fields; it was the line which ultimately led him to his last novel, the Good Utopia, *Island.* Meanwhile, if repelled, he was fascinated also by what he conjured up and let himself rip over Malthusian belts, *The Delta Mirror* and synthetic music.

> The scent organ was playing a delightfully refreshing Herbal Capriccio . . . "Going to the Feelies, this evening, Henry?" inquired the Assistant Predestinator. "I hear the new one at the Alhambra is first-rate. There's a love scene on a bearskin rug; they say it's

[1] London interview, 1961.

marvellous. Every hair of the bear reproduced. The most amazing tactile effects."[1]

Much in the book is crass or funny; much is horrible. Throughout there obtains the yardstick of the Aldous who admired Piero della Francesca for proclaiming all that is most admirable in man. The inhabitants of the World State of 600 After Ford have little left to be admirable about. Material security is complete; environment stabilised and safe (and superlatively hygienic); war is unthinkable, death not thought of; abilities and wants are bred to measure for one's station in life. There is no sickness, no old age, no solitude, no questions; no sleepless nights. Anxiety and depression are muffled by drugs that have no after or side effects and no one ever has to wait for the fulfilment of a desire. It is an existence without frustration, maladjustment, fear, rebellion, poverty or crime— there is no past, no art, no God.

A life-span without war, violence and the dread of cruel disease —is it not worth the silly slogans, the scent organ, the Feelies and the lack of an unknown freedom? But then the price—in our terms —is also the freedom to reject servitude, the freedom to choose, to grow, to change. The price is deep and graduated human relation- ships, is virtue, is courage, endurance, faith exchanged for uni- formity and spiritual squalor. There is no doubt on which side Aldous comes down.

"You all remember," [says the Resident Controller for Western Europe] "you all remember, I suppose that beautiful and inspired saying of Our Ford's: History is bunk. History," he repeated slowly, "is bunk."

He waved his hand; and it was as though, with an invisible feather whisk, he had brushed away a little dust, and the dust was Harappa, was Ur of the Chaldees; some spider-webs, and they were Thebes and Babylon and Cnossos and Mycenae. Whisk, whisk—and where was Odysseus, where was Job, where were Jupiter and Gotama and Jesus? Whisk—and those specks of antique dirt called Athens and Rome, Jerusalem and the Middle Kingdom—all were gone. Whisk —the place where Italy had been was empty. Whisk, the cathedrals; whisk, whisk, King Lear and the Thoughts of Pascal. Whisk, Passion; whisk, Requiem; whisk, Symphony; whisk . . .[2]

---

[1] *Brave New World.* Chatto & Windus, 1932.
[2] Ibid.

## Chapter Three

# Living

*BRAVE NEW WORLD* was finished by late August. "I have at last, thank heaven, got rid of it." Aldous wrote off his arrears of letters and threw himself into painting. "I'm taking a holiday from writing in painting in oils . . . a most exhausting process, I find, but extraordinarily pleasure-giving." So were the subjects he chose to paint, a swing in the garden, trees, a sea-shell and fan, portraits of his family and friends. No symbolism, no horrors, no abstractions: but joy and interest in the visible world and the problems of getting it on to canvas. What were they like, Aldous's pictures? Well, given his limitations (a Sunday painter with unpredictable sight) they were rather remarkable. Without any great claim to originality, they were not obtrusively derivative—though Aldous knew how to pick up a trick or two—and they had a certain personal quality. The colours are often subtle, the drawing a bit lop-sided; he took much trouble over composition. His paintings do what they did to him: they give pleasure. There is perhaps more than that in a few of the portraits. Three, the very charming one of Maria in a lamb's fur jacket and the heads of Eddy West and Gerald Heard—Gerald very Grand-Inquisitorial in sharp profile (all in Rina's possession), which I recently saw again, show a degree of physiognomic perception.

On the periphery, the life of the house went on. Friends had come and stayed, J. W. N. Sullivan, the second Mrs Arnold Bennett (now a widow), the children for their holidays. "Matthew exceedingly flourishing, I am glad to say; we are reading Monte Cristo aloud." Aldous attempted to help him with his Latin and to teach him the piano. These lessons were not a success. Aldous exhibited controlled conspicuous patience. He was easier with Sophie, a girl and a niece—responsibility at one remove. "To me," she says in a memoir,[1] "Maria and Aldous were a couple out of a fairy tale.

Maria so exquisite, always delicately scented, wearing lovely silks and furs, gardenias and coral ear-rings, and doing the craziest exercises on her bedroom floor . . . (They always had a passion for exercises, crazy diets, bizarre doctors etc.) Aldous was to me immensely long, wearing snake-skin ties in London . . . He was, at

[1] Written for this biography by Sophie Moulaert, the present Mrs Willem Welling.

times, quite conscious of me and very attentive and polite, always listening and answering my questions although he sometimes referred to me as a "female" which hurt my feelings very much. He used to come to my room and enjoy standing all my beloved dolls upside down. I would . . fly into a rage which left him baffled, and he would then at great pains explain to me that there was no good reason why dolls should *not* stand on their heads. I would think he was heartless.

. . Aldous and Maria were constantly present during my whole childhood. My parents being divorced, my mother always turned to Aldous for advice concerning my education and my future.

But Sophie too says that Aldous was "quite a bad teacher.

Although he enjoyed it . . . We worked together on Macbeth [that was some years later when Aldous was tutoring Sophie in Eng. Lit.]. After having me read a few lines, he would try to explain them to me but never went very far as he would digress on Shakespeare himself, and philosophy and politics and the fact that Macbeth was 'utterly un-understandable!'

Maria was often far from well (a delicate constitution: anaemia, fragile lungs, a queasy metabolism, not helped by not infrequent pregnancies—always interrupted—and severe attacks of migraine). When she felt ill, though, one knew it only afterwards—"I'm so much better." That summer Aldous tried to do something new about the anaemia which so far had resisted, he said, everything prescribed. He made Maria take dried animal stomach tissue. "I decided on the strength of the accounts I read in a medical paper . . the results have been excellent." For the time being.

They had not stirred from Sanary since April. Aldous had hoped to accompany Julian on his first journey to the Soviet Union, the book prevented it. He and Maria now proposed to go to New York in the autumn, but when the pound went off the gold standard in September, their plans changed. "Partly for reasons of expense and partly because I want very much to be on the spot when the crisis is being solved—or not solved! . . One develops a strong sense of patriotism when the moment comes . . ."

Thus Aldous went to England to stand by, followed some weeks later by Maria. They first put up in Dalmeny Court again, then moved round the corner into Rosa Lewis's Cavendish Hotel.

The [gods??] treated me very well this week for Aldous turned up for a night. [Robert Nichols wrote to the Heads on 3rd October] . . He's only gone about an hour ago . . . Aldous was in fine form though pale. He is more himself than ever; he really does now seem

in possession of his whole self. He is far and away the most intelligent
and humane man I have ever known save Henry [Head].

He goes on to comment on Aldous's range.

Here are some of the things we touched on—unemployment (effect
on character of workmen)—Crébillon—steam-cars—the nature of
music (pattern as opposed to content)—drug-taking in Siberia (consumption of a fungus and its effects)—the book of Job . . . the new
process for procuring petrol from coal by electrolysis . . . Siamese
cats—validity of different forms of experience . . . D. H. Lawrence—
Provençal poetry . . "Mistral must have been a silly old bird . ."—
Bolshevism—Noel Coward at Monte Carlo—alarming spectacle of
the scientists at the British Association—the popular Don Juan
played every November in Spain—modern free verse and T. S.
Eliot—the appalling fashionableness of drunkenness in the U.S.—
the difficulty of dealing with manuscripts sent for him to look over
. . . Homer, how sensible Homer is, how sane, what an enormous
gap there is till you come to another broad and wholesome writer—
he intoned Chaucer—Oh, and something else. We went for a walk
and looked at the sheep—I pointed out one like Wordsworth—he
capped it with 'in vagrant and in pensive mood'—and indeed that's
exactly how the old ram looked lying under a chestnut tree with his
head on one side, gently puffing—his slant eyes fixed on us. We
lingered quite a long time by the sheep—picking up conkers from
the chestnut trees—baubles he loves as I do for their beautiful rich
brown glossiness and their veining—but he is firmer-minded than I
am—I know they will fade in an hour and their lustre be gone, but
I carry them home, while he has the good sense to feast his eye and
finger-tips on them and then throw them away. He loves beauty
even more than I do. It's lovely to see him holding a split chestnut-
fruit in his fingers, close up to his face, admiring the dappled
treasure lodged in the pith as white as the flesh of a magnolia. By
the way his eyes are better. He's been seeing what he calls 'my two
dear quacks' in Westminster—Hitchcock and Duppock—or some
such names. They have soothed his blind eye by exercising it with
green light and he can now just see a little with it. They have also
given him very different glasses of immense power and a queer pair
which he calls 'my white-eyed poppies' which look like this

that is, they have a sort of pebbly lens in the centre
surrounded by a sort of silver shield. 'But,' he says, 'I
daren't put them on in public—they make every-
body laugh. I don't mind them laughing but there are tender-hearted
people who might be hurt at the notion that I was hurt . . .'
. . To return to the sheep. After we'd looked at them for some time
he said, 'You know the early Christians either had no luck or they

were very dense. Fancy choosing a sheep as a symbol. Gentle—yes
—but oh how stupid!!' He talked about the poet Beddoes too—how
good his letters were, how interesting, what a queer fellow he was.
I forgot how we got on to that. O yes, poets taking over scientific
discoveries, trying to incorporate the findings of their poems—what
a hash they usually made. I didn't bring up Goethe as an example
of the opposite because I don't think he really admires Goethe—
though he admired him more than he used to, finding him a bit
bookish I daresay—and he has been very nice about Goethe to me,
so much respecting my almost incessant admiration of Goethe. . . .

His taking to painting—for relaxation. 'But, my dear Bob, the
strain, the strain! It's so devilish exciting. And the discoveries one
makes! Quite ordinary, of course—any painter who knows his job
can put you up to the wheeze. But the thing is to discover them
for oneself. You can't imagine the lusciousness of putting on paint
. . . Well, one day I discovered that if you waited till your paint
was half-dry and then brushed it over—caressed it—with a dry
brush, you got the most marvellous effects—a bloom! My dear Bob,
I wouldn't have sold the excitement and the pleasure I had in
making that discovery for a million pounds. Incredible!' I really
think Aldous was more animated over this than I ever heard him
on any subject and, contrary to what people who don't know him
may well think, he can be very animated in conversation.

. . . Darling Aldous—the more I think of him the more perfect
he appears to me and the more I love him. And to think that I
once fancied I was and could be a greater writer than he. Benighted
and besotted idiot!

A good deal of Aldous's time in London then was taken up with
the business of Lawrence's letters, the rest he spent in libraries: he
had begun to ruminate an anthology of poetry with comments.
After the New Year they went back to Sanary for a quiet and
pleasantly industrious winter putting the idea on to paper—*Texts
and Pretexts*, the most serene perhaps of all his books. "A mixture
between an Oxford Book (tho' not very Oxonian in choice of
selections) and a book of essays. It's a pleasant thing to do and
should be quite agreeable, I think, to read . . . There's a great deal
of queer, good, interesting stuff in English poetry that never gets
into most anthologies . . ."

And what an appalling amount of bad stuff by even the best of
authors. "It's unbelievable what 80% of even Shelley is like. As for
Wordsworth, Browning, Spenser . . ."

Raymond Mortimer came to stay in February—"a charming
guest"—for the rest of the winter and early spring, Aldous and
Maria were by themselves, Aldous in good spirits, painting, working
hard. Aside from the anthology, he was thinking about his intro-

duction to D. H. Lawrence's letters—"a big job"—and re-reading his grandfather's life and works in preparation for the Huxley Memorial Lecture he had been asked to deliver. "He was really a very impressive figure . . . unquestionably the genuine article . . .

> Do you know the *Life and Letters* by my father? [Aldous wrote to Starkey] it's a good book. And the essays are first class and really astonishingly up-to-date. People try to make out that he was a dogmatical-materialistic old ass, who couldn't understand the finer shades. But it's not in the least true. He was quite as much aware of things as any of the Jeans-Eddington people. And how well he wrote! and what a heroic figure of a man! This century doesn't seem to breed them as the last did. But enough ancestor-worship!

Aldous could not really remember his grandfather who died ten months after his birth. T. H. Huxley's aura may have loomed more formidably over his childhood than it did over his brothers' who had known the private face of "the adorable 'Pater' ".[1]

*Brave New World* (published 2nd February) was extremely well received in England, selling 13,000 copies in the year and 10,000 the year after. It was not much liked in the United States, at first, pessimism and the guying of material bliss being still unacceptable at the time, and the sales were relatively minute. (Well under 3,000. The large, continuing, sales came later.)

Aldous's first American publisher was Doran. In 1927 the firm had amalgamated with Doubleday's. Aldous had weighed the pros and cons well—"are one's interests better looked after by an individual or a Ford factory?" and taken the line of least resistance. Now his Doubleday Doran contract was running out, nudged by Pinker, he was considering a change. This was talked about in London. Wheels turned within wheels. James Hamish Hamilton wrote by air mail to Eugene Saxton (then head of Harper & Brothers),

> Naomi [Royde-Smith, not Mitchison] the arch gossip says that Huxley is dissatisfied with Doubleday . . .

Harper's responded, so did other American publishers (Farrar & Rinehart are supposed to have been the main rival suitor). Cabled bids flew across the Atlantic, dealt with by Pinker in London while Aldous made up his mind in Sanary. Harper's terms were substantial. A three-year contract with a $21,000 guarantee to be paid

[1] Sir Julian Huxley, *Memories*, op. cit.

at the rate of $7,000 a year. But they were demanding six to seven books. These were presently reduced to five. Aldous's choice was influenced by his fondness for Eugene Saxton, who had been at Doran's in the early days. (The friendship began when they met —Aldous and Maria, Eugene and Martha Saxton—in New York in 1926 at the end of the Huxleys' journey round the world.) Pinker obtained some refinements in the Harper contract and it was signed on 9th February. (Seven years later Harper's were also able to take over the copyrights of all of Aldous's earlier books from Doubleday.)

By contrast the renewal of Chatto's agreement, due again that March, was by now a matter of course. (Incidentally, Aldous had fulfilled the last Three Year Plan almost *à la lettre*—one novel; one long story, novel-length by today's standard; plus three short ones; two volumes of essays and three miscellaneous slim volumes.) In commercial terms his books were doing well in England at the moment, better even than in the *Point Counter Point* year. It might be of interest to look at one complete account. Here are Aldous's gross earnings from books sold in the United Kingdom and the British Empire in the year ending 31st March 1932. (Ten per cent of these earnings went to Pinker, a good deal more to the Inland Revenue.)

|  | £ | s. | d. |
|---|---|---|---|
| MUSIC AT NIGHT | 481 | 17 | 6 |
| THE WORLD OF LIGHT | 77 | 15 | – |
| THE CICADAS | 113 | 5 | – |
| BRAVE NEW WORLD | 881 | 14 | – |
| 10,000 in 7/6 Ed. | | | |
| VULGARITY IN LITERATURE | 6 | – | – |
| BRIEF CANDLES | 8 | 6 | 3 |
| POINT COUNTER POINT | 86 | 5 | – |
| Phoenix Library Repr's | 360 | 18 | 6 |
| | £2,016 | 1 | 3 |

Chatto's present agreement, unchanged in terms of books (two novels plus three miscellany), raised the advance from £1,000 to £1,250 a year, and the initial royalty rate from 15% to 20%, and to 25% thereafter.

When Aldous had been long close to a piece of work, he liked to make a break by a few days' recreative motoring. This had all been very well in Italy, now he complained about the comparative paucity of art in Southern France. (Nîmes, Arles, Orange, he maintained, one should have seen before Italy, not after.) They decided on Cannes for the nonce. They drove off—it was mid-March—Aldous, Maria, a mutual friend, a very pretty blonde, and myself. Maria got us there, *porte à porte*, in two hours and fifteen minutes, or was it two hours and twenty-five? At any rate it was pretty good going. (How we all four fitted into the Bugatti, I can no longer say, except that our blonde friend was literally a light-weight.) During the drive Aldous appeared to be in a kind of speed-induced trance; only when we were coming down from the Esterel he began to point out landmarks and speak about the colours; when Maria hesitated about a turning, it was he who told her which way to take. This was most startling. One had learnt that when approaching Aldous one had to do what Roy Campbell had remembered and so exactly done, one had to make oneself known by voice. Maria had a quick way of identifying for him the person coming in, "Oh Eddy, there you are," "Oh Lewis, you're back already," —for Aldous was generally not able to distinguish a face on the other side of the room.

We put up at a comfortable and not fashionable hotel, very pleased by the Niagaras of bath-water (at Sanary one was always minding the level of one's cistern). In the evening Aldous and Maria went off to have dinner with H. G. Wells at his house near Grasse. It was to be their first meeting since the publication of the leg-pull, and Wells was supposed to have been very annoyed about the nature of Aldous's Utopia. (According to Gerald Heard, he wrote him a letter accusing him of "treason to science and defeatist pessimism"[1]; and Wells's old friend, Moura Budberg, used the identical word—in her deep, slow Russian voice—"H. G. was very cross, he said it was *defeatist*".) Aldous and Maria though went off cheerfully enough that evening and came back with nothing worse, as far as I remember, than a rather gossipy account of Wells's ménage. But to Harold Raymond[2] Aldous wrote a few days later,

> . . I'm glad the book still does so well. In Cannes we saw H. G. Wells who, I fear, wasn't best pleased with it.

Aldous enjoyed strolling along the Croisette, on the shop-side, peering into the windows, discoursing about women's clothes, economics, sex and fashions. One morning he spent at the aquarium at Monaco. We mainly ate Chez Oscar on the port of Cannes, a place that is no more, where the food was delicious. This was inconsistent. Aldous and Maria had a thing against good restaurants,

---

[1] Gerald Heard, "The Poignant Prophet", *The Kenyon Review*, 1965.
[2] Then head of Chatto & Windus.

grand restaurants they called them. Grand or granders was a word of theirs, granders might mean a first night or a white tie, "Is it going to be granders?" It had overtones of tolerant persiflage—grand friends were all right, even a grand party; grand restaurants were not. The expense, the disgustingly rich food . . . A liking for such indulgence really shocked the Huxleys. "He's the kind of man who likes grand restaurants," was near dismissal.

Later that spring Aldous and Maria went on a real journey. First to Brussels as they had been asked to dine with the King and Queen of the Belgians. Albert I, a man of diverse interests, had wished to meet Aldous and this was arranged through Maria's Uncle George Baltus. Aldous bought himself a pair of white kid gloves and they went off to the palace.

We dined en intimité [Aldous wrote to his father]; only Maria's Uncle . . ourselves, Willie de Grunne (who was at Balliol with Julian and Trev and is now the Queen's chamberlain) and a lady in waiting and A.D.C.

It went off "very pleasantly.

She [the Queen] is a really charming woman—a typical cultured idealistic Bavarian of the late 19th century generation, reminding me very much of Maria's aunts-by-marriage, the daughters of the sculptor Hildebrand. He is also sympathetic—a very thorough, rather ponderous mind, grinding exceedingly small and rather slowly. Curiously enough, speaking French with that typically royal German accent which distinguished royal English up to the times of Edward VII!

What really fascinated Aldous was that the palace "like all palaces,

was a bit mouldy in its splendour: actually moths flew out of the sofas when one sat down! A great difficulty was talking in the third person, which etiquette demands and which is directly cramping to conversation when one isn't used to it.

Etiquette equally demanded that one must never turn one's back upon the royal persons, leaving guests were required to vanish by walking backwards gracefully and straight to and through the doors. The King decided that Aldous should not be called upon to perform this feat and a compromise solution was arrived at. Their Majesties themselves got up at the appointed time and left their guests.

Raymond Mortimer joined Aldous and Maria in Belgium, and they went on to Germany together. They did some sightseeing at

Bamberg, Würzburg and Cassel, then to Berlin. I had gone there earlier and for about a week we coincided. Aldous was still full of the royal visit, the royal accent, the third person singular and the moths in the upholstery—he would beat the air thumping an imaginary sofa cushion. And the food had not been hot—the general way of palaces because of the great distance to the kitchens. On Germany he looked with a kind of aloof voyeurism: the gross-ness of the provincial crowds, the bulgy consumers of whipped cream in the cafés on the Kurfürstendam, the ubiquitous sign of the depression in the streets. It was, one must realize, less than a year before Hitler came to power. There *was* an ominous feeling about the country (I am sure this is not mere hindsight); in Berlin people appeared to be both restless and resigned, waiting for *any-thing* to happen, revolution from the extreme left or right, and in either case a cataclysmic breakdown of the social order. (Surely one of the reasons why Nazi rule became acceptable to the mass of the German people—impervious anyhow to the wickedness of what the Nazis said and did, and self-protectively ignorant—was because there was at first no apparent breakdown of the social order, which instead even seemed to have been saved.) Aldous and Maria met no educated Germans on that journey, they were tourists. For once they had come by train; I by car, and on the principle that any car was better than none, they submitted to be driven about in mine, a very old open Ford roadster. The radiator leaked so badly that it had to be topped up hourly from a tin. Worse: I was still on pocket money and could not afford to travel as I did; I had started from Sanary with a large drum of petrol (on tick—to be paid for on my coming of age) and this drum which had to be returned was now empty and rattled about in the dickey with unsuppressible din. This amused Aldous who chose to give me a hand with the water tin in front of the uniformed minions of the Eden Hotel. We drove to Potsdam, where Aldous did a minor verbal Taj Mahal on Sans Souci. Maria had bought a new Rolleiflex, I had a box Kodak, between us we took Aldous in front of the Old Residence, Aldous peering at a newspaper kiosk, Aldous skimming along the street in flapping overcoat and wide-brimmed hat, looking for all the world like Professor Picard. With Raymond we went to the Kaiser Friedrich Museum, to the Zoo, the opera (*Ballo in Maschera*); one evening we went to have a look at a large and glittering night club whose speciality was table telephones: middle-aged couples and a sprinkling of commercial blondes ringing each other up across the floor. The whole thing was of deadly vulgarity, a repulsive combination of facetiousness and lust—a Germanic Lyon's Corner House with the lid taken off and invaded by an infernal din of human shrieks and jazz. Aldous duly remarked how extraordinary it was and how depressing. (He did not venture again, this time, into the less orthodox regions of Berlin night-life.)

In June we were all back in Sanary (Aldous and Maria for a solid spell of time until December). Raymond had returned with them; Eddy West arrived from Knole; I, our house being shut down (my mother in a clinic, my step-father evaporated) was put up too. We made a quiet and, I think, extraordinarily happy house-party. Raymond, as Aldous has said, was a very charming guest, so was Eddy. Nothing much was happening. If we went out, it was for walks en famille and picnics. Eddy, who was working on a book, was given Matthew's room. (He was writing that remarkable, that very strange novel of his, *Simpson*, the story of an English nanny, which incidentally he finished eighteen months later, again in Sanary, in a house in the back country that belonged to D. H. Lawrence's friends the di Chiara's and was then inhabited by Eva Herrmann, the American artist, and myself.) Raymond and I fell into the routine of our industrious betters, he working on the material for a book on suicide he thought of writing, I hopefully filling notebooks. Maria loved Raymond and Eddy, and this made a circuit of affection; Aldous was very much at ease with them. He and Eddy talked music ("Eddy is a pianist nearly up to concert standards," Aldous would say with admiration); there was constant general talk about books and art. Aldous had the habit of airing subjects he was writing about in conversation. One remembers Ernest Hemingway's expressed dread of talking it out; Aldous did this with unconcern. Perhaps the passage *was* already on paper. Perhaps it was his way of working himself in. Aldous rarely talked about his work as such and so one often did not realize that he was quoting himself until months later when one saw in print an almost literal repetition of a passage heard. Now he would talk about Swinburne's peyotl trances and Shelley's dreamy vagueness in the words of the future *Texts and Pretexts*, and prequote with glee the lines of Coleridge that he regarded as the prime example of unsifted poetical rubbish.

> Why need I say, Louisa dear,
> How glad I am to see you here,
> A lovely convalescent;
> Risen from the bed of pain and fear
> And feverish heat incessant.

(Aldous still quoted Louisa Dear twenty-five years later in Holly-wood to Edith Sitwell.)

We were looked after breakfast, lunch and dinner. The delicious fried rabbit and zucchini flowers we took on picnics appeared and vanished without any of us lifting a finger. Beside Rina, there was Giulia, the cook, an Italian with an austere face and a fierce devotion to her masters (guests and friends were judged); and Camilla, a girl from a Tuscan village, more shy than sullen and of great good nature. Nothing, as I said, much happened. Suzanne's last word on her stay with Aldous and Maria in the 'Twenties was harmonious. *Harmonious*—looking back on it, I think of it as one of the happiest times of my life.

There was one event. A Sunday morning Raymond and I went on some errand into Bandol. We were strolling along the port in the sun. A bright little sports-car flashed past us with dotty speed, missed the turning and leapt into the sea. There it sat, stock-still and silenced in a flash, in twenty inches of water with the young man in his gay clothes at the wheel and the girl beside him in her dress laughing their heads off, waving at Raymond and me. It made his day, Raymond said. We told Aldous and Maria, they laughed with us and Maria said, "things like that *will* happen to Raymond".

Too soon we dispersed. The young men to England, I with the foolish or the enviable adventuresomeness of youth, to Istanbul.

Aldous sent off *Texts and Pretexts*, caught up with his reading, began and finished another play; painted. They built a small studio above the garage, white cube upon white cube, a structure of Moorish simplicity. Other guests stayed and went. They saw friends and new friends up and down the coast. Julian and Juliette, returning from an American tour, arrived on their first visit. The subject of the new play, *Now More Than Ever*, was high finance, with a Kreuger figure as the central character. This play was never produced, or published, and the typescript appears lost. (I read it at the time and retain an impression of it being rather exciting and without the ambiguities of *The World of Light*.) Aldous re-read *War and Peace*, "a great consolation and a tonic," and discovered Hermann Broch. He had already been impressed by Broch's earlier novel *The Unknown Quantity* (in the English translation); now *The Sleepwalkers* bowled him over. His face lit up when he spoke about it: *there* was a novel that had brought off complexity . . . I recall an image Aldous used—a skater seeing through the ice beneath him. To Martin Secker, who published Broch, he wrote,

. . I read the trilogy with steadily increasing admiration. It is the work of a mind of extraordinary power and depth, and at the same time of extraordinary subtlety and sensibility—of a philosopher who is also an artist of exceptional refinement and purity. It is a difficult book that makes great demands on the reader—nothing less than his whole mind at the highest pitch of attention . . .

The studio was finished. Flat-roofed it turned out to be stifling. Aldous painted nudes—one member of the household posing, another reading aloud. He was using gouache (I had brought Eva Herrmann from my travels, who became a great friend of the Huxleys and was experimenting with the medium then); Julian too was roped into the painting circle, Aldous persuaded him to try his hand at a still life he himself arranged. He so enjoyed doing things with Julian—the bond of affection, and shared interests between the brothers was visibly very great. In the Sanary summers a good many people came to lunch and dinner; once or twice a week Aldous and Maria dined out. Edith Wharton, Charles and Marie-Laure de Noailles, and Madame de Béhague of the Paris salon had houses at Hyères, where Paul Valéry and his wife and son spent the summer holidays. At St-Cyr were Meier-Graefe and his wife in their shaded *mas*; nearer home the Kislings at Bandol. Meier-Graefe was in his sixties, a man of vast presence (tall; a fine head; heavy beautiful hands), a life enhancer if ever there was one, a *viveur*, at the same time oddly delicate, moody, sharp, very difficult. Aldous had no more than heard of his main body of work (*Impressionism, Van Gogh*), but had read with some enthusiasm *The Spanish Journey* written in 1911 when Meier-Graefe had set out to praise Velasquez and stayed to discover El Greco. Meier-Graefe was a relentless worker; *his* hours were from dawn till about 4 p.m., sustained by fruit and pots of China tea, his output half a page a day. In winter he travelled, in summer he wrote. Unlike Aldous, to whom this would have been a shocking waste, his evening recreation was a game of bridge. One went to see the Meier-Graefes for tea or dinner out of doors on their terrace above a cypress alley. Bush, Meier-Graefe's wife, his third—she had eloped with him, running away from boarding-school—was very young, practically a girl, and already as competent as she had to be: driving the car, running the house hospitably, typing the books, managing at the same time to get on with her own painting and to be gay and giggly. Other eminent and elder men of letters were courting Bush and she always had a following as well of young and handsome men without literary pretensions. Meier-Graefe called her *Püppchen*, Poopers to Aldous. As the fates turned out, she eventually married one of the few contemporary writers, and the only one in the German language besides Kafka, whom Aldous admired, Hermann Broch. With the Kislings, Kiki and that force of nature Renée, there was not much contact. Aldous was not attracted by the robust sensuality of their style—those great feasts of garlic, fish and wine, the nights at *bals musettes*, the *couchages* that were not analysed in literary terms but blurted out—Aldous was bored, felt inadequate and withdrew behind polite French words. The Kislings shrugged off the Huxleys as bloodless intellectuals. Then one day Renée and Maria discovered their shared feeling for plants and cats, and Maria discovered Renée's Colette side, her exquisite perceptiveness of living things and the delicacy and humanity she was capable of. There sprang up between these two women an incongruous friendship (Renée Kisling looked like a splendid monster, a piece of archaic sculpture bedaubed in gaudy colours), a friendship all talk of gardens, offerings of fruit, sea-shells and scented herbs. But the bridge to Aldous was not flung.

It was at about that time that the Handleys too came into the Huxleys' lives. Len, Major Leonard Handley ex-Indian Army, and his wife Sally. The Handleys had been everywhere, tried their hand at anything. They had lived in Army stations, sailed with Chinese pirates, shot and filmed in the jungles of three continents, lectured to ladies' clubs in the U.S.A., got stranded in Panama. Wherever they went disaster overtook them. Lecture agencies failed, natives ran amok, elephants charged their cameras. They survived; just. They were always broke. Now they had taken a bungalow in Bandol with a view to mending their fortunes by writing. Len had already published one novel, *The Gay Sarong* (how that title entranced Aldous), Sally was working on scripts and lectures. She was in her twenties, blonde, willowy, very very pretty, chronically ailing and utterly intrepid. She was as disillusioned as the young women in the novels of Evelyn Waugh but without their vocabulary and sophistication and with a natural adherence to the morals and manners of the middle-class; hers was flat, non-cynical hopelessness camouflaged by a sense of humour that thrived in catastrophe, and she was one of the world's born story-tellers. Len looked kindly, loyal and conventional, and the first two he was. He adored Sally. They both wanted a child but their wanderings and strange luck were not conducive to completed pregnancies. (Happy to say, they eventually had a daughter.) Now the Handleys had taken a fancy to Aldous's work. They would walk over to La Gorguette, hang about the Villa Huley, babes in the wood that they essentially were, and stare at the gate. One day they were pulled in by Maria. Scheherazade began her tales, the looks did the rest, they were asked again. Soon they were friends. But there was something else—Sally was a Jonah. The well-serviced car that gave her a lift shed a wheel, the ships she sailed in sank, houses caught fire; it was no joke (I, too, came as near disaster as I'd ever care to on a little outing with Sally). The first time the Handleys asked Aldous and Maria to dinner, they had hardly sat down when a woman burst upon them meat-chopper in hand. She meant business. Maria and Sally protected Aldous while Len managed to disarm the woman which was not easy as her strength proved great—she was the femme de ménage who had turned murderous lunatic without warning. After gendarmes and ambulance had borne her away, they all went into the kitchen, very hungry now, and Sally set to retrieving a little supper over a spirit lamp. The spirit lamp upset. Oh yes, they managed to put it out, it was not really a big fire. Maria went home thoughtful.

It was one of the points about Sanary that so many people of wildly different ways of life were there at the same time. Painters had come since the turn of the century; later it was painters and writers, then more writers, some eminent, some beginners. Their language varied and their incomes and tastes. Some wrote more than others. Thomas Mann had lived in Sanary, and Brian Howard. They came by way of friends, through chains of circumstances. Katherine Mansfield's 1914-war winters led to Lawrence, led to the Huxleys, led to the Huxleys' friends. Sooner or later everybody met, *this* was the point: Sanary was no city—one newspaper kiosk, one post office, one paint-shop, two chemists, three cafés.

In these early 1930s there were two new literary ménages, one Anglo-American, one all American, the Connollys and the Seabrooks. Young Cyril, not yet thirty, before *Enemies of Promise*, before *The Rock Pool*, reviewing books (not every week) for the *New Statesman*, "with a book unfinished, beginning a second,"[1] and Jean, younger still—eighteen? nineteen?—with that slow erotic charm, talented, witty in her own right, but wilful, lazy, prone to discontents, self-destructive. There they were in that wind-battered house on the sea road east of Sanary in that time that is gone forever with their ferrets, "the English Rose . . . who saw three continents from a warm sleeve,"[1] and the lemur, "living for beauty—

> October on the Mediterranean, blue skies scoured by the mistral, red and golden vine branches, wind-fretted waves chopping round the empty yachts; plane-trees peeling; palms rearing up their dingy underlinen; mud in the streets, and from doorways at night the smell of burning oil. On dark evenings I used to bicycle in to fetch our dinner, past the harbour with its bobbing launches and the bright cafés with their signs banging; at the local restaurant there would be one or two "plats à emporter", to which I would add some wine, sausage and Gruyère cheese . . . then I would bowl back heavy-laden with the mistral behind me, a lemur buttoned up inside my jacket with his head sticking out. Up the steep drive it was easy to be blown off into the rosemary, then dinner would be spoilt. We ate with our fingers beside the fire,—true beauty lovers. . . .[1]

---

[1] *The Unquiet Grave*, Cyril Connolly, 1945.

The Seabrooks, Willie and his wife, Marjorie Worthington the novelist—a stiff, gentle woman with a soft voice and an unhappy face, were in their early middle-age; he on the affluent wave of international best-sellers, *Jungleways*, *Magic Island*, travellers' tales of his ventures into primitive societies, a man in the clutches of self-doubt and success. They were camping—with chauffeur, gardener, cook—in a barrack of a house on La Gorguette, high rooms dark with heavy furniture, the oppressive gloom of which they had reinforced with knives, masks and pieces of barbaric sculpture. Seabrook was a very strange man indeed (the rough diamond with the soft centre on the more obvious level) beset with inner problems. Like Jean Connolly, he bore the marks of American Prohibition. His great thing at the time was his exploits among the savage islanders. He would boast of having boasted to Parisian hostesses: "Reprenez donc un peu de rôti de veau, Monsieur Seabrook?" "Ah Madame, si vous aviez goûté la chaire humaine . . ." Yet he could feel very sorry for himself. He would lament his lack of intellectual and literary refinement, he was a craftsman, he would say, a cobbler, and he wanted to write like Tolstoy and like Aldous Huxley. Here his admiration was unrancorous and uncritical. "Mon illustre voisin," he would say to local tradesmen for the fun of it, "mon illustre voisin," in his very American French, "Aldóuss Usseley."

The neighbours became friends. Marjorie Worthington was an endearing creature once one got through her cloud of shyness, and there was something touching also about Seabrook, or a side of Seabrook. A number of disagreeable and sensational stories were going round about his sexual savageries, yet he never hinted at these practices to the Huxleys, and when dispensing hospitality to Aldous and other writers he could be meek with an *empressement* that was positively genteel. (Only once he made a very rum remark indeed to Maria in front of the gorilla cage he kept in the studio he had on the port of Toulon.) One consequence of the Seabrook-Huxley friendship was that Rina became engaged to the Seabrooks' young chauffeur, Emilio, a glib Italian.

The Seabrooks, the Handleys; not the Connollys. Between Aldous and Cyril nothing flowered then (their rapport came; but that was many years later). Why? Who else was there in Sanary at the time who could be called to anything like the same extent Aldous's peer? Cyril when he first came loved Aldous (these are his own words); had indeed come to live in Sanary to be near him; yet the response fell short even of the Huxleys' usual curiosity and kindness. Fan for fan, was Aldous not sensitive to the qualitative difference of Cyril's admiration? Not struck by his erudition, conversation, talent? Struck, yes. Not greatly interested, perhaps. What attracted Aldous then was the unfamiliar and bizarre—Willie Seabrook, Len and Sally were *terra incognita*; Cyril had gone through his own mill, College at Eton, Balliol. Cyril may have reminded him of the attitudes of his younger self which he was beginning to wish to slough off, aestheticism, pure art, the love of words; at thirty-eight Aldous at heart was no longer the literary dandy who had captivated Cyril's generation. Yet this cannot have been the whole story. Aldous still enjoyed, for instance, Raymond Mortimer's company. I rather think that the crux here was Maria and that it goes to show how much Aldous let himself be directed by her. When she did not choose to build his bridges, he was quite content to remain cut off. Now, Jean Connolly disliked Maria, who made her feel that she could never put a foot right. When she and Cyril dropped in they would be intercepted: *"Aldous is working."* Years after Jean still spoke of the watchdog with bitterness. In fact Maria *was* on her guard; Sally might threaten Aldous's life and limb, the Connollys were out for his time. Maria was also prejudiced. Neither she nor Aldous approved of their style of life; they did not see it as romantic or delicious. Eating your dinner with your fingers reading before the fire meant leaving grape skins and the skeletons of sardines between the pages. The ferrets stank; the lemur hopped upon the table and curled his exquisite little black hand around your brandy glass. Your *brandy glass*—exactly: liqueurs after luncheon. The Connollys did like grand restaurants. *And* they would not descend to any disguising of their tastes. People, as I have said, tempered their behaviour to the Huxleys' standards; the Connollys were more irrepressible and to Jean it would not have occurred to make friends on anything but her own terms. Maria would forgive you anything as long as you deferred implicitly to Aldous.

What matters, rather sadly, is that this casual coolness of the Huxleys amounted then for Cyril as rejection. It affected his own work. (He has written about his feeling of paralysis at Sanary by the thought of Aldous drumming away on his typewriter across the bay. He felt—again his printed words—a kind of mental poor relation.) And yet it was a fortuitous shutting out, a lapse in awareness—those elders, Aldous and Maria, too, were young still—it might not have been impossible to have broken through by some intuition or right word.

Autumn by the Mediterranean—reflections on the state of the world. To Naomi Mitchison, politically active (on the left) who sometimes challenged him, Aldous wrote à propos of the Scottsboro case, "It's terrifying what can be done by people who have the· monopoly of means of propaganda—private money grubbers in the U.S.A., Musso and Co in Italy, Communist party in U.S.S.R...

Yes, I perfectly believe that a lot of people are happy in Russia—because happiness . . is a by-product of something else and they've got a Cause . . . the working for which gives them happiness . . but it is always as history demonstrates, in the nature of a temporary intoxication . . . In Russia where propaganda is more efficient, it may last a bit longer . . . The next remedy is love, for an individual or for one's neighbours in general. This is the most powerful antidote against the misery of individual existence . . .

Well, well—it is all very obscure and distressing. [These are fragments from a very long letter] I wish I could even see clear into the economic problem. This system is bad, and on a large scale, seems not to work. But at the same time without some private property, what is to become of individual liberty? Private property is the only guarantee possessed by individuals against the tyranny of the State (and let us remember that the State is not an abstraction, but just Jones and Brown invested with power). Proudhon insisted on a limited amount of private property—and I think he was quite right. The difficulty arises in determining where the limits are to be placed. What a world!

In September the first edition of the letters of D. H. Lawrence, with Aldous's long preface, was published by Heinemann. The letters were a tremendous lot, as Aldous had written to Brett the year before:

> The early ones are particularly interesting and delightful—such high spirit: which he lost as he grew older and iller. The horror of that creeping disease! I am cutting out feeling—hurting passages, uninteresting bits and things which are repeated in several letters to different people. . . tho' it's often worth keeping repetitions because of the subtle variations . . .

For the rest, Aldous had kept editorial notes and comments to the minimum. The book did well. "Which I'm glad of for Frieda's . . sake:

> tho' the stupid woman is embarking on enormously expensive legal proceedings against L's brother now—quite unnecessarily in my opinion . . Her diplomatic methods consist in calling everyone a liar, a swine and a lousy swindler, and then in the next letter being charming . . Since L is no longer there to keep her in order, she plunges about in the most hopeless way. I like her very much; but she's in many ways quite impossible. She was only possible for someone who happened to be in love with her and married to her—and not only in love and married but, as Lawrence was, in some strange

way dependent, on her presence, physically dependent, as one is dependent on the liver in one's belly . . . I have seen him on two occasions rise from what I thought was his death-bed, when Frieda, who had been away, came back after a short absence. The mysteries of human relationships are impenetrable.

Matthew, aged twelve and a half, was moved to a new school, the Elmhirsts' Dartington in Devonshire, "an experiment which may, I think, turn out to be something very remarkable". As for the boy,

> Mentally he is the image of M's family—quick, with a remarkable intuitive power for grasping the essentials of a situation, a natural gift for living; but with a quite unusual incapacity to grasp and apply general principles . . . He is just the opposite of me; for he knows how to deal with people, but not with abstract ideas.

Joep and Suzanne came to stay for October. The weather was sparkling, they enjoyed a month of long walks and hard work. Joep did landscapes and portraits of Aldous and Maria (since destroyed by fire); Suzanne did the fine bust of Aldous, later cast in bronze; Aldous was inspired to paint a good many gouaches. He had begun to meditate his next novel. There were misgivings even then. He found it difficult to get under way, but hoped that one day the thing might flow.

> If it does start flowing [to Eugene Saxton in November] it might well be finished by the end of next summer.
> But this is all very uncertain and I shan't be able to say anything definite for another few months. If it didn't come satisfactorily, I shd ask Harper's to suspend all payments until such time as I was able to cope with the thing—abandoning myself to journalism while the novel ripened: for I know by bitter experience that I can't force myself to write anything that isn't ripe. I hope this won't happen: but if it should, well, then I'll ask Pinkers to make the necessary business arrangements to suit the situation. Meanwhile, I am just accumulating notes and writing experimental pages.

In December Aldous and Maria briefly went to London planning to be back for Christmas. But Matthew went down with influenza and they had to hang about. They were able to leave in time to reach Sanary for a small New Year's Eve celebration, dinner at the house with Charles and Marie-Laure de Noailles, my mother (temporarily restored to health) and me. We wore versions of evening dress and the character of the party—the Huxleys having announced their plan of leaving again almost at once on a long voyage, their second *tour du monde*, Rina called it—was festive and valedictory. Matthew had improvised decorations, a toy railway circuit on the dinner-table: you flicked a switch and a carriage laden with salted almonds, fruit or sweets came to a halt before your plate; it worked precisely and was a great success. After midnight Maria went into the kitchen and made some hard-boiled eggs which we ate then and there. This struck Madame de Noailles as an exotic lark. She would never dare, she told Maria, to put a foot into her own kitchen.

## Chapter Four
## Beyond the Mexique Bay

THE novel would not flow, Aldous abandoned himself to travel.
He and Maria sailed from Liverpool in January on the cruise
ship *Britannic* for the West Indies. They called at Barbados,
Trinidad, Caracas, changed ship at Jamaica and continued to
British Honduras and Guatemala. They went up to Quirigua, flew
to Copan, in the second plane ever to land there, and saw the
Maya ruins (their course is pretty well covered in Aldous's published travel journal). In March they were in Guatemala City;
there, at dinner with the Finnish Consul who happened to be an
English poet, they met Roy Fenton, the Consul's younger brother.
The meeting transformed their journey. Roy Fenton talked about
his coffee plantation on the slopes of the Pacific; Aldous, nostal-
gically, platonically, talked of the unattainable, of primitive
Mexico, wild Mexico, the country of *The Plumed Serpent*. On an
impulse Fenton said to him: Come with me and I will take you
there. It was both a friendly offer and a dare. What Fenton was
proposing was the overland journey to Oaxaca, the extremely
tough ride over the Sierra Juarez. Aldous said yes.

I found Aldous—charming. I found him—well— very open-minded.
[This is Roy Fenton speaking. Now; after these forty years]. In fact,
quite different from what I had expected from reading his books.
His attitude seemed to me quite humble at times. There was no
side. Yet one felt—from little things that peaked out from his mind,
that came out in conversation—that all the time he was exploring—
it was as if he were looking for something. How shall I put it? He
seemed to be looking for an experience.

It was Fenton who got cold feet. After another good look at
Aldous and Maria. He warned them. He made his conditions.
(Mexico was a rough place, a rough place struggling through rough
times. A man looking after his estate was very much a rule unto
himself, leading his men, going about armed, relying on his skills.)
Aldous and Maria would have to go into training. Fenton asked
them to come up to his *finca*, Progreso, for a couple of weeks of
riding and general toughening up. The three of them set out from
Guatemala City. Six or seven sweltering hours in the train to
Retalhuleu, transfer to a small Ford bus for the last twenty miles
to the coast. At last "we were in a street of decrepit shanties; there

were children in the dust and wandering pigs. Then, suddenly, vast and blank under the glaring white sky, the Pacific . . . Far out, a steamer lay at anchor . . . The air was as hot as fly-paper. A sentry in khaki, with bare feet and a two-foot bayonet at the end of his rifle, ushered us into a room, where a young *mestizo*, extenuated with heat and malaria and the unspeakable boredom of life at Champerico, very slowly did what was necessary to our papers . . .

"We walked out to the end of the jetty. There, twenty feet below us, a boat was wallowing among the rollers. One at a time, in an apparatus like a ducking stool, we were swung out into space and lowered towards the waves. When the boat heaved up within jumping distance, one jumped. A quarter of an hour later we were safely on board the steamer that was to take us up the Mexican coast."[1]

They landed in a rocky bay without a jetty. A whale boat took them from the ship to fifty yards off shore, at which point they and luggage transferred into a hollowed tree trunk, a kind of flat-bottomed canoe, like a coffin. Aldous described the process without turning a hair.

> You squat, cautiously balancing your weight; the coffin shoots forward on a wave and runs aground; then you wait till the retiring Pacific has left the sand relatively dry, and make a dash for it.[1]

In point of fact, according to Roy Fenton, Aldous had trouble landing. Presently a car took them as far as it could go. They reached Pochutla, one of those heart-breaking Mexican villages—the huge blazing plaza, the two or three Indian women squatting in the dust with half a dozen scrofulous tomatoes arranged before them in a pattern or some gory bits of meat in a cloud of flies, the bandstand and the painted church with the crumbling façade . . . They moved on. Another half-hour brought them to the end of the carriage road. Mules were waiting. At the house of the local bandit they got into gaiters and buckled on those enormous Mexican spurs. A bridle-path led them into the uplands. At first they travelled through a zone of *tierra blanca*, intolerably glaring slopes of white earth under a ferocious sun. Roy and Maria rode in front, talking; Aldous trailed behind. With his long legs, he was having difficulty in keeping on the mule. His feet were only a few inches from the ground and his spurs quite useless. Gaining altitude they came to a wood of low oak trees. "We were passing under very small stunted gnarled little trees [Roy talking[2]] in a white incandescent landscape that made Aldous screw up his eyes, and he looked

---

[1] *Beyond the Mexique Bay.* Chatto & Windus, 1934.
[2] Roy Fenton, talking to S. B. in 1968, '69, '71 and '72.

through a little telescope thing in his hand, a tiny telescope, which brought distance close up at the risk of not seeing the branches that were hanging in front of him."

He was still forty yards behind the others; Maria was still talking. "I found her an oddly contradictory character. At times I thought she was extremely solicitous for his comfort, and his welfare —*and yet!* At times a little bit inclined to be haphazard."[1]

Suddenly there was a great yell behind them and an OUCH! They turned to find the mule walking on and Aldous sitting on the ground.

He remounted. They climbed on. And then, almost suddenly they "were in perpetual summer. The mountain side was dark green with coffee bushes, and above the bushes rose tall trees, the larger of them survivors from the original forest . . . We were already on Roy's territory . . but the coffee *fincas* in these mountains are like small kingdoms . . ."[2] they were still more than an hour's ride from the metropolis of the estate, Progreso.

They found a comfortable house on a terrace at the head of a valley. The view was the stupendous one of those latitudes. The mornings were bright summer, the nights cool, the evenings perfect. Here Aldous and Maria rested for some weeks.

It was a place of seclusion and domestic bustle, of great natural beauty and of peace. Peace, in spite of the bandits and the revolutionaries roaming without, in spite of the flaring knife fights among the Indian hands. "The memory of Progreso has the romance and the peace almost of an hermitage; till I suddenly remember how we laughed and then I laugh again in memory of it. The parrot, the animals around the beds, and the dogs and the donkey . . ." So Maria later wrote to Roy. At once there had been a *rapport* between the three. Roy was still under thirty, strong, very handsome, very male; there was a man of action, who could cope with practical living, with danger, who was also kindly, thoughtful, who had read, who could talk; a complex man, one would guess —and a very unusual combination among Aldous's friends. No wonder that he was drawn to their generous host.

During the day Aldous and Maria pottered about on their own, watching the wheels of the estate go round, the *mozos* pruning the coffee trees with flashing blades, the women slapping their washing against the stones. In the afternoon Roy took them riding—"mule rides in the paradise of shade trees", in Maria's memory. And in Aldous's:

Towards evening, when the day had cooled off . . we would walk or ride among the *cafetales*. Our favourite path followed a level con-

---

[1] Roy Fenton talking.    [2] Aldous, op. cit.

tour line round the flank of the extinct volcano that dominated the estate, winding out on to projecting bastions and round again into the valleys indented in the mountainside. One walked through an undergrowth of dark and glittering coffee bushes, and out of the undergrowth sprang great trees, each tree a column standing isolated from all the other columns and visible, in this uncrowded forest, from its base among the coffee to its high green ceiling of spreading branches and leaves. It was the jungle, but domesticated; a vast essay in tropical landscape gardening, richly, romantically beautiful. I thought all the time of that passage in the Fourth Book of *Paradise Lost* . .

> *So on he fares, and to the border comes*
> *Of Eden, where delicious Paradise,*
> *Now nearer, crowns with her enclosure green,*
> *As with a rural mound, the champaign head*
> *Of a steep wilderness . . .*

At night the men talked. "Aldous had very strong views about certain things. [Roy speaking] But he didn't try to force them on you. He would simply give them as a factual thing that he felt very strongly. And at that time, it was in 1933, I felt, I knew, there was a deep worry behind his thinking . . . Of the future, of what the world was going to come to . . . The advent of Hitler and the Nazis. And that was *there behind a lot of his thinking*. He came back and back to it. In the most extraordinary contexts. We were discussing Mexican mythology, and the Spanish Conquest—Aldous was trying to look at some analogy with the present time. While I felt you couldn't equate the two civilizations at all. There was a barbaric element in the Aztec thing which fascinated Aldous. This queer cruel cult . . . He was all the time trying to find a way of seeing WHY they had evolved this philosophy of having to appease the sun by slaughtering so many people; not out of vengeance, not in anger, but because they felt they *must* appease the sun . . ."

Roy knew what they would have to face on their coming journey. "I was rather worried. Though I had been very surprised on occasions to find how tough both of them could be when it came down to physical discomfort. But we were going to pass through country in which there was absolutely *nothing*. Nothing between us and the place we were going to." Meaning no water? "We would be travelling for the best part of fourteen, fifteen, sixteen hours a day over country with NO water, NO shade, NO people."

In *Texts and Pretexts* the year before Aldous had written (having evoked Rimbaud)

. . There are hours and days, there are even whole epochs in the life of every human being . . when rest is the last thing of which soul and body feel a need; when all desire tends quiveringly towards a strenuous and exciting heaven.

The great morning came. They left in darkness. At 3 a.m. Roy, Aldous and Maria with two *Indios* on baggage mules.

. . Dark with a double night; for our road lay under trees, [Aldous distilled it in *Beyond the Mexique Bay*, in *Eyeless in Gaza*] and the black vault of foliage shut out the stars . . but the mules picked their way securely up and down the headlong windings of the track . . .

The air was deliciously fresh against the face and sometimes, in the darkness, one would ride through the perfumed aura of an invisible lemon tree . . . the scent . . was like the brief and inenarrable revelation of something more than earthly—a moment's ecstasy, and then, as the mules advanced, hoof after hoof, up the stony path, the fading of the supernatural presence, the return to a common life symbolically represented by the smell of leather and sweat.

The path climbed. When two hours later the sun rose they found themselves on an upland of bare rocks. Roy addressed them: "Now, we've got to 6,000 feet, and we have to descend into the valley of the Copalita river, which will bring us down again to about 1,800." They descended, slowly, very slowly, the most sheer steep slope of the Copalita range. Again, Aldous might be knocked off his mule at any moment by overhanging branches which he failed to see. They reached the valley by 8 a.m.—having covered only ten miles in five hours—and forded the river in the blistering sunshine. They dismounted and ate. Then the real business of the day began. Their goal, the goal they *had* to make before nightfall was San Pedro el Alto, the first inhabited place on their route. "I said to Maria, 'I'm afraid now comes the really tough part, we are now going to climb over the most vast bald empty mountain range, the wildest emptiest country on earth. And we shall have to be up to 12,000 feet before six o'clock this afternoon.' And this was about half-past eight in the morning."

The heat was tremendous.

. . The main range of the sierra was now before us; ridge above ridge . . . There was no shade, and the vast bald hills were the colour of dust and burnt grass . . . For five more hours we climbed uninterruptedly up one of the steepest paths I have ever seen. It was one of those vast chaotic landscapes that look as though they might go on for ever—a great desert of nonenity, endlessly not there, and empty, quite lifeless . . .[1]

[1] From *Beyond the Mexique Bay*, 1934, and *Eyeless in Gaza*, 1936. See Author's Note regarding quotations and sources.

Up and up they went.

> .. The sweat .. poured like water off [one's] face and soaked through shirt and cotton breeches . . . [one] could scarcely think or even see. The landscape seemed to advance and retreat before [one's] eyes, turned black and sometimes faded away altogether . . .[1]

"They kept on. [Roy speaking] They kept on; they never complained, they just kept on.

"And then we had a sudden relief—little donkeys appeared with the striped mail bags of the Mexican Federal Administration, carrying the mail from Oaxaca to the coast." [Roy speaking; now Aldous:]

> We drew aside respectfully .. Their long ears flapping at every stride, their slender feet twinkling in small precise movements among the stones, the little asses stepped delicately by, one by one, each under an enormous burden of red, white and green mail bags.

"And the two chaps [Roy again] who were shepherding them shouted Burr-rro! with that rumbling roll that keeps donkeys moving along the Mexican roads and ranges; and Aldous watched this and he took it up and got the greatest joy out of trying to roll his rr's as magnificently as the Mexicans. He shouted Burr-rro! The tremendous enjoyment he got out of that."

After fourteen hours in the saddle they reached San Pedro el Alto, a tiny village at the very top of the sierra, built on a knife's edge between two gulfs. The light was starting to go. It was still hot but the heat was a kind of veneer over an essential core of mountain cold. "And we got off our mules, extremely stiff so that you could hardly walk, extremely thirsty. Maria, poor girl, having a fearful battle with migraine. A terrible attack. We got the only shelter we could get, a store-room belonging to the village shop-keeper. It was extraordinarily clean, for what it could have been. We put down our blankets and things as best we could, and wrapped ourselves in every bit of wool we had brought. We asked the shopkeeper to let us have some supper. It took a bit of time coming. Meanwhile Maria lay down; Aldous and I went out for a stroll."

> .. The tiny plaza was like the deck of a ship, a flat space, thirty or forty yards from gunwale to gunwale, and on each side a drop; in the distance the mountains rolled away, crest after crest, like waves.
>
> Towards sunset, the boys of the village came out to play a kind

<hr>

[1] Ibid.

of football in the plaza—deck football; if you kicked too hard the ball flew over the edge and you had to scramble down a couple of hundred feet to find it. In the last, almost level light, the scene was curiously moving—had an intensity, somehow, the more-than-reality of a work of art. It was partly, I suppose, because there was no background. We were on a little platform at the top of every-thing, with only the sky all around us. Every figure stood out clear and rather flat in strangely significant isolation, against the pale bright vacancy. A donkey, tethered to a post and compact, self-contained, like Sancho Panza's ass in one of the Daumier paintings of *Don Quixote*; men passing, their heads stuck through the slits of their exiguous blankets, hunched and hugging themselves against the increasing cold; and in the centre of the narrow space the boys playing, brilliant in their white trousers and gaily coloured shirts, shining as though transfigured by the supernatural light of evening.[1]

All at once it was piercingly cold. They went back to their quarters. Supper was hot and remarkably good. The shopkeeper lingered to talk. Had they come far? Very far; from Europe. Yes, he knew about Europe . . . What chiefly interested him was the cost of the journey. "I gave him the figures—somewhat diminished, I confess . . partly from a certain sense of shame. Our host was doubtless one of the richest men in the village; but his whole annual income would probably not have bought a single first-class ticket across the Atlantic. He listened carefully: then, after a pause, 'I can't understand,' he said at last, 'why you should want to *gastar su capital* on coming to San Pedro'."[1]

Their beds were three wooden planks in the large freezing room. On these they slept quite soundly.

Next morning they washed in turns in a little basin outside on the stone parapet. They set off for another day's descending, climbing, descending, but the extreme desolation lay behind them. There were pinewoods, once or twice a stray dog slunk past. Aldous promptly ripped out, Perr-rro! That night they stopped at Ejutla, in relative civilization. They put up at the inn, found beds and bed-bugs. Before dinner Roy and Aldous went down to the bar. This was a crypt-like room with a sagging vaulted ceiling propped by thick wooden pillars. They sat down at a small table and ordered some beer. Leaning against the bar stood a smartly dressed young Mexican in riding-breeches drinking mezcal and boasting in a tipsy voice about the alligators he had been shooting in the swamps. Presently he turned, took in the foreign gentlemen and, with the slow formality of the drunk, asked them what they would have. Roy ignored him; the young man insisted. Aldous

---

[1] *Beyond the Mexique Bay.*

attempted some polite refusal in Spanish. The young man chose to take offence. He staggered forward, "*Ustedes me desprecian*". He crashed into their table and sent the drinks flying. His hand went to his belt. "Look out!" Roy yelled at Aldous, "get out of this, for God's sake!" Aldous, who was nearest to the man, jumped up and got himself behind one of the pillars. The young man fumbled out his revolver and waved it wildly. The proprietress screamed. The young man began to stalk Aldous. Aldous darted from behind his pillar and ducked behind the next one. It was a long moment. A shot went off as someone crashed a chair on the drunk man's arm —the bullet did not hit anyone and the man was quickly overpowered.

Next day there was a half day's ride to Ocotlàn from where they were able to take a train to Oaxaca. The adventure was over.

In *Beyond the Mexique Bay*, a few months later, Aldous wrote a fairly extensive account of those days. Curiously, the incident at Ejutla was entirely omitted. "It had been a damned unpleasant experience," Roy said; "and I wrote him twice after the book was published to ask him why." Aldous did not answer.

At Oaxaca they saw the archaeological ruins of Mitla and Monte Alban, then went north to Puebla and Mexico City. They looked at pyramids and ruins, met politicos and diplomatists and "a lot of literary gents—some charming and most intelligent," who gave Aldous a banquet. A Mexican gentleman sent in his card one morning, a Señor Eduardo Huxley, who wanted to know if he were a relation. Aldous decided that he was. "His grandfather, whose photo he showed me (taken in Ealing . . a man with . . a nose which 'seemed to me rather of the family type) was called Dr Edward Huxley . . born . . in 1825. His son, George Spooner Huxley, came to Mexico, married a Mexican, produced a family . . One brother, whose name I saw in the birthday book, was called Jesus Huxley! (Grand Pater wd have liked that, I think.)"

As usual, Aldous was describing it all in one of his travelogues to his father. He had been remiss on this journey, had not written for more than a month, not since they had left with Roy from Guatemala. Now, 29th April, he was making up for it, writing on board ship—"glad to be on the homeward road"—on their way to New York. His father never saw that letter. Leonard Huxley died of a heart attack on 3rd May 1933. The news awaited Aldous in New York. He and Maria returned by ship to England.

## Chapter Five

## 1933

"THIS is our permanent address and en plus—I hope it will be our address for a long time," Maria wrote from Sanary to Roy Fenton. "It is such a joy to be home. But Europe *is* in a mess." They had found Sanary, on their return in June, full of German writers at their first stage of exile. ". . so we cannot escape from that Barbarous German news. And France's great wall is terminated and she can now only be attacked through Switzerland . . . The dollar goes down the price of life goes up.

I am not sure that on the whole the wilds of Mexico and Mexican coffee plantations are not the best to live in at the moment where other problems are more vital than politics. . . . I . . think of the dark bushes the shade trees and the ravines—how lovely it all was —but very much a dream!

Aldous, still anxious to stave off his novel, was going on with the Central American book, "the travel book we both long for" (but his publishers, shaken by the slump, felt gloomy about the prospects of a subject book).

I am writing about our travels—that is, about everything from politics . . to art [Aldous to Naomi Mitchison] Tell Dick[1] to study the history of the five Central American republics. They illustrate very clearly the modern fallacy of supposing economics to be at the bottom of everything. In C A there were no economics, only evil passions . . . I was re-reading Wordsworth's account of his visit to France during the Revolution . . .

*The land all swarmed with passion, like a plain*
*Devoured by locusts. . .*

Which is exactly Europe in '33—the awful sense of invisible vermin of hate, envy, anger crawling about . . .

Yes, you may say by all means that I am not becoming a carthlick . . . I have never more passionately felt the need of using reason jusqu'au bout . . .

Do you think I am kind and unpossessive? Quien sabe? Perhaps I am only a person of rather delicate constitution who likes a quiet

[1] Lord Mitchison.

life. How senseless psychological judgements really are apart from physiological judgements! And of course I am also to a considerable extent a function of defective eyesight. Keratitis punctata shaped and shapes me . . .

Aldous snatched time for painting. "Like mad. Really it is an ideal art . . . (when one thinks of the horror of using a pen or a typewriter!)

I long, when I have reached a certain level of competence, to launch out on something more ambitious. It is deplorable that only bad painters shd now undertake important and intrinsically significant subjects and that good ones should live in terror of all that is obviously beautiful, or dramatic, or sublime.

It was a hot summer with a large crop of grapes and figs. The children had arrived, and strings of visitors. Maria watered her jacaranda trees, 5 inches high, grown from seed she had brought from Mexico. The house was full of their Central American trophies; Roy sent them sacks of coffee beans and a crocodile skin which Matthew unpacked on the station platform. The rubber boat leaked, Gene Saxton from New York—endlessly kind—arranged repair. The newest import from the U.S.A. was the Hay Diet, starch *or* protein at any one meal, faithfully imposed by Maria. So it was toast and rolls for breakfast one morning, two plain boiled eggs and no bread at all the next; a mound of spaghetti for dinner or bare roast beef. Rina married her Emilio, a rash young marriage; the Huxleys gave her the two John Collier portraits as a wedding present.

What with the economic slump and Rina's living out, Maria decided to manage the house with part-time help, and cook dinner herself. As their dining-room was upstairs and the kitchen in the basement, this entailed some not inexpensive alterations, turning the present kitchen into a dining-room and an adjacent verandah into a kitchen. They also switched from coal to the new bottled gas, and put a geyser in the bathroom. The new cooking verandah was long and narrow like a passage, as well as exposed to sun and cold.

. . I hope that the net result of all the changes [Aldous to Julian] will be that we can run the house more cheaply. At the present rate of exchange it costs a lot; but I hope that the French will find themselves forced off their perch of gold . . .

The Huxleys did not take much to the German refugees. "Rather a dismal crew," Aldous wrote to Julian, "already showing the disastrous effects of exile. Let us hope we shall not have to scuttle when Tom Mosley gets into power.''

One may find this callous; perhaps it was only candid. Those literary refugees were indeed the victims of barbarous events, forerunners of catastrophe; they were also our neighbours. They were men and women in a very unhappy situation, coping with the sudden and entire disruption of their lives: they had lost their homes, their language, their possessions (which in many cases meant their libraries); they had left friends and relatives in Germany who might be in danger and in concentration camps. Some of them, Jews and men of the political left, had escaped because they had to; others had *chosen* to go, or not to return, to Germany for moral reasons. (Thomas Mann, for one, and Meier-Graefe.) At the same time this particular wave of refugees was in an exceptionally privileged position—unlike the thousands, the millions, of fugitives to come, they were not hounded (for the time being) and they were not destitute. They had been unable to bring any money but they went on earning an adequate if diminished living from their translation rights, being well-known enough to have a sizeable English reading public. And, again by reason of their eminence, they were safe from the refugee's acutest anguish—papers. To be sure, they *were* beset by the recurrent problems of passport, visa, residence permit; but the problem got solved or shelved, often at the last minute, by Mrs Roosevelt or a Hollywood studio or (later on) by the popular front government in France.

The roll-call was impressive. The Thomas Manns, Lion Feuchtwanger, Franz Werfel with his wife, Alma Mahler Werfel, Bruno Frank and René Schickele had taken villas in Sanary; Heinrich Mann was at the hotel in Bandol, Arnold Zweig at a pension; Golo, the Manns' second son, lodged with the Seabrooks; Brecht, Emil Ludwig, Stefan Zweig came on visits. In their wake were wives, secretaries, translators, agents, fans. (The locals pocketed their rents and tips, and called them Boches, Jews, war-mongers and spies.) One might ask how they came to congregate at that one place. Well, they hadn't had much time to make a choice. They got into France because it had a land-border with Germany, and stayed because it had a democratic government; they went South because it was cheaper than Paris and because of the climate, and to this particular part of the coast because the Meier-Grafes were already there and because the eldest Mann children, Klaus and Erika, who had often been to see Jean Cocteau at Toulon, recommended it.

Aldous and Maria soon met about all of them at a monster garden party given by the Seabrooks. I remember it as an incongruous occasion. It was a broiling afternoon; tea and drinks flowed. Petit fours melted in the sun. Willie Seabrook, in the grip of a failure of nerve, had whipped off his shirt and confronted his guests in khaki shorts and hairy chest. Heinrich Mann, even more stiff and formal than his brother, arrived in a high collar and black coat, extending, like Monsieur de Charlus, two fingers to anyone offering to shake hands. Maria came with Guatemalan belt and Mexican satchel bag; Aldous, in white cotton from neck to heel, kept to her side; and so did the confrères, each holding court within a cluster of his wife and entourage. Only Feuchtwanger circulated, making the round of the younger and more attractive women telling them about his latest sales figures. Like Arnold Bennett and the transatlantic cable, his word-rate ran high.

What struck the Huxleys was the regard some of them had for themselves. They threw their weight about; they *were* pompous. Their womenfolk referred to them as *Dichterfürsten*, princes of poetry. And though united in their horror of the Nazis, they were far from being one big happy family; only Willie Seabrook would have dreamt of gathering them all in one front yard. They were roughly divided into two main clans. One, the *Haute Culture*, revolved round Thomas Mann—the Magician as his children called him—and his friends and peers; the other clan was dominated by Lion Feuchtwanger, and the bond between him and his satellites oddly enough was communistic leanings and/or financial success; each clan patronised the other. Both, with an *hauteur* worthy of de Gaulle, looked down upon the Anglo-Saxons—Aldous Huxley and his friends.

The *Haute Culture* formed a reading circle. Once a week Mann, Frank, Meier-Graefe and Schickele, in turn, read from work in progress to their families and an invited audience. I must give a glimpse of one such evening. It was at the master's house (a villa belonging, ironically enough, to the mother-in-law of the German Ambassador to Egypt). Thomas Mann sat at the centre of a high table on the terrace, his three colleagues beside him. Behind them were chairs for their wives and Erika Mann. In the grounds below this platform, on steps, cushions, garden bench spread the hoi-polloi—a Swiss woman poet, the younger Mann children, the Schickele's schoolboy son, a well-known English critic, Aldous and Maria, my mama, Eddy Sackville-West, Heinrich Mann's Juno-esque mistress and myself. Erika approached the platform bearing her father's manuscript. For some fifty minutes he read a chapter from *Joseph and His Brethren* in a not very carrying voice. Afterwards the high-table was served with Riesling and chicken salad. Some suitably graded refreshments—I seem to remember fruit cup and biscuits—were distributed among the groundlings. Only Meier-Graefe, impervious, pulled up a chair and made his young wife sit beside him, feeding her with white of chicken off his plate. It made Aldous's evening.

In the autumn Gerald Heard came to stay for some ten days. "very nice and more encyclopaedic than ever—also more pessimistic than ever, advising us all to clear out to some safe spot in South America or the Pacific Islands before it is too late. He enjoys his glooms: but the fact does not necessarily mean that the glooms are unfounded. The German spectacle is really too frightening." Aldous tried to do his bit by taking part in a Congress of intellectuals in Paris presided over by Paul Valéry. He came back from it shrugging it off, depressed.

Poor Seabrook had been in a bad way for some time, drinking too much, unable to finish a book. In October he decided to leave everything and go to America for treatment. "The Huxleys drove us to the Toulon railroad station in Maria's red Bugatti," Marjorie Worthington wrote in her memoirs.[1]

> Because she drove so fast, we reached the *gare* ahead of time and had to wait what seemed like ages on the dark platform for the Blue Train which would come roaring in from Ventimiglia at nine o'clock. I remember Aldous walking up and down the platform, talking a blue streak. Maria sat on a bench with Willie, consoling him, listening to him, mothering him. He often poured out his heart to lovely ladies, and this night there was a heavy load to unburden . . .
> . . I failed to gather what [Aldous] was talking about . . . he remained serenely on his own intellectual plane . . . that's where he was this night at the railroad station, seeing two friends off on a train, feeling very sorry for them but not able to cope with the emotions . . .

In November Eva Herrmann and I went to Madrid and the night before we left my mother had a small dinner-party with the Huxleys and the Meier-Graefes. Meier-Graefe tried to prepare us, talking of El Greco, of Velasquez, of Goya, his own first sight of them twenty years ago. He talked all evening—with such freshness and such fire that Aldous too was caught. Maria saw it and when we said goodbye lightly made a promise. A few days later a telegram from Sanary reached us in Madrid. The thin blue slip, survived by chance among my papers, recalls the pang of pleasure on first reading the unsigned message.

*llegaremos jueves besos*

*Arriving Thursday.* They came by air; we met them. The hotel was opposite the Prado, the weather autumnal, wind-swept, clear. Every morning we stepped across into those overwhelming halls. Aldous tried to see everything, even the vast collection of drawings

---

[1] *The Strange World of Willie Seabrook*, Harcourt Brace & World, 1966.

in the attics. El Greco had always fascinated him, now he was carried away by the astonishing variety of Goya—the garlanded girls, the portraits, the *Desastros de la Guerra*. Here was a man who had painted in turn the rulers, the *voluptés*, the horrors of the eighteenth century and who had lived long enough into the nineteenth to outlive Jane Austen by eleven years and Beethoven by one. We would leave the Prado full of talk, wild with eye-strain at about three o'clock and eat a good long Spanish luncheon at the hotel. Later in the afternoon we would gather in the Huxleys' room to read aloud the Spanish chapter of Buckle's *History of Civilization*. At sunset, at the hour of urban animation, we strolled the evening-streets; and night after night it would seem, we went to the theatre. This was Aldous's choice. And it was not that we were seeing Calderón or Lope de Vega—those plays were contemporary, if old-fashioned, drawing-room stuff, incredibly long-winded, with plots even Maria, who had startled us with a sudden fluency in Spanish, did not follow. The acting, so Aldous maintained, was superb. Dinner again at our hotel; Spain, in the second year of the Republic, was still a masculine civilization and we were the only *respectable* women dining in a public place. The others were mostly high-class German tarts in fox-furs (these were Aldous's observations). In this manner we spent the best part of two weeks. We went to the Escorial—it shook and depressed us, but how fascinated Aldous was by that monument to power and to death, how eloquent. Once we ate a freezing picnic in the clear light up in the Guadarrama; but what possessed our minds' dreams were our mornings, was the Prado, were those canvasses of kings and dwarfs and saints.

We also laughed a good deal. Maria dug up the louche advertisements in the evening papers for Aldous—"Masseuse *gran reacción...*" We laughed at nothing and at ourselves, at the contre-temps that are the travellers' lot, at my putting away so much of the Spanish food, at Eva's concern with comfort, at the Huxleys' economies that boomeranged. In a very hard slow train we went to Toledo for a few cold days; we went to Segovia and thence to Avila in a commodious hired car, having *proved* to Aldous and Maria that this actually cost less. They accepted the logic of the figures but this transport was so much more *agreeable* that their consciences still quailed. At Avila we were in the heartland of Castile—a November evening in grey walled streets that overwhelmed one with a sense of being outside our time. But there is another memory of the town of Saint Theresa. Beds. We stopped at the first inn. We walked into the lighted hall.

*¿Tienen habitaciones? Quieremos dos cuartos con dos camas cada.*

There were rooms. Upstairs Maria and Eva discovered that the sheets had been slept in. Horror. They pulled bells. No one came. In Spain at the crunch, they would pay no attention to a woman. Maria told Aldous that *he* must go. "You must be firm, darling. The porter understands English." We trotted after him. Arriving at the desk, Aldous turned and said in his bell-like voice, "Darling, how shall I put it?"

We had tickets to fly back from Madrid to Marseilles by Air France. When we got out to the aerodrome, the waiting plane was marked with the swastika. Lufthansa. (The German line alternated with the French.) Eva Herrman and I refused to travel on a Nazi plane. Aldous thought it was a pretty futile protest, but gave in to our emotional indulgence and eventually we were put on a Spanish plane. It was a small one and I cannot remember other passengers. The air was calm, the earth below looked tremendous; Aldous got out his notebook. I imitated him. Then something went very wrong indeed. The plane lurched sideways and dropped to about 25 feet. Lop-sided it proceeded to hug the coast line of the Costa Brava just clearing bathing-huts and cliffs. The engine noise was shattering. I looked at Maria for some reassurance, but her face had an inward look and her lips were moving; she was, she said matter-of-factly afterwards, composing herself for death. I looked at Aldous— he was being sick into a paper bag. The plane limped on for a full thirty minutes; it made Barcelona and we landed. Smiling German airmen in Lufthansa caps met us by the gangway.

That night, our last night in Spain, we had dinner in the Plaza de Cataluña. A bomb had just been thrown. A tram lay over-turned, people had been hurt, there was a lot of police. Aldous did not fail to remark on the waste and folly. "Everyone knows that home-made bombs have never been the *slightest* bit of use." What *was*? What was any use? We talked about the new Spanish Republic. Eva, rather warmly, expressed hopes—schools, the vote for women . . . Aldous let it pass. We talked of re-armament, of Germany— *What* was one to do? At what cost? At *whose* cost? It came back, our talk, as it still does, to the dilemma of the liberal. What Aldous said was abstract, far-seeing, aloof. In a way it was maddening. At last one of us said, "Well, if that's no good either, what would *you* do?" and Maria came in, "Yes, darling, do tell us."

Aldous's answer, his mood, his exploratory talk, I can no longer pin down. At the time it was startling. Up to a minute ago he appeared to be the man who said, "I have never more passionately felt the need for using reason *jusqu'au bout*." Now it was as if his points of reference had vanished. I wrote about that evening once before, in a travel book, twenty years ago (and twenty years nearer the event). I would be tempted to put it differently today, but find that first account, midway between the past and present, standing in the way. It will have to serve.

. . That night there was a new note. Benevolent rationalism seemed a little worn: there was a hint . . . that man was helpless indeed and therefore could be helped and help himself. It was not in anything that was definitely said, and I cannot remember words; only [that Aldous's] answer was disturbing by an undercurrent of thoughts yet unformed, a sense of tendrils on the move towards the unseen end of the stick, by something we were too shocked to recognize as hope.

Instead, one felt a sense of grievance at the shift from a trusted intellectual position (the first reaction of readers in the coming years).

. . Then the *paella* we had ordered arrived; we ate into the saffron rice, drank Manzanilla and talked of this and that, but again and again that night the conversation led to, hovered, and not quite stopped short, of some disquietening threshold. Once or twice, always in that graceful, courteous voice, a word was dropped from the upsetting vocabulary of the tract. The Self, the All, the One . . .

At one point the Hay Diet, of all things, set it off again. Maria noticed that rice *with* prawns and chicken was not at all the thing; Aldous said it didn't matter. Not matter? Don't you believe in it? Of course he didn't believe in it, Aldous said. Maria was shocked —But why on earth then have we—? "Well, because of the discipline, darling." And when I exclaimed at that, Aldous loud and clear said something about mortification. Rebelliously I stuck to the *paella*, and there came the intimation that this would shut one off from that which was not mentioned as surely as political passion. Next day we flew back to Marseilles by Air France.

*Beyond the Mexique Bay* had been finished a few days before Aldous left for Spain. (Too late for autumn publication—it came out the following spring; 1933 was the first year since 1920 Aldous did not have a book out.) Now he was digging himself in for a winter at Sanary with the novel.

## Chapter Six

## A Store of Gaiety . . .

FOR a time all went well. Aldous was writing apace; the stack of typescript waxed.

The theme, fundamentally, is liberty. What happens to someone who becomes really very free—materially first . . and then mentally and emotionally. The rather awful vacuum that such freedom turns out to be. But I haven't yet worked out the whole of the fable—only the first part.

At present this was no obstacle, the particular time sequence of the future *Eyeless in Gaza* led Aldous on into going ahead. The theme is presented in the opening chapter—we find Anthony Beavis, the central character (an unmarried man), in his house in the South of France in 1933, looking at old photographs, about to become aware of *the awful vacuum.* From this base in time the novel moved into various phases of Anthony's past. All action is precisely dated—November 6th 1902, June 17th 1912, December 8th 1926 and so on—but each period or episode is broken up into several chapters, and the order of these chapters is deliberately shuffled. Events begun in chapter five may be continued in Chapter X or Y. The conclusion of the fable—Anthony's future—was to be inserted in like fashion in due course of inspiration. As yet it was not revealed; Aldous did not see into post-1933 in fiction any more than he did in actual time. (Incidentally, I am convinced that it was this business of juggling with the dates which was Aldous's earliest *donnée* for this novel and that the opening of chapter one—"The snapshots had become almost as dim as memories"—was indeed his first line.)

Life in Sanary was quiet that winter and became more so when in February Maria went to London for medical treatment. I came to stay to look after Aldous under Maria's instructions. No man could have been more undemanding and more even-tempered, and during the day there were Giulia and Camilla to look after *us.* We ate breakfast, lunch and tea together, sometimes in complete silence. While Aldous wrote, I wrote (at Maria's desk, an essay on *Beyond the Mexique Bay,* then still in page proof). While he painted, I read aloud. We went for walks; at night I cooked our dinner which we ate in the new basement dining-room, facing each other across a wide table covered with green linoleum. I had been told to stir an egg yolk into Aldous's soup and smuggle cream into his vegetables, and this worked unless one got carried away. (Cream was hand-made by working butter and water through a gadget.) With dinner we drank a nice claret—a youngish Ste-Estèphe, home-bottled, that came by barrel from a négociant at Bordeaux my mother had discovered—and it was now that I might trot out some general question I'd been saving. Aldous's reactions were unpredictable. He could be quite marvellously set off by some congenial query about tadpoles or the doctrine of the Shakers; one fared less well when one really wished to keep him to the point. He was discursive, never argumentative; but he might stray anywhere, though he could be impatient himself with wide vague questions. Sometimes there was no response. Aldous would emit a kind of low-pitched *hmm* . . . It was not only as if he'd pulled the shutters down, whatever was behind the shutter had been withdrawn as well and was very far away; for the person in the room with him, there was nothing there. (Other people have talked of the prohibitive quality of that silence. He had other, peaceful silences.) Did he know what he was doing, as he had said to Dorothy Brett when he was a very young man?

The only outings during those weeks—apart from picnics in the winter sun—were driving Aldous to the dentist and a charity matinée at the British Vice-Consul's at Toulon where, without any preliminary fuss, he sat down and read the Dwarfs' story from *Crome Yellow* to a mainly female audience. Once Mrs Wharton, Edith Wharton, came over with her entourage. We were sitting round a tray of Cinzano in the sitting-room when Camilla announced luncheon. Aldous opened the door for Mrs Wharton and impelled her down the steepish stairs with gentle taps with his cupped hand on her behind. The entourage froze; Mrs Wharton turned her head, not abruptly, identified and gave him a sweet smile.

To me it seemed a good life, a writer's life. Aldous admitted to doing 500, 600, 700 words a day; yet he must have missed Maria, and if he was working too intensely to be very bored, he was certainly under-stimulated. Sure enough, Maria had hardly returned when they decided that he must have a break. Italy. Rome for Easter—showing it to Matthew "before Mussolini . . destroys it all in order to dig up more rubbish heaps of imperial glory". It should have been a radiant journey. It rained a great deal; the Fascist thing had become more open and unbearable; one saw too many places in too short a time. There were many good moments. Maria had gone ahead to have the Bugatti seen to at Nice. Aldous, Camilla who was to visit her family, and I followed in my car. (Camilla had consulted Maria in distress: what was she to do if she had to obey a call of nature? Aldous was briefed and every fifty kilometres or so suggested a stop to have a look at the view.) We spent the night at Nice; Raymond Mortimer was there and it was an animated dinner. Next day Aldous and Maria, Camilla and I, in separate cars, went into Italy. We managed a rendez-vous beyond Genoa and the four of us sat down to luncheon on a Ligurian waterfront (I mention it because of the way Maria turned an ordeal into a treat for that shy girl, Camilla). It was one of those trumpery election days and we were depressed by the strutting and the blown-up features of the Duce glowering from every hoarding, house and wall.

. . an organized attempt at apotheosis [Aldous to T. S. Eliot]—as for Caesar or Augustus. I happened to be reading Edwyn Bevan's *Later Greek Religion,* and his chapter on the deification of kings from Alexandrian times onwards was fantastically topical. One understands, in Italy and, I suppose, in Germany too, why the Jews and early Christians were so much concerned about idolatry.

We slept at La Spezia, strolling—Aldous in a mellow mood— late into the night (the rain had not caught up with us yet) and temporarily parted on the Campo Santo at Pisa the next morning, Aldous and Maria going on by way of the Etruscan cities to Rome to meet Matthew whose school holidays had begun; I to Lucca, depositing Camilla, thence to Florence to pick up Eva Herrmann. When we got to Rome the Huxleys, tempted by the new autostrada, had left for Naples. They had hardly returned—Bernini churches, a picnic at Tivoli, a visit to the truly idolatrous *Mostra del Fascismo* —when we all went off again on respective itineraries, the Huxleys to San Sepolcro and to Ferrara for the special exhibition of Cossa, Costa and Cosimo Tura. We converged in Florence and in no time at all, it seemed, we were back in the same small hotel in Nice—rather tired, rain-sodden and grumpy about having spent too much money.

Money. The house was not running itself noticeably cheaper with a succession of dailies. *Beyond the Mexique Bay,* out since April, was selling rather well considering the times. Aldous now could have enjoyed a small private income from his share, since his father's death, in Prior's Field school. After talking it over with Maria, he had written to his step-mother who was one of the governors of the school.

My dear Rosalind,
Thank you for your letter and the cheque. So long as the boys [Aldous's half-brothers, David and Andrew, aged 18 and 16] are

still being educated, I had rather not draw any money that may come in from Prior's Field, which I regard as a family thing rather than a personal one. I am therefore returning you the cheque and the receipt . . . Dear Rosalind, I hope that, if . . . the problem of the boys' education becomes more difficult, you will not hesitate to let me know; for I should like to be able to do anything within my power for David and Andrew . . .

Love from us both.

Ever your affectionate
Aldous

I have said nothing about Aldous's feelings and reflections after his father's death the year before. I do not know what they were. Nothing has come to light in his extant letters; letters to him were destroyed, and I doubt if many of his friends wrote to him in the accepted manner; it seemed to be an understood thing that one did not. Certainly one did not *say* anything. (I met them at the station a few weeks after, on their return from Mexico by way of London. Silence was expected. Very little came through even from Maria.) They had not reached England in time for the funeral. Leonard Huxley was buried in Surrey, in Compton churchyard beside Julia Huxley's grave.

In June of 1934 Aldous went to London on his own for a few days, then came back into the Mediterranean summer—the sequence of hot blue days and exquisite nights. The book still moved. The children were there, friends came: Robert Nichols, the Drieu La Rochelles, Victoria Ocampo, Clive Bell, Jeanne. The interests of the year were photographing insects through an enlarging lens, and human hands. Stimulated by Dr Charlotte Wolff,[1] whom they had just met, and her researches in that field, Maria collected prints of their friends' hands—a not unmessy process with a roller and thick ink. No-one escaped, not even the Hyères contingent arriving spic and span; Paul Valéry and Edith Wharton submitted. Afterwards the prints would be passed on to Dr Wolff and she and Maria would sit for hours poring over them. There were a number of young people in Sanary that year, some pretty girls, friends of Matthew's on one foot as it were, friends of his parents' on the other. How many picnics we had in those summer nights, in the woods under a moon, on beaches by a warm and phosphorescent sea. We drank planter's punch made from Aldous's

[1] Charlotte Wolff, M.D., F.B.Ps.S., author of *The Human Hand*, *A Psychology of Gesture*, etc., etc.

recipe, played games, the levitation game and Aldous and Maria's version of blind man's buff; Aldous sang:

*I'll sing you Twelve O*
*Green grow the Rushes O.*
*What is your Twelve O?*

At midnight we bathed.

"I wonder whether you could come," Maria wrote to Eddy Sackville-West, "and fetch a store of lazy gaiety to face the coming winter—it is more than gaiety in fact—it is serenity and detachment . . . The warm starry skies . . the scents and the peace . . with all my grapes ripening and the last tuberoses . . .

> You have never been here when the cumulative madness of five months of sun and country and stars make the world unreal in its pleasures and beauties—and when the northern sobriety is very northern and unreal indeed. I shall be so sensible this winter *but I am so happy now.*

They broke up early. Aldous needed a change of scene, wanted to do some articles, make some ready money. By 20th September they were in London. Four months, they planned. They found a flat, "a comic flat, 150 yards from Piccadilly Circus," Maria wrote to Roy, miraculously cheap: £5 a week. It was a studio under a raftered roof at 18 St Albans Place behind Lower Regent Street, with two large bedrooms: "a great deal of light . . much cupboard space. Of course we have to pay for this old-fashioned roominess by old-fashioned discomforts of heating by gas, no porter and no hot continual water. But it is very quiet, essential to peasants as we have become."

There was room for Rina (back with them for the time being); Aldous was able to do a bit of painting. "London is cheerful on the whole." He fell into his round—the novel, a little journalism, friends, walks in the park; Maria was suffering from her usual revulsion.

> My first reaction [still to Roy] are violent horror at the mechanization of the whole thing, the bad air and the, mostly, unfresh food. Also the amount of food appals me. The amount of unnecessary horrors invented to tempt humanity to spend its so bitterly earned money. The vulgarity of the crowds, its vacant look and its hustle in solid continuity in all the streets . . . How I hate it all. Passionately. But I will settle down to it . . .
> I wonder if you can imagine us here. I can imagine you so well

on your dare-devil tours which you combine with good business . . .
God preserve you of drought and storms. And above all from
drunken mozos. And from all the crocodiles and the chain of
horrors laying in wait for one in those countries . . .

To Aldous London seemed prosperous as well as cheerful: "The
English have convinced themselves that they're well off at the
moment and are acting accordingly—which appears to have the
same result as *being* well off." Julian had been made director of
the Zoo. "What good news . . ! I don't know what the disadvantages of the job are—but it seems to me to have a lot of advantages
from financial security to a house that . . compares not too un-
favourably with that of the gorillas!"

At this time, J. W. N. Sullivan, Aldous's old friend, was faced
with disabling illness as well as financial trouble being unable now
to meet a publishing debt. "I shall ask you to let me guarantee
the debt," Aldous wrote to Ralph Pinker, "or rather to pay it
provisionally out of any monies which may come into my account
with you.

. . I shouldn't want you to mention this arrangement to Sullivan,
of course. Merely tell him that the debt can be repaid in instalments
as he earns it. In this way he won't be worried . . .

In November Aldous and Maria came to one of their quick
decisions. They signed a seven-year lease for a flat, or set, in Albany.
This meant a permanent base in London. *If only one could spend half
one's time in each country*—libraries and intelligent, informed society
in England; warmth and country-life in Mediterranean France—
that old wish of Aldous's was being realized. Rent and rates came
to about £400 a year. They could always sublet the thing in summer
they told themselves; a set of rooms sounded less of a burden than
a flat or house. Again it was only a minute's walk from Piccadilly
Circus, again they were to enjoy unique urban quiet—no wheel
ever entered Albany, that private back-alley of Georgian houses in
the heart of London, the past abode of Byron, Bulwer Lytton and
the gentleman burglar Raffles. "Do you know Albany from literature?" Maria wrote to Matthew.

They furnished it cheaply. Second-hand tables and chairs, new
beds. They managed to get rid of their comic flat but this meant
moving out by mid-December. Suddenly they were under pressure.
Maria had to go into a nursing home for a few days; when she came
out she was not strong enough for all there was to do. Aldous was
beginning to sleep badly, a new experience and it upset him. Maria
thought that it came from his worrying over money, the cost of
setting up house on top of Christmas. They disapproved of the

whole business—the rich giving to the rich, spending money on things hardly wanted. But to their younger or less well-to-do relations and their poorer friends they would send cheques, most generous cheques. They never added up the total on a piece of paper. Aldous took mild sleeping pills, sipped Sedobrol; Gerald Heard advised breathing exercises:

.. of the Yoga sort with accompanying mental concentration and .. attempted elimination of irrelevant thoughts and feelings [letter to Robert Nichols] .. frightfully difficult and takes so long.

Presently Aldous was sleeping better again, but now Matthew arrived from school nervous and tired. After days of chaotic efforts they were in E2, their ground-floor flat in Albany.

They were at home on the afternoon of 31st December—tea at a round table that filled the darkish hall, sherry afterwards. People came and went, Aldous's step-mother, Gerald Heard, Evan Morgan (I think), Tommy Earp, Eddy West, Naomi Royde-Smith, Lady Ottoline Morrell, Ivan Moffat, Matthew's contemporary; Raymond Mortimer, Eva Herrmann, Marion Dorn, Ted McKnight Kauffer ... There were presents. Someone (Victor Rothschild?) had sent a handsome Strassbourg pie. Aldous and Maria did not approve of *foie gras*; for some moments its fate hung in the balance, then Maria said it would make a supper for Matthew, Raymond and Sybille. At one stage Lady Ottoline broke her string of pearls: large and beautiful pearls, if not well-strung, bounced and rolled over the floor like so many peas disappearing under carpets and the second-hand sideboard. We were on our hands and knees. Pearls collected in a saucer in front of Ottoline. But how many?—How many more had to be retrieved? Ottoline, quite unruffled, refused to count. Presently she took leave (pearls in a paper bag); we stood up, she made the round—the appropriate wish, the right remark. To me it was—in the great hooting voice—"You *will* enjoy the Strassbourg pie."

Afterwards Maria changed into a dressing-gown and we had supper in the bowels of the earth (in Albany, kitchens were either underground or on the attic floor). We drank champagne. We left in the small hours; Aldous came out with us for the night air. My car, parked in the front-yard beside the residents' Daimlers, would not start. Aldous and Raymond heaved to and pushed it into Piccadilly, broke into a run: they pushed and ran for a hundred yards till the engine caught. The car leapt forward and they fell behind; I waved, they waved, *Auguri*, we shouted, *Auguri!* Rather a nice beginning for the New Year, I thought.

# PART SIX

## Watershed?: 1935-1937

"Faith . . is the choice of the nobler
hypothesis. It is the resolve to place the
highest meaning on the facts which we
observe."

GERALD HEARD

". . the product, I suppose, of a
rationalist upbringing, I remain an
agnostic who aspired to be a gnostic—
but a gnostic only on the mystical level,
a gnostic without symbols, cosmologies
or a pantheon . . ."

ALDOUS HUXLEY, from a letter of 1962

"Ultimate reality cannot be understood except intuitively, through an act
of will and the affections. *Plus diligitur
quam intelligitur.*"

ALDOUS HUXLEY, *Grey Eminence*

## Chapter One

# E2 Albany, Piccadilly

SOON in the new year Aldous went over to Paris having rashly engaged himself to do some articles for *Paris-Soir* on the subject of *La France au seuil de l'année 1935*. He scurried about for a week interviewing schoolmasters and cabinet ministers, then returned to London exhausted and disgruntled for a breather. He started to sleep badly again. He worked, but the novel wasn't going and the flat, still far from finished, was a restless place. So he went off again to *La France au seuil* while Maria pulled things into shape. Albany was both rather wonderful and a bit preposterous. Their two front rooms were well-proportioned with high ceilings and tall windows, giving on, uncurtained, to the covered walk which, except that it was flanked by flower boxes, was like a promenade deck aboard ship. These rooms they made quite civilized; a handsome desk and deep chairs in one, Maria's usual wide bed and coral dressing-table in the other. The rest of the flat consisted of the entrance-and-dining hall already described, below a murky sky-light; a strip of a back-room where Aldous slept and a strip of a bath. The basement kitchen, down some twisty little stairs, was a mess of pipes with a coal-fed boiler in the middle which supplied hot water and erratic heating. Each Albany tenant was allotted a couple of servants' rooms three flights up under the eaves, connected to the master flat by a system of bells. There was also a system of rules, implicit and explicit, a statute in fact. You were expected to be waited on hand and foot.

Albany was founded in 1803. To obtain a lease you had to be a gentleman, a bachelor, and have no connection with trade. The vestibule off the main portal is still adorned by the busts of the more illustrious past inhabitants, Lord Byron, William Lamb, Frederick, Duke of York. You might not keep a dog, cat or parrot. The same goes for musical instruments (in the 1930s this rule was held to include wireless sets). The amendment allowing wives was passed in the early 1920s not long after the vote for women. Children were still out. Albany was always run by a gentleman trustee living on the premises. In Aldous's time it was a Captain Adams. The famous covered walk runs parallel to the Burlington Arcade from the main entrance in Piccadilly to a discreet gate into Vigo Street, fifty yards from Bond Street. Both ends were guarded by porters in uniform and top hats, the Piccadilly one day and night whereas the gate into Mayfair was left (shades of Caroline

Lamb) locked and private after 10 p.m. Tenants had a key. The porters were formal and friendly; if you were carrying a parcel, which wasn't very Albany in any case (though Maria appeared with vegetables in basket), you were relieved of it at the gate. Permit me, ma'am—whereupon the porter disappeared from sight into some subterranean passage like Alice's White Rabbit, and materialized again by your front door. They were three, one round and short and red, one built like a grenadier and a slight young man called Simpkins whom Maria took to in particular. Simpkins had a sister, Bessie, and soon it was arranged that she would come and do for the Huxleys for a few hours daily (Rina having returned to France and her Emilio). The rest of the housework and all the cooking Maria did herself (again not quite Albany). As for those servants' rooms, one they used for a box-room, the other Aldous and Maria in their kindness decided to lend to me (I had been living in digs and they wanted to save me money). The bells served. One for breakfast, two for a telephone call, three when the bathroom downstairs was empty (my attic room had only a cold-water basin and was lit—in 1935—by gas).

After Aldous returned from Paris for the second time, having finally got out of the French articles, the insomnia came back in force—he lay awake most nights, and next morning was hardly up to wrestling with the novel. Next night he could not sleep because of work undone—what *was* to become of them if he was unable to write? So the spiral went; every day he failed to get on better, the outlook seemed a little worse. On 25th February he wrote to Harold Raymond.

My dear Harold,
    I ought to have thanked you before for a very kind and generous letter—but this sleeplessness leaves one in a sorry state of incapacity to do anything. If, as I hope, I get over the state fairly soon, I trust to have the book finished by next autumn. Otherwise—God knows. Meanwhile, I don't want to let my indebtedness to Chatto's pile up; and, seeing that I can live on my own resources for a time, I think it will be best if you suspend payment till I get properly under weigh again.

Aldous tried country weekends, massage, vitamins, a hypnotist (who did some good but not at the right hours), went on with Sedobrol, that old French standby, a sort of Oxo cube with something soothing added (he would not let himself slide into sleeping pills, it was to be "the minimum of dope"). He persisted with Yoga exercises. Gerald Heard was very good to them, popping in and out almost daily, reassuring Maria. To him Aldous was able to talk. In letters too he touched on aspects of his trouble. Writing had its advantages, he told Bob Nichols, but offered no support "but what one can supply from within.

> when one's ill or unhappy, one needs something outside oneself to hold one up. It is a good thing, I think, when one has been knocked out of one's balance . . to have some external job or duty to hang on to.

What Aldous was looking for, I think, was some way of breaking through, some way of getting out of himself. Harold Raymond's wife, Vera, who was running the library at Bart's Hospital, suggested that Aldous should take on distributing books in a man's ward. He set off quite eagerly (by underground to the City) but the job turned out to offer small opportunity for practising the human touch. It was too rushed. What was required was quickness of feet and some memory for faces, though an easy manner and a ready word would not have come amiss. You were supposed to load up a trolley with books to suit all tastes, as well as books requested by individual patients on your last visit. With these you entered the ward at the stroke of 2 p.m. You went from bed to bed proffering and suggesting while fishing in the lockers for books to be returned. You approached the alert and tried not to disturb those who appeared asleep or sunk in lethargy. On the other hand you must not leave out someone because he had dozed off for just a minute. Some were vague, a few were very definite about wanting a work on wild flowers or the Amazon river or mathematics. Most were slow. There was some demand for "serious" books and more for romances than thrillers. You had to memorize requests, there was no chance to write them down as you had to be out of the ward by tea-time. So after your first round you galloped your trolley back to the library, which was quite a distance, through the corridors and up a baggage lift, filled up with the requests and galloped back again to leave the right book on the right bed just before the nurses came in with the trays.

Aldous tried his best. Vera Raymond and Maria tried *their* best to extricate him without making him feel useless. At last Gerald told him that it was all right to give it up. Maria and I took over the job and to Bart's we went (we were given a ward each) every Monday afternoon for the remainder of that winter and a part of the next.

It was Gerald, also, who persuaded Aldous to give one of the Sunday evening lectures at Dartington Hall as the Elmhirsts had asked him to do. He went down one weekend with Gerald and Maria. It was during term and they partly went to see Matthew. Now, on principle the school allowed a boy to work when and at what he chose. Matthew for the moment chose to concentrate on carpentry and the like (he did become an inspired *bricoleur*); Aldous was displeased and worried, probably thinking far too much ahead, coming out heavily on the side of family tradition. He spoke to Matthew, a rather delicate schoolboy as Aldous once had been, and Matthew who thought he had been doing all right (his headmaster thought he had) was upset. Aldous's visit, and the lecture which the school attended, was all a bit of an ordeal for him.

Aldous's subject broadly was the new idolatries. Science, he said, had produced a mental climate antipathetic to the religions of the old tradition. Meanwhile the impulses which make men religious still persist.

> . . Men still desire to be ascetic, still feel the urge to give to something greater than themselves . . they still hunger for certainty . . . the emotional substitutes for religion still persist but the intellectual premise in which the emotions could express themselves has been taken away. Those who in the past have worshipped supernatural beings now find it impossible to believe in their existence . . . and set up natural beings who are worshipped instead . . .
>
> . . They sing Te Deums at Mussolini's birthplace so that the living dictator is in competition with the old saints . . .
>
> Our problem therefore is to find a new religion that is better than the old in that it accepts science, and better than the new substitute. We want to live in a world that makes some sort of sense, we want to find some intellectual basis for our efforts, we want to know where we stand in relation to the universe at large.

Daily life was by no means all sackcloth and ashes. As usual in London, Aldous and Maria were surrounded by friends. Their most intimate at that period besides Gerald were the Hutchinsons, St John and Mary, and the McKnight Kauffers, Ted and his American wife, Marion Dorn. They also saw a great deal of Naomi Royde-Smith, who lived in what Maria called the *quartier*, and of course of Raymond and Eddy. There was usually someone for luncheon or tea, Moura Budberg quite often, Clive Bell, Bertie Russell, Tom Eliot, Naomi Mitchison, Vera Raymond, Madge Garland, May Voss. Hugh Mills, the playwright, then a very young man in advertising, called with his wife, Christina, leaving a typescript, asking advice. The Huxleys went out less because of Aldous's health, though they dined at the Hutchinsons' and the Kauffers', went to some of Sibyl Colefax's luncheons and to Ottoline's tea in Gower Street, saw Helen Anrep and the Kenneth Clarks; now and then Aldous would take one of his man friends to lunch at the Athenaeum. In Albany all meals but tea were eaten in the kitchen, Maria serving from stove to table which was quite a new thing then. (Some people, Aldous's cousin Jill told me, said that it was "beneath their dignity".) Once the Bernard Shaws came to luncheon and Mrs Shaw was put out by G. B. S. having to negotiate those stairs.

Maria was in one of her anti-food phases, anti-eating, anti-cooking, anti-cooking smells. She was very worried about Aldous without letting on and lived mainly on black coffee (still sent by faithful Roy, and unimaginably good even though Maria brewed it in a milk jug). What she produced for Aldous and her guests was simple and delicious—eggs poached in cream in those small china dishes, fresh vegetables, the good kinds of tinned soup, once in a while a chicken done in a cocotte (no roasting smell), smoked salmon, avocado pears. Good bread, good butter. Nor was it as extravagant as it may sound. There was a shop in Soho where you could get decent smoked salmon for four shillings a quarter of a pound (I used to be sent out for it when people stayed for supper). Maria *did* say, as she is quoted, "Such a saving to live in Albany—so convenient for Fortnum's." It's a bit misleading. She did use Fortnum & Mason's, but only for their wine (sherry, a little champagne, non-vintage, and some very modest claret; the wine department happened to be one of the most reasonable in London so was in fact a saving) and for the soups, the butter and the avocados, still exotic then, which the Huxleys had taken to in Guatemala. Her serious shopping Maria did in Soho street markets, wrapped in the blue Italian officer's cloak, made in Florence so many years ago, which she had not ceased to wear.

Although Maria never really got to like London she had the knack of making the best of things. When we remarked upon her stepping out into Piccadilly in slippers and dressing-gown to put a letter in the pillar box, she'd say, "but I'm in my *quartier*—c'est mon quartier".

One thing, I am sure, that was not right for Aldous was the room he worked in. That front sitting-room was a goldfish bowl. Not only was there the mildly distracting spectacle of the Albanites strolling up and down the covered walk, carnation in buttonhole, raising their bowler hats, but Aldous too, at his typewriter, was a sight revealed. (The typewriter by the way was tolerated; just. It was not so much the noise as the association with trade—might you not be writing business letters? The line was drawn at mine; Maria personally went to see Captain Adams. What did you tell him? we asked when she returned successful. "I gave him my word that you would only use it to write poetry."

Yet, I repeat, all was not sackcloth and ashes. Man, as Aldous never ceased to point out, is a multiple amphibian. Concerned about his relation to the universe at one moment, with other occupations and desires at the next. The Handleys were in England, on some disastrous lecture tour, turning up at the wrong hall on the wrong night, leaving their slides in taxi-cabs. As well as being amused by Sally, Aldous had mild designs "You'd better take her out to dinner, darling" said Maria. Their life in this respect was much as Aldous described it in *Point Counter Point*. The cure by affairs . . . Maria thought that he enjoyed such distractions, needed the change and his mind taken off his work. They amounted to very little, the distractions, and were either short or intermittent over the years. Aldous was never in the least involved. The women concerned were always very attractive in one way or another, some were beauties. Aldous had no fixations as to type or age. It might be a fluffy blonde just as soon as someone middle-aged and amusing. What Aldous offered, apart from the essential thing that he *liked* making love *and* made no bones about it, was friendliness, good humour, a measure of affection. What he did not offer was courtship. He would have grudged the *time*. Aldous seriously pursued only two women in his life—Maria and Nancy. So it was dinner and bed, or nothing. (It was rarely nothing: Aldous was seldom rebuffed; in that respect also the Nancy experience stood apart.) The logistics were largely Maria's. "You can't leave it to Aldous," she would say, "he'd make a muddle." She did it with tact, unbreachable good manners and a smile (ironic). She sent the flowers. Not actual flowers, that wouldn't have been Aldous's style, she saw to it that he sent a book. This he might inscribe with an elegantly turned allusive stanza of his own composition (in French: he still enjoyed *d'être un peu scabreux*). Maria did up the parcel. She did more than that. In a very subtle way she prepared the ground, created opportunities, an atmosphere, stood in, as it were, for the courtship.

Why did she do it? Well first of all, as she has said, for Aldous. For his work. It was also part of her generosity, and her sense of realism. "Surely, he'd get tired of only *me*?" Besides what did it matter? She really did not mind, Maria took what I should call the aristocratic view of sex. And she knew that she was wise—it never got out of hand. She did see to *that*. Not that it was necessary. And Aldous? Men have asked me: "Allowing one's wife to help one getting a girl—isn't that terribly undermining for a man?" They were shocked. Well Aldous did not feel in the least diminished, he never seemed to feel the need to assert his manhood. The situation would be unthinkable in many marriages; to understand it one has to look at it in the light of Aldous's and Maria's. It was a measure of how certain they were, and how free, and of the great niceness that there was between them. There was some brother and sister element in their relation: they could share each other's escapades. And this kept things in light perspective, protected Aldous from involvement. One might call it eating one's cake and having it. And why not? Maria would have said; it wasn't as much as all that, why grudge it to Aldous? And no one was ever hurt.

The women? One or two of them would have been glad enough to grab Aldous for good, but everyone understood soon enough that there was nothing doing. There was some resentment; on the whole the atmosphere of good humour and urbanity became contagious. Most of them were friends, devoted also to Maria. There was never any seduction of the innocent, anyone concerned was far too seductive to have remained single.

To return to Sally Handley. Here there must have been some initial misjudgement. Hers was not the aristocratic view. For once Aldous *was* rebuffed. She was deeply shocked. He took it with the best of grace, and so did she (remaining disconcerted). Aldous had stepped off a pedestal. What puzzled her most, she told me, was the delicacy of his approach—she could have dealt more easily with a straight pass. "You would have thought," she said, "he was a *Chinaman!*" I repeated this to Aldous (irresistible). The wretch went off to the British Museum to get a picture post card of some grinning mandarin which he sent to Sally, signed, "From your devoted Chinaman, A. H."

I should like to give a different glimpse of Aldous at that time. The Hutchinson's daughter Barbara had recently got married to Victor [Lord] Rothschild and Aldous often went to stay with them at Cambridge. Here Sir Isaiah Berlin first met him.

I expected to be overawed and perhaps sharply snubbed. But he was courteous and very kind to everyone present. The company played intellectual games . . Huxley plainly adored such exercises, but remained uncompetitive, benevolent, and remote. When the games were over at last, he talked, without altering his low, mono-tonous tone, about persons and ideas, describing them as if viewed from a great distance . . . He spoke with serenity and disarming sincerity, very simply. There was no malice and very little conscious irony . . only the mildest and gentlest mockery of the most innocent kind. He enjoyed describing prophets and mystagogues—but even such figures as Count Keyserling, Ouspensky and Gourdjief, whom he did not much like, were given their due and indeed more than their due; even Middleton Murry was treated more mercifully and seriously than in the portrait in *Point Counter Point*. Huxley talked very well: he needed an attentive audience and silence, but he was not self-absorbed or domineering, and presently everyone in the room would fall under his peaceful spell; brightness and glitter went out of the air, everyone became calm, serious, interested and contented.[1]

[1] *Mem. Vol.*

In March Chatto's and Aldous made their fifth agreement. The terms were the same as in the last, £1,250 a year etc., with one significant revision—three books in three years (one remembers the original six), works of fiction *or* non-fiction. For the first time since 1923 Aldous had no contractual obligation to produce a novel. The Raymonds' kindness and affectionate concern were a great help to Aldous and Maria (it went well beyond, and was different in kind, from a publisher's looking after an—in the long run— extremely profitable author). And it was never Chatto's who suggested suspending payments, it was Aldous who refused money during difficult times. This was necessary for his peace of mind; there were two unshakeable Huxley tenets: one educated one's children and one did not get into debt.

By the spring, without any attributable cause or treatment, Aldous was sleeping better; sleeping normally, Maria thought. He felt ready for getting back into the novel with a will. An acceptable sub-tenant was found for Albany, and in April full of hope they left for Sanary.

# Chapter Two

## "L'Année horrible"

MARIA wrote to Roy from France on 4th May, ". . you don't seem to have received . . my gloomy account of that winter, as grey as it was gloomy. But I shall not go back to that because now we are in the summer, in a bright country . . . Aldous . . is cured definitely cured, it seems since about a month. Work goes well and everything goes well.

Work goes madly as a matter of fact. He is finishing a novel already born when we were out to you so you see what it means: the strain was terrific. I am typing it out; some of it already, and that is always a sign that it nears completion. Apart from that we lead a peasant's life . . .

We have been reading chiefly easy or more difficult scientific books of interest to Aldous and which I read with great gusto . . .

I have done a lot of 'good-housekeeping' lately, I say with rather a sigh, for I do not like it and prefer weeding the garden, or mending fuses. We have had such an abundance of cherries that not with the help of all the friends and servants and neighbours have we been able to eat them, so they have been . . . made into jams . . This is all the harder work because my cook cannot read . . . so that I am often left with the boiling syrup literally in my hands. Last night we sat in the kitchen, I on a stool above the gas-range turning a lovely bubbling red juice in a copper saucepan reading aloud to Aldous who was sitting far below, a book on the history of philosophy . . . and the jam was not burnt.

. . But what is more comic still is that Aldous has decided to take violent exercise for the sake of his health and that that exercise is the most concisely found in the form of gardening. So he digs every spare inch of the ground and causes havoc all round him to the despair of the gardener . . . My despair is compensated by the fact that I believe it to be good for him . . . What a pity we cannot replace all that with some good riding in the cafetales.

. . We are going to South America in 1936, as surely as anything is sure . . .

I hope you will ask my boy one day to stay with you. He would adore it . . . But I wonder [if] with those wretched studies . . . he will ever have time to learn a bit about life.

Things were not quite as serene as Maria protested. Aldous's insomnia was at bay rather than cured, a matter of palliatives, of good weeks and bad. He was getting ahead—so many episodes to round off—the book was getting *long.* "I've been so busy with my bloody book that I've hardly painted at all." To Julian he wrote on 17th May,

> . . I have been dithering along with various downs as well as ups. At the moment, thank heaven, have an up in progress and am sleeping quite well with the aid of a wholly non-toxic mixture of calcium and magnesium, which, for some extraordinary reason, acts as a nervous sedative and mild hypnotic . . it's called *Calsédine* (made in France), does no harm, produces (so my doctor swears) no habituation, and leaves one perfectly fresh and cheerful in the morning. With its aid I do a fair amount of work—and about time too, as I have earned very little for a long time past. Have also taken to digging in the garden . . .
>
> . . I hope to get my book done by the end of the summer, if this beastly insomnia gives me the chance. It has been cold here and rainy, but pleasant . . . Mme de Béhague and the Noailles have gone—a relief, au fond: for, tho' nice, they have the rich persons' inability to conceive that other people have anything to do than eat lunches and teas in their houses.

The B.B.C., the previous autumn, had broadcast a series of talks on "The Causes of War", which, printed weekly in *The Listener,* attracted a good deal of attention and response. The speakers were Winston Churchill, Austen Chamberlain, Lord Beaverbrook, J. B. S. Haldane, W. R. Inge, then Dean of St Paul's, G. D. H. Cole, Aldous and some others, and most of them tried to come to grips with the acute question What Are We Going To Do About It NOW? Beaverbrook urged Isolationalism, Churchill said that Britain must be prepared to submit to Germany or resist, Professor Haldane proposed a League of Nations' curb on armament manufacture[1]; Aldous talked about the psychological phenomenon of war. Why do men and women make and accept war? "The causation of historical events is multiple . . .

> And yet strictly speaking all the causes of war are psychological . . . Wars are not *fought* by climates or political or economic systems, they are fought by human beings . . . the question of psychology inevitably arises. . . .

[1] H. J. Stenning's introduction to the published edition of these talks, *The Causes of War,* The Telegraph Press, New York, Dec. 1935.

Now Aldous had already developed this theme in *Beyond the Mexique Bay* in 1933. What he had said then, in a sixty-thousand words digression on war,[1] was that the fundamental problem of international politics was psychological, and economic problems secondary. "Our so-called wars of interest are really wars of passion —'*La guerre naît des passions*'.

> Interests are always ready to compound, passions never. You can always discuss figures . . ask a hundred and accept eighty-five. But you cannot discuss hatred, nor haggle over . . vanities and prejudices . . .[2]

Aldous cited Alain, the French philosopher, of whom it is reported that when in the trenches, his fellow soldiers complained of the miseries of war, he would answer: "*Mais vous avez eu assez de plaisir; vous avez crié Vive l'Armée ou Vive l'Alsace-Lorraine. Il faut que cela se paye. Il faut mourir.*" And who is it, Aldous asked, who enjoys these passions, the people as a whole or only the rulers? *Both* he believed to be the correct answer.

> It is the rulers of course who declare war . . . But rulers cannot carry on a war unless the ruled are moved by the same passions . . . the mass of people must . . imagine that they want the war; that the war is in their interest or at least unavoidable . . .[3]

The ruled are sometimes actually more war-like than their rulers, who find themselves reluctantly propelled towards a war which they would like to avoid.

> At other times, the ruled are less the slaves of national passion and prejudice than the rulers. Thus, I think it would be true to say that, at present, the majority of French and English people are more pacific, less dangerously obsessed by the Moloch-theology of nationalism, readier to think of international politics in terms of reason, than their governments . . . When the French populace was imbued with nationalism the bourgeoisie was pacific. Now that it thinks of freedom, in terms not of nations, but classes, the rulers are nationalistic.[3]

Fortunately, periods of intense general excitement never last very long.

> The social organism does not seem to be able to tolerate more than about twenty years of abnormal agitation. Thus, the thrilling, heroic

---

[1] Published also separately in *Life and Letters*, April 1934, under the title "War and the Emotions".
[2] *Beyond the Mexique Bay*. Chatto & Windus, 1934.
[3] Ibid.

period of the religious revival, set going by St Francis of Assisi, was over in less than a quarter of a century. The great animal that was Europe could not stand the strain of sitting up on its hind legs and performing primitive-Christian tricks. Within a generation it had settled down once more to a comfortable doze. Every violently exciting religious or political movement of history has run much the same course. It will be interesting to see whether the revivalist enthusiasm worked up by Communists, Nazis and Fascists will last longer than the similar mass emotion aroused by the first Franciscans . . . St Francis had no printing press, no radio . . . Nevertheless, it may be doubted whether [Hitler, Stalin and Mussolini] . . will really do better. . . .[1]

Yet while they last, *Il faut que cela se paye.*

What Aldous proposed, in 1933, was the calling of an official World Psychological Conference with a view of finding means to secure international peace. If the delegates agreed on—"what, alas, is sadly improbable"—their governments' need to discourage manifestations of collective vanity and hatred, they would be faced with a great many problems. How to prohibit activities that give great satisfaction? What sort of emotional compensation must be devised? How much excitement do people need to keep them contented and in health?

. . . There is a possibility . . that dislike and fear of Hitlerian Germany may result in a movement towards the unification, or at least the rational co-operation, of the other nation states . . .

In his talk on the B.B.C. (recorded, it would seem, sometime in 1934) Aldous's argument was on similar lines. "War is a catastrophe . . . And yet for every hundred people who kill themselves in peace-time, only seventy kill themselves in war-time.[2]

. . Man is a profoundly social animal . . . nothing brings [men] together more effectively than a common dislike for someone else . . . War strengthens [this] sense of group consolidation to the pitch of intoxication . . . War produces a certain simplification of the social structure . . and men are on the whole happier in a simple than in a complicated society . . . War begets and justifies . . violence, delight in destruction . . all the anti-social tendencies we have been so carefully trained to repress . . . The Barbarian and the sadist are strong within us . . .[3]

---

[1] *Beyond the Mexique Bay.*
[2] This fall in the suicide rate was already observed during the Franco-Prussian war of 1870 and again, more markedly, during the 1914-1918 war.
[3] Text taken from *The Causes of War*, The Telegraph Press, New York, 1935.

And while the pleasures of hatred are certainly not greater than the pleasures of love . . . they are greater than the pleasures of abstract and impersonal benevolence.

People can get more pleasure out of hating foreigners they have never seen than out of vaguely wishing them well . . . And governments foment nationalistic hatred and vanity. At school, children are taught to boast about their own nation . . . In dictatorial countries, this education . . . is continued by the State throughout adult life. In liberal countries, it is left to the voluntary labours of the Press . . .[1]

(Aldous did not love the Press and the Press did not love Aldous. The *Sunday Express*—under the editorship of James Douglas, he who said that he would rather give his child prussic acid than allow it to read *The Well of Loneliness*—once carried a two-page attack under the headline ALDOUS HUXLEY—THE MAN WHO HATES GOD.)

Aldous's answer on the B.B.C. was no longer the World Conference but long-term research into the human mind. History had shown, he said, that madmen and neurotics have been responsible for an enormous amount of mischief; we run danger even in entrusting our destinies to men who may be suffering only from the milder forms of neurosis. Research then into the psychological causes of war was urgent, but we must not look for quick results. "Those who have explored the unconscious are pessimistic about the immediate prospects of abolishing war." Winding up, Aldous stuck to the temperate long-range view, refused to raise (false) hope, spoke of fifty years of intensive research. There was something very very discouraging about that talk, and about the analysis of the war-disease in *Beyond the Mexique Bay*.

> *The best lack all conviction while the worst*
> *Are full of passionate intensity. . . .*

There is one passage we must note, in view of what was to come. Some listeners, he said, "may feel surprised that I have not spoken of the need for . . religious and ethical preaching against war". Such preaching might be desirable and do a little good, but it was off the point because man was not entirely or even mainly a conscious being. "The psychological causes of war have root in the unconscious." And what was to happen in the interval, during those years of research into that unconscious?

We must be content [he concluded] I suppose, to prescribe such political, economic and psychological sedatives as shall prevent the

---

[1] Text taken from *The Causes of War*, The Telegraph Press, New York, 1935.

patient from . . . committing suicide. If we can keep him alive long enough, the doctors may at last agree on the diagnosis and discover a cure.

*The hungry sheep look up and are not fed.* Aldous—inevitably perhaps —did not offer the listener anything he could feel or do. The paradox is that Aldous for his part at that stage was casting about for precisely that, for something to feel and do; he was holding the hero of his novel at a standstill for want of emotion and of action.

Meanwhile, on a day-to-day level, he would put in a small oar here and there. But the cool view still prevailed.

Old Henri Barbusse is trying to organize a mammoth congress in favour of peace [to Julian] . . His hobby is congresses . . . so he wants to have a really representative anti-war congress this time. His own left organization in France will of course be on tap . . . [he is also] going to try to get professional bodies—scientific, technical, legal . . This . . I very strongly urged him to go for . . if these congresses are any good at all they will only be good (because impressive) if they represent large numbers of respectable organizations. A peace demonstration would look serious if it were supported by the trade unions of doctors, engineers, lawyers . . and so forth in different countries . . . I am writing . . to ask you whether you think there'd be any hope of getting official representation from some important scientific body in England . .

Barbusse is "a dear old thing, indefatigable in verbiage and good works

. . droning interminably . . about the Social Consciousness and Russia —ignoring all facts and merely stating, again and again, what ought to be . . .

In June Aldous went to attend an international writers' congress in Paris. Among the ostensible sponsors were Gide, Priestley, Heinrich Mann. He came back indignant and disgusted.

I had hoped for serious, technical discussions . . [he put it to Victoria Ocampo]—but in fact the thing simply turned out to be a series of public meetings organized by the French Communist writers for their own glorification and the Russians' as a piece of Soviet Propaganda. Amusing to observe, as a rather discreditable episode in the Comédie Humaine; but it made one angry when one thought of what might have been done and wasn't, when one saw the cynical indifference of the Communist organizers to the wretched little delegates from the Balkans etc., who had been hoping for some serious effort on the part of other writers to understand their problems, and who found only . . endless Communist demagogy in front of an audience of 2000 people. One finds on these occasions all the worst aspects of religion—the refusal of some to use their intelligence, because they need the consolation of faith; and the cynical ambition of others, who don't believe anything but are anxious to rise in the Communist hierarchy. And everywhere a complete indifference to truth and the common decencies of civilized existence.

In July Eugene Saxton with his wife came to stay; Drieu La Rochelle was in the neighbourhood, other guests proposed themselves. Sanary life kept on much as before, but when sleep and work went badly Aldous felt hemmed in—no talks with Gerald, no prospect of interesting new cures round the next street-corner, only *Calsédine* to fall back on and the twice-dug garden.

It was after two o'clock. Anthony lay on his back staring up into the darkness. Sleep, it seemed, deliberately refused to come, was being withheld by someone else, some malignant alien inhabiting his own body. Outside, in the pine trees the cicadas harped incessantly on the theme of their existence and at long intervals a sound of cock-crowing would swell up out of the darkness . . .[1]

He took against the place (this was hard on Maria); talked of selling the house. The money spent on running it; money spent on so much else: doctors' bills, Sophie's education, helping Jeanne through difficult years; helping friends—no one in trouble, and so many of us were, was turned down but given often before asking; money going to unknown refugees. And no money earned. At this point Aldous and Maria got into a state about Matthew's future —School Certificate—University Entrance . . . His Headmaster's view was that the boy was not doing badly at all, was overcoming the handicaps of an unsettled childhood and (oddly enough) too many languages (Matthew was tri-lingual as a child, having French —in which he had done his first lessons—English and Italian, with some German thrown in by his Fräulein Bella); it would be wise, they thought at Dartington, to give him and the school a chance. (Actually Matthew had been with them for only two years and a half, which was about one term more than Aldous had had when he was whisked away from Eton.) Aldous disagreed. So, quite strongly, did Maria. As a child she had been quick and clever at her lessons. And then, what with the convent and the governesses and the quickness, and her visual turn of mind—for example, she

1 *Eyeless in Gaza*. Chatto & Windus, 1936.

could never get the words right in *Magic casements opening on the foam*—she *saw* sea and windows—she ended up with little education to speak of. She failed, we know, to get into Cambridge. Now history was *not* to repeat itself. If education was to Aldous what to most people is walking in the street *with* their clothes on, it was to Maria the personally unattainable ("he could never teach me to remember what I read in a book or spel") which one is jolly well going to make attainable to one's child. There was also this assumption: *Matthew is going to be a doctor.* (As Aldous had meant to.) This was never discussed; it was taken for granted.

Presently Aldous and Maria made a dash into Switzerland. They left in the Bugatti at 5 a.m. on a Saturday—500 kilometres in summer traffic—spent that afternoon and the whole of Sunday looking round Geneva and Lausanne, and were back by 9 p.m. on Monday night. The rush was an expression of their general state. They saw one school they liked very much, the Institut Rauch at Lausanne. Aldous informed Dartington that his son would not return next term. Dartington remonstrated and pointed out that the usual notice was required. There was correspondence. Aldous remained quite firm.

Matthew was not warned of the impending change. "Don't tell anyone, we don't want him to know," Maria wrote to Jeanne. Matthew left Dartington at the end of the summer term expecting to be back, not saying goodbye to his friends. His parents went to Geneva to meet him, another gruelling journey. The Bugatti started to boil—the radiator was ever its delicate point—and they had to limp home. Next morning at 6.30 they started again by train, twelve hours in a third-class carriage. They broke the news and introduced Matthew to the new school. He took it very well. On their return, fourteen hours, the train was packed and stank, they had to stand up in the corridor for half the way. Aldous went through his pockets but didn't have enough cash to change to second class.

Some weeks later Matthew came to Sanary for a long weekend, and they saw that he had adapted himself quickly. He seemed lively and was full of funny stories about the new place. "I am so relieved," Maria wrote to Jeanne. ". . What would we have done if he'd been unhappy or horrified?"

Maria's way now to keep things going was to live from day to day. When there was a good patch she made the most of it. At the heart of it all was still the novel; by then they rarely spoke about it to each other.

Ici les nouvelles sont bonnes [Maria wrote to Jeanne some time in September]. Aldous va bien et travaille assez bien. J'ai l'impression que ce roman se termine. Mais je n'en parle que très rarement. Il a des raisons multiples pour ne me mettre qu'en face du "Roman" accompli. Et je le comprends. Mais je m'en inquiète.

Toutefois nous sommes heureux, tranquilles et calmes.

And Aldous to Bob Nichols on 20th September:

> Here I'm hard at work on a novel that won't get finished. Expect to be in England in another month or so—unless of course we're plunged into war by then. In which case we shall probably all be dead. I wish I could see any remedy for the horrors of human beings except religion or could see any religion that we could all believe in.

(That we should all be dead at once in case of war was pure Gerald Heard—he was convinced that it would be incomparably more ghastly than anything before.)

What was going on in Aldous's novel? What was going on in Aldous's mind? We shall never be able to say. The perceptions, pointers, flashes that shape a work of art or shape a man are infinite and swift. All one can do is to attempt to trace some kind of pattern. "The theme [of the novel], fundamentally, is liberty. What happens to someone who becomes really very free ... The rather awful vacuum that such freedom turns out to be." For Aldous the aloof observer, the *littérateur*, the so-called cynic, it was in the day's work to write a novel about the vacuum, and leave it at that. As he had done more or less in *Antic Hay*. For Aldous the moralist, the man longing to make some sense of the world, the man who had said at Oxford, "I think the good will win at the end .. [if] the most persistent and tremendous efforts are made," for the Aldous who wanted to relieve the horrors besetting human beings, it was not enough. The vacuum had to be filled. Deliberately he renounced the winding up of the book in an artistically plausible way, and looked instead for a *helpful*, one might say a didactic, ending. Anthony Beavis would have to find something to feel and do that "we can all believe in". That *I* can believe in. Because with Anthony's predicament Aldous had built a model of his own.

> I sometimes have the disquieting sense that I am being somehow punished by so much good fortune [he had written earlier during the crisis]—that it is a scheme to lead me deeper into my besetting sin, the dread and avoidance of emotion, the escape from personal responsibility, the substitution of aesthetic and intellectual values for moral values—of art and thought for sanctity.

He was using the novel, using his *métier d'écrivain*, as a means of getting through—finding a solution in the novel would be finding a solution for his life. (At that point.) Maria was aware of this.

306

# "L'Année horrible" | 1935

*For a number of reasons Aldous wants to confront me with the finished novel, with the "fait accompli". Et je le comprends. Mais je m'en inquiète.*

Aldous projected himself into Anthony Beavis. He was not Anthony Beavis though he made use of a great deal of autobiographical data. Aldous and Anthony shared a background, had been to the same schools, same places, read the same books; in fact they shared a mind. *La bêtise ne fut pas leur fort.* Both possessed intellectual freedom. Otherwise there were basic discrepancies. Anthony lacked the two essential factors in Aldous's life, Maria and that very *métier d'écrivain*; he has no central attachment, and he is a sociologist who is able to write fluently, one of those novelistic transpositions of profession which seldom really work, he was a sedentary intellectual and all the rest but with the talent left out; and whatever it may be worth, that talent, it makes the difference in kind (*and* carries its own compulsions and exemptions). In other respects too, Aldous was not free like Anthony who had no domestic duties and a comfortable private income; Aldous was indeed comparatively free, being able to go or live where he pleased; but it was, and well he knew it, a precarious freedom. Last not least, Aldous was simply a much nicer man, young man, boy, than Anthony. Nor had he driven his best friend to suicide. That story of the betrayal was based on one he heard; nothing like it or remotely like it occurred in Aldous's life. (Once more the exigencies of fiction, the need to coarsen and to dramatize the fable.) There *are* other, marked autobiographical undertones. Brian Foxe, the young man who killed himself, was an admitted portrait of Aldous's brother Trev; Anthony's emotional paralysis dates from his mother's early death. Perhaps it had best be left by saying that Anthony Beavis was a much distorted portrait of Aldous by Aldous. "The school now," as Gervas Huxley said, "there is quite a bit of Hillside in *Eyeless in Gaza*, Bullstrode is straight Hillside—but no straight Aldous, oh no, no!"

Now in this context—to set the record straight—Mr Beavis, Anthony's father, was not straight Leonard Huxley, in fact was hardly Leonard Huxley at all. Aldous had not intended Mr Beavis to be like his own father.

The character came from an autobiographical poem by Coventry Patmore, called "Tired Memory". [He wrote to his step-mother in November 1936] . . the element of philology . . was based upon descriptions given by Frieda Lawrence of her first husband . . . the character yet has a strong resemblance to the parson in D. H. Lawrence's *Virgin and the Gypsy*, a figure who was actually derived from the same source. After that it became necessary to fix the personage in time, as the inhabitant of a certain epoch. And here, I am afraid quite unjustifiably, I made use of mannerisms and phrases

307

some of which were recognizably father's. I had not thought that they would prove recognizable to others and I am most distressed to find that they should have been.

Later Rosalind Huxley had a talk with Aldous on the subject. She spoke to him "about the excessive way he used traits of his father, and still more of Trev, then adding characteristics which were totally *alien*. To me he said how profoundly sorry he was . . . He made the same mistakes about other people, seeming curiously unaware that these things hurt people . . . but he was genuinely distressed and upset when they were mentioned. Yet he was the kindest and most considerate of people. I had a very great affection for him."[1]

Meanwhile it is still Sanary, September 1935. What is happening to Anthony as he lies sleepless in the Mediterranean night, listening to the cicadas who have ceased to charm? We do not know. Maria did not see the recent chapters (nor did anyone else). My guess, for what it's worth, is that Aldous had some intimation of where Anthony was going, but still could not see how to bring it off in terms of fiction—on that road to Damascus, whom was he to meet? The substance of this was getting ready to be tapped (had been tapped at other stages of Aldous's life—in *Antic Hay*, in *Those Barren Leaves*, that night in Spain). It was now, in this summer, that Aldous began to practice—with some difficulty—a kind of non-metaphysical meditation; what had started, at Gerald's instigation, as exercises in breathing and in mind control had led to this. It was his writing, however, which served him as the main discipline towards the break-through; at the same time, his writing, that is his circumstances and responsibilities, compelled him, unfortunately perhaps, to tap this thing in public and at once, when he was still not certain how to do it. Aldous had already gone a good way —on his own and with Gerald Heard, absorbing, using, at that point what Gerald had to offer—towards a "religious" solution. Now how to translate this into action? Aldous was yet to meet F. M. Alexander, Dr McDonagh and Dick Sheppard.

The Rev. H. R. L. Sheppard, Vicar of St Martin's-in-the-Field, Dean of Canterbury, Canon of St Paul's, a man overflowing with the love of his fellows, reckless in the expenditure of himself, orator, organizer, legend in his own life-time, a man who could make contact with every human being he met, the best known and most

[1] Rosalind (Mrs Leonard Huxley), in a letter to S. B., February 1970.

loved priest in England, whom when he died—early, suddenly, at
his desk in 1937—the country mourned:

> his coffin was followed from St Martin's . . . through the streets of
> London to St Paul's by a great concourse of every kind and class of
> men and women . . . the streets were lined as though for royalty . . .[1]

this man who "had built his whole life on the concept 'love one
another' ", who had been in the trenches in the first war and
appalled by the suffering inflicted by man upon man, became convinced that Christianity was incompatible with war, and decided
to make one great stand. In October 1934 he sent a letter to the
Press.

> The main reason for this letter . . is the fresh urgency of the present
> international situation, and the almost universally acknowledged
> lunacy of the manner in which nations are pursuing peace.
> The situation is far graver than we allow ourselves to acknowledge . . .
> I represent no Church and no peace organization of any des-
> cription . . .
> It seems essential to discover whether or not it be true . . that the
> majority of thoughtful men in this country are now convinced that
> war of every kind or for any cause, is not only a denial of Christianity,
> but a crime against humanity, which is no longer to be permitted
> by civilized people.
> Have we reached that state of belief?
> . . The idea behind this letter is not to form any fresh organization
> . . but to attempt to discover how strong the will to peace has grown.
> . . Would those of my sex who, so far, have been silent, but . . are
> willing to support a resolution as uncompromising as the following,
> send a postcard to me within the next fortnight:
> *We renounce war and never again, directly or indirectly, will we support or
> sanction another.*

Not a single postcard came for two days. On the third—the post
office had had to organize delivery—van-loads of sacks, sacks
crammed with postcards, postcards cascading over the floor. Over
a hundred thousand. "The first thing was to get in touch with all
those unknown people who had committed themselves . . .

> Thus it came about that an invitation to meet in the Albert Hall
> went out to every signatory . . . [in June 1935] Dick Sheppard was
> anxiously waiting in a room behind the platform . . wondering what
> was going to happen . . .

[1] Sybil Morrison, *I Renounce War: The Story of the Peace Pledge Union.* Sheppard
Press Ltd., 1962.

Presently they began to arrive, old and young men, but mostly young, in the end they were packed so tightly that there was no more room. The sight of that vast gathering of men . . keyed Dick Sheppard to his best . . he caught, held and deeply involved everyone in the great hall that Sunday. With him on the platform were Edmund Blunden, Siegfried Sassoon, [the Rev.] Maude Royden and Frank [Brig.-General] Crozier. There were to be other Albert Hall meetings, but never again one like this.[1]

That was the beginning of what was first called H. R. L. Sheppard's Peace Movement and later The Peace Pledge Union. (The pledge was later altered to a simpler form; the P.P.U. exists today.) Local groups were formed; Dick Sheppard got a number of people to act as sponsors. (The first of these were, besides those already mentioned, Storm Jameson, Ellen Wilkinson, Donald Soper, Laurence Housman, Eric Gill, Vera Brittain, John Middleton Murry, George Lansbury, Arthur Ponsonby.) Postcards still came in at the rate of 200 a day.

The Huxleys went back to Albany in October. At once Aldous had to cope with a three weeks of dentist appointments; then they went over to Belgium for the marriage of Maria's little sister, which "from a quiet affair [M to Roy] became suddenly a ceremony with show and friends and therefore us". (Rose, a ravishing young creature, perhaps the most wayward and ebullient of the sisters, was marrying the poet Eric de Haulleville.) And after that Aldous and Maria settled down "to live in London like hermits . . until the novel, which is going well, is finished.

You can probably picture my life, a constant refusal at the telephone to see our best friends who think they have a right to see us and who instantly think it is me who will not allow Aldous to go to them.

They did see Gerald, who in the meantime had become interested in Dick Sheppard's Movement. And it was he who brought in Aldous. Dick Sheppard recommended absolutes; absolutes, in Dennis Gabor's words, "so simple that a child could grasp them but only an angel could follow them". Aldous's great forte was complexity, he had been wandering for so long in his contrapuntal maze, that at this moment there was something irresistible in that difficult, angelic, simplicity. He went for it as one might for a

1 Sybil Morrison.

draught of spring water after a line of vintages. On 19th November he wrote those crucial words to Victoria Ocampo.

. . The thing finally resolves itself into a religious problem—an uncomfortable fact which one must be prepared to face and which I have come during the last year to find it easier to face.

"Meanwhile what an appalling situation we've all got ourselves into! Musso attacking Abyssinia: we using sanctions and so forcing the Italians to rally round Musso: the dictator's *amour propre* so . . inflamed . . that he can't admit any kind of defeat or make any compromise; and if he is forced into a corner he will act like Samson and pull the whole building down on his head—if he has to go, then let the whole of Europe go too!—It's the sort of behaviour one saw going on at one's preparatory school—and the whole world is threatened by it.

the only hope lies in the pacifists being better disciplined than the militarists and prepared to put up with as great hardships and dangers with a courage equal to theirs. Not easy. But I suppose nothing of any value is easy.

At the second big Albert Hall meeting on 27th November, Aldous *was* on the platform. He, like Gerald Heard, had become a sponsor of the Movement. On 3rd December Aldous gave the talk at the lunch hour meetings for Peace and Internationalism held weekly at Friends' House in the Euston Road.

. . Our end is peace. How do we propose to realize this end? . . If we want to be treated with trust and affection by others we must ourselves treat those others with trust and affection . . . We largely construct the ethical world in which we live. It is to a great extent a matter of choice whether we construct it as a world of fear and greed or as a world of trust and love . . . there is nothing inherently absurd about the idea that the world which we have so largely constructed can also, if we so desire, be reconstructed on other and better lines.
. . No end can be realized without appropriate means . . . No pacifist can permit himself to think in abstractions . . . war is a process of large-scale murder . . . hostile nations consist of individual men and women . . .

He went on to say—and *this was* the great turning point in Aldous's thinking—that the most propitious metaphysical environment for pacifism could not be humanism but a philosophy which recognized the existence of more than human spiritual realities. "Not, indeed a belief in any exclusive deity attached to any particular community or place—such a belief inevitably makes for war—but in a spiritual reality to which all men have access and in which they are united:

God . . regarded, and if possible experienced as a psychological fact, present at least potentially in every human being.

And Aldous ended this talk, "If enough people address themselves to living up to this belief, if enough people set out to experience [this] spiritual reality . . then there will be peace; for peace . . is a by-product of a certain way of life."

It is not certain who led Aldous to F. M. Alexander (Gerald? Bernard Shaw?) Anyway to Alexander he went in that same November and became his pupil. F. Matthias Alexander (1869–1955) of Australia, ex-actor, therapist, discoverer and teacher of the Alexander technique, author (*The Use of the Self, Creative Conscious Control, The Universal Constant of Living*, etc., etc.), who taught for some fifty years in England and the United States, of whom Leonard Woolf has said that he was a quack but an honest and inspired quack. G. B. S. and John Dewey had been his pupils. Now Aldous went, every day, applying himself to the difficult task of "kinesthetic" re-education, of learning how to walk, sit down, reach for a book, open a door, in a new, but only very subtly different, way. (As Shaw put it, "Alexander calls upon the world to see a change so small and so subtle that only he can see it".[1]) Aldous became convinced that Alexander had made a very important, in fact an essential discovery.

[He] discovered empirically [as Aldous put it in a nutshell 15 years later on in a letter to Dr Hubert Benoit] in experimentation on himself, that there is a correct or "natural" relationship between the neck and the trunk and that normal functioning of the total organism cannot take place except when the neck and trunk are in the right relationship. His findings have been confirmed theoretically by various physiologists and, in practice, in the persons of the numerous pupils he has taught . . . for some obscure reason the great majority of those who have come in contact with urbanized, industrial civilization tend to lose the innate capacity for preserving the correct relation between neck and trunk, and consequently never enjoy completely normal organic functioning. Alexander and the teachers

---

[1] As quoted in *The Resurrection of the Body: The Writings of F. Matthias Alexander*, edited by Edward Maisel. University Books, New York, 1969.

he has trained re-establish the correct relationship and teach their pupils to preserve it consciously. This, as I know by experience, is an exceedingly valuable technique. For not only does one have to become aware of the data of organic reality (to the exclusion of the insane life of phantasy); one also . . makes it possible for the physical organism to function as it ought to function, thus improving the general state of physical and mental health. (Incidentally, the "straight-spine" position so much insisted upon by the teachers of yoga is precisely the posture advocated by Alexander. The merit of A. consists in having analysed the essential factors in this posture and having developed a technique for teaching . . [it] . . .)

It was not at all easy to learn. Aldous—very willing, very patient —proved rather good at it. There he was practising away in Albany, how to place one's feet, how to get out of a chair. It became noticeable that he was holding himself differently—his movements looked deliberate and slow. Maria also went to Alexander, and they couldn't wait for Matthew to have a go at it. (He still dismisses it as "a rather expensive way to make a boy stand up straight". Alexander did not exactly run a charity institution.) Aldous eventually got the hang of it, re-conditioned his habits as he would have put it—in the fluid, unnoticeable way it was supposed to be; and he kept it up for the rest of his life.

Meanwhile Alexander sent him to Dr McDonagh. J. E. R. McDonagh, "that odd fish," who had a theory that many or most disorders were caused by intoxication of the intestines. "No wonder you are a sceptic if you poison yourself with butcher's meat." Aldous (and in due course Maria and the children) submitted to his treatment by colonic lavages, vaccine injections and diet. Aldous's life became exceedingly active. Committee meetings with Dick Sheppard, discussions with Gerald as to ways and means, planning a pamphlet for the Peace Movement, writing letters to the Press. In the morning he sat in his goldfish-bowl working away with a will. This was the time when the missing chapters, the clinching chapters, at last, at last, were flowing—the encounter in Mexico with Miller and Anthony's post-"conversion" diary, broken up into seventeen chapters (quantitatively about one-seventh of that very long book) and inserted here and there like the clues in a treasure hunt; a labour which must have given Aldous a certain satisfaction. (Originally he meant to finish with fewer and shorter diary chapters; it was Maria who after much hesitation, urged him to extend Anthony's *journal intime*. And it is rather interesting to read this journal straight.)

Aldous and Maria did no longer live like hermits in London, but they stuck to early evenings and tried to see only people relevant to his present concerns. They also tried to live economically (Aldous having published no novel for four years and no book at all for twenty months). Maria never looked at a taxi and often walked instead of taking the bus. They became more social for a few weeks when Dr Charlotte Wolff came over from Paris, at their suggestion, to collect prints of some interesting hands. Dr Wolff stayed in Dalmeny Court across the road, and the Huxleys put themselves out in the way of introductions. In the early afternoon when Aldous had gone off to Alexander, Maria would open the door to T. S. Eliot or Virginia Woolf or Lady Ottoline, and then go out herself. Presently one could perceive the doctor by the tall window poring through a magnifying glass into a distinguished hand in the waning London winter light. (Albany became censorious but was also somewhat intrigued.) As well as taking prints, the doctor did a kind of—very remarkable—psychological reading. Soon there were queues. She was bidden to Mrs Simpson's.[1] Aldous introduced her to Julian under whom she later made her studies of the monkeys' hands at the Zoo. (All this led not only to an interesting collection of records but to Dr Wolff's decision to base her future work in England.)

News of Matthew was good. (He did not come home that Christmas holiday.) The sudden change of school had done him no harm and he had got through an immense amount of work. "Aussi un rapport excéllent sur le caractère," (Maria to Jeanne). "Heureusement qu'il ne perd pas cela en grandissant." As a young boy Matthew had been remarkable for his openness and niceness; now, rising sixteen, it became evident that he was not going to lose his warmth and generosity of nature, nor his marvellous talent for spontaneous contact. The "nice" boy ultimately became an even nicer man.

No New Year's Eve party—but in January Maria was able to write to Jeanne, "The book is approaching its end. Aldous's health is good without being brilliant; but he is working enormously and he is calm and quiet.

> J'espère que cette année sera aussi différente de la dernière que possible. Je crois que personne ne peut se rendre compte de ce que toute l'année dernière a eu d'horrible . . .

The further I get away from it, the more I realize how horrible it has been. . . ."

---

[1] The present Duchess of Windsor.

## Chapter Three

## *Eyeless in Gaza:* The Nobler Hypothesis

Dear Gene,

. . Aldous really thinks he is going to answer your letter but I know better . . .

We believe that certainly the manuscript will go to Chatto's in the first week of March.

No the old enemy insomnia is checked and by the man Alexander but more of that later as I am trying to answer your letter point by point as an efficient secretary should, I believe, do.

Aldous does not wish to see the proof.

Alexander . . . certainly has made a new and unrecognizable person of Aldous, not physically only but mentally and therefore morally. Or rather, he has brought out, actively, all we, Aldous's best friends, know never came out either in the novels or with strangers . . . Probably you will think we have gone cracky, so did I think of Aldous until I saw the results and particularly since I went myself. It comes in the novel too. Oh, how I hate that novel. Except that now that it is finished I really don't care any more; but I did hate it. Not meaning that it is not very good; when I say I hate it it is for very different and personal reasons. The misery it has caused us and so on.

E2 Albany W.1
21 February 1936

So Maria to Aldous's American publishers. But meanwhile Aldous had engaged himself to do a pamphlet for the Peace Movement (Chatto's were to publish it, price 3d., royalties to the P.P.U.). The idea was to get it out quickly so he wrote it when he was still in the final stages of the novel. (The material was of course related.) The pamphlet was finished by 21st March, and a week later the last batch of typescript of the novel went to Chatto's. Maria wrote at once to Jeanne.

Chère Janin,

Here is our latest news. The book is finished. Aldous is going away with Victor for three days while I'm getting ready for the children. Je commence à m'en réjouir follement . . .

With what relief Maria was returning to the sweet ordinariness of life. The Hutchinsons are coming to tea, en famille, because it is their son Jeremy's twenty-first birthday ... She is thinking of going to Kew with Gerald—yesterday was so very fine—and taking a picnic lunch ... Tomorrow morning at ten Aldous will be off with Victor Rothschild "to visit centres of industry and low homosexuality at Nottingham". Now plans for the Easter holidays. Such an irresistible letter from Matthew yesterday. (I am translating and compressing freely.) He's asked a friend to stay, thinking we'd be in Sanary. May he bring him to London? What can I do? We can't say no—the first time he's asked us. I don't think we should *ever* say no. What about sending the two boys to Dalmeny Court— Sophie can have the sitting-room sofa—they have rooms for five shillings a night—*bain compris*—they might have their breakfast at a Lyons, and afterwards come here where all will be right and tight, and we can start the day. Matthew wants to show London to his friend. I shall lose a certain intimacy with him, which we renew at every holiday; but this is bound to happen one day, so I'm resigned.

There's the expense ... But I'm going to give up the idea of hiring a car ... It may all turn out cheaper in the end ... Donc je ne suis plus épouvantée. And Bessie (Bessie Simpkins who did the housework) speaks such pretty English, because she's Irish, that will be so nice for Sophie's accent. Adieu Janin et merci de me prêter ta fille ...

It all went very well (in spite of doctor's visits). Gerald had gone to Greece, such a pity for Matthew, but Gerald needed a holiday ... They went to see a Chaplin and a film by H. G. Wells, and spent Easter Monday Bank Holiday on Hampstead Heath. Sunday they had Matthew's Dartington friend, Ivan Moffat, for lunch, after which they went to the Zoo, followed by tea at Juliette's. At the Zoo, Aldous recited to the animals and teased the baboons with his umbrella. It was a gusty day and he was wearing his floppy overcoat and did look rather like a person out of Edward Lear. A string of sneering capering little boys attached themselves to his back, following him from cage to cage. Aldous appeared oblivious to their existence. (This is Ivan Moffat's story.) "He must have had eyes in his back—just as he was about to feed some monkeys, he whipped round and proffered the carrot to the little boys. They fled with shrieks."

The Huxleys had arranged to go to South America that summer, on the suggestion of their Argentinian friend, Victoria Ocampo, editor of the review *Sur*, literary and musical patron and a very great beauty in her time. Dr McDonagh advised against it, and in March Aldous cried off. ".. If the man weren't doing me so much good, I wd ignore what he says ... He says he can make a complete job of the thing if I have another treatment this summer. So I really have no alternative ... for I have no intention of relapsing into the condition I was in last year, if I can possibly help it." So in April, after the children were gone, Aldous and Maria went to Sanary for a short summer.

*Eyeless in Gaza* was published on 18th June. Ten days earlier Aldous had written to C. E. M. Joad to whom he had sent an advance copy,

> I'm very glad to know that you think the book's all right. I had lost all sense of what it was like—w'd have liked, if it had been possible, to put it aside and look at it again after two or three years. Wolves at the door imposed immediate publication and I let it go, feeling uncomfortably in the dark about the thing.

"We have no idea how it's doing," Maria wrote to Jeanne on 19th June, "but I'm almost certain it'll make enough to pay our debts [to Chatto's] and to keep us going for a year. At the moment we are still short, Aldous doesn't want to ask his publishers for anything before the accounts come in July, and we've given up the idea to fetch Matthew because of the expense." The book did better than that. The subscription (in England) was 4,000; with 26,700 copies sold by the end of the year. In other ways the reception, not unexpectedly, was very mixed. Readers often are disgruntled when their author ceases to provide expected fare. "Aldous," Harold Raymond once said, "shoots in front of his public flock. In a couple of years they have flown into his shot." Aldous's flock did increase after 1936, but some of it was a new and different flock. Then there were the critics . . . But that is literary history, not Aldous's. He had long given up reading anything about himself if he could help it.

What was the substance of *Eyeless in Gaza*? What, in essence, was it that Anthony at last believed in? The pacifist solution, certainly. The religious solution? Upon what ground or faith? What intellectual basis? Let us go to the book itself.

". . Swine will be swine." But may become human, I insisted. *Homo non nascitur, fit.* [From Anthony's Diary, 1st June 1934]

"It begins," he answered, "with trying to cultivate the difficult art of loving people."

"But most people are detestable."

"They're detestable, because we detest them. If we liked them, they'd be likeable."

"Do you think that's true?"

"I'm sure it's true."

"And what do you do after that?"

"There's no after," he replied. "Because, of course, it's a lifetime's job."

[Last chapter, 23rd February 1935]

Empirical facts:

One. We are all capable of love for other human beings.

Two. We impose limitations on that love.

Three. We can transcend all these limitations—if *we choose to*. (It is a matter of observation that anyone who so desires can overcome personal dislike, class feeling, national hatred, colour prejudice. Not easy; but it can be done . . .)

Four. Love expressing itself in good treatment breeds love. Hate expressing itself in bad treatment breeds hate.

In the light of these facts, it's obvious what inter-personal, inter-class and international policies should be. But, again, knowledge cuts little ice. We all know; we almost all fail to do. It's a question, as usual, of the best methods of implementing intentions.

[Anthony's Diary, 26th May 1934]

Mark . . began to laugh. Foresaw the time when I'd preface every mention of a person or group with the adjective "dear". "The dear Communists," "the dear armament makers," "dear General Goering." [Anthony's Diary, 20th May 1934]

. . Helen asked if I were happy. I said, yes—though didn't know if happiness was the right word. More substantial, more complete, more interested, more aware . . . [Anthony's Diary, 1st June 1934]

God—a person or not a person? *Quien sabe?* Only revelation can decide such metaphysical questions. And revelation isn't playing the game—is equivalent to pulling three aces of trumps from up your sleeve. [Anthony's Diary, Christmas Day 1934]

God may or may not exist. But there is the empirical fact that contemplation of the divinity—of goodness in its most unqualified form—is a method of realizing that goodness in some slight degree is in one's own life . . .

[Anthony's Diary, 21st September 1934]

And how had Aldous led Anthony to these convictions? Anthony, aged forty-three, at the point of deadlock, is sent off on an apparently futile journey to Mexico in the wake of his Draconian friend Mark Staithes who is going to assist one Don Jorge, a coffee planter, in a private revolution. Mark and Anthony ride across

the Sierra Juarez as Aldous had with Maria and Don Roy. They
spend a night in a place where the bar of their hotel is a crypt-like
room propped by wooden pillars. A drunken young Mexican
appears, offers a drink, is turned down and starts shooting up the
place. (It was now that Roy Fenton got his answer as to why the
Ejutla incident was left out in *Beyond the Mexique Bay*—Aldous had
saved it for the novel.) But the *mauvais quart-d'heure* in a traveller's
day had become a merciless exposition of *timor mortis*; Anthony is
shown reduced to quivering terror. "Don't, don't!" he cries as he
darts to take shelter behind a pillar. (In life it had been Roy who
shouted to Aldous to take cover.)

> . . Anthony imagined the revolver suddenly coming round the
> pillar . . A fear so intense that it was like the most excruciating
> physical pain . . . The noise of the revolver going off—that was
> what he dreaded most . . . The pistol went off . . the report was
> catastrophically loud. Anthony uttered a great cry . . shutting his
> eyes, flattened himself again the pillar . . .

And so on. Going once more recently through the whole thing
with Roy, we rather agreed that here was another example of the
genesis of fiction. Roy heard no great cry; Aldous, he maintains,
behaved sensibly, kept calm, though there had been good cause
for fear (Roy's own terror had been the possibility of Maria's
suddenly appearing). And yet, *and yet*—"Of course I don't know
exactly *what* went on in Aldous's mind as he was hopping from pillar
to pillar."

Ejutla was in passing. Next day, Mark Staithes has a fall and
is hurt. Anthony rides on alone in an attempt to reach an habitation
and get help. After two hours' riding over desolate country, "the
miracle happened. Coming round a bend in the track he saw advancing towards him . . a white man . . ." The white man raises
his hat. They speak. Anthony has met the catalyst. James Miller,
M.D., Edinburgh. He loses no time, on their way back to Mark,
Miller takes Anthony to task.

> "Well, Anthony Beavis . . what's your profession? Ever been married?
> You ought to have been. How old are you?"
> "Forty-three."
> "And look younger. Though I don't like that sallow skin of yours.
> Do you suffer much from constipation? . . and of course stiff neck
> . . lumbago. I know, I know . . . And the irony, the scepticism, that
> what-the-good-of-it-all attitude! . . Everything you think is nega-
> tive . . .
> "Oh, don't imagine I'm criticizing . . don't get it into your head
> that I'm blaming you in any way." Stretching out his hand, [the

doctor] patted Anthony affectionately on the shoulder. "We're all of us what we are; and when it comes to turning ourselves into what we ought to be—well it isn't easy. No, it isn't easy, Anthony Beavis. [Miller speaks with the friendly directness of the Quakers; now we are getting some straight McDonagh–Alexander]. How do you expect to think in anything but a negative way, when you've got chronic intestinal poisoning? . . at the same time stooping as you do. Slumped down on your mule . . Pressing down on the vertebrae . . . And when the spine's in that state, what happens to the rest of the machine . . .

". . . You've got to change if you want to go on existing. And if it's a matter of changing—why, you need all the help you can get, from God's to the doctor's. . . .

Now, this passage in the novel is not sudden for the reader, the bait was laid already by Anthony's post-Miller journal which, due to the shuffled time sequence, begins before the Mexican meeting. In the journal Miller comes and goes—his connection with Anthony unexplained for the time being—organizing a peace movement in England, teaching an Alexander technique, preaching by example. Miller is a saintly man, elderly, friendly, humorous, wise and blunt —forerunner of the Scottish doctor of *Island*—combining the conduct and ideas of Dick Sheppard with the theories of McDonagh and of Alexander (though *very* far from Alexander's rather epicurean way of life) and a good many concepts of Gerald Heard's.

"Speaking as a doctor [Miller concluded in the Mexican Sierra] . . I'd suggest a course of colonic irrigation to start with."

"And speaking for God," said Anthony . . "a course of prayer and fasting."

"No, not fasting," the doctor protested very seriously . . "only a proper diet . . As for prayer . . All that asking for special favours and guidances . . it tends to make one egotistical . . you're merely rubbing yourself into yourself . . . Whereas what we're all looking for is a way of getting beyond our own vomit."

And now we get a very characteristic passage:

Some way, Anthony was thinking, of getting beyond the books, beyond the perfumed and resilient flesh of women, beyond fear and sloth, beyond the painful but secretly flattering vision of the world as menagerie and asylum.

Anthony returns to London and the job of turning himself into what he ought to be. "It begins with the difficult art of loving people." He accepts help on *any* level: spiritual exercises, diet, physical training.

At today's lesson [Alexander] . . found myself suddenly a step forward in my grasp of the theory and practice . . . To learn proper use one must first inhibit all improper uses of the self . . . This process entails knowing good and bad use—knowing them apart . . . Increased awareness and power of control result . . trivialities take on a new significance . . Cleaning teeth, putting on shoes . . . Skill in getting to know the muscular aspect of mind-body can be carried over into the exploration of other aspects. There is increasing ability to detect one's motives for any given piece of behaviour . . . Also, one becomes more . . . conscious of what's going on in the outside world . . . Control also is transferred. Acquire the art of inhibiting muscular bad use and you acquire thereby the art of inhibiting more complicated trains of behaviour. Not only this: there is prevention as well as cure. . . There is an end, for example, of neurotic anxieties and depressions . . . In practice, neurosis is always associated with some kind of wrong use. (Note the typically bad physical posture of neurotics and lunatics . .) Re-educate. Give back correct physical use. You remove the keystone of the arch constituting the neurotic personality . . . Most of us are slightly neurotic. Even slight neurosis provides endless occasions for bad behaviour . . . Hitherto preventive ethics has been thought of as external to the individual social and economic reforms carried out with a view to eliminating occasions for bad behaviour. This is important. But not nearly enough . . . [We must find] a method of achieving progress from within as well as from without. Progress, not only as a citizen . . but also as a human being.

[Anthony's Diary, 3rd June 1934]

How hard though to achieve that progress—the vigilance, the patience, the continual saying No to habitual response.

Wouldn't it be nice, for a change, if there were another way out of our difficulties! A short cut. A method requiring no greater personal effort than recording a vote or ordering some "enemy of society" to be shot. A salvation from outside, like a dose of calomel.

[Anthony's Diary, 4th August 1934]

And what pitfalls. Meditation can become a bolt-hole from unpleasant reality, quietism mere self-indulgence.

"The contemplative life" It can be made a kind of high-brow substitute for Marlene Dietrich: a subject for erotic musing in the twilight. Meditation—valuable . . . only as a means of effecting desirable changes in the personality and mode of existence. To live contemplatively is not to live in some deliciously voluptuous or flattering Poona; it is to live in London, but to live there in a non-cockney style.          [Anthony's Diary, 17th September 1934]

Anthony has made a speech at a peace meeting . . . five hundred people in a hall . . some invincibly ignorant . . Afterwards Mark tells him,

"Might as well go and talk to cows in a field." The temptation to agree with him was strong. All my old habits of thinking, living, feeling impel me towards agreement. A senseless world, where nothing whatever can be done—how satisfactory! . . I caught myself taking immense pleasure in commenting on the imbecility of my audience and human beings at large. Caught and checked myself.
[Anthony's Diary, 20th May 1934]

And what if they understand, if they *are* convinced?

Very good meeting in Newcastle with Miller. Large and enthusiastic crowds—predominantly of the dispossessed. Note the significant fact that pacifism is in inverse ratio, generally, to prosperity. The greater the poverty, the longer the unemployment . . the more complete the scepticism about the conventional idols . . . A negative attitude . . Therefore not to be relied on. Negative pacifism and scepticism . . are just holes in the mind, emptinesses waiting to be filled. Fascism or communism have sufficient positive content to act as fillers. Someone with the talents of Hitler may suddenly appear. The negative void will be pumped full in a twinkling. These . . pacifist sceptics will be transformed overnight into drilled fanatics of nationalism, class war or whatever it may be. Question: have we time to fill the vacuum with positive pacifism? Or, having the time, have we the ability?          [Anthony's Diary, 4th November 1934]

We can only try. That, in the end, is Anthony's conclusion: We have got to try.

". . if you treat other people well, they'll treat you well."
"You're a bit optimistic, aren't you?"
"No. In the long run they'll always treat you well."
"In the long run," said Mark impatiently, "we shall all be dead. What about the short run?"
"You've got to take a risk."
"But Europeans aren't like your Sunday-school savages. It'll be an enormous risk."
"Possibly. But always smaller than the risk you run by treating people badly and goading them into war."
[Mexico, 7th February 1934]

The book ends with Anthony by himself. In a few hours he is
to speak at a meeting in Battersea. He has had a nasty anonymous
letter—We're going to get you, you pacifist skunk. Anthony begins
by being very frightened—physical violence, they're going to beat
him up; how will he face it? (the point was made, we see now,
behind that pillar at Ejutla). He is tempted to funk it. Why not
go back to what nature meant him to do, "to looking on from a
private box and making comments". Ring them up, a small voice
says, tell them you've got flu. He checks this "baseness". Now he
goes into a long meditation.

> "Unity." He was committed . . as a hand is committed to the arm.
> Committed to his friends, committed even to those who had declared
> themselves his enemies. There was nothing he could do but would
> affect them all . . For good, if what he did were good, for evil if it
> were wrong. Unity, he repeated.
> Unity of mankind, unity of all life . . .

Unity—and separation, diversity—the conditions of our existence. *Born under one law, to another bound.* The evil of separation
bridged by the act of love and compassion:

> . . Constantly obstructed. But, oh, let them be made indefatigable,
> implacable to surmount all obstacles, the inner sloth, the distaste,
> the intellectual scorn . . . Affection, compassion . . . Peace . . .

The clock strikes seven. Anthony emerges into the present—calm,
resolved, serene.

*Absolutes so simple* . . . Never again was Aldous to appear so single-
minded, so confiding, so unqualifying . . . But the resolutions of
*Eyeless in Gaza* remained.

It is a curious book. Aldous himself found it hard to see it whole.
There is much that is very good (that scene of the two children
sailing their toy ship in the night) and some things that are awful
with the deliberate awfulness Aldous used to drag into his verse,
the awfulness, indeed, he perceived to be a part of human experience. (How unnerved Maria was by that dead dog dropping
on to the roof.) One obvious defect of the book is the comparative
brand-newness of the "solution" inserts, the use made, compelled
by those wolves at the door, of too recent experience. The tract, it
was said, had got into the novel. Many readers of my generation
and antecedents, myself included, were put off, resentful even; the
book's qualities tended to get overlooked. The story, I think now,
is extremely well-knit, the famous jumbled time sequence *is*

effective, adding rather than detracting from coherence, adding to perspective. There is also an unobtrusive sense of period: one knows that this is 1902 or 1911 or 1926. The book's major fault seems to me its length. Too many points are made more than twice; too much is over-insisted on in the "unregenerate" narrative parts. Perhaps it was because Aldous, unable for so long to find the ending, went on and on about the things he knew. The impact at two-thirds or less the length would have been greater.

As concerns Aldous, *Eyeless in Gaza* was the expression of a stage in a lifetime of development. Aldous did not so much change—he went on. One stage, but a crucial stage; a point of no return. Aldous never went back on the convictions he had come to. The belief in the existence of a spiritual reality underlying the phenomenal world, imparting to it whatever value or significance it possesses. The belief that this reality can be experienced by anyone who so chooses. The concern with the present and the future of mankind —"the world is to a great extent illusory .. it is none the less essential to improve the illusion." The belief that desirable social changes can be brought about by changing the individuals who compose society. The continued emphasis on the need for knowledge and intelligence (directed by a disinterested will)—"for insensitive stupidity is the root of all the other vices". These, in a more complex, subtle and wide-ranging way, became the constants of Aldous's life, thought and work. In 1936 they were in parts still intimations of what he had not yet himself fully experienced but already believed to be attainable; circumstances and the first fine flush of Dick Sheppard's radiantly virtuous absolutes impelled Aldous to preach early what from that point on he practised. *Eyeless in Gaza* was the blue-print, as it were, of what Aldous set out to discover and to be. It was the expression of the nobler hypothesis.

> For faith is not believing something which our intelligence denies. It is the choice of the nobler hypothesis. Faith is the resolve to place the highest meaning on the facts which we observe.[1]

The last words of *Eyeless in Gaza* are: "He thought of what was in store for him. Whatever it might be, he knew that all would be well."

[1] *Prayers and Meditations: A Monthly Cycle Arranged for Daily Use*, edited by Gerald Heard. Harper & Brothers, 1949. Seven out of thirty-one meditations were written by Aldous Huxley. His friend Peggy (Mrs William) Kiskadden has the typescript of these. *Faith*, meditation No. 4 from which I quoted, is not by Aldous. (The ones by him are: *Being, Beauty, Love, Peace, Holiness, Grace* and *Joy*.)

# Chapter Four
## Striking Tents

A S for our winter plans, Maria wrote to Jeanne from Sanary in June, "I cannot tell . . .

> Je me laisse vivre au jour le jour et profite de la tranquillité et de la chaleur et de la gaîté de ce pays qu'il est bien possible que nous n'habiterons plus pour longtemps.

"I'm sure Aldous will sell the house at the first chance. Although he is happy and in good spirits, I have sometimes the impression that he's bored. He won't admit it; but I have reason to believe I'm right. He's hardly interested in painting anymore and only does it because there's nothing else for him to do."

Boredom? Flatness? Accidie? Or a sense of having reached the end of what that calm Mediterranean country had to offer him? Of having done with old habits and old friends, of being held back by their modes of thinking, living? An instinct for the need of a new framework, other stimuli? Aldous's health was all right; he was sleeping well, he was writing. Odds and ends for the Peace Movement, and *The Olive Tree*, another collection of essays (off his hands in August, published in December), some of it had already appeared in print: the ten-year-old "Crébillon the Younger", very characteristic of his manner of the period; "In a Tunisian Oasis", also of the 'Twenties and first published in *Vogue*; some of his finest critical work, such as the lecture on T. H. Huxley, the introduction to Lawrence's *Letters* and the essay on the painter B. R. Haydon, one of

> those indomitable madmen who have made the British Empire and English literature, English politics and English science the extraordinary things they are. Haydon was one of those glorious lunatics . . .

For that not very homogeneous collection Aldous now wrote three or four new pieces: a long discussion, "Writers and Readers", about the effects if any of the written word ("The propagandists of the future will probably be chemists and psychologists as well as writers . . .") and, close to his present concerns, the essay "Words and Behaviour" ("The most shocking thing about war is that its victims and its instruments are individual human beings").

It was particularly hot in Sanary that summer. The household was very quiet; Maria basking—she said—in laziness and peace. Actually she was struggling to acquire the alien skill of shorthand, and even found the time to type a chunk of a long novel I'd just finished. Alas she also passed the novel on to Aldous. It was a bad, empty novel, and he told me as much; on paper. Pages, hand-written, of analysis and good advice. I have them before me. He really did take trouble (though it was pretty shattering at the time). ". . lack of vital relationship between the characters . . . issues of little significance . . . the book needs to be simultaneously shortened and filled up . . ."

Matthew seemed to have taken a sudden step into grown-upness and he and Maria were pottering about a good deal on their own; he made, she said, "an adorable companion". Then this nice quiet life was idiotically shattered.

. . The earthly Paradise . . has been turned into a devilish hot turmoil. [Maria wrote to Eddy Sackville-West] One of my inter-ventions towards catastrophic friends has replaced the peace.

We expected to lunch . . a whole very energetic family of French people [Jean Coutrot, ex-pupil of the Ecole Polytechnique, one of the new French technocrats who acted as a kind of unofficial brain trust to the Léon Blum government, whom Aldous had briefly met in June at the Abbaye de Pontigny] . . at a quarter to two arrives a telephone message from the hospital at Hyères that they cannot come because they have had a motor accident and are lying there. Which made me feel very guilty as I had spent the morning saying that he was a wild driver . . . Scirocco in full blast, 36 [centigrade] in the shade and no lunch was not an ideal way to travel . . wonder-ing as to the full horror of the accident . . .

They were taken to the bedside of a very badly injured woman whom they had never met before, after which the hospital sent them on to break the news to relatives further along the coast. The Bugatti seized up in the heat, Maria left it and Aldous in a field, and

boarded the immense car of kind and stupid South Americans who I had stopped. Never have I been driven more slowly in my life . . .

Maria's letter goes on for some twelve pages; alas it is much too frank to quote. Enough to say that happily Coutrot was not badly hurt and that the woman recovered. For the Huxleys the turmoil did not let up for weeks to come; they were in for, Aldous ten, Maria ninety per cent, of hospital visiting, shopping, chauffeuring. Mme Coutrot and a son were put up at the Villa Huley.

When this subsided, in late July, time was almost up. There was one last Sanary picnic, an apotheosis of a Huxley picnic. It was a mid-day one and the site chosen by Renée Kisling an almost inaccessible cove beyond Le Brusc. A vanguard consisting of Maria, Renée, the two Kisling boys, tough little devils blackened by the sun, Matthew and myself, went early to bathe and reconnoitre. We left the cars on a promontory, Maria and the Kislings danced down a precipitous goat track, Matthew did creditably; I shut my eyes. Nobody expressed misgivings. Maria was in the kind of mood in which she let Aldous fall off mules. At noon Edith Wharton, Lalla Vandervelde, Paul Valéry and Mme Valéry, frail septuagenarians, shepherded by Aldous, were seen approaching the edge of the cliff. Led by the Kisling boys they undertook the descent. Dislodged stones rolled. Aldous managed with surprising tactile agility, the others seemed to do so by the force of the iron discipline bred into their class and generation—they made it. Mrs Wharton looked very flushed, the Valérys very white, but not by a word or smile did they betray the fact that anything more out of the way than walking from the garden into the dining-room had taken place.

Presently Aldous left Sanary. First he went to Brussels where Barbusse's big peace conference was now taking place, then, joined by Matthew, on to St Trond and to Holland, visiting Joep and Suzanne, re-visiting galleries (unadmitted, it was a farewell round), thence to England where Matthew sat for an exam and was put into the hands of Alexander and McDonagh, while Aldous began on his second lot of treatments and did some active work for the P.P.U. He gave a joint talk with Dick Sheppard at Friends' House, and saw a good deal of Gerald Heard. Gerald's predictions for the coming war were more than ever cataclysmic. There was no defence against aerial attack. Battleships were obsolete. The entire might of the British Home Fleet assembled in the Channel could be rendered helpless within one hour (this I heard him say with my own ears).

Maria, alone in the house in Sanary, began to go through her papers, through clothes and books, giving away here and there. "We *may* sell . . ." No offer had come, few people were confident enough to buy a house. "We *may* go away . . ." Go away, was what she said, not travel. "For long?" "Who can tell? We're gypsies." The American idea was already in the air. Maria always knew what Aldous wanted before he knew himself. She brought out the box with Aldous's letters, the letters he had written during their engagement that had come to her day after day in Italy; Aldous's love letters. She would take these with her. Now in those hot afternoons she read them again, untying, re-tying the bundles one by one; moved, at times amused. "How young we were." "There's so much about books!"

Then out came her journal—one knew that she had been keeping one, great spates typed at night, not regularly but continuously since their early married days in London. This Maria let me have a glimpse of, that is she allowed me to read two or three pages about a dinner party we had been at, and one other page—"you must stop there"—about an episode I knew about. I was immensely struck. Like her letters, it was obviously dashed off, straight off the fire, but with what feeling, what acuteness, the journal was pure first reactions, pulling no punches about herself or anyone, and there was a candour, a sharpness, a ruthlessness of insight that took my breath away. This may have been the way in which Maria talked to Aldous about their friends. I am sure that she must have let him read, and use, the journal. How I regretted then not being able to read more; how bitterly I regret now that the journal is no longer there to read. With it, an incomparable record of Aldous's life and circle has been lost.

In September Maria joined Aldous and Matthew in London. Albany was still sub-let so they settled down quite happily at the Mount Royal at Marble Arch in three adjoining bed-sitters with kitchenettes and baths—anonymous, well-heated, functional. Maria fretted about the extravagance, although the novel was doing very well, they were still anxious about money. "Because we have to spend so much on doctors," (Maria to Jeanne) "but we're really very fortunate to be able to have the doctors and enjoy the luxury of our three rooms." They were very busy.

We have spent the whole winter [September to December] in London where we worked like slaves. [Maria to Roy] Aldous for the Peace Pledge Movement with Dick Sheppard and I as secretary and slavy to those two men. But we were happy and comfortable. [Weather] grey and grey and grey . . luckily I was too busy to think of it.

Aldous, besides editing *An Encyclopaedia of Pacifism*[1] for the Movement, drafted letters, answered the questions (some hard, some silly) that came pouring in, made speeches standing on P.P.U. platforms holding his notes within an inch of his eyes. Maria was

[1] Chatto & Windus, 1937.

busy with a thousand errands, helping to set up some of the practical work that members were undertaking such as looking after destitute local families or released prisoners or guaranteeing maintenance to Jewish refugees. (Maria was not able to use the shorthand she had worked so hard at, Aldous had discouraged her—"He calculates that I will never be able to do more than 60 words a minute; he, speaking slowly, says 100 words a minute"—but she got through a vast amount of typing.)

Aldous made the speeches he was asked to. Yet he had doubts as to their effectiveness. Once he consulted Dr Charlotte Wolff. "He told me he was worried about making contact with people. That he didn't know—that he felt inadequate. How to make proper contact with individual people? And more so with the many? He wanted to be able to speak to the many. I tried what I could to reassure him—one felt naive in front of him, that's obvious—I told him that *his impulse was so strong* that it would be all right, that *some day* he would be able to."[1]

Aldous's own peace pamphlet, *What Are You Going To Do About It? The Case for Constructive Peace*, had come out six months ago. This was the gist of his argument.

> War is a purely human phenomenon. Animals kill for food . . fight duels in the heat of sexual excitement . . Man is unique in organizing the mass murder of his own species. War is *not* a law of nature. The old saw about the survival of the fittest is obviously nonsensical— active warfare tends to eliminate the young and strong . .; aerial warfare kills indiscriminately.

War is not a law of nature. War is an absolute evil. Yet war is made. What can we do about it?

> . . The Kingdom of God [cannot] be imposed on mankind from without, by means of change or organization (i.e. Marxian revolution) . . [Man] himself must work for it, and work for it not only as a public figure, but also in private life.
> . . The whole philosophy of constructive pacifism is based on a consideration of the facts of personal relationship between man and man.
> There are men who profess to be pacifists in international politics, but who are tyrants in their families, bullying employers, or unscrupulous competitors . . Such men are fools [to] suppose that it is possible for a government to behave as a pacifist when the individuals it represents conduct their affairs in an essentially militaristic way. Constructive peace must be first of all a personal ethic . . .

---

[1] From a recorded conversation with Dr C. Wolff.

.. Means determine ends .. the only right and practical policy is one based on truth and generosity.

How can such a policy be applied to the circumstances of the present? By the summoning at the earliest possible date of a world conference by the great monopolistic powers, England, France, the U.S.A. and Russia. "This, for instance, would constitute the only practical solution of the difficult problem of sanctions against Italy.

People of goodwill are painfully perplexed because it seems to them that sanctionist countries are on the horns of a dilemma. Either sanctions must be intensified, in which case it is probable that Italy will, in desperation, precipitate a European war; or else Abyssinia must be sacrificed, in which case a wanton act of aggression will have been rewarded at the expense of the victim. In fact there is a third and better alternative . . .

The world conference, given intelligence and good will, could settle not only the justifiable claims of Italy but of all other dissatisfied countries . . . The peace of Versailles, economically speaking, was a thoroughly bad peace . . . The immediate application of pacifist principles offers the hope of a solution of problems which, if they are left to themselves, may become insoluble . . . There would have to be new agreements on markets, tropical raw materials, currencies and tariffs, migration and territorial adjustments.

The greatest immediate sacrifices . . will have to come from those who possess the most. These sacrifices, however, will be negligible in comparison with the sacrifices demanded from us by another war. Negligible in comparison even with those which are at present being demanded by the mere preparations for war.

What of the League of Nations? There is, unhappily, much truth in the Italian contention that the League in its present form is . . controlled by the two great monopolistic nations of Western Europe, England and France. These nations are unwilling to sacrifice their present superiority and, though this superiority was won by the use of violence in the past, they prefer to seem righteously indignant . . at the use of violence by unsatisfied countries at the present time . . .

Pacifists in England now have one immediate task—"that time presses is, alas, only too true"—to persuade their government to apply the principles of preventive pacifism to the present international situation. Such a policy certainly has its risks. But anything else cannot fail to lead us into war:

. . We can break out of the circle. One generous gesture on the part of a great nation might be enough to set the whole world free. More than any other nation, Britain is in a position to make that gesture.

Which is better, to take a risk for a good cause, or to march to certain perdition for a bad one?

*One generous gesture might be enough to set the whole world free.* That was not an ignoble bugle call. The gesture, as we know, was not made. (Munich, whatever we shall decide that it has been, was not an act of constructive pacifism.) Men of good will fought or supported the war, that is, chose doing an evil thing that good might come of it, or worse be prevented. Some did so, pacifists of the previous war among them, because their abhorrence of Hitler's Germany was overriding (and that was something Aldous did not take explicitly into account), but for the majority the margin of choice, psychologically and materially, was very small indeed. Consequently, as again we know only too well, human beings everywhere were killed, maimed, bereaved; Czechoslovakia and Poland were *not* saved but underwent unspeakable suffering; the horrors of the torture camps and death camps continued and increased; when the German camps were put an end to—*one* war aim realized after what had been eleven years of possibly the greatest frightfulness of man to man in human history—Stalin's camps went on unliberated, unchallenged. The Allies dropped the Atomic Bomb on Hiroshima and Nagasaki. The H-Bomb did not take long to follow.

What might have been the course of events *if* the policies of the Peace Movement had prevailed? Would Hitler have been checked? Would he have been willing, even able, to call it a day? Is it conceivable that he and his hierarchy would have agreed to close Dachau, restore civil rights to Jews and dissolve the Gestapo, in effect to take steps to dismantle the dictatorial state?

And what if Britain had unilaterally disarmed, as was the stated policy of the Peace Movement? ("The political implications of pacifism may be briefly summed up as follows: . . . (5) Disarmament, unilateral if necessary."[1]) One obvious answer is that it was precisely because Hitler, misled by Ribbentrop and Co, believed that Britain would not fight that he advanced so freely towards war. Yet might there not have been a world of difference, of difference in kind, between not fighting out of self-interest or lassitude, and standing up against war actively, deliberately, courageously, risking the cost for the sole and professed reason that war is always

---

[1] *An Encyclopaedia of Pacifism*, edited by Aldous Huxley. Chatto & Windus, 1937.

evil? Might that not have been the generous gesture that set the
whole world free? Or would it have been the suicidal and quixotic
act that brought about our general enslavement? The question is
unanswerable because the premise is not there: unilateral disarmament on the part of any Western country carried out in the spirit
of the Peace Movement was inconceivable in the moral and
political circumstances of the time.

And yet there was then an atmosphere of hope and purpose
about the P.P.U. Membership increased; more eminent intellectuals, Bertrand Russell for one, joined the sponsors (he, with
Professor Joad, Rose Macaulay and some others resigned after war
broke out). Dick Sheppard stood for the Rectorship of the University of Glasgow as pacifist candidate with Winston Churchill as
his chief opponent and, against all predictions, won the election.
(He died before taking up the post.) Aldous's own work for the
movement was at times quite down to earth. "For instance," wrote
Gerald Heard,[1]

> he and I found out (it was easy to discover) how anxious the Nazi
> armament engineers were to get nickel, of which Germany was
> desperately short. The next thing was to see where the vital stocks
> lay—and that was in Canada. The price to corner the whole
> Canadian load was not much more than that of one of those floating
> steel anachronisms still then called Dreadnoughts. Through relatives
> we were able to get our brief but enormously important statement
> to the fatal Chamberlain. He sent back verbally the pet word of
> the purblind, "Impractical".

Naturally the Movement was attacked, and so was Aldous.
Leonard Woolf argued personally; C. Day Lewis wrote a pamphlet
(on current leftist lines) called *We're Not Going To Do NOTHING.*[2]
Aldous answered some of their points in respective letters.[3] How
out of tune he was with the political opinions of so many of his
literary contemporaries! Take the Spanish Civil War. In the
questionnaire published by Louis Aragon and Nancy Cunard,
*Authors Take Sides* (1937), 127 out of the 149 writers polled were
for the Republic; 5 for Franco; 16 either neutral or anti-war *per se*,
Aldous among them.

In December Maria's father, Norbert Nys, broke his neck. He
lived on, but in great pain. Maria went to him at Brussels. Back in

---

1 "The Poignant Prophet", *The Kenyon Review*, op. cit.
2 Published by *The Left Review*, 1936.
3 Nos. 393 and 404 in Professor Grover Smith's edition of the *Letters*.

London she went down with influenza, so did Aldous and Matthew though more lightly, and after this they decided on a break. Time, too, for Aldous to get back to his own work. Aldous and Maria returned to Sanary, Matthew to Switzerland (not to his strenuous school; after a successful exam he was to have a couple of months of rest and winter sports). Aldous, advised by Gerald, was thinking of continuing his son's education in the United States.

They found Sanary wind-still and quiet. ". . The avocado trees are so large and the sun is warm; mimosa and roses to welcome us. Alas, it will be to pack again as we are anxious to sell this house." (Maria to Roy.) They spent Christmas by themselves, all their friends, except Renée Kisling, wintering in the North. Maria was very run down indeed, to the point of admitting to a sense of perpetual exhaustion. Aldous was at the note collecting stage for a series of essays, *Ends and Means*, arising out of *Gaza* and the peace pamphlets, Maria reading to him for some hours daily. Their plans had crystallized.

> Now listen to our news. [To Roy on Christmas Eve] They are so exciting that I can hardly write about them. In March we go to the States; we mean to remain there some time. Perhaps nine months or a year and that is to include a visit to Mexico and to yourself if you will have us . . . We may be three or four of us so it will be a little more complicated than the first time we met . . The third may be Matthew who is a man of seventeen now and the fourth our very best and great friend Gerald Heard . . whom you would certainly like as much as we do. He, however, is a delicate man and we cannot expect to drive him as hard as we can drive ourselves.

On the same day Aldous wrote to Eugene Saxton:

> Thank you for the further information about colleges . . when we get across the Atlantic, I will have a good discussion and a look round. Meanwhile . . if Matthew is to have his educational visa and if, as seems likely, we ourselves stay for more than six months in America, it is necessary . . [to] have some kind of proof of my ability to support Matthew and myself while in the USA . . I think it would be best if Harper's were to write an official letter . . I expect that we shall be coming over in March.

And while they were away, the house might well get sold during their absence. Maria packed and stripped.

> Aldous spends his time tidying his cupboards and burning rubbish. [Maria to Jeanne] We mix old M.S.s with rosemary and thyme and it burns with a scent of poetry even when it was nonsense or old.

What wasn't burnt was given away.

> Sophie aimerait-elle un beau Shakespeare et tous les romans de Jane Austen?
> Veux tu des dessins (3) indécents? Tu pourrais toujours les vendre.
> Veux tu des livres français . . dédicacés que tu pourrais vendre?

Maria's father did not recover. Pneumonia set it and in January he died. Maria went to Belgium for the funeral. Mme Nys came to Sanary for a long stay. This had never been easy and became less so. Maria's childhood devotion to her mother had long given place to censure, irritation and consequent self-reproach. Maria had adopted Aldous's values. The root of the trouble was probably a certain smugness, a remorseless self-sufficiency that was a characteristic of the old European bourgeoisie. To be educated and materially privileged was not something due to one's good luck for which one was grateful and a bit ashamed, but one's right and positively a merit. It was a refusal of humility that made them impermeable, politically and individually, to the needs of others. To Aldous, Mme Nys's mould of mind was fascinating; to Maria it was a source of grief and conflict. Her letters echo with, "I ought to be nice to her, *pauvre femme*, I want to be nice to her . . . I ought to *think* nicely of her." It was a resolution broken a hundred times. Her mother had only to come into the kitchen, open her mouth . . . She judged people, often harshly; was interested in her food. "And yet, I am her daughter . . . I don't say 'I told you so,' because ever since I heard her saying it to Père, I decided not to do it. And I don't shrug my shoulders saying, 'Oh, all right, *all right*'. And I don't fling out of a room in a rage not quite slamming the door . . . But now I'm learning to be in the wrong and not to blame anything that goes wrong on someone else." Mme Nys never ceased to adore, though she criticised; Maria remained her favourite. For Maria there was also a constant element of pity in the relationship.

> Pauvre femme. Elle a peur des cambrioleurs qui l'assassineront, elle a peur de la guerre, elle a peur d'être seule.

Mme Nys was getting very deaf.

> I think it is my moral duty to buy her a hearing machine. But a good one costs 2,000 frs.

By the middle of February Aldous had written the first 10,000 words of *Ends and Means*; Maria from one day to the next was feeling well again; travel plans had reached a further stage.

. . Gerald Heard . . will be crossing with us, and we expect to be travelling with him in the USA. [Aldous to Eugene Saxton] He is the trustee for a big estate out West and has to wind up the affair, and we shall make our way by easy stages with him across the continent and probably find some place in the mountains of Montana to stay at during the summer . . . Gerald is a very dear friend of ours and a most remarkable man; I hope very much you will be able to do something with his books . . .

. . practical details . . We don't want, on this occasion, to stay more than a week or so [in New York], as we have to go southwards for Matthew's affairs and then a very long way north-westwards for Gerald's—and incidentally our own pleasure and instruction . . . We'd be most grateful if you could find us . . a couple of single rooms for Matthew and Gerald Heard, and a bedroom and sitting room with kitchenette, if possible, for Maria and myself. The position needn't of course be elegant, so long as it's fairly quiet. Then . . I'd be glad of a little advice . . whether it's better to get, say, a new Ford or a second-hand specimen of some larger and more majestic vehicle. I expect we shall need a small trailer for luggage. Hints on this subject will be most welcome . . that's the reward of previous kindness—to be asked to be kind again!

And Maria to Jeanne:

. . Nous acheterons une grande voiture. Nous voyagerons pendant neuf semaines avant d'arriver ou nous passerons nos vacances d'été. Nous irons dans le désert . . .

. . Notre départ est presque fixé. Possiblement le 31 [mars] sur la troisième de la Queen Mary. Il parait que l'on y est mieux qu'en seconde sur d'autres bateaux. En tous les cas, maintenant que je suis si bien portante je voyagerais même à fond de cale. C'est trop bête de dépenser son argent pour un peu de comfort. Et comme je ne connais pas les secondes je me contenterai des troisièmes. Je ne me mêle pas de cette question. Qu'Aldous ou Gerald décident. Je pense qu'à ce point de vue là, décisions, le voyage sera agréable car Aldous et Gerald décideront tout.

On the last day Maria gave the Bugatti to Renée Kisling. On 19th February 1937, Aldous and Maria left the Villa Huley.

Aldous was supposed to make a speech in London on the 25th, but was held up in Paris—"I was in the pink . . when an un-developed wisdom tooth brought me extremely low . . . [Aldous to Julian] I go into hospital tomorrow . . to have the thing hacked out."

335

Aldous arrived in London, still in pain. Once more they put up at their cherished Mount Royal. Albany was not let, they had as yet not found another tenant and had lent the flat to me; I had been living there since January, plying the typewriter in the goldfish-bowl. Now I didn't move out because Maria didn't think it sensible to start housekeeping for so short a time. This kindness had at least one fortunate result for them. Aldous's jaw was acting up again, and badly. A very pleasant young man who lived across the corridor in Mount Royal and to whom Maria in her way had spoken once or twice when taking in their milk, turned out to be a dentist. It was the weekend. He had one look at Aldous's Paris job, and did something effective then and there. On Monday morning Aldous went to his surgery. I wish I could recall his name because, as I repeat, he was a very pleasant man, but more to the point proved to be an extremely competent and up-to-date dentist. It was Tregar or something near it. He discovered abscesses at the roots and had to extract three more teeth. The whole job was done brilliantly; Aldous was very pleased and recovered quickly. T. and the Huxleys became more neighbourly than ever.

I remember Aldous being in a quiet, cheerful mood, going about his business with detached efficiency. He hadn't done any real travelling since Mexico in 1933 and he was looking forward to his nine weeks' motoring across a new continent. He did not give the impression of a man who was making a great decision. I don't think he thought about his going to America in that way. He was not attached to places—to suspend, at this point, such attachment as he had for family and friends, was a necessary, though almost certainly not conscious, step in his own development—there was little sense of parting. Move or Journey, whatever it might come to be, was in the lap of the gods, sufficient unto the day.

As for suspending his work for the Peace Movement, Aldous and Gerald, privately, were getting very very discouraged. They realized that in spite of so much present response there was no real chance of making the kind of impact that could push the government into action. There was plenty of fear of war but it was matched by fatalistic apathy. Not that Aldous was deserting the P.P.U. Gerald told him that he had shot his bolt and the most useful thing to do now was to re-state the case for peace by some sustained writing such as he was planning. Meanwhile Aldous was talking happily about the things he was going to see—National Parks, educational experiments, Professor J. B. Rhine's E.S.P. laboratory . . .

Matthew arrived (lodged in his own suite at Mount Royal), very pleased about it all, rather pleased with himself. He did not endear himself to Julian and Juliette by telling them in his elation that old Europe was finished.

If Aldous and Gerald did the planning—and went to the U.S. Embassy, the banks, the shipping offices—Maria carried out the detail. The packing. What to take? The minimum of clothes. Their own bedding. *Quite* a few books. What to leave behind? For Albany, too, was to be dismantled. (They were trying to get rid of the lease, with four and a half years still to run.) Maria had talked to a barrow man in Soho who not only would take their books away without charge but had promised her a pound or two for them. She asked me to be sure to stay in and answer the door-bell so as not to miss this golden opportunity. I implored her to let Percy Muir,[1] who happened to be a friend, have a look at the books first. Just odds and ends, Maria said, but consented because she didn't want to snub me. So Percy Muir appeared in Albany one morning. Aldous and Maria happened to be there. They watched him look at title pages, unhurriedly, concentratedly, one by one. There were 153 books in all. When Percy had finished he sat down and wrote a cheque. It was a handsome sum. Then he produced a folded sack—"just like a barrow man," said Maria. We helped him shove in the books and called a cab. Aldous and Maria remained gaping, though delighted, and a little doubtful if this hadn't been sharp practice—Are you sure your poor friend can afford it? Then Maria said, there was *one* thing off her mind now; I had shown such extraordinary business acumen that she would never have to worry about my future again. The 153 books were listed in Elkin Matthew's Catalogue of February 1937. The odds and ends in Albany included:

Matthew Arnold's Essays inscribed by his niece, Julia Huxley;
Clive Bell: some autographed copies, one signed by Jean Cocteau;
Russell Green's Newdigate poem "Venice";
Eric de Haulleville: Poems;
*The Hay Diet*, Maria's annotated copy;
Leonard Handley's novel, autographed;
Gerald Heard: one of his books with Aldous's notes;
Aldous Huxley: 1st editions of *Burning Wheel, Jonah, Leda*;
Aldous Huxley: sketch-book, described in the catalogue, ". . with two
   full-page pencil drawings, one of the interior of a railway coupé,
   the other of a landscape";
Julian Huxley's Newdigate poem;
Julian Huxley: several books, some with inscriptions;
Julian Huxley: a book inscribed to Matthew;
Leonard Huxley: *Life and Letters of Sir Joseph Dalton Hooker*, presenta-
   tion copy inscribed to Aldous;
Robert Nichols: poems signed;
Sacheverell Sitwell: poems signed;

---

[1] The bibliographer, and a director of Elkin Matthew.

Paul Valéry: poems, signed;
H. G. Wells: a presentation copy.[1]


As Elinor told Philip Quarles in *Point Counter Point*, Aldous had
no natural piety. At any rate, Percy Muir had known what he
was doing; "I wish," he wrote the other day, "that I had many
of the books now."


... The second week of March, the third, the fourth—last days.
Everyone was being extremely busy in the day time and in the
evening there were so many friends to see, but whoever came in
first from their engagements made for Maria's room—I too went
to Mount Royal every night whatever I had been doing and however late, it was not a time to be sensible or tired. There we talked.
Later still, I would walk back to Albany across Mayfair, across
Grosvenor, across Berkeley Square, thinking of what had been said
and not been said, through the wind-blown London night.

Maria was very divided. She, too, was looking forward, was full
of the car journey, the trailer, the new sights—they were gypsies!
—then she still had that taste for living, that *goût de vivre*. There
was also much anguish. (Gerald *had* alarmed them.) I saw her
looking at people she was fond of, and she was fond of so many.
There was Simpkins, the young Albany porter, who was saving to
get married and exactly the right age to be called up. There was
her own family. The guilt and misery of not being able to hand
out passages to America to everyone. (This was no personal failure
of nerve but a kind of rational conviction, reluctantly accepted—
Aldous said that Gerald was a remarkable man, so Gerald knew
what's what, and Gerald said that it was now possible to wipe out
life in a modern city in a matter of hours.) I never quite put the
question—Are you going for good? Matthew had been told that
they were going to see him into an American college. Would *they*
return? I don't think they quite knew, or wanted to know (although,
if this is not too fanciful, I think Maria *had* some premonition). The
point is that they were no more consistent than anybody else and
the war was not the only factor in the complex impulses that
prompted their going. ("Man is not an entirely or even mainly a
conscious being.")

A few weeks before sailing they made a decision within a decision.
Aldous wrote to his old employer Condé Nast in New York, and
the same night Maria sent a cri de cœur to Jeanne: "*Puis que nous
quittons l'Europe .. Je ne puis quitter tranquillement en vous laissant là.*

---

[1] The Elkin Matthew catalogue was kindly lent to me by a collector, Mr
Paul C. Jones, of Chagrin Falls, Ohio.

I want to write you a long and very serious letter. It's about America. Aldous and Gerald really think that the situation is getting worse and worse and that there may be a cataclysm before summer . . . This is something one should not talk about, there are so many people who cannot leave and it would be cruel to tell them about our fears. It's still possible that it won't happen, so why worry them pointlessly. Why worry Mère and Rose . . .

But as we are leaving Europe, I cannot go leaving you, you and Sophie, behind.

The letter to Condé Nast has gone off . . Aldous has asked him to find you a job in America . . if he does, you must come at once, Janin, without bothering about Sophie's school or the rent. If he doesn't, you must get ready all the same to leave at the end of term.

There followed instructions about ships, the quota, money, "We shall manage for you in one way or another.

If we were on our own, I don't think for a moment that we would leave. But we are not, anymore than you are; and wouldn't it be rather pointless to stay and risk so much when we happen to be among the very few free enough to be able to get away?

Don't tell Sophie. I don't talk war to Matthew. Remember what we thought of Mère when she did. I don't promise you an easy life, or a pleasant life, or riches, or anything. My one idea, and you must understand this, and give in, is to get you both into safety. Let me have your answer.

Aldous proposed that he should give me an interview, to be published the day after his departure. One afternoon we got down to it. Aldous perched on the arm of a chair with pad and pen. I was rather astonished when he started to forestall me. It was *he* who supplied the questions as well as took the note. There he was asking, scribbling, talking all in one, evidently an old hand at it; I had never seen him so efficient. He said a good deal more than he jotted down, but that's forgotten (I, too, possess no shorthand). The interview was never published for the silly and rather awful extraneous reason that someone pinched my typescript and tried to sell it to another paper. "Going to America?" Aldous said.

Q. Going to America? [Aldous wrote]
A. Yes.
Q. Lecture?
A. No. Learn. Not teach.
Q. Do you know US well?
A. Very little.

Q. What means of transport?
A. By car.
Q. Where going?
A. Across continent . . .
(I am transcribing a fraction only of Aldous's note.)

A. No very definite programme. But wish to see certain things. Esp.
  educational experiments.
Q. Are they more interesting than in Europe?
A. They are certainly more numerous . . .
Q. Do you intend to write while in US?
A. I hope that the material collected there may help me in com-
  pleting a sociological book I am now writing.
Q. What about?
A. About the means which must be employed if desirable changes
  are to be realized. Certain of the American experiments in . .
  industrial organization etc. should throw considerable light on
  this problem. The causes of the wrong functioning of society are
  numerous and the means for remedying this wrong functioning
  will consequently have to be of many kinds—political, economic,
  educational, religious, psychological, philosophical. To employ
  one means—e.g. economic change—without the others is useless.
  The problem must be attacked simultaneously on a number of
  different fronts . . . I am hoping to learn a lot regarding this in
  America. . . .
Q. Do you propose to write another novel?
A. I hope so. But I find it impossible to make definite plans in
  advance. It depends on circumstances.


" 'Depends on circumstances', you want to end on that?" Aldous
said he thought so.


Aldous, Maria and Matthew sailed from Southampton on the
s.s. *Normandie* on 7th April 1937.

I went to see them off. The luggage had gone earlier, and they
walked out of Mount Royal in mid-morning unencumbered.
Maria was wearing her Florentine officer's cloak. T. had left his
surgery to see them into their taxi. Aldous thanked him again
warmly, Maria embraced him. At Waterloo the boat train was
drawn up and we found the reserved compartment. Aldous seemed
calm and cheerful. We were still waiting for Gerald. (Christopher
Wood, their mutual friend, who was also sailing, had made his own
travel arrangements.) Minutes went. Gerald had told Maria that
one should treat a thing like going overseas with perfect equanimity,
it was not an occasion. She was sure that he was coming from

Bloomsbury by underground allowing neither more time nor less than he would for an everyday engagement. More minutes. There is nothing we can do, said Aldous. Maria spied a cluster of anxious looking elderly women on the platform. Below their overcoats they wore long skirts sweeping the ground. They must be some of Gerald's good women, said Maria. General anxiety increased. At last we saw him. The women stepped forward. Gerald, visibly put out, turned and got into the carriage. He sat down in a corner seat and pulled a curtain, his handsome inquisitorial profile stern and quiet. Maria went to the window with a conciliatory gesture, one of the women proffered a parcel. Maria signed to Gerald but the train pulled out. Luncheon presently arrived on trays. They had brought us pork chops in a greasy gravy which was as good an excuse as any not to eat. Thanks to Matthew, for whom naturally this was a great day, we got through the journey.

At Southampton we learnt that owing to some pettifogging squabble over harbour dues between the French and English the Normandie had not docked. She was lying in Southampton Water. Passengers were ferried by launch. It was a cold and longish ride on choppy waves. We were hauled on board. Aldous and Maria were at once escorted to a large and luxurious cabin (not the one they'd paid for: they were going tourist class) compliments of the French Line. They were also informed that they would have the freedom of the ship. Jeanne had sent champagne and some of this we drank now, Gerald reluctantly accepting a few drips. There was still an hour or more to go. Everything was entirely unreal. Gerald went to his own cabin. We wandered about the vast and brand-new ship, crossing and re-crossing public rooms, a gilded, throbbing, overheated limbo. Matthew drifted off. Every now and then Maria said, Eddy—you must give our messages to Eddy ... Don't forget to give our messages to Moura ... to Raymond ... Don't forget our messages to Vera ... To Naomi ... to Marion ... Give my messages to Bessie ... She did not say what messages. It seemed clear enough. When the bell rang for visitors to leave ship, I said farewell to Aldous. Maria came up to the open deck—it was night-fall now—from where one took the launch. I was a symbol, the last of Europe, the last link. At the end she gave me the dispatch case she was carrying. I was just able to undo it and get out their passports and a clutch of papers. "Oh, Aldous would have been so cross," she said. I was already down the gang plank when Maria took off her officer's cloak, keep this, she called and let it fall.

# PART SEVEN

## Caesura: 1937-1939

Just tired and busy and amazed and
amused and charmed and horrified.
MARIA HUXLEY, in a letter to the
Vicomte de Noailles

## Chapter One

## First Run Around

We have not had time to think about anything much. Just tired and busy and amazed and amused and charmed and horrified. No time to breathe and know what we think. That may come in some book some time.

THEY had had their days in New York (the Seabrooks, the Saxtons, strangers). "You have no idea how *famous* Aldous is here," Maria to Jeanne, "perhaps I shall end by being impressed."

They bought their car. A Ford. The four of them set off on their first rush across country. They went south—through Virginia, Georgia, Florida, Louisiana.

. . Have seen various seats of learning [Aldous's postcard to Julian, 7th May] from Charlottesville (mouldy) to Black Mountain (interesting), from Duke (a remarkable phenomenon) to Dillard, the negro coll at N Orleans (rather depressing) . . . Hope tomorrow to visit world's largest cavern—complete with elevator service . . and cafeteria.

. . But soon, as we reached through the tobacco country and the cotton country [Maria to Roy] . . the many heat waves began . : . So we got on pretty fast, through the swamps of New Orléans . . . Then we began crossing Texas; at leisure first when the country was rolling and scrubby and alive with animals and tortoises crossing the roads. But soon the desert grew more desertic, the roads dustier and the sun more and more vicious till we became almost hysterical and drove from air-cooled cinemas to air-cooled hotel bedrooms . . .[1]

Maria took against the car. Wheel and seats were at wrong angles for her, it was tiring to drive. After some five weeks on the road they reached Frieda Lawrence's ranch in the mountains of New Mexico, San Christobal, 8,000 feet above the valley of the Rio Grande. Maria weighed herself on arrival in a drug store at Taos, her weight was down to 98 lbs. with her clothes on. Frieda asked them to stay the summer; they accepted. She lent them a log cabin by a rushing brook. The first weeks were rough, a pioneer's existence; at times Maria thought that she would have to give up. But on 23rd June she wrote to Eddy Sackville-West,

[1] *Letters of Aldous Huxley*, from one of Maria's few published letters.

344

. . Sybille told you the mad situation I have gone and put myself
into. But now the worst is over, we are settled in, water flows, chimneys
draw, cleanliness reigns and peace too . . . Nothing seems to matter
much and I believe it is the terrific view from the hills that gives one
that calmness and serenity.


Maria wrote to several friends about that first summer; her
account to Eddy is the most candid. They understood each other
very well; he was one of the rare people Maria could complain to
and admit because she knew that he would not be too distressed.
"Dearest and most faithful Eddy," this letter starts (faithful because
*he* wrote regularly; some of their friends did not; there was a curious
barrier), and it runs to some 3,000 words.


I am happy to think that you enjoy Sanary [They had lent him
Villa Huley] . . That house and the walks were very precious to me;
the memory of them still is, and even Aldous's grudge against it
when he was ill has not spoiled it for me. You are right about thinking
that I am not very pleased with all this—but this is a secret—for in
reality I am always pleased enough with anything I get; not on
principle, just because it is in my nature to be so adaptable that
sometimes it shocks me. But we have been rushing too much and too
fast until we settled here: then until last Monday there was such a
terrific amount of work that I became very rattled underneath and
so tired that I don't know how much longer I could have carried
on. Now we are settled in a little mud-and-wooden house which has
a paper roof . . .
. . The views are surely described in Lawrence's letters and our lives
are going to be, I trust, monotonous. Aldous works in his bedroom
which communicates with mine through an arch. Matthew sleeps in
the sitting room which leads . . two steps down to the kitchen which
is so small that one of us has to sit on the steps for meals . . . Gerald
has a little hut on the other side of the stream and his ghostliness
comes and goes . . . Our watches have suffered from the altitude so
we do completely without and it is curious what a sense of time one
has anyways . . . Matthew, as well as doing carpentry and plumbing,
is doing algebra and American history; at night, while I wash dishes
(no servants whatsoever, and I cannot say I realized what that meant,
you would have to see me constantly with many brooms, I fear, and
not mind—I have six different kinds of brooms but this does not help.
They read aloud. We also have a bathroom [they had just built it
themselves, with Matthew doing most of the skilled work] and Aldous
insisted we have Butane, so now my life is comparatively grand. We
did depend on a little kitchen range which needed feeding with wood
constantly; not only heating us to a Dantesk degree but dirtying all

our gloves and rags and hands, not to mention the times I used to burn my fingers.

. . Frieda's lover, Angiolino, is so Italian that of course we have to humour him a bit . . . Fundamentally he is very decent and honest. How much they care for one another, or rather in what way they care for one another I don't know. I long to write and tell you more but shall wait until we meet again. This place, I mean Taos, 20 miles off and where we never go, is a nest of scandal and quarrels. Frieda has been, and still is, so affectionate and generous and warm-hearted that I do not want anything to come back to her which could be misinterpreted. You know how things come back, even from Europe and however discreet one is. There is however no scandals, no complaints to amuse you with; just the quarrels with her and Mabel Luhan who wanted to steal Lawrence's ashes from a childish little chapel Frieda built over them here . . .

. . The desert . . begins four miles from us . . pink on the barren soil, grey with the sage-bush, bright green in the irrigated oasis and then black cracks which are the running banks of the Rio Grande . . .

Frieda's life is extraordinary. She lives in such a primitive way that we can hardly understand it. Angiolino built her a concrete house . . and the sitting room is hung by all Lawrence's pictures. But the heart of the house is a large kitchen which has only a wooden range which heats, or rather tepids, a little bath water and which must be lit for every cup of tea. The easiness might be called messiness, the milk which comes . . from a pretty jersey cow is around in all forms of creams, and butters, and sour creams, and milks and what not . . . there are also the pig-bowl and the cat-bowl and the dog-bowl; many things to horrify me and shock me; yet she is essentially clean if you can imagine that; perhaps because she is a blonde. My greatest horror is to be asked to meals; it is then taken for granted that I do the washing up—I arrive with my rubber gloves—but the mess is such that if there were a heaven I deserve a bit of it for every washing up I do. Meanwhile there she sits, talking of Montaigne or Buddha or Mabel Dodge and making us all feel happy and at home. There is an art of accepting things from people which I feel I shall never acquire. I suffer a great deal when Gerald tries, and succeeds, in doing my housework. He is very very precious to us all in a different way, and we miss him. [He had gone off to Hollywood to stay with Christopher Wood.] A changed Gerald too. Grows a little beard which had to come off when he went to Chris; looks rested, without stressed hands, silent on the whole and drinking wine and water with every meal . . .

We took some pictures . . . so badly developed . . and upon this might come a long string of complaints about the barbarousness of America, about the inefficiency, about the junkiness, the backward-

ness and above all the poverty. But—I would not have missed this
life for anything . .

. . No American ever mends; they wear rags and holes; we stayed
at a school where the headmaster went to a picnic with a hole in his
trousers.

Frieda is continually visited out of the blue by vague friends or
strangers; they want to see Mrs D. H. Lawrence, and though she
complains she lets them. Then they bring her cakes . . and think
they have paid her for her trouble. They are the most casual and
tactless people I have ever known. Sometimes we suffer from it
too. But I firmly say Aldous is working . . . and I have already
learned to bear a stolid face . . But they don't mind finding me in
blue jeans, or in shorts and with a handkerchief of Aldous over my
head because I am dusting or going to my larder . . . My compromise
is to keep my toes nicely painted because my finger-nails have had to
go with so many other things. No housemaid's stockings, Eddy,
because I wear none . . but large heavy boys boots with hooks when
we go out for walks . . .

Please do not tire of writing again. At the moment you are the
only link, with Sybille who writes very rarely; it is curious how distant
and remote and unimportant Europe feels . . And yet I know I shall
be Europe-sick . . Never London, never England, never Paris, never
friends, I am afraid, but Mediterranean-sick, if you can understand
that. I am too busy with my family to miss people. I am only by
myself when I look out or wander round or drive to do the shopping.
Just like at Sanary my only lonely hours are the very early ones;
when the sun has risen over the plain which is brittle-clear, but we
are in shade and pines are dark, I sit on the porch and feel that this
is not my country. Unconquerable. Alien. Hating. The heat scorches,
the water floods and carries away, I can see the dust whirlwinding in
the plain . . .

Aldous, in the same month, was writing to Julian, "The country
is most astonishing and beautiful—but I don't know if one cd
stand it very long. I've never been in any place, except parts of
Mexico, which gave such an impression of being alien, even hostile,
to man."

While at the edges of the Mediterranean [Maria once more] the wild-
ness is sufficient to make one appreciate the toil and architecture
that goes into the terracing, the cypresses are signs of life . . the olives
are pruned and there is a clemency on the air I love. Yet, we are
told that "this country gets one." Yes, Matthew. But then he is
young and very different. And he still has to learn that peace and
not excitement are one's needs.

. . I had for two months about, no moment to my self nor no moments which were not under severe physical strain . . . It was a curious sort of hunted feeling. I was looking for some time to think and instead I was being hunted by time to do. It gave me a feeling like a Kafka book and I, even now, have not had time to know exactly what it was I wanted to think about. You'll probably laugh. But then, I never mind being laughed at.

This is all. The letter is written and the love is sent.

About two months later, Aldous had as good as finished *Ends and Means*.

. . I finished the copying four days ago [Maria wrote again to Eddy in what must have been latish August] Against time and with the electricity of the storms in all my fingers every afternoon—but it is done . . I think [it] is excellent indeed and shall long to know what you think about it. Now he is revising it, and, of course, there is more to do. But not so much that I cannot breathe or write to thank you for a letter . . .

. . Matthew has come back from Chicago and Gerald arrived from Hollywood and we were once more all gay and busy and how they talk! But, also, the more I know Gerald the more remarkable and lovable I find him. We all laugh and say he should not this and he should not that; and I tease him and scold him. Then I am mostly very impressed. When he left us it was as if ten Geralds had left us . . . he is gone again to Chris and to who knows how many other of his 'penitenti' . . .

. . On the 10th about [September] we go to Denver and buy Matthew his school outfit. He goes to a very nice school at Colorado Springs [Fountain Valley] on the 15th. Then we return here for a short time. To pack up and leave for Hollywood and meet Gerald.

. . Aldous and Gerald are doing a lecture tour (I call it their Mutt and Jeff) . . . Aldous had consistently refused to do it until he was told by Gerald, quite rightly, that this was such a good opportunity to get his ideas of peace across. So with the help of Gerald he signed his contract. It was not as fearful as some contracts can be. It will be nice for them being together . . but it binds them to this country until early January. I shall not go with them because it would be expensive and because, seeing that Aldous will be admirably looked after by Gerald, I think I can have a little holiday . . . I should like to be in a comfortable hotel in a country place where I know nobody and can have books. But it may . . work out that I shall go to New York to settle my sister who has come over . . into a flat and look after the child a little. They will probably be lost and also very busy. American life, I have discovered, is very hard on those who are not extremely rich. In spite of all electrical saving devices, work remains work and meals remain 4 meals a day. The life I have been leading here was a slight mistake; we none of us realized how much work there is going even at a minimum. But a good many women in America who are richer than we were when I first married work a good deal harder. I never had to do disgusting work; always in Europe we had at least a char.

. . Aldous and [G] must still prepare their lectures, they start in the West. I shall drive them about for the few, not too distant lectures. After the New Year, if they offer Aldous *tons* of money, he may work for the movies for a little while. Otherwise we shall travel . . .

I shall be glad to leave this place . . . I am rattled with the typing but it is not that either; nor doing most of Frieda's work. It is just that this place, in spite of the desert which is beautiful and the clouds . . is somehow empty and hollow . . . It did us all a lot of good. Until I started typing I had put on eight pounds . . . I often wish you were here; I have so few friends, sometimes ashamed of how I miss practically none of them, but I make up by caring very much about those I do care for. Being sad because you have stuck in your book. Knowing just what that means . . . I want to give you some advice about not squashing your sad thoughts under the novel, but coping with them. I always find I get over my sadness when I really look at it. But you are so far off . . . it is difficult enough to talk . . . those letters I rattle off with mistakes and bad grammar and so on; and when I think of how long Aldous takes to write a letter and of how many sheets he tears up I ought never to write at all. But what has one got friends for if it is not to expect them to like the news and over-look the rest.

In September the Huxleys loaded up the car again and left the ranch. They saw the Grand Canyon and what Maria called the view-places and arrived in California with a heat wave. They took a small flat in Hollywood. For the first couple of weeks they lived quietly, correcting the proof of *Ends and Means*. Then Matthew went off to his new school, and Aldous and Maria got into a whirl.

We have met here all the very eminent world of The Technical Institute of Pasadena [Maria to Roy], gone up Mount Wilson and looked at the sky with Professor Hubble, we visited the country and the prosperous ranches, we have met scholars on Bacon and novelists and sociologists and on the same day we have met Gary Cooper or Anita Loos or Charlie and the whole pattern becomes fantastic and improbable . . . We have seen . . the only Chinchilla farm in the world and the largest hogs, and the making of the Mickey Mouse films and working on orchids with mineral salts . . and oil drilling and hideous picture shows and the best and largest private collection

349

of French Modern pictures in the house of a nice mad-man . . .[1]
Yesterday we had a very *intellectual* dinner with Charlie Chaplin,
Paulette Goddard a very good and very handsome hostess and Upton
Sinclair one of the guests. Charlie . . did . . a mimic of Mussolini . . .
. . there are no buses or trams and distances so enormous taxis would
ruin us. But my chauffeur hours are not so bad as I get through a
good deal of reading. [When Aldous is at the dentist and so on] The
only misery can be the heat if I have to park in the sun . . .

The idea of making tons of money in the films had been started
by Jacob Zeitlin, the Los Angeles rare-books dealer, who had
written proposing himself as an intermediary. Aldous had answered
cautiously that he might be willing (later, they became friends).
Zeitlin suggested *Antic Hay*, "The Gioconda Smile", "After the Fireworks", *The World of Light* and possibly *Point Counter Point* and *Gaza*
as suitable for cinematic adaptation. The studios would have none of
it. "The best they cd do in Hollywood was to ask me to adapt *The
Forsyte Saga* for the screen :[to Julian] but even the lure of enormous
lucre cd not reconcile me to remaining closeted for months with
the ghost of the late poor John Galsworthy."
Aldous, however, did a radio interview. The fee was $750 and
Maria spoke of the unfair enormity of the sum. After two agents'
commissions and State tax, it dwindled to an acceptable $190.
They went on a jaunt to San Francisco with Gerald and
Christopher Wood.

piled in the same old Ford which goes as well as ever and drives even
more tiringly but I have come to terms with it now. [Maria to faithful
Eddy] We had a beautiful drive up . . stopping at Carmel . . sparkling
white sand and green shores and eucalyptus groves. Like a Boudin
under blue skies. At San Francisco the bridges were in their full glory
. . and we drove over and over them and walked about the town,
with a centre and shops and Italian and French food and compact
so that one could walk and take taxis . . . While Gerald and Aldous
went to their Guru to improve their souls Chris and I wandered and
drove about . . .
Then at night, the fogs came like serpents along the bay . . and the
ships hooted and searchlights flashed . . .
We drove back slowly through the big redwood trees . . . I cannot
give an impression of the old large sequoias. They like to stand in
clusters and it must have something to do with their agedness that
gave one a curious feeling. They are very impressive and the stillness
in those forests very moving.
. . We also went to San Diego . . [it] was to be a mixture of La

---

[1] John Davenport, I think.

Spezia and Toulon and a bit of Genoa (we have not yet learnt we are in America, it seems) and of course it was in fact the usual scattered untidy medley of wooden shanties with tin roofs and railways running in the street, then a large skyscraper, the best hotel and absolutely no centro della città to stroll in . . .

But the Zoo is the loveliest of all zoos—up and down a thickly planted sub-tropical park,

and the animals with fur healthy and shiny as that of a pet to a rich dowageress.

Aldous and Gerald had their first lecture in the Philharmonic Auditorium of Los Angeles in October. ("Aldous so slow and calm and passive, Gerald vehement and busy and coercive.") Presently the two men left for their tour "both in leather coats, small grey hats and umbrellas . . (at seven in the morning and chilly) . . They both promised not to die before I had joined them." Maria was to go east by bus as Gerald and Christopher Wood had terrified Aldous as to what would happen to her if she crossed the continent in the car by herself.

I would drown, starve in blizzards, be raped by hoboes . . . So now I have to sell the car here. I can't say I mind when I look at the map.

As for future plans. "Well, the Hollywood adventure is over. I loved it.

We were very amused, very interested and very cheerful and very well . . . Yet we are leaving it because it does not seem the place for us to settle down in . . . Now Marjorie [Seabrook] has come to the rescue as ever and it seems that Maryland, on the peninsula, would be . . perfect . . This here [California] is so far. So far, I suppose from Europe, or from New York or from I don't know what but it feels far . . . It will be Maryland probably and I like since ever that name. Only I do pronounce it like the French tobacco. Marylan. They don't understand me anyways. So I might as well have that pleasure to myself.

Mutt and Jeff came to an abrupt end. Poor Gerald slipped on snow in Iowa and broke his arm. Aldous took him to hospital and continued single-handed. "Very unpleasant for him . . very boring for me, as I find this process of lecturing extremely tedious. [to Julian] It was more tolerable when we were two and could throw the ball back and forth . . . I find myself often a bit overwhelmed by the curious rigidity and opacity of most human beings. There's

351

something dismally fixed, stony, sclerotic about most of them—a lack of sensibility and awareness and flexibility, which is most depressing. There seems to be nothing much to be done, beyond, of course, doing one's best to prevent the oncoming of mental sclerosis in oneself, to keep the mind open to the world and to that which transcends the world . . ."

Or as Maria put it, "Aldous tours the halls of America by himself and loathes human beings more and more in spite of all his theories and efforts. He, perhaps fortunately, is not so easily taken in." Whereas Gerald, "only wishes to see the good in people and then, when they say 'I am GOOD' he just believes it".

Aldous's lectures were on the lines of the book he had just finished and he was getting very bored with saying the same thing over and over again. There were compensations—in Chicago, he met Dr William Sheldon,[1] the man who evolved the psychological classification of individuals known as the Sheldonian Types, to whose work Aldous already then attached such great importance. "A very remarkable man . . ."

> In this country I have associated—by an odd series of accidents—mainly with doctors and astronomers. Very nice professions, both of them; for the doctors can feel they're doing good, while the astronomers can be sure that they're not doing much harm. There are not many other people who can feel the same. And then the mere fun of those trades! The experimental work on a new cancer cure which I saw being done—fascinating and exciting.

Maria meanwhile, in spite of exhortations, had started east by car. She was heading for New York where Jeanne and Sophie had landed a few months ago. Christina Mills ("the wife of the handsome playwright who sent us roses when they had no food") came with her on the first lap. "After two days of exquisite desert we reached Taos." Frieda and Angiolino "were so lovingly welcome and the stoves and fireplace were soon roaring and beds made in my little house and the stillness seemed stiller than it had been all summer. Next morning there was thick soft snow.

> There was no wind so Angiolino took me on a ride on the horses fattened and gay and when the sun came out and the distant desert was pink . . I felt this to be the most beautiful place I had seen. The snow was silent under the rapid horses and we came in as from a dream. [Maria to Eddy]

[1] Professor W. H. Sheldon, Ph.D., M.D., author of *The Varieties of Human Physique, The Varieties of Temperament, The Varieties of Delinquent Youth*, etc.

"But the next day brought an air mail letter from my sister. A very disappointing letter and it said, with many good reasons and sad words, that, unless it were to please me, she was returning to Paris. By the time I had read it . . the distance to New York stretched beyond end and the cautions I had about weathers and hold-ups seemed more real." Nonetheless, Maria went on next day.

. . Except for some moments of lonely fears and one bad incident of sticking in snow and slush, I got to New York in 5 days from there. I was cold and I was sad . . but the continual beauty of the whole country was the uppermost feeling. I was dressed in Aldous's Tibetan sheepskin . . but it was dry and it was fine. I drove from before sunrise to after sunset and got both the lights of pink in the skies. The whole of this continent is golden.

But through Arkansas I was shocked at the houses, huts rather, in which people are expected to live.

Aldous and Gerald were lost because their addresses had blown out of the window of my car when I opened it one night to ask the way.

Washington was my first large town . . and my sister met me there and we talked and I was even more unhappy at her decision which I had made plans to change. I could not ask her to stay to please me, but I had hoped to make her wish to join, in parts, our life . . . The next day as I again flew out of the crowded streets of Washington, or was it Baltimore? I was arrested by a handsome star-like policeman for speeding (I was) . . a chewing judge in a stuffy smelly shack back of the road made [me] pay 26 dollars; upon which I wept bitterly and had no handkerchief and felt ashamed and wept for a whole hour until we both realized that I was not weeping about the fine but about the miserable news Jeanne had for me. So you see how comic we must have been; still in the sheepskin and we stopped and hugged and everything was a little better. But not much.

A depressing and unsettling stay in New York. Next step, finding a place for Aldous to come home to. In December Maria moved into a little grey house on a Hudson estate, Edith Wharton country, "as ugly as can be but comfortable and well-heated . . very near the Seabrooks who are better friends than ever". Presently Aldous arrived; Matthew, who had telegraphed that he couldn't afford to come for Christmas, had been sent the 100 dollars for the fare— "Now everything is really better. I am reconciled to Jeanne's going [to Eddy] because she seems so happy at the thought that she looks twenty years younger than when I arrived. She has taken the whole trip not as a bitter disappointment but as a marvellous holiday and appreciates all that Paris can give her much more than she ever did before."

Now once more Aldous and Maria put their heads together as

to their own plans. Maryland was dropped quietly. On 15th December Aldous wrote to Harold Raymond as follows, "For the moment I have a respite [from lecturing]; but after the new year shall have to set off on my travels again . . . After that I expect we shall be heading for Europe, unless in the interval I get any news about a scenario I wrote while out in Hollywood. If there was a prospect of somebody wanting to do something with it, I might go back there for a bit . . ."

And Maria: "I wish you would come, Eddy . . I wish you would. Why not before you go to St Anton . . Come, and return with—us. But this last decision is not yet quite certain so you had better keep it a secret as Giulia [their cook at Sanary] would be too disappointed if it did not materialize."

By the end of the year it was still in the balance. "I wish I could say we were returning to the . . life in Sanary but we don't know . . [Maria to Charles de Noailles, 30th Dec.] It will not be certain for a few weeks . . Then it may be Sanary, it may be Mexico, it may be Hollywood."

It was in fact as close as that. Aldous might easily not have settled in America, gone back to Europe and thus to England and the war. (On that score everything was simplified for them by the facts that Matthew *was* in America and would stay to complete his education, and that Jeanne and her child *had* gone back.)

Ten days later it had swung the other way (for the present: essentially the decision was still open-ended). Aldous heard that a studio *might* take his scenario. "Our plans," he wrote to Jacob Zeitlin on 10th January, "have crystallized more or less . . After my last lecture . . we shall aim at Los Angeles." Meanwhile he set off again to speak at Washington, Philadelphia and Toronto. "Your letter sounds most ironically commenting on our present mode of life," Maria wrote to Eddy.

Erring and Erring Jews, as well as gypsies as well as bohemians is what we seem to be more and more. But *I* even more than the others because all the packing and all the rushing about is always mine. I suppose I love travelling . . . But as gypsy princess . . whereas I am turned into a gypsy cinderella.

Now there was to be more packing and more rushing. They acquired a new Ford—the first one had done 18,000 miles. "You know how I hated it but I have not had a repair, nor was I in trouble on the road ever." Presently they set out again for California by way of Colorado and New Mexico.

## Chapter Two

## Ends and Means

*E*NDS AND MEANS had appeared in England and the U.S.A. It is a book in which Aldous attempted to relate all social problems, the problems of international politics, of economics and education, to ethics; and ethics to his conception of the ultimate nature of reality. Our world is in a bad way, he postulated, what can we do to rescue it from its present plight?

*A desirable social order is one that delivers us from avoidable evils.* The means to achieve such an order must be multiple, and they must be the right means, means *good* in themselves. The obstacles, unfortunately, are immense.

Every road towards a better state of society is blocked, sooner or later, by war, by threats of war, by preparations for war.[1]

Yet war is not imposed on us by any kind of biological necessity.

. . Man has now little to fear from competition with other species. His worst enemies . . are insects and bacteria . . . For man competition is now predominantly intra-specific . . entirely gratuitous and voluntary . . we are wantonly and deliberately pursuing a policy which we need not pursue and which we have the best scientific reason for supposing to be disastrous to the species as a whole . . .

Another formidable obstacle to desirable reform is built into the existing order of things. To bring about radical reforms we would have to change first our "machinery of government, our . . administration and industrial organization, our system of education and our metaphysical and ethical beliefs.

. . Existing methods of government and . . industrial organization *are not likely to be changed except by people who have been educated to wish to change them.* [My italics] Conversely, it is unlikely that governments composed as they are today will change the existing system of education in such a way that there will be a demand for a complete overhaul of governmental methods. It is the usual vicious circle . . .

[1] All quotations in this chapter, unless indicated, are from *Ends and Means*. Chatto & Windus, 1937.

From which there is only one way of escape—"Through acts of free will on the part of morally enlightened, intelligent, well-informed and determined individuals, acting in concert."


*Ends and Means* became a kind of Bible to the Peace Pledge Union; unlike Hegel, *Mein Kampf* or Machiavelli, it had little influence on politicians or the masses; for the average sensual man it makes, like so much of Aldous's later work, disagreeable reading; it greatly affected some young men. Professor J. M. Tanner[1] speaks of the tremendous influence the book had on his generation (like *Crome Yellow* and *Antic Hay* on the one before)

> A tremendous influence on my actual life. I had been reading *Ends and Means* at Marlborough at the age of seventeen. Shortly afterwards I had an interview at Woolwich—I come from an Army family, my father had decided ... Some elderly military gents were asking questions.
> "What do you read?"
> "*Ends and Means, Point Counter Point, Eyeless in Gaza* is more serious."
> "What, no Buchan?"
> "Oh yes. I enjoyed that very much at prep school—stuff for kids."
> I was flooded by the realization: this won't DO. Wrote to Daddy that night. Then began doing medicine and physics.[1]


What is this world of ours—? Aldous asked. What is the sense and point of the whole affair?

> .. Is there any reason for regarding this world as superior to the world of earlier geological epochs? In other words, can evolution be regarded as a genuine progress? These questions can be answered, with perfect justification, in the affirmative. Certain properties, which it is impossible not to regard as valuable, have been developed ... The lower forms of life persist more or less unchanged; but among the higher forms there has been a definite trend towards greater control and greater independence of the physical environment. Beings belonging to the highest forms of life have increased their capacity for self-regulation, have created an internal environment capable of remaining stable throughout very great changes in the outer world, have equipped themselves with elaborate machinery for picking up knowledge of the outer world, as well as of the inner, and have developed a wonderfully effective instrument for dealing with that knowledge ...

[1] J. M. Tanner, M.D., D.Sc., M.R.C.P., Professor of Child Health and Growth, University of London. Talking to S. B.

Now, does the world *as a whole* possess value and meaning? And if so what is the nature and value of that meaning?

> This is a question which, a few years ago, I should never even have posed. For, like so many of my contemporaries, I took for granted that there was no meaning. This was partly due to the fact that I shared the common belief that the scientific picture of an abstraction from reality was a true picture of reality as a whole; partly also to other non-intellectual reasons. I had motives for not wanting the world to have a meaning; consequently assumed that it had none, and was able without any difficulty to find satisfying reasons for this assumption . . .
>
> For myself, as, no doubt, for most of my contemporaries, the philosophy of meaninglessness was essentially an instrument of liberation. The liberation we desired was simultaneously liberation from a certain political and economic system and liberation from a certain system of morality. We objected to the morality because it interfered with our sexual freedom; we objected to the political and economic system because it was unjust. The supporters of these systems claimed that in some way they embodied the meaning (a Christian meaning, they insisted) of the world. There was one admirably simple method of confuting these people and at the same time justifying ourselves in our political and erotic revolt: we could deny that the world had any meaning whatsoever . . .
>
> . . By the end of the 'twenties a reaction had begun to set in—away from the easy-going philosophy of general meaninglessness towards the hard ferocious theologies of nationalistic and revolutionary idolatry. Meaning was reintroduced into the world, but only in patches . . .

*Is* there a universal meaning? If so, can we reach cognizance of it? Aldous's present answer is affirmative. We can, if we choose, gain insight into the nature of ultimate reality. By liberation. Liberation from the prevailing conventions of thought, feeling, behaviour—by the practice of disinterested virtue. In other words, by goodness. And intelligence. There must always be the cultivation of intelligence.

> For insensitive stupidity is the main root of all the other vices.
>
> . . Love, compassion and understanding or intelligence—these are the primary virtues in the ethical system, the virtues organically correlated with what may be called the scientific-mystical conception of the world. Ultimate reality is impersonal and non-ethical; but if we would realize our true relations with ultimate reality and our fellow-beings, *we must practice morality* . . .

## Chapter Three

## Hollywood, California

ALDOUS and Maria got there in mid-February. "We were very gay and meant to be happy here where we arrived .. in a California so green that it took one's breath away. We found a house the next day and moved in just for Aldous to be ill."[1] A mild but stubborn attack of bronchial pneumonia. Three weeks in hospital. "He came back yesterday .. still has to stay in bed ... They found it was not T.B., so we were patient and are going on to be patient and we read till we have nothing left to read."[2]

Their house was a small furnished one on N. Laurel Avenue. Aldous was slow in picking up. Gerald Heard was living on a hill six miles away.

Today Gerald came with a little bunch of yellow flowers for Aldous and they were talking as passionately as ever and were happy with bread and honey for tea ... [He] looks extraordinarily handsome with a neat and full red beard .. His arm still is painful .. he does stoop terribly but otherwise seems very happy .. But I may be all wrong ... But then one knows the natural Gerald and forgets the 'become' Gerald.[2]

By April Aldous was doing a little painting and making notes for a future novel. He still had to lie down before dinner and was not allowed to go out at night. They saw a few friends, Edwin Hubble, the astronomer, and his wife Grace; Anita Loos, and through her some of the film world. "She is the doyenne of Hollywood, having started to write for the movies when she was seven," as Aldous had said, when he first met her in New York twelve years ago, in the letter that described her as so ravishing that one would like to keep her as a pet. Now she became one of their staunchest friends. They went for walks, with Gerald when possible, every afternoon.

You see the simple life we lead and very much like London, Sanary or wherever we go.[2]

Now it is spring ... It was the time of year we were in Central America [Maria to Roy]. How many years ago? How old are we fast becoming!

[1] Maria to Charles de Noailles, 6th March 1938.
[2] Maria to Eddy, 5th March 1938.

Plans were still fluid. ". . stay here till May. Go to the ranch [Frieda's] . . and when Matthew goes to College, return to Europe for a while. But that is not what my fortune teller tells me."[1]

Then came news that Maria's mother was ill in a Mexican hospital. Mme Nys had been travelling in Central America on her own all winter long with enjoyment and resource, "seeing everything plus all the things most people miss". Three days before returning to Belgium she was knocked down by a bus. Maria was on the point of going out to her, hesitated to leave Aldous, heard that she was out of danger. "But I may still have to go, and perhaps fetch her. The distance is that from London to Constantinople." (To Eddy.)

At Easter Lady Ottoline Morrell died in England. On 4th May, Maria wrote to Eddy. "Ottoline's death only reached us now and I daresay you don't know just how much she was to my life. In spite of the agonies of those young loves it was my greatest. And in those later years, in spite of a gap of coldness and distance, we had become devoted friends. I loved her dearly and am haunted by many thoughts. But they say she died peacefully, yet she did die suddenly. Is it to be wished for to die without a warning . . .? I hope she did not die of unhappiness. But none of these things we shall ever know. . . .

> . . . The doctor says [Aldous] is practically well. Yet I think he sometimes looks so tired. I hope all the tragedies for this year are over. Aldous's illness, Mother's accident and the irreparable death of Ottoline.

Then came a new prospect. Anita Loos rang up one evening asking if Aldous were approachable about doing the film script of *Madame Curie* for Metro-Goldwyn-Mayer. With Greta Garbo as Eve Curie. George Cukor, producer; Hyman, director—intelligent men whom Aldous had met at Anita's. (It was all due to her.) She now implored Maria to encourage Aldous to accept. "You will get enough to set you up for life, and I will protect you at the studio." Aldous was resting before dinner; receiver dangling, Maria went to talk to him.

"But *how* can I? And what can Garbo do in it? And anyhow I wouldn't be able to please them."

A moment later he caught fire. It *would* be interesting. One might do some scenes in the Belgian Congo, in Russia . . . show the use of radium in actual hospitals . . . Ideas flowed. They spent the rest of the evening talking. *And* it would be well paid, Anita

---

[1] Maria to Charles de Noailles.

had said so. No actual sum. It might be as much as 1,000 dollars a month, perhaps he should hold out for that; then they could save half of it, he thought. More than half, Maria said. Next morning he slept an hour longer. "He's got a good reason at last to get well," Maria wrote to Jeanne.

Financial security would mean very very great peace for Aldous. Gerald doesn't understand this, he thinks the old books will always bring in enough to live on . . But if Aldous were ill, that wouldn't be enough and God knows how much these illnesses cost . . . Since the insomnia I am always thinking about his worry and distress when he was afraid that he mightn't be able to earn any more . . .

Anita Loos had raised first hopes in May; for the next weeks nothing happened (as nothing happened—or ever did—about Aldous's original scenario which had brought him there).

Now Aldous is taking it all so seriously that I'm afraid he'll suffer horribly if there is a disappointment . . . He wants to project the passion of scientific curiosity, and the nobility of such a life [Mme Curie's], the significance of the discovery of radium, the humility and courage of that woman. Aldous wants it to be done properly and nobly . . . The great advantage of having Garbo is that she passionately wants to play that part; she admires Aldous and would do a bit more under his direction . . .

He talked of going to Paris himself to interview the Joliot-Curies, although Maria was not even certain if the doctors would allow him to do the work at all. What they were advising was an air cure in the desert.

Meanwhile (late June) they moved again. "We are in a very large house [N. Linden Drive in Beverly Hills] with a cool ground-floor and three bedrooms and a green bathroom and a yellow one for Aldous and Matthew and all the bedrooms have two beds for us to choose from. We had to move because of Matthew [home from school]. So now we enjoy a garden and two fountains in a little patio . . Aldous is . . working away steadily at the novel. Under a large blue umbrella and wearing a summer suit which I think is indecently transparent but does not seem to bother him. [Maria to Eddy] Our latest fad is homeopathy and it works really well. Aldous seems to be cured definitely . . . Though he does not look strong; He looks sad sometimes which he never did.

Matthew is so grown-up that we spent the afternoon trying out cars for him. He starts a summer course at the university tomorrow and is well and tall with a Leica camera hanging around his neck. I try to spoil him a bit now. It is the age when one really passionately wants some things and might as well have them. When they come too late it is like not having them at all. As if I now had all the pearls I longed for when I lived in Italy . . . If you see a film with Hepburn (not good) called Holiday please notice that all the jewels are real. Her diamonds glitter hugely and are lovely; and the pearls the other woman wears are real too. That is Hollywood. If I could tell a story without ruining it I would embark on a few . . .

X. is well and . . gay in spite of some disease he caught bathing (he telephoned to say it was not syphilis while I was having Krishnamurti in to tea) . . .

Would you like America? . . in the end, after some sufferances, you would certainly come to like it and be able to live here. You see it is so large that in itself is a horror at first. Now I even wonder whether . . Europe would not feel a bit cramping. Then the people are extremely tolerant. But you can't get that for nothing; they are also careless. And they are kind . . . And here we have quite a few friends who are what I shall, ridiculously, call (for the lack of a better word) "civilized". But I would not like the East. The people are more like the English and freezing . . . But here we have some Mediterranean ease and kindness. We have some friends. Not mere acquaintances. That is much after such a short time.

Indeed Aldous and Maria had already met or were about to meet in the months that followed the eight or so men and women who became their friends for life—the Hubbles, Edwin and Grace . . . Anita Loos . . . Rosalind Rajagopal who was married to a Hindu and founded the Happy Valley community and school at Ojai . . . Krishnamurti . . . Peggy Bok, later Kiskadden . . . Beth Wendel . . . Christopher Isherwood . . .

. . I used to long for Sanary. But now all that is over. I could live here without going back to Europe. I have made my peace with it. Which does not mean that we are not going back . . . Aldous will want to go back and I shall go with him. That horrid feeling that I cannot leave him. Yet all the time he was lecturing without me he kept well and caught his pneumonia with me sitting next to him! Ironic. Yet I know I am right too.

The years of adjustment were harder than Maria let us believe. Living in America, living there with the Englishness and intellectuality of Aldous and Gerald—to whom the mind was still very much its own place—and with a rapidly assimilating Matthew, Maria was in many ways alone. She missed the companionship of a woman with a shared past. She missed her sister Jeanne.

I know, Jokes Chérie, that if you knew the country, if you knew my friends, if you could love and understand all this, I would feel less pain in being separated from you. Even your short stay in New York helps me a good deal when I write to you because I know that you know what I'm talking about . . . But it is as difficult to imagine the West as it would be for a Londoner to imagine cypresses and olive trees.

The consolations were the new landscapes—the night sky—the growing love for the desert.

One night walking home with Aldous, Maria was struck by the thought that seeing Jeanne was an actual possibility. "J'étais obligée de m'arrêter. Je tremblais et je pleurais." The letter was written the same night. Come . . . Now . . . For a holiday . . a few weeks. It is easy—we are able to pay the fare. The film makes it all right. Aldous is for it . . . Come! The appeal was propped by practical details—Bring light clothes, leave Sophie in Sanary with Sybille (I was spending the summer in the Villa Huley, still unsold), book a passage on the fast ship, the fastest inter-continental train, you could get here in eight days or nine . . . (The distance then, only some thirty years ago, between Paris and California was formidable, heart-breaking, more so possibly than at an earlier age when people thought nothing of taking three days to get from London to Bath.)

Jeanne, taking up life again in France, did not come. Perhaps the scheme, in Chamberlain's word, was impractical. Maria answered generously, making light of disappointment. "But you must know that whenever you should want to come, *notre maison et notre cœur t'est ouvert.* You needn't give us notice; you needn't ask our advice. If you want to send Sophie, send Sophie. *Tu peux venir seule ou à deux, nues ou avec vos bagages* . . .

In July Madame Nys, convalescent, arrived from Mexico and stayed a month. Aldous's health was still much below par. M.G.M. at last made up their minds and a contract was signed. When the figures were out of the bag— $15,000 for eight weeks' work, Aldous and Maria were stunned. ". . $15,000—even with agents and taxes, it's enormous. But we're not celebrating or anything . . . I think that if destiny wants to present us with such a treasure it would be unreasonable to refuse. We have to envisage a long education for Matthew, and for Sophie too . . ."

So on the first Monday of August Aldous began his two months' stint at M.G.M. And what would they do after that? They would be rich enough to return, they might *like* to return, but—they had already cut themselves adrift—what would they be returning for? And was it worth it? Sanary for the winter? That would mean, Maria rationalized their thoughts to Jeanne, buying a car for three months' use. London?

What would we be doing and whom would we be seeing in London? So that journey would be a luxury and a caprice? It isn't as if Aldous could get a travel book out of it.

But what about returning for good?

At Sanary Aldous can only live part of the year, the working part; even so books are lacking. In London he can only live part of the year because of the climate . . . California—with its many disadvantages—combines some of the advantages of London and Sanary.

Anyway we can't go on like Lawrence, keep running off in search for the perfect place; it doesn't exist and it seems to me that at our age we ought at last to have found the tranquillity to stay where we are. I would understand a journey to an unknown country . . . where Aldous would find something new. In Europe there is nothing for him to do for I don't think he is going to start again losing his time preaching. If he wants to preach, let him publish his sermons . . .

So I've written to Sybille to find someone to buy [the Villa Huley] and at any price. [A week later she wrote to me again saying that Aldous and Matthew had decided to keep the house.]

At the end of his eight weeks Aldous turned in the finished script of *Madame Curie* (he thought it was rather good). The contract was not renewed. "They have followed their usual procedure [Aldous to Julian] and handed my treatment over to several other people . . By the time they are ready to shoot it may have passed through twenty pairs of hands. What will be left?" (Nothing. The film—new director, new script—was released five years later.)

Out of the blue, Maria, instead of the usual three or four closely typed pages, sent off a half sheet to Jeanne.

Aldous has absolutely no tuberculosis and it is true . . . It's some bronchial business . . . [the specialist] thinks it will be a matter of rest. He must lie down twelve hours a day. The climate here is all right. London or New York would be very bad.

I am so relieved that I realize [admit] how worried I was.

Whether they knew it or not, *this* determined their plans. The climate of Tucson, Arizona would have been even better. They would not have found there the other advantages they sought, libraries, intellectual stimulus, friends; the occasional chance to make some extra money in the movies. For the present they took a house on 1320 North Crescent Heights Boulevard. In 1925, Aldous had written to Bob Nichols, "when are you coming to Europe? I cannot believe that 622345678 Glen Av. Hollywood is a very salubrious address." *Tempora mutantur, et nos mutamur in illis.*

# Chapter Four

## 1938/1939

URING the Huxleys' first year and a half in America the news from Europe had been bad so steadily, had been so horrible, that, at a distance of some six thousand miles, it seemed too bad to be quite true. Until the Munich crisis.

This ghastly war came so close to being a reality . . . when it was over and we breathed again . . I thought of you, and all of you, as of ghosts. [Maria to Eddy] As of very ill people who had just escaped death . . . And how I did long to be with you and to know how it happened. How you stood it.

Gerald thought that they would close the frontiers and that no man could leave. And the fact that we "were safe" did not seem any comfort whatever . . Our thoughts and my wildest imagination strained to Europe. To Europe in general and to the face and moods of friends.

The radio spared us no . . details and no anxiety. On the worst day we went out . . to an Angricultural [*sic*] Fair. We had the radio . . on all the way and back and stopped to listen opposite the pigs. We were worn out by it. The distances made it worse I am sure.

Then I telephoned to my sister in Paris. It was marvellously clear and exciting and terribly sad. When it was over we both were (she wrote and told me) in despair. The distance seemed greater than ever . . . The child has not come. Had there been a war [Jeanne] would have waited too long. Now I know she will send her . . . I had a letter from Marion [Dorn] . . written while they waited in England for the first of October . . . And the letter from Paris from Charles de Noailles, waiting too . . And my mother's from Brussels and Sybille's from Sanary. No one taken in by words; no one wanting to fight. And now. What is the feeling? My sister writes from Paris that the detension was hysterically gay. As if there had been a war. Her concierge had just returned from a funeral; she explained that she could not feel sad. "Tout me semblait si beau, j'étais distraite, Madame. Les pavés gris me semblaient si beaux."

Meanwhile it is over. We are still ill with it. Aldous and Gerald would not admit it at the time. Gerald would hardly speak about it nor listen to the radio. He said we were mad. That was true, getting up all night and the real news coming in so early each morning . . . Then the disgusting pictures of gas masks; making people look like hogs. Now, this week, Aldous tells me, the pictures in *Life* are about the trenches in Hyde Park.

And then in California too life went on. The Huxleys had had to move in mid-crisis. Afterwards they discovered that they were in the ugliest house in Hollywood. It had a garden, though, "large and private like a Corot". Aldous at last was getting better. He was made to keep to his prescribed rest—ten hours at night, two in the afternoon. Rest without reading or talking. "He may listen to his radio in the afternoon, though technically he ought to sleep. I am rather annoyed with the doctors who were not at all precise about what they called taking it easy." All the same the week after Munich, because of their relief,

the four of us went on a little trip. Chris always sits in front with me while Aldous and Gerald sit and talk in the back. Chris has bought me an altimeter and we measured all our whizzings up and down. [We] went leisurely through a golden campagna like country with the stubble of barley . . then up into high country that was like Devon, apple orchards and all . . then moors and lakes like Scotland and wild duck and Gerald loving it. They were all delightfully homesick . . .

Aldous made up his mind. "He is going to start a short, easy, quick novel instead of going back to the big one he started . . . I think it is a good idea. So the other one can brew. [It never came to light] This one is about longevity, and is going to be comic too . . He is going to put in a lot about California life . . He is in a good mood." [To Eddy, 14th October]

## Chapter Five

## Private Miracle?

THERE had been for some time a great anxiety—submerged—in Aldous's and Maria's life. His sight. Since 1913 he had lived with it as a stationary affliction. This was no longer so. Such sight as he had was, in his own words, "steadily and quite rapidly failing. I was wondering quite apprehensively what on earth I should do." During his first autumn in America he had heard of a method of visual re-education, the Bates Method in fact, and decided to give it a try. The teacher, according to Maria, was so paralysingly stupid that Aldous did not go on, though he realized that there might be a lot in it. Now he found another man in Los Angeles. The first (extant) mention of the thing is a letter of Maria's dated 7th December 1938.

> Aldous goes on with his oculist and must be pleased with him. We don't discuss results every day; that would be agonizing. Especially as they vary so; but his theory is that what one can see once, one can see always. So now for the last three days Aldous has been able to see lines of "diamond type" which is so small that I have trouble reading it. He spends hours there, and at home he does exercises while he's resting; he looks at black. All this goes to show that there is hope . . .

Maria herself was none too well. "I've been so tired for the last month that in the evening I sometimes cry in my bath; not out of sadness but lassitude. My temperature is so low that it is ridiculous." Her life *was* tiring. To begin with there was all that driving (Profession: *Chauffeur*, she put down in hotel registers). Gerald would not permit himself to own or drive a car. "Out of humility . . . he will not see that this is actually an extraordinary indulgence." Nor does he "want to telephone or possess a telephone. So I not only have to refuse for Aldous but for Gerald. I'm their secretary." Now tomorrow, for instance,

> I shall drive Aldous to the oculist at 9.30. At 11.30 I pick up Gerald and leave him here; six miles each way. At 12.30 I fetch Aldous. He'll have lunch by himself and rest (because of the oculist he hardly works, *le pauvre*).

Meanwhile Gerald has to be driven to Pasadena because he wants to see their friends the Hubbles. He can't go on his own because he has no car, and he won't go with the Huxleys in the evening because he meditates from six to seven.

> It takes us three quarters of an hour in the mid-day heat. We can't stay long because I have to take Aldous out again. Then I drive Gerald back because he must be home on the dot of six p.m. for his meditation. After dinner I read to Aldous as he is not allowed to read at all for the moment. I even read him the newspaper at breakfast.

Maria's letters throw some light on the contradictions in the life of that extraordinary man who was Aldous's best friend.

> . . Tu sais combien j'aime Gerald et combien je le respecte et c'est autant plus triste de le voir rétrécir toute sa vie et toute sa philosophie comme il le fait . . .
> . . You know how much I love Gerald and how much I respect him [still Maria to Jeanne] which makes it all the sadder to see him shrink his life the way he does, and his whole outlook. And then he criticises the life we lead (because he loves us). He thinks that we are seeing far too many people and are not confining ourselves to those who want to save their souls . . . He thinks that Aldous has the right to say, as Gerald does, I'm too busy, my work is too important for me to go and see you . . . But I think that this is absolutely inadmissible *c'est orgeuilleux* . . . Then he thinks that I spend too much time learning what others feel and suffer, and that we often see people we don't really want to see out of politeness. But as we, and specially Aldous, are sometimes interested in going out into the world, it seems to me that we owe a certain politeness to the world. Gerald tells me that's my Latin education . . . I tell him that politeness comes from the heart . . . But then perhaps I do bother too much about people . . . looking into their lives. I ought to shut my eyes, I waste so much time . . but as long as it isn't Aldous's time. Fortunately he has such a capacity for "withdrawing himself".

Now Matthew is with them for the Christmas holidays, thin and low in spirits. They rush him to their doctors. The lungs seem all right. After he left (on New Year's Eve, Aldous and Maria having gone to bed at nine), he sent his mother a charming, reassuring telegram.

> Mathieu peut . . très finement me rassurer et me faire comprendre milles choses sans les expliquer définitivement; ce qu'Aldous ne peut ni faire ni comprendre.

In another letter Maria tells Jeanne never to misunderstand what may sound like criticism of Gerald. "I love and respect him and don't know what we should do without him and he is devoted to us to the extreme . . . He is impartial and just. Aldous *never* tires of seeing him and listening to him. He is able to be as silent or as chatty with Gerald as he is with me; and moreover Gerald stimulates him intellectually." Now look at the nice time they all had yesterday. After lunching at Anita's,

> we three went home for tea with toast and crumpets. Aldous *tout content*. Gerald reads till six, then meditates for an hour. At 7.15 he emerges and bakes, under my instructions, his first batch of bread. We heat up our supper and Gerald sets the table. Aldous comes down, all three of us in the best of humours. A & G discuss, always with the same interest, what they have been reading, while Gerald keeps an eye on his bread and doesn't burn it—at half past nine I drive him home. Aldous is already in bed, reading (he's been allowed to for the last few days). I still feel tired, but less than I did—anyway I think one has no right to be.

For Aldous's eyes *are* improving. Four weeks have passed—three hours at the "oculist" every morning—constant, watchful attention to right use.

> [8th January Maria to Jeanne] We have a definite improvement, though nothing spectacular as yet; what is certain is that even the right pupil is clearing up; the left looks quite cleared up but one must think that there is still some invisible opacity because he is still not able to read without fatigue. The *regard* is now that of his childhood photographs, and it moves me to see Aldous *looking at me* . . . Meanwhile he goes on with unbelievable patience . . . And its monstrously expensive . . .
>
> We are happier together than ever. I haven't written to you about this, but I think you must have guessed it from my letters. *Jamais en désaccord . . ni avec personne*—and he is becoming more and more patient.

## Chapter Six

## 1938/1939 II—Eat and Drink and Read Books

BY mid-February Aldous is able to report to Chatto's that he is hard at work. On a short phantasy, "a wild extravaganza .. but built up of solidly realistic psychological elements .. a most serious parable". After which he hopes to write eight lectures on religion to be delivered in Calcutta (yes—they were planning to go to India) "for a thing appropriately called the Gosh Foundation". The letter—Aldous's first, it would seem, since 18th November—is written on a typewriter with outsize lettering.

Their life became less enclosed. In March, a European visitor (the last?), Jeremy,[1] the St John Hutchinsons' son—"an adorable boy .. very amusing and intelligent . . . I'd like to keep him here for ever. It made me realize how exciting it would be to see other friends." (It was he and his sister who as children had dubbed Aldous the Quangle Wangle.) Aldous and Maria took him to the sights, Disney's studio, Hubble's telescope, and Chaplin took them all out to dinner at Earl Carroll's restaurant—"un floor-show—jamais j'en ai vu di'aussi belles filles; toutes presque nues et le dîner mangeable".

> For a young man it was all pure delight. [Jeremy Hutchinson writes] Maria so down to earth, so poetical, so full of humour and teasing, and of course for the adolescent so sexy . . . Within an hour of arriving .. I was being conducted round Forest Lawn with Aldous caressing the marble pink bottoms of the statuary and pointing out the "staggering sensuality" as the eternal Wurlitzer sounds came out from behind the trees. . . .
>
> I had been bitterly disappointed with *Gaza* and unsympathetic to religious experiences, but of course it was Aldous of the Essays, Aldous of day to day social contact, Aldous the apparent Saint .. gentle, inquiring, fascinating, and fascinated too with every fact, every thought, hesitatingly brought out with the amazed inflection of his voice .. Aldous the same with everyone—the black cook, the Japanese gardener, Charlie, Hubble, Gerald Heard, me . . . For a young man (and for a boy) he aroused a deep response . . . I loved them both. My whole memory was one of gaiety and stimulation.

Summer plans now. They would like to go to Frieda's ranch but

[1] The present Q.C.

Matthew wants a change from mountains—"He likes the sea and girls."

But presently Aldous has a relapse—extreme fatigue, a probable spot on the lung. "How *can* we go to Calcutta in six months?"

In April they moved house; again. To Pacific Palisades, a farther suburb of Los Angeles, 701 South Amalfi Drive. It was a real horror, far and away their most extreme. They looked on it with affection. As they lived there for three years it is worth a description.

It is a paradise we have this time [Maria to Eddy] A large rambling house in wood inside and out and Angiolino calls it the *wagone di terza classe*. And the man was German and collected horrors in European "kitsch" and specialized in women's bosoms. Pictures of women . . all over the place . . and statues of bronze . . Some we hid and when I got tired of hiding I hoped to get used to it and we did. Aldous turned the statues around when he preferred bottoms to breasts. But there are three sitting-rooms and a study for Aldous and a little bed and bathroom separate for Matthew . . . Aldous's room is small and we had to hire a hospital bed as . . nothing in the house fitted him. As a table de nuit he has a large safe . . inside he keeps books and I always fear he may pinch his fingers.

Then there is a bar in the cellar . . Covered with more bozomed women and clocks which tick up and down a fan on a naked lady and luminous dogs as lamps and . . a full-sized painting of a gorilla carrying a woman in a chemise to a very easily guessed purpose; there also stands a harmonium next to the gorilla. But the house we can laugh at and it is the garden which is the paradise.

We stand on a sort of island; high over the sea, over-looking steeply a very green valley with trees and a polo field and all around are the hills. They were very green and now are turning slowly to that dry gold . . .

And the garden is a garden. About five acres and filled with flowers and citrus trees and large Avocados now ripe and roses and gladioli and many flowers we don't know . . . We live as peacefully as in Sanary and the telephone rings rarely . . they all know that Aldous is finishing a book. Work is understood here.

[He] is working with determination to get his novel finished for autumn publication.

Anita Loos, in Santa Monica, was by Los Angeles standards a near neighbour.

One reason why we walk often at night. When she works at the studio all day it is the only time she has for walking. And it is not safe for her to walk alone so she brings a ridiculous little dog . . . She and Aldous laugh a lot; we are very fond of her. Otherwise we see no-one except often Constance Collier the old English actress. She is pretty grand and ridiculous and yet also witty and pompous. She is a dear and so proud when Queen Mary sends her signed photographs and messages ... The Chaplins we don't see often because Charlie is definitely working .. But we are good friends and Paulette is making quite a success ... of her movie career. The other careers being brilliant right away. I mean business and love and so on.

.. Of course we .. see Gerald less because he still won't have a car or drive somebody else's so he has to come and stay when he wants to see us as it is fourteen miles to his canyon each way. He is very well indeed and happy in his little cell adjoining Chris's house ...

To Jeanne, that same spring, Maria said about Gerald:

I think it's dangerous to live by oneself and with an *idée fixe* about continual meditation ... And yesterday, when I was driving him home, I asked him if he didn't have to get anything. No, he had all he needed, fruit, bread etc .. and when I pointed out to him that all of it was eight days old and that he really could afford to buy himself a piece of bread ... for him it's part of his Bovaristic image; part of the yogi and the saint etc ... poor Gerald and he is profoundly unhappy and sometimes I torment him by asking monstrously precise questions. He never answers me with a lie, but I find that he lies by omission. And all this saddens me because he is as miserable, in his sphere, as Mère is in hers. Mère has neither principles nor morality ... Gerald has them in abundance; Mère is lazy and allows herself to drift; Gerald works tenaciously at giving himself a positive direction; but they are both equally unhappy and I don't see that one of them does any more good than the other either for individuals or the world in general ...

May 1939. ".. Tell me all about England, about Europe. Are you getting used to living under continual threat?" Aldous was signing or soliciting affidavits, Maria again implored her family to come while there was time. Jeanne was not the only target. The Nicolas's house in Holland was only a few miles from the German border: those letters also rained upon Suzanne. She would answer that Joep had just accepted another big commission, was doing stained-glass windows in yet another church or public building, wouldn't hear of leaving—they had no capital, were unknown in the U.S.A. Leave it all, Maria went on, better poor than dead. We'll help you. At least send the children. *Now.* Encourage Mère to come. Aldous made legal and financial arrangements to get two Jewish children out of Germany whose mother had been a pupil of his mother's at Prior's Field. For the rest the Huxleys, like so many others, led a divided existence, resigned to uncertainty, now aware of danger, now getting on with things, looking the other way . . .

. . In the past year I have worn myself out so completely twice with anticipation of what might happen that I am now callous. [Maria to Eddy] Callous for what *might*—I don't suppose I could be callous to what is reality. But as it has not happened, maybe it won't ever. Of course they talk about it constantly and follow the papers and the radio and they mind terribly. But having minded more and more intensely and pointlessly, because it helps nothing, I was worn-out and I just listen to them. I mean chiefly Aldous and Gerald.

. . There are so many interesting things going on in America. And [Aldous says] it seems that Europe can be looked at better from far away. And it is strange that one needs no roots really if one tries living without . . . So you see what I mean about roots and patriotism and so on. But I see how much Bertie Russell suffers from the trees here not looking like so much cooked spinach. And I am sorry for him . . . But we live on as if there were no nightmare, and I suppose that is what you all do. Eat and drink and read books.

## Chapter Seven

## Private Miracle

HIS teacher that winter had taken him quite a long way, Aldous found. Then he met a disciple of the late Dr Bates, a woman, Margaret D. Corbett,[1] a genius of inventiveness, patience, intelligence and sympathy, Maria said, and devoted to her work. She proved perfect for Aldous. To her now he went six times a week. The lessons were not boring—"You are taught to *use* your eyes, taught *how* to read, to look, to drive." And, Maria added, Mrs Corbett helped anyone who needed it; for those who could pay her fees were reasonable while Mrs Bates in New York charged twenty-five dollars an hour.

Yesterday [4th May, Maria to Jeanne] he was able to read—not easily—the 15ft line at 15ft—that is normal, but hesitant, vision! It *is* a miracle!

And our old friend Constance Collier, too, who was nearly blind with cataract is rapidly regaining her vision. Now I begin to dare talk about it; even Aldous talks about it. The left eye has altogether cleared up. The right eye is clearing rapidly and above all he is able to move it, it moves back: you remember that as he wasn't using the eye, there was a marked strabismus.

And to Eddy three weeks later.

. . He has put on a lot of weight and with it a different air . . I cannot explain. If you saw Aldous you would understand—He is somehow smoothed out. His moods and his depressions have smoothed along with it . . . From having a vision of 15% he now has a vision of 50% and is making more rapid progress. So you see what that must mean to him. He can read even the paper without glasses, and above all he can read without fatigue. This is the great excitement of our life, and for me it will remain a miracle, and something to burn candles to the Virgin for.

And now Aldous, for his part, mentions it.

1 Author of *How to Improve Your Sight*, Los Angeles, 1938. Other literature on the subject: Dr W. H. Bates's own *Perfect Sight Without Glasses*, New York, 1920; *The Improvement of Sight by Natural Methods*, by C. S. Price, M.B.E., D.O. London, 1934.

.. I have been working on my eyes [he begins in a typical manner in a letter to his brother of 30th July] taking lessons in seeing from an admirable teacher here ... Optometrists loathe the method, because it endangers a hundred-and-fifty-million-dollar-a-year spectacle industry. Most doctors oppose it, because Bates's experimental work established unquestionably, it seems to me after reading his papers —that the Helmholtz theory regarding accommodation and refractive error is wrong. Still, the more liberal doctors have now got to the point of saying that it can't do any harm. Meanwhile there are the empirical facts which are those in my own case.

Aldous now gives the technical assessment of his improved vision. As the subject is extremely controversial, I shall transcribe it in full. For clarity, it might be best to begin by repeating his summing-up of his case (in *The Art of Seeing*) as it stood when he had partially regained his sight in 1913.

[The attack of *keratitis punctata*] left me (after eighteen months of near-blindness ...) with *one eye just capable of light perception,* and *the other with enough vision to permit of my detecting the two-hundred-foot letter on the Snellen chart at ten feet* [my italics].

[With spectacles, the good eye] was able to recognize the seventy-foot line at ten feet and to read tolerably well—provided always that I kept my better pupil dilated with atropine ... A measure of strain and fatigue was always present, and there were occasions when I was overcome by that sense of complete physical and mental exhaustion which only eye-strain can produce.

And in his present letter to Julian, Aldous specified the strength of the spectacles he had been obliged to use.

bi-focals, first of six and-a-half diopters of magnification, then of eight and ten diopters [in 1938], plus special reading glasses of fifteen diopters.

The letter goes on.

I am now wearing no glasses, seeing much better at a distance, reading, and all without strain and with a general improvement in health and nervous condition. I have just done the whole of the revision of my typescript (a very trying job, as you doubtless know) without glasses and .. without fatigue.

Meanwhile, the vision of *the right eye* [the *bad eye,* that had been capable only of light perception] has increased in the last three months, so that, from seeing the big 200-foot letter on the chart at three feet, *I can now read the 70-foot line at six feet* and large nursery print at the near point. The scar tissue is quite definitely clearing up, and I have good hopes that, if I persist, I may get back as much vision in the bad eye as I had in the good eye and that *the good eye may be pushed on from fifty per cent of normal vision (where it is now, having been raised from about fifteen per cent)* to something considerably nearer normal.

Meanwhile I have seen other cases responding in the same way. Constance Collier . . took the treatment for a cataract which had reduced one eye to a mere perception of light and darkness. After four months, she can now read normal print with this eye. Incipient cataracts clear up completely in as little as a month. Glaucoma is relieved very rapidly. I have seen several cases of children with squint completely cured . . .

And all through a perfectly rational and simple series of practices designed, first, to relax the eye and increase its circulation . . second, to train the mind to interpret what the eye sends it and not to interfere with the functioning of the eye by straining or staring.

What Aldous did not mention were the daily hours spent on learning those simple practices, the vigilance, the submission, the tough perseverance. *Not* to strain, *not* to stare, is as hard to learn for an urban adult as turning cart-wheels; harder. It needs a patience which, as Maria said, we would only understand if we ourselves had been half blind.

## Chapter Eight

## 1938/1939 III

"**I** AM asking myself—are we really going to run off to India? I think for us that kind of thing is over. Why not stay where we are?" Aldous took the point. "We might travel inwardly," he said, "instead of outwardly."

In June they heard that "Mère is ruined . . . She has played the market. We always expected to have to help her one day . . . We shall do it *de bon cœur*." (Mme Nys was not then actually ruined, though soon after they substantially had to help her, and this Aldous did to his last day.)

Kingsley Martin, of the *New Statesman*, wrote to Aldous taking him to task no doubt about his politics or lack of them. Aldous replied.

. . I don't know where you got information about Gerald and myself being about to start a community; it doesn't happen to be true. I can't speak for Gerald; but certainly I don't know nearly enough about many things to be able to embark on such a venture . . . This doesn't diminish my interest in such ventures; for I become more and more firmly convinced that it is completely pointless to work in the field of politics . . first, because one can't achieve anything unless one is in a key position, and, second, because even if one were in a key position, all one could achieve would be, at the best, a deflection of evil into slightly different channels . . .

. . Religious people who think they can go into politics and transform the world always end by going into politics and being transformed by the world. (e.g. the Jesuits, Père Joseph, the Oxford Group.) Religion can have no politics except the creation of small-scale societies of chosen individuals outside and on the margin of the essentially unviable large-scale societies . . .

Christopher Isherwood first came to Hollywood that summer, under contract to a studio. As an old friend of Gerald's he soon met Aldous and Maria who quickly became very fond of him. They liked him, as the saying goes, for himself. Oh, they knew he was *a* writer. There is an entry in Virginia Woolf's Diary (November 1938) which goes:

Isherwood and I met on the doorstep. He is a slip of a wild boy: with quicksilver eyes: nipped: jockeylike. That young man, said W. Maugham, "holds the future of the English novel in his hands."

376

Of that aspect of their friend's identity the Huxleys had but little idea. They had not read then *Mr Norris*, didn't know of Issyvoo.

In his turn he now recorded his own first impression of Aldous. An Aldous in his forty-sixth year. After remarking on that "extraordinarily sinister house which was built and furnished in a style best described as log-cabin decadent", Isherwood went on:[1]

> . . I had expected somebody resembling the skinny, thickly be-spectacled, spider-like intellectual of the early photographs . . . Aldous . . in the flesh was slender but not at all skinny, and the insect-look . . now seemed to me to be more of a bird-look, benevolent and quick with interest in his surroundings. He no longer wore spectacles. When he talked, his beautifully sensitive features seemed literally to shine with enthusiasm . . .
>
> Aldous's clothes were usually informal. But he wore everything well, and when he put on a suit he looked marvellously distinguished. It was not in his character to be consciously dressy; but he was never careless and I think he must have had a certain affection for some of the things he wore. For instance, he had kept a tie from Paris for more than twenty years and would remark that it was "like an early Rouault."
>
> Aldous had given up . . spectacles because he had become a convert to the Bates Method . . I have neither the authority nor the inclination to express a personal opinion on this subject; I merely record that I have seen people who were discussing it become enraged to the point of incoherence and I can well believe that it has sometimes been the cause of fist-fights.

Aldous's novel, *After Many a Summer Dies the Swan*, was getting written with the speed almost of *Crome Yellow*. On 25th July, the eve of his birthday, copy was ready and revised. Maria, on Mrs Corbett's advice, had learnt to touch-type just in time. Aldous said he didn't mind the mistakes as long as the thing got done. He had a horror of sending out his work, and even the *Madame Curie* script, with M.G.M.'s typing pool standing by, had been copied at home by Maria.

> I think we are pleased with it. [Maria to Jeanne about the novel] Matthew has been so nice. He finished reading it last night before going to bed. He said, "Well, I did enjoy that book, pop; very illuminating too!" What ease they have with each other.
>
> Aldous hesitated to give it to me, he put it off as long as he could . . I think it's because he was afraid I might criticise the cynicism with which he described stupidity. I, who know him so well, can feel underneath all his impatience and horror of stupidity . . .

[1] *Mem. Vol.*

And to Eddy,

It's in his most excellent manner—the brilliant fiendish manner. Funny—Indecent—Horrifying. Yet it is also, thank God, placated with the other side that is Constructive.

> *The woods decay, the woods decay and fall,*
> *The vapours weep their burthen to the ground,*
> *Man comes and tills the field and lies beneath,*
> And after many a summer dies the swan.

The Tennysonian lines from *Tithonus*, Tithonus to whom the goddess granted immortality but forgot to add eternal youth. Aldous's theme was time: a parable about the illusion, if you will, of purely quantitative time. However, in *After Many a Summer*, Aldous really did apply his principle of mixing all the categories, the book slides from slapstick into philosophic dissertation, eroticism, pastiche, esoteric moralizing. If it was a return to Peacock, it is very far out Peacock indeed. The essential theme is immortality and time, and the locale is Southern California. The "finer shades of the American language" were vetted by no less an expert than Anita Loos. There is much straight description, Baedeker in his heyday would hardly have been more accurate about the ride westward from Los Angeles railway station, the Union Depot.

The first thing to present itself was a slum of Africans and Philipinos, Japanese and Mexicans. And what permutations and combinations of black, yellow and brown! What complex bastardies! And the girls —how beautiful in their artificial silk! . . . the car plunged into a tunnel and emerged into another world, a vast, untidy suburban world of filling-stations and bill-boards . . of vacant lots and waste-paper . . and churches—Primitive Methodist churches built . . in the style of the Cartuja at Granada, Catholic churches like Canterbury Cathedral, synagogues disguised as Hagia Sophia, Christian Science churches with pillars and pediments like banks . . .

EATS. COCKTAILS. OPEN NITES.

JUMBO MALTS.

DO THINGS, GO PLACES WITH CONSOL SUPER GAS!

. . The car sped onwards, and here in the middle of a vacant lot was a restaurant in the form of a seated bulldog, the entrance between the front-paws, the eyes illuminated . . .

ASTROLOGY, NUMEROLOGY, PSYCHIC READINGS.

DRIVE IN FOR NUTBURGERS.

. . Mile after mile . . interminably . . .

CLASSY EATS. MILE HIGH CONES.

JESUS SAVES.

FINE LIQUORS.

GO TO CHURCH AND FEEL BETTER ALL THE WEEK.

. . A real estate agent's office in the form of an Egyptian sphinx.

JESUS IS COMING SOON.

BEVERLY PANTHEON THE CEMETERY THAT IS *DIFFERENT*.

. . Past a Rosicrucian Temple, past two cat-and-dog hospitals, past a School for Drum-Majorettes . . . Sunset Boulevard . . . Beverly Hills. The surroundings changed. The road [was] flanked by the gardens of a rich residential quarter. Through trees . . the façades of houses all new, almost all in good taste—elegant and witty pastiches of Lutyens manor houses, of Little Trianons, of Monticellos; light-hearted parodies of Le Corbusier . . fantastic . . adaptations of Mexican haciendas and New England farms.

For Aldous this was no mere exotic travel, it was a description of what was to become his home-town.

. . The houses succeeded one another, like the pavilions of some endless international exhibition. Gloucestershire followed Andalusia . . .

"That's Harold Lloyd's place," said the chauffeur . . "And that's Charlie Chaplin's . . That's where Ginger Rogers lives. Yes, *sir*."

And then we have of course the passing evocation of the Beverly Pantheon—Forest Lawn, the Western necropolis immortalized a few years later by another English novelist Aldous did not read (though he's been heard to say that he enjoyed *Vile Bodies*). Nightmare Abbey, where the house party and most of the action of the book take place, is nightmare castle, an almost undisguised version of W. Randolph Hearst's aberration, where the Huxleys spent a fascinated weekend. (Domestic details, such as cotton sheets in a house with an old master in the lift, were imparted in Maria's letters.) In fact Aldous came as near to making use of living models as he ever did. His Mr Stoyte, the boorish owner of the castle, maintains a private laboratory researching ways of prolonging human life; Hearst's fear of death was notorious. Hearst's young woman friend, Marion Davies, was, at least to contemporary Californians,

as recognizable as she is in Orson Welles's film [*Citizen Kane*]. And the wicked Dr Obispo is said to have been modelled after a Hollywood physician. The novel also includes Huxley's composite of two of Southland's leading educators merged into an unctuous college president named Dr Mulge, whose voice is a blend of vaseline and port wine. This did not endear the author to his models.[1]

On the "constructive" side, there is Mr Propter: Miller transmigrated from *Eyeless in Gaza* in the form of an American scholar. He holds forth on evil, time and liberation.

"I like the words I use to bear some relation to facts. [Mr Propter continued] That's why I'm interested in eternity—psychological eternity. Because it's a fact."

"For you perhaps," said Jeremy [the English high-brow].

"For anyone who chooses to fulfil the conditions under which it can be experienced."

"And why should anyone wish to fulfil them?"

"Why should anyone choose to go to Athens to see the Parthenon? Because it's worth the bother. And the same is true of eternity. The experience of timeless good is worth all the trouble it involved."

"Timeless good," Jeremy repeated with distaste. "I don't know what the words mean."

"Why should you?" said Mr Propter. ". . you've never bought your ticket for Athens."

From timeless good to longevitous wickedness—the Fifth Earl, a thorough-going autocrat with a nice turn of the pen and the tastes of the Marquis de Sade, the Fifth Earl of Gonnister who has succeeded in keeping himself alive and virile on a diet of raw carp gut into his two hundred and second year.

(Carp gut? "Well, that was just a fantasy," Aldous said in the London interview twenty years later on. "Incidentally, long after I wrote it, I read in some medical paper a whole theory about cholesterol being the villain in the whole ageing process. So it wasn't an entirely fantastic picture—I mean if we would find something to inhibit the formation of cholesterol, you *would* do something to increase life . . .") At a price:

. . The shirt, which was his only garment, was torn and filthy. Knotted diagonally across the powerful chest was a broad silk ribbon that had evidently once been blue . . He sat hunched up, his head thrust forward and at the same time sunk between his shoulders. With one of his huge and strangely clumsy hands he was scratching a sore place . . between the hairs of his left calf . . .

1 From an article by Aldous's friend, Lawrence Clark Powell, then Librarian of the University of California, "California Classics Reread" in *Westways*, December 1970.

Deathless, Tithonus became a repulsive old man; the Fifth Earl has turned into a foetal ape that has had time to grow up—evolution's finest joke. Dr Obispo breaks into a Mephistophelian laugh. The Fifth Earl growls and lunges at his female, then

> smoothed the broad ribbon of his order with the palm of his hand . . making as he did so a curious humming noise that was like a simian memory of the serenade in Don Giovanni.

Mr Stoyte finds words. "Well . . once you get over the first shock —well, they look like they were having a pretty good time."
*After Many a Summer*, in Maria's words, is "everybody's cup of tea in parts—but I can also see that it will be everybody's red rag in parts."

On the Sunday following Aldous's birthday and the completion of the novel, the Huxleys gave a big luncheon party. "Paulette [Goddard] brought a cake, a real birthday cake weighing 8 lbs., all white and inscribed '*Mon Coeur*,' that wasn't very explicit but charming in intention. And Charlot brought a case of Cordon Rouge, 12 bottles of Mumm's! Matthew said it was very good and dry. We had Helen Hayes and MacArthur, her husband, the Charlies, the Hubbles . . Constance naturally and Chris and Gerald and the Rodakiewitz's (Peggy and her second husband). In the garden. Hazel [the Negro maid Maria shared with Christopher Wood] came to help us and all that went admirably. They stayed till 7 o'clock and Charlie gave an exquisite performance; among other things a dance he is going to do with a balloon. They are going to start shooting next Monday. [Indeed, *The Great Dictator*] It will be the best thing he has ever done. Lillian Gish came later on and Orson Welles . . ."
As Christopher Isherwood put it, "One didn't think of Maria Huxley as being what is usually meant by a 'great' hostess; yet, in her charmingly haphazard way—by accident, almost—she created some historic parties."
There were a few more easy days. Aldous and Gerald do their spiritual exercises; Maria says she hasn't got the time so she is doing acrobatics instead. "Tell Sophie I can stand on my head now . . I think I was born acrobat." On Wednesday they are off to Santa Barbara where Rosalind Rajagopal and Krishnamurti are spending the summer. "He is charming and amusing and so simple. How he must suffer when he is treated as a prophet." Then Matthew needs a proper car. Maria proposes to buy him a new one—he ought to have the pleasure of a new car. "Aldous, curiously, turns

a bit childish, he wants me to pass my car on to Matthew and get a
new one for ourselves."

August, and everything overclouded once again by the one
anxiety. Aldous had been offered another job by M.G.M., the
adaptation of *Pride and Prejudice*; working again for a studio did
not appeal to him at all and he meant to turn it down. But in the
last week of the month, he accepted—to help even a few of those
who would be needing help, he wanted all the money he was able
to lay hands on.

Now it has happened, Maria wrote to Eddy after September 3rd.
"It still seems unbelievable. Certainly unimaginable. For two days
we were completely unexisting. I heard Chamberlain here in the
middle of the night as he addressed you in London . .

"By the time my family got up I was just capable of telling them.
Those hours had helped me to collect myself a bit. Though it is
so much worse for all of you in the middle of it, yet you are obliged
to do something—go or come or obey, whereas here we just listen
and cannot believe. . . ."

# PART EIGHT

## In Another Country: 1939-1945

". . Whereas here we just listen and
cannot believe."

MARIA HUXLEY in a letter to
Edward Sackville-West

# Chapter One

## Limbo

DURING the six years of the war, Aldous and Maria remained in Southern California. They did not travel; they moved house only once. Aldous started and abandoned one more utopian novel, found it hard to write, and during the worst time could not write at all, wanted to do something, did not know what; eventually wrote four books, three of them different in substance from what he had done before; ground out some work for the films when occasions arose. Matthew was drafted into the Medical Corps of the U.S. Army, became seriously ill, was consequently discharged. Maria's family took to the roads before the advancing German armies and there were many months with no news from them at all. Maria's health worsened; the doctors discovered signs of t.b., prescribed a very dry climate, and they went to live in a small oasis in the Mojave desert. There they led an existence of long solitudes punctuated by a little family life. Aldous saw less of Gerald Heard who was founding his own community, Trabuco College, gasoline and tyre rationing imposing separations in an area where distances were on an inhuman scale and public transport negligible; there were other reasons definable perhaps as shades of ideological estrangement. Aldous's own health continued precarious and he went through one long bad patch, a flare-up of the bronchial and other troubles. Such money as he was able to earn—and there were alarmingly lean years as well as very good—was needed for the responsibilities he kept taking on. Jeanne's child was sent over in time, lived with them, finished her education, went off to join the Free French forces. Joep and Suzanne Nicolas, too, had listened to Cassandra in the nick of time; Maria's mother and youngest sister with baby, after many hardships, reached the U.S.A. The two German Jewish children Aldous had tried to rescue did not, but they had got as far as England where his cousin Joan and her husband, General Buzzard, took them in and brought them up, Aldous contributing to their education. A large amount of Maria's time and energy was spent in trying to get food to Europe. Aldous persisted with his Bates training and saw Mrs Corbett when work and transport allowed. His sight continued to improve. And this, well beyond the purely personal level, was the most heartening thing for him in those years: one tangible hint that men could help themselves. His other solace was Maria, her unfailing devotion, companionship, lightness of touch.

Of the war, six thousand miles away, he would not speak at all. Not during the first bad years. On the day Paris fell, Anita Loos wrote later, his face was dead white and he bore the expression of someone who was peering into hell; but the talk that evening was mostly some scientific discussion between him and Edwin Hubble; nobody mentioned Paris. (The few references found in his letters are either remote and pessimistic or on the conventional personal level, expressions of concern for Julian's son, Francis, who was serving in a destroyer; Lewis Gielgud's safe escape from France.) What went on behind the silence even Maria did not always know, though some of it we can perhaps imagine. The consciousness—the consciousness of a sensitive if under-emotional man—that the victims and the instruments of *this* war *that is now* are living men and women; the consciousness of great present suffering that must be followed by yet more suffering. The sense of waste and folly. The sense of utter horror. Physical and moral. Unalleviated by any sense of right. For Aldous never changed the conviction he had arrived at: that war, in *any* cause, in *any* circumstances, must always by its own nature be evil and lead to further evil. When the war went badly, he grieved; when it went "well", he could not rejoice. He foresaw famine, massacres, destruction and whatever the present outcome, abolition of the decencies—an age of tyranny before us. Throughout, he remained unsustained by any sense of solidarity or achievement, of shared hopes and aims. Again, as he had been during the First World War, in a very different way, Aldous was cut off from the mass of his contemporaries.

He took no direct action. He did not preach on platforms, or sign manifestoes or write any more pamphlets or letters to the press. The way he chose now was oblique, less open—the long way round. The approach to the perennial philosophy is a quiet one. The first book he wrote, the book he found bearable—and useful —to write at this time, was the biographical study of a man who was a contemplative mystic who chose, for the greater glory of France, to immerse himself in power politics: a cautionary tale about the illusions of the human will and the horrors and catastrophic consequences of the Thirty Years' War. Aldous's own ends (in day to day conduct) might be defined as harmlessness: doing the work at hand, giving such individual material help as he could. His long-term end, his absolute end: discovery. The discovery of what we are. His life was mainly what, for want of a better word, we must call the inner life: a process of gradual self-transformation, the fruits of which are traceable, perhaps, in his books (Aldous left no journal) and were evident to those who met the man he had become. There were of course other, lighter, sides. The inner life was being refreshed by his curiosity about the outer one; and there was the daily fact that Aldous and Maria seldom ceased to laugh at themselves. In spite of the nightmare six thousand miles away, and in psychological distance immensely further still, there were pleasures. There was the Californian sunshine. There was the pleasure he took in the animals they kept, and in the two young human animals, a new nephew and niece; the pleasure and reassurance of the austere beauty of their desert landscape. Aldous's love and need of nature was greater even than the love he bore for art as a young man. As the turning points were passed and it became possible to believe in an end to the German terror and an end to the war itself, when it was evident that England would survive in far more than the physical sense and that in some parts of the world at least the chances for a tolerably free and decent life had not all been destroyed, Aldous's own mood lightened and he was able to advance again towards the serenity that was inherent in his nature.

What if Aldous and Maria had in fact returned to Europe in 1938 or 1939? Perhaps it might be worth thinking about for a few moments. Aldous appeared to attach little conscious importance to the matter; he never tried to justify or explain. (He did express the view that it was selfish of any woman, invalid or child to remain in Europe if they had the means to leave, because they would be using food and medical resources.) Yet might he not have been moved in part by the syndrome of the First World War which he did spend in England and in circumstances of much personal unhappiness—Trevenen's death, the desolation of Oxford, separation from Maria, reclusion in an underpaid and uncongenial job, the jingoism of the public mood, the prevailing hypocrisies that jarred so bitterly on his generation and the revulsion which brought forth such works as *Antic Hay*? For the older Aldous, too, *that* England would have been intolerably claustrophobic and distasteful, whereas now, in the present war, he and Maria would have been non-combatants living, very likely, in the country. Their physical danger would have been negligible. (Though of course they could not have known this while the Battle of Britain was on.) It is unsound to predict anyone's reactions but I doubt whether either of them would have been particularly affected by personal fear. (One recalls Aldous writing letters about French poetry to Juliette in 1917 while "being pestered by these German aeroplanes .. a fiendish banging of bombs eastward towards St Paul's ..".) Maria, though, would have had some very anxious hours on the days Aldous went up to London.

Food rationing, clothes rationing, shortage of drink, drabness and the rest wouldn't have mattered a scrap to them. On the contrary. And essentially they would have led the kind of life they led anywhere. Instead of talking to Edwin Hubble he would have talked to Julian, Joad and Haldane . . . It would have been marginally easier to go to see someone at an English university than getting to U.C.L.A. or Berkeley in war-time California. The Peace Pledge Union was soldiering on with admirable courage and good sense (and allowed to soldier on— up to a point—with no less admirable tolerance) for such things as a declaration of War Aims and a change in the policy of Unconditional Surrender. It is unlikely that Aldous would have been active in the first-hand ways of his novitiate in 1936 (though he never resigned his sponsorship of the P.P.U., indeed confirmed it by a letter in the 1950s), but he would have seconded the movement with the prestige and the respect he might well have held had he been present. Nor is it at all unthinkable that he might have filled some niche in the B.B.C. Meanwhile he would have written the same kind of books in a slightly different way. The intrinsic fact of war would of course have been unchanged. Yet nightmare at a lesser distance loses some of its obsessive power. To see people live through it, not as the doomed and passive victims in one's imagination, but with courage, humour, spirit, might have been revealing and consoling. By "being there" Maria would have been spared much anguish. One cannot speak for Aldous. There also remains the question whether, given their state of health, they might not have been killed off by six English winters. (Or perhaps their health might never have reached such a stage?) That, too, it is impossible to tell.

I have given an outline, a kind of scaffolding, of these years in Aldous's life. Years are made of days. In the three chapters which follow, I shall try to fill in some of these with glimpses from Maria's letters and with what comes through in Aldous's own, and with some eye-witness accounts.

## Chapter Two

## Pacific Palisades

ALDOUS had signed on with M.G.M. for *Pride and Prejudice* in August 1939. Now that the war was actually there, he felt he could not go on with it. He talked to Krishnamurti; he telephoned (with Maria on the extension) to Anita Loos. She wanted to know why.

"Because it pays fifteen-hundred dollars[1] a week," he answered in deep distress. "I simply cannot accept all that money to work in a . . studio while my family and friends are starving and being bombed in England."

"But Aldous," I asked, "why can't you accept that fifteen-hundred and send the larger part of it to England?"

There was a long silence at the other end of the line, and then Maria spoke up.

"Anita," she said, "what would we ever do without you?"[2]

On 10th September Maria wrote to Rosalind Rajagopal, ". . . Aldous has taken up his job and I am quite certain it was the right thing to do, for the moment anyway . . . he is going to do it good-heartedly . . . Tell Krishnaji. He was a great help. Tell him we thank him. He probably knows anyway."

After the first shock, after Poland had fallen but Western Europe was still ticking over, the Huxleys, too, succumbed to the lull. The R.A.F. was bombarding Germany with propaganda pamphlets, Aldous and Gerald took it as a hopeful sign. Sophie arrived safely in November. Waiting for her, Maria had promised Jeanne, "She shall never be lost, or lonely or sad." She was sixteen:

I hope she will be young and indifferent and discover her new life instead of regretting the old. I know that during the last war I had an immense indifference for it, was only out to discover life.

The Huxleys thought of adopting her. "In case we shall all be killed. We would want her to inherit the little we have with

---

[1] Upped to $2,500 in Miss Loos's text. The actual sum was $1,500.

[2] Anita Loos in *Aldous Huxley, A Memorial Volume.* Chatto & Windus, 1965; Harper and Row, 1966. Hereafter cited as *Mem. Vol.*

Matthew. We can count on Matthew treating her like a sister. But what if Matthew marries a wife who does not want to share with Sophie?"[1] Meanwhile she was to be called Miss Huxley. Then Aldous had the pleasure of a visit—all too brief—from Gervas. The Nicolases, Joep and Suzanne with their two small daughters, Claire and Sylvia, landed in New York. Next, "an unexpected piece of good news!" (wrote Aldous), Julian announced himself for Christmas. It was almost as if there were no war.

Maria had to "switch everything up and down the week because Julian kept contradicting his telegrams and letters . . And he had said that he wanted to see people . . At last he arrived, and he hurricaned us.

> But he was exciting and amusing and so nice. Even though he never realizes other peoples' existences. He must also be as strong as all of us put together . . . Well, I gave three parties . . . The last party was the largest and I stayed in my bedroom—like a queen you may say [this is to Eddy], but like a rabbit I think . . . When they had gone I collected the cigarette ends for 23 minutes . . .
>
> And so the nonsense went on . . . I could see Aldous was bored too. On my first evening I had seated Sophie next to Charlie Chaplin . . when to my dismay at the last minute and a flurry of white pleats she runs in to me and whispers she *must* sit opposite Charlie! You can imagine how that upset the orthodoxy of the never very orthodox table in my house . . . You see that my life was very complicated about nothing at all . . And Julian had to have a row of presents for everyone on Sunday when the shops were closed . . . And then he would insist on going on picnics at very early hours of the day—while my family would still be oversleeping and I would make breakfast in an aura of disapproval and grunts. But all went well finally. Julian loved us and we loved him. And he flew off on Tuesday.

Aldous's sight had so much improved "that Julian could almost not believe it . . . When I am tired or feel sad or depressed, it is always that which encourages me most."

Aldous's work on *Pride and Prejudice* stopped after the New Year. In February the studio recalled him for revisions; on half-pay. This turned out most welcome. The American royalty accounts came in and Aldous, for a wonder, read them. He knew that *After Many a Summer*, published in October, had already sold

---

[1] All unassigned quotations in this and the next chapters will be from letters by Maria Huxley.

10,000 copies. Now he found out that in spite of this he was in the red with Harper's, and to the tune of 9,000 dollars. (His old books had always been selling in England; in America they did not.) It was a blow. And not easily made up. Even if he did get a new job at a studio at full pay it would take—what with Federal income tax, State tax, agents' fees—about three months of film work. Meanwhile the future of the book-trade in England looked entirely uncertain. M.G.M. assured Aldous that they would always have work for him for the asking.

Which by the way is not just niceness on their part. [Maria to Jeanne] It's because Aldous has learnt to do their kind of thing extremely well, as he does anything he really wants to. The only thing I find that he has still to learn is to pay some attention to his own finances; the kind of surprise we just had simply shouldn't have happened. It proves that he doesn't even look at his accounts . . .

Nevertheless, Aldous did not accept any more film work for the next eighteen months. When *P. & P.* (M.G.M.'s working title for Jane Austen) was done with, he remained at home (he could never come to terms with the sealed windows, the air-conditioning at the studio) trying to work out a framework for a novel linking the present with a future: a forerunner, it would seem, of the Good Utopia, the antidote to *Brave New World*.

"We go for walks again, and there is some sense in our lives . . ." Maria could take Aldous to Mrs Corbett and the tailor and the osteopath; she took him and Gerald to have their hair cut: "They are equally difficult to get to the hairdresser, so I take them at the same time." She drove Sophie to her lessons. She (having been led to all their doctors) was now finishing her French schooling under private tutors, Aldous seeing to Eng. Lit.

I would like to save her [Maria wrote to Sophie's mother] all those painful experiences Lady Ottoline might have saved me at that age if she had taken the trouble to advise me . . .

One of the things Maria did not realize in her turn was the effect of that strange and gloomy house. Sophie usually went out with them in the evening, but

sometimes it was not possible and I[1] was terrified in that awful house at night. So it was decided to buy me a watch-dog. It was to be a great surprise and when it arrived, the surprise was mine, because they had bought me a toy-pomeranian, and I was of course

---

[1] From a memoir written by Sophie Moulaert, the present Mrs W. Welling.

expecting something like a German sheep-dog! Aldous adored this silly but intelligent little female dog. [But it was Maria who brushed it, washed it, fed it.] He would go on the floor to play with her, walk in the garden with her on a leash . . . and talk about the proper way of having her trimmed. He wanted to call her Mae West because she always wriggled her behind and was very seductive . . She was finally called Loulou after the cartoons of "Little Lulu" which Aldous followed. The evening Loulou joined the family, we went to show her off to Anita Loos who owned a male pomeranian called Cagney (after the actor). There was quite a large dinner party and everybody sat in a circle around the two dogs. Loulou was extremely charming . . Cagney was most disagreeable and growled. Aldous then revealed that Loulou had been acquired to be a wife to Cagney, but Anita told him that Cagney was castrated. Aldous was so disappointed that we all had to laugh.

Gerald, at the moment, was being difficult.

Il est d'une intransigeance incompréhensible, and [to continue in a free translation of Maria's letter to her sister Jeanne] Aldous says he has taken up the attitude of "the Buddhist Party", meaning that he's become as rigid as if he'd joined the Communist Party . . . Gerald has become the priest of this "party-religion" and so one may no longer laugh even about his person . . . He can't see us because he will not leave his house for more than two hours at a time because of his meditations . . . Meditation takes for him the place of drugs. When it's time he throws us out . . .

Aldous's own criticism was more general. Writing to Julian about Gerald's book Pain, Sex and Time, he said,

I have always thought it unfortunate that Gerald should have consistently chosen to employ historical and pre-historical terms for the discussion of psychological and philosophical problems. The result is a quite unnecessary confusion of issues and the casting of a haze of dubiety over matters of plain psychological fact . . .

Gerald's writing, or rather manner of writing, had ever been a stumbling block. In 1929, the year of their first meeting, Aldous had written to Robert Nichols:

I've not ventured yet to attack Heard's book. It seemed to be written in such a frightful way . . And anyhow does one—or ought one—to believe in these great generalizations? I make so many myself that I have a personal and intimate reason for distrusting them!

At present Gerald was beginning to give what Maria called lectures in churches. ". . Whether Hindu Temple or Baptist Hall, [he] has a large following. [This is again to Eddy] He speaks well, but we don't go often." When Gerald comes to the house they have "far more interesting talks than the preachings—quicker—less hammed—well, you know, and full of those facts that both of them always find everywhere . . . Chris Isherwood often joins us now; we like him very much indeed. On Tuesdays we all meet for lunch at a market . . and we can eat our vegetarian and medical faddist foods under olive trees. And talk for ever under umbrellas . . ."

Bertrand Russell was still being subjected to the abominable witch hunt that had arisen over his appointment to City College, New York.[1] Aldous sent him this note (19th March)[2]

Dear Bertie,
Sympathy, I'm afraid, can't do much good; but I feel I must tell you how much I feel for you . . in the midst of the obscene outcry that has broken out around your name in New York.
Ever yours,
Aldous H.

The phony war still held; able to write to France, Maria described an idyllic outing with their dog and goats:

Nous avons été en pick-nick avec les Rajagopal, Krishnamurti, leur petite fille et deux oies; nous avons apporté Loulou, Jaja et Blanchette . . nos petites chèvres . . .
Il y avait aussi des humains: Chris et Gerald et Peggy avec ses enfants et ses parents mais en comparaison des bêtes cela ne comptait pas du tout. Dans la campagne il faisait beau et doux et ensoleillé. Nous étions dans un bosquet d'eucalyptus sur une herbe succulente . . . Enfin c'était charmant . . .

In April the world changed. The German invasion of Norway and Denmark began on the 9th. Soon after, Aldous became ill. The trouble appeared to be some old and deep-seated low infection which now manifested itself in turns by intestinal upsets, urticaria, bronchitis, myocardiac weakness, and for the next three or four months Aldous was not fit enough to attempt any work. After

---

[1] See *The Autobiography of Bertrand Russell*, Volume II, Chapter II, George Allen and Unwin, 1968; and *The Bertrand Russell Case*, ed. by John Dewey and Horace M. Kallen, Viking Press, 1941.
[2] Published in Russell's autobiography as above.

the invasion of Belgium there was no more news of Maria's mother, or of Rose and Eric de Haulleville and their baby; after the fall of France there was no more news from Jeanne. Weeks later, they had word that the Belgian party had left Brussels on foot in the general exodus, and after frightful days on the road—machine-gunned from the air, caught in a panicking crowd—had got to Bordeaux; and that Jeanne had been out of Paris when the Germans came.

. . We heard from them briefly . . . [Aldous to Julian, 7th July] we were making arrangements to get money through, when the curtain drops again. Goodness knows where they are now . . . and goodness knows how or when any communication is to be established with them. For the moment no money can be sent . . . And, of course, if the war goes on, there will be famine conditions in Belgium by the winter.

Aldous was now in the hands of Christopher Isherwood's Austrian doctor, Kolish, slowly getting better under his (rather experimental, I gathered) treatment, and trying to get over his inability to write.

. . all political and social speculation looks silly and irrelevant before the ink is dry on the paper. However, I seem at last to have something significant crystallizing in my mind—something which may permit itself to be written. I hope I may soon be well enough to begin . . .

In July I arrived in California (a refugee—having been in France, with a minor anti-fascist record, at the time of the German breakthrough and got away on an American ship). I found Aldous and Maria very changed. There was of course Aldous's new sight—there he was without his spectacles, walking, reading (still holding the print close to his eyes), but this was not as impressive as it might have been because of his looking so drawn and strained, like a man with a great burden of unhappiness severely locked away. I had often seen him look ill or withdrawn or quietly sad, but even during the great insomnia of 1935 he had always kept his air of equanimity. And poor Maria was so thin, so worn, so nervous—and so resolutely cheerful. One felt that everything was too much for her, physically too much, every minute. It was of course a deeply unhappy time for most of us, but it seemed to me that the Huxleys were almost deliberately, if not consciously, putting themselves under the greatest possible strain, submitting themselves to some rigorous process of repression; a process, I thought even then, that must have been of longer standing, must have ante-dated the catastrophic news of the last weeks.

Their house indeed was sinister, and quite unfunny. They did not live on stale crusts and squashy fruit, or shut their doors at fixed hours, yet there was now in their life (unlike before and unlike later on) something of that same element of *retrécissement* Maria had commented on in Gerald's. The ease had gone, the blessed lack of tension. What had been a framework was now a timetable. Start for Mrs Corbett; start for Dr Kolish; dinner not in the cool of the evening but on the dot of 7 p.m. Bedtime at ten. Most of it *was* imposed by geography or health, but there was rigorism in the execution. Maria's protectiveness, that had been so discreet, was now compulsive. There were a number of taboos. "Don't talk war to Aldous." One had to accept everything American, never show longing for Europe— . . *je regrette l'Europe aux anciens parapets . . . that* was unmentionable. I *could* not have spoken of the war to Aldous; once I manoeuvred our mutual English friend, Allanah Harper, into asking him, "Aldous, don't you want England to win? Wouldn't it be *better* if England won?" Aldous remained mute for a second, then he said in a colourless voice, "There won't be any England as we knew it". To Maria, Europe had already become unreal, a remote hell. Allanah who had come out of France with me had brought her dog; this Maria could not understand. I explained that since one had been *able* to take the dog, it would have been wrong and cruel, quite apart from any personal attachment, to have abandoned him. She would not see it. "You could have brought a baby instead." "Maria, what baby?" "*Any* baby." Go up to a Frenchwoman with a pram, "Madame, donnez-moi votre bébé, je le porterai en Amérique"? Maria remained convinced that this could and should have been done.

Yet they doted on Loulou. This funny little thing was the incongruous element in their household. When Gerald came, the dog would sit on his lap—it was a kind of dare. I can still see Gerald, rocking to and fro in a wicker-chair, talking a blue streak to Aldous, clasping the toy pom to his knees. (If one wants an idea of the cadences and subject matter of his conversations, one should go to Christopher Isherwood's novel *Down There on a Visit* and listen to Augustus Par.) Aldous and Maria were now vegetarians. One could not get out of them how much of it was due to diet and how much to not eating living things. At any rate, unlike Gerald, they still ate fish. There were meat and wine on the table for Matthew, Sophie and unregenerate guests. Life was being kept resolutely "normal" for the young. Matthew had just come home for the summer months (having got through his second pre-medical year at Colorado University), was taking some scientific course and going about quite independently with his friends. Sophie had passed her *baccalaureat* (at the Lyceé Français in New York where Maria had taken her during the bad days in June). "What good it will do her now, I don't quite know!" wrote Aldous. Maria wished that Sophie, too, would study medicine —it was a way to anything: even writers such as Maugham and Céline had begun by being doctors. Sophie thought she'd like the stage and enrolled as a dramatic student at the Max Reinhardt School at Hollywood.

In August Aldous began research for *Grey Eminence*: a mass of reading on the religious and political seventeenth-century background, most of it aloud by Maria (they got through five volumes of Bremond's—admirably readable—*Histoire du Sentiment Réligieux en France*, Gustave Fagniez's huge and indigestible work *Le Père Joseph et Richlieu*, and so on and on). By the end of September Aldous started writing. ("The whole story has an obliquely topical interest," he wrote to Harold Raymond, "for Joseph was as much responsible as anyone for prolonging the Thirty Years War, which is in the direct line of ancestry to the present disasters.") The atmosphere became more relaxed; they went again for their long walks on beach and hills, and visited such Huxleyan haunts as the pier at Santa Monica where Aldous would consult the lady fortune teller (The World's Largest Drug Store came later on).

In October, after the first full month of the Blitz on London, Aldous wrote this much to Lewis Gielgud:

> As for the future—*quien sabe*? The one enormous lesson of it all . . is that unless things are done in time, the most ghastly events will occur. There is a tide in the affairs of men—which no politicians ever take. There were 15 years after 1918 during which something cd have been done, either along purely Machiavellian lines or else along lines of genuine co-operation. Nothing was done and the world drifted into the state of a man with a neglected cancer, who will die if he is left alone and will die under the knife if operated. The fable of the Sibylline books is appallingly apposite—less and less at a higher and higher price . . .
>
> For the rest one tries to alleviate, however infinitesimally, some tiny fragment of the general misery; one writes . . . one tries to understand a little of this extraordinary universe . . .

The year's money troubles were not over. Aldous's British agent was Ralph Pinker, head of J. B. Pinker & Sons, "one of the two or three oldest literary agencies in London—highly regarded and supposedly uncorruptible." (I owe the inside of this story to Cass Canfield of Harper's, whom I shall be quoting.) Pinker's elder

brother, Eric, founded the American branch of the firm in the
1930s.

> . . Eric Pinker seemed to me a kind of "Mr Salteena" but agreeable
> nevertheless—a sporty type with gambling proclivities. Things went
> along well with him until E. Phillips Oppenheim could not collect
> from Eric $100,000 owed in royalties. Eric was sentenced to a term
> in Sing Sing . . .
>
> A year or two after Eric's release I lunched with his brother, Ralph,
> at the Savoy in London. This was a bibulous and sentimental
> occasion. Ralph elaborated on how many of the great authors who
> let the Pinker agency take care of their affairs had stuck by him.
> This affected him deeply.

However, by the summer of 1939 even Aldous noticed that
Ralph Pinker's payments were short of nearly £900, and wrote
him a stiff letter.

> . . I am at a loss to understand why money which was paid to you
> on my behalf as much (in some cases) as a year ago should still be
> withheld from me . . .

To this and other letters there had been no satisfactory answer.
In October Julian cabled that Pinker's was going into liquidation.
Like his brother, Ralph had hung on to some of his clients'
earnings and was in due course sentenced to a term in Wormwood
Scrubs. "The Pinker situation sounds fantastically worse than one
could have imagined," Aldous wrote in December when the
details had come in.

> . . I suppose the poor imbecile started speculating to offset an
> overdraft and didn't stop till he'd reached minus thirty-six thousand.
> It is difficult to see how else he could have spent so much, seeing that
> he has always made an excellent income out of his business . . .

Some of Pinker's clients were badly stung; so Aldous was relatively
lucky to get away with a loss of £500.

News again of Maria's family—two long and wonderfully vivid
letters from Rose—all were re-united in Sanary for the present,
though fearing re-patriation to Belgium by Vichy France. "But
one of my brothers-in-law [young Eric de Haulleville] cannot live
long," Maria wrote to Eddy,

> Because the strain of the walks and nights and starvations and fears
> has ruined the heart and the kidneys. He is a surréalist poet and had

to drop, along with a bicycle, all his manuscripts . . that must have broken his heart too.

And Jeanne was married again. To Georges Neveux (at the Mairie in Sanary). The Huxleys started cabling money . . .

During the Presidential Elections in November (Roosevelt *v.* Wendell Willkie) when the rest of the European colony was putting their hopes on F. D. R., Aldous remained wearily aloof—one *politician* against another . . .

Before the end of the year, Maria wrote one of her summing-up letters. She was sending a Christmas hamper to Eddy and Raymond Mortimer, "if it ever gets there, remember it was sent with love and melancholy . . Melancholy because it is really impossible to write anything. Yet I think much about you and all the unguessable part of English life becomes like a burden." But the letter went on. She told Eddy about Aldous's illness, "Such a good excuse to lead a quieter and quieter life." But he is cured now. About his work, "It is the first work he has been able to do since the war. It means he can work now in spite of the war." And he found the book "more difficult than he thought he would; the arranging and presentation at the right place." About the Californian seasons—"It is the time when fires destroy whole hillsides and villages. And the air crackles with electricity . . ." About Matthew, who will be with them for three weeks again at Christmas.

> He has become such an adorable person—his intellect . . has solidified, and he is so like Aldous, and so like Julian too, that it makes me laugh. He writes articles on population which he sends to Aldous, and short stories which he sends to me.
>
> . . We all live far, and all are ridiculously busy. Last year and for the whole year I was so rushed and driven that I don't think I could have kept it up and remained quite sane. Now Aldous is better and Sophie has a car . . .
>
> We have both changed a good deal. Aldous definitely smoother and more relaxed and even more gentle and so well looking, whereas of course I have not got any younger; women don't!
>
> . . Then when it is over, we cannot probably make up for it; we shall be completely out of the most fatal years of our lives and there will be an uncommunicableness that only a long long time can make up. [Sad to say, Eddy and Maria only met once more, and very briefly.] I went through it after the last war; when after five years of growing-up and roaming through the world I found my grandmother again whom I admired and loved. They had worked hard on the spot under the invasion. Very important work for soldiers in German prisons; and I came back so futilely busy living a selfish girl's life;

I did not even realize at the time why I was so out of tune, tactless and thoughtless; it took many years to make up for that. But of course it is highly improbable that we shall want to go to Europe ever.

There was one piece of news Maria had not been able to give Eddy. In France, on Christmas Day, Jeanne had had a baby.

Jeanne, wisely, had not told them before the event. Then, with communications as uncertain as they were, Aldous and Maria only got the news of Noële Neveux's birth in March.

. . I am very near the point of tearing my heart out with hesitation and imagination. [To Eddy] In three successive days I have heard that my sister in Nice had a baby; that the baby was between life and death for three weeks, and when the telegram announcing its survival came, it went on saying "Send us food."

And my mother's letter begs for food and all the packages are stopped by the blockade!

. . Another ray of hope is that we might get them all over here.

But if we do succeed in getting them over here, who is going to keep them all? Should I ask Aldous to work for them? Should I leave them in distress and hunger while we live in comfort? Aldous is feverishly lost in finishing his book. Gerald is much too busy preaching. Krishnamurti is full of sympathy but cannot make my decisions for me. So here I am telling you about it who are under God knows what circumstances in England. For the news was bad tonight. [15th March] It comes on those loud excited voices and yet I must know before I go to sleep because sometimes too it is good. And you have fog and too many clouds for attacks.

. . I do find letter writing extremely difficult now . . one's feelings are so . . strained and also changing . . outside circumstances alter so rapidly . . . But when you say you like to hear from me that pleases me . . . Those very far days when we seemed so young are far enough gone for me to say how fond I was of you . . . I remember one cold night when the lights had gone out and we sat under capes and coats and you said that when we were both eighty we would reminisce. Well, now I am not eighty but one hundred and eighty. So excuse the affection I express . . . It is not very well in keeping with the rules of English reticence. But then, nor am I English. Never very English, was I? Nor did the English like me. I think you were an exception.

My heart is as heavy as my grandmother's heart must have been. And I think we must get used to that too. Never will our hearts ache less . . . Once last week, it was so beautiful as I drove down through

the canyons covered with white scented brush, that I think I sang . . .
But it was not happiness or light-heartedness. Something very
different. Nor did it last.

And to me a few days later, Maria wrote (I had left California
the month before):

> It is horrible to be asked for food and not be able to give it. I know
> you can imagine the situation. Now that Jeanne has that baby too,
> it is tragic. Tell Suzanne that the baby is saved. The cable said,
> "Noële sauvée mais envoyez nous nourriture." You can imagine
> what I felt like. I am torn between asking Aldous to help and you
> know at what cost that is. He has never been willing to "make
> money" for ourselves and now to "have to make money" for my
> family is too much to ask him. He feels strongly about asking favours
> from people too and so on. Also if I were not busy and striving and
> pushing all the time, they would all forget and let go and nothing
> would be done . . . The same is happening now. Poor Aldous.
>
> I know that if I cannot get the affidavits, I can ask the Saxtons or
> even Willi [Seabrook] . . . When I say I can ask that means I feel I
> may ask . . Curiously enough there are so many people I *cannot* even
> ask. One has the answer before asking.

Then came some details about how often to send food, and about
money because I had heard about a way of sending parcels from
New York.

> We ought to send once a week, don't you think. (Eddy liked the
> canned ham and butter.) Chocolate is what my mother asks for.
> Some disastrous letters arrived at the same time as the telegrams.
> Obviously the situation has suddenly become much worse. Ask
> Suzanne to read my mother's letter. It is very touching. But we must
> get them out too. God knows how I will manage that. I am terrified
> of the burden.
>
> If you have any bright ideas about their coming over, let me
> know . . . I am very anxious . . . but I think I let myself be less
> destroyed by things now than I used to. All the teachings have
> taught me that little anyway.

And again to me a few days later:

> I know how awful asking is; that is why I so often overdo helping
> people; to spare them the asking . . . Everyone encourages us to get
> all of them out. Except Anita and her brother. Who also made us
> waver for a day when they said the first duty etc. but Aldous says
> that we only hesitated because there was nothing immediate to do.

The minute we could do something we did [everything] to further the chance of getting them out . . . I believe we may succeed . . . I want to sleep and forget a while. I still can sleep as many hours as I can get . . .

Georges Neveux will get help here because "he is an honourable man" as well as everything else . . . isn't it the most wonderful thing to be able to trust people. I think it must be a better feeling than being trusted. I feel it so anyway. When those one loves or even friends come up to scratch. But how painful, how uncomfortable when one fears they may not . . .

. . If you have time, in your troubles, wish me well in my undertaking. Eric died. Good night.

Eric de Haulleville died at Vence, like D. H. Lawrence. He was not yet forty.

Presently, Aldous spoke the liberating word. He told Maria casually, "If they weren't your family but six Chinese who had only us to save them, we would do it." Maria in her immense relief reported it at once in a letter to Suzanne.[1] *He* was confident and calm. "But—why hasn't it occurred to him to tell me this at once?"

I who was in despair believing that the whole decision was to be my own.

He thinks it inconceivable that I hesitated; he thinks we've only got to live like poor refugees because we *are* refugees, which is quite true after all. De là à mourir de faim, il dit, qu'il y a du chemin.

And the week after in a hand-written scribble to me:

. . So many unnecessary complications . . . Now I hear that Rose is pregnant too! One cannot judge them but it is difficult to understand. And tonight as I was listening to short waves, I was haunted by the Greeks . . . [April 1941—the war had reached the Balkans] The news . . . [illegible] a new type of horror . . .

Sophie is more seriously in love than ever. She does not tell me.

[1] Maria's letters to her sisters were always in French; whenever their contents are essential to the narrative, I have—freely—translated them. My decision to leave some letters, or passages of letters, in the original was based on two reasons. Maria's French had a very particular flavour and some of the things she wrote would have lost the shade of meaning she intended in translation; she would either have left them unsaid or put them in a different way in English. So the choice was really between leaving out such passages or keeping them in the original. My second reason was that consistent English would not have been true to the essentially bi-lingual nature of the Huxley household. When alone, Aldous and Maria usually spoke French to one another.

But what a muddle we are all in . . . Oh, I am well again. Not my health—my interest somehow. I understand Virginia. [We had just heard of the death of Virginia Woolf.] For I suppose she did it deliberately. Only now we must not do it any more. I have learnt it is not a way out—there is no way out—I can't even say it is frightening, just tiring, tiring . . .

Joep and Suzanne Nicolas, in New York, were working hard to establish themselves. Joep was getting big commissions, such as the stained-glass windows for Holland House, Suzanne had orders and gave sculpture classes, but to do their work they needed a studio, materials, assistants, and they had to live (at a certain standard). They asked Aldous and Maria to help them out with $500 a month for the next four months. They did. (This was faithfully re-paid after the war.)

Aldous was due to enter his seventh Three Years' agreement with Chatto & Windus. The sixth, in 1938, had been identical with the one before (made at the time he was stuck with *Eyeless in Gaza*), three works of fiction or non-fiction within the three years and an annual advance of £1,250. Now the situation had changed. For one, with the collapse of Pinker's, Aldous was without an agent. This was of little matter. For some time already he had had no literary agent for America (though indeed he used one for his film jobs) and had been dealing with Harper's directly. He was very glad to do so from now on with Chatto's, as in fact he had long done for all practical purposes. Ralph Pinker had earned his salt only with translation rights, and translation rights were at a standstill. The two things that had really changed were that Aldous could no longer bind himself to writing even one book every year, and that Chatto's were no longer able to let him have any regular income whatsoever. (Wartime regulations did not allow advances to be paid to a non-resident author; all he was entitled to receive—ahead of actual earnings—was £50 for a delivered MS.) His English royalties for the year, moreover, had shrunk to £843 before taxes.

The crisis about their coming . . . has been crowned by their refusal to come. [Maria to Sybille in May] I had a letter which explained why yesterday. A very nice letter from Georges who must be a very decent man and Jeanne is well with him. They won't come because he won't be a refugee on our shoulders. He does not think it is fair. And I can sympathize so readily with that. But I shudder at the future unknown to us all.

Then there is Rose who won't come because she wants to stay with her friends, and particularly with one friend. Mother can't bear to be separated from Rose's child. Meanwhile, one, the quickest and smallest (two I mean) of Mrs Ebert's food parcels arrived. [A woman in New York who managed to get food into France from Portugal.] . . I did send mother some money via a Quaker friend just when you told me you could do it . . Now, because . . of the great possibility of France and the U.S. finding themselves at war it seems to me urgent I should send more money. I herewith enclose a cheque for five hundred dollars. Send it to Jeanne Neveux, Villa les Flots . . Sanary. If you think it better to send in smaller sums or wait or anything else do. I trust your judgement entirely on these matters. I have an adorable photo of Jeanne with Noële who is now quite well though miniscule. A lively-looking adorable little child. And a photo of Georges with her. I like his face very much.

. . The book is almost finished; one can say it is. We went on a holiday thinking it was, then Aldous started changing some things. He will probably go into the movies for a bit. He is extremely well . . . Matthew will be back. I believe I am very tired but otherwise all right. I long and long to get away and hide but probably it must be from myself I should hide to get a rest. Too much imagination and too much concern for other people's business. We are again in love with the Mojave desert where the flowers have grown in such profusion this rainy year . . .

. . We don't see Eva [Herrmann] often but it is always nice to see her. We were polite to the Feuchtwangers and the Manns live exactly opposite so we meet on our walks. The poodle has been shorn . . and looks much nicer . . .

Indeed, the Sanary pattern had curiously repeated itself, the Thomas Manns in Pacific Palisades, Bruno Frank in Beverly Hills, Heinrich Mann and Feuchtwanger—in safety after hairbreadth escapes—working at M.G.M. (Like Goethe, Mann liked to be attended by a faithful black poodle; we rather had it in for Nicko, the present one, because he made up to everyone when the Magician's back was turned: by his side, he cut us.)

In June Aldous had the sad news that his Aunt Ethel Collier, The Dragon, the youngest of T. H. Huxley's daughters, had died at the age of seventy-five. "Dear Dragon . . ." He wrote an affectionate letter to his cousin Joan (still minding his two refugee children) talking of Aunt Ethel's noble stoicism, light-heartedness and humour.

*Grey Eminence* was finished and Aldous uncertain what to turn to next. By July,

Aldous, poor Aldous is making a little urgently needed money at the Fox studios . . . [to Sybille] he is correcting proofs which come in

like punishment. And that combined with the movie work is a lot
for him. But this time he is doing some sort of nonsense for Fox and
Fox is nice. They don't expect him to go there and sit every day, so
our life is much as ever.

. . A long letter from Victoria [Ocampo in Buenos Aires] . . she is
running some sort of French review as well . . . Malraux is at
Roquebrune having escaped from a prison camp. There is a price.
Usually ten thousand francs. Once in unoccupied France apparently
they are left alone . . . As for the Russian affair none can even guess
at the truth or the future.

. . Matthew is working with Mr Barrett's tools in his house. [Mrs
Barrett was a very nice woman who cooked part-time.] Loulou and I
are looking out of an undimmed dining-room window towards a
placid sea and many swinging trees and clouds . . . I have always
had this tendency to look out of the window for ever and was already
laughed at when I arrived in England with the last war.

. . Oh wooden shacks! I could fall in love with them too! And we
may still escape into one bang on the desert slopes of these hills.
But I should not whisper about it! It was so beautiful last time I went,
I almost could not return.

. . From Marjorie [Seabrook] regular letters . . . But I don't understand Americans. Why they have no money and why everything.
They bob up and down like mad corks. We may bob up and down
in our hearts but anyway the polish on the shoes was always there
and shiny.

Gerald and Christopher Isherwood and all that gang have gone to
a camp with some Quakers and others and are having prayer meetings
and talks for a whole month. We are going to Rosalind [Rajagopal]
for the weekend. She and Krishnamurti and the children have been
away for a month and we have missed them a great deal. Her blue
innocent eyes . . . Now it is time for me to go and fetch his lordship
and we come back via the barber and the tailor. It is very like being
in a job suddenly. Aldous actually gave Antonio [the gardener] some
shoes he should have had two years ago. Still some from England I
believe. But so we become avaricious too. The Mrs Ebert packages
were ruinous but you should have read the letters they sent when
receiving the food. Their news is good and Jeanne is happy. They
all tell me how nice he is and he does look it.

More photographs had arrived and again Maria says how much
she likes Georges Neveux's face.

To me like a monk's face yet he is anything but a monk so I am
wrong.

. . . My mother and youngest sister . . are expecting their papers to
come to the U.S. [To Eddy six days later] . . even through the help

of some people in Washington it seems eternally slow . . . I also hear that the Quakers are coming home because they cannot get food in to feed the children. Meanwhile we are full of hope again for England. That is to say I am. I never dare say what Aldous thinks because I suppose I don't always know, but it seems as if she has at last got a worse stick to beat them back with.

. . His biography of Father Joseph . . I was astonished to see with what interest Matthew read it, and continuously, for three days. I expected him to be bored . . I, on the contrary, thought it pretty tough reading because of the packed historical background so incongruously mad; but it may have been because it is just the sort of thing I cannot remember. Gerald likes it immensely and it is the first book of A he has liked whole-heartedly; but that is special too.

Now that the book is finished he could not write another though he thought he had an idea. He says he cannot sit down and write fiction in the middle of it all and so well I understand . . . No money of course comes to us from England . . .

Maria mentioned The Dragon:

. . She wrote the most free letters . . Small details one does not think about . . She had remained in London all the time in her large lonely house. Maids extinguishing fire-bombs in the garden as silently, I suppose, as English maids do everything.

Iris Tree, too, friend of Aldous's London youth, had drifted to California.

We see [her] a lot and she gets interesting letters from her son. [Ivan Moffat] Do you know him? He must be very intelligent . . He is a friend of Matthew's and we liked him . . . Iris herself is full of charm and sweetness; the vagueness does not matter. She lives in a tiny house with two enormous dogs and no money to feed herself yet always enough for the dogs and the vets. She goes to stay in the forest and breaks all the rules by feeding bears honey and milk on her back porch but she gets by with everything. She found a tame blue-bird that had settled on her hand from nowhere . . She lives next to our friends the Krishnamurti bunch and you know the horror Brahmins have of dogs . . But they forgave Iris for bringing the dogs and sitting all over their car, leaving trails of smell and white hairs . . . K. has travelled everywhere and speaks all the languages which is so nice too. One single language becomes very boring.

Christopher Isherwood had written to say that Gerald's prayer camp was being a success: he was radiantly happy and radiantly well in spite of the heat because the camp was interesting and everything was going well. So that is good. They are released on the 7th [August] and will all come here on the 8th . . . I must say they are doing pretty well to be able to correspond. When I was in my convent and we were "en retraite" we could not send or receive letters . .

Eva [Herrmann] is still painting and living in lonely comfort in a too large house and overspending as usual. But she is nice. Then there is Maugham whom Gerald sees and who came here and who asks us to lunch . . he seems . . much mellowed and gentler though tired. . . Tonight is one of those rare occasions when Aldous went to dine with the Ronald Colmans. You must know him on the pictures and he is a nice man. But Matthew was here and he is so grown-up now that I could not resist having too much of a head-ache to go out. It is the rarest thing for me to have a free evening.

One might note here that with the Huxleys *nice* was a strong word used with deliberation. When Aldous said that someone was a nice man, it meant a good deal; as for instance in his letter of 1918 when he speaks of "the marvellous niceness common to all Beerbohms".

I have a comic little dog now which I spoil and Aldous spoils. . . While I type its hair gets caught in my fingers. And she is a great nuisance . . It is because she looks like a fox and has such impertinent and observing eyes that I cannot resist her.

Matthew is back from college as adorable as ever only more so and handsome . . But I don't know much about him. He is affectionate and easy, yet reserved. He seems so definite and yet so muddled and imprecise and yet intelligent. I wonder what his life will be. I cannot guess but would not be surprised if he surprised us all one day.

When we left Raymond thought it would be Aldous and Gerald who abandoned me for a column in the desert. Now I have fallen in love with a "Cabonan" in the middle of the desert . . .

Send us your news, dear Eddy . . . Raymond never writes at all so I don't either. You give him the news and my love . . . That is best. Nor have any of the Hutchinsons ever answered me and it is best to leave that too. Naomi writes. Do you remember Naomi Royde-Smith? You liked each other.

Dined with father and mother Mann, last night [To Marjorie Seabrook, 4th September] Golo was there [Thomas's second son, the professor]; trying to keep up the grumpiness of an honest philosopher. Mony, the one whose husband was drowned under her eyes, was there and completely silent. Matthew, so alert and trying so hard to talk to Madame: they liked each other so that was all right. Aldous had on a new suit, his first in America, and I could not keep my eyes from him . . . All the old ones are tight and shrunken but nice too in a way. Mann himself has learned English admirably and reads it with interest. He was peaceful and pacifying; she was hating and violent and we would not discuss it; besides to be rude about America while you *have* to remain in it. Eva was there.

. . I can't urge you to come here [California]—so many people detest it. Though, if I dare to presume to say so, they are all wrong. And Sybille is a silly little snob about it—so don't believe her.

Aldous, in his better suit no doubt, had been conscientiously attending Sophie's every public theatrical performance at the Reinhardt School. "He never excused himself," she wrote, "because of work—or because it bored him. One evening I found on my pillow a little note saying: 'Ce soir j'ai été fier de toi. A.' " Nevertheless, not wanting "to be a burden to them any longer—they were spending lots of money and energy on all the family and friends," Sophie decided to give it all up and went to take a secretarial course. In October I had a dispirited letter from Maria:

. . Avarice will have to play a bigger and bigger role in our lives [after talking about people using air-mail stamps] . . . God will help us I am sure when the slump comes and there will be no more movies . . .

I have heard today to my great relief but with a growing sense of responsibility that the Visa Department at Washington have cabled mother and Rose and Olivia their visas for this country. I was very worried about their situation as Belgian refugees in France . . . Only the great problem will only begin once mother and Rose are here . . . But I am trying hard not to think of anything before they are here. Except that I have knitted each of them a jersey like yours.

. . You have often scolded me about mail: now . . . it is worse than ever. We are looking out only for the French mail and for a letter from Washington . . . Flying thoughts in my heart are still so fond, but they never materialize. The loathing of letter writing grows. I also cannot bear writing about myself any more. Chiefly because what we do is so unimportant and unamusing . . . So the day will soon come when I write nothing at all to nobody . . . Now I still make an effort . . but it won't be possible much longer. Then there is of course the dreariness of the actual typing. The noise and the hours I spend at it. Now I seem busy too. Aldous has had to go back to the studio but it won't be for long. We have been often to stay with Rosalind and Krishnaji in Ojai and to see Gerald who now lives in Laguna. Chris [Christopher Wood] has bought a most lovely and comfortable large house there, very Italian looking . . .

Hazel the black one has accompanied them and even you would approve of the cooking. Chris has a wine cellar with a key and Gerald's bed (they got the furniture with the house) is pink and blue cretonnes all padded and stitched. The dining-room is an octagon with large windows onto the sea, very civilized.

Reading aloud a life of Tolstoi after having read some of his journals. What a strange man . . . Much more passionate than I realized. To myself, War and Peace for the 5th time . . .

Got hold of Marjorie's story at last. Excellent, don't you think? I hope you will see her a little . . Do be a bit nice and consoling . . . Aldous heard from Jeremy [Hutchinson] who is stationed in Portsmouth Virginia while his boat is being repaired. He is a lieutenant and has a wife, Peggy Ashcroft, and a three months baby and sounds sad but peacefully so. A letter from Eddy same as ever and one from Raymond. Very affectionate but differing much in opinion, he says, with Aldous and Gerald and regretting *that*. Sad too, but again, peaceful . . But above all an affectionate letter. Dear Raymond. He sent his most beloved pictures to America for safe-keeping with a friend and they all burned, in the friend's flat.

. . Sophie does secretarial courses—so anyhow she won't ever quite be one of the starving actresses but will be able to type for a crust of bread and a bad bed in a tenth-rate boarding house if the very worst comes to the very worst. Perhaps I am gloomy but perhaps tired because it is late and I shall go to bed.

In November Aldous, for the first time since 1934, wrote again to his unmet correspondent Starkey; a long letter about war in which he stated some of his most consistently held views. ". . when war is waged on a large scale and for a long time between equally matched powers, all attempts at a solution of the problems involved become equally disastrous.

Thus, it is clear that to make peace now with the Germans on their terms will lead to catastrophic results. And to go on fighting until the Nazi regime is overthrown . . . will lead, in all probability, to results hardly if at all less catastrophic. We live under the illusion that all problems are at all times susceptible to a reasonable satisfactory solution. They are not.

And he said this on pacifism. "In wartime . . psychological conditions

are such that the application of pacifism to politics is for all practical purposes impossible. There can only be the personal pacifism of individuals. That . . such personal pacifists cannot produce any large scale amelioration of social conditions is obvious. Nevertheless, they fulfil a real social function, particularly when their pacifism is based upon a "theocentric" religious experience. The world would be even more horrible than it actually is, if it were not for the existence of a small theocentric minority working along quite other lines than the anthropocentric majority. It is immensely to the credit of the English and American governments that they should have recognized the existence of personal pacifists, and provided for their functioning as integral parts of the democratic society. No democratic society can exist without an opposition—the ordinary political opposition, and an infinitesimal opposition of men and women who are simply not concerned with the things that preoccupy the great mass of human beings . . .

The men and women of the margin, as Aldous called them in *Grey Eminence*.

. . England and America owe an incalculable debt to the Quakers for the way in which they have educated successive generations of rulers to realize that a theocentric opposition is a thing of enormous value to the society containing it . . .

Good must be worked for (as he again developed in *Grey Eminence*) by individuals and organizations small enough to be capable of moral, rational and spiritual life.

Aldous now had the bad news about Drieu La Rochelle. He explained it to himself in a letter to Julian.

My old friend Drieu has, alas . ., become, as the new editor of the *Nouvelle Revue Française,* an ardent advocate of collaboration. He is an outstanding example of the strange things that happen when a naturally weak man, whose talents are entirely literary, conceives a romantic desire for action and a romantic ambition for political power and position. Rushing in where angels fear to tread, he does the most insensate things. It is the greatest pity; for there was something very nice about Drieu and I had a real affection for him. We occasionally hear from Charles de Noailles . . . The family camps in a few rooms of their huge house in Paris . . .

*Grey Eminence, A Study in Religion and Politics* had been published in October. It is the history of a man who set out to become a saint and ended up as Richelieu's right-hand man; François Leclerc du Tremblay, known in religion as Father Joseph of Paris and to anecdotal history as l'Eminence Grise, who began life as a mystic and got involved "in more and more frightful power policies, which resulted in the destruction of a third of the population of Central Europe, guaranteed the rise of Prussia . . . paved the way for Louis XIV, the Revolution, Napoleon and all the rest". Father Joseph, who had been a pupil of Benet of Canfield, was a man of genuine spiritual gifts, without desire for personal power; what moved him was nationalism, the passionately held conviction that the glory and supremacy of France were willed by God—the French were the chosen people. A barefooted Capuchin monk, Father Joseph never ceased to practise great austerities; part of his days and half his nights were spent in prayer and contemplation. And after prayer and contemplation,

back he had to go to the hideous work to which his duty to the Bourbons had harnessed him, the work of spreading famine and cannibalism and unspeakable atrocities across the face of Europe . . .[1]

To the very end he made a desperate effort to make the best of both worlds. Needless to say, he failed. He failed because this *must* fail—and that is the dominant theme of Aldous's book. What made him write it?

No episode in history can be entirely irrelevant to any other subsequent episode. But some events are related . . more significantly than others. This friar . . . we shall find if we look into his biography a little closely, [that] his thoughts and feelings and desires were among the significantly determining conditions of the world in which we live today . . . [They] led to August 1914 and September 1939. In the long chain of crime and madness which binds the present world to its past, one of the most fatally important links was the Thirty Years War . . . [Father Joseph] was one of the forgers of one of the most important links in our disastrous destiny; and at the same time he was one of those to whom it has been given to know how the forging of such links may be avoided. Doubly instructive in the fields of politics and religion, his life is further interesting as the strangest of psychological riddles . . .

Aldous finished his present movie work in November "—tiresome work, but unavoidable, since Books at the moment don't keep wolves very far from doors, and the movie work is on the whole preferable to the continual shallow improvising of articles and stories . . ." Presently he was able to write to Julian, "I have started preliminary work on a new book, a kind of novel."

---

[1] *Grey Eminence.* Chatto & Windus, 1941.

# Chapter Three

## Llano del Rio

TWO months later the novel began to flow. ".. Enfin ça marche. He always has trouble at the beginning." Maria to Suzanne. "He breaks off, starts again, change—dropping the idea that seemed so good a few weeks ago."

One present concern was Matthew. The doctors found him in such poor health—anaemia, low blood pressure—that he was forbidden to return to college and ordered at least a year of rest and feeding up. Hard on him, Maria said, as it isn't natural to live at home at his age. (Rising twenty-two.) Luckily he appeared to be looking forward to his leisure and cheerfully settled down to a regime of reading and nursery food.

Aldous was writing, well enough to do just that, for the rest his own health was ticking over. To Suzanne, Maria for once took off the lid. "Je me suis tout à coup rendu compte que probablement il ne sera jamais vraiment normal.

I fear that for the whole of his life he will never be really well. I don't think he'll even mind. He is more and more absorbed by his books and ideas. And a nice walk once a day. He doesn't even notice that he hasn't used his hands or his body for the last two or three years. The slightest effort, the slightest change in routine brings about a relapse, depression, fatigue. The one thing that consoles me is that it doesn't seem to bother him. He isn't quite aware of it, I think.

It is discouraging for me—I felt very sad the other day when I had realized that it might be like this for ever . . .

I telephone for him. When Loulou barks at night I have to force myself to shut her up, I even hide her under my sheets. I'm always full of apprehension and remorse. One has to plot to make him go to bed early or keep his siesta as one does for a child. Because he won't even bother to think about such things, or to plan and organize. At the end of a day this can be as exhausting as physical work—only I have to admit that I think he is happy. That is to say: relatively.

He's recovered from the shock of the Japanese war [Pearl Harbor], and the moment his work gets going he is so absorbed that he forgets the world. He forgets Mère, and Noële and Matthew, and the house and our bank account, and to take his medicine and not to tire himself and to answer his letters.

I believe that he is outside life more than he ever was. There used to be a time when he made some kind of contact through his curiosity about material things . . . Now when I try to reach him, I'm reminded of the fishermen in the Bible . . . But he is so touching, because he is trying so hard to help me, he wipes the plates for instance when I'm washing up . . .

The note of discouragement, in another key, is sounded in a letter of Aldous's (to me; à propos of something I had written about *Grey Eminence* and Mr Micawber). "I was born between two worlds, one dead, the other powerless to be born, and have made, in a curious way, the worst of them both.

For each requires that one should be whole-heartedly *there*, at the moment—with Micawber, as he is and for his own sake, while he is drinking his punch: with the Clear Light of the Void as it is and for its own sake, in an analogous way. Whereas I have always tended to be somewhere else, in a world of analysis, unfavourable equally to Micawberish living, Tolstoyan art and contemplative spirituality. The title of my first book . . *Limbo*, was, I now see, oddly prophetic!

Slowly, quietly, they had been going on with their idea of moving into the desert. The wooden shack was bought, made habitable and a second little house was a-building. The original house, not quite a shack, stood under a clump of large trees beside running water—an irrigation ditch planted with poplars; there were fruit trees and almond trees and vines, and this was what had caught them, this and the beauty of the Sierra far away on the horizon. On 11th February 1942 they left the monstrous house in Pacific Palisades and moved into the Mojave, to Llano.

That is, Maria and Matthew went to get things into shape, Aldous followed when the new house was ready and meanwhile stayed at Eva's. Gerald, too, was building; a monastery, as Aldous called it. The official name was Trabuco College. He and Maria drove over to see the site. "It is a huge estate," Aldous wrote to Christopher Isherwood, ". . in a very beautiful, rather English country-side behind Laguna . . . one rather serious problem will be communication with the outside world. The nearest store is about twenty miles away . . ." (The war-time rubber shortage was just starting.)

In March Aldous did some movie work (on *Jane Eyre*), and when that was done moved out to Llano. Some time before this he had already come to an impasse in the novel and laid it aside for the moment. Instead, he had started on "a little book of pure utility," as he wrote to Eugene Saxton, about the Bates Method.

"I am anxious to get this out pretty quickly; for the optometrists are lobbying their hardest . . to get it legislated out of existence, nominally because the teachers of the method are 'unqualified', actually because theirs (the optometrists') is an overcrowded profession and they fear the inroads of rivals who may cause a diminution in the sale of optical glass. A little book by a reasonably sane and responsible person might help to keep this unquestionably very valuable technique alive and contribute towards its official recognition as a branch of education . . . The title I have chosen is *The Art of Seeing*."

Llano was still far from finished—water problems, lighting problems (they had to generate their own electricity)—but there was a marvellous sense of solitude.

Car l'immensité et la nudité d'un désert se sent même sur une route encombrée de camions de l'armée; c'est quelque chose de pénétrant comme des ondes invisibles. . . L'hombre entoure la maison et les feuilles sont encore jeunes et d'un vert que l'on peut croire transparent. Car je n'habite pas un désert, j'habite une oasis. [Maria to her niece, Claire Nicolas.[1]]

There were nine kittens playing under the trees while rats gambolled in the little cellar below. "Matthew is with me. He is happy here and his room is large and green, a Chinese green . . . he has his encyclopaedia, we each have our own. Opposite is Aldous's room where he works, it is the sun-burnt colour of the drawing-room in Sanary, with book shelves and ten windows . . but with shutters like European windows . . . He has a Louis Philippe desk with brass feet which we replaced with castors. Because we are putting everything on castors. The kitchen table and the beds and the desks. Of course the beds roll away when we make them, and the dining-table too when the meat is tough and I hope Aldous's desk won't roll off into the desert . . .

". . To the East, among the poplars and the vines, one jump across the brook, you would find a little house, white inside and out, stuffed with wall-cupboards and easy to sweep. That is my house . . I cook in an aquarium, I am the fish and outside are the mountains and the snow and the plain and the leaves that shade us, for the trees are very big. My bedroom is minute—if I want to sit by the window I must roll away the bed . . . Above is a blue attic with a very long bed, like the bed at Sanary. That is for Aldous. But under the thickest and greenest of the poplar trees there stands a silvered caravan which might comfortably house one day a young poet . . .

[1] Claire White (Mrs Robert Winthrop White), the writer.

". . There is no prospect of getting new tyres so we use our car only when strictly necessary and then so slowly that I risk falling asleep and into a ravine. Fortunately this obliges us to stay here where I am so happy."

The Nicolas children, Claire and Sylvia, were talented and precocious girls. To Claire, the prospective poet of the silver caravan, Aldous sent this message.

Aldous has asked me to tell you that he advises you to write "poetry" strictly in accordance with the rules. He would like you to follow these with great care because he says this leads to an enrichment of the language. The most difficult for example are sonnets. Take Hérédia. Since you like Rimbaud at the moment he advises you to study him à fond so that you will realize that *he* did not allow himself any liberties . . . Aldous thinks that you have enormous facility and talent and that you've got to exercise restraint in order to achieve *quality* . . . Il t'embrasse en confrère.

In another letter to Claire, Maria formulated advice to the rebellious young. "From your letters and your poems I would guess that you were *distraite, rêveuse et révoltée*. Am I right? Vague and dreamy because a poet wishing to escape from life; in revolt *because* of life; and here lies the great danger.

Life is and will be the reality. Rebels are ineffectual, unless they manage to put their feelings in a harness . . . What I'm trying to say to you is that you will have to live this life for a good many years, with human beings as they are, and with humdrum tasks—but tasks which if they are not performed will take on a terrible importance . . . For, to give you an irritating example, the over-independent artist who doesn't wash, smells; the one who leaves his drawings all over the place, loses half of them. The brilliant and egotistical creature who enchants in company has no friends and is wretched at home . . . Rebels never succeed in making their Peace with life, they end up by being obliged to live on the Charity of life. And it is just that which one must avoid. Read biographies. Read the biography of Verlaine, of Rimbaud. After that, I hesitate, but, Claire, do try to understand, read the lives of the saints. You see it's quite a programme. Adieu ma chérie.

Ta Coccola.

At Llano, in his ten-windowed room, at his roller-skating desk, Aldous worked so well that he had finished the new book, *The Art of Seeing* in July, and then went back almost at once to the deferred novel. And now there was the sudden news that Rose, too, was married again and actually *in* America.

. . by some miracle of which we haven't yet heard the details, [she] managed to get on to the S. S. *Drottningholm* with her husband [Billy Wessberg] and baby. They are now in New York.

Another piece of good news, Aldous went on, "was a cable from M's mother, saying that she expected to get to Lisbon this month —after 18 months of wrestling with visas, etc., and more than a year after we had aeroplane tickets for her passage."

Meanwhile Aldous went off to a seminar at Gerald's.

. . He is delighted . . and Gerald writes me just as enthusiastically about Aldous; Aldous says that Gerald is at his most brilliant and Gerald says that Aldous is in his very best form and *full of* initiative; this is startling . . . This is the best news I could have and perhaps once again they will become the devoted friends and work together as they once did. The split, although never actually mentioned, always made me sad and seemed so unnecessary. [Maria to Rosalind Rajagopal.]

And in August Mère arrived in New York. "I know what would give her the greatest pleasure in the world," Maria wrote to Claire.

If you could get her interviewed and have the interview published with her photograph! Do you see? She always suffered from being nobody and this is perhaps the one occasion in her life. I suppose I could arrange it here . . but Aldous wouldn't understand, would be horrified etc. But I can see nothing bad about it. You must know some journalists? Mother of four daughters—refugees during the last war—dramatic escapes—mother-in-law of four remarkable men, Aldous, Joep, Eric and Georges; all well-known. You yourself known, well, what more can a newspaper want?

Three attempts to get to America go wrong; the tickets I send to Bordeaux never reach her; Washington loses her papers; a second lot of papers arrive the week America enters the war; we give up all hope—and *here* she is.

Staying in the studio of her sculptress daughter; going to live in the oasis of a desert (romantic description) with another daughter. One grand-daughter is a pupil at Max Reinhardt's (sounds more romantic than secretarial course and Sophie still goes there some-times). Well, you see. I think it's a brilliant idea and Mère would adore it.

414

# *Llano del Rio* | *1942*

At Llano the summer, their first desert summer, had been very hot.

. . terribly hot, but I stood it. [Maria to Sybille] Aldous and Matthew were away for most of July and half of August which helped . . . He spent three hard weeks at Gerald's monastery and only lost a bit of weight . . . Then at the end of August came a terrific storm . . now the nights are long and cool . . .

But the news. Oh dear. It is so good that as we confided to each other yesterday, it is rather disquietening. We were walking towards sunset, the Joshua tree immensely slender and tufted, Loulou ahead, Tom the cat behind and we shared our thoughts.

Because Aldous is very very well. Stood the summer without a murmur . . The eyes are improving; the book on the eyes is coming out this autumn. The novel is progressing well. The moods are excellent and his interests are growing to such an extent that I am amazed. He does pick the figs for his own fun; he goes and gets the tomatoes; does all the drying in a box outside his terrace . . . He makes his bed so well that I only go up once a week to change it. He scrapes his shoes on the irrigation days before coming in and he shakes the carpets every morning without being asked to. He loves it all and for the first time knows the joy of things growing and of doing with his hands; that is because he sees better, I am sure.

Then Matthew . . is helpful with ideas that he never puts into practice. Luckily he drinks so much milk and cream that even if he does not like my rapidly improving cooking I know he is well enough fed. Now he will have to go to the army soon; he is a non-combatant as his plea for objection was refused; the only choice being prison, and Matthew and Aldous and me, all three thinking that useless; nor has the child the strength, morally as well as physically, to go through with that. But we have had difficult days over it. Everyone has. He may go to U.C.L.A. for a term unless they call him up before. I don't know.

Maria was writing the day after her birthday and described how she had spent the eve in Los Angeles with her devoted friend Pepe (Weissberger) distributing fruit from Llano.

. . Some delicious, some beautiful, but never both at the same time— huge, lusciously rosé bunches of grapes that taste of nothing but remind one of the passage in the *Après midi* . . . Mrs Corbett with a note from Aldous was the first stop. Then Mrs Barrett's German shoe-making friend, and Mrs Wallace the fat cook you remember, then to my mad French dress-maker . . . then a long dash to the negro quarter where my dear old Hazel received the largest case . . .

but she, typically of her kindness, had gone to hospital giving me up and assisting a dying friend. Then [spending the night in Hollywood] I did a very unusual thing. Matthew had left a detective novel about; I was curious, I looked, I read till 3.15 and . . it was so bad I could not understand or believe it—so ignorant and stupid . . . I was more than a year older by the time my birthday came, and after some medical visits and shopping [I] came home to Aldous for a walk and dinner and a quiet desert night. We now have a huge, blue enamel bedstead standing in the middle of the desert and it looks quite well really. Misses a *pot de chambre* or an immense clock to make it quite a Dali, and a shell. Eva telegraphed, and Anita. That was nice. I was astonished. I forgot all about it till I got your letter from Aldous.

The bedstead was not the only outdoor objet d'art at Llano. In the middle of their yard, on the trap-door over the pit that housed their generating engine, stood a terra cotta bust of Gerald Heard. This ensemble was referred to as Gerald's Tomb. Maria had broken off the letter; she went on next day:

Mañana es otra dia, to the extent that the tomatoes have ripened, the peaches too; that I shall have to think of peeling them for preserving and so on—basketsful of tomatoes and I feel it is my duty to turn them into tomato purée . . There is no doubt that transportation is getting scarcer and scarcer and that this winter we may get stuck for vegetables and fruit . . So I sit for many hours in my cool kitchen through which the desert extends . . and peel and core and chop. But the sun does the rest. I just put out some sliced peaches covered with honey and they go into a contraption Matthew made with glass and mirrors and black paint and out comes the jam . . Sun cookery is Aldous's hobby, marvellous because it isn't tiring. He puts the teapot in the box in the morning . . . soft eggs take two hours . . .

. . We read aloud a good deal but not your style of books . . . No more time to knit . . Rose's little baby will need some and I wonder when I will do that . . . Why, oh why, must they go in for procreation so in my family? But the whole of America is doing it; I'm haunted by the pregnant women, they are all young, even childish . . They will be bad mothers and be divorced many times and so what of the little children? But all that is in the ways of the world. Our cat must have a wife and they will have babies too, and really it is very cruel not to allow Loulou to have them. When all is quiet . . birds come; they come in the evenings to drink as we are one of the only pools for many square miles; the road-runner has a little chick running after it for many weeks; the quails with long families in their coveys, pheasants yesterday from the next ranch and gluttoning on the grapes; ugly young ones; but the migrating birds stop. Six ducks one evening with blue-tipped wings and then, making me think I had gone mad, five large white cranes in our dark apple tree! Such is desert life. I delight in it. It seems utterly inexplicable when all the papers and magazines and friends are filled with the horrors of war and internal stresses. When Matthew himself may have to go any day and when food has to be sent to Jeanne and in Belgium my family is starving and sick. They are sick all around us; we don't have to think so far, and most people so unhappy, so muddled; so craving and scrambling that it is truly inexplicable that we should have so much and I so much delight. Because if it is egoism it is certainly a form which does not hurt anyone. Nor was I any help to people when I got all excited and distressed and muddling. So now I live this mood until another time may or may not come. Perhaps you do not understand, perhaps you disagree, perhaps you condemn. But I have sent a letter you asked for and I know that you will always be fond . . . Don't forget to write at Christmas! Let us be conventional about traditions.

Maria ended this letter—a long one even for her, of which I have transcribed about one-third—with this passage:

Mother is in New York. With Suzanne at the moment, proposing, on my suggestion, to come and live with us. I trust and hope that we will behave well and stand it. I think so. And the day may yet come when Aldous and I will be alone in our desert as it was meant; by us; because who knows about fate.

The little book of pure utility came out in October in America (and in England some months later selling 10,000 copies in the first few days). Aldous had written *The Art of Seeing* to repay a debt of gratitude:

. . gratitude to the pioneer of visual education, the late Dr W. H. Bates, and to his disciple, Mrs Margaret D. Corbett, to whose skill as teacher I owe the improvement in my own vision.[1]

There was also his hope that the book might suggest help to the thousands and thousands of people who suffer from eye defects and do not get complete relief from spectacles. (He was not offering help or cure, it must be made clear, for any of the acute diseases of the eyes that are treated by surgery or medication, but confined himself—as reputable teachers of the method do—

[1] This and subsequent quotations are from *The Art of Seeing*. Chatto & Windus, 1943.

to the much more commonplace visual defects now treated by means of lenses.) I shall attempt to sum up, in compressed form, Aldous's case for the Bates Method.

> *Medicus curat, natura sanat* . . the whole scope and purpose of medicine is to provide sick organisms with the internal and external conditions most favourable to the exercise of their own self-regulative and restorative powers.

It remains to determine what *are* the most favourable conditions for a given disorder.

In the early years of the present century Dr W. H. Bates, a New York oculist, became dissatisfied with the ordinary symptomatic treatment of eyes. Seeking a substitute for artificial lenses, he set himself to discover if there was any way of re-educating defective vision into a condition of normality.

As the result of his work with a large number of patients he came to the conclusion that the great majority of visual defects were functional and due to faulty habits of use. These faulty habits were invariably related, he found, to a condition of strain and tension . . . Other causes, he found, were strictly psychological: grief, anxiety, irritation, fear may cause a temporary, or, if chronic, an enduring condition of mal-functioning.

Dr Bates discovered that, by means of appropriate techniques, the condition of strain could be relieved. When it had been relieved—when patients had learnt to use their eyes and mind in a relaxed way—vision was improved and refractive errors tended to correct themselves . . .

Now, it can be laid down as a general physiological principle that improvements in the functioning of a part of the body always tend to be followed by organic improvements within that part. The eye, Dr Bates discovered, was no exception to this general rule. When the patient learnt to relax his tenseness and acquired proper seeing-habits, the *vis medicatrix naturae* was given a chance to operate—with the result that, in many cases, the improvement of functioning was followed by a complete restoration of the health and organic integrity of the diseased eye.

Now if this is so, why is there such widespread, to put it mildly, scepticism about this method in the medical world? One answer, Aldous said, can be summed up in three words: "habit, authority and professionalism.

> [orthodox] symptomatic treatment of defective sight has been going on for a long time, has been carried to a high degree of perfection,

and, within its limitations, is reasonably successful. If it fails in a certain proportion of cases to provide even adequate palliation of the symptoms, that is nobody's fault, but a condition inherent in the nature of things. For years, the highest medical authorities have all asserted this to be the case—and who will venture to question a recognized authority? . .

Another stumbling block (beside the opticians' vested interests) is the very fact that the Bates Method lies outside the pale of recognized medicine—an open invitation to charlatans to cash in.

. . There exist, scattered about the world, some scores or perhaps hundreds of well-trained and thoroughly conscientious teachers of Dr Bates . . But there are also, unfortunately, a number of ignorant and unscrupulous quacks, who know little more of the system than its name . . . no standards of competence are legally imposed upon [them] . . .

As for potential patients,

Visual re-education demands a certain amount of thought, time and trouble. But thought, time and trouble are precisely what the overwhelming majority of men and women are not prepared to give, unless motivated by a passionate desire or an imperious need.

Aldous draws an analogy between Bates and the treatment of infantile paralysis developed by Sister Elizabeth Kenny. Both methods "protest against the immobilization of sick organs. Both insist on the importance of relaxation. Both affirm that defective functioning can be re-educated towards normality by proper mind-body co-ordination. And, finally, both work."

*Work if you work.* Having stated the case, Aldous got down— he tried to keep the book as brief and clear and practical as he could—to the actual techniques of teaching the eyes to move and relax, the Batesian exercises of palming, shifting, flashing, the way to read, or to watch a film, without strain. Never mind the medical hypotheses on which the theory is based, is his refrain, our knowledge of the human mind-body *is* limited, theories may be inadequate or turn out wrong: does it matter as long as it works in practice?

. . Bates's theory of accommodation may be as incorrect as were the eighteenth and nineteenth-century explanations of the efficacy of lime-juice in cases of scurvy. Nevertheless scurvy was cured by lime-juice . . .

(In this context it is worth mentioning that during the war Mrs Corbett and her teachers were training young men who had been turned down by the U.S. Navy and Air Force but were determined to have another try. "They are so anxious to normalize their vision," Aldous reported to Julian,

> that they are ready to take a lesson every day and to practise intensely for hours at a stretch. The result is that scores of them get through their tests after only a few weeks, sometimes even a few days, of training. The doctors still oppose the whole method on *a priori* grounds; but a number of air force and navy officers responsible for recruitment are now actually recommending young men who can't pass the tests, but whom they would like to have, to go and get themselves normalized by Mrs Corbett. In another twenty or thirty years, even medical orthodoxy may come round to it.)

Mme Nys was about to start on her journey West. Maria sent her a warning word.

> . . J'ai un peu peur que tu ne devines pas la simplicité de notre vie. Car, par exemple, pas de radio; impossible de lire au lit parceque la machine qui produit l'electricité est précieuse et caduque. Nous mangeons très sainement mais vaguement. Enfin c'est solitaire, et nous y tenons . . .

In October she arrived. Inevitably, perhaps, the old conflict flared up again. "Mère hasn't been here a week," Maria wrote to Suzanne, "and already I have become insufferable, irritable and nasty.

> . . The presence of the poor woman, so sweet and calm now and full of good will, is enough to make me shrivel up like a spider . . . *Que faire? Que faire?* I had the best intentions in the world . . And I reproach her with exactly the same faults which she makes rise in me; and I look at myself with horror.
> I fell under the spell of this desert and thought I'd become an angel. At the first temptation I find myself as intolerant as ever. When I'm with Mère everything goes to pieces, Mère who hasn't spoken ill of anyone yet, who hasn't done any harm to the dogs or the cats, or to Olivia who adores her, or to Aldous or to me. And I can find neither affection nor tenderness for her in myself. As soon as she is out of the house, I'm filled with repentance and pity; as soon as she comes through the door again and opens her mouth, I find something to make me boil with anger . . . So it is easier to preach to others than to behave well oneself. Remember the letter I wrote to Claire—I could weep with shame . . .

Poor Mme Nys did not love the desert, and this saddened and upset Maria. Mme Nys didn't like the vague and healthy eating habits or having to read by candle light. Least of all she liked the solitude. This was the kind of situation that arose:

> Mère offers to bake us a cake. Instead of saying Yes—because I know that she's longing for some—I say of course you can bake a cake but don't do it for us as neither Aldous nor I want to eat any cake. Which is true. But couldn't I have pretended? To anyone else I would have, out of sheer politeness . . . but there is a demon in me which interferes . . . Hélas!

Now Matthew went down with acute appendicitis. Luckily he happened to be in Los Angeles and could be operated on within hours. When he came home again, Aldous and Maria had decided to set up Mme Nys on her own. "My mother came, I failed, and she went," Maria wrote to me. "A passage we might as well forget. As she is now very agreeably and satisfactorily living in a little apartment in Beverly Hills near the Library and has already many friends.

> . . Alas Rose has also decided for the $n$th time that mother is impossible in the house. I do so wonder if the poor woman does realize . . . I can't say what it is that turns me into a shattered bundle of nerves.

Aldous, who always treated his mother-in-law with the greatest courtesy, sent this little note in December:[1]

Chère Mère,
    Grâce à mes dix jours de travail chez Fox, je me sens (ce qui est très à propos à cette saison) un peu riche. Je vous prie donc d'accepter ce petit cadeau du Père Noel cinémafotographique; et j'espère que vous trouverez quelque chose de joli pour pendre à votre Christmas Tree, ou pour mettre dans le bas des autres.
                                    Affectueusement,
                                                            Aldous

Rose's little girl, Olivia de Haulleville, a charmer but a handful, was spending the winter at Llano while Rose was expecting another baby[2] by her second husband. Matthew was drafted into the Medical Corps of the U.S. Army (having done his pre-medical years at Colorado University) and was off to his training

---

[1] Unpublished.
[2] A boy. Sigfrid Wessberg. Maria was godmother.

in Abilene, Texas. (Maria, in a letter to me dated 8th March, set down the family news, or newses as she sometimes spelt it.)

. . Matthew takes it all in his stride and is filled with his usual interests . . . He looks handsome and is very happy because he has found an adorable woman to love. I shall have few letters of course. In spite of being as Blimpish as you are some times he is interesting and liked. So we laugh together and also listen to him. I miss him a lot but am so very pleased at the whole solution of a difficult situation and am glad if he is strong enough now to stand the life that all other men must have to stand.

Aldous is admirably well and is writing the best novel yet. He is also enchanted with all our houses and gardens and sheds and trees, and several times a day he goes visiting the large irrigation reservoir which a silver mill pumps water into . . . He is also very anxious to plant vegetables and so it shall be . . Once more, but without the interest, you would find me painting the artichoke leaves . . . Everyone talks of the food shortage which here is more serious than in town and we fare badly always but what of it; I know we won't starve just as I knew we would always have enough money until Aldous got ill and frightened me in his insomnias and there were so many people to support. I hope he will not frighten me into planting beans . . . Since Matthew went, Sophie has been staying here . . . She has typed [parts of] Aldous's novel beautifully and retires each night to read Havelock Ellis and burns a huge log fire that scents the mild air wafted into my windows . . .

From Jeanne no news whatsoever since the total occupation of France following the Allied North African landings last year. Her last letter was dated 29th November.

And all my letters were returned; even some things sent 1941 Xmas! Rose, I don't know, I see her so little. I think she loves the new blond husband who is very authoritative . . . 6 foot high and 34 years old.

And the books we read are fascinating and we do every evening after dinner as ever . . . Read W. Sheldon's last book on Temperaments and you will see why you need privacy and I am driven crazy by my mother and why Aldous cannot take physical exercise . . .

There are few news . . We rarely go to town . . Now we go next week and visit Ojai, we saved our gas for that. We are better friends all the time with Rosalind and Krishnaji and miss seeing them. Then Aldous goes to Laguna to visit Gerald who now owns a large monastery on top of a beautiful hill . . He is happy as far as I can make out but I have not seen him for more than a year. Gas and other things. We write sometimes.

As it turned out both Aldous and Maria went to see Gerald at Trabuco in April.

.. And he was sweet. [Maria to Rosalind] He is very, profoundly, sad. Poor Gerald. He feels he muddled many of his friendships and does not understand . . . Aldous will stay with him in May and he asked me to go and so now slowly he may have his family back. I told you he sees the swami . . .

Matthew was now transferred from Texas to Denver, Colorado, to start training as an Army laboratory technician. This was excellent news as it was the work he wanted. Then, hardly started, he caught measles, followed by a throat infection. Aldous was worried. "Measles is a horribly treacherous disease", he wrote to Julian, ". . and I hope very much that this may not prove to be something unpleasant with long-range consequences.

.. One can only pray that the army doctors aren't merely pumping him full of toxic sulphanilamide for lack of knowing any other treatment—which is what so many medicos do nowadays, since the sulfa drugs became fashionable. They even give sulfa-pills to six months old babies for a cold in the head. The cold is short-circuited of course; but so is the baby . . . One day I should like to write a little book on fashions in medicine . . . fortunately no animal species possesses anything approaching the toughness of man.

Now something rather sad was happening to Aldous, although they did not realize it at the time. "A ridiculous accident", wrote Maria; "he was doing some weeding . . and getting a poisoning of the skin comparable to poison ivy. Not knowing anything about it except that there is no poison ivy here, we neglected it." Aldous's blood stream became infected and he had to leave the desert for Los Angeles and treatment. Matthew meanwhile in his army hospital was severely ill. They *had* pumped him full of sulphanilamide—and this on top of massive immunization shots for tetanus, typhoid, smallpox and the rest. Shots, as Aldous said, which don't do one much harm if one is strong, but which, if there is a constitutional weakness, may play havoc. Matthew got worse and the doctors believed that he had rheumatic fever; then again that he had not. After seven weeks of it, still undiagnosed, he was medically discharged from the army. He had lost forty pounds and reached home in June in a very low condition.

Aldous, too, had returned to Llano, believing himself cured of the skin trouble. Twelve hours later it flared up—very badly—and he had no choice but to leave again. It was thought that the thing had been brought on originally by his handling of some particularly virulent kind of burr weed, and that he had become allergic to the very presence of this weed which was quite common in the desert. Maria stayed on without him "because Matthew has to be looked after, also because I love it."

On 26th June Aldous's old friend Eugene Saxton died. Aldous wrote to his wife, ". . I always thought of him as one among the best of my friends.

> It was as though he possessed some quality stronger than absence and distance—an essential lovableness and reliability and warmth . . . In a curious, hardly analysable way Gene was, for me, a living proof of the triumph of character over matter . . .

Slowly, Matthew improved. Aldous, inoculated, was back at Llano: "Gay in spite of the poison-ivy-poison which is at last subsiding." (It was not.) "We are all three very happy and sometimes I wonder at it all." (Maria to Rosalind in July.) Their friend Peggy[1] came to stay with them.

> . . The visit was a great success. She looks as fresh and pretty as any girl in love and we were very gay and it was like having one of my sisters here. (I suppose you know that she is going to marry the doctor [Kiskadden] *I* wished for her two years ago—rather frightening . . . He impresses one as being extremely nice . . .) Her visit was most valuable as she saw many ways to improve my treatment of Matthew . . who has a great affection for her.
>
> We are reading the autobiography of Nehru.

Then Aldous went off for two weeks at Trabuco.

> He likes it there [still to Rosalind] and is fairly well looked after, not as well as when he goes to stay with you. There is another seminar and he goes earlier to see a man, Evan Wents . . It is nice to think that he and Gerald are good friends again. Gerald was for so long stimulating to Aldous that when there came a lull I was sad. Now it seems they are very pleased with each other and so I keep out of it all. I gather it is entirely intellectual and on "principles". But that is all right too . . .

What is one to think about that "lull", that intangible rift between Aldous and Gerald Heard? My guess is that the cause of it was that Aldous would not go along with Gerald's personal involvement in the religious life—the preaching in temples, the assumption of spiritual directorship; Aldous, to put it very bluntly,

---

[1] Peggy, the future wife of the late Dr William Kiskadden, had already been a great friend of Gerald Heard's in England (when she was Mrs Curtis Bok) where both had been connected with Dartington.

could neither believe in or approve of Gerald as a guru figure. Both he and Maria saw it as a grave mistake and feared for Gerald. What, if anything aside from "theological" argument, ever came into the open, I do not know. Most likely Aldous silently withdrew; while Gerald, affected by implied disapproval and the loss of coadjutor or disciple—both implausible roles for Aldous—may have seen it (this is guesswork) as a typical failure to commit himself. Whatever happened, there never was a break, the whole thing *was* a lull, an estrangement; it was bridged and their friendship survived, though their companionship, I believe, never quite returned to what it had been during their last English and their first American years.

In 1943 Maria, too, took to spending a few days now and then in what they called Gerald's monastery.

. . Aldous says Gerald has the whole thing, ways of life as well as philosophy, very clearly worked out and on the tips of his fingers which I gather means "tip of the tongue" and that people here find it extremely stimulating . . .

. . It is an extremely beautiful place [to Sybille] and the little convent is built rather like an Italian one. The bells ring and we slip into the Oratory wearing blue jeans and red dresses . . . Iris Tree—the irresponsible Iris—has been out there for three months, most reliably preparing the meals. Deliciously out of beans and starch with sometimes the help of a Boulestin cookery book. She is always on time and always plentiful and angelic. An untidy and sometimes a little dirty angel with blown hair at the early morning meditation . . . She writes hymns in the morning sun and runs wildly with the goats in the afternoon. But she is tired as we all are—and weather-beaten—as we all are even more.

The botanical intolerance started up each time Aldous went back to Llano, disruptive to his work and to their lives. For the rest of the summer he drifted about from place to place, undergoing new treatments, always expecting to be cured and able to return next week. In the autumn he and Maria moved into a furnished apartment in Beverly Hills and tried to make the best of it. At least it was restful to be able to sleep all night without "rushing a flash-light at the howling coyotes", Maria wrote to Matthew who had remained at Llano, "lovely but lonely". Sophie, too, had an apartment in town and was earning not the stale crust of Maria's prediction but an agreeable independent living.

[She] is very pretty, very well, very nice and very happy. She is secretary at Warners for all the dubbing in French and is much appreciated. In fact she is much more than a secretary and loves it and works very hard and very willingly. She has her hair done at Sax's and buys fourteen dollar shoes . . .

Before the year was out, Aldous had got within forty pages of the end of his novel: all but the epilogue to *Time Must Have a Stop* was written. He was still waiting to go back to Llano, but his particular weed was slow to die. It was so strong, Maria wrote to me sadly on 13th December, that it had resisted the first snows. "The Christmases that I thought would string themselves out on a desert gold and silver for the rest of my life till we reached the golden little cemetery above us have already been interrupted . . ."

The weed gave up and Aldous and Maria had a long, quiet winter and spring at Llano. The novel was finished in February. Rose's husband was taken for the army, Rose with her two children moved into the desert, to a small house six miles away Aldous had bought. Matthew was well enough to stay in town. When he came out to see his parents every other week or so, he would bring their provisions—a shopping list, Maria sent him, has turned up amongst his papers. A shopping list can be more individual than a love letter.

30/Jan/44
Lettuce (2 as I cook it) romaine,
those snub-nosed little squat
2 artichokes
2 bunches of small carrots and fresh radishes.
And pears and a few tangerines and apples.
Also CHEESE. And a loaf of bread.
And, if possible, a bottle of Nestlé coffee.

Matthew was well enough in fact to return to the university, take his degree and get down to his medicine. He had been on the point of going back to Colorado when it all came out (the Huxleys, it may be remembered, had always counted on their son's medical career)—Matthew did *not* want to be a doctor, had never really wanted to be one, and his pre-medical years had made him loathe the whole idea. Aldous and Maria were badly shocked. At themselves. How *could* they have been so obtuse? They said yes at once. So Matthew was now looking for a job on the technical side of the movies. (At the same time Aldous and Christopher Isherwood were working together on an original film story. The studio never bought it—perhaps it was too good; Matthew, however, eventually landed a job as reader at Warner Brothers.)

On Easter Day Aldous wrote to Cass Canfield, the president of Harper's, who since the death of Saxton was dealing with his affairs:

> . . I hope to be able to get down to a project which I have had in mind for some time, which is an anthology with comments, along the lines of *Texts and Pretexts*, but devoted to what has been called the Perennial Philosophy—the Highest Common Factor underlying all the great religious and metaphysical systems of the world. It would bring together, under a series of headings, quotations from Western and Oriental sources of every period . . .

Grace Hubble kindly and most competently did most of the proof corrections of *Time Must Have a Stop*. "Professional proof reading", Aldous wrote her, "has now reached a pitch of ineptitude undreamed of in happier times and my own talents in this direction have not improved correspondingly . . ." Relieved of this chore he was able to begin work on the anthology in May.

Almost at once he interrupted himself again to write the article on William Sheldon's classification of human types[1] which he always regarded as of extreme importance and as the first serious advance of the science of man since Aristotle. Sheldon, after some forty years of research, has devised a typology based upon three factors present to a varying degree in every individual. To these factors he gave the names of endomorphy, mesomorphy and ectomorphy. The endomorphic physique is soft and round and dominated by the digestive tract; the mesomorphic hard, heavy-boned and dominated by the muscles; the ectomorphic is a linear physique, like Aldous's, with slender bones, stringy muscles and a thin-walled gut. Each of them is very closely correlated with specific patterns of temperament—viscerotonia, in Sheldonian terms, somatotonia and cerebrotonia. Now *all* three physical factors are constitutional components in every individual, although in very varying combinations and degrees. Sheldon evolved a system of calculating the relative amounts of each component by dividing the body into five zones, taking a number of measurements of each and subjecting the results to certain

---

[1] *The Varieties of Human Physique* (1940) and the companion volume, *The Varieties of Temperament* (1942), followed by *The Varieties of Delinquent Youth* (1949). Though the closeness of the relation between physique and temperament is still a matter of controversy Sheldon's classification of physique is now a standard part of Human Biology and occupies a chapter in a principal current textbook *Human Biology* by G. A. Harrison, J. S. Weiner, J. M. Tanner and N. A. Barnicot (1964).

mathematical procedures which yield a three-digit formula expressing the amount of each component present in the organism measured.

> Thus the formula 7-1-1 indicates that the individual . . exhibits endomorphy in the highest possible degree, combined with the lowest degree of mesomorphy and ectomorphy. In practice, he would probably be extremely fat, gluttonous and comfort-loving, without drive or energy, almost sexless . . How different from the well-balanced 4-4-4, the formidably powerful and aggressive 3-7-1, the thin, nervous, "introverted" 1-2-7![1]

"For the first time", [Aldous to Grace Hubble] "the old insights and intuitions about the different kinds of human beings have been clarified and put on a firmly objective and measurable basis." And to E. S. P. Haynes:

> . . All other psychologists are merely psychological, and talk as though the mind were unrelated to its muscles, intestines and bones. Sheldon considers human beings as they really are—psycho-physical wholes . . . The gut of a round fat man, like G. K. Chesterton, may be as much as forty feet long. The gut of a thin man, like myself, may be as little as eighteen feet long and weigh less than half . . It would obviously be miraculous if this physical difference were not correlated with a mental difference. And yet these asinine psychiatrists and sociologists continue to talk of minds and characters as though they existed in a vacuum.

The question now posing itself is whether these physical differences are unalterable and absolute? Is there any way—hormone therapy, dieting, exercise—by means of which the physique of, say, a 1-1-7 can be changed into a 7-1-1 or 3-4-3? "The answer would seem to be no. An individual's basic formula cannot be modified . . .

> . . Our fundamental physical pattern is something given and unalterable, something we can make the best of but can never hope to change.[1]

Something we can make the best of. Or, by refusing to acknowledge it for instance, the worst.

> For example, less than ten boys out of every hundred are sufficiently mesomorphic to engage with even moderate success in the more

---

[1] Aldous Huxley, "Who Are You?" *Harper's Magazine*, November, 1944.

strenuous forms of athletics . . Hence the almost criminal folly of encouraging all boys, whatever their hereditary make-up, to develop athletic ambitions . . . A rational policy . . would be to tell all boys the simple truth, which is that . . excellence [in the more violent sports] depends primarily on a particular inheritance of size and shape, and that persons of other shapes and sizes . . have as good a right to realize their own *natural* capacities . . .[1]

And this leads of course to one of the most serious problems of society—individuals with an inborn propensity to violence.

There exists . . a certain percentage of people, [Aldous to Julian] . . "Somatotonics" . . who are constitutionally aggressive, who love risk and adventure . . who lust for power and dominance, who are psychologically callous and have no squeamishness about killing, who are insensitive to pain and tirelessly energetic. How can these be prevented from wrecking the world?

Sheldon's concept of constitutional analysis, Aldous held, has provided us with a new and extremely efficient instrument for thinking about human affairs. (Aldous's own article was published in *Harper's Magazine* with "pictorial comments" by James Thurber.)

At Llano at the moment all was well. In June Maria wrote to Matthew that Aldous would like to plant two fig trees. "He has seen some advertised at ten dollars a piece. Apparently he has been longing for years to get them." Then the weed returned and he was chased away. Once more it was the pattern of last summer and autumn: flight; inoculations; hopeful return; flight. Only now, having kept on the town apartment, Aldous had a place to escape to.

. . Really quite large [Maria to Sybille] two large bed-rooms, large sitting-room and dining-room, and Matthew lives in it all the time. I keep my respectable clothes there and as I never wear them they never wear out and it is a great economy. And Aldous keeps his hat there . . .

South Doheny Drive is a street astride the demarcation line between Los Angeles and Beverly Hills. The Huxleys' apartment, number 145 1/2 was on the West side and had a Beverly Hills

---

[1] "Who Are You?"

postman; the East side had a Los Angeles postman who simply consigned any letter, book or contract with a Beverly Hills address to the dead-letters office. Aldous thought it was "preposterous" that one postman would not walk across the street, or the other make no effort at an interception.

For his birthday, Aldous was at Llano. Matthew had sent him some Corelli records which he unwrapped and played before the day. Maria wrote to him, "I don't suppose you knew it was Aldous's 50th Birthday yesterday? The only mail was a letter . . saying that the story [the movie story] is not selling."

Summer 1944 and news at last from France. Paris had been liberated. Jeanne, Georges and Noële were there. "A postcard to say they are well. Alive anyways. How protected we have been." Sophie came out to Llano to announce her decision to join the Free French forces and return to Europe. She expected opposition. Instead, Maria leapt out of her chair and cried Bravo. Aldous agreed to let her go. ("In his absent-minded, cool and charming way." she wrote, "I knew he loved me. I amused him . . .") Presently she left for a training camp in Baltimore. Matthew sent her off with an orchid, her first.

> Sophie went off in a glory. [To Sybille] After those . . five years all ended in perfection . . . She is leaving with nothing but good memories from this stay in a country that will become a fairy-tale episode in her life . . . Now she has gone back to Jeanne and what? Perhaps a man, devotion, self-sacrifice and a perfect mother and wife. It would not astonish me.

Now Rose's husband in turn was medically discharged from the U.S. Army "and they are living happily ever after—we hope. They paint, they sculpt, they sing and they admire their children. Olivia goes to the local school in a yellow bus but speaks French at home and has an English accent."

In November the doctors allowed Aldous to return to Llano for the winter. And now he did something he had often longed to do, he learnt to drive. Maria taught him.

> . . Yes, it's wonderful about the car. [To Sybille] He will not take a licence or drive on the main highways and in town but he adores it and still likes speed. Nor did he ever make a mistake; not when learning to back or enter the garage. Even the cattle stare in wonderment when he drives through them and our gate neatly into a crowded garage. And he smiles and his cap is always on one side or the other for the setting of the sun and you know how comic and rakish and adorable he looks then. Also like a little boy because he is very preoccupied to do it well—and does.

Christmas they spent with Rose, and Maria was able now to describe it to Jeanne:

> . . un beau Noël chez Rose. We are all so fond of one another that it was charming and even Mère (who is no longer afraid of us and therefore not on the defensive) has become a good kind granny to the children who adore her . . . [Rose's boy] Siggy is superb, and like Holbein's portrait of the little English prince in red and gold. Olivia will have looks . . . Rose was beautiful . . .

And on their way home, Matthew told Maria "avec une conviction qui faisait pitié, 'If I could have a wife like Rose I would be happy.' . . . He has a horror of divorce and loves family life just as though he'd been brought up with brothers and sisters."

January 1945. Once more Maria sent me her news report from Llano.

> . . The spring is in full sweetness. A spring with snow in the mountains, water in the rivers and green over the desert . . . So we are lazy as in the Sanary winter days; all the more in the expectations of Mistrals. Mistral there and Mistral here. One's fate, even in winds, varies little. Now I hate it less. It has so many values in summer for coolness and windmills.
> My mother was staying here and Rose came with the children . . .
> I have patience with my mother too and can be fond of her now, after 46 years, which is a great relief.
> Aldous is just finishing another book. A fascinating one: a Text and Pretexts of Philosophy. It will be out in the autumn and very much your cup of tea even though you may not agree with it. Philosophia Perrenis. (It would be unlike me to have spelled it properly.) Then he is going to have a painting bout. He has not painted since we are in this country and now is going to try . . . His skin is getting steadily better and next year we hope not to have to go away in the summer . . . We have long walks in the evenings and after dinner we read. But we dine very late and until then we live in our houses. The nights under the same roof but the days well apart . . .
> Since my cure I am less abominably tired . . .

This is one of Maria's rare references to her health. Very few people knew that there had been anything to be cured.

> . . My health is excellent again. It is a bug with a tail; a flagellate and has a face like a tadpole. Usually . . makes children ill but not

grown-ups . . . It caused all the fatigue, the stupidity, the discouragement, the pains and discomforts. After a week of atabrin,
which the soldiers take in the Pacific, I was . . so stimulated instead
of sleeping fourteen hours a day I could not sleep at all. All the
energy has come back . . . This is the most wonderful climate and
life for health. We shall all live to be two hundred and shall we want
it then? Do I want it now? Shall I ever want it? At the moment it
would feel like a punishment but I must say I never think about it.
Used to bother me and horrify me when I was always tired. But it is
one of the old habits you teased me about—living in the present.

. . How much one fundamentally alters I do not know. It seems
that things which were always there come up in turns. Sometimes
they wilt, sometimes they grow . . . It is just this getting older . . .
which gives you some steadiness. If one can get old without resentment or holding back I believe it is worth much more than the
beautiful losses. I know I feared it for a long time. Then I forgot
about it because I was so busy with other things . . .

Every three weeks Matthew comes for a long weekend and has
plans. Now he is installing an invented telephone . . . He is full of
wonderful ideas—usually too wonderful . . . We adore each other in
a comic and in a tender way. And sometimes we insult each other
because the dishes are badly wiped or washed or there is some ash
on the table. He is as finicky as I am but we each have our specialities
as well as a great many in common. He and Aldous are excellent
friends and then, we think he is a queer fish! I don't really know.
Because he is both reserved and not at all. And he has queer lazinesses
and absences; and then is the most conscientious and thoughtful
person.

He reads trash for Warner Bros. But earning his living and finding
that he is very much appreciated . . . Many women but thank God
no wives or babies. His chief interests are social and political. Very
active . . . I am nice and see the likeable side of every new woman:
even when one had greasy hair! He is very "sérieux" and could lack
a sense of humour if he did not have to live with me who let not a
blimpishness pass and he is good-natured about it . . . He is also
good looking in a very strange way and . . that straw hair is now
much darker . . . He is bound to go to New York . . He has too
much of Aldous's integrity for me to ever give a thought to the dangers
. . . I think it will be "girls"—il a d'ailleur de qui tenir.

I have a little more patience with cooking and don't mind any
more . . . No meat for either of us. Eggs from our chickens and a
wonderfully healthy bread. Cream for Aldous and our complete
satisfaction with monotony.

Gerald we hardly ever see . . . We see Christopher Isherwood. He
is a sort of habitué sans habitudes. Part of the family. But no successor
to Eddy—or Raymond. Somehow those days are all over . . .

Eva . . . I asked her whether she would like to come to a séance which a famous man whose name I do not know is offering to give us in our flat . . . Only eight people. I never went to a séance except the sitting we had with Mrs Garrett and that was not successful.

. . May the horrors of this world not disturb your peace-of-mind. It is the most haunting world and particularly haunted me while the Germans re-advanced. Now it is relieved a little . . . That peace will be a misery and misery. Nothing but overwhelming pity if one went back. I read about it a bit. But one can only have a true picture through experience . . .

. . Now it is bed-time. A bed which stands in a bow-window and looks out onto the stars. But not until the eyes have travelled up the dark trees which are like fountains towards the sky; more beautiful than with their leaves even . . . Then, further, the snow-covered hills. The nights are usually very still; even if the wind blows during the day. So I look out and the silence is so silent it will mean much. Tomorrow I will have a long day . . . Then Aldous will come back late with news and books from the library.

## Chapter Four

## *Time Must Have a Stop*

"WHICH of your novels, Mr Huxley, has been most real to you?" John Chandos asked in 1961. "You mean the actual characters?" said Aldous. "The actual characters, and the ambience—is there any one novel that became most alive to you?"

"In a way—somehow the one—*Time Must Have a Stop* was the one I most enjoyed doing."

Whereupon Chandos asked about the Fifth Earl and carp gut and living to a hundred, and Aldous had to say, No, no, not that one; and we heard no more.

*Time Must Have a Stop* took nearly two and a half years—more than the actual writing time of *Eyeless in Gaza*, a book twice the length; two and a half years, that is, passed between start and finish. But the interruptions here were external interruptions—beneficial if anything to the book a-simmering—due to other work and ill health. Although he ran into trouble now and then, Aldous was never intrinsically held up. From the beginning he knew where he was going and what he wanted to say. There remained the—horribly difficult—job of finding the way of doing it. The novel was perhaps his most integrated one to date and it does not lend itself to anthologizing. In spite of extracts from note-books and the usual discursive dialogue, the burden is conveyed essentially by a story, and Aldous's own summary of it says about as much—or falls as short, as anyone's.

. . About half way through the story, [to Cass Canfield] which I have deliberately kept light, with events on a small scale minutely described, the principal comic character dies, and all that follows takes place against the background of his posthumous experience, which is, of course, wholly and disquietingly incompatible with the life he was leading . . . The other principal character is a very precocious and talented boy of only 17 during the main story—whose date is 1929—and whom we meet again in an epilogue, of present date, as a young man, maimed in the war, and concerned with the problem of the relationship between art (for he is a poet) and religion, the aesthetic and the spiritual life. Altogether it is an odd sort of book; but I hope it has come off.

Later he was heard saying once or twice that he thought it had. To Ted Haynes he wrote at the time:

# Time Must Have a Stop | *1945*

I am very glad you liked the book. I liked it pretty well myself—
though I remain sadly aware that I am not a born novelist, but
some other kind of man of letters, possessing enough ingenuity to be
able to simulate a novelist's behaviour not too unconvincingly. To
put the matter physiologically [Sheldonianly], I am the wrong shape
for a story teller . . .

Aldous's later books are fully acceptable, and intelligible, only
to those who have had, or wished to have, some intimation of
what Jeremy Pordage, in *After Many a Summer*, dismissed with
distaste as *timeless good*—it is a matter of having bought, or of
having at least the intention of buying one day, your ticket to
Athens. What Aldous was trying to say—in differing ways, on
differing levels of intensity, is what he began to say in *Eyeless in
Gaza*. Does *Time Must Have a Stop* bring home the walled-in daily
nonsense of the lives of most of us? How credible, how capable
of moving—transforming moving—is the character of Bruno,
Bruno Rontini, the enlightened and, thereby, the *good* man?
How potent is the scene where Bruno has the flash of insight
about Eustace Barnack who will die in a few hours, or the scene
where he first reaches the boy Sebastian, or the last scene where
Sebastian adult meets his father? Do the chapters of the after-
death experience come off? For a (personal) answer one has to
read the book. I shall only quote two passages. One because it
gives the key to Aldous's choice about his own writing during
the later half of his working life; the choice to withhold some
substance or vitality from his writing for the sake of something
else. Bruno Rontini and Sebastian have been talking about poets
and writers. They express their knowledge of reality, Bruno has
been saying, but themselves very rarely act on their knowledge.
Why not?

"Because all their energy and attention are absorbed by the work
of composition. They're concerned with writing, not with acting or
being. But because they're only concerned with writing about their
knowledge, they prevent themselves from knowing more."
   "What do you mean?" Sebastian asked.
   ". . You know in virtue of what you are; and what you are depends
on three factors: what you've inherited, what your surroundings
have done to you, and what you've chosen to do with your surroundings and your inheritance. A man of genius inherits an unusual
capacity to see into ultimate reality and to express what he sees. If
his surroundings are reasonably good, he'll be able to exercise his
powers. But if he spends all his energies on writing and doesn't
attempt to modify his inherited and acquired being in the light of

what he knows, then he can never get to increase his knowledge . . .
he'll know progressively less instead of more."

The other passage is the last two paragraphs but one in the novel.

Sebastian smiled and, standing up, ran a finger-nail across the
grille of the loud-speaker.

"One can either go on listening to the news—and of course the
news is always bad, even when it sounds good. Or alternatively one
can make up one's mind to listen to something else."

*Time Must Have a Stop* was published in America in October
1944 (where it sold at once some 40,000 copies) and in England
in the February following.

Spring 1945: news coming in from the continent of Europe.
Drieu La Rochelle imprisoned in France waiting to stand his
trial for collaboration. "When I read of this," Aldous wrote to
Victoria Ocampo, "I thought of the possibility of escape by
suicide."

And now it has happened. I had known him and been fond of him
since 1919, and these last tragic chapters of his life, with their
violent ending, make me feel very sad as I think of him.

There was news of Rina (her own name, one might recall, was
Rontini). Rina was re-married, to Marcel Eustration; had spent
part of the war in Sanary at Renée Kisling's, heroic in procuring
food for Jeanne and other friends in desperate straits. When her
husband joined the Maquis, she had gone to work on the land
to help feed his comrades. The Villa Huley had been sold. (It
was uninhabitable in war-time, converted as it had been to bottled
cooking gas: there was no gas.) Jeanne had bought another house
for them instead, La Rustique, on the main road between Sanary
and Bandol, and transferred the furniture. Rina and Marcel were
living there at present. Here is Maria's first letter:

Chère, chère Rina, Tu ne peux croire combien j'ai été touchée en
apprenant par Madame Neveux l'amitié et le devoument que tu as
eu pour elle et pour moi durant ces horribles années de guerre. Je
sais que tu habite maintenant La Rustique . . je m'imagine que tu
t'assoie dans les grands fauteuils, à la table en verre . . et cela me
donne envie de pleurer.

J'ai souvent pensé à toi avec tendresses car nos années de jeunesse
ne peuvent s'oublier: lorsque nous voyagions ensemble dans la Fiat

et dans la Bugatti. Lorsque tu étais avec nous à Londres et à Paris. Lorsque tu soignais Pussy et Miquette . . . et je suis toute heureuse de savoir que . . tu est restée parmis mes affaires à Sanary et si amie avec ma sœur.

Ici nous menons une vie bien différente de notre vie en France . . .

Maria describes their life at Llano, their animals and cats, the desert flowers, the poisonous snakes they meet on walks.

. . Mathieu est un très grand garçon qui aura 25 ans la semaine prochaine. Mais nous avons encore toujours des fraises pour son dîner d'anniversaire . . . Il a été dans l'armée pendant quelques mois seulement y étant tombé gravement malade. Maintenant il travaille dans un studio de cinéma . . je ne sais pas ce qu'il fera après la guerre.

Then she talks about Aldous, his health and work. He has written many new and successful books and a few stories for the cinema.

Mais cela ne lui plait pas . . . Rose habite à 13 kilomètres d'ici . . Sa fille a déjà sept ans, le petit garçon et tout blond et gras et rose . . .

J'espère que tu aura le temps de m'écrire et que tu me donneras toutes tes nouvelles . . . concernant ton mari, nos amis et ta famille en Italie. Je n'ai encore rien reçu de Mme Peterich [Costanza] mais je sais que Monsieur Fasola est mort. Je n'ai plus de nouvelles d'Angleterre. Le Comte de Noailles m'écrit que Monsieur Mortimer était à Paris et un homme très important maintenant dans le journalism. "Il Signorino Duca" [this was the Italian household's nickname for Eddy Sackville-West, who sometimes had the look of a fragile and ageless princely child] parle à la TSF et m'écrit quelques fois. Mrs Hutchinson jamais . . . Mme Gielgud va bien . . . Le fils aîné de Madame Kisling est Pilote Français dans un camp américain . . . Ma sœur Nicolas est à New York . . . Monsieur Seabrook est remarié et Madame Sybille est à New York. Eva à Hollywood.

Mais la première de nous que tu reverras sera Sophie . . car elle est dans l'armée Française . . . Je termine en t'embrassant très très tendrement et en te remerciant de toute ton amitié et de ce que tu as fait pour nous. Je t'envoie un tout petit colis de chocolat; nous ne sommes jamais trop vieux pour cela. J'écris à Marcel par le même courier . .

Ta Maria

A few weeks before the armistice in Europe, Aldous finished *The Perennial Philosophy*. Its greatest merit, Aldous wrote to Starkey, "is that about forty per cent of it is not by me, but by a lot of saints, many of whom were also men of genius." By Chinese Taoist philosophers, by followers of Buddha, by Christian mystics; by Lao Tsu, Asoka, Plotinus and St John of the Cross, by François de Sales, by Eckhart, St Teresa, by Boehme and George Fox, by William Law, by Christ . . . It was useful, Aldous thought, and timely to show precisely what the best and most intelligent human beings had agreed upon in the last three thousand years. "Seeing that it is perfectly obvious that we shall never get more than a temporary truce until most men accept a common *weltanschauung*." For the blurb (which he re-wrote) Aldous insisted on the insertion of this line,

Mr Huxley has made no attempts to "found a new religion".

". . it may take the wind out of the sails of some of the ecclesiastical critics who will want to say that I am another Mrs Eddy."
*The Perennial Philosophy* is about the nature of ultimate reality and the ends of man, about how to apprehend this reality and to attain these ends.

But the nature of this one Reality is such that it cannot be directly . . apprehended except by those who have chosen to fulfil certain conditions, making themselves loving, pure in heart and poor in spirit. Why should this be so? We do not know.[1]

Aldous, who has been accused not only of being another Mrs Eddy but of letting down the intellect, goes on:

It is just one of those facts which we have to accept, whether we like them or not and however implausible and unlikely they may seem. Nothing in our everyday experience gives us any reason for supposing that water is made up of hydrogen and oxygen . . Similarly, nothing in our everyday experience gives us much reason for supposing that the mind of the average sensual man has, as one of its constituents, something resembling, or identical with, the Reality substantial to the manifold world; and yet, when that mind is subjected to certain rather drastic treatments, the divine element, of which it is in part at least composed, becomes manifest, not only to the mind itself, but also, by its reflection in external behaviour, to other minds.
It is only by making physical experiments that we can discover the intimate nature of matter and its potentialities. And it is only by making psychological and moral experiments that we can discover

---

[1] This and subsequent quotations are from *The Perennial Philosophy*. Chatto & Windus, 1946.

the intimate nature of mind and its potentialities. In the ordinary circumstances of average sensual life these potentialities of the mind remain latent and unmanifested. If we would realize them, we must fulfil certain conditions and obey certain rules, which experience has shown empirically to be valid.

. . few professional philosophers and men of letters . . did very much in the way of fulfilling the necessary conditions of direct spiritual knowledge. When poets or metaphysicians talk about the Perennial Philosophy, it is generally at second hand. But in every age there have been some men and women who chose to fulfil the conditions . . and of these a few have left accounts of the Reality they were thus able to apprehend and have tried to relate, in one comprehensive system of thought, the given facts of this experience with the given facts of their other experiences . . .

The fulfilment of the necessary conditions—it always comes back to that; the steps we must take to annihilate, however gradually and painfully, the self-regarding ego: self-will, self-interest, self-centred thinking, wishing and imagining.

Extreme physical austerities are not likely to achieve this . . . But the acceptance of what happens to us (apart, of course, from our own sins) in the course of daily living is likely to produce this result . . . self-denial should take the form, not of showy acts . . but of control of the tongue and the moods—in refraining from saying anything uncharitable or merely frivolous (which means, in practice, refraining from about fifty per cent of ordinary conversation), and in behaving calmly and with quiet cheerfulness when external circumstances or the state of our bodies predisposes us to anxiety, gloom or an excessive elation.

Also:

Sufficient not only unto the day, but also unto the place, is the evil thereof. Agitation over happenings which we are powerless to modify, either because they have not yet occurred, or else are occurring at an inaccessible distance from us, achieves nothing beyond the inoculation of here and now with the remote or antici-pated evil that is the object of our distress. Listening four or five times a day to newscasters and commentators . . . St John of the Cross would have called it indulgence . . and the cultivation of disquietude for disquietude's sake.

. . The twentieth century is, among other things, the Age of Noise. Physical noise, mental noise and noise of desire . . . All the resources of our miraculous technology have been thrown into the current assault against silence . . .

. . One of the most extraordinary, because most gratuitous, pieces of twentieth-century vanity is the assumption that nobody knew anything about psychology before the days of Freud. But the real truth is that most modern psychologists understand human beings less well than did the ablest of their predecessors. Fénelon and La Rochefoucauld knew all about the surface rationalization of deep, discreditable motives in the subconscious, and were fully aware that sexuality and the will to power were, all too often, the effective forces at work under the polite mask of the *persona*. Macchiavelli had drawn Pareto's distinction between "residues", and "derivations"— between the real, self-interested motives for political action and the fancy theories . . . Like Buddha's and St Augustine's, Pascal's view of human virtue and rationality could not have been more realistically low. But all these men, even La Rochefoucauld, even Macchiavelli, were aware of certain facts which twentieth-century psychologists have chosen to ignore—the fact that human nature is tripartite, consisting of a spirit as well as of a mind and body; the fact that we live on the border-line between two worlds, the temporal and the eternal, the physical-vital-human and the divine; the fact that, though nothing in himself, man is "a nothing surrounded by God, indigent of God, capable of God and filled with God", if he so desires.

To be filled with God. And what is the point of that? The average sensual, the average rational man may ask. Aldous attempted to give an answer in *Grey Eminence*—where there is no vision, the people perish . . .

A totally unmystical world would be a world totally blind and insane. From the beginnings of the eighteenth century onwards, the sources of mystical knowledge have been steadily diminishing in number all over the planet. We are dangerously far advanced into the darkness . . .[1]

And yet even now

the existence at the heart of things of a divine serenity and goodwill may be regarded as one of the reasons why the world's sickness, though chronic, has not proved fatal . . .

"But the goods of eternity cannot be had except by giving up at least a little of our time to silently waiting for them." Not merely on the economic level income must balance expenditure. Just as "we cannot put forth physical energy unless we stoke our body

[1] *Grey Eminence*.

with fuel in the form of food [or] . . utter anything worth saying, unless we read and inwardly digest the utterances of our betters. We cannot act rightly and effectively unless we are in the habit of laying ourselves open to leadings of the divine Nature of Things . . .

> This means that the life in which ethical expenditure is balanced by spiritual income must be a life in which action alternates with repose, speech with alert passive silence . . . "What a man takes in by contemplation," says Eckhart, "that he pours out in love." The well-meaning humanist and the merely muscular Christian, who imagines that he can obey the second of the great commandments without taking time even to think how best he could love God with all his heart, soul and mind, are people engaged in the impossible task of pouring unceasingly from a container that is never replenished.

Aldous, for his part, had learned this early. *Silently waiting, Taking time to think*—hours of solitude and quiet were part of the disciplines of his profession. In his later years the disciplines served other ends as well. I think that Aldous, unlike Gerald Heard, did not meditate in any formal, stated way, only that in his later life not all his private hours were spent over typewriter or note-book—how often Matthew or Maria had come upon him, sitting quietly, head in hand . . .

That Maria, for her part, followed—possibly preceded— Aldous on this road there is no doubt. But she only spoke about it obliquely; spontaneous, and articulate, though she was, her medium was not words. The question of her beliefs was made more complex by her cradle Catholicism—her Catholicism discarded, her Catholicism retained. Christopher Isherwood, who loved her well, once said, "What Maria believed in nobody knew. Certainly not in words.

> 'Off to Trabuco, Chris?' she asked me.
> 'Not this week. Oh, no.'
> Maria: 'Why?'
> 'I'm so fed up, sick and tired of hearing them yacking about God.'
> Maria like lightning. '*How* I understand you.' "

That June the Huxleys were still in the desert but it was becoming evident that Aldous would never be rid there of the botanical allergy. What happened next, Maria related in a letter to Rosalind.

> We have actually bought, rather suddenly and vaguely the most hideous little house at Wrightwood . . It is twenty-three miles from

here in the hills above us next to Big Pines. A small [mountain] resort with crowded ugly cabins though not of the lowest type. All facilities such as water, electric light, gas deliveries . . a very good little store.

For there were other grounds that made Llano difficult to live in: periodical water shortages, the great heat in summer, the capricious electricity supply.

One day we went for a walk, enquired to rent, saw a house which was the right size, furnished and clean and in three days we owned it.
Then we discovered it was monstrously painted and shaped and draped; stupidly and lazily kitchened and bathroomed; and sadly that the two upper bedrooms were really very small and Noah's arky . . .
Wonderful walks and flowers and surprises of just escaping to tread on a rattler [a rattle snake] and running nose to nose with a mother and baby bear; not so nice and I was terrified because of stories Frieda [Lawrence] told me about mother bears.
. . Meanwhile Aldous is full of energy and initiative and with white paint he has done very good alterations. I laugh when I see the smears and the crusts and the brush hairs and his finger prints and the paint over the floor and his face! Also he has painted at last a very good and lovely picture . . .
. . I tell you very secretly that this wonderful place [Llano] is for sale again . . . Pangs of regret for the beauty—should it be allowed to play such a part in one's life?

The first post-war visitor from England arrived in July. "Madge Garland,"[1] a very old friend, of the fluffy pretty type who worked on *Vogue* for years. [Maria to Rosalind]

Still pretty and gay but so serious, so much more with a sense of values and that sadness in her eyes which so many seem to have. But she was also kind and sweet in the old days; only more so now; none of that malicious wit and brilliance of that milieu in our young days. She thought Aldous was wonderfully "transformed". Not only changed and looking well and so on. But transformed. I forget so often how badly he did see. How green and stoopy he used to be . . .

And this is Madge Garland's own account.[2] "It was quite extraordinary—when I arrived, Maria took me out into the garden at Llano. Aldous was pottering about across a little bridge: he called

---

[1] The present Lady Ashton.
[2] In conversation with S. B.

out, 'Hallo Madge.' He *saw* me. Then he crossed the narrow plank bridge without stick or specs."

10th August 1945. Aldous writes to Victoria Ocampo: "Thank God we are to have peace very soon.

> But . . peace with atomic bombs hanging overhead . . National states armed by science with superhuman military power always remind me of Swift's description of Gulliver being carried up to the roof of the King of Brobdingnag's palace by a gigantic monkey: reason, human decency and spirituality, which are strictly individual matters, find themselves in the clutches of the collective will, which has the mentality of a delinquent boy of fourteen in conjunction with the physical power of a god.

14th August 1945. Maria to Jeanne:

> Janin, ma Chérie! Le jour de Paix est arrivé . . . It has been official for the last 4 hours. This is something one will not forget! Everybody was smiling—or crying. There is much grief made harder to bear by this exuberance of deliverance. All the shops closed spontaneously . . Mère brought me roses . . . I went to a little church in the Mexican quarter, and I was moved in that poor church because the people were really praying . . .

# PART NINE

## Sufficient unto the Day: 1945-1951

"One is compelled willy nilly to adopt
the advanced Christian attitude of 'one
step enough for me', for the good reason
that circumstances don't permit the
seeing of a second step, much less the
distant scene . . ."

ALDOUS HUXLEY in a letter to
Naomi Mitchison

# Chapter One

# Wrightwood

IN August 1945 Aldous and Maria went out to camp in their new house. Wrightwood stood at an altitude of 6,000 feet in a landscape of pinewoods and sage brush, below a chain of close and spectacular mountains. The nights were noisy with the yelpings of foxes and ranch dogs. It was their first American summer of 1937 all over again, chaotic and strenuous as the settling in at Frieda's ranch. The wooden house was not insulated, the electric light unconnected, Aldous's future room still a stable; workmen appeared, vanished within a few hours; there being no window-glass to be had, they used windows lifted from Llano. "Please," Maria wrote to Rosalind, "like it when you come."

Aldous loved it from the first. "Aldous loves the mountains wherever he sees them. His enthusiasm for the walks are like those of a little boy and make me think how strongly he remembers the holidays in Switzerland with his mother.

> [I] for choice would go back to the expanses reminiscent no doubt of the plains of Flanders—which does not mean that I am not perfectly happy here. You know how happily I can fit into any situation which is not London—or Paris—or New York . . . The altitude used to make me sick but that is better and can be taken care of.

Throughout it, workmen's clatter, hayfever—the form his allergies took that year—Aldous was working away on a slim book on science, liberty and peace. Daily living had become easier within weeks of the end of the war; gasoline flowed again, Maria got hold of five tyres and the promise of a reconditioned engine ("Krishnaji will drive me to the garage"). This new mobility made them more busy and restless, "the long monotonous stretches are no more . . ." But the overwhelming thing, "the actual joy, each day, is peace. Bad as it is. Ominous too as it is. But to know that they are not burning, smashing, torturing at the moment, is a continual and active realization."

*The Perennial Philosophy* was published in America in September, and sold 23,000 copies within weeks. (Pleasing to Aldous, Maria wrote, as an "expression of interest in it".) Matthew had become

446

an American citizen, and went off to the University of California
at Berkeley to continue his education, specializing now in Latin-
American studies.

[He] has been the big happiness and joy of my life lately [Maria
to Sybille] because he very rapidly has become just the sort of man
I wanted him to become. Self-assured; and self-directed. Definitely
on the side of all that we care for and his personal integrity is beyond
doubt. He will make small mistakes; not big ones—I think . . . His
health is excellent . . . I suppose that you think me quite a doting
mother—but Aldous has turned into a doting father. And Matthew
is extremely useful to him sometimes. Helped him out instantly over
a deep jam in the Alice situation. Then Matthew presses him to more
activity than he would have otherwise in worldly matters.

The Alice situation: Aldous had been asked to work with Walt
Disney on a film about *Alice in Wonderland*—part a cartoon version
of Tenniel's drawings, part flesh-and-blood episodes from the life
of Lewis Carroll, the Rev. Charles Dodgson. The project came
off and Aldous and Maria returned to their town apartment for
November and December. Aldous thought that something rather
nice might be made out of it—Dodgson, the "fascinating mid-
Victorian eccentric" and "the old, unreformed Oxford of the
eighteen-sixties".

. . My mother was brought up there as a child—[he wrote to
Victoria Ocampo] and incidentally Dodgson, who was a passionate
amateur photographer, made a number of delightful pictures of her,
some of which are reproduced in the volume of Dodgson's letters to
his child friends. Also my aunt, Mrs Humphry Ward, lived there
as a young married woman and has left a very lively account of the
place in her *Recollections of a Writer*. [Which Maria was then reading
aloud] It would be nice to be able to reconstruct the university of
the period, with its long-drawn struggles between Tory High
Churchmen and Liberal Modernists, under Jowett and Pattison.
But, alas, there is no time in an hour of film—and even if there were
time, how few of the millions who see the film would take the
smallest interest in the reconstruction of this odd fragment of the
past!

All the same, Maria said, "this is the first movie he likes doing".
When it was over they retreated once again to Llano for the
winter and spring. In May Maria sent off one of her situation
reports, this time to Harold and Vera Raymond, apologizing for
Aldous's silence. It used to be my business, she said, "writing the
letters to friends. Now I have hoped he did some of it because I

have been so busy . . . But this evening [Aldous was in town] I long to write to you both and give you the many messages which I know Aldous too feels for you.

. . Perhaps Aldous never writes to Gervas either. His very favourite cousin. But then: we are all so busy . . . Nor is anything improving here with the strikes. There are no queues because nothing is rationed and therefore one just simply does not get anything that is short. There is a double kind of black market here; the regular one and the one which is just favouring the habitual customer—which is fair. But desert rats as we are, no one has our customship and it is lucky that we need so few things . . . You say you just received my parcel . . It must be the Xmas one. I am very discouraged with sending to England as such a small percentage arrive . . Particularly in London . . I spend my whole days making parcels . . Since last year when France was opened I have not stopped or relaxed. Luckily for me the countries did not open all at once. Then the needs grew less urgent while others grew so much worse. Belgium is now actually flourishing. In France my sister can get along fairly well too. She has a delicate little girl which complicates matters. And now I do all I can for Italy. [For Costanza Fasola, for Rina's family, for so many others.] There also it is disheartening because so much is stolen . . . And I know that I have stood in front of my table with the weighing scales for as many hours as the continental mothers have in their queues . . but with the difference that I did it with joy . . .

Has Aldous told them that they usually lived in a desert and that "we loved it? That it was [and the *was* crossed out and made into *is*] the most beautiful place on earth?" But now they are thinking of selling because there is this new house in the mountains.

We shall go there soon . . . our dearest friend Krishnamurti will be there all June . . .
. . We are a gay and intimate family. Matthew is very different. Yet he has so much of Aldous, the kindness . . . Yes, Aldous still has no glasses. In fact he sees better and better. Enough now to drive the car on these country roads. He can read large print with the eye that was blind. If you notice on the photographs, the eyes are never retouched now . . . He is planning two novels. I suppose he told you at least that. But we are not planning to visit Europe. Sometimes I long to. To go to Florence again. To see the roofs on the French houses. The mists over the dark tree trunks of the London Parks. We are not likely to go soon. Mostly because we cannot bear the miseries. The begging officers in London streets after World War I were bad enough. And the Viennese. So we just went where there

were no beggars and forgot. Now the despair will be in every country
. . . also we think it is not fair to go and eat your food. Certainly one.
day we shall go back. To visit or to stay . . .
. . My little niece is upstairs [Olivia] . . and I can hear her sleep.
She has come to keep me company. It helps remarkably . . I do not
like to be entirely alone somehow even though there are not the
ghosts of the flat in Albany. [Maria used to be certain that E2
Albany was haunted; indeed during the time I stayed there alone I
was uneasy, without tangible cause, every night.] But only cats are
little company. All the dogs have died. Many cats too, but we have
two left . . . snakes, thieves, coyotes, even owls; just the desert. It is
hard on those soft little things. And I mind very much each time.
We started out with eleven [cats] and added up to fifteen . . . and
only two left. One is pale and streaky ginger with golden eyes . . .
Here ends the paper and the tales but never the many messages of
good wishes and much love that we send you both and to the boys
too . . .

It was Aldous who felt aloof and gloomy about Europe. As
Maria had said about him earlier in the war: "Aldous has no
wish to go to England any more. He loved Italy, he loved France,
but his home-sickness was only for England. That has gone now.
It's dried up." To Victoria Ocampo he wrote:

Yes, how remote it seems, the time of our first meeting, and what a
strange, unsatisfactory kind of existence I was leading! And what a
strange Decline-and-Fall world it was we were living in! What
Europe must be like now, after the Fall, is hard· to imagine. And of
course it must get much worse . . . as the hunger grows more intense
in the coming months. I was sent a number of French books recently
—all rather horrifying, I thought. Novels about the Resistance—
half heroism, half unutterable moral squalor; essays by existentialists,
which are just Kierkegaard without God and also without genius.
I hope, and presume, that there must be something better . . .

*Science, Liberty and Peace*[1] came out in America that March and
in England a year later. It said, Aldous thought, some things
that needed saying, "absurdly simple things such as 'the Sabbath
is made for man, not man for the Sabbath', things which men
of science like to forget because it is such enormous fun inquiring
into the processes of nature and designing bigger and better
gadgets that they do not wish to realize that human beings are
sacrificed to applied science . . the pious talk about science serving

[1] Written at the request of Nevin Sayre of the Fellowship of Reconciliation
to whom Aldous made over the royalties.

mankind is (as things are at present) pure nonsense and hypocrisy
. . . I have said all this as drily and unemphatically as possible,
as nothing is gained in this sort of case by rhetoric."

The slim book opens with this paragraph:

> If the arrangement of society is bad (as ours is), and a small number
> of people have power over the majority and oppress it, every victory
> over Nature will inevitably serve only to increase that power and
> that oppression. This is what is actually happening.[1]

*Actually happening.* In 1946? In 1900. That paragraph was
written not by Aldous but by Tolstoy some seventy years ago.
No social evil, Aldous then went on, can possibly have only one
cause. "All that is being maintained here is that progressive science
is one of the causative factors involved in the progressive decline
of liberty and the progressive centralization of power, which have
occurred during the twentieth century."[1] Now is there any way
in which the advantages of a new technology can be enjoyed
without consequent loss of freedom? "My own view," says Aldous,

> which is essentially that of the Decentralists, is that, so long as the
> results of pure science are applied for the purpose of making our
> system of mass-producing and mass-distributing industry more
> expensively elaborate and more highly specialized, there can be
> nothing but ever greater centralization of power in even fewer
> hands. And the corollary . . is the progressive loss by the masses of
> their civil liberties, their personal independence and their oppor-
> tunities for self-government. But here we must note that there is
> nothing in the results of disinterested scientific research which makes
> it inevitable that they should be applied for the benefit of centralized
> finance, industry and government. If inventors and technicians so
> chose, they could just as well apply the results of pure science for the
> purpose of increasing the economic self-sufficiency and consequently
> the political independence of small owners, working either on their
> own or in co-operative groups, concerned not with mass-production
> but with subsistence and the supply of the local market . . .
>
> . . Ralph Borsodi's studies[2] have shown that mass-producing and
> mass-distributing methods are technologically justified in about one-
> third of the total production of goods. In the remaining two-thirds,
> the economies effected by mass-producing are offset by the increased

---

[1] *Science, Liberty and Peace.* Chatto & Windus, 1947 (and subsequent
quotations).

[2] Ralph Borsodi—set up a "School of Living" in the East (U.S.) in the
1930s to do research into methods of small-scale production and decentralization.

cost involved in mass-distribution over great areas, so that local production by individuals or co-operating groups, working for a neighbourhood market, is more economical than mass-production in vast centralized factories.

But of course, as Aldous pointed out, it is highly unlikely that this so desirable process of decentralization and de-institutionalization will be carried out. *Quis custodiet custodes?*

. . What is needed is a restatement of the Emersonian doctrine of self-reliance—a restatement, not abstract and general, but fully documented with an account of all the presently available techniques for achieving independence within a localized, co-operative community . . .

Inevitably we come to the results of pure science as applied to war. Armaments, as Aldous pointed out, are the only goods that are given away without consideration of costs or profits.

Modern war is, among other things, a competition among nations as to which can hand out, free, gratis and for nothing, the largest amount of capital goods in the shortest time. These capital goods are all maleficent and unproductive; but the thought occurs to one that something resembling wartime prosperity might be made permanent if there were more giving away at cost, or even for nothing, and less selling at a profit and paying of interest.

To this Aldous added a warning note. If it were to happen we should find ourselves with a political system approximating state socialism. Preferable, most likely, in some ways to the present dispensation. But

we must remember that any government enjoying a monopoly of political and economical power is exposed to almost irresistible temptations to tyranny.

There is no way of escaping Acton's dictum.

. . The most important lesson of history . . is that nobody ever learns history's lesson. The enormous catastrophes of recent years have left the survivors thinking very much as they thought before. A horde of Bourbons, we return to what we call peace, having learned nothing . . .

If our rulers were sincere in their desire for peace, "they would do all they could to by-pass the absolutely insoluble problems of power by concentrating all their attention . . on the one great problem which every member of the human race is concerned to solve . . . The first item on the agenda of every meeting . . should be: *How are all men, women and children to get enough to eat?*"

During the first half of 1946 Aldous was engaged in short-term work, articles for *Vedanta in the West*, a series of essays for the *Encyclopaedia Britannica* (finally not published). In June he started on a film version of his 1921 short story, "The Gioconda Smile". He was working with Zoltan Korda, Alexander Korda's brother, and found this very pleasant. "He is a nice, intelligent fellow," he wrote afterwards to Anita Loos, "and we were able to co-ordinate our respective specialities of writer and director without the interference of a producer. Consequently the work was done quickly and efficiently, without being held up by retired button-manufacturers using the Divine Right of Money to obstruct the activities of those who do the actual work."

In July Aldous and Maria moved up to Wrightwood again, where the house had become livable enough. The place was agreeable, Maria wrote, "but there is no immensity . . . The beautiful desert is out of my life though it will never be out of my inner eyes." In the evenings they were visited by a charming racoon who took food from their hands. "He holds it in his front paws and carries it to the bird-bath to wash it before eating." Deer trustingly came down the slopes at night, but also swarms of large mice who settled in the caravan, and there was always the fear that Aldous might step on one of the rattle snakes on his walks. After dinner they re-read Proust—alas, their enthusiasm of twenty-five years ago seems incomprehensible now, almost inexplicable. What does Georges think of Proust? Maria inquires of Jeanne (in fact twenty years ago, Aldous had already asked himself this question). "The most curious feature of [Proust's] mentality is his complacent acceptance of the 'intermittences of the heart' and all the other psychological discontinuities which he so subtly and exhaustively describes.

> No author has studied the intermittences of the spirit with so much insight and patience, and none has shown himself so placidly content to live the life of an intermittent being . . . *The idea of using his knowledge in order to make himself better never seems to have occurred to him* [my italics].[1]

In August they are expecting Suzanne and her girls. Maria had not seen them for six years; of Claire and Sylvia, Aldous

---

[1] "Personality and Discontinuity of the Mind", *Proper Studies*, 1927.

had only had brief glimpses when they were little: now they were young women, twenty-one, eighteen. They drove all the way from New York through the height of the American summer in an old station wagon loaded to the gills with Suzanne's statues. Joep Nicolas had gone to Holland for his first post-war show, and the party was escorted by Claire's fiancé, Bobby White. One morning early in mid-country they saw a notice stuck against a tree:

SUZANNE C'EST ICI

"We arrived [Claire wrote[1]] while Aldous and Maria were having a breakfast of stewed fruit, delicious bread and tea. Aldous came like a huge insect out of a tiny pod, his silver caravan, I was struck by how much more handsome he had grown since those years ago in Holland when his forehead was tensely furrowed and his posture stooped (. . as a child I was taken along on a sight-seeing tour and remember his knocking his head on all the doors and his passionate interest in unicorns . . .) Maria, looking at my now husband Bobby asleep in a hammock, whispered to Suzanne: 'Comme il est beau, on dirait un Picasso!' and little Olivia said: 'Qu'est-ce que c'est un Pique Oiseau?' "

Soon they were all in a great bustle. Aldous sat to Suzanne for a head, then Maria; Sylvia painted, Bobby sculpted. Claire wrote and drew. Very sweet, amusing, talented girls, Aldous called them, the elder a wraith-like being, the younger with her feet firmly planted on the ground, the two "equally gifted and charming, and equally unaffected and unspoiled." Claire was a little afraid of Aldous, "feeling one must talk—on those marvellous family walks in the mountains—whereas with Krishnamurti . . I was terribly relieved at not having to say one word and feeling completely at ease. I got my first rise out of Aldous, typically, by a naïve remark. These salt blocks in the meadows for the cows, were they for making salt butter rather than sweet butter? Actually what happened was that Sylvia adopted Maria and was relaxed with Aldous who delighted in her and said she had the same figure as Maria at that age." Indeed Aldous was enchanted and amused, Maria told Jeanne, describing what she called "ce centre de travail et de joie.

I cannot tell you the pleasure these three "sisters" are giving us (for Suzanne seems to be her children's age, and they seem to be nearly hers) . . . Les enfants sont belles et gracieuses . . douces,

[1] Claire Nicolas White in a letter to S. B. 1969.

intelligentes et facile à vivre et affectueuses. Je ne sais pas combien Claire est fiancée mais . . elle a bien choisi. Et tous travaillent et ne parlent que de travail. On croirait à peine à une réunion de trois femmes. Elles ne boivent ni ne fument et ne semblent s'intéresser à aucunes sottises de leur âge. Je trouve que Suzanne a une chance incroyable. Et qu'elle les as joliment bien élevées. Suzanne elle même est heureuse parcequ'elle travaille.

And what they have seen of Suzanne's work is good, very good, "Pas de génie peut-être mais de premier ordre quand même." It is difficult to believe this about one's own sister, but Aldous says so too. And what does she look like now, Suzanne, who used to turn all the heads? "Elle est mince . . . Son visage est beau—je trouve qu'il a gagné de la personalité en vieillissant." Her English is excellent with a slight accent, a Dutch accent. "It seems we have the same voice on the telephone. Matthew falls for it.

Nous nous ressemblons tellement—et si peu. [This was exactly true.] Suzanne est plus vivante, je crois. On se connait si peu . . .

The girls adore Rose, are for ever running in and out of her house, painting away on her verandah, roping in Siggy and Olivia, sketching wherever they go . . .

They all tell me that Rose is happy. And I know that this will please you, Janin. That her life is agreeable and amusing . . .

Maria, so concerned about Rose with two small children, a husband out of work and practically no money, would like to believe it. "Bobby and the girls dream of living in the desert on love and spring water . . . And that old wash-tub of Rose's, the tub with the mangle—*my* nightmare is the thought of that weekly wash—well, it's precisely that old wash-tub which enchants Suzanne!" Aldous's head has started very well; but poor Suzanne does not foresee the difficulty she is going to run into with Maria's.

I give an impression of being young; but then, in detail, the face is tired and shows its age, 48, and Suzanne, whose mind is still full of the me of her youth, is lost. I am not telling her this but I can feel it.

Now for glimpses of Maria by Suzanne. In the evenings, of course, one read to Aldous. Tolstoi. "Poor Coccola who did not see very well and, because of the Bates system, wouldn't wear spectacles, tried to hold the book close to her eyes and then far again, and was enchanted when we took her turn . . . She was tremendously active, living entirely on her nerves . . . using the

454

money saved by having no domestic help to send parcels to an Italian orphanage . . . And all those fortune-tellers—she and Aldous were fascinated by fortune-tellers. And yet Coccola would go and pray in that little Mexican church . . and read St François de Sales . . . Once she said to me 'If I weren't married to Aldous, I would be a Catholic.' . . She also admitted that she suffered from not having developed a talent of her own. Instead she devoted herself body and soul to Aldous's talent . . . But then there is his *gentillesse* for her—the way he comes running from his study when she gets home from marketing and relieves her of the parcels . . ."

Presently Claire's fiancé had to return to New York; Aldous commissioned him to sculpt a new bird-bath which paid for his train fare. In the midst of it all, Aldous finished the *Gioconda* script and switched to the stage version and to note-taking for a novel about fourteenth-century Italy. In the intervals he wrote several long letters to his brother about world affairs, letters to Middleton Murry about demoniac possession, to Cyril Connolly about Palinurus, to Professor Rhine about para-normal perception and to Anita Loos about the toughness of the problems of the stage. To Victoria Ocampo, who had asked him for an article on T. E. Lawrence, he demurred: he had read a quarter of the *Seven Pillars* some fifteen years ago.

. . I found it as hard to read now as I found it in the past . . . even in his writing, Lawrence was a man of the conscious will. He *wanted* to write well, and he wrote about as well as a conscious will can make one write. But the consciously willed style always . . stops short of the best, the genuinely good. It is always what the other Lawrence calls "would-be" . . . not all artificial styles are of the "would-be" variety. To some people it comes natural to write artificially; they are artificial with freshness and unction—like Milton, for example. Nothing could be more artificial than "Lycidas", but nothing could be more deeply spontaneous, less of the surface. "Lycidas" is as much a product of the Tao as are the "wood-notes wild" of more natural poets. But with T. E. Lawrence I never felt any freshness or spontaneity . . . freshness, the free-working of the Tao, the something not ourselves that makes for beauty and significance—these are the things I find myself valuing more and more in style. And these are the things I don't find in the *Seven Pillars*, which I read with admiration for the man . . . As a character, I find Lawrence extremely interesting . . . If one wants a demonstration of the basic *misère de l'homme*, one could hardly choose better than Lawrence; for he had everything that the human individual, as an individual, can possess —talent, courage, indomitable will, intelligence, everything, and though his gifts permitted him to do extraordinary, hardly credible things, they availed him nothing in relation to "enlightenment", "salvation", "liberation". Nothing burns in hell except self-will says the author of the *Theologica Germanica*. Lawrence had a self-will of heroic, even of Titanic, proportions; and one has the impression that he lived for the most part in one of the more painful corners of the inferno. He is one of those great men for whom one feels intensely sorry, because he was nothing but a great man.

In a letter to Victoria earlier in the year (also à propos of the *Seven Pillars*) Aldous had explained the lines guiding his own reading. ". . I don't read very much in the way of general literature. My eyes make it impossible for me to keep up . . .

and at the same time my primary preoccupation is the achievement of some kind of over-all understanding of the world, directly and, at one remove, through the building up of some hypothesis that accounts for the facts and "saves the appearances". Most of the limited reading I am able to do is aimed at the refinement and clarification of the guiding hypothesis. In regard to belles lettres— outside the few stupendous things, whose periodical re-perusal throws fresh light on the central problem—I read what chance brings to hand, paying attention only to what contributes in one way or another to the furthering of my underlying purpose.

Asked by the honorary librarian of the Peace Pledge Union to write a preface to the translation of Godel's *La Paix Créatrice* Aldous replied (in an unpublished letter of 16th September) that he would think about it. Meanwhile,

I feel more and more that the best way of advocating and securing peace at present is to insist in and out of season on the world's basic and most difficult problem—that of feeding a population already too large to feed adequately and destined to increase from two thousand millions to three thousand millions in a lifetime. Everybody wants to eat. All the resources in intelligence and good will are needed to make it possible for everybody to eat. Power politics guarantee that the world shall *not* be fed properly. Human beings seem incapable of coming to an agreement except in the face of a common enemy—and the only common enemy who is not another human being or society is hunger. Only by concentrating on the basic problem of humanity can we by-pass the non-basic problems, those of nationalism and power.

And to Julian, that same autumn, he put it rather more succinctly:

And of course this business of population is the one thing these bloody politicians should be thinking about at this time . . . Poverty

in the midst of plenty is largely bosh. There is poverty in the midst
of poverty . . . All this criminal haggling as to who shall bully whom,
which is all the peace conferences can think about, seems pretty
silly to say the least. Just gangsterizing while the world starves . . .


The happy families left Wrightwood for Los Angeles in late
September ("beautiful abandoned Llano was passed on the way,
with its gardens brimming with fruit" [Claire]). Suzanne's show
opened at the Taylor Galleries on 3rd October. "A good show,
with some excellent things in it, and we rounded up quite a good
collection of people," Aldous wrote to Anita Loos. "Let's hope
to goodness they will do some buying and ordering of portraits.
Grace and Edwin were there . . Constance has been a great help
and stand-by . . ." The three sisters went to live in Mme Nys's
Beverly Hills apartment, eating their suppers at Aldous and
Maria's. At noon once or twice a week, as was the Huxleys'
custom, they met at the Town and Country Market—that
pleasant, shaded place at Fairfax and Third—Aldous and Maria
had a friend there, Yolanda, an Italian woman with a lively face
and eyes and worn scrubbed hands, who ran a spaghetti and
fried chicken stall. She came from Rome and had married an
American, Louis Robert Loeffler. They first met at one of Swami
Prabhavananda's services at the Vedanta Temple of which
Yolanda was a member. At the market she found time to sit
with the Huxleys over their coffee, the three of them talking
away happily in Italian. It was at Yolanda's one day that,
according to Claire,

> Sylvia and I spotted Stravinsky whom we had met at a friend's
> party and had both flirted with, I think. We went over to talk to
> him, and Aldous, with his usual courtliness, joined us and introduced
> himself by saying, "I'm a friend of Victoria Ocampo's." This is how
> their great friendship began.


Presently the Nicolases ran out of money. Claire decided they
must all take jobs.

> I found one in the papers for Sylvia as an usherette in a local movie
> house and for myself at the Marian Hunter book store. Could not
> persuade Suzanne to be a cashier in a restaurant. For one month
> Aldous went every night to fetch Sylvia after the evening show and
> walk her home. I think he found it terribly amusing to escort her in
> black satin pants and a green military type jacket with huge padded
> shoulders, her uniform.

457

In December they had saved enough money and drove back to New York. (A hazardous journey with half a ton of sculpture in the car and a difficult boy for escort, a beau of Sylvia's who had turned Buddhist and refused to consult a map. In Texas their station wagon overturned: much against the odds, humans and statuary escaped uncrushed.)

Aldous learned that Julian had been elected to the director generalship of Unesco. He was delighted and sent a letter of good wishes and hopes. Might it not be possible for Julian to persuade the technologists that human beings have certain physical and psychological needs, and that applied science should serve those needs?

> The ideal would be if technologists and pure scientists could meet, consider the human situation, evaluate human needs in the way of food, clothing, shelter, peace, individual liberty, group self-government etc; and then frame a policy of research designed to fulfil those needs.
>
> E.g. it is perfectly obvious that atomic energy, being generated from uranium, which is a natural monopoly, is a power-source no less politically unsatisfactory than petroleum. Like petroleum, uranium may occur within the territories of powerful nations—in which case it increases their power and their tendency to bully others; or it may be found within the borders of weak nations—in which case it invites aggression and international chicanery, as is now the case with the oil of the Middle East.

Now how about developing a source of power which is *not* a natural monopoly? Nor a wasting asset, like uranium, or petroleum, or even coal?

> The most obvious power source hitherto inadequately exploited is wind. I gather that the experimental wind turbine which has been producing fifteen hundred kilowatts in Maine has proved entirely satisfactory. If scientists genuinely wanted to contribute to peace and well being, they can collectively and intensively consider the yet more efficient development of such wind turbines and thereby end natural monopolies and remove one of the standing temptations to aggression, war and foreign burrowing from within. But they prefer to concentrate on atomic power, which creates unparalleled temptations . . .

That winter Cyril Connolly came to California, the first English (non-expatriate) writer after the war, the first to see Aldous, their first new meeting since those barren encounters at Sanary in the past. So much had happened. Cyril had gone on from the love of his youth for the early books ("the brilliant destructive period"), had felt let down by *Point Counter Point*, had pounced on *Eyeless in Gaza* with a savage parody, and then become captivated again by *Ends and Means*, which he reviewed, and been "strangely moved by passages in *After Many a Summer* and almost all of *Time Must Have a Stop*."[1] Meanwhile Aldous had written a fan letter to the author of *Palinurus* (there was a distinctive flavour about its *Weltanschauung* which, like Byronism, might become contagious— "future historians of literature may discover lingering strains of palinuremia"). And now here they met. "I loved him again," Cyril said; and in print, "I was at once struck by the strange new quality of sublimated sensuality, intellectual pity, spiritual grace . . ."[2] He found nothing Americanized about Aldous (". . unlike the younger expatriates, he speaks better English than you or I, with a silvery and almost extinct intonation—sounding the 'o' in petrol like a bell").[1] Hollywood, Los Angeles, Aldous's environment, Cyril like so many Europeans found unlovely, alien— "those who have loved the Mediterranean will not be reconciled here and those who really care for books can never settle down to the impermanent world of the cinema . . ." Yet there are exceptions, he goes on to say, and of these Aldous is the most remarkable.

> The California climate and food creates giants but not genius, but Huxley has filled out into a kind of Apollonian majesty; he radiates both intelligence and serene goodness, and is the best possible testimony to the simple life he leads and the faith he believes in, the only English writer, I think, to have wholly benefited by his transplantation and whom one feels exquisitely refreshed by meeting.

One day after the two men had been lunching together, Cyril had a dream in which Aldous appeared to him in a blue light and from which he woke with an extraordinary sense of serenity and consolation. When he told Aldous about it, Aldous said very simply, "Yes, I thought about you a good deal. I felt you were unhappy."

In January 1947 Aldous and Maria began the process of moving their possessions into Wrightwood: they were pulling out of Llano for good. (Though it was still unsold and hard to sell.)

"First night in Wrightwood," Maria wrote to Jeanne on 26th

---

1 Cyril Connolly in *Picture Post*, 6th November 1948.
2 Cyril Connolly in *Horizon*, No. 93/94, October 1947.

February, "since it has become my only refuge; and I am sad."
But now that they have put in central heating and gas and
Aldous's very special light-bulbs, it really ought to be quite satisfactory. And there is the good news that Matthew has just had his
degree at Berkeley, "an excellent degree . . one couldn't do better.
I am proud and happy." *But*: Matthew got himself involved with
a woman who adores him and he not, "and he doesn't seem to
be able to get rid of her." And Aldous has been in a muddle over
the dramatic rights of the *Gioconda*. It is sorting itself out but
has made him nervous and tired. And he had strained his heart
again in the autumn and doesn't seem to get over it. Maria's
next letter a week later is even more discouraged. Aldous has a
toothache, his general health *is* low and Wrightwood so ugly and
the house uncomfortable and too small and there is no proper
help. "I often ask myself why life should be so complicated for
two people of simple tastes who are rich and free? It must be
our fault somehow . . . If only Aldous would take a secretary or
perhaps a taxi once in a while . . . But then we've just been
spending so much on this house . . . I try my best to *feel* as reasonable as I appear and keep telling myself that even if we are going
to live here for the rest of our days, time passes quickly. Too
quickly to waste it over the hundred and one things I do . . .
Forgive this letter . . it's only to you that I dare open my heart . . .
It must be largely fatigue. I'm constantly struggling with details:
you see, Aldous *will* not have anything to do with practical and
financial matters. He doesn't want to talk about them, he doesn't
want to *think* about them . . . And yet he has an excellent practical
intelligence on the rare occasions he chooses to employ it." Now
they've been asked to go to Russia for the Quakers. So interesting
. . . "I should like to go; with Matthew for instance. But for Aldous
at the moment it's out of the question."

Jeanne for her part was in London. She had not returned to
journalism after the war but had decided, on Aldous's advice, to
acquire an entirely new trade. Her little girl Noële had begun
life with defective sight, she had been able to help her with the
techniques from *The Art of Seeing*, and so became interested in the
wider applications of the method. Now she had gone to be trained
as a Bates teacher by the Misses Scarlett, who were practising in
Portman Square (with Aldous and Maria commenting on her
every step from California). In a third and even more open letter,
Maria admitted that she herself was taking Bates lessons again
as she had been seeing very badly. "Reading lately has been
torture.

How well I understand what you say about nervous fatigue . .
Sometimes I have the sensation that if I were pushed a little further,

or a little faster, I would go mad. Whereas I *can* cope with physical fatigue. I have no longer any trace of tuberculosis and though I definitely strained my heart several times this winter, I seem to have recovered from both these troubles. (Obviously, you must not say a word of this to *anybody*, so don't even refer to it in your letters . . . I couldn't bear the offers of advice and help . . . Je m'arrange très bien pour me soigner en secret.)

What with a house in the country and a flat in town and Aldous the most absent-minded of men, this isn't too difficult.

. . Il est si bon et si affectueux que toute ma vie en est comblée. Mais la fatigue causée par les êtres humains m'est insupportable et insurmontable. Une promenade m'est *tout*. This, by the way, is one of the reasons why I'm so afraid of a journey to Europe. Which in any case is out of the question for me for at least another year . . .

How she envies Jeanne. To be able to do work of one's own. Whereas, "I don't see how I can ever stop being general maid. If we lived in Los Angeles all year round, we could have domestic help; even here we could." It's the double existence, one day here and one day there, "it's our love of LIBERTY that makes me a slave. So I cannot complain . . it's voluntary . . and so calm to be alone all day and so nice to be à nous deux at night . . . And now I must go to bed.

Je vais me coucher tout en sachant que je ne verrai même pas les trois étoiles habituelles . . . je me souviens qu'un hiver à Londres dans un troisième étage d'hôpital je me suis liée intimement avec le haut d'un arbre denudé, sur un ciel rose de brouillard . . la beauté de cet arbre était intense et amical. On peut trouver son plaisir partout et toujours.

Meanwhile Aldous was still struggling with *The Gioconda Smile*: ". . this translation and development of an old theme", he wrote to Leon M. Lion who had produced *The World of Light* in London, "into and through two different media . . a play and also a movie script . . ." He was finding it interesting as a literary problem but was growing tired of "the endless jig-saw puzzle and carpentry work . . . Also . . one gets tired . . of having to express everything in terms of dialogue. This would be all right if one were Shakespeare . . . But not being Shakespeare, and working in the realistic medium of the modern play, one has to stick to conversational verisimilitude and to be, therefore, even less poetical than one is capable of being in narrative . . ." Aldous had not yet had any theatrical opinion, but feels that he has learnt a good deal by the current experiment and will not, in future, "make as many obvious mistakes as I made in my first essays."

And then this job is done and Aldous's health is better and his mood is gay. On their evening walk he tells Maria that this morning, 19th March, he has sat down to his new novel. He speaks about it with passion. Fourteenth-century Italy, the age of *Decameron*, the Black Death, the condottieri, Sienese painting . . . "Petrarch will be a character in the novel . . disguised, of course . . and Catherine of Siena . . . The real saints, Aldous says, are so much more improbable than anything one could invent.

> It must be sad for him [Maria to Jeanne] to talk to someone who knows so little about the fourteenth century . . . But he assured me that he never misses his brilliant friends . . . He doesn't want conversational fireworks any more . . . Aldous, you know, has become a very remarkable human being . . . I wish you knew him now.
>
> But often we just have fun on our walks, or we're silent; today was different.

Only a few days later, Aldous has his doubts, he wonders whether he knows enough about the period. "Going to the other extreme," he writes to Anita, "I think perhaps I may write something about the future instead . . a post-atomic-war society in which the chief effect of the gamma radiations had been to produce a race of men and women who don't make love all the year round, but have a brief mating season. The effect of this on politics, religion, ethics etc. would be something very interesting and amusing to work out."

Aldous had just signed his ninth three-year agreement with Chatto & Windus. The eighth in 1944 had been identical with the seventh in 1941—no fixed number of books, no annual advance. Now there was one last change: a flat royalty rate of 20% on non-fiction as well as fiction. He and Chatto's continued to enter into an agreement every three years for the rest of Aldous's life. The terms never changed and I shall not refer to the matter again.

In April Maria was still very dejected. "Aldous tells me that my spirit is broken. It happened slowly but surely . . . whenever I dare hope to have some time to myself, or allow myself some personal interest, I am punished. Whenever I relax my tension vis à vis of Aldous, he falls ill or over-tires himself or something . . ." On 9th May Aldous left Wrightwood and his desk—he is on salary again, this time at $1,560 a week. They are going to shoot the *Gioconda* this summer with Zoltan Korda directing and Charles Boyer in the principal part.

Matthew had prospects of a job in the East and was ready for a change of scene. His young woman was still clinging. Aldous himself took a hand in engineering a smooth and sudden departure. One dead of night, Matthew, solo, was sent off in his car to New York with parental blessings. On arrival, at Suzanne's, he found a letter of admonishment from his mama:

> . . It is an encouragement to marriage to keep such an affair going . . . the minute it becomes as domestic you give hopes . . . Remember that for the future and I hope this chapter is closed and that you are already in the arms of a plump, gay and unfaithful blond!

She also advised him to write only once, ". . that is, an answer to the first letter she will probably send after the break."

Claire Nicolas was officially engaged now to Bobby White, the grandson of the late Stanford White, the New York architect. "An aristocratic family, in the American sense," Maria wrote, "which means among other things, well brought-up . . important after all . . . Bobby is charming and has an enormous talent . . ." The wedding was in July. The Huxleys did not go because of Aldous's work at the film studio, which was expected to go on all summer; besides "we have less and less desire to travel."

Aldous had some recent news of T. S. Eliot from Ted McKnight Kauffer whom he answered, "I'm glad Tom Eliot was well when you saw him.

> He is a man for whom I have always had a great affection, (though I have never been very intimate with him, in spite of nearly thirty years of acquaintance) as well as a profound admiration.

In July Maria wrote to Matthew, "Strange, sad news—Gerald has said that God's will was to end Trabuco and Trabuco ended . . .

> A very nice man called Kelly came to tea and told us all about it . . . He spoke with no resentment or judgement. But there is no doubt that Gerald really made a mess of the whole thing, chiefly by having favourites and then dropping them to take up another and so often making the dropped favourite despair of everything and leave Trabuco and God; forgetting that God and Gerald were not the same thing.
> . . Peggy had heard vaguely and did not know it had happened yet. It transpired that Gerald was even more of an autocrat than we had thought: and more self-satisfied too . . .
> It is sad . . . Poor Gerald, I suppose.

Seen from the side lines it makes a queer story. Perhaps Gerald Heard's[1] biographer will be able to sort it out clearly and charitably one day. Trabuco itself was eventually acquired by the Vedanta Society.

By September the *Gioconda* film was done and Aldous pleased with the final version which, "thanks to the untiring resourcefulness of Zoltan Korda, came through the cutting rooms without losing anything from any of the essential scenes [To Gervas]." The one unfortunate thing was that the title had been changed, as nobody was supposed to have heard of the *Gioconda*. "The all-powerful Jewish gentlemen in charge of distribution have elected to call the thing *A Woman's Vengeance*, and there's nothing to be done about it." To his brother-in-law, Georges Neveux, Aldous wrote a detailed description of the cast in which he said, "Boyer a su créer une atmosphère de tendresse très simple et sans aucune sentimentalité." (Neveux—author of *Plainte contre Inconnu*, *Zamore*, etc., adapter of the French dramatic version of *Anne Frank's Diary*—was for his part translating and tailoring Aldous's *Gioconda* play.)

In the course of the year Aldous wrote an article, "The Double Crisis", some 10,000 words long, about a subject to which even politicians and industrialists have since had to pay at least lip-service. Twenty-five years ago very few people thought about it or considered it worth thinking about. The subject is ecology. The human race, Aldous postulated already then, is passing through a time of demographic and ecological crisis. There were in fact, he said, two crises—a political and economic crisis of which we were conscious and which was being discussed, and a crisis in population and world resources of which "hardly anything is heard in the press, on the radio or at the more important international conferences. The Big Three or Four hardly deign to discuss it . . ." Indeed so feeble was the interest that Aldous had some difficulty in getting the article placed. One editor of a large-circulation magazine turned it down with the private comment that its hot air content was high. What Aldous was insisting on was (*a*) that world resources were inadequate to world population, (*b*) that world population was rising, (*c*) that the discernible upper level problems could not be solved without reference to the problems that were shaping up in the cosmic and biological basement.

. . *Après moi le déluge*. Industrialism is the systematic exploitation of wasting assets. In all too many cases, the thing we call progress is

---

[1] He died in California in the summer of 1971.

merely an acceleration in the rate of that exploitation. Such prosperity as we have known up to the present is the consequence of rapidly spending the planet's irreplaceable capital.

Sooner or later mankind will be forced by the pressure of circumstances to take concerted action against its own destructive and suicidal tendencies. The longer such action is postponed, the worse it will be for all concerned . . . Overpopulation and erosion constitute a Martian invasion of the planet . . .

. . . Treat Nature aggressively, with greed and violence and incomprehension: wounded Nature will turn and destroy you . . . if, presumptuously imagining that we can "conquer" Nature, we continue to live on our planet like a swarm of destructive parasites— we condemn ourselves and our children to misery and deepening squalor and the despair that finds expression in the frenzies of collective violence.[1]

1 "The Double Crisis", first published in *World Review*, 1948, republished in *Themes and Variations*. Chatto & Windus, 1950.

## Chapter Two

## Reversions

AND then they do decide to go to New York—Aldous's first move after nine and a half solid years of California. They left on 15th September, by car of course, staying with Frieda on the way. A month later Maria writes to Rosalind from West 59th street: "We are not lost or dead or even tired. We are simply having a wonderful adventure on this glorious Eastern shore.

> . . The journey was fascinating . . usually it had been winter when I drove across . . . The climate was kind; the trees green and heavy with fruit and there were flowers in little old-fashioned gardens. We right away forgot the West and the deserts.
> . . We are far from that now. Because we also drove through the large cities which always have parks and rivers for the rich and slums and smoke for the poor . . . Then New York was horribly disappointing at first because our large-roomed and beautiful flat is also horribly old, dilapidated and not organized for a tidy person such as myself. By now, of course, all is perfect. The view over all the roofs and the sun pouring in is what matters most.
> May I tell you that I have an absolute horror of California. I would not mind if I never went back . . . *nothing* there holds me, nothing invites me back. And I would have no more qualms if I lost Wrightwood with the books and the kitchen than I had when the house in the South of France went . . . Seen from here . . it seems quite a mad life. Not the years at Llano. Those were peaceful.
> . . I can't tell you how well Aldous is. [The life] we are leading . . is very far from our lazy, now I almost think self-indulgent California life. He seems stimulated by the climate, the people and things.

In the morning Aldous went down and had breakfast at the Automat where he could get tea and porridge. Victoria Ocampo was in New York. He ran into John Gielgud—who was playing opposite Judith Anderson[1]—"looking romantically battered." There were Julian and Juliette—on their way to a Unesco Conference in Mexico—Julian "better and more relaxed than I had expected he would be under the strain of his job . . ." There was an unexpected meeting with Gervas, travelling on tea business

---

[1] In Robinson Jeffers' adaptation of *Medea*. Gielgud played Jason, Miss Anderson, Medea.

and "nicer than ever"; and when those six united Huxleys—
Gervas, J. & J., Aldous, Maria, Matthew—were having dinner
at a restaurant, in walked their young cousin Jill, arrived that
afternoon from England with another party (promptly abandoned). She found Aldous rounded out, "much less up in the
air than he used to be . . ." And Gervas found that he still had
"that tremendous zest—that gift of being interested in everything—almost too much so . . . But the lovely air with which he
talked and talked about all those things . . . One wasn't frightened
by that extraordinary knowledge he had—he brought one *into* it
—did you feel that? And people think of him as aloof. He wasn't
really, you know. *He was more and more concerned.* And how nice
Matthew was to him—I took a very good view of Matthew."
(Who was about to start a job with the Elmo Roper polls and
had found himself a nice apartment in the West Seventies.)

Fridays to Tuesdays Aldous and Maria spent at the Nicolases'
who now lived at Islip, on the South shore of Long Island. "Today
[13th October] is Sunday at Suzanne's. Victoria and her sister
came for the day and are resting . . .

It is a very large house, full of their paintings . . and so very comfortable as well as agreeable . . . We walk to the sea and in the parks
of the neighbouring houses . . . Claire is living a charming life; the
husband sculpts, she writes . . and their house is a small one standing
on the estate of their parents [the Stanford Whites] whose grandfather owned and built the mansion—everything is so much more
like Europe; it might bore me later—so far it is like being at home;
I meet old-fashioned English people who might be all Aldous's
aunts; and very intelligent and sober at that.

I like the different look the faces have in the street, and the vacuity
of the faces of Los Angeles crowds grows more and more so in
retrospective. However, all this does not mean that we are here for
ever. Aldous has a novel to finish; and after all I have a house . . . I
wonder about the apples. Rose wrote there are a great many . . now
is the time to pick them . . . It seemed to me always ridiculous that
people should need holidays . . . until America put me to work. So
now I am having what every American woman talks about—and
enjoying every minute of it . . . Wonderful also to be so near Europe
that all I have to do is walk into a grocery or Bloomingdale, order
the food for Europe and it is gone. No weighing and strings and
papers to glue. It seems so easy and I feel so near! Near what is
difficult to tell you.

The dam is broken, they are up to their plans again. Thinking
of the Argentine: "Victoria has often asked us. Now we shall go."
But the ships are booked up till the autumn of 1948. So they think

of taking the car and crossing Central America from the Pacific. "Would it tempt you?"

They left the East in the middle of November. On 3rd December Maria wrote to Matthew from the Los Angeles flat.

Darling Matthew, I want to tell you that Aldous is wonderfully well, full of spirits and "happy to be back". I don't mind about "being back" because it is now so obvious that I must revolutionize our life that all will be well in the end. For that reason alone I am glad we went. I was slowly getting obsédée by the narrowing of my life . . . now I give it no more thought because it will change. Not suddenly, that it can't, but it will.

So think of us quite happy here. Aldous is working well [on the post-atomic-war novel; Catherine of Siena abandoned] and reading quite a bit in spite of going to Mrs Corbett every day and I go to Miss MacGavin [one of Mrs C's assistants] every day. You see, I already indulge myself too . . . Aldous also goes to [Dr?] Leaf every day; there is no doubt that . . . treatment is immediately resultful for Aldous's coughs. That time it was the allergic cough, this time it is the last bit of bronchitis which left after two treatments; but Aldous goes every day of this week all the same. There have been dentists too . . .

In the evenings they are being very gay.

Monday night dined at Constance's [Constance Collier] who risked having the Chaplins and the Colmans. Charlie always refused to see Ronnie. While Ronnie has a rather sentimental admiration and love for Charlie. Charlie very Left and provocative and Ronnie very Right but never picked up the gloves Charlie threw quite unnecessarily several times—people have such a need to air their views always. But all went well; they were very polite to each other at first but luckily their children are of the same age and play together. So very soon that table of old people (except Oona) was dotingly talking of their children . . . Aldous and I could not get a word in about you because you were definitely out of date. Then Charlie did the usual acting but with much tact and let Ronnie tell and act (very badly and shyly) about his Othello film. Charlie was stupendous doing the Chopin film . . .
Benita [Colman] very beautiful in her plantureuse way and not ashamed of being the Juno type; beautifully dressed in the only dress I admired in New York in a Saks window . . Her warm voice, her healthy laughter . . and the kindness with which she extremely tactfully brings Ronnie out and to the fore. They are

obviously two very happy ménages. And all under the grand wing of Constance . . . And Aldous ate a slice of ham . . .

Yesterday we stayed at home, today we had a most delightful dinner with the Stravinskys. Berman[1] only there . . And I must say it was delightful to listen to Stravinsky. He pours out—what pours is very intelligent—it is often very new—sometimes quite difficult to explain but always immensely worth listening to and the French, not perfect, is intelligent and colourful. There were also books, and reproductions; and everything. A vegetarian dinner for Aldous, just right, simple, good. She is so easy and very nice. Berman, I don't know. Clever, certainly. He showed us a whole book of drawings from Mexico. Competent, but not nice. Somehow—méchant. An unpleasant line, harshness . . But the house is nice, easy, straggling, full of things . . . Stravinsky is so extremely polite, I suppose the old school of politeness but quite all right and unnoticeable at the same time. Then suddenly at ten, they asked me if I wanted some champagne? It startled me so much. Of course I said no, so did Aldous, but when they opened it all the same we of course had it and it was such a symbolic thing somehow. We quite easily and unostentatiously drank each others health—but I felt it was a gracious act of hospitality and also a gesture of particular friendship. I believe they have real friendship for us. We like them very much.

And who else do you think has come back into our life—Gerald. Not only physically (he has bought a house in the Valley, where Ventura and Sepulveda meet) but actually he has already asked Aldous twice to go for walks with him. And he is so nice and there is so much of the old Gerald in him *without* the old tension in the hands and eyes! So we are very happy about that . . Dear Gerald, perhaps he has gone through enough hell by now.

. . . I realized more and more during the journey how little I liked California. Even the sun I loathe and it gives me head-aches and the way of life with distances one cannot walk, with help who will only work eight hours a day [or not at all] . . . It is very unfair because the sun is wonderful for Aldous's eyes. He knows it. But Mrs Corbett says the eyes are very good and that the holiday did him, the eyes, a lot of good. Aldous says no; so I suppose he knows best . . He lost a bit of weight . . now he has porridge every morning because I noticed he liked it at the blessed automat.

. . We have not started readings yet. We shall get a gramophone tomorrow to take with us. Both Peggy and Stravinsky recommend a small portable Philco which Aldous heard in the shop and liked so don't criticize it to him. I hope it has *volume* because that matters so much to Aldous that it makes the neighbours' life intolerable . . . Good bye my darling. I wish I were Suzanne and saw you for weekends!

---

1 Eugene Berman, the Russian painter and stage designer.

Then after two weeks of Wrightwood, Maria wrote to Matthew again: "This is a letter to ask you to help me . . .

. . My behaviour during the last five years has become apparent to me . . . for some unknown reason I have been piling upon myself a kind of punishment which took the form of work, physical work that is. I should have realized that indirectly it was a much greater punishment on Aldous who thereby lost help for his own work. When we cleared out of the desert I thought we got out of the situation; but because I had not understood my own psychological reasons, or because there were some unconscious reasons as well . . the situation remained the same.

Because I personally disliked Wrightwood and all mountains I punished myself by trying to live here for Aldous's sake. It is now clear that Wrightwood is going to be a much greater burden than Llano because not only do we both feel the altitude but because the snow and ice make an extra problem . . We have to keep [the house] warm all the time so that it does not freeze. I can rely on no one for friendship or money to turn everything on and off. No one . . has time to be conscientious . . . We made a mistake when we thought we could find help here . . . Even if we could find help, that fact that we live irregularly means we have to pay it for doing nothing . . . or not get it when we want it . . . The same problem in town; the laundry cannot call, the milk neither . . .

We are doubling expenses of living, that is evident. We have here a great capital engaged which would have been well employed if we had been living here most of the time. The house is superbly equipped for permanent residence. *But*, Aldous needs to work for the movies to make a living—he says so in so many words. When there is snow we don't wish to live here, when it is too cold we don't wish to live here. When we *do* live here we are always rushing to town [the best of two hours' drive] for my dentist or Aldous's or something. It is restless . . . For a long time I have felt it catching up with me. For a long time I have told all of you in a joke or in despair that I was going mad; mad or ill, it will be one or the other and now I know it and I told Aldous and we are going to sell Wrightwood.

We must centralize our efforts . . . It will be very hard to find a house in town. It may even be entirely too expensive. But this time I hope I will remember that perfection is out of the question. That I must stick to essentials. Aldous's needs. That I do not need a wonderful kitchen . . . The entire mistake in this house is that I perfected it so that I could run it. I am through with running houses myself. We shall take holidays in expensive hotels . . This habit of economizing on ourselves is ludicrous. And my freedom, my strength, my gaiety are really Aldous's. So I am going to indulge in it. While I punished myself he bore the consequences. Why I have felt the need of punishing myself is fairly clear to me, no need to waste time over it; stupidity, selfishness and misunderstanding are at the base of it.

(By the way, do not think I am ill—[Dr] Hawkins thinks me better than I have been for a long time, so all I do is preventive. Hawkins is *very* clever with me in many ways I notice . .) But to remain well, I know better than any doctor can tell me, that *I must stop.* Just as I knew better than any doctor, when I was young, that I was not going to die unless I did stop. You can trust me to keep fit for Aldous's sake.

In town we shall need something like the house on Crescent Heights. Everyone is very kind and will help. Peggy and Bill [Kiskadden] understand. And Stravinsky has been curiously kind and considerate to me; gone out of his way to be kind about nothing in particular as though he had a second sight about my despair. Because despair it was . . .

Now come figures about what Wrightwood has already cost them. Bills for 20,000 dollars. "Plus all we forget. Shall we ever get it back? We are incapable fools.

. . . Please wish them all a happy Christmas . . Don't spend too much on anyone. You are not rich and we are not either. Aldous has to earn every penny of it.

Then it is Aldous who goes on, in hand-writing, on the same page:

Dearest M, I know you will approve this necessary decision. The next problem is to find something in town . . .

We saw "Monsieur Verdoux" the other day. What an aesthetic mess! He passes from a mime about murder which depends on *not* being taken seriously, to attempts at serious psychology which are supposed to be taken seriously & consequently make the murder-farce seem intolerable—because after all murder once removed from the world of childish make-believe, is not conceivably a subject for comedy. One feels terribly sorry for Charlie—such talents, such a mess—in art no less than in life. And all because he refuses to take anyone's advice about anything, but believing that, like the Pope, he is infallible.

Love from

Aldous

(Here one might note that Chaplin, in his autobiography, records that Thomas Mann and Lion Feuchtwanger gave him a standing ovation at this same private showing of *Monsieur Verdoux*.)

Aldous published no new book in 1947; Harper's, however, brought out *The World of Aldous Huxley: An Omnibus of His Fiction and Non-Fiction Over Three Decades* with an introduction by Charles J. Rolo, and Suzanne's bust of Aldous on the cover. And in February 1948, both Chatto's and Harper's published the *Gioconda* play (Harper's, confusingly, under yet another previous title, *Mortal Coils*).

In January Aldous gave a quote to the publishers of *Our Plundered Planet* and at the same time wrote to Fairfield Osborn, the author: "The great question now is: will the public and those in authority pay any attention to what you say, or will the politicians go on with their lunatic game, . . ignoring the fact that the world they are squabbling over will shortly cease to exist in its old familiar form, but will be transformed, unless they mobilize all available intelligence and . . good will, into one huge dust bowl . . .

I have been trying to put this question . . for the last year or two—even succeeding in planting it in the *Bulletin of the Atomic Scientists* this summer, pointing out that, while mankind could do very well without atomic energy, it cannot dispense with bread. But hitherto I have had no audible response from any quarter. I hope very much that you, with your scientific authority and your beautifully organized collection of facts, will be able to make some impression in influential quarters . . .

. . I see this problem of man's relation to Nature as not only an immediate practical problem, but also as a problem of ethics and religion. It is significant that neither Christianity nor Judaism has ever thought of Nature as having rights in relation to man : . You will find orthodox Catholic moralists asserting . . that animals may be treated as things. (As though things didn't deserve to be treated ethically!) The vulgar boast of the modern technologist . . that man has conquered Nature has roots in the Western religious tradition, which affirms that God installed man as the boss, to whom Nature was to bring tribute. The Greeks knew better than the Jews and Christians. They knew [about] hubris towards nature . . . Xerxes is punished, not only for having attacked the Greeks, but also for having outraged Nature in the affair of bridging the Hellespont.

But for an ethical system that includes animate and inanimate Nature as well as man, one must go to Chinese Taoism, with its concept of an Order of Things, whose state of . . balance must be preserved . . . Whitman comes very close to the Taoist position. And because of Whitman and Wordsworth and the other "Nature Mystics" of the West, I feel that it might not be too difficult for modern Europeans and Americans to accept some kind of Taoist philosophy of life, with an ethical system comprehensive enough to take in Nature as well as man. People have got to understand that the commandment, "Do unto others as you would that they should do unto you" applies to animals, plants and things, as well as to people; and that if it is regarded as applying only to people . . then the animals, plants and things will, in one way or another, do as badly by man as man has done by them . . .

On the 22nd of February 1948, Maria wrote to Matthew:

I must tell you of a great event—the book was finished last night. Aldous arrived in the kitchen saying he was late for dinner, which I had not realized, and then, walking around as you know he does, he suddenly said, "I think I finished the book!"

It was *Ape and Essence,* his second Utopia, the gruesome Utopia set in an enclave of survivors after atomic war.

. . I decided I would read it all night. Take coffee and then take the manuscript to bed. Of course Aldous said no and silly and so on. But after dinner he asked me, "We might read it aloud if you like." This is the first time he allowed me to read anything [of his] aloud, except the play.

And then we settled down in our first class carriages. Aldous's is long and comfortable and he can stretch out, but usually I wriggle and get cramps because mine is that silly short green sofa . . but the first time I moved was at page 70 and Aldous thought of going to bed which I would not—he gave in easily and we finished at one thirty. It read for four hours and a quarter without a lag of interest . . .

My feeling was awe when I had finished. Not fear and horror . . that was coming in waves during the reading; but awe at the possibilities and at Aldous. He looked so well and pink and rested from lying down . . in his blue jersey and the cotton blue shirt . . Though he so often looks old now he looked young and a bit shy and pleased: you know his air of a little boy. Honest, innocent, humble and so clever and knowing so much.

. . All you have been told about [the book was] the destructive side, and it is also constructive. It is also in a very interesting medium. The scenario form giving room for very beautiful descriptions of nature, for music, for poetry. Excellent medium for cutting out all that he does not actually need and for getting in, via the narrator, all he needs to say. Then also a very clever use of the religion that prevails. But I won't spoil it. I shall have an extra copy made and sent to you at once . . .

Aldous is so sweet. When we had finished I was dazed of course, I had . . a violent head-ache in the eyes . . and I felt sick. All I could say was, "Well, I am impressed."

But when I came up with my hot-water bottles he was walking around still in his blue jersey and asked, "What do you think of it? Is anything wrong? Must I change anything?" "No!" Most emphatically . . . Not that I am a good judge but often my quick reactions do help him to see something. His corrections go farther and deeper than I can see for myself. But this . . size, shape, form . . is absolutely perfect.

At first the typescript made me halt and read it badly; I was also nervous—that I would spoil it for him. But then . . I got so deeply interested that it read well and fluently... I had not even remembered to drink any coffee . . . Oh, and when I think what I am made to read sometimes. Those interesting books so buried in twaddly language. Or those odious personalities coming through what they say about others . . .

I suggest you read it when you have *time* . . not at night, when you have been tired . . If you had someone to read it with it would add to the pleasure I believe. Aldous enjoyed my reading of it; I am astonished he often says he likes the way I read—*when* I read properly. Knowing him so well and every thought and his language too, I suppose it was much as he thinks it aloud. I suppose about forty or fifty-thousand words.

*Ape and Essence*—the form, a scenario (a rejected script rescued on its way to the studio incinerator); the time, the post-atomic twenty-first century; the setting, the Los Angeles plain. "Dissolve to street: under the porches of ruined filling-stations lie heaps of human bones . . ." "Cut to medium close shot of the Unholy of Unholies . . ." It is some decades since the Bomb, "the Thing", has wasted most of our known world; active radiation has ceased, but food is still short, and everything else. The books from the former L.A. Public Library are used to stoke communal ovens; labour gangs dig up and plunder the corpses of the dead. Four babies out of five are born deformed and are destroyed (and their mothers savagely punished); sex is loathed and feared, only periodical public orgies are permitted by Church and State.

> *But man, proud man,*
> *Drest in a little brief authority—*
> *Most ignorant of what he's most assur'd,*
> *His glassy essence—like an angry ape,*
> *Plays such fantastic tricks before high heaven*
> *As make the angels weep.*

The state religion is a cult of Belial, government absolute by a hierarchy of castrated priests. The Arch-Vicar, a figure reminiscent of the Controller in *Brave New World*, explains the new theology to the explorer from unbombed New Zealand. All things foreseen by Belial inevitably come to pass:

> "The overcrowding of the planet . . . the land . . ruined by bad farming. Everywhere erosion . . the deserts spreading, the forests dwindling. Even in America, even in that New World which was once the hope of the Old . . . Bigger and better, richer and more powerful—and then, almost suddenly, hungrier and hungrier. Yes, Belial foresaw it all . . . The New Hunger . . of enormous industrialized proletariats, the hunger of city-dwellers with money, with all the modern conveniences, with cars and radios, . . the hunger that is the cause of total wars and the total wars that are the cause of yet more hunger."

And remember this, the Arch-Vicar adds,

> ". . even without the atomic bomb, Belial could have achieved all his purposes. A little more slowly perhaps . . men would have destroyed themselves by destroying the world they lived in . . . From the very beginning of the industrial revolution He foresaw that men would be made so overwhelmingly bumptious by the miracles of their own technology that they would soon lose all sense of reality. And that's precisely what happened. These wretched slaves of wheels and ledgers began to congratulate themselves on being the Conquerors of Nature. Conquerors of Nature, indeed! In actual fact, of course, they had merely upset the equilibrium of Nature and were about to suffer the consequences. Just consider what they were up to during the century and a half before the Thing. Fouling the rivers, killing off the wild animals, destroying the forests, washing the topsoil into the sea, burning up an ocean of petroleum, squandering the minerals it had taken the whole of geological time to deposit. An orgy of criminal imbecility. And they called it progress. Progress! . . . Progress and Nationalism—those were the two great ideas He put into their heads . . ."

You mean, you think—it was the *Devil*? says the explorer from New Zealand.

> "Who else desires the degradation and destruction of the human race?"
>
> "Quite, quite," Dr Poole protests. "But all the same, as a Protestant Christian, I really can't . . ."
>
> ". . Well, what are the facts? . . Nobody wants to suffer, wants to be

degraded, wants to be maimed or killed . . [yet] the overwhelming majority of human beings accepted beliefs and adopted courses of action that could not possibly result in anything but universal suffering . . The only plausible explanation is that they were inspired or possessed by an alien consciousness . . .

". . consider all the other evidence. Take the First World War, for example. If the people and the politicians hadn't been possessed, they'd have listened to Benedict XV or Lord Lansdowne—they'd have come to terms, they'd have negotiated a peace without victory; but they couldn't, they couldn't. It was impossible for them to act in their own self-interest . . the Belial in them wanted the Communist Revolution, wanted the Fascist reaction . . wanted Mussolini and Hitler and the Politburo, wanted famine, inflation and depression; wanted armaments as a cure for unemployment; wanted the persecution of the Jews and the Kulaks; wanted the Nazis and the Communists to divide Poland and then go to war with one another. Yes . . He wanted concentration camps and gas chambers and cremation ovens. He wanted saturation bombing (what a deliciously juicy phrase!); He wanted the destruction overnight of a century's accumulation of wealth and all the potentialities of future prosperity, decency, freedom and culture. Belial wanted all this, and, being the Great Blowfly in the hearts of the politicians and generals, the journalists and the Common Man, He was easily able to get the Pope ignored even by Catholics, to have Lansdowne condemned as a bad patriot, almost a traitor. And so the war dragged on for four whole years; and afterwards everything went punctually according to plan . . . men and women became progressively more docile to the leadings of the Unholy Spirit. The old beliefs in the value of the individual human soul faded away; the old restraints lost their effectiveness; the old compunctions and compassions evaporated. Everything that the Other One had ever put into people's heads oozed out, and the resulting vacuum was filled by the lunatic dreams of Progress and Nationalism . . ."

The Arch-Vicar chuckles shrilly.

". . Take the scientists, for example. Good, well-meaning men, for the most part. But He got hold of them all the same—got hold of them at the point where they ceased to be human beings and became specialists. Hence . . those bombs . . .
". . And finally, of course, there was the Thing. Unconditional surrender and bang! . . ."

The Post-the-Thing community in *Ape and Essence* is unspeakably bestial, unspeakably horrible. Affection, joy, compassion have withered, only hunger, fear, lust, cruelty, malicious glee are left. Aldous strained to pile horror upon crass horror—the narrator's blank verse, the Arch-Vicar's donnish discourse, alternate with scenes of orgies, whippings, cruel ritual, presented in the harsh distorting medium of black musical comedy. The book, it always seemed to me, achieves a high degree of unbearableness. Unbearable: is it correspondingly effective? (It appears to be very much so among American students today, the one book by Huxley to which the majority of them profess itself to be able to "relate". Matthew, in his own twenties at the time he read the advance copy, recoiled and wrote a long argumentative letter to his father.) Aldous wrote the book as a warning—*this* is what human beings are capable of becoming, *this* is the degradation we may reach . . . Yet beside the undoubted element of prophecy, there is also one of hindsight in *Ape and Essence*. Aldous chose to postulate (with all the artifice this entailed) his diabolical community in the future. Why? Unutterably horrible though they are, the doings of those post-atomic apes of California don't come near the toll of pain, waste and final human outrage that had already happened in places such as Auschwitz.

Maria said that she looked with awe at Aldous. It is hard to imagine her reading this book to Aldous, stretched out on their long chairs in their wooden house at Wrightwood, hard to imagine Aldous asking for this particular book to be read to him. One must suppose that if he could bear to write it, he could bear to hear it. Did Maria protest too much about the pleasures of that reading?

# Chapter Three

## "As If We Had Never Left"

ALDOUS and Maria were at Wrightwood; Aldous, not ready to embark upon another book, thinking about a film. "On Saturday Anita, Paulette [divorced from Chaplin, remarried to the actor Burgess Meredith], Burgess and the Huckles came out to lunch [Maria on 12th April] . . because Burgess wants to make a scientific film on hypnotism, Aldous to write the story. Aldous saw demonstrations here by a man who uses hypnotism to short-cut psychoanalysis and deals very successfully with sleep." Meanwhile Zoltan Korda proposed a script of another old short story of Aldous's, "The Rest Cure" from *Brief Candles*, to be filmed, if all went well, with Michèle Morgan, Alexander Korda putting up the money. And after that perhaps, they might do *Point Counter Point* . . .

> Aldous is entirely thinking and behaving as if we had never mentioned selling Wrightwood. [Maria to Matthew] So I let him be. If he likes it that much—Well, I'm quite prepared to enjoy its good sides . . . Please do not mention this. I know when it is dangerous to disturb Aldous. This is one of those times. If I bothered him about selling the house or reminding him of it, he might have a new type of allergy or something else which would necessitate an immediate and prolonged stay at Wrightwood. Do we know what tricks we play on ourselves?

Tricks or not, a couple of weeks later Aldous went down with virus pneumonia. This, however, was efficiently dealt with and for once did not seem to bring an aftermath. Nor did it interfere with the plans which sprang up like a sudden wind. The Korda brothers decided that Aldous should write the screen play of "The Rest Cure" in Italy, paying for the story rights by financing his and Maria's journey. "The Rest Cure" was the elaboration of an anecdote that had happened to a woman who lived opposite Costanza Fasola's, and the Kordas wanted Aldous to give it an up-to-date Italian post-war background. Aldous said yes; Cunard promised a passage for mid-June. On the 10th they were at the St Regis Hotel in New York (Aldous attending a round table conference on modern art got up by *Life* Magazine.

Meanwhile *The Gioconda Smile* had opened at the New Theatre in London on 3rd June, with Clive Brook as Henry Hutton,

478

Pamela Brown as Janet Spence, Brenda Bruce as Doris Mead
and Noel Howlett as Dr Libbard. The notices were mixed (good
in the *Mail*, the *Standard* and the *Spectator*, poor in *The Times* and
the *New Statesman*).

Aldous and Maria sailed for Cherbourg on the *Queen Mary*. On
the second morning out Maria, after breakfast in bed and Aldous
standing by in a dressy suit, scribbled a note to Matthew, "My
Wild Western Bovarism did not really work." Dissolve and cut
to Jeanne Neveux's journal. Tuesday 29th June 1948.

> Ils arrivent! Nous sommes à la gare St Lazare. Georges, Sophie,
> Noële et moi. L'attente est longue, nous n'avons pas le droit d'aller
> sur les quais, et nous les guettons—Aldous est le plus grand.

There is Juliette, too, waiting by the exit. Cut to Georges Neveux's
journal.

> Enfin les voici. J'ai lu tant de lettres de Maria à Jeannot et si
> longtemps vecu au milieu des souvenirs et des livres d'Aldous à
> Sanary, que j'ai l'impression de les voir sortir non de l'inconnu,
> mais du fond de ma mémoire. Aldous ressemble assez à sa photo,
> Maria ressemble à Rose; même sourire, même conversation sautill-
> ante qui n'écoute jamais la réponse mais qui épie sur le visage de
> l'interlocuteur le reflet de ce qu'elle vient de dire.

They are borne off to the Neveuxes' flat in the rue Bonaparte,
between St Germain-des-Près and St Sulpice.

> Everybody is tired. We go to bed quite early. Maria is to have our
> room (Jeannot and I moving into my study) and Aldous to sleep in
> Noële's room . . . Noële. Maria has given her a wristwatch. A real
> watch. Noële is very surprised to see the hands go round all the time.
> The idea of those hands never stopping disturbs her.

The Neveuxes ask in French writers who want to meet Aldous. "Il
est fêté." Maria goes off to see their old friend Mimi, Lewis
Gielgud's ex-wife, at Passy. Aldous and Georges are asked to do
a talk on the French Radio. It is to be recorded Sunday evening;
in the morning they rehearse.

> I suggest a number of questions to Aldous. He nearly always rejects
> them. He does not want to take too definite a position on any point.
> He is afraid of being cornered, pinned down like a butterfly on the
> cork of an idea. He slips through our fingers, takes wing, becomes
> vague, alternates.

And above all he dreads irony. Why? Because for so long he himself used to handle irony with such skill . . .

At last we manage to set up four large pages, a long dialogue which we copy out and read aloud in turn, straight-faced like two popes . . .

Afterwards they go out with Maria, are photographed outside the *Deux Magots*, look at the *Musée d'Art Moderne*. On the way back, Georges and Aldous go and have a look at the inside of the Church of St Sulpice and the frescos by Delacroix which seem to Aldous (and to Georges as well) *"bien emphatiques.*

On our return, Aldous becomes animated, smiles, charms. He recites Mallarmé, Rimbaud, Shelley. (Il a un certain respect devant l'obscurité poétique. Ça, c'est la zone sacrée, que son esprit scientifique n'a jamais pu entamer. Et c'est de cette zone là qu'est sorti son mysticisme actuel.) 5 Juillet. Il me parait d'une grande modestie naturelle. Et cette modestie n'est pas le revers d'un orgueil dissimulé, mais le complément, le gardien de son travail. Ça le dérange dans ses opérations intellectuelles de se sentir vu et commenté. Les articles qui paraissent sur lui, il ne les lit jamais. Le livre qui vient de paraître à Paris sur lui, je le lui ai acheté. Il l'a soupesé, regardé avec méfiance, et reposé. Il ne l'a pas lu—pas même feuilleté. Il m'explique que ça ne pourrait pas lui être utile.[1]

On 9th July, the evening French Radio broadcast the Huxley-Neveux conversation, Aldous and Maria left for Siena. Now Maria sends some scrawls to Matthew.

. . It is as if we had never left. There are two worlds, and will remain so . . . We don't miss the orange juice, the ice-water, the cellophane wrappings, we laugh at the flies in the streets, the smell of urine, the horse-dung . . I also hope that you will marry a European, selfishly but perhaps also for your pleasure: the difference is infinite and I think for the better.

. . Aldous is at his best for health but annoyed at having to work and it is a shame when you see the pleasure he gets out of wandering in streets and the churches and the museums and countryside . . . it seems more and more inconceivable to live in California. Jeanne

---

[1] Thus Aldous did not as much as cut the pages of a book about himself. Since the publication of this book in England, I am often asked about the effect on his work of adverse criticism of the calibre of Wyndham Lewis's devastating use of the first page of *Point Counter Point* in *Men Without Art* or Cyril Connolly's parody of *Eyeless in Gaza*. I am almost certain (one cannot prove a negative) that he never read either. "Were they kept from him then?" No. Aldous omitted to read about himself partly out of a protective instinct for his work (he would ask and take advice, but did not believe in the constructiveness of most published comment), partly out of natural incuriosity and detachment.

and Costanza made it so clear to me. Now I even doubt the only favourable angle—that is climate. For as they point out Aldous was *never* ill in Europe—and certainly this European climate, so much more temperate, has so far produced *no* allergy—*no* cough—*no* hives—*no* skin troubles and, what he minds most of all, *no* hayfever. Of course winters are cold, but again everyone agrees that with money one can buy fuel—no more black market, so no unpleasant business relations . . . So now there is our *great plan* for which we begin to prepare now—next May you either quit or ask for a six months vacation—so we three can leisurely explore Italy or maybe Spain. We take a new Ford with a four-shift gear box (essential) and an extra loud horn, and at the end of it we decide on where we should live—probably in Sanary . . . This is not considering politics— how can one—tell me what you think and that you will love it . . . I will buy you rings and belts and shirts, Aldous will adore to show you everything—it is touching to see how he enjoys it, every leisurely look at paintings and statues, and how gay and well he looks. Yet sad, because I notice how little he sees, and how much he deserves to see.

By chance Georges Neveux was also making a film in Italy and arrived in Rome with Jeanne and Noële. Aldous and Maria joined them on 2nd August. They stayed at the Hôtel de la Ville above the Spanish Steps, the Huxleys in a suite on the eighth floor (booked by the Rank organization) with a terrace of incomparable view.

The four of us dine at the Grappola d'Oro. [Georges Neveux's journal] We drink to our reunion. *"Enfin nous voici en Europe,"* says Maria. "In Europe at last." Which goes to show that for the Nys sisters Europe is Italy . . .
5th August. [Jeanne's diary] We dine at Professor Cherubini's (the Marquis de St Amour), Costanza's first lover . . .
18th August. Georges and Aldous . . dine in the charming little Trattoria of the Via del Boccaccio where the cinema people go, Rossellini, Magnani. Afterwards we go every day . . . 19th August. Maria has gone on a jaunt to Naples with Rina's sister . . .
19th August. [Georges] Never met—never imagined even—a being of such exquisite elegance of feeling. Aldous's inexhaustible *gentillesse*, so natural so light, that it becomes almost invisible . . .

On the 22nd Maria writes to Matthew, "I cannot tell you how happy we have been here . . . the ease of the country . . .

There are many drawbacks. Such as the inefficiency and the dishonesty which in Naples reaches a point that is haunting—but one does not have to live in Naples . . .

Jeanne and Georges. The more we go on the more we are united in friendship, tastes, views on life etc. and also with our love for the child whom they bring up without an error.

24th August [George's journal] Aldous is not well, Maria had to go to a dinner at the Boccaccio . . and he dines all alone, on his vast terrace above the illuminated city of Rome, off a biscuit and an apple out of a paper bag.

He's delighted to have a visitor . . lively, gracious, mischievous. He reminds me of an old comedian playing tricks on an invisible schoolmaster. But his cheeks look hollow and he must have had a bad day.

On the 28th they left together by bus for Sanary, spending the night in Genoa.

At Sanary, Aldous and Maria found a house waiting for them. When Jeanne had sold the impracticable Villa Huley during the war, she had saved furniture and books and re-arranged them in La Rustique, the new house she had bought for them. The curtains were hung, the walls had been re-painted in the old colours; Rina was there, come to look after them:

Darling, now we are really at home. [Maria to Matthew] This house is so like the other without the disadvantages, that we forget it is new. All our things are there—cups, plates, books—it all seems very natural. Same old mosquito nets over the same old beds. Large rooms. Divine bathing—effortless swimming in a temperate sea which is just right. Sun air water wind combine to spoil us. Rina runs the house; she took time off from her own in-laws . . . The people in the village ask after you, and Renée is just as ever—I like her as much—and so would you . . .

Sophie came to join them. In the evenings they read aloud. The letters of Mademoiselle de Lespinasse, Benjamin Constant, Diderot, Barbey d'Aurevilly, Novalis, Valéry, Baudelaire; Georges reading.

2nd September. [Georges] Aldous is installed on the terrace just outside his bedroom door. He is typing away at the end of his film.

4th September. Aldous has found a stack of canvases—his own paintings of fifteen years ago. Strange canvases . . . Evidence of his first effort towards the external world, towards contact . . . And now all day I hear the sound of hammering—Aldous and Maria hanging those paintings . . .

The one thing that really moved them was the discovery of their old walking sticks in the cellar which suddenly reminded them of all their walks in the past. And at once they set out on a long cross-country ramble.

Aldous and Noële adore each other. Yesterday Noële did her daily eye exercises under Jeanne's instruction. Aldous sat down beside her and, keeping time with her, went through exactly the same movements. A charming little scene . . .

10th September [Jeanne] Today in the lovely shady garden we fêted Coccola's 50 years.

Rina has made our stay a paradise of grace and comfort.

Walking sticks and canvases—there was something else that Aldous re-discovered. The year before he had published an article, "If My Library Burned Tonight".[1] "Fortunately for me, it never has," he wrote; "But I have moved house sufficiently often and have had enough book-borrowing friends . . to form a pretty good idea of the nature of the catastrophe." Happily, books are replaceable—at any rate the kind of books that filled the shelves of *his* library. Aldous had never had any use for the collector's point of view, or the collector's items.

> It is only about the contents of a book that I care, not its shape, its date or the number of its fly-leaves. Fire, friends and changes . . can never rob me of anything that cannot . . be restored in fullest measure.

Indeed; but what about such contents as one's annotations? What Aldous found again among his books in Sanary was the copy of Maine de Biran's *Journal Intime* extensively annotated by himself. Biran had always interested him; now the recovered journal became his spring-board for the long study of the philosopher that he presently began to ruminate.

By mid-September the film script was done and on the 19th Aldous and Maria left for Paris—a short fortnight at Mimi Gielgud's, interrupted by a couple of days in Brussels. Then England. On 2nd October they arrived in London (put up at Claridges by Rank Films). What Aldous thought and felt about this first return after eleven years, I have not the slightest idea. It is one of the things one encounters when trying to find a sequence in a life—three different views of some, possibly trivial, event on a given day, and so many many days unremembered, unrecorded. This, so far, seems to be the case about that return to England. I have come across no relevant letters. Julian, at Unesco, and Juliette were out of the country. Eddy Sackville-West, whom they saw, is dead. Georges and Jeanne had stayed on at Sanary. I was in Italy. The friends who did see Aldous then are no longer able to make a clear distinction between that

---

[1] *House and Garden*, 1947, republished in their *Weekend Book* of 1969.

visit and his many later ones. (There is a postcard from Maria to Betty Wendel from Rome, "We are leaving Italy too soon to suit us and are moving northwards . . . all rather sad.") They stayed in London for about three weeks, saw a good deal of Harold and Vera Raymond (and had looked forward to doing so), Aldous made a brief appearance on the B.B.C. on *In Town Tonight* and saw a performance of *The Gioconda Smile* which was still running. (The play in fact did very well, with an eventual full nine months in the West End.) We do not know what Aldous felt—nothing very much I would suspect; that return to England unlike some of his later ones was no sentimental journey—but we do know how he appeared to one of the most intuitively acute of his contemporaries: he was interviewed by Cyril Connolly.

If one looks at his face one gets first an impression of immense intelligence, but this is not unusual among artists. What is much more remarkable and almost peculiar to him is the radiance of serenity and loving-kindness on his features; one no longer feels "what a clever man" but "what a good man", a man at peace with himself . . .[1]

They talked about their contemporary world—the bomb, radioactive contamination, famine, the possible technical and scientific solutions; but the real problem, Aldous said, would always be the soul of man and the ignorant cravings for pleasure and power which destroy it. They talked about baroque funeral sculpture; they talked about religion. And here Cyril seems to have managed to pin Aldous down to an unusual degree. He asked him how close his own brand of neo-Brahminism or Vedanta came to Christianity, Aldous answered:

"I am not a Christian," he said, "but if I were, the sect which would appeal to me most would be the Quakers. They seem to me to be nearest the original truths of Christianity . . . As for my own religion—there have always been people who have tried to approach God without an intermediary; these mystics have been found in every church, but unfortunately it's very difficult to become one."

The interview took place in Aldous's sitting-room at Claridges. "He dressed," Cyril wrote,

like an Argentine dandy who moves between Oxford and Rome, and he is adored by Chaplin and other Hollywood magnates, but

[1] The interview appeared in the now defunct *Picture Post* with some very characteristic photographs of Aldous in the act of talking, by Elizabeth Chat.

often inaccessible to them. He eats fish, but not meat; will drink wine, but not spirits; goes to bed early, studies paintings corner by corner through a magnifying glass, enjoys seeing his old friends. Yet I know no-one more desperately concerned about the state of the world.

From Maria, there is one fragmentary line about London to Matthew, "But oh—le temps retrouvé."

In November they were back in New York. There they spent some weeks and intended to stay longer as Aldous had encountered an eye specialist, Dr Gustav Erlanger, who had done experimental physiology in Germany and London and developed a method of treating eyes by iontophoresis. Aldous began the treatment and thought that it resulted in a slight clearing of his old opacities; but he went down with severe bronchitis and had to desist. He returned to California and was ordered a three months' stay in Palm Desert. There he and Maria settled down in a furnished bungalow at the Sun & Sage Apartments, Aldous trying his hand at an adaptation for the stage of *Ape and Essence*.

## Chapter Four

# Domestic Seesaw

ALDOUS'S bronchitis slowly wore off in the dry air and warmth of Palm Desert. Just as well to be there, as it turned out, for the rest of California that winter was having what Aldous called preposterous weather. The orange and the lemon groves were frozen; snow kept falling in the foot-hills, there was deep snow over the Mojave, five feet of snow at Wrightwood, with their house disappearing under a drift—"Well, we are lucky not to be inside it." Aldous is writing to Matthew. A long letter of paternal advice—should he change his job? There is the short-range prospect, says Aldous, of being condemned to a period of donkey work. Donkeyishness can be high even in "such apparently lively work as literary journalism. I remember the . . asininity of doing 'shorter notices' of bad books on the *Athenaeum*.

But the donkey work has got to be done and, in the nature of things . . it will be the new boy . . who has to do it . . I should, if I were you, certainly not be too much in a hurry to turn down the research job in the Conservation concern . . . it won't offer much scope for your gifts; but if there is a fair prospect of the job leading to something of greater interest and authority in the future, I am sure you would be well advised to accept it. [etc., etc.]

No more talk about Matthew's taking six months off to travel Europe with his parents, that great plan has slid into oblivion. He took the new job (with the Fairfield Osborn Conservation Foundation in New York) and stayed in it for the next three years. Aldous had finished the stage version of *Ape and Essence* (never performed) and some essays for his next book, one of them, "Death and the Baroque", inspired by the Italian tombs he had visited that summer, to appear at once in Cyril Connolly's *Horizon*; and was turning now to the material for his study on Maine de Biran. In February he writes to Julian,

. . The prospects of reconciliation between East and West seem to be about on a par with the prospects of reconciliation between Christendom and Islam in the twelfth century. The best that can be hoped now is what happened then—a state of hostile symbiosis . . whereby the irreconcilable antagonists bound themselves, as a matter of practical utility, to respect one another's spheres of influence.

Man's life span being as long as it is, I suppose one cannot expect any major change in thought-patterns and behaviour patterns to take place in under one or two centuries.

*Le Sourire de la Gioconde*, in Georges Neveux's adaptation, opened in Paris in February (a moderate success).

Eventually the Huxleys went back to their apartment in Beverly Hills. Aldous hears of the death of his cousin by marriage, Ted (É.S.P.) Haynes. "The last time I saw him, in October, he remarked that he expected that he would die in the spring. He was a good prophet. Modern circumstances are such that we shall not look upon his like again; for he belonged to that curious and very delightful species of the English Eccentrics . . .

> Our world is too tidy to admit of marvellous disorder, the Dickensian leisureliness of an office such as Ted's. His death marks the passing not only of a friend, but also of an epoch of history and, one might almost say, a character in fiction.

On one of their evening walks, Aldous and Maria saw a house and garden in a quiet street. "Last night we were suddenly tempted", Maria wrote to Jeanne on 1st May.

> . . It is built in a way we like [all ground-floor in an inoffensive neo-Spanish style] it should be within our price . . there should be room for Noële. Would it look to you as if I were abandoning Europe? I think I could do as much for Noële here, perhaps more. Remember Sophie . . . If Noële could come . . . for her education, her health. She seems to be so near to us, so near to Aldous spiritually, intellectually . . .
> *Will* we buy a house in Los Angeles? I have an impression that we shall not settle again in France . . . I do not understand why I feel this—I have often had what I call a *"savoir"* an "I know it" . . . Aldous et moi, nous nous *voyons* ici dans nos vieux jours. Or ils sont bientôt là les vieux jours.

A week later they have plunged. "Coccola will have told you," Aldous writes to Matthew,

> The house—large, commodious—the garden—with big trees and plenty of space and privacy—and the location—in that curious country lane between Santa Monica and Melrose, full of huge estates and enormous trees—all seem ideal. And the price—ten thousand down with thirteen thousand to pay in ten years at $135 a month, is considered reasonable by all sensible people with whom we have talked. So there we are.
> I hope we shall be able to dispose of Wrightwood this summer. Nice as it is, it imposes too much of a strain . . .

Soon after they went up to Wrightwood for the summer. Krishnamurti will again be in the neighbourhood. "Aldous is in a happy mood, working hard and gaily. I . . well, rather moth-eaten; I have to admit it." Maria had a temperature which persisted through the summer and was dreading their next major house move, "the sheer muscular fatigue"; and there is more *va-et-vient* than ever; a few days in Los Angeles every other week or so. But they got a new car while they were about it, "I don't know why that means so much to me?" An Oldsmobile, 135 h.p. Rocket engine; no gear shift. By July they were able to spend the odd night in the new house.

Our house in town, 740 North Kings Road, L.A.46. WEbster 3 0455, has not yet had a defect [Maria to Matthew]. It is *large*; at last I feel at home again . . . The drains would not take a garbage disposal under 350 dollars so I do without . . It's still all up in the air. But we *love* it. We both purr in it. It is extremely cool and livable. Nothing too ugly. Nothing wildly pretty but all livable.

Edwin Hubble, the astronomer, received an honour from the Institut de France; Aldous composed his letter of acceptance in French. "We had a lot of fun over that because Aldous ended the letter à la façon de Gide.

So we knew there could be no error. When in doubt Aldous always goes back to that. The only letter I believe he ever had from Gide. [Who had ended it with "sincèrement votre" than which nothing could be more idiosyncratic.] But we composed the right thing, I believe, except for one sentence; but I did not insist . . And after all he is a foreigner, I mean Edwin. Their cat came and bit my legs. He is a strange cat.

This is perhaps the place to mention a comment Maria made, also to her son, on the company they kept. "Only the first-rate [intellectual] world is difficult . . That is why I learned to shut up so long ago—from the day I was sixteen it was first-rate most of the time. The second-rate bores *me*. And I shut up for another reason."

Aldous was asked to make some recordings,[1] and chose to read the story of the dwarfs from *Crome Yellow*, "Sermons in Cats" from *Music at Night* and the posthumous experience passage from *Time Must Have a Stop*. He wrote this comment on his own voice for the sleeve.

[1] For a company called Sound Portraits formed then by two young Californian sound technicians, Mr and Mrs Barron.

For me, these records possess a certain historical . . interest. For, unless my ear and memory greatly deceive me, the way I speak is practically identical with the way my mother and her brothers and sisters spoke. Language is perpetually changing; the cultivated English I listened to as a child is not the same as the cultivated English spoken by young men and women to-day. But within the general flux there are islands of linguistic conservatism; and when I listen to myself objectively, from the outside, I perceive that I am one of these islands. In the Oxford of Jowett and Lewis Carroll, the Oxford in which my mother was brought up, how did people speak the Queen's English? I can answer with a considerable degree of confidence that they spoke almost exactly as I do. These recordings . . . are documents from the seventies and eighties of last century.

Wrightwood le 7 septembre
Darling . . [Maria to Matthew] we are breaking up here . . My desk has gone, so has my bed . . The books have yet to go and Aldous's desk . . Now there is no hope that we can sell the place so we shall shut it up; cut off water and gas and not come up at all during the cold weather. If we go to Europe as is decided next May, therefore to New York next April to have a month with Erlanger [the eye man] it will be shut a great deal . . you who like it so much may use it some day—or we may another summer—but that seems a long way ahead . . .

Aldous . . is of course less bouncingly well because of pushing to finish the work. No-one else would notice it but myself . . . We are all breaking up soon. Radha and Rajagopal go East on the 14th . . Rosalind and Krishnaji leave Wrightwood on the same day. So that will leave us free to leave as soon as it suits Aldous. Usually he has to leave about this time of year as the sage-brush is blooming, but so far the allergy is just in his nose and throat at the end of the day and does not keep him awake at night so we may stay until the M.S. is completed. I read most of this last Essay [Maine de Biran] which is one of his best ones.

Then we shall rush down, I with relief and delight. I really wonder what some of my friends mean when they say that Aldous does all I want . . When I think that I lived in this place for five years . . . I pray that the dampness of Kings Road will not be bad for Aldous. It is curiously damp . . . The large garden is watered a lot and the whole street has gardens . . also it is on the ground floor—how awful if we had to move another time . . .

# Chapter Five

## Themes and Variations

HAVING hung on at Wrightwood well into October, Aldous and Maria made the move for good into North Kings Road. Here, with the last book off his hands, he was able to turn to other matters, Orwell's *Nineteen Eighty-Four*, Julian's recent articles on Russian genetics in *Nature*. "Have you read them?" he asked Matthew. "If not, do so.

> They are extremely interesting and contain a vast array of facts. The picture he draws is extremely depressing. One of the significant facts is that Russian geneticists no longer use the word "hypothesis", but always refer to "doctrines", exactly as the Schoolmen did in the thirteenth century. I suppose they will end up in the same sterility . . .

To Orwell, Aldous wrote this letter.

> . . I had to wait a long time before being able to embark on *Nineteen Eighty-Four*. Agreeing with all that the critics have written of it, I need not tell you, yet once more, how fine and how profoundly important the book is.
> May I speak instead of the thing with which the book deals—the ultimate revolution? The first hints of a philosophy of the ultimate revolution—the revolutions which lie beyond politics and economics, and which aim at the total subversion of the individual's psychology and physiology—are to be found in the Marquis de Sade, who regarded himself as the continuator, the consummator, of Robespierre and Babeuf. The philosophy of the ruling minority in *Nineteen Eighty-Four* is a sadism which has been carried to its logical conclusion by going beyond sex and denying it. Whether in actual fact the policy of the boot-on-the-face can go on indefinitely seems doubtful. My own belief is that ruling oligarchy will find less arduous and wasteful ways of governing . . and that these ways will resemble those which I described in *Brave New World*.
> I have had occasion recently to look into the history of animal magnetism and hypnotism, and have been greatly struck by the way in which, for a hundred and fifty years, the world has refused to take serious cognizance of the discoveries of Mesmer, Braid, Esdaile and the rest. Partly because of the prevailing materialism and partly because of prevailing respectability, nineteenth-century philosophers and men of science were not willing to investigate the odder facts of

psychology. Consequently there was no pure science of psychology for practical men, such as politicians, soldiers and policemen, to apply in the field of government. Thanks to the voluntary ignorance of our fathers, the advent of the ultimate revolution was delayed for five or six generations. Another lucky accident was Freud's inability to hypnotize successfully and his consequent disparagement of hypnotism. This delayed the general application of hypnotism to psychiatry for at least forty years. But now psycho-analysis is being combined with hypnosis; and hypnosis has been made easy and indefinitely extensible through the use of barbiturates . . Within the next generation I believe that the world's rulers will discover that infant conditioning and narco-hypnosis are more efficient, as instruments of government, than clubs and prisons . . . In other words, I feel that the nightmare of *Nineteen Eighty-Four* is destined to modulate into the nightmare of a world having more resemblance to that which I imagined in *Brave New World*. The change will be brought about as a result of a felt need for increased efficiency. Meanwhile, of course, there may be a large-scale biological and atomic war—in which case we shall have nightmares of other and scarcely imaginable kinds.

Thank you once again for the book.

For the present there were no very fixed work plans. Another original script for the films, possibly, with Christopher Isherwood. "If I don't succeed, I suppose I shall have to take a job in some studio . . ." Aldous's post-war income from English book sales was fairly high, if uneven. From £970 in 1936, up to over £3,300 in 1948 and to nearly £5,000 in 1949. But at this point the pound had been devalued.

The new book, *Themes and Variations*, contains perhaps some of Aldous's finest work. The four variations on art and artists—on El Greco, Goya, Death and the Baroque, Piranesi's Prisons —have the elegance, the range and sparkle, the contagious ardour, of the Aldous of the 1920s, with the confluence of ideas enriched by experience and compassion, the intellectual play sustained and clarified by unitive philosophy. The heart of the collection is the study of Maine de Biran, "Variations on a Philosopher". I often regretted that it was not given the impetus of separate publication. Slightly longer than *Ape and Essence*, twice as long as *Science, Liberty and Peace*, it could well have stood on its own, a little book to be carried about, travelled with, annotated, as Aldous had annotated his copy of Biran's *Journal Intime*. It is, I think, an extremely stimulating piece of work, leaping as it does to every kind of question (without coming up too readily with the literary or the preachy answer), lucid, yet aware of the unfathomably queer and complex facts of human existence. The life and works of Biran, a "spiritual positivist", were made to set off a man with Aldous's particular compass and talents: the man of letters who would keep breaking his own pattern, the man congenitally interested in science who was not a scientist, the man of thought who was not a professional philosopher; the man of religion who might not be pinned down to dogma or creed. "Variations on a Philosopher" is about man's nature and man's destiny.

> [Maine de Biran] is turning into a consideration of life in general [Aldous said to Hubble in mid-writing] as exemplified by what that particular man and thinker did, felt and thought, and also by what he didn't do or feel or think—for what is left undone is often as significant in a biography as what is done . . . I have become fascinated by the individual's relations with history and culture—the extent to which a man is in and out of history, like an iceberg in water . . .[1]

(Biran's own contention was that the individual's relation to history and society was normally that of victim to monster.) A major section of the biographical essay, Aldous's first, deals with Maine de Biran as "a Moralist, Metaphysician and Candidate for Salvation", a philosopher whose philosophy, spiritual positivism, was based upon carefully observed psychological facts:

> facts which, unlike almost all his immediate predecessors, unlike many of his contemporaries and successors, our philosopher takes as he finds them and refuses to explain away in terms of something else. For him, there is no hierarchy of facts. One datum of immediate experience is just as good as another. A fact belonging to the inner world is not less of a fact than one belonging to the outer world . . .

As a young man and during his early middle age, Biran—like Aldous—had been "never indeed a dogmatic atheist, but profoundly an agnostic. He wished and hoped that there might be a God and was only waiting to find some compelling reason to believe that there was. 'If', he wrote, 'If I ever find God and the true laws of the moral order, it will be by good fortune, and I shall be more credible than those who, setting out from a set of prejudices, tend merely to establish these prejudices by means of a theory.' A profoundly honest man, our philosopher knew that, if one is to explore the unknown, one must not start by pretending that it is already known . . ."

---

[1] This, and the next, quotation from "Variations on a Philosopher", *Themes and Variations.* Chatto & Windus, 1950.

# Chapter Six

## 740 North Kings Road

MATTHEW HUXLEY was in his thirtieth year when he gave his father occasion to write him the following note.

9 December 1949

Dearest Matthew,

Your letter arrived this morning and gave us the greatest happiness, both on account of the news it brought and on account of the way you conveyed it. After thirty years of it, I can say I am definitely for matrimony, and I am sure that, if Ellen is all that Suzanne tells us she is, you too will be of the same opinion in 1980. Keep us posted on what's happening and on what you plan. Meanwhile this brings you the paternal blessing and every best wish for the happiest possible Christmas.

Your loving

Aldous

After a quiet first winter in their new house, Aldous alternately reading for the historical novel he never wrote and working with Christopher Isherwood on a script they did not sell, Aldous and Maria went to New York for Matthew's wedding. They had been delighted for their son; now they were enchanted by the girl. She was Ellen Hovde, daughter of Professor Bryn J. Hovde, president of the New School for Social Research. They found her charming, intelligent, life-enhancing, with great good looks thrown in. They also found a curious affinity, between Ellen and Maria, between Aldous and Ellen, it was hard to say who took most to whom; and meanwhile the two young people, as Aldous observed, were wildly in love with each other.

Matthew and Ellen went off to Europe and the Villa La Rustique at Sanary (looked after by Rina) and a round of family visits in Belgium and France. Aldous and Maria spent a busy five weeks in New York, taking the new eye treatment with Dr Erlanger. *The Gioconda Smile* was to be put on in the autumn and Aldous was discussing and resisting changes proposed by the producer Shepard Traube. On the 9th May they sailed, again on the *Queen Mary*, and on the 14th stepped off the boat-train at the Gare St Lazare a few minutes before midnight. The three Neveuxes, with Sophie and Sylvia Nicolas, were there. "Tout le monde,"

Georges noted, "est ému." How true this must have been. No one had spoken of emotion on the first return two years before, the show of feeling became possible on the attenuated occasion. The weather was icy, taxis were found and the Huxleys conducted to their hotel, the Paris-Dinard in the rue Cassette, two steps from Jeanne's. Another stay in Paris: three weeks of museums, walks on the quais, theatres (Claudel's *L'Otage*, *Othello* in Georges's translation), a family celebration of young Sylvia's birthday. Then Italy: Siena, Rome. In early July Paris again and Aldous on his way to London, Maria on hers to central France where Georges and Jeanne have taken a house for the summer.

Julian and Juliette were in their Hampstead house and Aldous stayed with them. Maria sent minute details about tailor, shirtmaker, dry cleaners; Juliette was asked to keep him on a strictly vegetarian diet. ("I generally disregarded these instructions," Juliette writes, "and at the end we found that Aldous had put on a little weight.") What Aldous promised himself, besides English clothes, were new quacks. (He used the word without derogatory intention: "Don't wait," Aldous and Maria would say, "go and see a doctor or a quack at once.") He might go down to Brighton for a day or two to see Wilhelm Luftig who uses light therapy, plus homoeopathy . .

. . There is also another unorthodox eye man, called Brooks Simpkins, who has written a very good book on the mechanics of vision . . . He lives at Eastbourne. And perhaps I can look in on him too. And talking of unorthodoxies, I am asking a curious and interesting Danish acquaintance of mine, Dr Christian Volf, who is an expert on hearing, to send me, care of you [Julian], one of the special recordings he has made for relief of sinus trouble. One listens through ear-phones to a record of synthetic sounds in the lowest musical octave and the effect is to give an intense internal massage, vibrating the bones of the skull . . . I have heard of many people who keep sinusitis at bay simply by listening to the record every morning before breakfast. I am hoping that this thing may give you some relief from your miseries in this field. If, as I hope, Volf comes to London . . we will have a talk with him.

Aldous made some comment about that second return in two letters (one during, one after) to Christopher Isherwood.

. . England is much more cheerful than it was 2 years ago . . . Life is easier . . . Saw Stephen Spender several times—white-haired and wonderfully distinguished looking . . . expect to see Tom Eliot tonight and Cyril Connolly tomorrow. Poor Osbert has got Parkinson's disease . . . Edith a monument . . . Sybil Colefax, bent

double with her broken back, but indomitably receiving guests and
going out. The Jowitts—occupying an amazing Victorian-Gothic
apartment in the House of Lords, reserved for Lord Chancellors. All
very much *Le Temps Retrouvé*. "I show you sorrow and the ending of
sorrow"—with no ending in sight, of course, for any of us.

At a luncheon at Raymond Mortimer's Cyril made the follow-
ing remark (I am reporting this exchange exactly as he told it),
"Longevity is the revenge of talent upon genius."
Aldous: "Who said that?"
Cyril: "I."
Aldous: "When?"
Cyril: "Now."
Aldous: "I think we must all applaud." And they clapped.
Julian and Juliette gave a family party—twenty-seven Huxleys
with their wives and husbands. ". . It was a pleasant and touching
experience," Aldous wrote to Peggy Kiskadden. "*Not* a bad lot,"
he kept saying to Juliette, "not a bad lot at all."
At the end of July Aldous went to join Maria at Sanary. They
remained there for the whole of August but without the sense of
rediscovery of the last time. There was a heat wave; material
existence had become completely normal ("How amazingly tough
the French way of life has proved itself!")—but somehow it did
not interest them very much. Julian and Juliette came; so did I.
On arrival I found Aldous doing a sister Anne—standing on the
lookout for a buyer who was to turn up that morning. They had
taken against the house and were determined to sell. (There was
indeed an odd sense of double *déjà-vu* about the place.) The buyer
did not come. In September they went to join the Neveuxes at
Julliac in the Limousin.
It was a cool old country house, if somewhat primitive, and
the five of them had an idyllic ten days in that prodigal region
of France—sitting under trees, picking mushrooms in the fields,
descending into grottoes, subterraneous rivers, magic caves at
Lascaux, Rocamadour, Padirac, Les Eyzies . . . In the evenings
Georges and Jeanne were introduced to the latest of the Huxley
interests, dianetic sessions. There was also their first meeting with
Dr Roger Godel, physician and philosopher, and his wife, Alice,
who came all the way from Paris to meet Aldous.
The rehearsals of the *Gioconda* in New York were going badly
and Aldous decided on an early return. He and Maria left Juillac
on 10th September (it was probably then, on their way north,
that Aldous stopped and had his hard look at Loudun). In Paris
they put up at Mimi Gielgud's flat in Passy (a faithful friend
though long divorced from Lewis). "Dear ones," Maria scribbled
to Matthew and Ellen, "tomorrow at 8 a.m. we are off.

Everything has been quite an excitement as this day a woman
appeared with money in her hand to buy Sanary—so we sold for
2 millions, 5,000 dollars. Not good but good riddance!!

So the looking-glass Villa Huley was sold, as Jeanne put it, for
a mouthful of bread. The original house had cost them about
30,000 dollars. Thus Aldous and Maria achieved the near impossible—a loss in real estate in the South of France.

On 22nd September, Suzanne on board, they sailed back to
America. They found the *Gioconda* "in the most frightful mess—
the actors at daggers drawn with the director-producer, the
rendering of the play unsatisfactory in the extreme . . ." (Aldous
to Harold Raymond) Betty Wendel found him "enraged by
changes that had been made without his consent. New York
friends advised Aldous to demand that the opening be postponed,
and that he should fight it out." Instead, the play duly opened
on 3rd October (with Basil Rathbone as Hutton, Valerie Taylor
as Janet Spence). Aldous did not go to the first night but, terribly
nervous according to Suzanne, stayed at his hotel until he was
telephoned that it was an apparent success. Next morning the
notices in the *N.Y. Times* and *Herald Tribune* were bad. And a
few days later Aldous and Maria drove off to California.

". . The *Gioconda* is dead," he wrote to Anita Loos from North
Kings Road in November. "The move from the Lyceum to the
Fulton [theatre] coinciding as it did with the universally bad
businesses during election week, brought the receipts down to
about seven thousand dollars . . So Traube decided to shut up
shop . . . Now it is dead, it is dead, I suppose, for keeps.

. . It is a bore; for I would have enjoyed making some easy money.
Now I must settle down to some honest work—and perhaps some
dishonest work in the movies, if I can find it, which isn't so easy
nowadays.

What was it like, the play, and what is it about?

. . the story has been developed in such a way [Aldous's own
summary to Leon M. Lion in 1947] that the man who is falsely
condemned for his wife's murder (. . the original short story . . was
based on the Greenwood case of 1920) finds an internal solution by
the acceptance of his fate, while the woman who actually did commit
the murder and who seems to have successfully got away with it,
refuses to accept the real state of things and thus breaks down into
madness. By dividing the stage in the last act, I contrive to show,
without interruption, alternating pictures of the one character on
what, in spite of the circumstances, is the up grade, the other on a
descending spiral . . .

So here we have a strong dramatic situation backed by the
psychological spectacle of a conversion, a condemned man in his
cell, seen modulating from stark fear of death to near serene
acceptance. The play reads very well and its potentialities were,
one is told, admirably brought out by the London production of
1948.

Since *Grey Eminence*, since Maine de Biran, Aldous was looking
for some historical or biographical theme that would bring grist
to his mill. Now he began to work on the material for that strange
and revolting seventeenth-century episode, the diabolical possessions of Loudun. How did that come about? he was asked by
John Chandos in 1961.

Years and years ago I read the account in Michelet's book *La
Sorcière* of the Loudun case, and was interested—and incidentally
found, when I came to look into the documents, that it was extraordinarily inaccurate, I mean [chuckle] this *great* historian was very
slap-dash—and then I thought no more about it for many years,
and then quite by chance I picked up in a second-hand bookshop
the . . reprint . . of the autobiography of the prioress. And one of
Surin's autobiographical things, and the late seventeenth-century
book by [Pastor] Aubin which is an account of the whole episode.
And reading those I was so fascinated—there was such extraordinary material there that I began collecting it, and found in fact
that no historical episode yet has ever had so much documentation.
There are autobiographical statements by the prioress, by Surin; a
great many letters; all the exorcisms were taken down in shorthand,
and a great many of them were printed. And a great many still
remain unprinted. I have never read any of the unprinted material
because I just can't manage those things. But I don't think it would
have contributed anything. Most of the exorcisms were very like
one another . . .
Then there were a great many accounts by outsiders who came to
look at the possessions—I mean Loudun became one of the most
popular tourist resorts of the seventeenth century. People went from
all over the continent to see these nuns rolling about on the floor and
screaming obscenities—it was the greatest fun.
. . So there was a great deal of material quite easy to get hold of.

It was also a great deal of material to get through (Maria still
did much of the reading); days immersed in that labyrinth of
witch-hunts, devils and hysteria were followed by other explora-
tions in the evening, probings, by other means, into the workings

of the sub-conscious and the super-conscious mind, the experimental sessions that became a standing feature of North Kings. Usually it was a Tuesday. First the participants would eat dinner at the counter of the World's Largest Drug Store, then assemble in the long main-room of the house, the music-room. Here—always game to try out anything that might come up, and what did not come up in Southern California—they would flash bright lights, make magnetic passes, turn on records of strange sounds, put the visiting hypnotist or medium through his paces. They would go into it with passionate interest but also critically, accepting that there might be fraud or multiple explanations. It was Aldous's open mind working both ways. That winter it was dianetics (which he thought might shed some useful light on the possessions of those nuns of Loudun). L. Ron Hubbard, the founder of the therapy, came to North Kings in person. The subconscious (if his theory may be roughly summarized) is presumed to function on several levels. There is a cellular level as well as a cerebral level. The cells are able to record words heard in sleep and even in pre-natal life. These recorded words, "engrams" in dianetic jargon, can act as obsessive commands—much like post-hypnotic suggestions—on an individual throughout his life.

. . The sub-conscious seems to take these verbal commands literally and unreasoningly, without regard to their context. [Aldous to Dr Roger Godel] The result can be disastrous, both mentally and physically. (If this is really the case, we may have here the rationale of magic spells, curses, anathemas and the like.)

Hubbard's therapy consisted of a procedure, called "auditing", which aimed at bringing those fatal recorded words and phrases into consciousness (and this without deep hypnosis or the standard psycho-analytical process). A patient who had brought his engrams to the surface was called "a clear". Aldous and Maria had three or four sessions with Hubbard. He and his wife came to dinner, "stiff and polite" the first time, bringing two pounds of chocolates which Maria described as *inutile*.

. . Up to the present I have proved to be completely resistant [Aldous wrote to Jeanne in an unpublished letter]—there is no way of getting me on to the time track or of making the subconscious produce engrams. Furthermore I find that there is a complete shutting off of certain areas of childhood memory, due, no doubt, to what the dianeticians call a "demon circuit" an engrammic command in the nature of "don't tell", "keep quiet", etc. Maria, meanwhile, has had some success in contacting and working off engrams and has been back repeatedly into what the subconscious says is the pre-natal state. Whether because of dianetics or for some other reason, she is well and very free from tension . . .

In any case, he concluded, the thing seems to be worth looking into and experimenting with.


They had settled into their pleasant, dignified, new house—respectable, Maria called it. It was certainly more conventional than either Llano or Wrightwood, where a tent pole had propped the ceiling of Aldous's room and the silvered caravan stood outside their door. It was comfortable, unpretentious, adapted to their needs—Aldous's study, the music-room, a breakfast-room, an arbour to sit out in. There were gadgets of all kinds, many contrived by Matthew; and Maria had at last succumbed to regular domestic help; indeed soon they were to have an excellent French cook. They still nipped out to their neighbourhood barbecue and there were the luncheons once or twice a week with the Stravinskys and a group of friends in the open air at Yolanda's in the Town and Country Market—booths and tables under pepper trees. The regulars were Robert Craft, the Reverend James McLane and his wife, an Episcopalian priest Aldous and Maria were fond of (great theological arguments went on) and a very young man, now Dr James Brainard Smith, who minded boutique (his words) for Mme Stravinsky and who recalls the arguments and the pleasantness of it all. These might be joined on any day by Peggy Kiskadden, by Gerald or by Betty Wendel or Christopher Isherwood. In the afternoons to book-shops and the L.A. Public Library, all blessedly within walking distance so that Aldous could go on his own, look into windows, browse among the shelves at his friend Jake Zeitlin's on Cienega Boulevard . . . To Mrs Corbett, for Aldous's eye training, they would go by car, and afterwards he and Maria would go for a stroll in "our cemetery", Rose Dale Memorial Park, a rural oasis a few miles south of mid-town Los Angeles, quiet graves below immense old palm trees . . . Then home. Friends for tea . . . Music . . .

# PART TEN

## "I Will Show You Sorrow . . .": 1951-1955

. . There remained with him . . a
haunting sense of the . . transience,
the hopeless precariousness of all merely
human happiness.

ALDOUS HUXLEY in *Grey Eminence*

Each man's life is also the story of
Everyman.

IRIS ORIGO

# Chapter One

## Summer 1951–Winter 1952

Aldous has been on and off his book [*The Devils of Loudun*, Maria wrote to Matthew in March 1951], ever since he started it. He feels in an off mood and that he never has anything to say. It is a horrible shame that that play collapsed. He did deserve to earn some easy money.

MARIA assured him that if he never felt like writing a book again he still could earn his living with lectures and articles and so on; "not movies obviously as he has been trying in vain to get a job since we are back and *nothing* turns up. Anita tried . . Now they are dithering about some readings with Ethel Barrymore . . ."

A bad kind of flu was going round Los Angeles; Aldous and Maria caught it. The flu settled on Aldous's right eye, the bad eye, and for three days it was red and painful. Then the flu cleared up but the eye remained red, uncomfortable and vision deteriorated to nothing. This happened on 4th March. A month later "the eye was still no better," Maria wrote to Matthew in May,

. . though Aldous had gone to a very good specialist and been given drops of cortisone with the approval of Bill [Kiskadden] and [Dr] Hawkins and assent of Aldous. On April 24th this same excellent oculist put in some drops which were supposed to tear apart some old scars covering the pupil, this meaning that Aldous would see better. If it worked on the right eye it was to be tried on the left eye. The doctor had talked Aldous into trying this, without bullying him. The results were: for five days . . great redness, no vision and above all pains in the eye, the head and the neck. Psychologically it was the worst thing I have ever gone through. The pain would of course have been nothing had not Aldous been frightened and hating the doctor. The doctor telephoned from the hospital where he had fallen sick that it would be nothing, that obviously the medicine had been too strong, that the only thing to do was compresses. But of course and very naturally Aldous was frightened, very naturally I was equally frightened, and upset to see Aldous walking up and down, holding his head impatient, enraged, in fact so different from himself.

Bill came to see us on the Sunday and was definitely concerned; not because it was dangerous, but because one never knows. Once in a while things do turn out badly and Aldous is so evidently a *personage difficile* . . He was so rattled. It really was horrible.

Now [in mid-May] all is well. That is: the doctor will never try the rough medicine again . . . The eye is not *quite* recovered . . But in two weeks with Aldous's full wish, they are starting the gentle cortisone drops in the left, that is, the good eye.

Peggy is going east next week . . She will tell you about this; in fact I want you to ask her . . It is always interesting to hear two sides of a story . . Bill took it seriously enough to talk to Hawkins and tell him to look after Aldous properly; that is to come to see him here and take his time with him rather than slicing him between all the crowds in the office . . . For more than a week I thought I was very ill; then I discovered it was just the anxiety . . . Now we are well and happy and hopeful for the future. We plan nothing except a nice trip for the summer.

Aldous indeed was able to get on with his book, but had to say no to an invitation to go to India with his new friends the Roger Godels. Matthew and Ellen were expecting a baby in the autumn. Maria wrote, "I have so much peace at heart since you are married. One does not know one's preoccupations till they are over; as with Aldous's illness . . .

But now all *is* normal. Vera Stravinsky rang up . . they could not bear going to another cinema, could they visit us? So I said yes the programme would be good but not the refreshments and they came at 9.

We are very fond of them, Stravinsky still looks like father and is very sweet really; always the same programme. Stravinsky, Bob Craft—almost an adopted son of theirs, 26 and very clever, knows everything, terribly nervous and not a pansy—and Aldous stay in the music room and Vera and I stay around somewhere else . . They play music and we chat . . Last night [12th May] Stravinsky arrived in an enchanting costume . . narrow effect in little blue jeans, and a blue jean zipper jacket open on a deep red wine jersey and silk scarf tied with pin. He looked enchanting and was really pleased with himself. I must not forget the always white socks and sandals. I do not know what he makes me think of, a voltigeur in the circus, a leprechaun with the little elegant legs or what? a cyclist? And Aldous *will* turn the heat off when I am gone and poor little Stravinsky shivers and dares not ask and Aldous notices nothing. So finally he came to sit on my bed, and Vera inside the open window in a decolleté dress under a lace shawl and velvet bows in her hair looked immense next to the little shivering elfish man. I am very fond of him and I like her and we are good friends. Bob too is very nice . . . They are all going to Venice where the world première of the opera on the *Rake's Progress* is taking place in September. [It was Aldous who had suggested that W. H. Auden should write the libretto.] I wish we could [be] there.

Gerald Heard had published an article on Flying Saucers, on which Aldous commented to Matthew: ". . in spite of Gerald's bad writing, there may be something there after all. I have no settled opinion so far, but keep my trap shut and wait." To Maria, the saucer business seemed "wildlier than we will ever grasp.

They may just be radar vortices, if you know what *that* is. I did not till two days ago when we walked with Gerald. These are just a vortex undetectable except by radar . . . then Aldous muddles it even more by telling me that we are only vortices but with a little more to it. And I give up.

Aldous had long been taking great interest in the Happy Valley School at Ojai, a small co-educational, non-sectarian and, of course, non-segregated, secondary school founded in 1946, of which he with Krishnamurti and Rosalind Rajagopal were the original trustees. The motto was *Aun Aprendo*, I Am Still Learning. Rose de Haulleville's girl Olivia was being brought up there; Maria hoped that Matthew would send his children, "Such a strong and happy atmosphere in the place . . . they have a Russian cook who is also a virtuoso on the piano; it sounds mad but it works." This June Aldous delivered the Commencement Address. *Aun Aprendo*—the process, he told them, goes on from cradle to grave and, doubtless, beyond. Or at least it ought to. Alas, in practice . . . "In all too many cases men and women do not wish to go on learning . . . They are like the young man of that ancient limerick . . who

> . . . . . *said 'Damn,*
> *It is borne in on me that I am*
> *A creature that moves*
> *In predestinate grooves;*
> *I'm not even a bus, I'm a tram!'*

And those people do not even say Damn."

Now they are all beginning to think about Christian names. This was Aldous's first contribution. "Dearest M, [to Matthew

in an unpublished letter] Coccola tells me that you're floored for
a name for the cub. Seeing that we embarked on the Evangelists
with you, might not Mark be a possibility . . ? Or if it's a girl,
there is Margaret—except that Miss Truman got there first. Or
Frances,

which was my mother's second name, as also the name of Matthew
Arnold's youngest sister, who was alive when you were born and
wrote me a letter to say how pleased she was that you had been
called Matthew. My mother's first name, Julia, is also good. So is
Elizabeth . . Or perhaps you had better do what was done in the
case of the royal children of France—they were not named at all
until a state baptism at five years old. Till then the Dauphin was
called Monsieur, the elder daughter Madame, the second daughter
Petite Madame . . . (We know all this as we are reading aloud a
charming book, made up mainly . . from the day-to-day journal of
Jean Héroard, the resident physician of Louis XIII. It gives a
fascinating picture of nursery and adult life at the beginning of the
seventeenth century . . .)

When you are next at a news-stand, invest fifteen cents in a copy
of the latest "See" magazine . . There is an article by Gerald
embedded in the midst of twenty-six (I counted them) nearly naked
women, whose photographs constitute the rest of the magazine.
Gerald's bearded image sits there like St Anthony in the midst of his
Temptations—or is it a prevision of the homosexual's purgatory,
innumerable bosoms and not a boy in view.

This letter was dated 1st July. On the 27th, Maria had to write
to Matthew and Ellen as follows:

My darlings, I am sorry to have to give you less good news than
usual but that right eye of Aldous's had an unaccountable flare up
since ten days ago . . So we had a sad birthday and when your little
gadget came this morning [a pocket telescope] it was wildly welcome
but sadly so; as if you had guessed the need of it.

. . . He was working well, very hard, I think too hard, and was very
cheerful . . . Dow diagnosed iritis . . also telling Aldous he would not
suggest removing this or that part of the eye. (I cannot quote in
medical terms). This rather frightened me . . I wondered if Dow
was preparing him for something very bad . . Hawkins . . suggested
a consultation of other doctors to which we agreed. He however
put Aldous on a general antibiotic drug, chloromycetin, in case there
should be some smouldering infections of flu left. This was Wednesday. Last night about five there was enough improvement for us all

to hope that this general antibiotic was having good effects. So we were cheerful. Aldous slept very well until four; then woke up in great pain . . The trouble is that they cannot even give soothing treatments, no nursing or calming the eye seems possible.

I would not have written all this to you if your little parcel had not arrived this very minute and made us feel sad. Aldous is now sleeping with some aspirin.

The question is not . . whatever . . caused it—that would be a useless squabble . . Aldous is obviously one of those people on whom the usually successful treatments have unaccountable effects. Dr Volf, that charming man who has the deaf-curing, sinus-curing record is here for two days and according to his diagnosis Aldous is otherwise perfectly healthy, unusually so for a man of his age; so I hope that he will very soon now overcome this. I will let you know if it should not get better.

Three or four days later, Maria wrote again.

Aldous has had a terrible time. *Very much pain.* Now pain is over but congestion and inflammation still there—will last for weeks— Peggy and Bill a *great* stand-by. Do not worry about doctors—we have the best—all that is possible is being done . . . poor poor Aldous—it was terrible—now it is sad—we live in a dark house. We walk at night. He cannot work—I try hard and have much help. I *never* leave him. We read—he dictates—but of course it is not the same—poor poor Aldous, but he is patient . . sometimes very depressed—I am full of courage and not once was I [word illegible]— except on the night *before* it started—enormous fear—I knew something serious was coming . . . Iritis *and* glaucoma—if it recurs it means operation to relieve the tension . . . Aldous knows *Nothing of This.* Never mention anything specifically. It may be all right. Rose was here—she said "Ce n'est pas juste."

Unless you hear again it means progressing well . . .

Then to Jeanne on 2nd August:

After some frightful nights and days, I believe the menace is passing . . . if there hadn't been a slight improvement since 2 o'clock this morning, and if the improvement does not keep up, they will have to operate, an iridectomy . . . He has suffered terribly . . . for ten days, the last two days and nights were the worst—in spite of all the science . . . It is a consequence of the flu in March, iritis can also be a consequence of keratitis, which he did have forty years ago. Now no news will be good news. Otherwise Mère will write to you . . .

And on 18th August at last, to Matthew and Ellen:

Well, my Dear Ones, I will write a real letter . . that of course means Aldous is better—poor Aldous, we shall never quite know what he went through. If he knew himself it might have helped—I mean I am *sure* that he was afraid of going blind, but he did not know he was afraid—I even suggested it. One time I suggested that *I* was afraid because in spite of what the doctors say one did not know what might happen—but it definitely brought no response. And I can *tell*. After 32 years I really can tell whether he is consciously worried-afraid. I think he feared for the good eye—and who would not? But oh! how he would not even tell myself that . . . The oculist agreed it was all right not to tell Aldous about the possibilities as long as he could tell me. I had warned him I was tough—but it is very extraordinary that a patient should not wish to know exactly the possibilities—the worse ones—of his case. I find it better to know because one is prepared for the lesser ordeals.

But Aldous is much better today. Tomorrow he proposes to write a little in the morning . . .

From then, Aldous got well quite rapidly. (Though the affected eye, his bad eye, never properly recovered.) Maria says nothing of the hypnotic treatment which Aldous mentioned when all was safely over. (" . . I live in fear of a recurrence—tho' hope for the best," he wrote to Dr Roger Godel in December.) He had in fact two or three brief hypnotic sessions with the head of the Psychology Department of U.C.L.A. which "undoubtedly helped me to sleep and to deal with the pain." He was not himself, he said, a particularly good hypnotic subject, but could get at least into a light trance.

Moreover, [this is from a letter written the summer after in another context] by means of auto-hypnosis (which is an art not too hard to acquire if one has a good hypnotist for a teacher) and by treatments from Maria and our friend LeCron, the psycho-therapist, I was enabled to get over the very considerable apprehension which accompanied and followed the iritis—apprehension that the good eye might be involved and lose much of its vision . . .

. . the benefits due to hypnosis are due fundamentally to the fact that it is accompanied by a high degree of relaxation, mental and physical. The ego is able to let go, to get out of the way, to stop interfering . . .

It was during the period of relaxation and relief after the iritis that Aldous and Maria were able to talk as follows. (In the remote past in Sanary, Maria once told me that there had been a third Huxley brother. "We don't speak about it.") Now, in the letter about Aldous's recovery, she said this to Matthew and Ellen:

> [A few nights ago] I dreamed about Trev—at breakfast I asked more questions about him than I ever had—Aldous knows little enough about the causes of his death . . [Trev] was at a nursing home at the time while he and the family were on holiday in Scotland. There was some trouble with a woman . . . and also his graduation marks had been far below what he could have expected. He was very brilliant . . . Talking about [Aldous's] going blind, I asked who was there to comfort him, Aldous said, "People were very nice—and *there was Trev*." So Peggy comes to tea and says you want to call the cub Trev. *DO*. We asked Aldous—it was so easy just after the morning's conversation—he would like it very much—and Matthew-kins, they say you are as [utterly illegible word] as he was—and Aldous says that Julian would like it too. I have wanted to suggest it long ago but feared you would think it too unusual. So write to Aldous what you decide. What about his "layette" have you bought it? May I pay for it? . . .

Three days later, Aldous took it up, beginning with a preamble, "I forgot . . to ask how you stood financially in regard to the blessed event. Please remember that, if you should need anything to cope with the emergency, I shall be only too proud and happy to advance it . ." He went on (in an unpublished letter),

> I have been thinking more about names and asking myself why, in the event of the cub's masculinity, we shouldn't think of my brother Trev. Trevenen has the defect of being a bit out of the ordinary, but the merit of being euphonious and of commemorating a very rare being, whom we all loved . . .

A couple of days later Maria ran into "Lola the wonderful fortune teller who I thought was dead, but she is not practising anymore . . . But I did see an astrologer . . more educated and therefore less fun . .

> but [he told me] there is more money in 1952 than there has been for some time and 1953 is really the money year. So we breathe a little more freely in anticipation . . yet how it goes—and now more doctors, more medicines, more treatments of all kinds. But so far we have at least got it. More than some people have . . .

On 20th October Mark Trevenen Huxley was born. Matthew telephoned the news to California early in the morning. His father wrote:

Dearest M & E,
I'm suddenly reminded of a letter I wrote to Arnold Bennett thirty-one years ago, in response to a note of his about Matthew's arrival—a letter in which I remarked that we literary gents might talk about our creative efforts, but that after all these creative efforts were pretty feeble in comparison with what our wives and le Bon Dieu contrived, between them, to achieve! Best love to all three of you.

And Maria,

God bless you Matthewkins—and Ellen and our little cub. It is already as if he had always been there and his name is so familiar in Aldous's voice—I hope that even if Trevenen is his second name you will use it—Aldous so definitely expects it—and it is a very pretty name. He was that before he was born—our cub . . .
Aldous almost fell out of bed rushing to the phone—he guessed it was you—and he is so happy—he suddenly kissed me this afternoon and called me granny . . . How soon can we expect photos—I can "see" you three—and Ellen and Trev in her arms—as if I had been there. Ellen has a way of looking down which is so beautiful. In fact, this is as important to us as to you, Matthewkins, even though it is all your own and we are so far away . . . Are you Christening him? I mean—in some religion?
I hope you can write soon—I have of course a most terrific head-ache—now realize how anxious I was—Goodnight My darling—

"Darlings—" in a large faint hand, the words painstakingly, legibly formed, "you are going to have a funny letter and I don't know how to begin because I feel shy and also want to be diplo-matic—you see the limelights have been *on me* and you know I make faces . . ."
It was a letter from hospital, and the first Matthew and Ellen heard of it. The letter went on—five passages of re-assurance and admissions. There had been a cyst—Hawkins just kept at me— the usual paraphernalia of surgeons—it was done at a wonderful moment, Aldous being better than ever and taking his oxygen treatment from the maid who is a treasure, Bill Kiskadden keeping an eye on him. I shall recover 100%, there will be no recurrence. P.S. Will they telephone Constance Collier who will hear it any-how and better from us direct—and just minimize it all you can.

On 26th January Aldous wrote to Jeanne (unpublished).

> Maria is back at home and is getting on remarkably well, gaining strength every day. The doctors are confident . . . No radiation will be necessary.
>
> . . Rose is now with us here, which is a great comfort, as she drives the car . . & looks after things in a general way. In a few more weeks I think that M will be back to normal, able to do everything . . .

But the cyst had been found to be malignant and the prognosis was not good. The Kiskaddens knew this. So did Maria.

Aldous had finished *The Devils of Loudun* while Maria was in hospital. The typescripts have gone off, she reported in her first letter from home, now Aldous hopes to start soon on a film about Gandhi with Gabriel Pascal, the producer of Shaw's plays, and it might be necessary to go to India. By March, in fact, they were able to go on a short trip to the Arizona desert, Maria driving.

> . . particularly wonderful at this time of year, with snow on the higher mountains . . . and, in the warm plains, an immense profusion of wild flowers, which come rushing out after the spring rains . . . [Aldous in a long letter to a new correspondent, Mrs Elise Murrel, whom Maria called "our un-met psychic friend in England"] And here and there, in the most arid and naked plains, spring the desert lilies . . with grey green leaves and a pyramid of perfumed blossoms, snowy white with green veins on the outside of each petal. It is an unforgettable spectacle—the good will of life, the tenacity of it in the face of the most adverse circumstances, the patience of it (the lilies will lie dormant for as much as ten or fifteen years, if there is a drought ). . the profusion, the beauty. And the yearly miracle takes place in an enormous luminous silence. Huge spaces completely empty of human activity, flooded with light and enclosed in an immense crystal of silence, to which any sound—the song of a bird, the noise of a passing car or plane—is completely irrelevant. It remains unflawed . . .

# Chapter Two

# Watershed

WELL worth looking into and experimenting with—that, so far, had been Aldous's approach to dianetics and to how much else. One has to dream, as he said once or twice, in a pragmatic way. Now, there appears an escalation in his interest, one might almost say his need, for these pursuits, a precipitation set off perhaps by the events of the last months, a change from curiosity to conviction. Maria filled a supple role of leading and at the same time waiting. Since her return from hospital Aldous had been treating her with hypnosis, helping her greatly, he thought,

. . she has been in strikingly good psychological shape, with a serenity and a cheerfulness which have undoubtedly contributed to her excellent recovery.

Indeed, he had "become a rather good hypnotic operator . . ." (There is a corroboration by Stravinsky,[1] ". . Aldous's friendship was a great comfort to me, and more; Aldous is a healer, a skilful masseur who cured me of insomnia . . .") At present, however, it was the "E" Therapy that Aldous and Maria were absorbed in. This therapy ("E" for entelechy, or if you like, the informing spirit), though akin to dianetics, had been evolved from early Buddhist texts by an Oriental scholar[2] whom they knew, and was a therapy supposed to reach and affect the "deeper self". This self, Aldous expounded, "can generally be relied on to come up with something useful to the organism, if it is politely asked to do so—

e.g. some memory which requires to be talked out several times until there is no further emotional reaction to it, or else some symbolic image which may not seem significant at the moment, but will often turn out to make sense later on. This method of approach is, I believe, much better than any course of suggestions pushed in by the operator, or than a too busy probing of analysis. There is a part of the subconscious non-self which is much less stupid than the self and

[1] Igor Stravinsky and Robert Craft, *Dialogues and a Diary*. Doubleday, 1963.
[2] A. L. Kitselman.

personal subconscious, and can be relied upon to provide help if asked . . .

. . . The procedure is actually a form of meditation, in which the meditator does not work alone, but is helped by the questions of an auditor. Why these questions should be helpful I do not exactly know. But the fact remains that they seem to assist the mind in its task of standing aside from the ego and its preoccupations, and laying itself open to the eternal consciousness. In a number of cases which I have seen the results have led to a remarkable increase in insight and improvement in behaviour.

There is a good deal more about this subject in Aldous's letters (from which I quoted fragments), to Julian urging him to have a go, to the Godels, later on to Dr Humphrey Osmond. Aldous's concern went beyond the immediate therapeutic results; the year before he had been working "with an interesting man, who was used, as a youth, as a hypnotic subject by a systematic investigator and goes down, under passes and suggestions, to a very great depth of trance—depths which are most uncommonly met with in ordinary hypnotic practice.[1]

The reports from these depths are most curious . . .

. . . Everything seems to point to the fact that, as one goes down through the subliminal, one passes through a layer (with which the psycho-analysts commonly deal) predominantly evil and making for evil—a layer of Original Sin, if one likes to call it so—into a deeper layer of "Original Virtue", which is one of peace, illumination and insight, which seems to be on the fringes of the Pure Ego or Atman . . .

Maria meanwhile was dealing with the thing in her own way. Aldous, she wrote to Jeanne, was quite evidently "blocked" and will take a long time to reach his "E" or deeper self. Whereas,

I, they say (and I know it's true) have a *rapport* with my "E" . . One feels oneself guided. I've always been profoundly convinced that we are guided; and had personal experience of it. During the first

---

[1] Aldous's interest in hypnosis began early. In 1937 he had published an article on the subject in *Nash's Magazine*. "The very pleasant young man", whom I called T., who was Aldous and Maria's neighbour at the Mount Royal Hotel in London during that spring and who rescued Aldous from the consequences of the botched operation on his jaw in Paris, did not entirely agree with the article and said so to Aldous. Aldous told T., who is of course Mr. Boris Trainin, the Harley Street dental consultant and analytical psychologist, that he very much wanted to be hypnotized but had never succeeded, and he asked him to try. "It occurred to me [in B.T.'s own words] that the previous failures might have been due to a wrong approach—i.e. asking him to lie down . . . I got him to stand up and you might say I took him by surprise. He was an excellent hypnotic subject. This first experience may have been the basis of his later development in this field."

years of our marriage I used to say to Aldous (without knowing what I was saying) "God's hand will show the way"—it was about material matters then. When I knew him better—thought I knew him better—I didn't say it so clearly any more. Now, all this is so evident between us . . . I think with this therapy we may have got a simple and rapid way of getting to what the yogi recommend us, and the saints. E Therapy, like dianetics, is not an *end*, but at present it seems to be the best *means* . . .

And last Tuesday they had had another meeting of "interested and serious friends", LeCron, the psychotherapist and the Hixons, their dentist friend and his wife, "a very intelligent medium", with Aldous giving magnetic treatment to Mrs Hixon. And now, Maria went on "I must come to another aspect of all this. Aldous.

. . You do know for how many years we've loved Aldous and known his goodness and his sweetness and his honesty—but you also know how tiring, in spite of all this, he was to live with—sad to live with. Well now, he is transformed, transfigured. What I mean to say is that this change has been working in an intangible way and for a very very long time but that the result has suddenly exploded—and I say *exploded*. Aldous no longer looks the same, his attitude is not the same, his moral and intellectual attitude, his attitude to animals, people, the clouds, to the telephone ringing (and that's going very far)—no, let's go further and say that he even decides his own decisions—*qu'il répond du tac au tac à des articles insultants; qu'il se fait payer son dû et demande que l'on lui rende des services*—but he also *offers* his services, whereas up to now he has always been content to offer a little money rather than to pay with his person, or rather with his soul. At last he has reached the point of putting into constant daily practice everything he wants to practise, and this even without realizing it . . . He goes to doctor's meetings, he went to defend a friend of Matthew's in court; he telephones Mrs Corbett to ask how she is—he eats Marie's dinners with pleasure, even orders them . . .

. . His search for this road, we know, did not only come out of his philosophical interests; he helped himself by psychological experiments, by spiritual exercises . . . what we shall never know is where this virtuous circle begins and ends. My illness, which might have muddled and blackened and exhausted everything, has been both the starting point and the arrival of this development. Which once more goes to show that every experience has some positive value and that we must accept it constructively.

Aldous's illness, already, was a great step for us in the good direction—or let us say, an enlightenment . . And it encouraged me a good deal. We need not fear anything . . .

Next Tuesday we are going to make an experiment I suggested and

Gerald will be here, but I don't know if this will be good or bad.

This letter to Jeanne was dated April, and in May Maria wrote that very curious one about her own visionary experiences to their "psychic friend", which Professor Grover Smith includes in Aldous's *Letters*. It begins:

. . Thank you for answering my question about prayer. I suppose I know all the answers in my head, but I only understand them when I know them in my heart; but that is all right too. Lately I am much more settled in my answers, and more believing in them. Just sometimes experiences are unbelievable because oneself is the experiencer when it seems that others would be more suitable—and deserving . . .

In the midst of all this Aldous went to see China Lake, the U.S. Naval Research station in the desert (he never missed the chance of any kind of sight, be it laboratory or sewage plant). "A thousand square miles of testing grounds. Sentries and F.B.I. men to check everybody going in or out . . ." Aldous was shown everything from million-volt X-ray cameras to refrigerated vacuum tanks and the insulated town

. . of twelve thousand inhabitants, mostly PH.D's, entirely air-conditioned, in the middle of the most howling of wildernesses. The whole directed exclusively to the production of bigger and better rockets. It was the most frightening exhibition of scientific and highly organized insanity I have ever seen.
One vaguely thought that the human race was determined to destroy itself. After visiting the China Lake Research station, one feels quite certain of it. And the whole world is fairly crawling with physicists in barbed wire compounds working three shifts a day *ad majorem Diaboli gloriam*. What a relief to turn to the book by [Konrad] Lorenz . .! Consider the wolves and the jackdaws . . .

Matthew was offered an interesting and well-paid job in an international organization, gave up his present one, found that the offer depended on further departmental decision and was left dangling. His father urged him to come out to California with Ellen and the baby on a long holiday. ". . Install yourself here, where I am sure you can make yourselves reasonably comfortable and have a reasonable degree of privacy [unpublished letter of 20th June]

Don't consider problems of expense. Your living won't cost much and money exists to be spent for productive purposes—and what purpose can be more productive than acquiring strength of body and peace of mind for a new beginning? . . . As for the job—it will come in due time. There are moments in life when it is imperative to behave like Mr Micawber and wait for Something to Turn Up, not try too hard to turn it up oneself, as though one were looking for a centipede under a stone.

Aldous, for his part, was in a similar position, the film on Gandhi for which he had been waiting these four months—"the haggling has been going on since February"—having been called off. Disappointment, vexation, but he tried to make the best of it. "I . . shall have time and peace of mind . . ." He also was at last getting the better of his chronic bronchitis by a pressure-breathing treatment with a new device, an apparatus attached to a portable oxygen tank, which he could take at home. Maria confirmed to Jeanne that both she and Aldous are admirably well, that Aldous is enlarging the range of his occupations, is speaking on the radio, appearing on television and on platforms. He has agreed to give a lecture on Art in Washington in 1954, "and even thinks that he might be able to talk instead of read. Which is an enormous step. In the past he simply would have ignored the possibility of doing such a thing."

Maria's letters this summer always come back to the main theme. To Jeanne she writes: "I am much comforted to know that you are interested in spiritual things. Because for a long time now it is only this which interests me and I feel entirely cut off from those who do not share this in the ultimate sense.

Of course there are a thousand ways or rather as many ways as there are human beings, of being spiritually concerned. But if it's totally lacking I have no more contact. Rose is much nearer to it than you would think—by way of the Catholic side. Suzanne, on the contrary, is very far, I think; but the worst situation is Mère's. If there is time I'll talk to you about Mère . . .

. . First of all I must tell you that pure "intellectuality" is as much an obstacle as anything else . . its a *barrage* . . .

. . *Savoir et pouvoir*—to know and to do—are two different things . . . And we must look everywhere to find what we are looking for . . . The Perennial Philosophy is the most helpful . . . And yet I've got to tell you what Krishnaji indefatigably repeats—that it is in ourselves that we shall find the answer if we know how to listen. Where Krishnaji doesn't give us any help is in learning to listen and how to prepare the ground. Krishnaji has so well understood the error of Theosophical directions by the . . Masters etc that he himself will indicate no system. And yet we are all so buffeted by the speed of living that it seems to me that a technique is necessary to eliminate the *fragmentation, the unnecessary tensions,* caused by the details of daily life . . You and I, and certainly women, have a more cluttered life than the men of our class. When their work, which is essentially concentrated while ours is dispersed, is over they are able to sit back, they've earned their living. Whereas you have to be at the disposal of your husband, your children, the housekeeping, have to pay the bills, go to the hairdresser and the cleaners, sew a button . . even to ask someone else to sew a button is a distraction and interruption . . .

At this point there did come one indeed, and Maria had to resume her letter a few days later.

I think that what I meant to tell you is that it was probably the search for their E—in that useful terminology of the E therapy— which made those so-called bigots always run to church. The silence of a church, and perhaps even the monotony of the litanies and the prayers prayed by the lips only, may calm the conscious, send it to sleep, so that we may arrive at the unconscious. So we should not criticise those pious old women too much, for as soon as one criticises one feels oneself superior and by this alone buckles oneself into an armour impenetrable even to our E.

Then, going back to the perennial philosophy, Maria speaks of Aldous's talent for choosing "important, comprehensible and practicable passages.

. . [his extracts from] William Law, for example, have moved me so much, while read as a whole he is unreadable, at least to me. The same goes for Benoit who is often arid, and also for Godel . . .

. . I hope that if ever you feel a need for calm, for silence, such as I had in the desert, you will go and sit in a corner of St Sulpice and forget everything that may be troubling you. You will be surprised how much this will calm and "enlighten" you . . . I remember some of my most difficult moments, physically and emotionally—in New York with Sophie [in 1940] for her *bachot.*[1] The real war had started, but I'd promised to take her, I travelled under pressure, no news from Europe, worried about Aldous, with Sophie anxious about her exam, anxious about you, Mère and Rose, and you all God knew where. Well, it was in the cathedral, where I went to burn a candle for Sophie's success, that I found re-assurance—and I was far from realizing then how this could be possible . . . I think you understand what I am trying to tell you.

---

[1] Argot for *baccalaureat.*

It was possible, even natural for Maria to write like this to Jeanne, herself open, alert to new theories and practices. How to approach a young man confident in the ways of the world? How to approach Matthew? Finally she wrote him a very long letter. It is the letter which began with, "Why, why in the world did Aldous choose me of the many prettier, wittier, richer etc girls? Why in the world did he come back to fetch me after two long years . . .? Knowing all the time . . that he could never teach me to write poetry or remember what I read in a book or spel . . ." It is the letter first mentioned, in the context of 1918, in the chapter called Strain. These questions were Maria's *entrée en matière*, the matière being the E therapy and all it stood for, and it now went on:

He told me yesterday [in 1952] that I *was* very pretty when I was young . . but I doubt it, I would have known it then, and the photographs would show it now. Anyway one does not choose and wait so long or stick so long to a woman who was pretty once.

And why did I who was horrified by those Garsington men (and women) I who was so squashed by the English and terrified of·them, why did I let Aldous approach me . . ? Why, because, though I was not then in love with Aldous, even though he was in love with me, we could see all the underlying possibilities which are really facts. He could sense, shall we say, instead of see, that in spite of all he had been told, I was a steady one, and I could sense that I would be entirely devoted to his service for the rest of our lives. In fact we were fated to each other. And where psychology comes in is that we *acted* on it. And later on, in spite of life with a big L, we still stuck it out. Nothing is always perfect for anybody. So Aldous had to put up with me and I had to put up with him, or rather we had to put up with the difficulties life with a big L, as it does everyone else, got us into. Why we managed is because, underneath, our psychological sensitiveness knew better. Now, you are going to receive the same pamphlet[1] that Aldous sent Julian. Do read it; and do re-read it. Also re-read my letter after you have faithfully read the pamphlet; then you will say (because one needs some kind of speech) that our E's functioned. And that is what we think of yours and Ellen's.

Aldous's E functions chiefly in his work. But now, by developing it . . it works more and more in everyday life . . Aldous in fact, is being spontaneous . . . Aldous who could never *say* the right thing (I mean in the psychological sense and strains), now cannot say the wrong thing—and what is more, bubbles with the right things at the right moments and with the most difficult people and in the most difficult circumstances and in the most unaccountable positions. I

[1] A. L. Kitselman's on "E" therapy.

will add to all this that his health has immensely improved with the treatments, but to that must be added that now he himself takes them, orders the new [oxygen] tanks, in fact he *runs himself*. In fact he lets his E or super-conscious run him. There is no more a blockage between him and his super-conscious.

In my case, all the attempts at the hand-writing, hand-reading, interest in fortune tellers, the fact that they read so well for me and *through* me; the fact that I do immensely know all the time what people feel, unfortunately too much sometimes . . (of course there is a reverse side to my medal as well) . . my spontaneity . . the fact that in a whole life I cannot remember quarrelling with anyone (Ottoline when I was 17, because she said I flirted with Philip who was . . not more interested in me than in every other young woman . . .). You probably never stopped to realize the terribly difficult position of an upstart little refugee getting away with the prize of the artistic English world—and keeping her prize—and at the age of twenty and without any schooling except failures. I did not ever come down to their levels of malice or sex, but that does not mean that I ever rose to their heights of intelligence and brilliance. Now, do you not realize that something helped us stronger and better than ourselves. Certainly not my *intelligence*; nor Aldous's. And from the E (to use the jargon, one must use some) everything is explained and explainable. And what an interesting novel; to write the life of people backwards, tracing their E. (It would have to be called something else, for public consumption—do not think we have become Faddists. Less than ever. We eat and drink and think and sleep and walk and work as everyone else does). In my case with more realization for the steps I take, and fall down upon too. But with no more despair and recrimination. I really have become patient. And those nerves were so very superficial. *I tremble to know* how you will both take it. Because we would lose nothing by your criticism as we know your affection is unlimited, but we would retard your realizing what we think is so important to realize. By putting you against it. And of course experience is the only thing . . I . . have always known it; Aldous knew it when he wrote *The Perennial Philosophy*, but at one remove so to speak; intellectualizing the whole thing. But it was in him; a few of us, Aunt Mary, and all his family, knew the treasure there was in Aldous, I sensed it, always as well as *knew* it, it was always ready for me, *under*, the superficial denseness, as superficial as my nerves and yours, but whereas one can get at nerves more easily by medications and by conscious will, one cannot get at that other thing so easily. Now the treasure is flowing in torrents of gaiety and openness, just sift it out while keeping in clear cool water. And as you can expect when the clearance hits Aldous it *is something*. Nothing ever was much buried in me, nor was there so much to reveal; but there is an easing for myself and all others which you would appreciate more than anyone else. And I *could* have been very ill and tiresome after the operation; some people remain rather stunted in their movements. Yesterday I actually managed to stand on my head again (it needs a terrific *stretch* in the arm). So you must *one day*, for we are as patient as we are trusting, come and see what you think of all this for yourselves and Trevenen.

Now, I hope this does explain a bit more. We are still using doctors, we are still using Bates, we still are imperfect, but we are at least working on improving ourselves, our output, and we do think there are many ways, and many of them unexplored, and their results are widely and wildly fascinating and worthwhile . . I know, you are afraid we go off the rails—don't. This has come to Aldous's help because *his* danger was that the rails would stop in front of a cement dam. You said as much when you were nervous in Wrightwood, that he was just "sitting looking at his own navel" *that* was the danger. Whether navel or otherwise, let us all look as far as we can and that is unlimited.

As our loves,

Coccola.

Here one might come in with a fragment of corroboration by Aldous. "There is a striking phrase by von Baader", he wrote to Alan Watts, "the German philosopher of the Romantic Era, who emended Descartes' Cogito ergo sum to cogitor ergo sum—we think only in so far as we permit ourselves to be thought by the immanent and transcendent X."

And this is how Rose—whose own marriage had gone to pieces —saw her sister and brother-in-law at this very time (in a letter to Jeanne).

. . . Maria et Aldous vont tous deux remarquablement bien. Très calmes et très, très gentils et compréhensifs . . . Leurs études les passionnent et semblent leur apporter beaucoup de paix. Ils sont si gentils l'un pour l'autre que cela me réconcilie avec la vie: il y a donc des couples heureux. Leur maison est un succès et enfin digne d'eux.

A visit by Joep and Suzanne now, on their way back from a journey in Mexico. They found Aldous in good form and Maria more willing to let herself be waited on. Suzanne, too, approved of the new house and the presence of a really first-rate French cook—Marie Le Put, a Bretonne and a very kind and intelligent woman. The Nicolases joined the round of Stravinsky luncheons ("for Igor one had to have French wine, whereas ordinarily one drank California wine"), gramophone music, walks. They did not take part in the Tuesday evenings, in what Suzanne calls "les séances de spiritisme et de chiromancie."

After they had left, Madame Nys sprained her arthritic shoulder and a less harmonious family note is sounded by Aldous letting off some steam to Matthew and Ellen (in September)

> . . . she is making use of her trouble to get as much attention and service out of both Rose and Coccola as she possibly can. Rose had to rush in from the desert over the weekend . . and C is kept on the hop all the time, fetching, carrying, shopping etc. This wouldn't be so bad, if it weren't for the continual stream of emphatic and self-contradictory talk . . and for the elaborate and preposterous schemes and plots which BM [Bonne Maman] has only too much leisure to hatch. Coccola has never had a wide margin of reserve strength to draw upon, and since her operation this margin has shrunk to a point where her mother (who, for all her age and her rheumatism, has far more physical energy than her daughters) can easily push her over the edge . . .

The problem, Aldous goes on, is a difficult and many-sided one. There is first of all the psychological problem of an old woman who has consistently refused to be anything in life but a tourist.

> BM resolutely declines to do anything useful, to co-operate in any way which would entail her making compromises and suiting her own convenience to that of others . . . Because she reads the *Figaro Littéraire*, she feels herself immeasurably superior to the general run of her neighbours . . She has quarrelled with the local Catholic church and so cut herself off from the social and benevolent organizations which it sponsors and in which she could certainly have found something interesting and useful to do. Age and disability make the full life of the tourist impossible for her; and she now spends her energies brooding and making life intolerable for Coccola and Rose. What can be done I don't know . . . In no circumstances would I think of installing her in this house. She would drive Coccola to death or madness in a few months, would make it impossible for me to do any work . . .

This last more than anything makes one realize what a penetrating personality Mme Nys has been. "Suzanne", Aldous concluded, "may consider herself extremely lucky to be three thousand miles away . . ."

Aldous's friend Larry Powell, Librarian at U.C.L.A., asked him to give a talk on Bernard Shaw. Alas, Aldous replied, he felt wholly unqualified to talk about G. B. S., "whom I don't know at all well—perhaps because I have never found him very interesting. Did he, after all, ever know anything about human beings?"

In October, publication of *The Devils of Loudun*. The long, laborious job that promised, as Aldous said in mid-writing, to turn into something very substantial. It is a psychological study of "one of the most fantastically strange stories in all French history—the story [as he described it to Harold Raymond ten years before] of the demoniac possession of the nuns of Loudun,

> which begins with fraud, hysteria, malicious plotting; goes on with the commission of a monstrous judicial crime, the burning of Urbain Grandier, as the supposed author of the possession; continues posthumously with more diabolic manifestations and the bringing on to the scene of Father Surin, one of the most saintly ecclesiastics of his age, who tries to exorcise the Abbess of the convent . . . [and] by a kind of psychological infection, himself succumbs to possession and becomes half mad, but with perfectly lucid intervals, in which he realizes the full extent of his misfortune. Surin remains in this state for nearly twenty years, but finally emerges into a serene old age of something like perfected sanctity, during which he writes some of the most important spiritual works of his period . . .

And nearly twenty years later, Aldous went on in the London interview, "The strange thing is that the whole Loudun affair is interesting only if you take the two sides together.

> If you take the case of Grandier, and then the case of Surin. Between them, the two episodes describe the religious life on every level— from the most horrible to the most sublime. The whole gamut of religious life is set forth in a kind of parabola in these two episodes. Now the really extraordinary thing is that as far as I know I was the first person to bring these two episodes together in a single volume. Plenty of French people have written about Grandier, and in recent times about Surin, but nobody has thought fit to put the two cases together . . .
>
> This is the whole message of this extraordinary episode—religion is infinitely ambivalent. It has these wonderful sides to it, and these appalling sides . . .
>
> And here is a story which is strictly historical—and I really never departed from the historical documents—which is at the same time a parable. And *this* is what I'm looking for: an historical or biographical medium in terms of which I can think about all sorts of general subjects.
>
> I do strongly feel that philosophical and religious ideas are better expressed not in abstract terms but in terms of concrete case histories

.. If you can find the right kind of case history .. And this .. is why I am looking for another biographical historical personage or episode on which to hang my ideas . . .

Before the turn of the year the long expected arrival of Matthew with his family. Matthew was still between jobs, the delicate baby in poor health, Aldous, though fighting bronchitis, at work again —on the scenario of a popular film on the sun, a bread-and-butter job. Once again, life with Aldous and Maria is seen through a young woman in their household, Ellen, their daughter-in-law (older than Suzanne at Paddington, younger than Jeanne or myself). ".. It's fascinating to see what can be recalled and what is gone.[1] I have strong visual pictures, almost like a camera— Aldous doing his Bates eye exercises in the patio outside his study door; Maria darting about, her feet scarcely touching the ground, as she sprayed Air-Wick throughout the house because someone had smoked a cigarette; Marie Le Put, smiling and smiling and making madeleines or a soufflé (my God, the Huxleys ate well! .. the inside of their huge freezer, stuffed with breads and meats— they had given up being vegetarian on doctors' advice, and switched merrily over to the side of the carnivores; they even used to sneak hamburger to the Rajagopal's cat, because the poor thing was given only vegetables).

I suppose you have written about Maria and cars? I was astonished by her expertise with them . . . the incongruity of her small, feminine self being able to listen to her car engine critically, whip it into a garage, and give the mechanics a complete run-down on what was going on and how she wanted it adjusted.

They had a ring-toss game for Trev, a wooden rabbit with long ears and a set of rope rings you were supposed to toss on to the ears.

Aldous was deadly at this game—he was so used to concentrating what sight he had, when he wanted to use it, that he simply never missed. Though at other times of course he would run into things . . . Kings Road was a dark and gloomy house, with long corridors, not much sunlight . . .
We saw many people. They were tremendously hospitable, even to people they didn't know. Maria was major-domo and screened the visitors, but with so much tact and charm that everyone without exception felt better about themselves by the time they left . . .

[1] The present Ellen Giffard writing to S. B.

Maria drove them out to Pasadena for tea with Edwin Hubble, "the astronomer of Palomar . . Fred Hoyle came too, being very intelligent and very bumptious,

the screaming was intense. Except for Hubble, that gentle, warm, touching man—in the middle of all the complex talk he wandered outside, came back to urge us all out ". . to see the evening star".

Edith Sitwell was in Hollywood that winter, and, as Ellen put it, "was around a lot. Maria would groan privately and say that Edith had always been in love with Aldous and wanted to marry him; Aldous said nothing, but was obviously enjoying himself.

He and Edith spent a happy day together touring Forest Lawn cemetery; they said they got treated with a lot of interest because they were both old enough to be serious candidates for a plot. They crowed when they found out that the bridal chapel was heated by heat generated by the crematorium.

And there were of course the North Kings Tuesdays. Aldous would take Matthew and Ellen to the pre-séance dinner at the mammoth drug store (mixed grill and phonograph records). Maria did not come: she never ate on Tuesdays.

. . She was in her element, very good at these things, completely in tune with her unconscious—Aldous went at it without preconception and with immense good will, but he was passive; his imagination didn't run naturally along those lines.

After these glimpses, Ellen sums up her main impression of that time. "Aldous and Maria dealing with being parents and parents-in-law and grand-parents, all three unfamiliar roles to them. They included us in their circle, were terrified Matthew wouldn't approve of the Tuesdays, doted on Trev, worried about Matthew's future, opened their hearts to me in the most generous way, suffered from their loss of privacy, couldn't believe how much we ate, thought us rather 'square', offered tremendous intimacy and openness. Maria never knew when to stop giving and start protecting herself, which would make her cross and exhausted at times—and she was full of forebodings about her health (typically, she discussed this with Marie the cook and not with the family; she had the deepest, strongest relationships with her servants [here I profoundly agree]. There is nothing she wouldn't have done for them, or they for her). So we got to know each other, and dealt with a lot of anxiety, and had great times together, and my remembrance is of untold tenderness and grace and love and good will . . ."

Matthew and Ellen left before the spring. On 25th February Lewis Gielgud died. His death came as a shock, Aldous wrote to Juliette, "we had been friends for half a century". And to Naomi Mitchison, that other companion of his young years, he wrote a month later,

> His going seems curiously hard to take in . . He had been part of my Order of Things . . ever since we first met as new boys at our preparatory school in the autumn of 1903. He was a gentle man as well as a gentleman, with all the qualities of humaneness connoted by both expressions.

Lewis Gielgud—who at Eton had learnt Braille in order to be able to write to Aldous. Aldous too had been a faithful and affectionate friend. He was always that; in his great friendships and his lighter ones: inseparable by distance, time and the widening spaces of his own development. The thought that had flashed through Gervas's mind in 1914 as they said goodbye on the platform of King's Cross, cogito*r*, the thought which Gervas, as Aldous saw it now, had permitted himself to *be* thought—"If one survived one would never have to bother about communication with Aldous, there was something imperishable there," proved true. They all lasted as long as life, kept a freshness at the rare encounters: the friendship with Lewis, with Gervas (theirs was a double tie), with Eugene Saxton, with—to lesser degrees—Evan Morgan, Robert Nichols, Tommy Earp, the affective, companionable, exploratory friendships of his youth and the two great formative friendships of his maturer years, D. H. Lawrence and Gerald Heard. And now he was within weeks of one more of these precipitatory compatibilities, a relationship, this time, with a very much younger man whom he came to hold in affection and admire, Dr Humphrey Osmond. (One does realize that Aldous's most intimate friends, though men of high intelligence in their different ways and men of human quality [Lawrence of course stands entirely apart], were not the masters, the highbrows, the literary mandarins of his time, not, though he knew them all and was fond of many, Bloomsbury, not the Sitwells, not Morgan Forster or Tom Eliot.)

Dr Osmond, an English psychiatrist, was working at the time in a state mental hospital, Saskatchewan, on the Canadian Prairies. He, with Drs John Smythies and Abram Hoffer, were doing research in schizophrenia in the course of which they had been using mescalin. A paper setting out some of their findings had been published in medical and scientific journals. These Aldous read. He sent a friendly letter to the young doctors. Humphrey Osmond, who had kept a copy of *Texts and Pretexts* by him on Atlantic convoys and who had just read *The Devils of Loudun*, answered. Aldous wrote again. A month later, unexpectedly, Osmond had to attend a meeting of the American Psychiatrists' Association in Los Angeles. As unexpectedly, Aldous asked him to stay at North Kings. Later on he was told how it had come about, how at breakfast one morning Aldous had looked up and said, " 'Let's ask this fellow Osmond to stay'," and that Maria replied, " 'But he may have a beard and we may not like him.' Aldous thought for a bit, and said, 'If we don't like him we can always be out.' "[1]

On 3rd May the young man arrived. Feeling very shy. Maria, of course, put him at his ease. She told him that he and Aldous, being Englishmen, would get on. "To Maria, Englishmen were largely incomprehensible except to each other."[1] (How true this was.) Then, "Aldous glided towards me from the cool darkness of the house into the sunshine of the front porch. He seemed to be suspended a fraction of an inch above the ground like one of Blake's allegorical figures . . ." They got on. Humphrey says that what struck him from the beginning was the kindness and tolerance of this man, whose writings had led him to suppose that he would be "disillusioned, cynical and even savage". Or solemn. Humphrey took Aldous along to a session of his learned conference. They were standing in the foyer "when Aldous's voice cut through the hubbub like a knife-blade, 'But Humphrey, how incredible it is in a Marxist country like this . . .' It was 1953 at the height of the McCarthy era . . ." Inside the hall, Aldous sat "paying the keenest attention, crossing himself devoutly every time Freud's name was mentioned . . Here was a congregation, including many pious Freudians, so Aldous was kept busy. Luckily my psychiatric colleagues were so absorbed by the incantations that no one noticed him."

Mescalin, so far, had not been mentioned between host and guest. Mescalin, one might briefly recall, is a mind-altering substance, derived from the Mexican root peyote, that causes hallucinations, visions and dreams. It was first classified in the 1880s by a German pharmacologist, Louis Lewin, who divided all mind-altering agents into five groups: *euphorica, inebriantia, hypnotica, excitantia* and *phantastica*. Mescalin and LSD belong to the *phantastica*. Mescalin was synthesized about 1918. LSD—lysergic acid diethylamide—a synthetic, was discovered only in 1943.[2] By the 1950s mescalin had been experimented with on and off for the last seventy years, by Havelock Ellis, Jaensch,

[1] Dr Humphrey Osmond, *Mem. Vol.*
[2] By the Swiss scientist Professor A. Hofmann in the course of work on ergot derivatives.

Weir Mitchell among others. A number of psychologists and alienists had taken it in the hope of coming to a firsthand understanding of their patients' mental processes, but these were a small and limited category of guinea pigs, and the material collected was still very inadequate. Aldous offered himself as a possible new subject. He has given his reasons for doing so in a letter to Dr Osmond (10th April 1953) which it is rather essential to read if one wishes to understand what followed.

> .. It looks as though the most satisfactory working hypothesis about the human mind must follow, to some extent, the Bergsonian model, in which the brain with its associated normal self, acts as a utilitarian device for limiting, and making selections from, the enormous possible world of consciousness, and for canalizing experience into biologically profitable channels.
>
> Disease, mescalin, emotional shock, aesthetic experience and mystical enlightenment have the power, each in its different way and in varying degrees, to inhibit the functions of the normal self and its ordinary brain activity, thus permitting the "other world" to rise into consciousness . . .

Now Aldous comes to what for him was the basic problem of education—"How to make the best of both worlds—the world of biological utility and common sense, and the world of unlimited experience underlying it." He believed that a complete solution of this problem could only come to those who had learned about "the third and ultimate world of 'the spirit', the world which subtends and interpenetrates both of the outer worlds. But short of this ultimate solution, there may be partial solutions, by means of which the growing child may be taught to preserve his 'intimations of immortality' into adult life.

> Under the current dispensation the vast majority of individuals lose, in the course of education, all the openness to inspiration, all the capacity to be aware of other things than those enumerated in the Sears-Roebuck catalogue which constitutes the conventionally "real" world. That this is not the necessary and inevitable price extorted for biological survival and civilized efficiency is demonstrated by the existence of the few men and women who retain their contact with the other world, even while going about their business in this. Is it too much to hope that a system of education may some day be devised, which shall give results, in terms of human development, commensurate with the time, money, energy and devotion expended?
>
> In such a system of education it may be that mescalin or some other chemical substance may play a part by making it possible for young people to "taste and see" what they have learned about at second

hand, or directly but at a lower level of intensity, in the writings of
the religious, or the works of poets, painters and musicians . . .

Once under the same roof, however, the two Englishmen
needed Maria to get it going. She told Humphrey Osmond that
Aldous was waiting to take the mescalin, was looking forward to
it and that his doctors had no objection. Aldous had already laid
on a dictaphone for the occasion. Humphrey Osmond, who had
misgivings—What if it didn't work? What if it worked too well?
—could see no decent way of backing out. "Aldous seemed an
ideal subject . . . in spite of remarks that I sometimes heard about
'unfortunate mystical trends in his later years' I found him, both
then and subsequently, shrewd, matter-of-fact and to the point . . .
[and] Maria eminently sensible, and we had all taken to each
other, which was very important for a good experience . . ."[1]

Thus it came about [Aldous speaking[2]] that, one bright May
morning, I swallowed four-tenths of a gram of mescalin dissolved in
half a glass of water and sat down to wait for the results.

The session lasted for about eight hours. Dr Osmond and Maria
remained with him throughout. They, it goes without saying, had
not taken the drug. The experience was of profound significance
to Aldous. This he tried to put across in a small book, much
debated, *The Doors of Perception*.

[1] Dr Humphrey Osmond, *Mem. Vol.*
[2] *The Doors of Perception*. Chatto & Windus, 1954.

# Chapter Three

# The Door in the Wall

HUMPHREY OSMOND left. Aldous and Maria went off on one of their car journeys—three weeks, five thousand miles, of nature and national parks in the vast American Northwest. From Cœur d'Alene, Idaho, they sent a postcard to Anita Loos.

> *There was a young lady of Bute*
> *Who was so indescribably cute*
> *That, each time she came out,*
> *All the boys gave a shout,*
> *With the Lesbians hot in pursuit.*
>
> Love Aldous

What more can one add!! M.

After their return Aldous was ready to get down to the small book. He finished it in a month. "So we are happy and working [I had a note from Maria] .. Last Sunday we had a fête, Aldous's 59th birthday." (The Hubbles, Stravinsky, Gerald, Eva Herrmann, Christopher Wood.) Work continued. Opportunely, *Life* Magazine asked Aldous to do an article on parapsychology.[1] Matthew and Ellen were expecting a second child. What a good letter, Aldous said as he read the news.

What good children, I thought. [Maria to Ellen] What treasures ...

With Matthew between jobs, the young Huxleys had been having the devil of a year but were getting the better of it now by making their own decisions. Matthew chose to specialize in a field that interested him and was given a scholarship at the Harvard School of Public Health. Once more, Maria was trying to impart to them something of what she had learned—about the give and take of marriage, about how to live—letters impelled, one feels, by a great urge and written in a tempo that is not that of the young and well. Perhaps that terrible year has brought them something, she wrote, "no experience, however painful, is not without its own reward: to Matthew it may have brought a patience towards grown-ups; and when he will realize that no one 'Knows better' but that we all 'Know differently', he will

---

[1] "A Case for Esp, Pk and Psi", *Life*, January 1954.

have reached what Aldous has reached now. And I believe that
Matthew may reach it at a very much younger age than Aldous
did."

Last winter already they had been "enchanted and surprised"
by him and Ellen. "Never did you refuse to look at the things,
however mad or new which came your way when you were
staying with us." And once we realize, Maria went on, about
this " 'knowing different', then we can apply to ourselves that
which we can use, rather than waste our energies to teach others
what we think we know better. Others can only use what we
have to give if we let them use it in their own way. Of course
one must also understand that some things might be left to the
one who does them best . . in practical matters for instance. You
cannot pack properly and leave it to Matthew." Yet even there
they have a warning in her and Aldous's life.

> Since I was exactly sixteen, I lived with those who could "think
> better" and also "speak better" . . but there was one field in which,
> when we were young, Aldous always turned to me—psychological
> matters. He used to say I was his personal relationship interpreter—
> and probably because he relied on me then, I took over too much;
> his efforts grew less and less until he gave it up almost completely
> and had to start the whole thing from scratch almost, about four
> years ago—I *could* have used my mind with more precision had I
> exercised it more—until that age my studies were very satisfactory . . .
> Aldous is both being more and more practical and needs *no* inter-
> preter ever now with human beings. It is a bit late for me to start
> training my mind in memorizing quotations which Aldous has at his
> fingertips, but I am sure that somewhere I am "still learning" . . .

As ever the letter is packed with fifty other things: from Sophie
being off to Ceylon on Unesco business, and the Kiskaddens
well and cheerful, to Ellen's health—"Relax in a room as silent
as can be, and pile cushions *under* as well as over the telephone . . .
but then we are so much older and of a different period that I
do not realize what you need . . . I wish I were the useful type of
Grandmother . . . My cooking is getting rarer and worse. [their
French paragon did not come every day] Luckily Yolanda is
reconstructed now and cool and open at night; the Stravinskys
send their love." California has been hotter than anyone can
remember but she stood it well, so now they *can* go to India any
time Aldous wants to. He has finished his article on mescalin.
Hutchins is reading it and was enormously interested and is
going to try to get the psychology department to take an interest . . .
"Magic," the letter ends, "is advancing."

That was Robert M. Hutchins, then a director of the Ford

Foundation, now President of the Center for Democratic Studies at Santa Barbara, whom Aldous had been trying to persuade, now with Alan Watts, now with Dr von Bertalanffy,[1] now with Julian, to carry out a variety of projects—research into the phenomena of the human organism as a whole, research into the role of language in international affairs, into non-verbal, non-conceptual education. The latest idea, suggested by Drs Osmond and Hoffer, was to record mescalin experiments with some fifty people of outstanding and diverse abilities. Hutchins himself was generally willing but unable to override objections from the heads of the concerned departments, the mesozoic reptiles, Aldous called them, who would not touch anything faintly controversial with a barge pole.

Hutchins's comments on how relentlessly Aldous pursued all technological change.

He dragged me to Hollywood to meet a man who had a device that would slow down a phonograph to half speed and thus permit far longer and cheaper records . . .

He dragged me to lunch with the founder of the Ampex Corporation to hear the tale of building an airplane untouched by human hands that could fly to any destination without a pilot . . .[2]

But he always raised the question of advantages or disadvantages to human life; once when someone held forth about the wonders of modern communications, Hutchins heard Aldous reply,

"When we didn't communicate with Japan, we didn't go to war with her, either."

During the summer the Huxleys got themselves involved in a farcical imbroglio. "Were you with us at Bandol when at the Casino there was a Fakir called Tahra Bey, sticking pins and needles and doing terrific other tricks?" Maria wrote to Matthew.

Well, Tahra Bey has become a friend in distress. He is an M.D. of the faculty of Paris and Turkey (?). He is here and Aldous had a long talk with him . . . He is giving a show on Wednesday and we are all going . . .

Maria has been very busy [this is Aldous, to Humphrey] trying to help a man we met twenty years ago . . a Lebanese doctor who learned all the tricks of the dervishes and has made a living all these years by giving demonstrations of being buried alive . . . A charming

[1] Dr Ludwig von Bertalanffy, the Austrian biologist, author of *The Problems of Life*, London, 1952.
[2] Robert M. Hutchins, *Mem. Vol.*

man—but unfortunately he contrived to spend more than two years in London without learning one word of English. This somewhat cramps his style when giving demonstrations here. He has been swindled right and left . . . he is finally in the hands of some Armenians . . . pork manufacturers, with a farm where five thousand sows work overtime eating the garbage of the city of Long Beach . . . our poor friend . . who was brought up in Armenia . . despises them as *marchands de cochons* and won't accept them as interpreters.
So his performance is a chaos of incomprehensibility . . .

And so it would appear, from accounts of persons on the scene, was the tale of Aldous and Maria's intervention: hilarious but too chaotic to relate here.

Now Julian appeared, on his way to Australia. "Julian came and went like a dream" Maria wrote to Matthew and Ellen. ". . Every minute of his stay was perfect and I believe he enjoyed it as much as we did. Poor Julian . . whenever he is not talking about his own affairs—and I must say very interesting—he has such a sad look in his face, perhaps that is why he must keep his mind crammed and crammed with outside business. But he looked well and was very calm and peaceful and *so like* little Trev —did you also notice that? . . Julian did not once *really look* at Aldous, ask how he was, what he was working at etc, really it is very extraordinary."

Their own great excitement was a new car. An Oldsmobile again, and "really almost everything that the advertisements say about power brakes and power steering is true. I was upset for 3 days at what it cost and could not sleep. Now it has all settled down—except for paying of course."

Edwin Hubble died on 28th September, very suddenly on his driveway in his car. Besides their own sadness Aldous and Maria were much concerned about his widow, their friend Grace.

Two years earlier, the Huxleys had decided to take out their first papers, to apply for American citizenship that is. They had been living in the United States for fourteen years. "We were *de facto* Californians, and it seemed the proper thing to become *de jure* Americans." According to Betty Wendel, their chief reason was that Matthew, himself a citizen since 1946 and raising an American family, would have liked his parents to do so. In the spring of 1953 Aldous and Maria had put in their final petition, and on 3rd November they came up for the routine examination

on the American Constitution and other matters which immediately precedes the ceremony that would make them U.S. citizens.
Betty Wendel and Rosalind Rajagopal were their character
witnesses. It was a Tuesday and they set out before eight o'clock
in the morning, taking Betty in the car.

Aldous looked *so* English [she writes in an unpublished memorandum
to S. B.], sitting by himself in the rear seat, those long legs folded,
arms outstretched, head tilted back in the posture that signalled his
willingness for small talk. And Maria looked so Maria at the driver's
wheel, not completely disguised as an American businessman's wife
by her dark blue suit and hat, white blouse, white gloves within reach
for changing from chauffeur's pigskin. I presented each of them with
a handkerchief with M.N.H. and A.L.H. embroidered in red, white
and blue, immediately placed in pockets with monograms showing.
To me the night before there had come a basket of champagne splits
with the Maria-Aldous bookplate affixed. On the back of it Maria
had written—legibly, ceremoniously: "Good health to you from two
very old friends and very new CITIZENS."

Maria had been coached for the looming examination and it
worried her that Aldous had not given her homework a glance.
"Aldous, are you *sure* that you know American history?"

"Reasonably sure."

"Do you understand the principles and the form of government?"
(In the rear-view mirror she saw him nod his prodigious head and
smile.) "Of course they'll see how intelligent *you* are, and they won't
question you the way they'll question *me*."

He teased her. "The examination can be as thorough or perfunctory
as they choose to make it."

"They won't make it perfunctory with me," said Maria.

Aldous laughed. "They might ask you to swear that you speak
English, but even if you fail to prove it, darling, *understanding* English
is good enough. You can nod your head in English, can't you?"

"Now you're making me cross."

He leaned forward and patted her shoulder. "Your mother and
Rose passed with flying colours. It's in the genes."

Presently they reached their destination, a court and offices on
a floor of the Rowan Building in Downtown Los Angeles.
(Rosalind Rajagopal was waiting.) "And there we were, Maria
and Aldous standing in a line that led to an information desk
with men and women of all ages and nationalities, flanked by
their character witnesses to whom they spoke in foreign accents
from slight to very thick." Betty and Rosalind were led off to
separate cubicles where anonymous men asked them how long
they had known Aldous Huxley? Was he, to their knowledge, a

man of good morals? regularly employed? on good terms with his neighbours? Did they know whether he had any pressing debts? Aldous and Maria meanwhile, having proved quite easily that their knowledge of the Constitution was sufficient, were required to fill in one more questionnaire. Among others, it contained these questions:

(*a*) Are you prepared to serve in the U.S. armed forces?

(*b*) Are you prepared to do non-combatant service in the U.S. armed forces?

(*c*) Are you prepared to do work of national importance under civilian control?

Aldous and Maria answered No to the first two questions and Yes to the third. They were summoned to a court room. A judge was on the platform, Aldous and Maria stood before him. (Betty was seated directly behind them and later made a verbatim note.)

The Judge: Mr Huxley, would you not bear arms in the United States Army?

Aldous: No.

The Judge: Would you not drive an army truck transporting armaments?

Aldous: No.

J: If the enemy were approaching your home, in defence of your wife and in self defence, would you not pick up a gun and stand by your front door, ready to fire?

A: I would not have a gun in the house.

J: Would you be willing to make bandages for the wounded.

A: Yes.

J: Would you serve in the Red Cross, as an ambulance driver?

A: If the question applies to my willingness, yes.

J: It does, Mr Huxley.

After the same questions had been put to and answered in the same spirit by Maria, the judge asked them whether their objection to bearing arms was based on religious beliefs? On philosophical convictions, Aldous replied and Maria followed .suit. Religio-philosophical? said the judge. No, purely philosophical.

Now, in 1946 there had been a U.S. Supreme Court decision to the effect that a person objecting to bearing arms might none the less become a citizen. The judge explained, in what Betty describes as regretful tones, that this decision had been superseded, or was held to have been superseded by most lawyers, by the McCarran Immigration Act of 1952 which denied citizenship to any person refusing to bear arms for any reason other than *religious beliefs*. "The judge then gazed at Aldous with the deep respect to which he was accustomed and asked if he was not a religious man? Aldous said that he was indeed a religious man; his opposition to war, however, was an entirely philosophical one.

"The judge sighed. Maria whispered, 'Aldous, do say it's for religious reasons, let's get it over with.' Could he give his personal definition of conscientious objection? asked the judge. Aldous changed his stance from languid to making a stand, he looked directly at the judge, his face and hands became mobile (Maria perked up), his voice was at its most melodious . . . He smiled as he said that at the age of 59 it was unlikely that he would be drafted and have to claim exemption as a conscientious objector. Any trace of irony was gone as he went on to explain that his personal definition of pacifism was a deep conviction of the evil of war based on his philosophy, and not on the tenets of any religious belief, his own or that of any church or creed. Maria looked disturbed, but only for a moment. The judge sighed again and asked Aldous to consider the possibility that his philosophy was an extension of religion."

Aldous stuck to his guns. At the end the judge had no choice but to adjourn proceedings. "Aldous looked at his watch, not closely enough for him to see the time, but as his signal to Maria. 'I think we must be going,' he said to the judge, and then he reached across the table on the platform to shake hands. The judge gave Aldous printed sheets of paper, complete with addressed envelopes, and said 'I will send my report to Washington. At your convenience there will be a special hearing to determine what procedure will grant you naturalization. I am sorry that *postponement* is necessary.'

"Maria said, 'Thank you, your Honour.'

"When they left the building Aldous's face was white. He said with an entirely uncharacteristic show of feeling, 'They don't want us here!'

"On the way uptown there was little conversation. All three of us sat up in front of the car and I felt in the middle of more than the seat. Aldous loosened his necktie, ran his fingers through his hair, wiped his forehead with that foolish souvenir handkerchief from me. Worse, in the refrigerator at home lay three splits of champagne for a celebration luncheon. As we were nearing my house, Maria asked Aldous if he would rather go straight home, and he said, 'Yes, I would.' Stupidly I said, 'But we're having crab salad . . and brie cheese and melon.' 'Can't we have it tomorrow?' Maria asked. 'Not the same crab,' I said. Aldous said, 'I very much want to go home and go to bed.' Maria said, 'Betty, you understand, don't you?' I understood everything except the McCarran Act, and having seen leaving the building goodness knows how many brand new United States citizens happily chattering in the languages of their native lands now that they were Americans. None of them looked distinguished . . a few struck me as shady characters up to no good in our melting pot."

A few days after, Aldous wrote to Cass Canfield asking for his advice. "The current situation, so far as we are concerned, is as follows. We shall be called up for further examination, probably within three or four weeks.[1]

> If the examiner finds our position acceptable, we shall be allowed to proceed with our naturalization; if not the petition will be rejected.
>
> If it is rejected, we shall, I suppose, return to the status of resident alien. But in practice it will be difficult, perhaps impossible, to return to this country if we should ever leave it. Now I have various engagements in Europe next spring and do not wish to cancel them. Moreover the situation of not being wanted and not being able to come and go at will is one I would not be prepared to accept.
>
> So if the petition is rejected, I should feel bound, albeit with great reluctance, to wind up our affairs here and leave the country . . .
>
> . . The whole business has its absurd side, since it hardly seems probable that the armed forces would be very keen on having either Maria or myself in their midst. However, a law is a law.

They went off for a couple of weeks in Northern California. Here Aldous gave his first lecture on a subject that more and more engrossed him, Non-Verbal Education, the training, that is, of the human entity by psycho-physical procedures. He spoke once at Palo Alto, once at a women's college (Mills), feeling, he said, like Daniel in a lionesses' den, a prey to innumerable questions about all that is knowable and a good deal that is not. For the rest they drove about enjoying that incredibly beautiful countryside. Aldous's work plans were quite unsettled. He might try to do some more short stories or novelettes, he wrote to Harold Raymond, or might try his hand on a book on human beings and what, if anything, can be done about them. "I have written one chapter of it and have others in my mind." (I think that the chapter may have been "Education of an Amphibian" which appeared later as the lead essay in *Adonis and the Alphabet*.) Alternately he might sit down to something he has had in his head for a long time, a novel extending from the mid-nineteenth century to the present.

It was only in December that Aldous mentions that Maria has had to have X-ray treatments and is going to have more. In two letters, to Humphrey Osmond and to Eileen Garrett, he speaks of

---

[1] Unpublished letter of 7th November.

how very badly the rays affect her, of the intolerable nervous strain, the physical exhaustion. There is not a word about it in Maria's letters to her family. (Only to the unmet psychic friend in England did she write already in October, "I am well too, but suddenly X-ray treatments come to shatter the wellness.")

Matthew had had a daughter, Tessa, in the autumn. First photographs arrived in the New Year, and Maria wrote

Matthew darling . . . Ellen my sweet—How beautiful those children are! Aldous's first remark was, "Aren't you proud of them?" And in the middle of dinner he suddenly interrupted the music to say, "I can't get over the beauty of those children." . . It is more than beauty, it is peace and strength already that radiates from them—and *gay* happiness too. How we love you and what happiness your little family brings us. I can see what it means to Matthew to have you all. Did you see how little Trevenen crosses his legs just as Aldous does and already did in his 6 year old photo—and the repose in Trev's hands when he sits with you and Tessa . . . I am so grateful for everything . . . It is not good manners to say such things. I shall not say them again probably . . .

Aldous for his part had been moved to write:

Dearest M . . . I must say that between you, Ellen and you have done us proud. What really beautiful little human beings! "Heaven lies around us in our infancy"—and one can go a step further than Wordsworth and say that heaven sometimes seems to appear in us and through us. They really look like angels—though I suppose both have their share of original sin . . .

Presently Edith Sitwell, touring America, arrived again. Here is an original diary entry of Betty Wendel's.

Los Angeles, late afternoon of Thursday, Jan 14th.
With Maria and Aldous to visit Edith Sitwell . . . very high up in the Sunset Towers [then the tallest apartment building in Hollywood] Edith Sitwell in a garnet coloured robe . . centers a great divan, after indicating chairs that Maria and I should take, side by side, back of her, out of her sight. Without being told to do so, Aldous sits on the floor at her feet, suddenly becomes an English schoolboy, his sixty years gone except for twelve or thirteen, as he gazes adolescently up at his elder, enquiring about Osbert . . Sacheverell . . .
After being given glasses of sherry, Maria and I are ignored, while Aldous and Miss Sitwell chat and sip their sherry, poured from a bottle that stands on a table with another bottle of identical size,

containing ink. Maria whispers to me, "He's always like that with the Sitwells." Out of sight, out of minds that are in England, there is no danger of our being overheard.

"Some more sherry, Aldous?"

"A little more thank you, Edith."

Maria suddenly rises and utters a sharp warning. "Edith! don't give Aldous *ink* to *drink*."

"Goodness!" says Miss Sitwell, "Let me get you another glass."

All at once reminded, Aldous looks from the face of Maria to that of his watch. "I'm afraid there isn't time, dear Edith—"

We thank Miss Sitwell for letting us come. After a private leave taking of Aldous, she asks him to come again.

"I'll bring him whenever he likes," Maria says, "and then fetch him."

For Aldous, quite an amount of external activities: on 31st January, with his new book about to come out and his article on ESP in *Life* Magazine to be reprinted in the *Reader's Digest*, he answered questions on TV; the night before he had appeared on CBS with Dr Gustaf Stromberg of the Mount Wilson Observatory, "a nice old Swedish astrophysicist." (He was so good, Maria said, that Vera Stravinsky brought him a bunch of flowers.)

The new book was *The Doors of Perception*. The battle over the Bates Method is mild in comparison to the battle over Aldous's attitude to mescalin and later LSD. I certainly do not have the competence, nor the desire, to put forth an assessment or a personal opinion. My job at this stage—I shall have to come back to the subject—is to point again to the more ascertainable facts. (The *extent* to which his writings, and example, can be held to have been causative factors in today's drug scene is difficult, perhaps impossible to tell.) What did Aldous actually try to say, and why? What did he not say? *The Doors of Perception* is a short book, not hard to read (though hard to read perhaps with an open mind).

Aldous first took mescalin in 1953 when it was not exactly a household word. (Odd how often this reserved and quiet man would get himself into the thick of things ahead of his time.) He took the drug, under medical supervision, with a view to extending knowledge about the workings of the human mind. The book, essay rather, is an account of the experience itself with reflections on its philosophical, aesthetic and religious implications. It is a curious little book written, I would say, with utter sincerity and simplicity (though the simplicity of a very intelligent man), written, too, with evident passion—this whole thing was very

very important to Aldous and had moved him deeply—but the passion is balanced with detachment. It reflects a heart and mind open to meet the given, ready, even longing, to accept the wonderful. *The Doors* is a quiet book. It is also one that postulates good will—the choice once more of the nobler hypothesis. It turned out, for certain temperaments, a seductive book.

Now, what Aldous experienced under the drug was a change in *everyday* reality. Unlike other mescalin takers before him, he had no stupendous visions, saw no landscapes, geometrical structures or enormous spaces; *he* looked at familiar objects, his typing table, the books on the shelves, his flannelled legs, three flowers in a vase, and they were transfigured. The books glowed, the flowers shone:

> . . I was seeing what Adam had seen on the morning of his creation—the miracle, moment by moment, of naked existence . . . flowers shining with their own inner light and all but quivering under the pressure of the significance with which they were charged . . . Words like "grace" and "transfiguration" came to my mind . . .
>
> . . Being-Awareness-Bliss—for the first time I understood, not on the verbal level, not by inchoate hints . . but precisely and completely what those prodigious syllables referred to . . .[1]

He looked at a table, chair and desk, and the three pieces came together in a pattern that might have been by Braque or Juan Gris—but as he looked

> this purely aesthetic, Cubist's-eye-view gave place to what I can only describe as the sacramental vision of reality. I was back . . in a world where everything shone with the Inner Light, and was infinite in its significance. The legs, for example, of that chair—how miraculous their tubularity, how supernatural their polished smoothness! I spent several minutes—or was it several centuries?—not merely gazing at those bamboo legs, but actually *being* them—or rather being myself in them; or, to be still more accurate (for "I" was not involved in the case, nor in a certain sense were "they") being my Not-self in the Not-self which was the chair.

And again,

> . . Today the percept had swallowed up the concept. I was so completely absorbed in looking, so thunder-struck by what I actually saw, that I could not be aware of anything else. Garden furniture,

[1] All quotations in this chapter are from *The Doors of Perception*. Chatto & Windus, 1954.

laths, sunlight, shadow—these were no more than names and notions . . . The event was this succession of azure furnace doors separated by gulfs of unfathomable gentian. It was inexpressively wonderful, wonderful to the point, almost, of being terrifying. And suddenly I had an inkling of what it must feel like to be mad . . .

Confronted by a chair which looked like the Last Judgement . . . I felt myself all at once on the brink of panic. This, I suddenly felt, was going too far. Too far, even though the going was into intenser beauty, deeper significance. The fear, as I analyse it in retrospect, was of being overwhelmed, of disintegration under a pressure of reality greater than a mind, accustomed to living most of the time in a cosy world of symbols, could possibly bear. The literature of religious experience abounds in references to the pains and terrors overwhelming those who have come, too suddenly, face to face with some manifestation of the *Mysterium tremendum* . . .

Now in what way can a drug, a bio-chemical intervention, bring about this change in the quality of perception? Aldous inclined to a belief in the validity of a suggestion of Bergson's as expressed by the Cambridge philosopher Professor C. D. Broad, a suggestion that the function of the brain and nervous system and sense organs is, "in the main *eliminative* and not productive. Each person is at each moment capable of remembering all that has ever happened to him and of perceiving everything that is happening everywhere in the universe. The function of the brain and nervous system is to protect us from being overwhelmed and confused by this mass of largely useless and irrelevant knowledge, by shutting out most of what we should otherwise perceive or remember . . and leaving only that very small and special selection which is likely to be practically useful." The assumption, in fact, that the brain transmits consciousness, rather than the assumption that the brain *produces* consciousness. From this it would follow, Aldous carried on, that each of us is potentially Mind at Large. "But in so far as we are animals, our business is at all costs to survive.

To make biological survival possible, *Mind at Large has to be funnelled through the reducing valve of the brain and nervous system.* [My italics] What comes out at the other end is a measly trickle of the kind of consciousness which will help us stay alive on the surface of this particular planet . . .

. . . Most people, most of the time, know only what comes through the reducing valve and is consecrated as genuinely real by the local language. Certain persons, however, seem to be born with a kind of by-pass that circumvents the reducing valve. In others temporary by-passes may be acquired either spontaneously, or as the result of deliberate "spiritual exercises", or through hypnosis, or by means of drugs. Through these . . by-passes there flows . . . something more than, and above all something different from, the carefully selected utilitarian material which our narrowed, individual minds regard as a complete, or at least sufficient, picture of reality.

Mescalin, for instance, reduces the supply of sugar to the brain. The brain is an organ that is in constant need of sugar. What happens when the normal ration is reduced? Aldous summarized what had happened to the majority of those (still few) who had taken mescalin under supervision,

(1) The ability to remember and to "think straight" is little if at all reduced . . .

(2) Visual impressions are greatly intensified and the eye recovers some of the perpetual innocence of childhood . . . Interest in space is diminished and interest in time falls almost to zero.

(3) Though the intellect remains unimpaired . . the will suffers a profound change for the worse. The mescalin taker sees no reason for doing anything in particular and finds most of the causes for which, at ordinary times, he was prepared to act and suffer, profoundly uninteresting. He can't be bothered with them, for the good reason that he has better things to think about.

(4) These better things may be experienced (as I experienced them) "out there," or "in here," or in both worlds, the inner and the outer . . . That they are better seems to be self-evident to all mescalin takers who come to the drug with a sound liver and an untroubled mind.

. . . When the brain runs out of sugar, the undernourished ego grows weak, can't be bothered to undertake the necessary chores, and loses all interest in those spatial and temporal relationships which mean so much to an organism set on getting on in the world. As Mind at Large seeps past the no longer watertight valve, all kinds of biologically useless things start to happen. In some cases there may be extrasensory perceptions. Other persons discover a world of visionary beauty. To others again is revealed the glory, the infinite value and meaningfulness of naked existence . . .

"This is how one ought to see," Aldous kept on saying during the experiment, "this is how things really are." And yet there were reservations. For if one always saw like this, one would never want to do anything else. Just go on looking at a flower, a chair, at flannel. But what about other people? they kept asking him. What about human relations? One ought, was the recorded answer, "to be able to see these trousers as infinitely important and human beings as still more infinitely important."

One ought—but in practice it seemed to be impossible . . . (how I longed to be left alone with Eternity in a flower . . and the Absolute in the folds of a pair of flannel trousers!) I realized that I was deliberately avoiding the eyes of those who were with me in the room, deliberately refraining from being too much aware of them. One was my wife, the other a man I respected and greatly liked; but both belonged to the world from which, for the moment, mescalin had delivered me—the world of selves, of time, of moral judgements and utilitarian considerations, the world (and it was this aspect of human life which I wished, above all else, to forget) of self-assertion, of cocksureness, of overvalued words and idolatrously worshipped notions.

Meanwhile Aldous's question remained unanswered.

How was this cleansed perception to be reconciled with a proper concern with human relations, with the necessary chores and duties, to say nothing of charity and practical compassion? The age-old debate between the actives and the contemplatives was being renewed . . . Mescalin opens the way of Mary, but shuts the door on that of Martha . . .

And now to the great drug issue itself. In the simplest terms, is it good, is it right, for people to have recourse to these Artificial Paradises (or Hells), or is it wicked, futile, destructive? Aldous's answer was that temporary escape from selfhood in one way or another *is* inevitable, and that therefore we had better see to it that the means of the escape shall be physically harmless, morally desirable and socially undisruptive.

. . Most men and women lead lives at the worst so painful, at the best so monotonous, poor and limited that the urge to escape, the longing to transcend themselves . . is and has always been one of the principal appetites of the soul. Art and religion, carnivals and saturnalia, dancing and listening to oratory—all these have served, in H. G. Wells's phrase, as Doors in the Wall. And for private, for everyday use there have always been chemical intoxicants. All the vegetable sedatives and narcotics, all the euphorics that grow on trees, the hallucinogens that ripen in berries . . all . . have been used by human beings from times immemorial. And to these natural modifiers of consciousness modern science has added its quota of synthetics—chloral, for example, and benzedrine, the bromides and the barbiturates.

Most of these . . cannot now be taken except under doctor's orders, or else illegally and at considerable risk. For unrestricted use the West has permitted only alcohol and tobacco. All the other chemical

Doors in the Wall are labelled Dope, and their unauthorized takers are Fiends.

We now spend a good deal more on drink and smoke than we spend on education . . .

Alcohol and tobacco—". . Lung cancer, traffic accidents . . millions of miserable and misery-creating alcoholics . . ." Yet the problem, "it goes without saying, cannot be solved by prohibition. The universal and ever-present urge to self-transcendence is not to be abolished by slamming the currently popular Doors in the Wall.

The only reasonable policy is to open other, better doors in the hope of inducing men and women to exchange their old bad habits for new and less harmful ones.

Some of these other, better doors, Aldous hoped, would be social and technological in nature, others religious, psychological or athletic.

But the need for frequent chemical vacations from intolerable selfhood and repulsive surroundings will undoubtedly remain. What is needed is a new drug which will relieve and console our species without doing more harm in the long run than good in the short.

A drug not only harmless and cheap to produce, but a drug with a constructive side, able to cause "changes in consciousness more interesting, more intrinsically valuable than mere sedation or dreaminess, delusions of omnipotence or release from inhibition." Did Aldous say that he considered mescalin to be such a drug?

Although obviously superior to cocaine, opium, alcohol and tobacco, mescalin is not yet the ideal drug. Along with the happily transfigured majority of mescalin takers there is a minority that finds the drug only hell and purgatory. Moreover, for a drug that is to be used, like alcohol, for general consumption, its effects last for an inconveniently long time.

But chemistry and physiology, he goes on, are capable nowadays of practically anything and can be relied upon to produce something at least more nearly ideal than what we had to make do with "in the wine-bibbing past, the whisky-drinking, marijuana-smoking and barbiturate-swallowing present."

Did Aldous say that mescalin was a completely harmless drug?

To most people, mescalin is almost completely innocuous. Unlike alcohol, it does not drive the taker into the kind of uninhibited action which results in brawls, crimes of violence and traffic accidents. A man under the influence of mescalin quietly minds his own business. Moreover, the business he minds is an experience of the most enlightening kind, which does not have to be paid for (and this is surely important) by a compensatory hangover.

Innocuous, then, to *most* people. Any warnings about others? Once or twice Aldous referred to the fact that the stuff must be taken in good health, under proper conditions and in the right spirit. He did mention the *sine qua non* of a sound liver.

. . The drug brings hell and purgatory only to those who have had a recent case of jaundice, or who suffer from periodical depressions or a chronic anxiety . . .

The warnings are there, though rather casually dispersed about the text; the proper conditions, the right spirit are only implicitly specified. Aldous used to say that he never thought of his potential readers as this would only interfere with his mental processes. If he addressed himself to anyone it must have been some shadowy beings very much like himself. He was also quite sceptical as to the influence, if any, of the (literate) printed word. Would it— and should it—have occurred to him that the contents of *The Doors* might trickle within the reaches of the half-baked, the under-educated, the unstable and indeed the pre-experienced, the young?
We do find this:

. . Of the long-range consequence of regular mescalin taking we know very little . . the available evidence is still scarce and sketchy.

Today we stand two decades later. In *The Doors of Perception* Aldous drew on what he had been told by workers in the field, on what he had read in the scientific literature to date, and on the one experiment upon himself. (It might be as well to anticipate and put on record here that later he took mescalin twice again and LSD and related substances at least seven, and possibly nine, times; which comes to nine to eleven times in all in ten years and a half.)
Lastly, did Aldous say that an experience under drugs could be a mystical experience? He did not.

I am not so foolish as to equate what happens under the influence of mescalin or of any other drug . . with the realization of the end and ultimate purpose of human life: Enlightenment, the Beatific Vision. All I am suggesting is that the mescalin experience is what Catholic theologians call "a gratuitous grace," not necessary to salvation but potentially helpful and to be accepted thankfully . . To be shaken out of the ruts of ordinary perception, to be shown for a few timeless hours the outer and the inner world, not as they appear to an animal obsessed with words and notions, but as they are apprehended, directly and unconditionally, by Mind at Large—this is an experience of inestimable value to everyone . . .

. . . the man who comes back through the Door in the Wall will never be quite the same as the man who went out. He will be wiser but less cocksure, happier but less self-satisfied, humbler in acknowledging his ignorance yet better equipped to understand the relationship of words to things, of systematic reasoning to the unfathomable Mystery which it tries, forever vainly to comprehend.

The response to the book when it came out was anything from excitement, discriminate and indiscriminate, moral and intellectual disapproval, shrugging-off, embarrassment. Drugs, dope, are emotionally charged concepts about which many of us have conditioned, and possibly quite sound, instincts. Yet it was not so much for advocating drugs that Aldous was decried in those early years. What people shied away from—or were attracted by—was the unfamiliarity, the way-outness of the whole thing. Really Aldous was proving himself too amphibious by half; from enfant terrible of *Antic Hay* to psychodelic acolyte he had been slipping through everybody's net. Self-respecting rationalists saw fresh evidence of quackery and intellectual abdication while the serious and religious were bothered by the offer of a shortcut; but I rather think that the people who were most angry were the aesthetes who were really outraged by Aldous's attempt to put art in its place. True enough he had paid the obvious tribute, "What the rest of us see only under the influence of mescalin, the artist is congenitally equipped to see all the time . . ." But look at *this*.

. . What sort of pictures did Eckhart look at? What sculptures and paintings played a part in the religious experience of St Joan of the Cross, of Hakuin, of Hui-neng, of William Law? . . I strongly suspect that most of the great knowers of Suchness paid very little attention to art . . . Art, I suppose, is only for beginners, or else for those resolute dead-enders, who have made up their minds to be content with the *ersatz* of Suchness . . .

The passages found most enraging were those where Aldous gazed with such rapture at the folds of his old grey flannel trousers. Those magic waves, those depths—

. . how rich, how deeply, mysteriously sumptuous!
. . . "The nearest approach to this," I said, "would be a Vermeer."

Grey flannel—how dared he? And thereby hangs a small tale. After she had read the book, Betty Wendel asked him, "But Aldous dear, you were wearing your blue jeans that morning. I saw you." So he did, said Aldous. "Maria made me change it in the M/S. She thought I ought to be better dressed for my readers." Oh, what a disservice she did there to Aldous! Blue cotton, blue linen, light-washed, sun-rinsed—who has not seen those transfigured in impressionist and post-impressionist paintings; postmen's trousers, French railway porters' tunics, are magical almost by definition. How much more tolerable, more comprehensible, Aldous's raptures might have appeared had he only been allowed to admit to his blue jeans.

Washington was taking its bureaucratic time and by the end of January no news had come yet as to the next step in the Huxleys' citizenship application. Since they were supposed to go to Europe in April, it was "all very tiresome," as Aldous wrote to Matthew, "all the more so as we have got into this imbroglio quite gratuitously and of our own volition." This was certainly true. There were no material reasons for them whatsoever to change their status. The U.S. visa they had been granted in London in 1937, an immigration visa, was still valid and would be valid *in perpetuum*. A large number of persons have entered the United States with such a visa and resided there ever after without applying for naturalization. There are no strings attached. The Huxleys were free to work, take paid employment, acquire property, travel; only upon leaving for another continent they required the formality of a re-entry permit. If they were guests, they were fully paid up guests being subject to both Federal and State income tax. The only things they could not do were to vote, run for political office or enter the civil service. As for non-material reasons ("We are *de facto* Californians . . ."), it does seem gratuitous that a man of Aldous's a-nationalism and detachment should have chosen to make that kind of gesture of commitment. Well, it was not to be. In February there was still no news from Washington. "If papers come through," Aldous wrote again to Matthew, "well and good; if they don't, well and good also. Still I wish we hadn't let ourselves in for this bother and confusion." A few days later he and Maria decided to drop the whole thing. They renewed their British passports and, resuming their *status quo ante* of resident aliens, applied for U.S. re-entry permits. These they received at once. No problems ever arose from their shelved application to become Americans. For the rest of his life, Aldous came and went at will. He remained what *naturaliter* he was, an evolved Victorian Englishman at home in the second part of the twentieth century, at home in Southern California, who walked alone.

# Chapter Four

## 1954–1955

THAT whole business, on top of so much else, had been a strain for Maria. So were their travel plans—the Middle East: Egypt, Jerusalem, the Lebanon; Cyprus, Greece. "Je n'ose m'attendre à trop de bonheur", she wrote to Jeanne in early March, "*rien* ne marche facilement, ni agréablement en ce moment." Aldous has no book in sight, and is depressed . . Finances are low . . Fortunately Eileen Garrett's foundation is paying their passages . . . They may go to Switzerland as well, to see Jung who has asked them. "Perhaps in Switzerland—the country of good doctors—they may have different views on the subject of my health, which should be useful."

When it was brought home to Aldous that Maria might not be fit enough to undertake such a journey, he fell ill himself. He took to his bed for two weeks (Maria told Ellen). Indeed, we play strange tricks upon ourselves. Only a few friends knew that Maria was very ill. The Kiskaddens knew, Humphrey Osmond knew. Her family in New York and Europe feared but did not really know, as they had not been told. Aldous was given opportunities both for knowing or not knowing.

In the event, Maria's doctor told her that she and Aldous might as well go; so in March they went off to New York. There Aldous went down with a new attack of his bronchitis. He recovered enough not only to carry on but to start a new book, a short novel, a tale, which he managed to write—on ship-board, on hotel balconies, in gardens—at odd moments during the summer. On 7th April they sailed for Cherbourg on the *Queen Elizabeth*. Once more they arrived in Paris in the evening, once more there was the family reunion at the station, the taxi ride to the hotel. Maria looked radiant, very much *en beauté* (a press photograph taken as they stepped off the ship is there to prove it); Aldous looked ill. At the Hôtel Pont Royal they all went into the bar downstairs and had a bottle of champagne. "Joie de les revoir," noted Georges Neveux. "Mais inquiétude." There was an undercurrent of anxiety—Aldous had to have an oxygen cylinder in his room for his pressure-breathing: had it arrived? Maria had an appointment with a specialist the following afternoon.

Next day they lunched together. "La joie de les revoir continue. [G. N.'s journal for 13th July] Aldous encore fatigué. Maria toujours pleine d'allant."

547

That afternoon Maria went to see (the late) Professor Mondor, the eminent French specialist who was still practising. Jeanne, with Noële aged thirteen, sat in the waiting-room. Nothing was said to, or before, the child but the experience haunted her for many years and may have played a part in the grave illness that followed some months later. Georges telephoned Professor Mondor in the evening. "He told us the truth," Jeanne noted simply. And Maria, too, had wanted to be told just that. (Mondor was a noted Mallarmé scholar, the two men knew of one another and he spoke openly to Georges.) "You must tell *me*", Maria had said to him. "You must *not* tell my husband. My husband has a book to finish and must have peace of mind." Rarely, Mondor said, had he met such fortitude.

That night Maria had dinner on her own at Georges and Jeanne's (Aldous was having a tray in bed at the hotel). She talked to them—her one and only time—of what was in their minds. She told them that she knew the seriousness of her case; she told them that she had become indifferent to the thought of dying. She expected death and was preparing herself. "But I can't give in, as I mustn't die before Aldous. How would he manage without me? It would be wrong of me to die before Aldous—I should have failed in my duty to him." And of course it must all be kept entirely from Aldous. And she talked to them, Georges says, in the calmest manner, in a peaceful, undramatic voice, sitting in their bedroom on the edge of a chair, interrupted now and then by Jeanne's having to answer the telephone. "So I must fight inch by inch, day after day, to keep alive so that Aldous will have me with him all his life, so that he shall never have to do without me . . ."

> Elle parle de sa mort [Georges wrote in his journal] comme on discuterait de l'opportunité et de la date d'un voyage, calculant au mieux et avec réflexion. Quelle femme extraordinaire . . .

On 19th April Aldous and Maria flew south to attend Eileen Garrett's symposium on Philosophy and Parapsychology at St Paul-de-Vence. Professor H. H. Price of Great Britain read a paper on Philosophic Implications of Paranormal Cognition, Gabriel Marcel of France on Intersubjective Approach to Survival, Aldous on A Visionary Experience; there were papers and discussions by doctors and psychologists and philosophers from America and Switzerland and Germany . . .

> . . no conclusions, of any kind, of course; [Aldous wrote from St Paul to Humphrey Osmond] but a lot of interesting things were said and there were occasions to greet very remarkable people. I liked

especially Price, [C. J.] Ducasse, Marcel and [C. W. K.] Mundle . . Bender of Freiburg, Martiny and Assailly of Paris. Bender has a case of demonic possession on his hands, which exceeds in horror and in duration anything met with at Loudun—13 years of blasphemy, split personality, stigmatization . . . and still no end in sight . . .

Both Aldous and Maria had a great affection for Eileen Garrett, and she for them. She spoke to me of Maria's tiredness at that time. "You should go home, my darling," Eileen told her. But Aldous wanted to go on travelling (wanted everything to be normal). She spoke of how much Maria did—"Always, always—Aldous not realizing it." Of her hinting that he did not know how to love, and Maria giving her one of those lightning straight looks and saying with utter conviction, "Oh yes, he does!" She spoke of her own answer to Maria's great anguish, What will happen to Aldous? "It will turn out right."

On 3rd May the Huxleys flew to Egypt to keep the engagement that meant most to Aldous, a stay with Dr Roger Godel at Ismailia, where he was the Médecin en Chef of the Suez Canal Company's Hospital. They had met in France in 1950 and corresponded since. A very remarkable man, Aldous had outlined his expectations to Humphrey Osmond, "a heart specialist who makes extensive use of psychological methods, a doctor who is an eminent Hellenist, respected by other Greek scholars, and finally a Western scientist who is interested in Enlightenment and has written some interesting essays on 'L'Expérience Liberatrice.'" He was not disappointed.

At last we have again found peace [Maria scribbled off to Matthew and Ellen]—the first since before I started packing and passports in L. A.

We arrived here last night after only 7 hours of excellent flight, in the middle of a desert on the banks of the canal. Flowers, lawns, silence and our dear friends the Godels. Now I know I am tired but Aldous is well again.

And Aldous on 9th May.

We have been here nearly a week—a very extraordinary place in company with a very extraordinary man. The house stands on the edge of the canal (it was built originally for the Empress Eugénie at the time of the canal's inauguration), and the ships pass practically through one's bedroom—enormous tankers going to or coming from the Persian Gulf, liners . . cargo boats of every shape and size . . .

Every day Aldous, disguised as a visiting doctor, went to the hospital with Godel.

.. It is a liberal education to accompany him through the wards with his interns and the young doctors who come from France or Lebanon or Greece to be his pupils. He succeeds in being . . . a physician who is also a philosopher and psychologist. Where patients are responsible for their own illness—and how many of them, here as elsewhere, are psychosomatics!—he treats them physically with all the resources of modern medicine, but tries at the same time to get them to recognize and, in so doing, to get rid of the underlying causes . . . He does it by Socratic questioning—often through an interpreter, for the poorer patients speak only Arabic—and it is wonderful to hear him patiently eliciting—exactly like the Socrates of the Platonic dialogues—fundamental answers about soul and body, about appearances and reality. And the thing works; for he gets amazing cures and enjoys a prodigious reputation. In himself he is a quiet gentle man . . .

And all this knowledge, Aldous added, "is applied in the most intelligent and humane way, for the service of his patients." One can imagine how captivated Aldous was, how satisfied by the nature of this work—at last something constructive, something worth doing, being actually done. "It would, I believe, be a wonderful thing if you [Matthew] cd come here for a few months and work with him."

Aldous and Maria really longed to bring this about. There was so much to be learned . . . Godel occasionally did take laymen pupils—there would be room for Ellen and the babies—"the project is something you shd consider seriously . . . Even if you cd not get a scholarship it wd . . be worth thinking of coming here independently, as an educational investment . . . So ruminate and digest and make inquiries." And Maria in a (published) P.S. "This is a dream which I feel will materialize . . . I have not known a place and people so congenial at the same time. The beauty of the place passes belief, also the gentle climate . . . Perhaps we may even return for some weeks next year . . . I suggest that though it will not be necessary Ellen and I sell (not even pawn) our jewellery and Aldous his typewriter and the car and everything—because this seems the best idea for us all."

Maria had come to see Godel. They had some private talks— a part of her conscious preparation. Aldous later thought, and Jeanne, that this had been of great importance to her. To Matthew she wrote again after they had left Ismailia, "The greatness of Godel is not only to be a great doctor that people fly to consult but also a good man and a wise man."

On 11th May they went to Cairo. (Their first time.) "One can really form no idea of Egyptian art, wrote Aldous, until one sees it in the mass and at its best—the museum is fabulous, the pyramids . . beyond description . . ." Then Jerusalem, Beirut, Damascus . . . "Oh! everything has been such an education", Maria wrote,

Such discoveries in all directions, as we knew nothing of the Middle East. Now we—not just jokingly—talk about retiring in the Lebanon which has a better climate than the South of France, is cheaper, and much more up to date than Egypt and is no volcano of politics . . .

Cyprus, Istanbul, Greece—also for the first time. From Athens Aldous wrote a very sombre letter to Eileen Garrett. ". . It has been a very wonderful journey through space and time—wonderful but very depressing; for I have never had such a sense of the tragic nature of the human situation, the horror of a history in which the great works of art, the philosophies and the religions, are no more than islands in an endless stream of war, poverty, frustration, squalor and disease.

One sees the misery of the Egyptians huddled about the pyramids, the hopelessness of the inhabitants of Jerusalem for whom the holiest of cities is a prison of chronic despair, punctuated by occasional panic when the hand grenades start flying. And it must always have been, like this—little islands of splendour in a sea of darkness,—and then, during the times of trouble, darkness unmitigated for a few centuries. The Near East is one huge illustration of the primal tenet of the Buddha: "I show you sorrow and the ending of sorrow" . . .

From Athens they flew to Rome. On the telephone (I was living there at the time) Maria said, "Oh, *I'm* very well indeed," quickly, emphatically, making quite sure that one would not ask again. "Aldous is superb." In the evening I walked up the Spanish Steps to the Hôtel de la Ville where they had two rooms with a view. It was so—Maria had used the only word. I had not seen them since Sanary in August 1950: Aldous had changed. It was so evident, so disconcerting, that had it not been for his voice, Maria's presence and a kind of continuity in their atmosphere, one would have had the sensation of being, not with another man, but with another version of the man, a double, a brother. Now the point was that Aldous never *really* changed; he oscillated: no woman could have been more *journalière*—absurdly young, graceful, animated one day; sallow, tentative, withdrawn the next; his

pendulum might swing between the casual dandy and the old
man of Thermopylae. He did change, somewhat, in 1936 after
he had been taught by F. M. Alexander; he was changed a
good deal by the Bates treatment. *This* was a change in kind,
perceptible to begin with on the physical level. (I am putting
down what is only a personal impression, but it was a very
definite one.) Aldous looked robust; substantial; very much all
there; he had in fact filled out, though this was not in the least
like the thickening of middle-age (he was going to be sixty next
month) it was more like the filling out of a boy who is coming
into his own. If he looked young—he did—it was no longer
touching or unfledged young, but the youthfulness of full powers.
Never before had I seen Aldous look less vulnerable (nor since).
He was as gentle as he had been in all his phases, yet behind it
one felt authority. And there was a sleekness, a smoothed-outness;
he was glowing with it, as it were, and this had an extraordinary
peace-inducing effect as though one were sitting—if this is not
too fanciful—at the feet of a large and benign cat.

Yet he was not in the least remote. Pleased to be in Rome, he
talked about what they were going to see, he talked about their
journey. They had been overwhelmed by Egypt—the lighting up of
Aldous's face as he flung out his hands and said "staggering";
disappointed by Greece. Several times he used the word squalor.
And I, while talking away myself, even then was trying to sort
out this new thing, trying—how stupidly—to find words, waiting
to put them before Maria. The summer before she had written
to me, "We are still exploring . . . also now exploring psychology
and para-psychology—*much further* than hands [those palm prints
they used to pore over in the Thirties with Charlotte Wolff]—
but they were the first steps." I had read the passage the way one
reads a letter . . . During that stay in Rome—two short weeks—
I understood a little what Maria meant. They *had been exploring*.
And whatever it was they had found, Aldous had tapped something, made a breakthrough. Into what? A potential Aldous? An
altered mode of being? How can one *say*. It was—obviously—on
a non-verbal level. There he *was*; and what he was, one felt,
was in some new way extraordinary. (Being with him had a
profound influence on me, of a kind that would be hard, and
that I don't really wish, to define. It lasted for some time, wore
off, at one point went into reverse, has not worn off entirely.)
Many of us in the course of our lives have found ourselves briefly
in the presence of a being of another order. The order might be
of various kinds but it is always *other* and always, unless we are
too besotted with cocksureness, recognizable. It is not usual to
make such a statement about a man who is the subject of a (I
hope detached) biography as well as an old friend, yet I think

Matthew, Maria and Aldous in the early 1930s
( Photograph by Dorothy Wilding )

Aldous, Sybille Bedford, Eva Herrmann
at Sanary on the Riviera, 1930s

*Left:* Aldous, climbing in the Sanary back country, 1930s
*Centre:* Raymond Mortimer at Sanary
*Right:* Eddy Sackville-West at Sanary

Picnicking in Switzerland
*en route* to Italy, summer 1926:
*left*, Aldous and Maria;
*below*, Aldous and Rose Nys

Aldous and Maria and the Bugatti,
travelling in the south of France circa 1931

Aldous and Maria *aux vendanges*, pressing the fruits
of their grape harvest, California, 1940s

*Left:* Aldous and Gerald Heard at Duke University, North Carolina, 1937
*Right:* Aldous and Anita Loos, California, late 1930s

Maria at Amalfi Drive, Pacific Palisades, circa 1942

Aldous with Rina Eustration, Marseilles, August 1950

Aldous and Maria in Siena, 1948

OPPOSITE: Aldous in April 1948

North Kings Road, Los Angeles, circa 1952:
*from left*, Aldous, Ellen, Maria, Marguerite
(Mère) Nys, Trevenan, Matthew

Aldous and cat circa 1952 in California

Laura and Aldous in Italy, 1958

Laura and Aldous listening to music
at Deronda Drive circa 1959

Quote . . . unquote

Aldous in April 1958
(Photograph by Philippe Halsman)

Aldous at Saltwood Castle, Kent, August 1963

that I should not leave unsaid that in Rome I had such a
flash of recognition about Aldous. It is superfluous to add that
it had nothing to do with the quality one commonly associated
with Aldous, intellectuality. Sitting with him, the images that
rose unwilled to my mind were sleek herds in serene countrysides.
(This was not quite easy to understand or to convey, and when
in due time I took it to Maria, I left-handedly said something
about cows which took a moment to put right.) Maria, now, I
did not find changed—she was herself to an *n*th degree. In appearance, she still looked as she had at Cherbourg, *en beauté*, animated,
gay, with sudden sinkings into tiredness.

On their daily level, magic, to borrow Maria's saying, certainly
was advancing. It had become as casual as taking aspirin. "You
don't sleep well? Aldous, do give Sybille some of your Mesmeric
passes." *Animal Magnetism*, I shied like a well-trained Pavlovian
dog. Is *that* respectable? Aldous wrote down two books to read.
("You ought to be able to get them from the London Library.")
And Esdaile; I should read Dr James Esdaile on anaesthesia by
hypnosis. We didn't get down to magnetic passes in the first week,
but what Aldous, rolling up his shirt-sleeves, gave me was a very
competent spinal pummelling (against tension). He did this with
his right hand only, while the fingers of his left rested lightly on
the base of my neck like a violinist's hand on his keys. Aldous,
what is that for? "Ah," he said, "I haven't the faintest idea, that's
where the abracadabra comes in." At sunset we went up to the
Roman roof above my flat where I had made a garden. On a
slanting ledge I had built a stack of scrubbed empty flower pots
resting on ochre tiles. "Now, this is *very* mescalin," said Aldous.
At dusk we watched the opening of some large white moon-
flowers on a trellis; I told him that what I loved to look at most
though were their leaves. Aldous seemed pleased with this and
quoted a *haiku*.

> *The flowers are easy to paint,*
> *The leaves difficult.*

Their days were long with sight-seeing. (It was hard to believe
that Aldous should have required an oxygen cylinder six weeks
ago, and yet he had. In fact, the new robust look notwithstanding,
that swing between decent health and ill remained.) A friend
drove them out to Frascati and Tivoli, Tarquinia and Etruscan
tombs—"wandering through the ripening wheat," Aldous wrote
to Matthew, "and popping down into the rock-hewn chambers
with their still gay paintings of hunting, wrestling, dancing, even
copulation and sodomy . . ."
Their niece Claire White was there, her husband having had

a Prix de Rome. "They came for dinner," Claire wrote in a letter to me fifteen years later,

> . . . Maria looked so frail . . I suddenly realized how terribly much I loved her and offered to walk Aldous about Rome to spare her fatigue, but she fought this off energetically. "It's much more tiring to be at home doing the housework," she said.

They went to see the international exhibition at the American Academy.

> . . Aldous praised each young artist he liked with such kindness. Maria suddenly looked at me and said—"Tu es une femme forte, comme Ellen." But oh the exhaustion with which she walked home after that, barely able to lift her feet but still only concerned that Aldous should not stumble across a stone.

At the end of their first week Aldous and Maria went to Florence for a couple of days; they went to say goodbye to Costanza. Costanza Fasola, the first friend of their Italian youth, was dying of cancer of the lung.

One evening as we were beating our way through the noise up the Via Babuino, Maria spoke of a friend of theirs who happened to be in Rome. (It was the young woman who had taken them to Tarquinia.) Perhaps I'd like to meet her? This she let fall so lightly that at once I was all ears. Maria never forced, she suggested; one was left to choose. If there was no response, she withdrew. (Where her sisters were concerned, this was not always so.) In the sound-shelter of a café in Via Due Macelli, she came back to it. Their friend was a rather remarkable woman, interested in "our kind of things". An Italian, Aldous took it up, a musician, concert violinist, who had become a practising psycho-therapist—"She uses this rather curious method . . and I must say it works . . I'm glad to say it doesn't take seven years on the couch . . ." The one thing I became obscurely certain of was that Maria wanted me to meet this friend.

The friend was Laura Archera. A couple of evenings later, followed by Aldous and Maria, she came to my flat in Via della Fontanella, not the forbidding esoteric therapist I had half expected, but a young woman, feminine, high-spirited, full of life and warmth. (She has herself described our meeting—with a touch of extravaganza—in her book on Aldous.) The most incisive memory of that first evening for me was what passed between her and Maria. It was night, we were all up on that roof terrace, my friend Evelyn Gendel put a kind of lucky-dip question to

Aldous: When does a grasshopper become a locust? Aldous took a deep breath. "Ah—" he said. "Well, now—" he said. "This is a very interesting question. My grandfather used to puzzle . . ." Aldous got under way. Maria and Laura disappeared. They had gone below to talk. They talked for a long time.

Up here the Roman night was what such nights can be. No traffic sounds could reach us. There was a scent of honeysuckle, jasmin, tobacco flower. There was darkness and patches of luminous leaves; to the north, almost on top of us, rose the cupola of one of the twin churches in Piazza del Popolo; to the east, across a gulf of night, one could see as far as the Pincian Hill; above us, garlands of vines and in their interstices the sky. There was Aldous's voice . . . Below in the quiet flat Maria was still talking to Laura. And I knew as surely as if I had been there that Maria was speaking at last about her illness.

Soon after I saw Laura Archera again—friendship came almost at once, Aldous and Maria having acted as the catalyst; Laura thought that they had wanted us to meet because she might be able to help me (I was struggling with a book and a multitude of anguishes); this indeed she did. Yet I am still convinced of what had been already present in my mind that night, that Maria was thinking a good deal further ahead.

Then, we finally did get down to the magnetic passes. Again no insistence, less than a hint by way of Maria; and I caught on that this was something Aldous would enjoy doing. I was very willing. (Before it, I'm ashamed to say, I dodged into the kitchen and quickly swallowed a glass of wine.) I lay down. Aldous stood over me making slow wave-like motions with his arms. Maria and Evelyn Gendel went on talking in another part of the room. I shut my eyes. Aldous in a slow seductive voice began the incantations.

Presently you will be going out . . . You are going to spend a cheerful evening . . .

And then tonight you are going to have a deep deep sleep, a restful sleep, a deep refreshing sleep . . .

You are going to spend a cheerful evening . . .

I did not feel drowsy, I felt alert and peaceful. The sound of the words was soothing, full of promise, already I could feel the quality of that delicious sleep.

And presently we did go out, and it was a cheerful evening— dinner with Aldous and Maria in a trattoria, in a pool, as it were, of their own quietness, with the Italian waiters putting forth their *gentilezza* (but that was the *old* Huxley magic working as it had in all those years and times), a night stroll afterwards . . . How

one wished to remain in those hours! All the same I went home
as for a treat. The deep sleep did not come. I did not sleep at all.
Not a wink. An entire night of quite cheerful if rather astonished
wakefulness. I didn't sleep the second night, and very little in
the third. We were all more amused than distressed, though
Aldous was a bit puzzled and concerned; Maria advised against
our trying again. Later I learned that the same thing the other
way round had happened to Laura Archera some years after
in California; *she* remained in a somnabulistic state days after a
round of Aldous's Mesmeric passes. She has told the story charmingly in her book,[1] and the gist of it was that Aldous had forgotten to wake her up.

At the time *Helen of Troy* was being filmed at Ciné Città, with
1,200 extras, Wooden Horse and all, and of course Aldous went
to have a look and as he did so he was recognized. (By Maurice
Zuberano, assistant director, who kindly wrote to me.) ". . The
writer of the screen play had laconically put down the words 'A
baccanale takes place.' I asked the director if he had ever been
to a baccanale and he said 'No,' he had been born and raised
in a small town in the Middle West. I had been born in New
York City but I did not know what they did at a baccanale either.

I was about to embark on a research trip when I looked up and saw
a tall man watching us shoot a battle scene on the back lot. I
recognized him as Mr Huxley . . . He was unattended so I offered
to show him the studio. We then took each other to lunch. He
showed great interest in my problem and went on for hours relating
what he knew about baccanales. As a result our baccanale was so
successful that the crowd people could not stop when the director
cried "cut" . . .

And then it was the last evening. ·18th June. Sunset on the
roof, dinner near Piazza Colonna. Afterwards I went with them
as far as their hotel. At the door, Maria turned from me. "We
don't have to say goodbye," she said, "we've had our goodbye."
On the ship, on the *Normandie*. She did not have to say it. She
was gone. Aldous telephoned next morning. They were going to
Paris for a couple of weeks, then south to the Drôme to spend the
long holidays with Jeanne and Georges in a little country town
called Dieulefit. It would be a nice change, he said, to be sitting
still, he was looking forward to doing a piece of honest work.
Later perhaps they might pop down into Provence . . . Perhaps
we would meet later in the summer. He made some joke about

[1] *This Timeless Moment: A Personal View of Aldous Huxley.* Farrar, Straus & ·
Giroux, 1968; Chatto & Windus, 1969.

the demons that interfere with sleep. And now they'd have to be off to the airport. Maria did not come to the telephone.

The house the Neveuxes had taken at Dieulefit was old and spacious, standing amid lawns and trees like an English country house. The Huxleys arrived on the 3rd of July. Aldous was enchanted; he installed himself in this garden, typewriter on knees, and got going again with his book. "Through the Wrong End of the Opera Glasses" was his working title; it became *The Genius and the Goddess*. But Maria had grown not only very tired but extremely nervous, as if she had something on her mind. Georges' and Jeanne's journals show that there was great tension in the house, an undercurrent of desperate unhappiness. Again and again Jeanne refers to it as the tragic summer. They did not speak of it at the time, Maria would not have it. And there was Aldous to consider, and the child Noële.

> Aldous tape à la machine et adore le parc. [Jeanne's Diary] Maria n'est pas heureuse, c'est pénible. Elle est inquiète et d'un commun accord nous ne parlons pas de ce qui nous hante . . . et de notre impuissance. Je me sens coupable d'être bien portante. Mais nous faisons des promenades. Coccola cueille des fleurs et a toujours cette grâce qui est sienne.
> . . . Pourtant Aldous semble ravi [Georges' Journal] il travaille dans le jardin et nous avons deux bons moments—la promenade sur la chemin de la crêe (ce pays est beau) et le soir la lecture à haute voix.

It was always Georges who read to them. This year, André Maurois' life of Victor Hugo.

> Il y a le thé de cinq heures [Jeanne] que Noële a tant aimé avec eux—mais maintenant Noële c'est la jeunesse et la vie . . .

Three weeks of this. On 23rd July they drove south to Vaisons-la-Romaine for the Festival. Georges' play *Zamore* was being given in the Roman Theatre next day. Sophie had come down from Paris, and Rina with her husband from Marseilles. They had taken lodgings in a vast Renaissance mansion in the old town. After the play there was a dinner party. They returned to Dieulefit and celebrated Aldous's sixtieth birthday. Rina came back with them. There was no telephone in the house. On the 28th, Maria spoke not to Jeanne but to a friend of Jeanne's, Marcelle Rodenbach, telling her that she was concerned about some symptoms; Mme Rodenbach arranged for her to telephone in private from somewhere. Next day Maria was able to get on to Professor Mondor in Paris, who told her to come to him at once. The Huxleys decided to leave. Aldous was disappointed, perhaps shocked. He had been so well there, he said over and over again, but softly, so as not to upset Maria. Next morning, 30th July, they left in the Neveuxes' 2-*chevaux* for Valence to catch the Paris train. "Ce départ dans la panique", wrote Georges, "a quelque chose de déchirant."

Professor Mondor advised Maria to return to America and her own doctors as quickly as she could. That was 1st August. They were not able to book any definite passage. Aldous left for London and stayed with his brother and Juliette. Maria remained in Paris on her own. ("I have no links with England," she had written the year before to Elise Murrel, "nor in fact many links at all.") So she stayed in Paris, the close-aired empty Paris of the August holidays, wandering about the streets, eating in students' restaurants. In the evenings there was Sophie.

One afternoon in the Hampstead garden Aldous told Juliette about Maria's symptoms. Juliette, alarmed, asked him if he were not worried. " 'Oh no,' he replied lightly, 'it is not at all serious.' "

Maria herself made light of her premature return to Matthew and Ellen. ". . I really long to be home and the only doctors I like are my L.A. doctors . . ." she wrote. She hopes that New York will not be boiling, though at any rate the Warwick will be air-conditioned. "We won't stay long but we must see *you* (Let us swear to each other that if anyone has a cold we don't let Aldous approach them, even you or Ellen or Trev or Tessa) . . . Paris is expensive . . . Eileen is ill at St Paul . . . I want to see Jeanne again, who has been wonderfully kind and patient . . ." An old old friend, Luigino Franchetti, passed through Paris and they had dinner together. "Luigino was touching in his affection . . ." But it was Sophie who spent all her spare moments with Maria. (She was tied in the day to her job at Unesco.)

> I think [Sophie wrote] that we were never more close to one another as during these days. I knew how ill she was. She did not know that I knew. Never once she complained or said a thing, but one evening I arrived at the hotel and found that she had ordered whisky and I was very surprised. Maria said very simply that she thought I would be hot and tired and might enjoy a drink (which I did). I took my glass and before I had had one sip, I saw that Maria had completely finished hers and that horrified me. I remarked upon it with amazement (she never drank) but she apologized and said that she must have been absent minded. I realized how distressed and "angoissée" she must have been.

Once they played tourists and took a *bateau-mouche* down the Seine and there, gliding on the river, Maria told Sophie how Aldous had proposed to her on the lawn at Garsington.

Finally they were able to get passages for 21st August on the *Mauritania*. On the 16th Jeanne travelled up to Paris to spend a few days with Maria. "We do not talk much. Maria does a lot of unnecessary errands. We spend hours at the hairdresser's. And I leave again. *Nous avons tenu bon toutes les deux . . .*"

Rina also came. Arriving at the Hôtel Pont Royal after her night in the train, they told her at the desk, "Mme Huxley? Left by air." Rina experienced a moment of blank desolation. Shocked though she was, she had the wits to seek out Sophie at Unesco —Maria had merely flown to Nice for the day to see Eileen Garrett. So in the evening Rina took the bus out to Orly and waited, and saw Maria arrive, walk alone, unutterably tired, touched her arm at the exit and saw her face change. Rina stayed with her three days, sleeping in the same room in the hotel. Maria saw her off. After they had parted, Rina inside the station heard steps, saw her again—Maria had stopped her taxi and run back to embrace her once more.

(Later she found an envelope: reimbursing her fare and the words, "For Rina because she knows that friendship never can be paid.")

Maria had sent a little fur jacket of hers to a shop in the rue St Honoré. She was very attached to it as it was a present from Aldous.

When she went to retrieve it, [Sophie wrote] she found the shop closed for the rest of the month . . She was frantic. She made any amount of démarches to try to get the shop opened and regain the coat, all without result. I tried to calm her and I said I would send it on to her, but she was very upset at the thought of leaving it behind. Finally she had to, and I later on got the coat, and sent it . . and Maria had her little coat back. But the energy and will she put into moving heaven and earth to retrieve that coat . . .

And on 21st August Sophie took Maria to the Gare du Nord and put her on the boat train. ". . As in a bad melodrama, we met friends on the platform and . . had to make polite stupid conversation with them. It was horrible. When the train pulled out, Maria was at the window crying. That was the only time she let herself go in all those days. I ran along the train as it pulled out and shouted to her, 'Ne pleures pas, voyons, tu sera avec Aldous dans quelques heures et c'est tout ce que tu désire.' She smiled then, 'Tu as raison, je suis une idiote,' and she waved . . . That was my 'vision' of Maria, wearing a silly little hat and leaning over the window of a departing train."

Aldous was on the ship at Southampton. Together they sent off a postcard.

Non posso dimenticare tua cara presenza a Orly e a Parigi.
A l'année prochaine,   M.

Aldous echoes,

A l'année prochaine, cara Rina,
Aldous H.

They landed on 27th August and remained in New York for fourteen days. Nobody had a cold and they were able to spend the time with the children and grandchildren. One night Matthew and Ellen took them down to the Battery; "New York est si belle!" Maria wrote. On 7th September they were back at North Kings Road and Maria began a series of X-ray treatments. On the 26th she and Aldous got away for a weekend with Rosalind at Ojai. "Krishnaji is here," Maria wrote to Jeanne. "I feel so much more calm . . . Aldous is admirably well, and stimulated and optimistic. On Thursday he is leaving for Washington and New York, by air, for 10-12 days, and alone! 1) Because it costs too much for two. 2) Because without me it's easier for him to stay with the professors. 3) Because I can't leave my treatments here."

So on 1st October Aldous gave a lecture in Washington at the Institute of Modern Art, went on to New York and on the 5th flew to Durham for the same lecture at Duke University. Aldous and J. B. Rhine had met once before, on the Huxleys' very first trip across the continent in 1937.

The second visit [Professor Rhine wrote me] I had arranged . . . I found the English Department extremely eager to have Aldous . . and although he mentioned that he had not done much university lecturing, he consented to read a paper he had just written on visionary experiences. It was about the time he was especially interested in mescalin, but the paper was not directly concerned with that.

I recall that the anticipatory enthusiasm . . was great, and the largest hall on the Campus was completely packed.

Aldous had just come from the North . . at any rate he was dressed in woollen clothing, and the night was unusually warm . . I recall the doors were open, but it was still much too hot for his clothing. The chairman was dressed in summer clothes. I suggested to Aldous that he take off his coat, but he was reluctant. I took the chairman aside and . . asked him to lead the way by taking off his own coat. And there with that university audience (of pre-Hippy days at that) the two men marched onto the lecture platform with their jackets over their arms. It put everyone at ease immediately, and, anyhow, the audience was completely captivated. Aldous was a person, as you know, whom it was easy to like spontaneously. His gentle dignity and a suggestion of frailty, that perhaps came from his vision, made one lean a little his way in a helpful attitude.

During the reading some of his papers got out of hand and fell to the floor, . . and I know that everyone in the audience felt just as I did—they wanted to jump up there and help him. I myself was deeply impressed by the hold which he had upon that audience, by the remarks that followed in the days succeeding, coming even from persons I would not have expected would listen to such a topic. The next night he was scheduled to lecture at the University of North Carolina, and again the night was hot, and again he read his lecture in his shirt sleeves. In the hour that followed a discussion was held in the student lounge, Aldous sat in a big armchair, surrounded by piles of students on the floor, in every sort of posture, eagerly trying to catch every syllable. I remember that Aldous led a sort of parade back to my car when we had to leave.

. . . I like to think that these contacts with the students at Duke and U.N.C. must have impressed him with the warmth and appreciation American students so readily extended to him. To me it was a phenomenal experience indeed.

Aldous dovetails with (to Humphrey Osmond after his return) "Frightful heat in Washington and at Duke—97° with 96% humidity. But there were nice people in both places."
A few days later *The Genius and the Goddess* was done.

Aldous has just finished his best ever (I believe) long short story. [Maria to Matthew] 30,000 words and Oh Darling, there is Trev in it. I read it in M.S. . . it seems much "stronger" than anything else . . .

And a little later:

I can't help feeling that this love for Trev extends and makes the story so good—will make all of them so good . . . Because it *is* a great step ahead, or rather à-haut.

Aldous himself thought that the story had a good easy flow. ". . the easiness, I may say, [to Ian Parsons] was horribly difficult to get, and I have been writing and re-writing the thing for months, before, during and after our trip in the Near East."

Now Julian in transit blew in and delivered a lecture to the American Humanist Society. "He was sweet," Maria wrote to Matthew on 21st October, "though, poor man, how antagonizing he can be.

> And how ludicrous too when he talks as if only he were right—he shuts up even eminent people by contradicting something they know much better, and everybody knows too . . I was rather appalled, because even if he had been corrected on practical things such as time-tables . . he carried on repeating the correction as if he had always known. It must be a form of neurosis . . And he is *fundamentally so tired*. The actual delivery of the talk was excellent as well as natural (but rather too low-brow): dignified, clear, steady . . .

Humphrey Osmond was expected in November. "We plan more mescalin and a tour in the desert." Maria had decided to take the drug with Aldous. But when Humphrey came—it was their second meeting—Aldous had a mild bout of shingles, and Maria was under X-rays once more and suffering from a very painful lumbago (Aldous had lumbago too, "stealing my thunder," Maria said), so neither of them was fit enough to try mescalin. Humphrey experimented with Gerald Heard[1] and Hoynigen Huene, the photographer, instead. In Aldous's presence, ". . both of them very interesting [Aldous to Matthew and Ellen] albeit in rather different ways. Huene's reactions were wholly aesthetic, Gerald's mainly verbal and mediumistic—with other personalities talking through him from a variety of mental levels . . ."

(At this point, *The Doors of Perception* had been reviewed in *Pravda*. "It is like a parody of Dialectical-Materialist denunciation written, not by Orwell, but by someone a good deal less clever . . . [Aldous to Ian Parsons] Heavily funny—but how extremely depressing! For there is not the slightest evidence of any wish to discover what the other fellow is trying to say . . ."

Then much to their regret Humphrey went back to Canada. ". . he is a very remarkable young man, whom it is both a pleasure and a stimulus to have around . . . very able, imaginative and energetic, with a wide-angled intellectual lens . . ." What Maria said about him was, "Humphrey makes life more passionately interesting but busy. We both have a deep affection for him and miss him." And some weeks later, ". . We love him dearly—one does." While he was there she had spoken to him

---

[1] Gerald Heard, at least in his article in the *Kenyon Review* of 1965, puts the date as November 1953.

openly. About her concern for Aldous—"knowing that her time was short." She had said to him, "Aldous is a good man." (Humphrey later wrote to Aldous that he was so filled with grief that he wept for half an hour.) By this time Maria had begun to warn some of her friends. At the end of November Aldous had asked Betty Wendel to read the MS of *The Genius and the Goddess* and to meet them next day for luncheon at the Town and Country market to discuss the book. There Aldous asked her whether she would consider collaborating with him on a play dramatization. Betty burst into tears, overcome by the compliment (this is her own account). Aldous asked her to work on her own for a few days, roughing out ideas for construction. It was very important to him, he said, to have her write the stage descriptions for the sets, as he did not visualize anything and wrote all his descriptions of places from those he had actually seen and remembered. Betty did an outline of the play, and she and Aldous began working separately and together on the actual script. While this was under way, Maria asked Betty to lunch with her alone at the market, not letting Aldous know. "She told me that she was very ill and had been told in Paris that she was coming home to die. She had not told Aldous. She asked me to keep working with him, even when she became bedridden." (Some time before, Maria had written, "Betty Wendel is a wonderful friend and far from being a fool in spite of so much real *sweetness* and *kindness*.")

On 10th December Maria wrote to the children in New York. "Aldous is working passionately without taking a breath [extending his paper on visionary experiences into what became *Heaven and Hell*]—making up for so many months of travelling." But, "It is sadder and sadder that we live so far apart, and nothing is going to budge Aldous from California; nor would any of us dare move until he wanted to—not only because we think he deserves having the few things he wants but also 'because it doesn't pay to have one's will'—I found that out so long ago . . ."

*1st* January 1955. Maria writes a long hand-written letter—they are all by hand now—to New York.

My first love, my first thoughts to you as well as to Aldous, my 4 Darlings, and my very first letter . . .

But Christmas "was *not* very gay. I re-developed that lumbago . . . so things were a great chore. My maids are touching . . . Betty Wendel is our good angel . . ." She and Aldous had dinner alone on Christmas Eve then went over to take parcels to Mère and Rose and her children, and on Christmas Day they all came to a late lunch: "Marie is a genius because the skin of the turkey still crackled; they all ate well and went off to the cinema while Olivia walked with me. But I was getting older and miserabler by the *minute, everything* ached . . . Then I was better until yesterday when I was again 1955 years old, but Aldous repeated treatment and gave me a lot of suggestions so I slept like a log and have the courage to write . . ."

Also to write to Jeanne to rejoice with her over the recovery of "our Noële" from a long and inexplicable illness.

A few days later "a remarkable personage, called Captain Hubbard," turned up in North Kings Road—"the scientific director of the Uranium Corporation, who took mescalin last year, was completely bowled over by it and is now drumming up support among his influential friends . . ." "He has everybody's ear [Maria wrote] because instead of being a cranky literary man he is a nuclear physicist, a businessman, a millionaire and an ardent catholic. He gives the mescalin in small doses . . . Aldous and Gerald and himself took it last night. I was too pained and drugged to take it. And Aldous says it was totally different from the first time and as immensely important . . ."

This was the second (and apparently last) time Aldous took mescalin. He had telephoned to Humphrey in Canada for his approval. ". . since I was in a group [Aldous wrote to the Godels] the experience had a human content, which the earlier, solitary experience . . did not possess. For five hours I was given a series of luminous illustrations of the Christian saying, 'Judge not that ye not be judged,' and the Buddhist saying, 'To set up what you like against what you dislike, this is the disease of the mind.' "

Now this letter to the Godels was dated 10th January and it said first:

> . . . I think so often . . . of our stay in that magical house by the canal . . . and of our long talks, while the ships glided silently past the windows . . .
>
> Here [we] have been well—but not exuberantly so. Maria had to have a long series of X-ray treatments, which achieved the desired results . . . Recently she has been having recurrent and very painful lumbago—which now seems to be yielding to treatment . . . However, in spite of everything we are happy. I have done a great deal of work . . .

On the same day Maria wrote to Ellen:

> Aldous is still well and very cheerful. So is Gerald, and we walked with him yesterday, then he came home for tea and a "hypnotic instruction" by a record which sent him sound asleep, and he was refreshed for our dinner at the Stravinskys. We are such a happy

family with the S's. Vera and myself always the only women—red wine of good quality—only just enough of the main course but a large dessert . . . then music and books. They have wonderful art books. He works *very hard* and all those concerts are for the sake of money. They spend every penny and sometimes more but live easily. Vera has a one-man show in Rome and Aldous is to write the notice. We love what she does.

. . . Can you take a holiday, just all of you? We could meet you anywhere you choose—South of the Grand Canyon? Taos?

. . . We are rejuvenated by our new diet. I wish Matthew would try it for 3 days. [There follow two pages of charted meals which read like some resurrection of the Hay diet] Gerald won't; he's too much of a priest to give up his carbohydrates, and Mère is too much of a gourmet . . .

Two days later Aldous wrote to Humphrey, "Poor Maria has still got the lumbago. We have begun ultrasonic treatment . . . [by] one of the new German machines, and I hope very much that this may do the trick." And Maria to Jeanne on 13th January, ". . all our news is good at present: Suzanne and all her offspring, Mère, Matthew too . . ."

But on 16th January Aldous wrote to Humphrey:

Maria has just left for a couple of days at the hospital, where the doctors want to run a series of tests to see why, as well as this long drawn lumbago, she has been running temperatures every evening. I suppose it is some infection in the intestine or kidney, and hope they will be able to put their finger on it and get rid of it; for she has had much too long a siege of pain and below-parness.

While Maria was away Aldous worked on the play with Betty Wendel.

My Darlings . . . I have been stupidly careless with that lumbago [Maria reassured Matthew and Ellen on 18th January] so I am at the Good Samaritan again. It is hard on poor old Poppa—I wasn't much use with a back-ache, and now he must foot the bills . . .

There followed minute instructions for a present she wanted Matthew to get for a friend of his who was off on a long journey; and this is what Marie Le Put told me about her visiting Maria in hospital. It was a very cold day. "Elle m'a touchée—mon manteau—'Marie, est-ce que vous êtes assez couverte?' Toujours pour les autres, *toujours* . . ."

Maria returned on 22nd January. Some liver trouble was found, Aldous wrote Humphrey on the day, "but the doctor seems to think that much of this will disappear spontaneously as the result of helping the back. I think she is also embarking on a treatment of some kind. So I hope all will be well within a short time . . ."

Only a few days later Maria went back to hospital for more treatments. On 30th January Aldous still writes to Matthew and Ellen that he hopes "when they are over, next week, she will really start to get better." A day later he wrote to Eileen Garrett that the news hasn't been too good of late. "So please, dear Eileen, pray and think for the best outcome."

On 3rd February, he writes to Humphrey, ". . the news here is discouraging. Maria is not getting better . . ." Then two days later, poor Aldous at last is told, and Aldous sees. He wrote at once to Matthew, asking him to come. He wrote to Jeanne. That letter began:

> Je t'écris du fond d'une immense tristesse. Maria est très malade, s'il faut croire aux médicins, sans espoir. Elle rentrera à la maison après-demain car elle sera plus heureuse chez elle.
>
> Pense à elle avec tout ton amour, et à moi aussi,
>
> Aldous.[1]

Peggy Kiskadden (abroad these months) flew back from the Middle East when her husband cabled her and arrived in time to see Maria on her last day in hospital. Maria greeted her with an affectionate, mischievous smile, "I *knew* you would come," She said. "Aldous is letting me go home, isn't it kind of him?" and that afternoon Maria telephoned to Betty Wendel.

> She said to let me talk to her without interrupting because it was the last time she would ever talk to me. She asked me to keep Aldous working and gave me other instructions. The last thing she said to me was "Always, have a fresh ribbon on your typewriter so Aldous won't have trouble reading."

From hospital Maria wrote once more to Jeanne. The letter bears this postscript.

> Quant à toi Janin—nous savons ce que nous savons. Ne sois jamais triste *pour moi*.

---

[1] "I am writing to you from the bottom of an immense sadness. Maria is very ill and if we are to believe the doctors, there is no hope. She will be coming back to the house the day after tomorrow as she will be happier at home.

"Think of her with all your love, and of me too, Aldous".

Maria came home to North Kings Road on Monday 7th February. Rose was in the house, and Helen Halsberg, the nurse who had looked after her in 1952. Maria asked for the door of her room to be kept open so that she could hear the movements in the house. Aldous went over to an ironmongers and got rods and rings, and hung up a curtain in her doorway. In the afternoon their therapist friend, Leslie LeCron, came in for half an hour, put her into hypnosis and gave her some suggestions. Aldous repeated these suggestions later in the evening and from that time on she was free from any distressing symptoms.

It is Aldous who set everything down in an account he wrote afterwards for Jeanne and Julian and Juliette, for Gerald and Humphrey, of which copies were sent to a few other friends. (The account is published in full in Laura Archera's book as well as in a footnote in Aldous's collected Letters. I shall only quote essential passages.)

Matthew arrived on the Tuesday morning. Maria "was still able to find a great and fully conscious happiness in seeing her son . . .

> I [Aldous] spent a good many hours of each day sitting with her, sometimes saying nothing, sometimes speaking. When I spoke, it was always, first of all, to give suggestions about her physical well-being . . . I would suggest that she was feeling, and would continue to feel, comfortable, free from pain . . . These suggestions were, I think, effective; at any rate there was little pain . . .[1]

These suggestions for physical comfort were followed each time by much longer suggestions addressed to the deeper levels of the mind.

> Under hypnosis Maria had had, in the past, many remarkable visionary experiences of a kind which the theologians would call "pre-mystical". She had also had, especially while we were living in the Mojave Desert . . a number of genuinely mystical experiences, had lived with an abiding sense of divine immanence . . . This was the reason for her passionate love for the desert. For her, it was not merely a geographical region; it was also a state of mind, a metaphysical reality, an unequivocal manifestation of God.
>
> In the desert and, later under hypnosis, all Maria's visionary and mystical experiences had been associated with light . . . Light had been the element in which her spirit had lived, and it was therefore

---

[1] "It was only during the last thirty-six hours that sedation (with Demerol) became necessary."

to light that all my words referred. I would begin by reminding her of the desert she had loved so much, of the vast crystalline silence . . of the snow-covered mountains at whose feet we had lived . . . And I would ask her to look at these lights of her beloved desert and to realize that they were not merely symbols, but actual expression of the divine nature; an expression of Pure Being, an expression of the peace that passeth all understanding . . . an expression of the love which is at the heart of things, at the core, along with peace and joy and being, of every human mind. And having reminded her of those truths—truths which we all know in the unconscious depth of our being, which some know consciously but only theoretically and which a few (Maria was one of them) have known directly, albeit briefly and by snatches—I would urge her to advance into those lights . . .

So the days passed . . . her surface mind drifted further and further . . so that she no longer recognized us or paid attention. And yet she must have still heard and understood what was said; for she would respond with appropriate action, when the nurse asked her to open her mouth or swallow. Under anaesthesia, the sense of hearing remains awake long after the other senses have been eliminated . . Addressing the deep mind which never sleeps, I went on suggesting that there should be relaxation on the physical level and an absence of pain and nausea; and I continued to remind her of who she really was—a manifestation in time of the eternal, a part forever unseparated from the whole, of the divine reality; I went on urging her to go forward into the light.

When Mère came, she found her peaceful, "Maria est très calme, couchée dans son beau lit blanc . . . Je la suppose calme sous la présence d'Aldous. Rose dit que s'il elle parle c'est en français . . ."

Suzanne arrived on Thursday. Maria opened her eyes, "et gentille comme toujours elle me dit, 'Tu as un joli chandail.'" Then Maria said, "Vous êtes tous là. Comme à St Trond. C'est comme la mort de Bon-Papa."

A little before three on Saturday morning the night nurse called Aldous. "I went and sat by Maria's bed . . . I told her that I was with her and would always be with her in that light which was the central reality of our beings. I told her that she was surrounded by human love and that this love was the manifestation of a greater love, by which she was enveloped and sustained. I told her to let go . . . She knew what love was, had been capable of love as few human beings are capable. Now she must go forward into love . . . And she was to forget, not only her poor body, but the time in which that body had lived. Let her forget the past, leave her old memories behind. Regrets, nostalgias, remorses, apprehensions—all these were barriers between her and the light.

Let her forget them . . . 'Peace now,' I kept repeating. 'Peace, love, joy *now* . . ."

Matthew was with them.

Those last three hours [he wrote to Ellen afterwards] were the most anguishing and moving hours of my life. It was just Aldous and Peggy and I. Peggy had put out the night nurse. And Aldous was whispering to her all during the time. Whispering the lesson of the *Bardo Thodol* . . . but framed in such a moving and personal way— illustrations from their lives together and incidences . . . and her own revelation of what the *Tibetan Book of the Dead* speaks about. "Let go, let go . . ."

. . . It was over so quietly and gently with Aldous with tears streaming down his face with his quiet voice not breaking . . .

Maria died at six o'clock in the morning on 12th February.

Maria was buried on 14th February in Rose Dale Memorial Park at Los Angeles. Aldous made the decision. Everyone thought, wrote Matthew, that Aldous would be the one who'd break down. "No, it was he, far more than any of us who held the family together . . It was his example that kept Bonne Maman going so wonderfully." Aldous decided that there should be some kind of service to satisfy Rose, Suzanne and Mère. Matthew believes that Aldous himself desired this. Matthew and Peggy saw to the arrangements. For some reason they stopped short of a Catholic ceremony. The service was conducted by their friend, Father McLane, a High Episcopalian, who was grief-stricken himself and who, in Matthew's words, "with almost unbelievable tact pro- duced something so moving, so suitable to Coccola that even I who hated the whole idea was satisfied.

I now feel that the service had one profound and valuable effect—it acted as the great, the last catharsis, a kind of full stop, from which one *has* to look into the future; though the past is illuminated by the beauty and sweet remembrance of that being who for thirty years was the closest being in my life.

Throughout the ceremony, it was Aldous, frail as a ghost, who gave his arm to Mme Nys and who sustained her. The next day he and Matthew went away together.

## Chapter Five

### "*Telle qu'en elle-même . . .*"

"WHAT is to become of Aldous? That is the greatest single question which is facing us." Matthew, point by blunt point, tried to work it out:

> The immediate short-range problem [he wrote to Ellen on 17th February] from now until April when he intends coming to New York for the spring and summer with us in New England.
> 1) It looks as if I will not be able to persuade him to have anyone in the house with him. While the mechanics of running the house are working out very well—Marie [Le Put] will be there four times a week etc—he is not covered from 3.30 pm until the next morning. Quite apart from the gloominess of the empty house, there always exist . . problems and emergencies . . that Aldous will not be able to cope with. Possibilities: a full-time individual, or a part-time individual who comes in for the afternoon and evening, say, 2-9 pm. Or what he's presently thinking of, a pansy-boy—which he can't stand—but it doesn't have to be a pansy—to tootle him round in the car twice a week for a couple of hours . . .
> The long-term problem. 1) This depends of course on where *we* are going after I leave H.I.P. at the end of the summer. Ideally, I think very definitely on Aldous's part, he wishes that we could come and live here in Los Angeles.
> . . My thinking on the subject—I *must* have a job, but not just any job, but a job in terms of a career etc etc.
> . . Would *he* be willing to move himself? I think he would: he gave me an indication when we were talking over what might happen to 740 [North Kings]—he thought he might move to a service type apartment or hotel, leaving us the house . . The house which in 4 years will be paid for . . .

Humphrey asked Aldous to come and stay with him and his wife in Canada; Frieda Lawrence asked him to the ranch. Anita Loos cabled offering financial help . . . Aldous resumed work with Betty Wendel on 23rd February.

> Wednesday 23rd was the first day that we took up where we had left off. [Betty's diary] When I arrived Aldous said that he would like to have some music. Maria had always put on the record player for him. He had difficulties starting the machine—he fumbled with

the arm—dropped it on the record—I felt I could not make a move to help him; at last he got the music going.

Presently Matthew had to leave. Practical arrangements were made more or less on his lines—Marie Le Put to cook and leave food four times a week; Onnie Wesley, "a dear kind coloured woman," to see to the house on one or two other days; a friend of Gerald's to drive Aldous on three afternoons; and an old Dartington school-fellow of Matthew's, Marianna Schauer, to come on alternate days for secretarial work and reading aloud. As for the rest . . . The evenings, as Matthew put it, were uncovered. He could do *nothing*, he wrote to his Aunt Jeanne, but respect his father's wish for solitude. "I had to overcome my fears and leave him alone in the house." Aldous had said to him, "For the moment, I think, I will stay here with my work."

No book in hand. He persisted with the play, carried on with some essays and the notes on the Utopian theme that had so long pursued him; thought—the suggestion was Gerald's—of writing something about death (anonymously), the whole problem of death "and what can be done by those who survive to help the dying, and incidentally themselves". One thinks back to the boy of seventeen who struck by blindness retired into work.

He wrote to his friends, responded to their letters. Frieda he told how often while he was sitting by Maria's bed he had thought "of that spring night in Vence twenty-five years ago." (Frieda wrote to her sister Else, ". . Maria Huxley is dead. A true true friend . . .") He wrote to Maria's family, the family that had become, that was, in the deepest sense, his own. To Claire, the published letter in which he says, ". . in so far as I have learned to be human—and I had a great capacity for not being human—it is thanks to her." To Sophie, this unpublished one:

I can't write a long letter—but am sending this little note to tell you that the thing which gave Coccola her greatest happiness during the last month of her life was the news that you were going to get married. She loved you and longed for you to be happy in growing to your full stature, in becoming your best, completest self.

Telle qu'en elle-même l'éternité la change,[1] she hoped that you will become telle qu'en elle-même l'amour, la tendresse, la joie, la douleur, la change.

Be as loving, sensitive, understanding and brave as she was—and be as happy, both of you, as we were.

All my love

[1] This is of course a—slight—variant of Mallarmé's line; a line which had long haunted Aldous.

To Yolanda, their friend of the market stall, he took a copy of his account of Maria's last days. This gave her the courage to come to him with something else. First she asked him not to be angry about what she had to tell. He promised. Whereupon she produced four hundred dollars in clean notes (Maria used to pick up dirty change with a tissue). This was her story. Last September Maria said to her, "Yolanda, you are worried." Yolanda confessed to business trouble, money trouble. How much? Maria asked. Fifty dollars? Five hundred? "Oh," Yolanda said, "she had no money sense!" So there it was. Maria lent her the four hundred she needed, and now she was all right again, but Aldous must not mind that it was done behind his back. Aldous cried.

To Rina, he wrote first of all of the affection Maria had borne her; in Italian, he told her about the last days. And now "mi adatto ad una vita amputata. Non sa che cosa farò eventualmente. L'ultima malattia è stata, grazie a Dio, breve e poco dolorosa . . . La fine è stata tranquillissima."

# PART ELEVEN

## Soles Occidere et Redire Possunt: 1955-1960

"I don't think . . that we can be
really happy until we have nothing to
rejoice at—nothing, that is to say,
specifically *Ours*."

ALDOUS HUXLEY

". . he always returned to the single
theme that dominated his later years:
the condition of men in the twentieth
century."

SIR ISAIAH BERLIN

## Chapter One

## "Meanwhile Life Continues . . ."

ALDOUS stayed on alone at North Kings for over two months. On 19th April he and Betty Wendel finished their first draft of *The Genius and the Goddess* play; next day he left to spend the summer in the East. He travelled, the way he knew to travel, by car. Rose was going to drive. In Maria's car, the last new Oldsmobile. The afternoon before he went to tea with Mère. "J'ai constaté sa bonne mine," she wrote to Jeanne, "son calme, et certainement son soulagement de quitter la maison." He left her the itinerary of their route so that she could follow them on the map. It was the extreme southern route, by the tip of Texas, the longest to New York and one that he had never taken, a point not lost on Mme Nys, who wrote how glad she was that Aldous would be spared "les souvenirs d'une route connue." Betty came to see them off. They were taking a picnic basket and a great many books.

Rose was a little nervous. She told me. She hoped Aldous would like her driving. She wondered what it would be like sitting side by side with him all the way across the country. [It was not only, one must remember, that Rose was so much younger than all her sisters but that up to then anyone's contact with Aldous with a very few exceptions—Gerald, Humphrey, and even there, I would say, not a hundred per cent—had never been quite direct, with Maria always the conductor who got the circuit going.] Rose laughed when I presented them with a bottle of sherry each. When Aldous was out of earshot she said she would probably have her sherry alone and would need a drink at the end of the day. Plans had been carefully made; so many miles every day, reservations at motels . . .

Frieda, for once, was not at the ranch but in Texas, and so it was made natural for Aldous to avoid Taos and travel instead by way—a huge way—of Phoenix and El Paso down to Port Isabel on the Gulf to see her. From there they made their way up to Washington, D.C., more or less following the coast, by Houston, Baton Rouge, New Orleans, Mobile and, after crossing Florida, Savannah, Charleston. Aldous turned out very sweet and companionable. They would start at about nine in the morning, stop for a picnic lunch, and they did drink their evening sherry together in one of their cabins at the motel. From New Orleans

Mère had word that Aldous was beginning to press on—"Il trouve le pays trop grand. [Mme Nys to Jeanne] Ce n'est pas le pays, mais l'absence de Maria et qui s'aggrandira d'heure en heure."

After twelve days and four thousand miles of it, they reached Washington. A couple of busy days—luncheon at the Indian Embassy, tea at Dumbarton Oaks, a visit to the National Institute of Mental Health, and on to New York. Aldous had been lent George S. Kaufman's apartment on 1035 Park Avenue (Rose went on to Suzanne's) and there he settled down for the next eight weeks. "I live," he wrote to Betty, "in a style to which I am not accustomed—

> pent house with terraces overlooking the City, French butler and wife (admirable cook), Siamese cat and an enormous library of plays, mutely urging me to work—which I am doing now, like mad, for I cd do nothing en route. Have revised the first act and am now doing the second . . .
> . . Anita . . very sensible about producers, directors, actors etc . . .

He allowed himself one more interruption, a meeting of the "nut-doctors" at Atlantic City. From there—the American Psychiatrists' Association meeting—he wrote to Humphrey on 11th May. He was staying at an hotel called the Marlborough-Blenheim.

> Here I am in this Dome of Pleasure, floating midway on the waves, where is heard the mingled measure of the Electric Shock Boys, the Chlorpromaziners and the 57 Varieties of Psychotherapists. What a place—the luxury of early Edwardian days, massive, spacious, indescribably hideous and, under a livid sky, indescribably sinister!
> I am under the protective wing of a bright young researcher . . . They steer me through the tumult and introduce me to the Grand Panjandrums, who mainly speak with German accents and whose names and faces I can never remember for more than five minutes.
> . . Tomorrow we have an evening party with speeches about mescalin and LSD, at which I am supposed to hold forth for 10 minutes.

Humphrey came to New York later in the month for a few days and Aldous saw as much of him as he could. On the whole he kept himself busy in every available way. "I am leading a horribly social life," he wrote to Betty, "too many lunches and dinners, even when the people are pleasant and interesting there is apt to be an expense of spirit." And of course there were negotiations about the play—these were to go on for a long time to come; now Aldous arranged for Helen Harvey of the William Morris Agency to represent him and Betty and draw up a financial agreement. "We will split the hypothetical royalties," he wrote to her, "as you suggest—twenty-five and seventy-five. I hope they will be *very* large." This broke down as fifty per cent to Aldous as author of the novel on which the play was based, with the other fifty per cent divided half and half between Aldous and Betty as co-authors of the play. They agreed to share all expenses and they were to have equal rights and equal billing. On 2nd June he telegraphed for her. She arrived on the 6th. They sought every conceivable advice. "There were meetings, meetings, meetings," Betty said, "talk, talk, talk." At this point Alfred de Liagre, who had produced most of Van Druten's plays, became interested. (He "is pleasant and a gentleman, and has a record of successes," Aldous wrote.) They conferred with him in Betty's room at the St Regis Hotel.

Delly [de Liagre] is handsome, stylish, rather formal [Betty's journal]. About four o'clock I asked if he would like some tea and he said he would love tea. He looked as if he was expecting me to phone for room service and appeared a little surprised when Aldous got up, opened my cupboard and produced an electric kettle, tea bags, cups and saucers, a grocery box of lump sugar, a package of cookies. Aldous told me to go on with play talk while he made tea. Delly quickly subdued his chic and urbane manner and matched Aldous's cosy simplicity. But at another meeting, which lasted until evening, as I was asking Delly if he would like a drink, he quickly got to his feet and insisted that we go downstairs to the King Cole Bar; I suppose he was beating Aldous to a trip after Scotch in my cupboard.

De Liagre suggested changes in the play which the authors half-heartedly agreed to work out, and Betty returned to California without anything being signed and sealed.

During this period Aldous wrote across the Atlantic to Elise Murrel (Maria's "psychic" correspondent):

Dear Friend,
   ... Meanwhile life continues in its new, amputated context. Quite apart from everything else. there are certain mechanical difficulties; for, as you probably know, I am pretty blind and depended on Maria for many things requiring sharp eyes, such as driving a car, reading aloud, looking after the practical affairs of life. My old

friend Eileen Garrett—Irish like yourself, and a medium, and now the head of the Parapyschology Foundation, which finances research in ESP phenomena and organizes discussion of them by philosophers, psychologists and medical men—told me something very interesting about Maria the other day. M. has appeared to her several times since her death, and particularly vividly on two occasions, when she said two things which Eileen didn't understand, but which M. told her to pass on to me without fail. First "I didn't hear the whole of the Bardle" (this was how Eileen heard the message) "but the effect was to lull me and to carry me through, so that I was still with it on the other side." The other was, "I found the Eggart (again Eileen's version) very helpful."

Now, Aldous went on, he had *not* told Eileen about Maria's last days, had not explained that he had been repeating to her what resembled in a certain way the ritual for the dying described in the *Bardo Thodol* or *Tibetan Book of the Dead*, "and the word which Eileen interpreted as Bardle was obviously Bardo: for M. knew the book well and had a great feeling for it . . . As for Eggart —that was obviously Eckhart, whose tremendous phrase, 'The eye with which we see God is the same as the eye with which God sees us,' I had repeated.

Eileen also said that M. had always appeared in the midst of an intense ruby glow (the light of love, I suppose; for she was enormously capable of love); and that she seemed to be less attached to things here, less possessive about those she had loved, than anyone she had ever seen in this posthumous condition . . . Eileen's feeling was that she would not remain in this region for long, but would press onwards in the knowledge that she could do more good that way than by hanging about on the fringes of our poor old world . . .

Aldous mentioned Eileen Garrett's rapport with Maria to several people, Grace Hubble, Ellen, Jeanne (to whom he wrote, "Eileen . . se trouve assez souvent en contact, spontanément, avec Maria—la trouve heureuse, légère, gaie, jeune et extraordinairement *libre*"). And yet at about this time when Constance Collier's friend, Phyllis Wilburn (Constance had died in April while Aldous was en route), talked to him about survival and asked outright, "Do you believe in life after death?" Aldous answered "I do not know."

At the end of that long letter to Elise Murrel, though, we find a key passage:

I don't think . . that we can be really happy until we have nothing to rejoice at—nothing, that is to say, specifically *Ours*. Only then do we begin to have everything, impartially—the entire visible universe and the invisible too—being happy in all the countless reasons for happiness that exist in a world of infinite depth and beauty and significance, and not unhappy in the particular reasons for our own misery, however terrible they may be . . .

Of course, he ended, this is easy to say but "dreadfully hard to practise . . Illness (which is death in life) is much harder to cope with than death (which is life in death)."

At the end of June Aldous moved to New England with Matthew and his family. They had taken a house for the summer at Aldous's instigation, a beautiful eighteenth-century house called Newcomb, under great trees, on the banks of a tidal river, at Guilford, Connecticut. Aldous paid the rent (never mind if it's steep, "my *Esquire* articles will make it easy"). Matthew, working in Public Health at New Haven, commuted; Aldous was finishing off *Heaven and Hell* and spending his spare time with Ellen, their old affinity flowering in the daily companionship; the countryside was green, the township pleasantly rustic.

. . Aldous and I shopped together [Ellen wrote to me] and talked about food a lot, and discussed the children an incredible amount, and the weather almost constantly. It was atrociously hot and humid; the air simply sat there being re-breathed and getting damper . . . ["The hottest summer in the history of Connecticut," Aldous recorded] I made him a pair of pedal-pusher style shorts out of a pair of his old pants. He wore these a great deal, looking completely unselfconscious and at the same time like a stork wearing shorts. Edward Lear would have done a devastating drawing of him.
He worked, or foozled, in the mornings. Foozling, which was his term, was a way of avoiding work, and meant tickling the inside of his nose with opened paper clips—sometimes his desk was *covered* in opened paper clips—or recording bits of poetry, philosophy, literature that he liked, onto his dictaphone, and then playing them back again. But work he did, of course, and actually claimed that he became physically ill if he didn't work a good part of every day.

Little Trev and Tessa, though flourishing, were a handful. "How I admire people who can cope with children!" Aldous wrote to me." Ellen and Matthew do so remarkably well.

But, my goodness, how clearly (because they exhibit human nature with the lid off, or rather before the lid has been put on) children illustrate the four Noble Truths of Buddhism. Life is sorrow. The cause of sorrow is craving for individualized existence—and do they crave, poor little things! The extinction of craving puts an end to sorrow. And the means to that extinction are the prescriptions of the eightfold path. The path, of course, is out of the question for children, and all that can be done for them is to screw some reasonably acceptable persona over the seething mass of craving and aversion, which constitutes the human being in the raw . . .

"Lunch was always interesting," Ellen continues. "Aldous used it as a time to unwind, and would muse aloud about what he had been writing, or thinking about, or what was in the morning's mail, or what we would do in the afternoon." *How* like the summers at Forte, the summers at Sanary (*mutatis mutandis*) . . .

We both suffered from shyness, [Ellen] and our intimacy was often oblique. I remember particularly a lunch when he suddenly started to speak about visiting a medium in New York (I had picked him up at the station that morning). The medium had gone into trance and contacted Maria, and Maria had then poured out her feelings of love toward him, and told him that these feelings had widened into a completely accepting, non-clinging love . . . they would never lose each other, or what they had had together, and she now wanted to assure him that he had her permission and encouragement should he ever want to love someone else, and marry again. I realized that he was not only fascinated by the experience but also that he was, in his way, telling me that Maria would have wanted him to remarry, that he wanted to, and that he wanted my permission too. I was very moved, and told him that anyone who had participated in such a love would only be confirming that love by loving again. He agreed and seemed satisfied . . .

(Ellen had no idea that Aldous might be meaning something quite specific.)

We drove in the afternoons . . I was a horrible driver . . Aldous was my teacher . . he had a way of trusting me to do everything properly—when I slid, sweating with tension, into a tight parking space, he would pat me gently and say ". . . masterly, my dear, masterly!" I owed all my confidence to him. Anyway, we used to pack Trev and Tessa, and usually the cook's child too, into the back seat, and take off to the beach, to see Gillette's Castle, to visit neighbouring towns, to buy ice cream, to simply drive through the countryside . . he missed nothing and never seemed to tire of toodling around.

Once we rocketed up to Boston. I was delivering him to some conference or other, but we went a day early so we could see the

Fine Arts Museum and the Gardner and go to a play. He was fantastic with maps and deadly accurate about where we were at all times (I had never been to Boston, much less driven there), so he did all the navigating and enjoyed it enormously. I'm sure you have been through plenty of museums with him . . we simply galloped along, A. with his largest magnifying glass at the ready. I would read the labels, he would study the painting; he absorbed so much in such a short time that I felt I wasn't reading labels fast enough sometimes; later he would go on about the painting as though we had stood there for an hour. We went to an outdoor theatre in the evening. I don't remember the play, except that it was a Restoration comedy thing and it was very well done and some of my friends were in it—I mention it only because Aldous had such a good time, and I have one of those indelible mental-pictures of him standing backstage, hat pushed back onto the back of his head, a can of beer in his hand, laughing and talking with the actors . . . he was suddenly 25 years old.

Our other big activity in Guilford was walking. Matthew generally arrived back from New Haven in time for a glass of sherry and a talk with his father. I had a bath and changed—unbelievable luxury for me, I was used to cleaning up the children and feeding them and preparing dinner all at the same time. Now the cook did it, and the children ate in the kitchen, and we were served in the dining room, all elegant and civilized. After dinner we walked, as I said—my God he liked to walk. We knew every path and road intimately, and every silo, every cow, every bit of landscape. The air was so warm and damp that it was like walking through molasses, even late at night . . .

The *Esquire* articles, which helped to pay for cook and rent, require an explanation. Aldous had had a windfall. He had been approached at the beginning of the year with what he called a most surprising offer—"to send a monthly essay on anything I like to *Esquire*, that curious magazine which combines naked girls, men's fashions and a certain amount of literature. It is the only periodical, outside the most poverty stricken highbrow class, which will print an essay." (Two of his, "Sludge & Sanctity" and "The French of Paris", had already appeared in *Esquire* in 1953.) He accepted. "Thanks to the nude ladies, they can pay very well." In fact they paid him a thousand dollars an essay. Pretty high pay at the time, if not in *The Saturday Evening Post*, *Life* or *New Yorker* bracket; and extravagantly high, on the mass market, for that kind of writing—think-pieces they were called—published without interference. The money was very welcome, but, best of all, the arrangement gave Aldous a platform: the editors were as good as their word and he was able to write about anything he felt that needed saying—warnings about over-

population, spoliation of our resources ("we are living like
drunken sailors, like the irresponsible heirs of a millionaire
uncle"), the misapplications of technology, about censorship by
commercialism, warnings against the doctrine that in this universe
of ours anybody can get anything for nothing. It was literary
journalism at its most ungratuitous, for the last thing Aldous
aimed at, the elegance and agreeable jugglery of these essays
notwithstanding, was to adorn or to fill space. The first of the
series appeared in July 1955 and continued with hardly a break
until April 1957. The titles were part of the sugar-coating—
"Usually Destroyed", "Doodles in the Dictionary", "Canned
Fish", "Where Do You Live?", "Madness Badness Sadness",
"Back Numbers" etc etc.

Aldous stayed in New England for two months, interrupted by
some days and nights in New York, a trip to Boston and one to
Maine to attend one of those parapsychological gatherings he was
getting addicted to, Dr Henry Puharich's Round Table Foundation at Glen Cove.

> . . some days . . in the strange household assembled by Puharich . . .
> [to Eileen Garrett] Elinor Bond doing telepathic guessing . . .
> Frances Farelly, with her diagnostic machine . . . Harry, the Dutch
> sculptor, who goes into trances in the Faraday cages and produces
> automatic scripts in Egyptian hieroglyphics; Narodny, the cock-
> roach man, preparing experiments to test the effects of human
> telepathy on insects.

Aldous watched, open-minded certainly, not particularly credu-
lous. "It was all very lively and amusing—

> and, I really think, promising; for whatever may be said against
> Puharich, he is certainly very intelligent, extremely well-read and
> highly enterprising. His aim is to reproduce by modern pharma-
> cological, electronic and physical methods the conditions used by the
> shamans for getting into a state of travelling clairvoyance and then,
> if he succeeds, to send people to explore systematically "the Other
> World". This seems to be as good a new approach to the survival
> problem (along with a lot of other problems) as any of the rest, and
> may yield some interesting results.

And now we have only Aldous's own letters—often so resolutely
on the surface, at times lightningly unreticent—to reflect his
moods. In his birthday letter to Julian he was able to strike this
positive note:

> Dearest J,
> Many happy and happier returns! Yes, it is hard to feel old—to be

quite *sérieux*, as the ageing bourgeois ought to be! We both, I think, belong to that fortunate minority of human beings, who retain the mental openness and elasticity of youth, while being able to enjoy the fruits of an already long experience . . .

Yet the month after he wrote to Humphrey:

I too have had a birthday, this very day.

How soon hath Time, the subtle thief of age,
Stol'n on his wing my first and sixtieth year!

How little to show! One ought to have done much better. But perhaps it's never too late to mend. And what sad, sad, strange experiences since my last birthday, which was in France!

And to Ralph Rose (the author of a stage adaptation of *After Many a Summer*):

. . This has been a hard time for me too. There seems to be no remedy except to learn somehow not to identify oneself with the pains and losses one has to suffer, the bewilderments and darkness one has to go through—to accept them realistically as things that happen, but not permit oneself to be equated with them, not to forget that they do *not* constitute the entire universe and that we are capable, even in disaster, of being impartially aware of all the other non-disastrous aspects of the world.

To Eileen Garrett, very ill in France, some lines (in the course of a very long letter) showing his belief in the efficacy of benevolent thought, of prayer if you wish:

. . These last days I have been thinking of going with her [Maria] to your room at Le Piol and laying on hands. I hope the thought may have had at least some tiny influence for the good of your health.

To Noële Neveux, fourteen years old, he sends a warning against Proustian indulgence.

Hélas, le temps ne se retrouve pas . . . Rome, Dieulefit, tout le passé—il ne faut pas essayer de les revivre à la manière de Proust.

Instead, he tells the child, we must use the lost time in the present with the given facts of *now* and *here*, and in that way we might come nearer, perhaps very much nearer, to timeless eternity and to those whom we have loved and who have gone from us into death.

And embedded in a letter to one of his strangers, Mrs Barry Stevens, we find a confirmation of his long true ignorance (or his own conviction of it). Telling her that his wife died early this year, he speaks of her "four or five months of seemingly perfect health last summer, when we travelled in the Near East and in Europe."


At the end of August Aldous returned to California, making his own arrangements with some firmness. He was going by air (the car to be driven back eventually by some reliable person). Both his domestic helpers happened to be off on holiday; Aldous wrote to Marianna Schauer, Matthew's young friend who had been dealing with his post:

> Dear Marianna,
> I am not supposed to know (since both Rose and her mother seem to think that I am too frail to take it!), but I actually do know that things are going very badly—Rose being ill etc. They both seem to be exceedingly disturbed about (a) the cleaning of the house, (b) the fact that neither Marie nor Onnie will be on hand when I arrive. Let us deal first with (a).

There follow commonsensical instructions about engaging house cleaners. ". . I do not want Rose, her mother and/or Peggy getting hot and bothered about something which can be handled so simply by a cleaning firm. If any of them start making a fuss, say that these are my instructions . . . I know you can handle this with tact and firmness—both of which seem to be needed at the moment!" And let nobody bother to meet him at the plane. As for Marie Le Put and Onnie's being away, he could easily manage breakfast and lunch for the time being and go out for dinner either to a restaurant or to friends. "So don't let anybody worry about that . . ."

On 1st September he was back at North Kings and to much the same life as he had led there in the spring. (The house, he wrote to Humphrey then, "is full of the presence of an absence.") His existence was compartmentalized, no one was allowed to see more than a part of it. Work solitary or with Betty in the morning. Marianna three afternoons a week. There wasn't much secretarial work, Aldous being very well organized with his letters.[1] They talked over tea. He asked questions about her life, her child . . . They went for drives, to tea at Mme Nys's, to shop at Farmers' Market or browse in bookshops on La Cienega. Some evenings he remained alone in the house, others he spent with friends, at the Wendels', at Peggy and Bill Kiskadden's, the Stravinskys', with Eva Herrmann. "One never asked where he was going or where

---

[1] Marianna Schauer, the present Mrs Newton, talking to S. B.

he had been", Betty said. Friends drove him home at night but he would never allow himself to be seen into the house.

There was a long dark drive with an irregular surface from street to home [Dr James Brainard Smith writing to S. B.] and yet he, without cane or whatever, was quite firm about sending me back to the car and *not* being led up it home. Not at all! And waited for the car to leave.

At the best of times Aldous had appealed to the maternal, the fraternal, the protective instincts, and now there were a good many people who could see themselves in the role of taking over. But Aldous was determined not to be looked after. As an adolescent he had shrunk from the help waiting for him in vulnerable positions. Later he became able to take help, physical help, daily and unremittent, from one woman (his brother Trev may have been, up to a point, another exception). Now he was quite deliberate in his intention to forego this help, not to allow that pattern to be repeated. He had received in the fullest measure what can be given by one human being to another, now he was going to learn to do without. He did not wish for anything like an attempt at emulation of Maria. And not for her sake, for his own. Here was something that went well beyond his need for privacy and the wish not to be fussed over; it was, I am convinced, part of a process towards renunciation. Quite rightly, from their points of view, Matthew, Julian, Juliette, his friends, were deeply and affectionately concerned. The Julians were in England, Matthew was tied to his job in the East, while Aldous by health, habit and inclination was tied to California; and it was in California that gently but unmistakably he drew a line, the invisible chalk circle: so far and no further.

Within a week of his arrival there occurred one of those frightful sudden California bush-fires that can ravage a whole countryside with such appalling swiftness. "Santa Barbara is surrounded by flames. Last night all roads going north were closed . . ."

Aldous's doctor, to whom he had gone for a check-up, declared him healthy; "I manage to do a good deal of work—mostly of a very exasperating kind." For they were by no means rid of the play yet; at the moment he and Betty were revising their revision, putting back some of the characters they had been persuaded to take out during the summer. *The Genius and the Goddess*, the novel, Aldous's first for seven years had come out (in June) and was doing very well. (A good start in America; twenty thousand copies sold in six weeks in England and a second printing ordered.) The novel, Aldous's shortest, is also his most un-Peacockian. The confluence of associations is there all right—that was as particular to him as breathing—but the dialogue and its apparent digressions are astringently subservient to the action. And he appears interested in telling a story, a story *sub specie aeternitatis* to be sure. The book is very far from what Cyril Connolly called the early brilliant, destructive period; the analysis of human motive remains ruthless, but the keynote is compassion, loving, not detached, compassion. (One interesting, technical, feature of the novel is that it has an all-American cast and setting, effortlessly as a matter of course, not Americans characterized as such but Americans as members of the human race.)

I am glad you liked the little book [Aldous wrote to me]. It was a favourite of Maria's, in its manuscript form. As you say, one could have gone on with it almost indefinitely; but on the whole I think it is better that the rest should be silence.

It was the last book of Aldous's Maria read. (". . . it seems so much stronger," as she had written to her son, ". . . a great step ahead, or rather à-haut.") Edwin Muir, too, thought it the best thing he ever did.

His original title had been "The Past Is Prelude", more expressive of mood and theme than *The Genius and the Goddess*; at one point it became "Through the Wrong End of the Opera Glasses" (the main action being seen through receded time) which was discarded because of length. One may well ask why Aldous spent so much time on dramatic versions of his books. For one thing, he never let go of his *ignis fatuus* of the successful play ("which ought not be beyond one's competence", he declared when he was still an usher at Eton), the long stage run that would set one free, not now from actual financial worries because he had not had any to speak of since the end of the war, nor free from work as he would always work, but free to work at his own pace. According to Betty, he very much wanted to see a play of his produced and produced well. ("If one could see one's own dramatic ideas well realized . . the thrill would be enormous," as he had said twenty-five years ago when *Point Counter Point* was on the stage.)

He talked to me about all this many times. [Betty] When crossing the ocean he had seen people reading his books, but they hadn't changed their expression turning pages, nor did they applaud at the end of a chapter, or walk away from their deck-chairs telling someone else about the book.

And yet he was so obviously bored by the mechanics of play writing—all this jigsaw work—unfortunately necessary. Never, for all his persistence, had there been less a man of the theatre.

> About the sets [Aldous to Betty]. I confess stage sets have always left me profoundly indifferent. As long as they are not monstrously ugly or monstrously silly . . I don't care what they are like, provided they permit the story to be told . . .

All that is required is efficiency. ". . I had the hideous experience [in *The Gioconda Smile*] . . of what happens when you try to change a scene very rapidly by mechanical rather than optical methods.

> Lights can go on and off in 1-100th of a second. Curtains take 5 seconds at least, and the setting up of realistic scenes may take long minutes. Hence I approve the idea of doing . . . with a minimum of machinery and a maximum of lighting effects. My own conviction is that no play (I am not speaking of a spectacle—ballet, musical comedy act) was ever made or marred by its setting . . .

Betty also remarks that Aldous, though perfectly aware of the power of dramatic critics, was no more concerned about them at the writing stage than he was about the book reviewers. Now, how did she and Aldous organize their collaboration? At their meetings—and in Aldous's long memoranda—they threshed out scenes; Betty, he insisted, was good at construction and at visualizing; she went off to write, then brought back her text to Aldous. "I loved his dialogue and he liked mine after he had inverted my sentences. After a while I started inverting my sentences myself and then Aldous inverted them back to where they had been at the beginning . . ." Most of their troubles with prospective directors arose from the fact that there was a play within a play. The outer play, they called it Conversations, consisted of Old John Rivers, the narrator, talking to a friend about the eminent physicist, the genius of the title, whose assistant he has been and in whose household he has lived as a very young man. The talk takes place the night of Christmas Eve in the present year of grace. Does his friend want to hear the official fiction, Rivers asks, the official biography, or the truth?

> "The trouble with fiction is that it makes too much sense. Reality never makes sense."
> "Never?"
> "Maybe from God's point of view. Never from ours . . . In the raw, existence is always one damned thing after another . . simultaneously

Thurber and Michelangelo . . . The criterion of reality is intrinsic irrelevance."
. . "To what?"
"To the best that has been Thought and Said . . . Oddly enough, the closest to reality are always the fictions that are supposed to be the least true." He leaned over and touched the back of a battered copy of *The Brothers Karamazov*. "It makes so little sense that it's almost real. Which is more than can be said for any of the academic kinds of fiction . . . More than can be said even for biography fiction . . ."[1]

The reality, the one damned thing after another, are acted out in the main, the inner play. De Liagre and other advisers felt that the Conversations should be shortened. "I seemed to be alone in clinging to the Conversations, [Betty] not only because they contained the most brilliant of Aldous's writing but also because they bridged the going from comedy to tragedy and back to comedy, and because they were in themselves dramatizations of the inner play. I suppose Henry James was right in defining the art of play-writing as a process of jettisoning the cargo so as to save the ship. But too much cargo was jettisoned. The version approved by Aldous and me has never been produced (or has not up to now). I am unconvinced, as Aldous was unconvinced, that the ship needed saving . . ."

By October they had done with the new revision; but a director, Joseph Anthony, whom Aldous had waxed enthusiastic about, had meanwhile taken on another engagement supposing—wrongly —that the authors would not mind delay.

Aldous at this time was busy with extensive reading for a talk —that grew into a long essay "Gesualdo: Variations on a Musical Theme"[2]—he had promised to give at one of Robert Craft's Monday evening concerts at the Southern California Chamber Music Society, a talk about the court of Ferrara and the "utterly amazing musical style" of the madrigals of Carlo Gesualdo, the psychotic prince of Venosa who had murdered his wife. Aldous delivered the lecture on 27th October.

. . When he spoke of Gesualdo's special brand of 16th century eroticism, [Betty's journal] the audience, mostly music lovers who sit with their eyes closed, or hands over face, or reading the score, tittered then laughed out loud. Aldous went on and on with story after story about the composer-flagellator . . increasing laughter sweeping through the auditorium . . . After the lecture when we were waiting to drive Aldous home and his admirers had dispersed, only

---

1 From the opening of *The Genius and the Goddess*, the novel not the play.
2 Published in *Adonis and the Alphabet*. Chatto & Windus, 1956.

one young man, very earnest and erudite, was lingering. He asked Aldous to tell him where he had found so much data on Gesualdo . . . Aldous mumbled about journals and letters. The young man asked where they could be read. Aldous said to telephone him. Safely in my car, he said, "I have done the most dreadful thing—and I'll be caught . . . I was carried away and invented all those stories except the first one. Never have I done anything so preposterous. Oh dear!"

Now another glimpse of Aldous, this time through Rose. On her birthday, he telephoned Mère asking himself to tea with Marianna, "sa gentille secretaire . . .

> Et voilà Aldous qui s'amène avec une énorme boîte sous les bras [Rose de Haulleville to Jeanne] . . . un superbe manteau sport . . . Il était allé avec Marianna dans un magasin choisi par lui, "Gifts for Men", c'est à dire pour tapettes mais où il y a des choses charmantes, et là lui-même a choisi ce manteau. J'étais émue aux larmes, surtout, lorsqu'il m'a dit que c'était pour les jours froids et venteux du désert. Tu vois comme il est adorable, et tâche de nous remplacer Maria, mais avec tact et simplicité et sans sentimentalité. Il semble heureux; plein d'humour, et très décidé de ce qu'il veut et ce qu'il ne veut pas. J'ai admiré chez lui son nouvel aspirateur, dernier modèle et un nouveau deep-freeze . . . Il est si beau à regarder, fort à l'aise se balançant un peu comme les éléphants et de temps en temps un geste de ses belles mains . . . D'une certaine façon je le trouve "libéré." Comprends moi bien! Quant à moi je suis encore toute perdue . . .

In November Aldous mentions that he is about to deliver a lecture "at the Swami's Tiny Taj Mahal" in Hollywood. This was the Vedanta Temple of Swami Prabhavananda, Christopher Isherwood's Swami, of whom Gerald Heard and Aldous saw a very great deal during their first years in California.[1] Shortly before Christmas Aldous, with Gerald and two others, took LSD for the first time. This he described at length to Humphrey Osmond (number 730 of the published Letters). Here I will refer only to his reactions to music.

[1] Swami Prabhavananda was good enough to receive me in 1969. He said, "Aldous was my disciple, he was initiated by me." I asked if I might have some particulars and the Swami told one of his monks, "May we have the file for Aldous Huxley's initiation." But there was no file. They kept no records at the Temple at that time. "A brilliant mind," the Swami said, "and a noble soul." He then expressed some discreet criticism of Aldous's experiments with LSD. This he mitigated with: "He had to follow many roads."

We played the Bach B-minor suite and the "Musical Offering," and the experience was overpowering. Other music (e.g. Palestrina and Byrd) seemed unsatisfactory by comparison. Bach was a revelation. The tempo of the pieces did not change; nevertheless they went on for centuries, and they were a manifestation, on the plane of art, of perpetual creation, a demonstration of the necessity of death and the self-evidence of immortality, an expression of the essential all-rightness of the universe—for the music was far beyond tragedy, but included death and suffering with everything else in the divine impartiality which is the One, which is Love, which is Being or Istigkeit. Who on earth was John Sebastian? Certainly not the old gent with sixteen children in a stuffy Protestant environment. Rather, an enormous manifestation of the Other—but the Other canalized, controlled, made available through the intervention of the intellect and the senses and the emotions. All of us, I think, experienced Bach in the same way . . .

The effect was quite different when they tried music of a lesser magnitude, a record of traditional Byzantine music, the Greek version of Gregorian:

To me at least, this seemed merely grotesque. The single voice bawling away its Alleluias and Kyries seemed like the voice of a gigantic flunkey kowtowing before a considerably magnified Louis XIV. Only polyphony, and only the highly organized polyphony (structurally organized and not merely texturally organized as with Palestrina) can convey the nature of reality, with its multiplicity in unity, the reconciliation of opposites, the non-twoness of diversity . . the Love which is the bridge between objective and subjective, good and evil, death and life.

. . . Meanwhile let me advise you, if ever you use mescalin or LSD in therapy, to try the effect of the B-minor suite. More than anything, I believe, it will serve to lead the patient's mind (wordlessly, without any suggestion or covert bullying by doctor or parson) to the central, primordial Fact, the understanding of which is perfect health during the time of the experience, and the memory . . of which may serve as an antidote to mental sickness in the future . . .

Aldous added that he felt it would be most unwise though to subject a patient to sentimental religious music "or even good religious music, if it were tragic (the Mozart or Verdi Requiems, or Beethoven's Missa Solemnis). John Sebastian is safer because, ultimately, truer to reality."

And in January 1956 Aldous once more took mescalin (it must have been his fourth time; there was a third in October 1955 to which I shall return). The present experiment was designed to test a possible short-circuiting of the mescalin effect by a new tranquillizer, Frenquel; it was conducted by two M.D.'s, Dr Howard Fabing of Cincinnati and a young pharmacologist, Dr Barbara Brown, and is again described to Humphrey in the Letters.

By the end of the month Aldous had finished off his current volume of essays; Betty was in New York to see to their play business and new hope sprang in the shape of a young director, Arthur Penn, whom Betty was highly recommending and whose suggestions seemed constructive.

# Chapter Two

## Adonis and the Alphabet

THE sequel, to a certain extent, to *The Doors of Perception* was published in February 1956; it is well summed up in Aldous's own words, to S.B.

> I have a long essay coming out . . called *Heaven and Hell*, about visionary experience and its relation to art and the traditional conceptions of the Other World. It springs of course, from the mescalin experience, which has thrown, I find, a great deal of light on all kinds of things . . . I spent a good part of this summer writing a series of supplements or appendices—on painters such as Géricault and Georges de Latour [and how succinct and penetrating these are]; on popular visionary art (pageantry, theatrical spectacles, fireworks, the magic lantern, coloured movies in certain of their aspects) and the technology connected with it; on the bio-chemical conditions of visionary experience and the rationale, in terms of modern pharmacological and physiological knowledge, of traditional ascetic practices. It has been interesting to write . . .

And later in the same year *Adonis and the Alphabet*[1] appeared, a volume which contained, besides some of the *Esquire* contributions, two major essays, on the potentialities of education—what can we do about teaching man to fulfil his contradictory roles? *Man*, Aldous said over and over again, *is a multiple amphibian*. It was the development of what he had tried to grapple with already thirty years ago—*Oh, wearisome condition of humanity, Born under one law to another bound.*

> . . Simultaneously or alternately, we inhabit many different and even incommensurable universes . . man is an embodied spirit . . . [he] is also a highly self-conscious and self-centred member of a sociable species. We live in and for ourselves; but at the same time we live in and, somewhat reluctantly, for the social group surrounding us. Again, we are both the products of evolution and a race of self-made men. In other words, we are simultaneously the subjects of Nature and the citizens of a strictly human republic . . .
> Below the human level amphibiousness presents no difficulties. The

[1] The American title was *Tomorrow and Tomorrow and Tomorrow.*

591

tadpole knows precisely when to get rid of its tail and gills, and become a frog . . . With us, alas, the case is painfully different . . .[1]

We have to deal, to take but one of our problems, with "the troubles of an ape that has learned to talk—of an immortal spirit that has not yet learned to dispense with words." Yet words *are* necessary. Without words no scientific theories, no philosophy, no law, and without these we should be nothing but Yahoos. (Moreover, there is the basic twentieth-century fact that we live in a world where ignorance of science and its methods is the surest, shortest road to national disaster.) There is no substitute, Aldous goes on, for correct knowledge, and in the process of acquiring that knowledge there is no substitute for concentration and prolonged practice. Except for the unusually gifted, learning must ever be hard work. "Unfortunately there are many professional educationists who seem to think that children should never be required to work hard.

Whenever educational methods are based on this assumption, children will not in fact acquire much knowledge; and if the methods are followed for a generation or two, the society which tolerates them will find itself in full decline.

We are human because, at a very early stage in the history of our species, our ancestors discovered a way of preserving and disseminating the results of experience. Take classical education:

"The literatures of Greece and Rome provide the longest, the most complete and most nearly continuous record we have of what the strange creature *Homo Sapiens* has been busy about in virtually every department of spiritual, intellectual and social activity. Hence the mind that has canvassed this record is much more than a disciplined mind. It has come, as Emerson says, into a feeling of immense longevity, and it instinctively views contemporary man and his doings in the perspective set by this profound and weighty experience. Our studies were properly called formative . . . because their effect was powerfully maturing. Cicero told the unvarnished truth in saying that those who have no knowledge of what has gone before them must for ever remain children."[2]

So far so good. Yet if the letter is essential, the letter also killeth—"the paradox may be expressed in the statement that

[1] "The Education of an Amphibian", *Adonis and the Alphabet*. Chatto & Windus, 1956.
[2] Aldous, in "Knowledge and Understanding", is quoting from Albert Jay Nock's *Memoirs of a Superfluous Man*.

the medium of education, which is language, is absolutely
necessary, but also fatal, that [its] subject matter . . which is con-
ceptualized accumulation of past experience, is indispensable, but
also an obstacle to be circumvented.

> "Existence is prior to essence." Unlike most metaphysical proposi-
> tions, this slogan of the existentialists can actually be verified. "Wolf
> children," adopted by animal mothers and brought up in animal
> surroundings, have the form of human beings, but are not human.
> The essence of humanity, it is evident, is not something we are born
> with; it is something we grow into. We learn to speak. We accumu-
> late conceptualized knowledge and pseudo-knowledge, we imitate
> our elders, we build up fixed patterns of thought and feeling and
> behaviour, and in the process we become human, we turn into
> persons. But the things which make us human are precisely the
> things which interfere with self realization and prevent under-
> standing. We are humanized by imitating others . . . by acquiring
> the accumulated knowledge which language makes available. But
> we understand only when, by liberating ourselves from the tyranny
> of words, conditioned reflexes and social conventions, we establish
> direct unmediated contact with experience. The greatest paradox
> of our existence consists in this—that in order to understand, we
> must first encumber ourselves with all the intellectual and emotional
> baggage, which is an impediment to understanding . . .[1]

What we must do—in Aldous's contention—is to balance that
baggage with other, non-verbal, methods of education, by techniques for rediscovering "within ourselves . . a virgin not-mind
capable of . . response to immediate experience." So far unfortunately organized education has done very little to help us in
this task and we shall have to discover and re-discover the
educators in psycho-physical health—F. M. Alexander, John
Dewey, Yoga, Zen . . .

> . . The notion that one can educate young people without making
> any serious attempt to educate the psycho-physical instrument, by
> means of which they do all their learning and living, seems on the
> face of it radically absurd. Looking back over my own years of
> schooling, I can see the enormous deficiencies of a system which
> could do nothing better for my body than Swedish drill and com-
> pulsory football, nothing better for my character than prizes,
> punishments, sermons and pep talks, and nothing better for my soul
> than a hymn before bed-time, to the accompaniment of the har-
> monium. Like everyone else, I am functioning at only a fraction of
> my potential.

[1] "Knowledge and Understanding."

## Chapter Three

# Here and Now

DURING the third week of March of 1956 Aldous wrote to his
friends Humphrey and Eileen about this and that; nearer
home he appeared to be taken up by new activity about the
play: Arthur Penn, a prospective director, arrived from New
York and Aldous dined with him at the Wendels' on the 15th.
On the 16th and 17th there were long meetings with Penn and
Betty at North Kings (which went well, Aldous having taken a
liking to the intelligent young man). In the afternoon Aldous
went and bought himself a new shirt, a cowboy shirt with a gay
pattern. On the 17th he dined at the Kiskaddens'. On 18th
March, a Sunday, Arthur Penn came again to the house and
after he left Aldous sat down and wrote one of his detailed
memoranda to Betty about changes in the play; over the telephone he told her that he was going away for a few days and
would she please carry on the talks with Penn. Then he went
out and had lunch with Gerald Heard and they, too, talked
about this and that. When Marianna Schauer turned up for
work the next day, 19th March, she found the house empty:
she became at once intensely worried as she had known Aldous
to be "the most considerate of men" (he had in fact written to
her not to come, the letter through some muddle had been
delayed); later that afternoon Betty, working on their notes, was
rung up by someone asking whether she had heard the news?
The radio had just been announcing that Aldous Huxley had
got married to Laura Archera.

In the same way the news reached Matthew in New York.
(And Mme Nys in Beverly Hills.) In Europe it was published
next morning first in the *International Herald Tribune* and was
soon conveyed to Julian and Juliette, to Jeanne, Suzanne . . .
Meanwhile, within the hour, Betty's house became a storm centre
of information seekers. United Press telephoned. Matthew telephoned. Anita Loos telephoned from New York, and Aldous's
dramatic agent; Peggy Kiskadden telephoned and other local
friends—not one of them would believe Betty, that Aldous had
never as much mentioned the name.

In due course Aldous's letters from Yuma, Arizona, dated 19th
March, arrived.

Dearest Matthew and Ellen,

As you have probably read already in the papers—for the press was on hand within two minutes of our signing the licence—Laura Archera and I got married today . . . You remember her, I am sure—a young woman who used to be a concert violinist, then turned movie cutter and worked for Pascal. I have come to be very much attached to her in recent months and since it seemed to be reciprocal, we decided to cross the Arizona border and call at the Drive-in Wedding Chapel (actual name). She is twenty years younger than I am, but doesn't seem to mind. Coccola was fond of her and we saw her a lot in Rome, that last summer abroad. I had a sense for a time that I was being unfaithful to that memory. But tenderness, I discover, is the best memorial to tenderness.

You will be seeing her in April, when we come East,
Ever your affectionate,

Aldous

On that same evening and in the same vein, he also wrote to Julian and Juliette, Mme Nys, Rose, Peggy, Betty, Jeanne: to her he started baldly,

Je me suis marié avec une jeune femme italienne, de 40 ans, Laura Archera . . . Maria l'aimait et je sens qu'elle approuverait ce mariage qui n'est pas une infidélité à la mémoire de notre vie ensemble, mais la commémoration, la continuation de cette tendresse de tant d'années.

En attendant je suis toujours, chère Jeanne, ton très affectueux frère

Aldous

Amd a week later there was this word to Anita:

Thank you for your sweet message, which greeted us on our return from the local Gretna Green—to which I had resorted in the naive hope of conducting my private affairs in privacy . . . We w'd have done better to have had a slap-up affair at St Patrick's with Cardinal Spellman officiating and Claire Luce as bridesmaid.

. . . But tho' I deplore the circumstances, I don't regret the event. Laura is very much all right.

They had met originally—Aldous, Maria, Laura—in 1948 when Laura, impatient of postal communication, had driven herself out to Wrightwood to get Aldous interested in making a film with her in Siena. She arrived in what her friends called *Laurissima*, a fast and temperamental old car, and there, greeted in Italian and following Maria down a corridor, "suddenly we were standing at the bathroom door.

> There, for the first time, I saw Aldous: unreasonably tall, washing his hands in a sink too little and too low, his strange light eyes looking at me, curious and amused, through a romantic lock of hair.[1]

Sporadic friendship followed mutual liking; the Huxleys became interested in Laura's techniques in psycho-therapy and had a go at it (Maria first, to try her out for Aldous, "My dear," she said "you do this very well"; Aldous in an attempt to regain access to some blanks in childhood memories—this did not work; it was he, instead, who sent Laura to sleep). They met again, though not often; all were busy, travelling. Six years later came the Roman encounter. They did not correspond. Laura returned to Los Angeles on 12th February 1955, a few hours as it happened before Maria died. Presently she wrote to Aldous; he replied, asking her for luncheon and a walk.

> I had many questions in my mind about Maria and he answered them without my asking . . .[1]

In the two months that followed Laura went to see Aldous quite often. "He was going through the most difficult period of his life," she wrote in her book.

> . . I saw then, for the first time, how Aldous applied his philosophy: Live here and now . . be aware of what is going on now. "Let go" . . .
> He succeeded much of the time. Once in a while he would lapse into a depressed silence. He did not speak much about his pain; he only said. "It is like an amputation."[1]

Nothing that had happened to him was allowed to be turned into self-pity. Aldous's own first, and only, mention of Laura before their actual wedding day occurs in a note to Marianna Schauer written from South Carolina in April 1955 on his drive East with Rose. He had forgotten his address book, would she please send him:

Kiskadden—phone and address.
Gerald Heard—phone and address.
Kent—phone.

---

[1] From Laura Archera Huxley's book on Aldous, *This Timeless Moment: A Personal View of Aldous Huxley.* Chatto & Windus, 1969; Farrar, Straus & Giroux, 1968.

Archera—phone.
LeCron—phone.
Betty Wendel—phone and address.

During the summer Laura had been in New York; Aldous joined her, from New England, for some days or weekends. And in the autumn and winter after his return to Los Angeles:

> .. in the evenings he spent at home I was often there .. we would speak of everything under the sun. I was then very active in psychotherapy. We discussed that; we listened to music, experimented with cooking. Marie Le Put, the lovable and wise Bretonne who had helped Maria, came three times a week .. We always found delicious dinners ready in the refrigerator. ("Monsieur is eating so much," she said .. She did not know that often there were two eating her meals.)

## In October Aldous had taken mescalin with Laura present.

> I decided it might be interesting [he wrote to Humphrey Osmond] to find out why so much of my childhood is hidden from me, so that I cannot remember large areas of early life. So I sat down to a session with a woman who has had a good deal of experience with eliciting recalls and working off abreactions by the methods of dianetics—which do in many cases produce beneficial results, in spite of all that can and must be said against the theorists of dianetics and many of its practitioners . . .

Laura, who had not taken, or seen anybody take, a psychedelic drug, asked him if there were anything she should know or do. Nothing, Aldous told her, "Just be as you are."

> I arrived at Aldous's home about nine o'clock. Aldous took the pills . . .
> . . . partly due to my experience in psychotherapy, I had expected—in spite, alas, of trying not to expect anything—that Aldous might speak of Maria. I had hoped he would . . .
> During that first [LSD] day the thought of Maria was often present. We were in her house, where nothing had been changed . . We had been silent for a long while listening to music. Now the record came to an end—I wanted to stop the machine to avoid the .. click of the automatic stop. To do this I had to walk a few steps . . . towards the record player. As I took the first step I felt suddenly that Maria was present. Present, but not outside of me—present in me. Amazed and fascinated, I knew that I was walking as Maria—that she, not I, was walking. It must have been at the third or fourth

step toward the record player . . that his voice reached and touched my shoulder. Extremely firm and gentle, the voice said, "Don't ever be anyone else but yourself."

Aldous did not have to remind me of that again.[1]

Again their attempts to recapture Aldous's childhood failed. ". . Very soon I gave up trying as I became aware that something awesome was taking place. I did not know what it was, but I felt that one had no right to disturb what was happening with the usual recall techniques of psychotherapy . . ."

. . there was absolutely no recall [Aldous's own account to Humphrey]. Instead there was something of incomparably greater importance; for what came through the closed door was the realization . . . the direct, total awareness, from the inside, so to say, of Love as the primary and fundamental cosmic fact. The words, of course, have a kind of indecency and must necessarily ring false, seem like twaddle. But the fact remains . . . The result was that I did not, as in the first experience, feel cut off from the human world. I was intensely aware of it, but from the standpoint of the living primordial cosmic fact of Love. And things which had entirely occupied . . . my attention on that first occasion I now perceived to be temptations—temptations to escape from the central reality into false, or at least imperfect and partial Nirvanas of beauty and mere knowledge . . .

Another thing that I remember saying and feeling was that I didn't think I should mind dying . . .[2]

At one time in 1955 Aldous had asked Laura lightly, "Have you ever been tempted by marriage?"

I had never been asked that question in such a charming way . . .

. . . [It] launched me into an autobiographical narration of some aspects of my life. It ended with the mention of two men—but these are other stories.

What had chiefly kept her from marriage, she told Aldous, was a fear she had of losing her freedom. Brought up as a musical prodigy on the violin, giving concerts, studying *"avec rage"*, her childhood and youth ruled by the disciplines of practice and performance, watched over by a loving and, one would guess,

[1] From *This Timeless Moment*, as all following quotations unless otherwise stated.

[2] The complete accounts of the experiences of that day can be found in Laura's book and in Aldous's letter to Humphrey Osmond.

possessive Italian family, Laura had been almost completely deprived of free activity of any kind (reading was regarded as a
sort of luxury, "like going to a masked ball"); and when at length
she did attain a degree of freedom, it was "not by the usual
rebellion . . . but by unflinching arduous work". Much later—
during the war in fact—she gave up the whole thing, her career
as a virtuoso, feeling that it was too life-devouring; and after
trying her hand at various things—breeding poodles, becoming
a professional film-cutter—found that she had got a second major
talent, psychology and its applications. She remained, she says,
attached to freedom in an almost compulsive way. Thus when
Aldous spoke of marriage, it was evident that for her this was not
an easy matter. As the months passed, though, the decision came
to look less formidable. One evening (according to Laura, in
January 1956) they were having dinner at North Kings. Aldous
mentioned his lecturing engagements in the spring.

> "It might be nice to be in Washington for the cherry blossoms,"
> he had said nonchalantly earlier. And then, as if picking up an
> interrupted conversation, he said briskly, "Well, now, what about
> plans—shouldn't we decide the date we are going to marry?" The
> tone was light and gentle . . .

By then they had been spending more and more time together,
had made a few short journeys; Laura had seen the way Aldous
ordered his days—marriage, at that point "would only have been
a confirmation". (To me, shortly after the event, Laura wrote,
". . it evolved as naturally as a Bach fugue.")

> . . Aldous continued, "Don't you think we should get married?"
> His tone was now more pressing, but not too pressing—he was not
> going to force an answer if I were not ready for it. (. . I think he was
> incapable of forcing.)

At length Laura answered. "I think it is very logical," she said.
So Aldous's choice was Laura, was not one of the candidates
resolved to enter upon a life of service—Laura Archera with her
misgivings and determination to cling to independence. What she
brought him was youth, drive, courage—her very particular blend
of inspiration and bravado in taking life head on; she brought
her Latinity; intuition, once more, rather than knowledge; discovery, challenge, *Le vierge et le vivace et le bel aujourd'hui*—renewal.
Off they went eventually to Arizona and the Drive-in Chapel.
In Laura's car, Aldous wearing perhaps the new sports shirt. The
forseeable slap-stick procedure, complete with random witness and
confusion over the ring, is described in Laura's book. At one point

she lost her nerve—might Aldous not expect from her "the same total dedication? I loved him and did not want to disappoint him." And now it was too late and public to go into this. She only managed a quick aside, " 'You know, darling, I love others too.' " Aldous with marvellous calm, shot back, " 'It would be awful if you didn't.' " After the ceremony they went to the nearest restaurant; they had hardly sat down when two local reporters swooped down on them. "Aldous was surprised and dismayed . . . [he] gave little satisfaction to the newsmen, but, we heard later, the news was on the radio within an hour.

> I was not worried about my family hearing the news. Aldous had written my father a month before and had received his answer. Ginny [Virginia Pfeiffer, Laura's greatest friend, in whose house she had been living for many years] knew that we were getting married . . I had taken it for granted that Aldous had made a similar arrangement. I did not quite realize that it was in Aldous's nature to act first and speak later . . .

Now she was a bit flabbergasted to hear that to Gerald yesterday Aldous had been talking about cockroaches and telepathy—"but not of our marriage!

> I thought Aldous seemed worried out of proportion by the sudden appearance of the journalists. As soon as they left, I understood why; he had not told his son yet and was deeply distressed . . .

They drove to the next resort and rented a bungalow. Did any thought of his own father come to Aldous's mind as he now addressed himself to the task of writing those letters? When Leonard Huxley had married again in 1912, his intentions, it has been said, were casually, or clumsily, revealed, and for his younger children at least there was an element of shock. (Aldous himself, though he insisted that there wasn't any one-to-one relation between Mr Beavis and his parent, worked off the theme of father breaking the news to son in *Eyeless in Gaza*.) The position of course was different. When Leonard married again, Aldous was an adolescent and his sister still a child; there could be no question now of Laura making another home for Matthew, a man in his mid-thirties and a father in his own right. The boot, here, was on the other leg: Matthew at his mother's death, if in psychological more than practical fact, must have felt that it was for him to continue her role as Aldous's shield. A natural role, on his side, given his affectionate nature and profound concern, and a role in which he had been trained implicitly since childhood by Maria. That this would never become quite feasible, second or no second marriage, because Aldous did not wish to accept protection—open and entire—for a second time, and because he too, like D. H. Lawrence, if in a different way, was a man who "needed to have a woman back of him", may already have been partly evident to Matthew. Only the situation would have been so very much more acceptable if the ground had been prepared; a post facto announcement by those we love is always hurtful. The actual mischief was caused by the media. Was Aldous to blame for not having thought of himself as newsworthy? (One remembers that when he met Stravinsky at the Town and Country Market, he introduced himself to the maestro as the uncle of Claire and Sylvia Nicolas.) Was he to blame for having misjudged the apparent obscurity of an improbable Western wedding-mill? However, the pouncing of the media would not have mattered if Aldous had exercised, not foresight about the workings of the press, but insight about human beings—Laura had told *her* best friend, had thought it proper for Aldous to bring in her father (by some elegant formula no doubt, and short of asking for her actual hand)—people like to be allowed to feel a part of things, and if Aldous's handling did turn out not to have been the most considerate to Matthew, it was also not the fairest one to Laura. Surely it might have been a good deal easier for all concerned, if his friends had already met Laura, seen them together, even if, or because, this would have led to talk? But then one of the few things Aldous was passionately attached to was his privacy (not withstanding the paradox of what he was capable of putting into a novel). In the event, the bad start was mitigated by the almost general good will. After an initial tremor, families and friends were glad to be able think of Aldous as no longer on his own. He and Laura returned to a North Kings filled with flowers and an accumulation of affectionate messages and good wishes.

## Chapter Four

# 3276 Deronda Drive, L.A.

FIRST recorded introductions were to Betty and to Mme Nys.

Monday, 26th March [Betty's journal]: Lunch with Aldous and Laura. I felt strange arriving at Kings Road. Passed the house and left the car on the street instead of parking in the driveway. When I rang the bell Aldous came to the door, as usual. We went no further than the living room instead of his workroom. In a moment or two Laura joined us. She came towards me with outstretched hand. She looked very serious. Aldous was completely at ease, I was not at the beginning. Laura said that Aldous had spoken of me often; I could *not* say he had spoken of her.

Laura told Betty that she had read the script of the play and how much she liked it and hoped they would continue to work on it together. A little girl of four ran into the room, she was one of Virginia Pfeiffer's two adopted children whom Laura was helping to bring up.

They began to tell me all about Yuma and the Wedding Chapel. Laura stopped looking serious after a little while. We talked and laughed . . .

"Not as old friends of course . . It was much too soon for that, but as new acquaintances who were getting on well together. And it was the start of a new and lasting friendship." After lunch Virginia Pfeiffer came to the house—" 'Ginny', Laura's great friend—a pleasant looking, dark haired, dark eyed woman."
Mme Nys wrote to Jeanne that she found it "tout à fait normal qu'il refasse sa vie." Laura telephoned her, thanking her "de mon gentil message, demandant si je pourrais les recevoir l'après-midi.

Aldous m'apportait des roses du jardin. J'ai embrassé Laura en lui souhaitant la bien venue . . . Aldous *si beau*, calme et communicatif. Assis à côté de moi, j'ai tout à coup dit à la jeune femme—Venez vous asseoir aussi à mes côtés et la main dans la main je les écoutais . . .

In the evening Mme Nys telephoned Matthew as he had asked her to. "I said, it is hard for Laura to fill that place . . . It is up to *us*, not to make the comparison."

In April Aldous with Laura went off to lecture, first at Lexington, Kentucky, then at Washington and Baltimore. They went on to New York to meet Matthew, Ellen and the children, and a number of Aldous's friends. (One of them told me how Aldous, helping Laura into her coat, said over her shoulder with great glee, "Laura does things in phases. She has had music. She has had dogs. Now she is—temporarily—having husbands.") After their return to Los Angeles Aldous, not yet settled in a book, was thinking of doing something practical about the population problem with Bill Kiskadden, who had been twice to India and Indonesia within the last three years and had "returned with a very urgent feeling that something more should be done about [it] . . than the writing of yet another report." What they thought of doing was to make a few pilot films for exhibition, by mobile projectors, in Indian villages. ". . . audio-visual propaganda . . to reduce the Indian birth-rate," Aldous wrote to Julian.

. . Kiskadden has asked me to ask you if you would also give your name, so as to lend weight to the organization . . . Kiskadden is extremely *sérieux*, a great virtuoso surgeon, who has now, in his early sixties, turned to population control as the work of the rest of his life. He is a man of great determination . . .

Meanwhile Aldous had read the American Academy of Science's report on the genetic effects of radiation. How wonderfully close, he remarked, modern history is coming to the phantasies of the *Arabian Nights* and *Grimm's Fairy Tales*—

the stories of the fishermen [to Matthew] who let the djinn out of the bottle and couldn't put it back . . . the more philosophical variant of the three wishes theme, W. W. Jacobs' "The Monkey's Paw", where the old people wish for a hundred pounds and get it, thanks to the magic paw, as compensation for the death of their son. Atoms will give us all the power we want, but at the price of multiplying the number of monsters and, perhaps, bitching up the whole human species.

Laura could not get herself accustomed to living in North Kings, so they found another house: high up in the Hollywood hills, in wild country. They would be within a few hundred yards of Virginia Pfeiffer's house, Aldous wrote to Matthew, ". . where there is a swimming pool, along with Virginia's adopted children, to whom Laura is much attached." On 16th July they moved.

Aldous, sending his new address to Humphrey, seemed delighted. 3276 Deronda Drive. Fire bricks to walk on,

> . . virtually no smog and an incredible view over the city to the south and over completely savage hills in every other direction, hills which remind me a little of Greece in their barrenness . . . Moving has been a job, and it will be a while before things are in order . . .

For Laura was completely redecorating the house, making of it something light and bright. She was dreaming of "a marvellously shining white surface.

> To throw out a new carpet [which had come with the house] would seem a needless extravagance to most husbands, but Aldous generously agreed . . .
> Aldous was fascinated by reflections of light, and that floor became an unending source of pleasure. Sometimes, coming home late at night, we would delight in finding the moonlight reflected on the living-room floor as on a pond.

They decided not to sell North Kings before the end of the summer so that Ellen and the children could use it for a holiday. ("Matthew, poor wretch, has to remain in New Haven where his boss's unexpected retirement leaves him in charge of the office.") Aldous, too, was busy and beset with dead-lines: three long articles for *Esquire* in one go, owing to the editorial time-table, and there was still much to be done to the play. No, he wrote to Humphrey, he could not manage to take part in the series of half-hour television shows on CBS; and even if he had unbounded leisure he would decline on second thoughts—unwelcome publicity, people stopping one in the street to say how much they liked, or disliked, what you said. Particularly annoying after a TV show on mescalin.

> Mescalin, it seems to me, and the odder aspects of mind are matters to be written about for a small public, not discussed on TV in the presence of a vast audience of baptists, methodist and nothing-but-men plus an immense lunatic fringe, eager to tell you about *my* revelation and to get hold of the dope on its own account. One gets plenty of lunatic fringe even after . . a two and a half dollar book . . .
> . . . I had a letter a few days ago from Mauritius, from a gentleman who went out there twenty years ago to achieve enlightenment and . . has now written the most extraordinary book on the world's history, and will I please write an introduction . . And I say nothing of the gentleman in Chicago who has discovered the Absolute Truth and sends letters and telegrams about it to President Eisenhower and Bertrand Russell . . . nor the young man from Yorkshire who ate a

peyote button . . . and for three days heard all music one tone higher than it should have been . . .

As you say . . we still know very little about the psychodelics, and, until we know a good deal more, I think the matter should be discussed . . in the relative privacy of learned journals, the decent obscurity of moderately highbrow books and articles. Whatever one says on the air is bound to be misunderstood . . .

(*Psychodelics.* "About a name for these drugs—what a problem!" Aldous had written to Humphrey a while ago. Could they call them psychophans? or phaneropsychic drugs? "I have looked into Liddell and Scott and find that there is a verb phaneroein, 'to make visible or manifest,' and an adjective phaneros, meaning 'manifest, open to sight, evident' . . . or what about phanerothymes? Thumos means soul . . . and is equivalent of Latin animus. The word is euphonious and easy to pronounce; besides it has relatives in the jargon of psychology—e.g. cyclothyme. On the whole I think this is better than psychophan or phaneropsychic . .

> *To make this trivial world sublime,*
> *Take half a gramme of phanerothyme.*"

However, Humphrey Osmond stuck to the name he had originally come up with ("To fathom Hell or soar angelic, Just take a pinch of psychedelic.") Psychedelic—to Aldous psychodelic—it became.)

Busy; and at peace. "I, too am well," Aldous wrote to Victoria Ocampo during the summer, telling her that he had married a young Italian woman. ". . She gets on very well with my friends, and they with her. I am very sure that you will like her. The terrible sadness of Maria's last months . . [has] retreated, and my memories of her are now happy, grateful, happy memories. And that she survives and develops, I feel sure . . ."

Aldous enjoyed Ellen's stay with Trev and Tessa, and the ensuing family whirl—Rose and her children also camping in North Kings, outings with Virginia Pfeiffer's little boy and girl, hospitable gatherings round her swimming pool—and at the same time (with workmen still in his own house) he was beginning to come to grips at last with the long-hatched Good Utopia.

I am now starting to work [to Humphrey] on the play revisions as well as on my phantasy, which begins, as I make notes, to take the rudiments of shape.

Even so he was still undecided whether to get on with it "full blast," or to tackle a dramatic version of *Brave New World*— *B.N.W.* "might be very profitable. Or it might not . . ."

Frieda Lawrence died on 11th August. "How strange their

careers were!" Aldous was later moved to write to Victor F. White.[1]

The coalminer's son escaping, via Frieda, into the larger world, beyond his social conditioning. And the Richthofen, who had somehow blundered into marriage with possibly the dullest Professor in the Western hemisphere, escaping, via Lawrence, into that same world and into an old age in that New Mexico desert which was, in some sort, a projection of her own deep nature. How improbable! But that is the charm and horror of human history: the impossible actually happens—all the time.

In September Julian and Juliette came for a fortnight's visit. The house was still unfinished.

. . We had the big bedroom downstairs [writes Juliette[2]]—no cupboards yet. Laura left after three days, taught me to drive that panther of a car, and went off with Ginny to the desert. Aldous took us to San Diego [to the incomparable zoo] to Disney Land, to see his friend Grace Hubble, the musician Porter . . I cooked for him and Julian, we fed in the little kitchen—very happy. Lots of talk between J. and A. . .

The brothers did the scientific sights, the new Salk Institute at La Jolla, John Lilly's experience with dolphins, which meant long expeditions by car "on the great speedways of California [Julian in his *Memories*[3]]. Juliette was often driving Aldous's leaping car with her heart in her mouth, amazed at Aldous's grasp of the map and his perfect direction: he had an unfailing memory of the landscape and of the maze of Los Angeles' motorways." They went to see the animal experiments at the University of California. These must certainly, wrote Julian, give the rats pleasure, and Aldous enlarged upon this to Humphrey:

. . rats and cats and monkeys with electrodes stuck into various areas of their brains. They press a little lever which gives them a short, mild electric shock—and the experiment . . is evidently so ecstatically wonderful, that they will go on at the rate of eight thousand self-stimuli per hour until they collapse from exhaustion, lack of food and sleep. We are obviously getting very close to reproducing the Moslem paradise where every orgasm lasts six hundred years.

---

[1] The late Dominican philosopher and psychologist, author of *God and the Unconscious*, etc., etc.　　　　[2] In a letter to S. B.
[3] Sir Julian Huxley, *Memories*, Vol. II. Allen & Unwin, 1973.

"Though perched on the heights above Los Angeles, Aldous was far from leading a hermit's life.[1] While we were with him, there was a stream of visitors—Linus Pauling, Gerald Heard, Christopher Isherwood, Romain Gary . . Lesley Blanch . . Professor Harrison Brown, population expert . . Dr William Kiskadden . . Bertalanffy, Alistair Cooke . . . Aldous was the fulcrum of the conversation . . . He seemed to radiate what journalists now call *charisma*, which added quality to the moment, as we sat around on the terrace of his little house, watching the wide evening sky."

After the Julian Huxleys leave, Aldous is distractedly busy making up for time—he has got to write the outline for a TV film on over-population and a speech on the History of Tension for the N.Y. Academy of Sciences, and there is his usual article for *Esquire* as well as the first act of a musical comedy version of *Brave New World* to get on with. (Musical comedy, "for everybody tells me that [it] can never succeed as a straight play.") The Utopian phantasy has to be laid aside for the time being. In October he and Laura fly off to New York for his speech on the 18th.

Our time in New York was a bit strenuous [to Humphrey]. The NY Academy . . have a publicity man so marvellously active that, on my arrival, I found no less than seven radio and TV appearances lined up for me, at hours ranging from six thirty in the morning to eleven fifteen at night. The conference on meprobamate [the tranquillizer] was quite interesting and I made some pleasant acquaintances—Dr [F. M.] Berger, the inventor of Miltown, and Dr James Miller, who heads a . . group at Ann Arbor, investigating human behaviour and trying to establish some kind of common language among psychologists, chemists, economists, sociologists and ministers. A commendable project . . .

(One eminent bio-chemist, according to Aldous, suggested—not entirely playfully—that the United States government should make a free gift to the Soviet people of fifty billion doses of the tranquillizer.)

Then within days of his return to Los Angeles Aldous left again for St Louis to attend a seminar on human potentialities, returning the same Saturday to do a TV show with Gerald the next day. He was obviously going through a streak of exceptionally good health (partly due perhaps to his desire to keep up with Laura; though he appears to have out-done her. "On these exhausting days [Laura wrote] when we returned to the hotel to take a breath and get ready for dinner, Aldous took me to my room, saying, 'You rest a little, darling. I am going to take a turn around the block and will be back in time to change my suit.' ")

[1] Julian Huxley, op. cit.

In December he did catch a bout of flu ("feeling low and mouldy"), but emerged before the year was out—the first act of the musical *Brave New World* was finished; Matthew had accepted an excellent new job; Mme Nys continued to report to Jeanne with unabated goodwill: "We must rejoice to see Aldous so calm and in such good form . . . I told him *combien Laura était bonne et gentille . . . Chaque fois que je la revoie je me réjouis qu'Aldous l'ait rencontrée.*" "May 1957," Aldous wrote to Humphrey on post-Suez Christmas Day "be as happy as the lunatics in the world's chanceries will permit . . ."

To Julian and Juliette he had this to say in January,

What we are paying for four hundred years of white imperialism— and how long, to all appearances, we shall go on paying! Asians and Africans do not forget and are so far from forgiving that, if they can thereby do some harm to the ex-imperialists, they will blithely damage themselves, even commit suicide. If I can spite your face I will cut off my nose. There is no appeal from these passions even to self-interest . . And the trouble is that these deep rooted passions can now be implemented in violent practice. The great truth enunciated by Hilaire Belloc:

> *Whatever happens, we have got*
> *The Maxim gun, and they have not—*

has unhappily ceased to be true. *They* now have the Maxim gun— and unless the West is prepared to out-trump the gun with atomic missiles, *they* will soon be in a position . . to win all the "little wars". If I remember rightly, Nostradamus prophesied that in the year two thousand or thereabouts, yellow men would be flying over Paris. It may easily turn out that he was right.

The Bates system once more has come under attack, this time in England through an article in *People* by Philip Pollack, a Helmholtzian oculist (obviously, Aldous thought, of the old school "who regard the eye as an optical instrument and take no account of the mind-body with which it is associated"). Aldous writes to Ian Parsons that he thinks it best to do nothing about the whole business.

. . *The Art of Seeing* is about the mental side of seeing and the improvement of function—not by "exercises", as Pollack likes to call them, but by training in relaxed activity. *Even if there are no physical changes in the eye, seeing can be improved by proper function.* [My italics] This is something which someone who has never thought in terms of psychosomatic medicine cannot understand.

Aldous goes on to point out for the record that he has "never claimed to be able to read [without spectacles] except under very good [light] conditions." Incidentally he had just embarked on a new treatment aimed at getting rid of some of the scar tissue on his corneas—a combination of diet and the administration of a sulphur compound "(eyes with cataract and, in general, most sick and ageing eyes, have shown to be short of sulphur, which is normally in rather high concentration in the eye tissues) . . . The man who has developed this treatment is a very experienced old ophthalmologist, who has had many successes, both with cataracts and corneal opacities. It would be wonderful if the treatment had even a very small effect . ."

In February Aldous learned that his *Esquire* articles had to come to an end—the magazine was changing its format, more pictures, less reading matter.

. . Evidently the majority of the public don't want to read, and now that so many cents in the advertising dollar go to TV, the magazine publishers (with the resounding crash of *Collier's* and *Woman's Home Companion* still ringing in their ears) must do everything in their power to increase circulation . . .

. . So this convenient and well-paid pulpit has been pulled out from under me. I regret it very much . . .

Aldous agreed to work once more, briefly, at a Hollywood studio, UPA, doing an outline for an animated cartoon of Don Quixote; then involved himself—"goodness knows why"—in yet another dramatic project, an adaptation of *After Many a Summer*. One cannot say that he went into it with eyes shut. ". . This theatrical world is dreadfully exasperating [to Anita Loos]; and if I didn't have other things to do, I should find my present, small involvement in it very nerve-racking. To write a play is certainly to ask for trouble."

No clinching offer had been made yet for *The Genius and the Goddess* (Alfred de Liagre was still interested, and Arthur Penn; and Binkie Beaumont was thinking of doing the play in London). Now Courtney Burr, producer of *The Seven Year Itch* and *The Bad Seed*, came up with an advance of $3000 and a definite production date. Betty sped off to New York.

Delly had been the one Aldous and I most wanted to produce that poor, poor play. And when Burr offered us that advance and promised us the world, we still wanted Delly to co-produce, and he was willing, but Burr wanted to go it alone . . .

By the end of March the agreement with him was signed.
Aldous, still in pursuit of staging *Brave New World*, wrote to

Robert Craft about the music. Whom would *he* advise? There was Leonard Bernstein of course, and someone had suggested sending the thing to Rodgers and Hammerstein.

> Needless to say, if the maestro felt inclined to take some time off to do something light—a little ballet music for the brave new worlders . . . I would be only too happy. But I hesitate to ask him—wouldn't want to do so before finding out what you think.

Stravinsky, apparently, did not take it up, for ten days later Aldous wrote to Leonard Bernstein. "As a very busy man with a large correspondence, I can well understand your annoyance at receiving yet another letter from a perfect stranger. But at the risk of being a bore . . ." (No composer for *Brave New World* has been found to this day.)

In April Aldous spent a week lecturing in San Francisco and at Stanford; in May, without Laura, he flew East, first for a weekend with Matthew and Ellen, then for lectures at Washington and the University of New Hampshire. In New York he talked to his new producer—"We have an excellent leading lady, Nancy Kelly, but not yet a leading man . . ." and saw people in various Foundations in the hope of getting someone to sponsor a TV documentary on over-population.

> . . (We have a little Foundation of our own, called Population Limited, rich in talent—my brother Julian, Harrison Brown, Kingsley Davis, the sociologist, Fred Zinnemann, the film director, Bill Kiskadden—but poor in money.) . . . I have written a synopsis of a film on Egypt—because it is better to attack the general through the particular, and because Egypt is a particularly painful case . . . Everyone agrees that the population problem is the most important problem of the present century; but nobody wants to get in trouble with the Papists . . .

On 15th July Aldous and Betty were summoned to New York to attend the first reading of the play.

# Chapter Five

## A Misadventure

AS matters turned out, Aldous was kept in New York through the worst of summer until late November. I shall not attempt to give more than an outline of the dismal tale. Things looked wrong from the beginning. Aldous and Betty found out that Courtney Burr, behind their backs, had engaged another collaborator (Alec Coppel) who was to be given programme credit and to whom they were to pay a quarter of their royalties. Betty wanted to go home then and there; Aldous persuaded her to stay. Now Burr, at first so enthusiastic about the play, changed his mind, insisting that it was unproducible in its present form. Aldous, on the assumption that he must know less than the professionals, reluctantly agreed to have the play re-shaped. Coppel dropped the play-within-the-play and turned out a weak domestic comedy with a single plot line and a happy ending; "a fairly slick piece of conventional craftsmanship," Aldous called it, but without depth and a weak and "somewhat phony" ending. He was assured by the experts that the new play was a better piece of dramatic writing and much more likely to be a commercial success. "Once again I made the enormous mistake of believing them."

Aldous and Betty, at the producer's request, were kept busy through the gruelling summer writing and re-writing and re-writing dialogue and scenes in an effort to infuse some quality and substance into the new version. "It was a pretty hopeless task," Aldous summed it up four months too late, "but I did my best. I listened to the suggestions of those whom I mistakenly believed to be more competent . . ."

He and Betty were at the Shoreham Hotel on West 55th Street, each in a bed-sitter with kitchenette. (By contract they were to receive $20 a day each for their living expenses. "Burr kept off paying us [Betty]; but at last began to do so when rehearsals started.") There was little time to see friends or do other things. In the evening they would often eat at one of the smaller French or Italian Westside restaurants; Aldous, in spite of heat and irritation, with a healthy appetite. When they got tired of each other's company, they would cook themselves a mess of vegetables on their hot-plates. (Aldous indeed had started eating meat again some years before, but as far as I know never tried to cook it.) On home nights he was apt to appear in Betty's door, steaming plate in hand—"If I give you half my mushrooms, will you let me have one of your artichokes?" and withdraw again to his own quarters with the loot. On the whole, he said, New York was not too bad; only four or five really equatorial days a month. He managed to go to the—"beautiful"—loan exhibition of French paintings at the Metropolitan, and look at the big Picasso show at the Museum of Modern Art "(what a lot of slapdash shoddy stuff surrounding the twenty or thirty masterpieces!)" Once or twice Laura came East to see him, and in September stopped on her way to Italy where she was going to remain with her father in Turin until the opening of the play.

One muggy day Betty, returning to the hotel, was met by the manageress, a kindly lady, in a state of agitation.

"I'm so glad you are back, Mrs Wendel—have you seen Mr Huxley?"

"No."

"Well, he is up on the roof—and he ought to come down!"

Betty asked what was the matter.

"You'll *see* when you get up there."

From the tenth floor, where Aldous had his apartment, an iron stairway led to the roof—tarred and pebble flooring, a safety rail of sorts, clothes-lines, some tattered canvas chairs—there in the blazing sun was Aldous, barefoot, but otherwise completely dressed in a suit with the collar turned up, his long arms widespread and flapping as he was slowly revolving on his own axis, looking for all the world both like Don Quixote *and* the windmill.

"Aldous!" Betty at last managed to call out. She could tell that he had heard her by the changes in the tempo of his flapping, but he did not speak until his slow rotation let him face her again. Then he said, "This damned suit won't get dry."

"How did it get wet?" Betty asked; then, gathering her wits, "Why are you drying it *on* you?"

Still flapping and revolving, Aldous said, "I washed it on me under the shower and then trotted up here. The label says 'Wash & Let Drip Dry.' The only other suit I have for this damned heat is at the cleaners."

Eventually Burr's new director, Richard Whorf, arrived and the situation—"after weeks of irritation and ineptitude"—seemed to look a little brighter. But now new changes were suggested and "summarily made—mainly consisting of cuts, which reduced many scenes to a kind of digest of themselves." Rehearsals began in October, and on the 13th of November the play opened at New Haven, Connecticut, with Nancy Kelly as Katy, the English actor Alan Webb as Maartens, and Michael Toland as young John Rivers. The week after it went on to Philadelphia. (After the first or second night there, Aldous sent a letter to his leading lady which is of interest because of what he so openly says about D. H. L. and Frieda. He was distressed, he wrote, to think that he had failed in the play to make his conception of Katy, the goddess, clear to her. It was very clear to him because he used to know very well a specimen of the breed.

This was Frieda Lawrence, the wife of D. H. Lawrence. I think I told you the other day about the miraculous way in which she raised Lawrence almost from death when he was ill with influenza (superimposed upon . . TB) in my house. Katy's miracle with Henry is merely a transcription of what I myself saw, thirty years ago. (Incidently the miracle was chronic. Thanks to Frieda, Lawrence remained alive for at least five years after he ought, by all the rules of medicine, to have been in the grave.) Frieda (and Katy is a non-German and less Rabelaisian version of Frieda) was a woman of enormous strength and vitality, completely untouched by the neuroses of the Age of Anxiety. Everything that Katy-Frieda does, she does with her whole heart. With a whole heart she loves and admires her genius and with a whole heart she quarrels with him. (Frieda used to throw plates at Lawrence, and Lawrence threw them back at her. I have spared you this!) Again, it is with a whole heart that Katy-Frieda looks after her man when he is sick, and it is with a whole heart that she makes fun of him when he is being peevish or ridiculous. Frieda and Lawrence had, undoubtedly, a profound and passionate love-life. But this did not prevent Frieda from having, every now and then, affairs with Prussian cavalry officers and Italian peasants, whom she loved for a season without in any way detracting from her love for Lawrence or from her intense devotion to his genius. Lawrence, for his part, was aware of these erotic excursions, got angry about them sometimes, but never made the least effort to break away from her; as he realized his own organic dependence upon her . . .

Frieda . . was profoundly matter-of-fact, accepting events as they were given, in all their painful or delightful confusion. She had little patience with idealism or exalted ethical systems. Her essentially realistic view of life was expressed in Shakespeare's words in *King Lear*—"Ripeness is all." This ripeness of realism made some people feel, at a first meeting, that she was rather rough and even a little heartless. But her teasing . . was always profoundly good-natured. She would speak ironical words, but out of a depth of human kindness and sympathy. Another characteristic trait was her child-likeness . . product of her capacity . . for living fully in each successive moment, as a child does. And this gave her a certain superficial air of inconsistency . . . Finally, she had the most sovereign disregard for what people might think or say about her—a disregard based upon a certain native aristocracy, on the confidence of a very rich personality in its own essential rightness and excellence. This meant that she was never anxious, never apologetic, never tense or nervous. She did everything—baking bread, scrubbing floors, making her own clothes, tending the sick genius—with the unhurried, easy serenity of the heroines and goddesses of the Homeric myths. Her speech reflected the same spirit. She spoke slowly, deliberately, relishing the words she used (for she had a great command of language, even in a tongue which was not her own) . . .

At New Haven, the producer engaged yet another expert who wrote new lines and one entire scene; these were rehearsed—in secret—at Philadelphia. Aldous found out and "This final outrage was too much even for my long-suffering nature". He left for New York to consult his lawyer and his agent,[1] Betty remaining as his watch-dog. Meanwhile the unauthorized lines and scene were actually played on the last night in Philadelphia. On 23rd November Courtney Burr tried to keep Betty away from the performance on a pretext, but she went (upheld by Laura and her own husband, Sanford Wendel, who had arrived and rallied). On the 25th the play went on to Boston. Aldous, on professional advice, sent the following telegram to Burr on the same date.

You have flagrantly breached your minimum basic production contract with us by inserting material and making changes in the play without our consent . . . and have further and in various ways conducted yourself arbitrarily without regard to our rights as authors . . . we hereby demand that you correct the foregoing breaches within three days. If you fail to make such corrections within that period, all your rights in the play shall automatically terminate . . . Beth Wendel will remain in Boston during the three day period with authority of both of us to attend rehearsals and grant script approvals.

Aldous Huxley   Beth Wendel

On the same day Aldous exhorted Betty by letter to get hold of the script. "The only hope—and in view of what these people are it is rather a slim hope—lies in having a script, of which the more important parts can, if necessary, be photostated, so that we can produce them as evidence of what we have agreed to. They will of course want to discuss things; but my advice, and the advice of Helen [Harvey] and the lawyer, is, Don't. Just ask for the script."

Burr actually did remove the unauthorized material before the

---

[1] Mr Arnold Weissberger and Mrs Helen Harvey, who was then running the William Morris Agency.

end of the Boston run (4th December), but then inserted scenes which had already been vetoed by the authors during rehearsal. Aldous gave up and returned to California, having demanded that their names be taken off the play. *The Genius and the Goddess* opened on Broadway on 10th December, Aldous Huxley and Beth Wendel appearing on the playbill. The play closed on 14th December after a run of five nights.

Helen Harvey, fifteen years later, made this comment (the actual business correspondence is already destroyed) ". . I do recall that the production was horrendous. Many of the people involved were as incompetent and inefficient as is usual around the theatre, and Aldous Huxley simply could not believe that these professionals really didn't know what they were doing! So he went on re-writing, re-thinking and re-doing, until he himself was just as confused as the rest of them."[1]

Aldous, then, peacefully ensconced once more in his Hollywood hills, wrote an article, "Postscript to a Misadventure," then thought better of it, decided to leave ill alone and put the MS into a drawer. A copy of it survived at Matthew's; there are one or two nice bits which Aldous, I am sure, would not mind being published now. "This story," he wrote, "a very commonplace one, as I am assured by those who know their Broadway—has several morals.

> First, even during the frenzies of production, the writer should keep his artistic head and retain what I may call (since "the courage of his convictions" is not the right phrase) the obstinacy of his intuitions. Second, he should be extremely sceptical of any claim to superior wisdom on the part of those who call themselves experts . . . Third, if he wants to go on writing plays, let him have them produced in some place where the costs are less exorbitantly high than they are on Broadway . . . exorbitantly high costs . . create, in the minds of all concerned, the anxious sense of being embarked upon a very dangerous and deadly serious adventure, where humour and light-heartedness are as much out of place as they would be on a burning ship in the middle of the Pacific Ocean. A play should have something playful about it. But how can anyone feel playful about a hundred-thousand dollar investment? In the grimness of these desperate theatrical gambles the amenities of life and even its common decencies are apt to go by the board.

His private post-mortem Aldous wrote to Betty in a letter of 15th December. ". . all's well, or can at least be made fairly well, that ends badly.

---

[1] From a letter to S. B.

Weissberger has advised strongly against suing for damages, and I shall follow his advice. If the expense money can be extracted from these people, it will be a small triumph. If not, then it will be another loss that has to be written off. I have already had to write off four months of time . . . My motive for leaving the play at Philadelphia was disgust—the feeling that I didn't want to be associated any further with people who had broken their word and violated their written agreement. Writing articles and suing for damages, would be a kind of continuance of that association in negative terms, and I don't want to get involved in that.

Meanwhile what a comfort it is to be doing some kind of useful and interesting work once more!

There remains one question—what about the play? The final version of *The Genius and the Goddess* as written by Aldous and Betty? This version exists, but the question cannot be answered because (to date) it has never seen the foot-lights of an English-speaking stage.[1]

---

[1] It was televised in Australia, and in Germany and Switzerland in Herbert E. Herlitschka's translation.

## Chapter Six

## Towards a Topian Phantasy

FOR the next six months, the first half of 1958, Aldous stayed put, writing away quietly. He finished *Brave New World Revisited*, his short book—of some effect, he hoped—on the problem of freedom in an age of over-population, a series of articles— he called them that rather than essays—on governmental and economic power and all the means for reducing psychological resistance, from brainwashing and advertising to (potentially) drugs and hypnoapaedia, and about what might be done to counteract these menaces by holding on to old fundamentals— "Every human being is biologically unique . . . The Sabbath is made for man"—and by new methods of education. He had also polished off a commissioned article for *The Saturday Evening Post* on the social and ethical implications of psycho-pharmacology.[1] It was work which Aldous could turn to at almost any time, material he had at his finger-tips, though it always remained hard labour to shape it into a lucid ("snappy" he hoped) and convincing form. And did it convince? *Was* it to some effect? Did his exhortations ever reach the right men in the right place? These were questions he was much aware of. "And, over and above the normal difficulties,

> I have to wrestle with the problem of not seeing properly [to Humphrey]—which makes all research and consulting of notes such an enormous burden. Which is all, no doubt, ultimately All Right— but proximately pretty fatiguing!

Julian touches on this in his *Memories*.[2] "How Aldous managed to absorb (and still more to digest) the colossal amount of facts and ideas which furnished his mind remains a mystery . . . Maria devotedly read to him for hours at a time; and with his one good eye, he managed to skim through learned journals, popular articles and books of every kind. He was apparently able to take them in at a glance, and what is more, to remember their essential content. His intellectual memory was phenomenal, doubtless trained by a tenacious will to surmount the original horror of threatened blindness . . ."

[1] "Drugs That Shape Men's Minds." October 1958.
[2] *Memories*, Vol. II.

"But I am sick and tired of this kind of writing," Aldous said to Ellen when *Brave New World Revisited* was finished. Yet at least these months were even ones, a stretch of time without major anxieties or upheavals, no house move or hotel existence, and above all good health at home. Laura was doing her share for Virginia's children as well as being extremely busy with her patients. (Laura, Aldous said to Christopher Isherwood, "is becoming a walking Grotto of Lourdes.") It was in this New Year's Honours that Julian received his knighthood—"I'm delighted," Aldous wrote to him, ". . and hope that . . you will be able to feel as happy about it as I do." The one bad personal news was Bill Kiskadden's cardiac operation in February, a most frightful operation Aldous called it. "He has recovered—but is still in a sadly diminished state . . ."

Mme Nys, too, was coming out of a time of illness, "thanks to God, to Rose, to Laura and to Aldous."

"Laura telephoned . . ." "Quick dinner with Aldous and Laura before the theatre . . ." "Aldous et Laura dinent chez moi . ." ". . asked to lunch at Mrs Pfeiffer's . . ." "Laura has given [Maria's] Oldsmobile to Rose." "Dinner *en ville* with A & L, followed by a concert, Boulez, Stravinsky . . ." "Laura, without my having asked, took me to the cemetery on Maria's name-day." "Aldous came with books . . . brought flowers . . ." The letters to France are full of such amiable odds and ends, implicit reassurance to Jeanne.

Everybody seems to come out of this pretty well. What of Mme Nys? Was this Mère, the woman who had caused those agonizing conflicts in Maria (her favourite, her beloved daughter), and provoked so often even Aldous's strictures? The personality that arises from the correspondence appears a good deal more tolerant and sympathetic. Were they unjust to her, or had she mellowed? (Did not Maria write, only so lately, "Ma mère est devenue une femme bonne et douce"?) Matthew always loved her; she adored him (and had devoted herself to him when he was a little boy at St Trond). She was less pleasant to one or two of her grandchildren and she certainly made life exceedingly hard for Rose. Perhaps something of the truth can be got hold of in Jeanne's mature reflections: Mère was horribly difficult, horribly exigent and touchy in everyday life; she talked too much, she would not listen, she was always right—*Mère est odieuse!* the sisters used to cry. One could not live with her; they loved her from afar. (Mark that, unlike Maria or Rose, Jeanne and Suzanne were seldom under the same roof with her.) Yet she was also good and generous and resolute and capable, and these virtues she deployed particularly on what Jeanne calls the grand occasions: Mère was at her best in crisis, illness, war. Uncommonly self-centred, she could transcend self-interest—Elle avait des élans grandioses. She had profound affection and respect for Aldous; and after Maria's death recognized his choice and need, and accepted it with grace and fairness.

In the spring, with *Brave New World Revisited* off his hands, all was serene enough for Aldous to return to wider latitudes, yet he still found it hard to get the Utopian novel flowing. The present difficulty was not the subject matter, which was so very near his heart—and Laura's—a society in which serious efforts are made to realize human potentialities of sanity and happiness; nor the locale—a hypothetical island between Ceylon and Sumatra which due to a lack of harbour had had the historical luck of escaping colonialism; the difficulty was the working out of a story line to hold the thing together.

I don't know yet [to Humphrey in June] if I have a satisfactory fable, or how much of a fable will be necessary, or . . how reluctant people will be to read material which isn't straight story telling . . .

Meanwhile he went on feeling his way into the book— ". . the only thing is to go ahead, one step at a time . . ." He was also finding himself involved once more with the stage. The play was his, Laura was the producer, an undaunted one as it turned out. She put on *The Gioconda Smile* at Los Angeles through thick and thin, as Aldous said,

. . Like the generals of earlier days who used to have horses shot under them in their decisive battles, she has had about six complete casts shot under her in the course of her campaign—only to come up with better replacements, so that now we have a first-rate collection of English actors, highly competent and thoroughly trained . . .

Aldous attended rehearsals, listening with closed eyes (and congratulated his leading lady, Sylvia Marriot, on being word-perfect from day one). The play opened at the Beverly Hills Playhouse on the last Friday in June, (the Stravinskys in the audience) and ran for about six weeks, losing, as Laura put it, "a little bit of money".

The second half of 1958 was spent travelling. The Brazilian government invited Aldous to visit the country, he and Laura left for their first long journey together in July. They flew to Lima by way of Mexico City and spent some time in Peru. In

August they arrived in Rio de Janeiro where Aldous received a tremendous reception (one newspaper carried a daily column about him headed *O Sabio, The Sage*) and had to submit to interviews, official luncheons and a lecture at the Foreign Office. Then came the sights; they were taken to Brasilia, which expectedly he found inhuman, to Bahia, to São Paulo, and were flown up the Amazon in an army plane to the Matto Grosso to visit a tribe of stone-age Indians. They landed, unannounced, in the middle of the jungle and were swarmed upon by a horde of brown, stark-naked, friendly, shouting people, every one of them a good two feet shorter than Aldous, who moved about them fascinated, "all his antennae out." (It was he, before Laura did, who saw that they all had vaccination marks on their arms.)

. . a frail-looking white man . . came out of the jungle [an anthropologist officer of the Indian service]. He looked at Aldous as though he had seen an apparition . . . [He] stopped dead for a moment . . approached, "Uxley? Uxley . . . *Contrapunto* . . ." and burst into tears of joy. The two men embraced. Aldous, too, was moved . . .[1]

From Brazil to Lisbon. To Turin; to Sicily. To Turin again to celebrate the 80th birthday of Laura's father. In October, on his own at first, Aldous went to London. It was his fourth visit since the war; and for Julian it was "as always a time of intensified activity, social as well as intellectual.

. . Breakfast might go on to mid-morning before we tore ourselves away from these wonderful exchanges of ideas—how I wish I had had a tape recorder! . . .
From these encounters, I always returned to my work stimulated and refreshed, my mental and spiritual batteries recharged. I cannot remember a single subject, even in my own speciality, on which Aldous was not sufficiently informed to enable us to discuss it competently, enriching my own thinking in the process.[2]

Social and intellectual. Aldous saw old friends: Rose Macaulay (who died two days later); Bertie Russell; E. M. Forster; Tom Eliot ("who is now curiously dull—as a result, perhaps, of being, at last, happy in his second marriage"); Cyril Connolly (who interviewed Aldous for the *Sunday Times*[3]); Yvonne Hamilton,

[1] Laura Huxley, op. cit.
[2] *Memories*, Vol. II.
[3] Published on 19th October 1958.

ex-Franchetti, ex-Palavicino of the young Florentine days; the Provost of Eton, Noële Neveux . . .

. . London looks curiously old fashioned after São Paulo and Rio— not a skyscraper to be seen and amazingly little re-building . . .

Noële, Jeanne's little girl whom he had not seen for these four years, was rising eighteen and at boarding school.

London yesterday to see Aldous. [Noële's journal] Zoo and National Gallery. A strange feeling—Aldous hasn't changed, he is only a little older. The English climate does not suit him. Rather shy at first with me, who, in a way, is a witness of another part of his life. But I soon find again the essential Aldous . . . He is very elegant in a dove-grey suit, red tie, and a new wrist-watch he is unable to read.

Aldous appeared on a Brains Trust programme with Julian and Professor Ayer, and was interviewed by John Lehmann on TV.[1] On the Brains Trust, Aldous remained rather effaced, prodded now and then by Julian who kept trying to bring him in, only warming into animation by a question on metaphysics. On television he looked robust and sleek against a silvery, birdlike John Lehmann, and was very fluent. Writer to writer, they talked a good deal about the novel. He had always felt, John Lehmann said, "that it is really as a novelist you should be thought of first. Would you agree?"

Aldous: . . . I would certainly like to have written a very good novel; I don't think I ever have . . .

J. L.: . . . how delighted we all were with those early novels of yours in the twenties, you seemed to us the most sophisticated, witty entertainer, a debunker bringing things down to earth with a bump, particularly sex. But even then I felt . . . your desire . . to discuss strange ideas was very much in evidence. Did you have a feeling that you wanted to teach then, as well as to entertain?

Aldous: Well, I think I had a—always had a feeling that I *wanted* to learn, and maybe that this was the most effective way of learning— I mean, it is very often that the fact of getting things down is the best way of clarifying one's own mind. Maybe I am a little bit *pedantic*, but this has always been my desire, to learn, to explore.

J. L.: And when later on the—shall we say—the teaching side in your novels seemed to grow stronger . . . were you working out these new ideas of mysticism and the divine ground for yourself in these books?

[1] Broadcast on 12th October 1958.

621

Aldous: Yes, I—my problem has always been, of course, to find if possible some balance between the two sides. I don't think I've succeeded very well always, I think I have once or twice succeeded pretty well—not perhaps to my whole, entire satisfaction . . .

J. L.: You say in one of your essays that Balzac almost ruined himself as a novelist by trying to stuff everything into his novels . . . banking, science, politics, industry, mysticism. Were you conscious of—of this difficulty, this danger yourself?

Aldous: Well, it's certainly a temptation to which I've been very much subject . . .

John Lehmann asked him if he had lost faith in the novel?

Aldous: Not at all.

J. L.: And you don't think that the novel as an art form is on the way out?

Aldous: Well, a lot of people like to say so, but I cannot see any reason why this should be true; I think people will always go on using the narrative form, because it is the most extraordinary form . . . there are no rules, except to *do it well*. And I think people will continually adapt the narrative form to the problems which confront them at a given moment in history.

J. L.: Yes, but in a recent essay of yours you do say that serious novel writing was facing a very difficult future; and might have, in fact, to—to go onto gramophone records?

Aldous: I mean this is an economic problem . . . there is such a thing as may be called an economic censorship . . . and it's very grave . . . possibly, spoken literature may be a way out of this.

J. L.: It would be bound to change novels, wouldn't it, if they became spoken?

Aldous: I don't think you could have a very long novel. I think you could have shorter pieces which might go. I don't know. It is just a suggestion I made.

John Lehmann asked if it wasn't perhaps that other difficulties were more serious today for the novelist?

Aldous: . . There are—what may be called social difficulties. I was reading just the other day as I was travelling through Sicily, reading Trollope's *Framley Parsonage* and thinking how wonderful it was for novelists in those happy days to have a completely rigid framework. Everybody knew exactly where they stood, and it was possible to make your comments from an accepted ground—

J. L.: And that's quite gone today.

Aldous: It's quite gone today.

In due course they went on to lysergic acid, Wordsworth, heightened perceptions, tranquillizers—"You do of course anticipate this world . . of drugs in *Brave New World* to some extent," said J. L. Yes, said Aldous, but he projected these things five or six hundred years into the future—

> It is rather alarming to find that only twenty-seven years later quite a number of these forecasts had already come true, and come true with a vengeance.
>
> J. L.: Are you going to write a postcript to *Brave New World*?
>
> Aldous: Well, I've written a few chapters on the things which have already come true . . the menaces to individual liberty . . I think . . very grave threats, which although they may not be acute, particularly in the democratic countries, are potentially very grave indeed.
>
> J. L.: And unforeseen by you in *Brave New World*?
>
> Aldous: Some of them were foreseen and I think some of them I didn't have the imagination to foresee but I think there is a whole armoury at the disposal of potential dictators at the moment . . .
>
> J. L.: Do you think that can be mirrored in art? You say somewhere . . that art and the novel can't really cope with some of these problems that face the world today.
>
> Aldous: Well, I think there are very great difficulties in putting certain problems into the form of art . . . take the fact for example that poetry has very seldom had anything very significant to say about money.

And before the round-off, "Are you going to write some more novels?"

> Aldous: Well, I'm trying to write one, I've just begun one.
>
> J. L.: Can we ask what its subject is?
>
> Aldous: . . . it's a kind of reverse *Brave New World* . . . an extremely difficult thing to write . . it's much easier to write about negative things—
>
> J. L.: It's an ideal?
>
> Aldous: It's an ideal. But I hope not a stratospheric ideal, what may be called a Topian rather than a Utopian phantasy, a phantasy dealing with a place, a *real* place and *time*, rather than a phantasy dealing with *no* place and time.

Now Aldous, after nearly two years of uninterrupted decent health, was again beginning to feel far from well; apparently it was not the English climate. Julian's doctor diagnosed a stone in the bile duct and prescribed drops and diet. Laura joined Aldous on 21st October and a week later they went to Paris.

Rue Bonaparte—Jeanne and Georges, not seen since 1954. Aldous goes alone at first, next day with Laura. Julian and Juliette are in Paris, too, and four of Aldous's five nieces, and Virginia Pfeiffer. There is a family luncheon in rue Bonaparte followed by a mass outing to the Impressionists at the Jeu de Paume, but Aldous feeling ill, looks ill; Georges finds him listless, Jeanne is upset and unhappy. Aldous refuses to talk on the radio, to appear on television; the one thing he was intent on was going to the Louvre lit up at night ("As soon as he puts foot in a museum, he comes to life" [Georges Neveux's journal] but the one evening he was free of the engagements heaped upon him was a Tuesday and on a Tuesday the Louvre, as they only realized in the taxi, is shut. Georges persuaded him to give at least one interview— "pour marquer son passage" (with A. Parinaud for *Art*). The three men met for luncheon at a bistro in the rue de Verneuil and here again Aldous came out of his shell. "Il est éblouissant —enfin il se reveille . . ."

But two days later he is down with mild flu or a bad cold and has to postpone his and Laura's departure for Italy. On their last night a small farewell dinner at the Neveux's with Sylvia and Sophie and her husband, Willem Welling. Georges described the end of it thus:

> Au moment de se séparer Aldous, qui est le dernier à partir, me regarde. On se regarde en silence. Il a comme des larmes aux yeux. On se donne l'accolade. Dans l'escalier il se retourne et me fait un grand geste vague . . .

In Venice Aldous went down with influenza and stayed in bed for a week. Later in the month he had to give four lectures (partly in Italian), the first in Turin, the second in Milan, the third in Rome. Here he had a relapse; bed again until he "had to creep down to Naples and there, hardly able to stand, deliver my final lecture." (One can see that Aldous would fulfil his engagements; why he let himself in for such increasing numbers of them is a more complex matter.) He and Laura flew straight back to Los Angeles, cancelling New York as Aldous feared the cold, it being now December. On arrival he felt so low and weak that he went into hospital for tests. It was found that the London diagnosis of a gall stone had been wrong.

> . . The main trouble [he wrote to Julian and Juliette on 14th December] seems to be the chronic emphysema in the right lung, aggravated by the flu. I'm taking the pressure breathing treatment that helped me so much in the past . . .

The weight loss is probably due to emphysema—tho' conceivably there might be TB [tests later showed that there was not] . . . No indication of cancer, I'm glad to say, and all well with heart, kidneys and pancreas.

And to Humphrey Aldous wrote a few days later that he was already emerging from his hideous state of tiredness and pleased to be back in the sun, able to do some honest work for a change —free at last from the swarm of interviewers who had plagued him both in South America and in Europe.

I was simultaneously touched and appalled to discover that I am now, as the result of having been around for so many years, a kind of historical monument, which sightseers will come quite a long way to inspect . . In Brazil it was as though the Leaning Tower of Pisa had just come to town . . and even in Italy I found myself talking to full houses in large theatres. It was really very odd and embarrassing.

## Chapter Seven

## Father to Son

ALDOUS recovered quickly. "Working hard and eating normally . . . regaining weight," he wrote to Julian in January 1959; his troubles must have been due to too much travelling and too much talking, on top of his old smouldering bronchitis. But now something else was happening that brought much sadness to them all: after nine years and many of them happy, Matthew and Ellen's marriage had gone wrong; they were about to part, at least for the time being. Their trouble does not concern us here except in so far as it affected Aldous. Enough to say that the fundamental cause was probably the kind of temperamental difference which two people do not mind when they are young and much in love, and are unable to put up with when they are older, yet not old enough to have come to tolerance and give and take. Aldous, who had come to that stage, was very much affected. "Your letter and Ellen's made me very sad," he wrote to Matthew the day after he received the news. He asked Eileen Garrett for advice about anything useful he could do.

. . Each of them has written; so I understand the story in its main outlines—the friction of dissimilar temperaments—Ellen spontaneous and adventurous, Matthew with his tendency to be rigid, rather censorious . . . But the details and the nature of the crisis which brought the trouble to a head are obscure to me . . . Ellen tells me that you discussed the whole thing with her and that you had been in touch with Maria in regard to what was happening. I should be grateful for any help you can give me, any advice you can offer as to the best way of helping them . . .

. . The news of the rupture has left me very sad; but sadness does no good and the problem now is to discover the best way of mending or ending, of changing circumstances within the marriage or outside it.

To Matthew he said more:

. . probably what you have decided is the best course in this unhappy situation. I know very well what you mean when you talk about dust and aridity and a hard shell that makes communication in or out extremely difficult. It was something that made the first part of our marriage difficult at times; but Coccola was very patient and in the long run I learned to get through the shell and let the dust be irrigated. Unfortunately, when you were a child, I was predominantly in the dust-crust stage, and so, I'm afraid, must have been—indeed, I know that I was—a pretty bad father.

And now what is to be done? . . .

Meanwhile would it be possible for you to get away from the office for a few days and fly out here? The tourist flights are relatively cheap and I will treat you to the ticket. So do come here if you can . .

We would love to see you—and Ellen too, if she can come later on, when you or someone else can be with the children. It is quiet on the hill here and, in spite of smog, the sun still shines—a statement that carries more than a meteorological meaning.

I shall say nothing to Mère or Rose about all this, unless and until you want me to do so.

Laura sends her love, as do I.


A month later Matthew had not come; Aldous, who had accepted a visiting professorship at Santa Barbara for the spring semester, now spent two nights a week there. He urged Matthew to come out and meet him, but heard nothing for some time. Probably the best that can be done now, Aldous wrote to Eileen, "is to salvage a friendly relationship between E and M, and to see that the children get as good a psychological break as possible . . ." In April he had a letter from Matthew which made him feel that something better was beginning to emerge "from the sad confusion of the situation.

. . To become capable of love—[Aldous wrote in his answer] this is, of course, about two thirds of the battle; the other third is becoming capable of the intelligence that endows the love with effectiveness in an obscure and complicated and largely loveless world. It is not enough merely to know, and it is not enough merely to love; there must be knowledge-love and charity-understanding or prajna-karuna, in the language of Buddhism—wisdom-compassion. People have been saying this for the last several thousand years; but one has to make the discovery oneself, starting from scratch, and to find what old F M Alexander called "the means whereby," without which good intentions merely pave hell and the idealist remains . . ineffectual, self-destructive and other-destructive . . . It has taken me the greater part of a lifetime to begin to discover the immemorially obvious and to try, at least, to act upon the discovery. I hope it will take you only half a lifetime and that you will emerge from this excruciatingly educative ordeal with enough love and understanding to transfigure the second half.

To Humphrey Osmond, who had seen a good deal of both Matthew and Ellen, Aldous wrote that he, Humphrey, had

summed up their problem only too well. "Inhabitants of different
. . worlds *can* live happily together—but only on condition that
each recognizes the fact that the other's world is different and
has just as much right to exist . . . as his own . .

> . . there can be something very stimulating and liberating about
> the experience of being joined in a loving relationship with somebody
> whose universe is radically unlike one's own. . . I remember a very
> touching passage in one of my grandfather's letters about his own
> obtuseness—the obtuseness of an immensely intelligent man of the
> highest integrity—in relation to his wife's insights, immediate,
> non-rational and almost infallible, into human character . . .

In April Aldous went to New York now to receive a prize, the
1959 Award of Merit for the Novel by the American Academy
of Arts and Letters, then under the presidency of Mark Van
Doren. It is a reward that goes to a novelist once every five years;
Aldous's predecessors were Ernest Hemingway, Thomas Mann
and Theodore Dreiser. The prize, a gold medal and a thousand
dollars, was presented to him by Malcolm Cowley at a joint
ceremonial of the Academy and the National Institute on the
20th of May.

As his first semester at Santa Barbara was coming to an end,
Aldous was able to stay on in New York for ten days, Laura with
him. Both attempted what they could. Matthew's cousin Claire,
much on the scene, thought that Aldous was very fair, very just
—equally concerned for both ("Laura was feeling sorry for Ellen
and I vehemently took Matthew's side"). "I wish our last evening
had been less sad," Aldous wrote on his return to Deronda Drive,
"but sad it was. All that can be done is to try to make the best
of a bad job.

> I think the idea of calling in a lawyer to draw up some kind of a
> written agreement is good. Once it has been drawn up, you will
> both know where you stand. Ellen will know where she stands in
> relation to the future, to the overall situation. And you will have the
> knowledge that she knows, will have a framework within which you
> both can function, and . . play the day-to-day situation by ear, so to
> speak, without having to spend energy, and create friction, by having
> to insist on the overall situation and future contingencies. It will
> mean, I hope, that you will be able to meet with one another . . with
> the same preoccupation—the day-to-day well being of the children
> within a long-range scheme which has been worked out by a third
> party and which both of you accept.
>
> . . I hope, that both of you will be able to follow the gospel injunc-
> tion, "Judge not that ye be not judged"—one of the most important

and significant sayings in the whole corpus of Jesus's teaching. You will not have to judge Ellen for her reluctance to think of the future and the overall picture, and she will not have to judge you for what she regards as an undue preoccupation with things which, to a person of her temperament, seem merely mechanical, organizational, abstract . . . As in all human situations, there is a paradox here. "Judge not" . . . And yet, at the same time, choose what seems to be right, reasonable, decent. In other words, judge but don't judge—judge in the sense of discriminating, but don't judge in the sense of condemning. Even where there seems to be a moral evil, don't judge in a condemnatory way . . .

It is over half a century since Aldous's mother's last letter: "Do not be too critical of others, and love much." To his own son, he continued,

. . Huxleys especially have a tendency not to suffer fools gladly—and also to regard as fools people who are merely different from themselves in temperament and habits. It is difficult for Huxleys to remember that other people have as much right to their habits and temperaments as Huxleys have to theirs . . . So do remember this family vice of too much judging . . . Write to me from time to time to let me know how you are faring.

Aldous's own summer plans—after one more lecture on the 2nd of June, "my last, thank goodness"—were to get down "seriously and continuously" to the novel. As he was due for his second semester at Santa Barbara in September, he had three, not quite clear, months in hand. Georges Neveux was considering a French adaptation of *The Genius and the Goddess*. "Vous repensez à ma malheureuse pièce . . ." and here Aldous, too, was thinking again about that wretched play. He and Laura arranged a reading of it (in its original form) at the house. They had good actors; one of them Allan Napier who had played Everard Webley in the London production of *Point Counter Point* and taken part in Laura's Los Angeles *Gioconda Smile*. They read the play (he told me) to a private audience of about a dozen people, read it to a snore-snore obbligato by a fat woman who had gone to sleep and who was supposed to be a prospective backer. But the general effect was quite good, thought Aldous, who afterwards buckled down to make a number of new cuts, shortening the play by some fifteen pages. (Soon after he made what I think is a pertinent comment on an aspect of dramatic effectiveness. "Mindlessness and horror," he wrote about a film that had its quota of the latter,

. . Mindlessness and horror are all right provided that they be shown in relationship with the mind and the good that will keep the world from collapsing. Consistent mindlessness, such as one gets in Tennessee Williams' plays, becomes a great bore and is also completely untrue to life. (A Williams play about mindlessness cd not be put on the stage except by a lot of highly intelligent people displaying all the qualities . . so totally absent in Williams' picture of the world.) Why intensely mindful people shd choose to portray only mindlessness is a psychological enigma . . . In doing so, they deny themselves, make the survival of humanity as a species completely incomprehensible . . and narrow the scope of art as a commentary on life.

One August night, on one of his solitary walks in the dark, Aldous stumbled over the kerb of the road and fell some eight feet on to a terrace below. It was a nasty fall in a steep and hazardous place, and it seemed a minor miracle to those who knew it that he got off with shock and a jolted back, trifling in comparison to what might have happened. Laura thought that he was mainly saved by his state of physical relaxation in falling. Aldous expressed himself profoundly grateful for a really providential escape. "If ever guardian angels were on hand, it was on that night," he wrote to Matthew.

A couple of weeks later, "as good as new," he was working away again on the Utopian novel.

.. wrestling with the problem of .. [not] becoming merely expository or didactic. [To Matthew] It may be that the job is one which cannot be accomplished with complete success. In point of fact, it hasn't been accomplished in the past. For most Utopian books have been exceedingly didactic and expository. I am trying to lighten up the exposition by putting it into dialogue form; which I make as lively as possible. But meanwhile I am always haunted by the feeling that, if only I had enough talent, I could somehow poetize and dramatize all the intellectual material and create a work which would be simultaneously funny, tragic, lyrical and profound. Alas, I don't possess the necessary talent . . .

Alas also, time was getting on. In a few days Aldous would have to turn his attention from the novel to the autumn's lectures at Santa Barbara.

# Chapter Eight

## Santa Barbara—Professor at Large

IN the past and particularly over the last years, Aldous had been lecturing with increasing response and ease in a good many American universities; Santa Barbara now was his first experience of a visiting professorship. U.C.S.B.—University of California at Santa Barbara—had invited him to give a course for two semesters. From February to May, and again from September to December of 1959, Aldous delivered a lecture every Monday afternoon, followed the next day by a seminar. "My modest theme is 'The Human Situation.'" During the spring semester he attacked it on the large-scale level—planetary resources, population growth, advancing technicalization, suicidal traditions of nationalism and so forth. He had put in a great amount of work collecting and organizing his material so that he was able, as he now preferred to do, to speak largely *extempore*. People gathered around him on these two weekly days and he had "to do a good deal of gibbering on the side—so much, indeed, that, last week, I almost lost my voice.

However, everybody seems to like it, and if I were to accept all the invitations that come pouring in, I should be talking non-stop for the next two years . . .

There were indeed full houses, great appreciation (I was told), but also opposition; some came from the English department, some from the metaphysicians . . . (One present faculty member, Donald Lent, who was a student at the time, wrote to me about the University, as he saw it, making a couple of mistakes: "They loaded the course on how good students' grades were, so you had a dull, efficient lot by and large—also amazingly brash; one pre-med student would preface his remarks with, 'well, you writers may think that, but *we* scientists think such and such'; another student . . suggested in a paper that went on for over an hour [Huxley-time burning up, I kept thinking] that the solution to the population problem was not birth control but the 'humane' killing off of the aged who filled our hospitals and rest homes . . . The second mistake was that they placed a professor in charge of the course. He saw that people did those awful papers and were graded etc . . .")

In the autumn semester, Aldous talked about The Human

Situation on the small-scale level—the make-up of the individual,
his latent potentialities and what we might do about their realization, the relation between concept and datum, the nature of
art . . . "It is an impossibly large project—but worth undertaking,
even inadequately, as an antidote to academic specialization and
fragmentation."

Worth undertaking . . . There is, on yet another level, something that remains of Aldous's passage in a few individual lives.
Ten years after—if for once I may be allowed to intrude what
was then the future, the better to conjure up the past—ten years
after, Aldous and Maria's beloved friend Rosalind Rajagopal
brought together some of the men and women connected with
Aldous at Santa Barbara in 1959. The meeting took place in the
house of Rosalind's daughter and son-in-law, Radha and James
Sloss at Hope Valley on a night in January 1969. There were
some twenty of us; we ate together and drank wine—the house,
in that quiet countryside, was spacious and attractive; our hosts'
two adolescent children, so well known to Aldous, intelligent and
graceful; animation, friendliness, generated. Later we settled in
an informal circle. There were present Dr Elmer Noble, University Chancellor in Aldous's first semester; faculty members;
board members of the Ojai Happy Valley School; members of
the Platonic Academy at Montecito[1]; as well as two or three
people who happened to be both Santa Barbarians and Aldous's
friends. Dauwe Sturman, Professor of English and Philosophy,
the man originally responsible for getting Aldous to U.C.S.B.,
took the chair (such as it was)—a youngish man, lean, very
Nordic, being in fact of Friesian extraction, who gave the
impression of combining a very acute mind with quiet, straightforward benevolence. Under a window halfway down the room,
sat Jack Wilkinson, Professor also of English and Philosophy (at
Montecito)—a little older apparently than Sturman, well-knit,
of middle height, extremely intelligent, who spoke extremely well.
Opposite him, Howard Warshaw, painter and Professor of Art,
a big, dark man, brilliant, quick, coming in again and again
with expressive brio. Everyone in that room had something to
say; some spoke once, some often; there were no interruptions, a
flow rather from solo voice to confluence, orchestral progression,
initiated and sustained by these three men, Sturman, Warshaw,
Wilkinson, who between them carried the evening.

There was no tape recorder (we decided against one). It was
not essentially what was said—though some of it was fireworks—
that was significant, but the kind of people who said it (Aldous

[1] "The Platonic Academy among the gardens of Montecito" was what
Aldous liked to call Robert Hutchins's Center for Democratic Studies.

had had that knack of attracting quality, not only intellectual but human quality) and the way in which it was said: the undercurrent of emotion. How should we proceed, Sturman had asked me when we formed our circle? Did I want to ask questions, had I brought notes? No notes, no questions—let the thing develop. Warshaw began by telling an anecdote and it being taken up, a reminiscence here, fond recollection there—small things we know —Aldous's willing chauffeurs, his interest in cars, in gadgets, his knowledge of the map. It was usually Laura, they reminded one another, who drove him to Santa Barbara, the some eighty miles from his L.A. hilltop, on the Sunday night; or if she was too busy he might take the bus, or get a lift—"But, Aldous, how *did* you get here?" Oh, he said, pleased as punch, "I just thumbed a ride." They talked about his voice, his courtesy; his utter professionalism . . . "but without assumptions—he always remained a private person." His patience and politeness with the students, his ceaseless moral and intellectual energy; the ways, outlandish to Americans, in which he arranged his practical existence. He always put up at what they described, marvelling at such frugality, a fire-trap hotel, "the dear old Upham" (a wooden structure indeed, but really a charming, chintzy, old-fashioned residential hotel frequented by elderly gentlewomen). And those walks! how he *insisted* on walking. Well, at least this was in Santa Barbara, whereas in Los Angeles . . . And we recalled that several times Aldous had been arrested—let's say on the point of being arrested —by the police when out on his evening walks . . . Yes, and not only at night, once in mid-afternoon on Wiltshire Boulevard he had been stopped by the law: "Mister, where's your car?" and the silvery English voice, "I haven't got a car."

On Monday morning he would usually be fetched from the hotel by Eric Petrie, an English academic and husband of the sculptress Marie Petrie, for whom Aldous sat for his portrait bust.[1] Mrs Petrie put him in a swivel-chair fixed to a revolving platform where she could look at him from all angles by giving the chair a push from time to time. Whoever had an hour to spare would come to the studio to listen to the captive Aldous who would talk about Vedanta, Brazilian architecture or the Pill— "Why don't they put in a few vitamins, that might be a way out for the Catholic Church?"—talk, as he was pushed from one profile to the other in his chair, about Pavlov, Schweitzer and Toulouse Lautrec, never stopping as he whirled. Luncheon afterwards at the Petries' under the figtree in their garden with some

---

[1] A very fine head, now in the possession of the late Marie Petrie's grandson, Mr Brian Petrie, in London. (A cast has been acquired by the Los Angeles County Museum.)

eminent or amusing person to make a fourth. Later they would drive him to the campus (Marie Petrie coming in the back of the car, saying she needed the extra twenty minutes of looking at Aldous's head and ears).

The lecture, full houses—students, staff, the public (Santa Barbara intelligentsia flocking in) . . . He used few notes—in very big letters—spoke—dispassionately in manner—about ecology . . dwindling planetary resources . . . Some said Aldous was crying wolf . . . How *much* he anticipated, his *concern* about the human condition—*that* came through. And yet, another day, privately, he might retail, full of glee, some piece of hair-raising lore. Before the bomb, before population catching up, he said, returning from some scientific conference, "there will be this virus conveyed by air travel. Ah, the little microbes will get us first!" There had been opposition to Aldous's appointment; not everyone at the University was pleased; some of the metaphysicians looked down their noses, calling his stuff old hat. Had anyone listened again to the recorded lectures? Not yet. This was the first time, really, that they were talking away like this; one could not have done so before, not a few years ago, not so soon after his death . . . Now, it was not too late—the memories were there, rediscovered, fresh. The meeting[1]—or what should one call it? a party, group interview, memorial service or a séance, this fraternal and spontaneous evocation of an extraordinary man? (thus had Gervas Huxley evoked the Hillside schoolboy, the young man at Oxford) perhaps symposium serves—well, the symposium then entered a discursive, intellectual phase. Aldous's metaphysics. What exactly did he believe? And how did he believe? The ends of man, Enlightenment, the Divine Ground—this Taoist agnostic whose element was not rock but water, this inveterate empiricist, this modern saint, who never ceased to ask "Where are we going?" who had also said that one must dream in a pragmatic way—was he moved by choice, by will, by faith? (Perhaps a part of an answer not given that night can be found in *Island*: "Believing in eternal life never helped anybody to live in eternity. Nor, of course, did *dis*believing. So stop all your pro-ing and con-ing (that's the Buddha's advice) and get on with the job.") Later still the talk curved back into the personal, the reminiscent past. It was Santa Barbara that had given Aldous his first honorary doctorate. He

[1] There were present at this meeting, besides our host and those already mentioned, Professor Garret Hardin, biologist and author; Mrs Hardin, Mrs Noble, Mrs Warshaw, Mrs Wilkinson; Katherine Peak, Aldous's fellow board member of the Happy Valley School; Frank Lacey, director of the school; Harriette Van Breton; Aldous's old friend Eva Herrmann; and of course Rosalind Rajagopal and her sister, Mrs Louis Zalk, and S. B. The date was 31st January 1969.

seemed *delighted* . . . He stood up in his new gown on the campus platform in the open air giving his acceptance address, his hair blown in the autumn wind . . . But later in the semester, he turned up for his lectures without the doctor's gown. "Oh!" Aldous said, "Well, Laura uses it for sun-bathing . ."

## Chapter Nine

# Menninger Foundation—Professor at Large

THE Julian Huxleys came for Christmas. Deronda Drive, which had still been in the making during their last visit in 1956, had reached its definitive stage; there was no spare room and they put up in a small hotel at the foot of the hill. Laura fetched them daily. "On approach, the house [through Juliette's eyes] looked like a squat grey toad, but inside it was charming. Laura had furnished it beautifully—white rugs, a large bed downstairs ensconced in a window, nylon curtains of many colours, a dining-table of shining black, white sofa and armchairs. Aldous had his room upstairs next to the second bathroom, and his study on the mezzanine floor—very *encombré*." (According to Mère, the number of Aldous's upstairs rooms was *three*; "small rooms, but not *mesquin*"; what she regretted was that he could not step from study into garden.) "The view incredibly lovely, over the whole plain, glittering at night with a million lights. Racoons came . . and were fed milk . . ." It was a Californian Christmas and they were able to swim in Virginia's pool. "Laura driving, though it was only 5 minutes walk. J. and I often walked back.

On Christmas Day lunch at the house with Mme Nys, Rosé, the Capitano [Angelino Ravagli, Frieda Lawrence's third husband]. We exchanged presents; I can't remember *what* book A gave Julian . . . Mme Nys very lively. It was a happy day. We all sat outside in the sun.

Gerald Heard and Christopher came in one afternoon; there was at least one dinner-party with Romain Gary and Lesley Blanch, "Laura a good hostess, and the food nice"; all too soon their time was up. "It was wonderful having you here," Aldous wrote, "and I wish it could have been longer."

January and, for Aldous, back to the Utopia—"the writing of which presents extraordinary difficulties". For Laura it was back to psychotherapy. Her work was most stimulating to Aldous, who transcribed some of her methods straight into the novel. She had, he said, "remarkable results in many cases: for she seems to have an intuitive knowledge of what to do at any given moment, what technique to use in each successive phase of the patient's mood and feeling." Among other things she had been using LSD "in a few cases where the method seemed to be justifiable."

636

Incidentally [to Humphrey], what frightful people there are in your profession! We met two Beverly Hills psychiatrists the other day, who specialize in LSD therapy at $100 a shot—and, really, I have seldom met people of lower sensitivity, more vulgar mind! To think of people made vulnerable by LSD being exposed to such people is profoundly disturbing. But what can one do about the problem? Psychiatry is an art based on a still imperfect science—and as in all the arts there are more bad and indifferent practitioners than good ones. How can one keep the bad artists out? Bad artists don't matter in painting or literature—but they matter enormously in therapy and education; for whole lives and destinies may be affected . . But one doesn't see any practical way in which the ungifted and the unpleasant can be filtered out . . .

At this time Aldous asked Matthew's advice upon a point of business. The University of Texas had approached him—indirectly—about some of the manuscripts and literary correspondence in his possession. "This might be a good idea—sell some MSS now and put the money into the children's trust fund. What do you think?

I won't make any move until I hear what you feel about the matter. I've no idea what sort of price the U of T will pay: but if they offer a fair sum it might be a good idea to dispose of MSS rather than await my demise . . .

Matthew—as this would have benefited *his* children—did not respond, and, unfortunately, ironically, no action was taken in the matter.

Aldous's finances, incidentally, had been in a healthy state for quite some time. Between 1955 and 1958 his annual income from Chatto & Windus, U.K. and translation rights alone, averaged nearly £5,000. In 1959, he had just heard, the precise sum was £7,239—"a most surprisingly good showing". American royalties fluctuated, yet, again on the average, seldom fell below 75% of English ones. And on top of this, there were his not inconsiderable lecturing fees.

Present life was quiet. "Rose has retreated again to the desert—waiting for a very hypothetical job as a member of an archaeological expedition to Yucatan with 2 gentlemen from Texas. Bonne Maman [an Aldous view of Mère] flourishes under the stimulation of successive disasters in France—the death of Camus, . . the Fréjus dam break, the news of which in the *Figaro Littéraire* . . excites her and keeps up her morale like a shot of adrenalin . .

What a strange creature! But what a blessing that it takes so little—the account in a newspaper of a French catastrophe (it has to be

French: nobody else's catastrophes cut much ice)—to keep her in good shape.

The Utopia was getting on—300 pages typed in February—though with no end in sight. "Heaven knows how much more there will be . . ." He had still not solved his main technical difficulty.

. . I became disturbed by the low ratio of story to exposition and am now, after discussing the problem with Christopher Isherwood, trying to remedy this defect by the introduction of a brand new personage . . .

(Could this character have been wicked, clever Mr Bahu, the envoy from the Bad Island?[1])

After more than a year of separation, Matthew and Ellen's dilemma had not been resolved. Aldous took a hand, writing to Ellen. ". . I had imagined that by this time you would have come to some definite decision—either to make a reconciliation or a definite break . .

. . This half way position with one foot in a marriage and one foot out strikes me as profoundly unsatisfactory—especially for Matthew who is essentially a family man with a deep wish for roots and stability and on whom the present arrangement imposes a rootlessness and a homelessness that for him are peculiarly distressing . . .

. . . Rose evidently feels very strongly that you should decide in favour of reconciliation. If you find it emotionally possible, I would also be for it—but I don't think it should be forced . . . The important thing, however, is to decide. If there is anything I can do to help you to come to a decision, let me know.

The decision was made, and it was to break. ". . there is no consolation," Aldous wrote to Matthew, "only the reflection that a mending . . on any basis short of a heartfelt 'marriage of true minds' might be an even sadder thing for all concerned.

The problem now is to make the best of the situation . . . [I] can only hope that you will soon be able to create for yourself a new home base, with its own internal relationships of love and affection, from which you can relate yourself to the children. *Their* well-being will be enhanced by *your* well-being: so it is as much for the children's sake as for yours that I wish and hope for your future happiness.

---

[1] C. I. does not remember.

And for the same reasons, I hope for Ellen's future happiness. Her letter to me was full of sadness . . .

> *Nel mezzo del cammin di nostra vita*
> *mi ritrovai per une selva oscura*
> *ché la diritta via era smarrita.*

Each of you must find a way out of the dark wood, for your own sakes and for the children's. And if I can help in any way, that is what I'm there for. Whatever may have happened on the level of the previous generation, the family still persists in Trev and Tessa . . .

There seemed to be almost nothing, wrote one of his medical friends, Max Cutler,[1] about which Aldous could not be curious. Yet on that vast circumference through which his mind swept, there were sectors of particular concern: health, for instance, and the whole issue of medicine . . . "I had of course, before I went blind, intended to become a doctor" Aldous, for his part, said in the London interview of 1961. "I presume that if I *had* gone on with it, I would have gone into medical research. I don't think I would have been a very good *practising* doctor—Why? Well, I don't know that I would have been good enough in the personal relationships, which I think are tremendously important in a good doctor: I mean, I was diffident and shy and awkward then, I think I've slightly improved with age—but I think I would have been a fairly good medical researcher, I think I would always have been very interested in the research part of the thing . . ."

The following, for instance, had happened a few years ago. In Philadelphia in 1957—at the time of the unfortunate opening of the play—Aldous saw a young doctor he had known in California, Robert Lynch, who was experimenting with what at his hospital they called the French Cocktail, a mixture of chlorpromazine, phenacetin,[2] aspirin and demerol compounded by a French doctor and used for producing a form of hibernation. Administered in large doses, the Cocktail reduced temperature to ninety-two and lowered metabolism. A friend of Dr Lynch's, another young doctor, was afflicted with a horrible cancer of the lymphatic system, resistant to radiation, grown to the size of a football in his chest. Experts gave him a few months to live. Aldous and Laura urged trying the French Cocktail.

. . I argued [to Humphrey] that, since the cocktail greatly reduces the metabolic rate and since cancer cells require a great deal of

---

1 Professor Max Cutler, the eminent cancerologist.
2 *Or* Phenergen: the prescription differs in Aldous's relevant letters.

nourishment and probably don't like cold, there might be a chance of the malignant cells dying or being checked in their growth, while the healthy cells survived the hibernation process.

. . . We suggested combining semi-hibernation . . with intensive hypnosis, talking to the cells . . . wildly unorthodox . . . but conceivably it might work.

And it did. The summer after, Dr Lynch gave Laura the results. They were "extraordinary—complete disappearance of the tumour, acceptance of the young man as a full-time intern at the U of C hospital at Berkeley, complete recovery of weight, strength, vitality."

So when the Menninger Foundation, a major centre of psychiatric training in America, invited Aldous to spend two months with them in the spring—visiting Professor, no special duties, "just hanging around and occasionally talking"—Aldous accepted with much pleasure. ("It will be interesting, I think, to penetrate the holy of holies of American psychiatry.") What he was actually being offered was the Sloan Professorship of the year, and he proposed to deliver a few lectures on subjects connected with psychology and discuss "the art of writing case histories" in a seminar. As to practical matters—

I shall be coming alone; but it is possible that my wife might come for a short time during my stay at Topeka—in which case she wd probably go to a hotel.

What I would like is a small apartment or motel room with a kitchenette. (One gets very tired of restaurant food, and I wd like to be able to make my own culinary mess when I feel like it. So a little kitchen wd be a *sine qua non*.)

Aldous arrived in Topeka, Kansas, in mid-March. The Middle West was under 18 inches of snow about to melt and "one waded about in rubber boots like a salmon fisher". He found "a vast psychotic population at large and in a dozen hospitals," an enormous hospital, a veterans' hospital, Dr Menninger's private hospital, schools for delinquent boys, for backward children, a large staff "—a lot of very able people . . (Gardner Murphy, Bertalanffy, for example) . . and some hundred and fifty young MD's and PH.D's taking a three years' course." Aldous was free to go anywhere, see anything he wanted.

. . much to admire [he wrote to Juliette] and also not a little to shake my head over in incomprehension. E.g. they treat hospital patients in a rational way, attacking their problems on all the fronts from the nutritional and gymnastic to the psychological: but their private patients they treat in the grand old Freudian way . . . by psychology alone, and psychology of only one, not too realistic brand. Very odd . . .

In what he regarded as the good hospitals, everything was done at once: psycho-therapy, work, play and music therapy, chemo-therapy, vitamins, diet . . "they really get to work on the person from every angle; and then you have a chance of getting the person out in quite a short time . . ." Aldous talked at some length about the subject a year later at the London interview. Strict Freudians can't really *do* very much with psychosis, he said. "There is no doubt that the whole organic approach is gaining ground—

I think it's pretty clear now that schizophrenia is an organic disease . . of chemical origin . . . and probably one could find chemical means of coping with it . . .

"The other day I was talking to Dr [William] Sargant who is the chief psychotherapist at St Thomas's, he uses entirely organic methods. And gets very good results. He wouldn't dream of using the sort of Freudian methods, because they just don't work . . But there is no *doubt* that we *are* on the threshold of some *very important changes* in treatment of mental disease . . .

"I was never as intoxicated by Freud as some people were, and I get less intoxicated as I go on. I think he omitted too much from his purview of human beings . . . We do know very well that there are many things on the neurological and bio-chemical level which *profoundly* affect our lives. But Freud—although he did himself say that finally all nervous disorders would turn out to be organic—he did say that in the meanwhile . . . we could treat them successfully by purely psychological means—I think this is absolutely *untrue*.

"His followers of course dogmatically insist upon this, in the most ridiculous way, the orthodox Freudians. Well, thank heaven, most psychotherapists are *not* orthodox Freudians now, they are eclectics and making use of organic and chemical methods, and psychological and sociological methods, which guarantee a cure which a pure Freudian just doesn't get with his eight years on the couch.

"As I said, I was never very intoxicated by it, and more and more as I learn what is happening now in the field of neurology and bio-chemistry, and in the general study of the human physique and the classification of human types, I feel more and more strongly that you have to have the total organic approach. We *have* to see the thing as *a totality*—we *have* to make the best not only of both worlds, *but of all the worlds.*

"*Man is a multiple amphibian who lives in about twenty different worlds at once.* [The italics are in Aldous's voice] If anything is to be done to improve his *enjoyment* of life, to improve the way he can realize his desirable potentialities, to improve his *health,* to improve the *quality* of his relations with other people, to improve his *morality,* we have to *attack on all fronts at once.*

"And the greatest, and what may be called the original sin of the human mind is *sloth,* it's over-simplification. We *want* to think that there is only *one* cause for every given phenomenon, therefore there is only one cure, *there is not!* This *is* the trouble: no phenomenon on the human level, which is a level of immense complexity, can ever have a single cause—we must always take at least half a dozen conspiring causal factors into consideration . . . The trouble with the Freudians is that they took only *one* set of factors into account, and of course their system doesn't work at all well.

". . . This is the sort of intellectual and scientific correlate to my feeling that the highest forms of art are those which impose harmony and order upon the greatest number of factors . . ."

Later again Aldous was to write on the subject in *Literature and Science*; here, and in the lectures he gave in the autumn following his stay at the Menninger Foundation, he developed his thought on these lines:

. . The interesting thing is that the ego remains very much what it was in Homer's day. It is this conscious, fairly rational creature which uses words, which is analytical, which pursues its own self-interest. It is the person, in the words of Robert Louis Stevenson, "The person with a conscience and a variable bank balance." But around this ego, around this person . . there are a whole lot of "not I's" . . .[1]

There are, for instance, Até and Menos.

Well, who and what is Até?[2] In the Greek tragedies the word stands for disaster, but in Homer the word stands for "the state of mind" which brings on disaster . . . the state of infatuation, the state of mind which leads to all kinds of absurd things against our own interests, things which make no sense to us whatever, and yet we still do them. And Homer personified this . . as an alien, supernatural force which came into man . . . Now, Homer . . makes it quite clear that there are also positive interventions from the

[1] "The Contemporary Picture", 2nd Lecture by A. H. at M.I.T. 13 Oct. 1960.
[2] "Ancient Views of Human Nature", 1st Lecture by A. H. at M.I.T. 5 Oct. 1960.

supernatural world. In general these . . are made in the form called Menos, and Menos is that kind of accession of power and eagerness and strength and vitality which permits us to do the impossible. Even animals are capable of experiencing Menos. Horses every now and then . . do the most extraordinary things in the *Iliad*. Homer would have said that any particularly good idea . . any remarkable action of great insight, is given to us *from the outside* by a god who breathed his Menos into us . . .

. . . Today of course . . .[1] we speak about [Menos and Até] in terms of an active, dynamic unconscious. It's remarkable how recent this idea is. We now take it completely for granted, but actually it is an idea which William James dates exactly. [He] attributed the beginning of the new psychology, with its stress upon the dynamic unconscious, to the publication of a paper in 1886 by F. W. H. Myers [setting forth a theory of the sublimated self; later developed in Myers' posthumous *Human Personality*]. Myers was a profound student and describer of the unconscious mind, and I regard him as one of the best . . .

Nine years after Meyer's paper, after experimenting with novel therapeutic techniques, Freud published his first book and formulated his famous theory of human behaviour in terms of libido, repression and a dynamic unconscious. Myers' fame became completely eclipsed. Yet Freud's hypothesis, Aldous thought, was less complete.

. . . for unlike his older English contemporary,[2] he paid very little attention to what may be called the positive side of the unconscious. Myers was more interested in Menos than in Até; Freud's primary concern was with the state of mind that leads to disaster . . . As a research physician, with a large clientèle of hysterical and neurotic patients, he had ample opportunities of observing the destructive activities of Até, very few for observing the influxes of Menos, the visitations of the Muses . . or the admonitions of the kind of daimon that spoke to Socrates.

. . . Freud,[3] so to speak, is talking all the time about the basement downstairs with the rats and black beetles, whereas Myers is largely concerned with the floors above the ground floor where the ego lives, and he would agree, I would think, with the mystical point of view that the topmost floor of these upper levels has no roof to it and is open to the sky.

[1] 2nd M.I.T. Lecture.
[2] *Literature and Science*. Chatto & Windus, 1963.
[3] 2nd M.I.T. Lecture.

# Chapter Ten

## Reprieve

AFTER the six weeks at Menninger's, more journeys, more lectures: Berkeley, Idaho State University, the University of Arizona. It was well into May before they were settling down again, Aldous hoping to get on with his book, Laura to start one. For Laura had decided to write. One Sunday afternoon two young English scientists had come to tea to discuss ways of setting up some useful project. ". . It was a question of large sums of money, committees, laboratories and it seemed hopelessly long before any of this would have a practical application.

> I . . could hardly imagine a million dollars, or a million people, but I was very clear-minded about the individuals in question—quietly self-liquidating in streets, hospitals and prisons, long before the project would even be out of the organizational stage.[1]

The scientists left. " 'Those are bright young men,' Aldous said. I was seething with impatience. 'Yes, they are bright—but it will be years . . .' And even before I had time to co-ordinate my thinking, I heard myself suddenly announce, at breathless speed, 'You know what I am going to do? I am going to write a book. I am going to make a book of my techniques—and everybody can use them right away, without a committee, and without a million dollars. And I am going to call these techniques, *Recipes for Living and Loving*.' " Aldous was delighted. A wonderful idea, he said, and a very good title. That was the beginning of *You Are Not the Target* by Laura Archera Huxley.

In a letter dated 18th of May, Aldous told Matthew that he hoped to finish *his* book before the next load of engagements in September; told him that Mme Nys was having dizzy spells and Matthew had better write to keep her cheerful; expressed pleasure about Matthew's plan to join an expedition to the Brazilian jungle, and enclosed a $20 bill for some vast and learned book he wanted sent. It was the usual even-toned and friendly letter, and no one could have told that Aldous was going through one of the most shattering experiences there is. He had just been in hospital for tests, and been given the diagnosis of a malignant tumour on the back of his tongue. Radical surgery, which might

[1] Laura Archera Huxley, *This Timeless Moment*.

have left him more or less speechless, had been recommended, or rather pressed on him as both urgent and inevitable. Aldous was against this, or at least against an immediate decision; so was Laura. And it was largely thanks to her quick good sense and resolution that he was spared this fate. She helped him to get dressed and actually whisked him out of hospital in the luncheon hour.[1] Then she telephoned Aldous's friend Dr Max Cutler for an appointment. They went on 19th May. Aldous asked, "Isn't there something else that can be done?" Cutler advised him to take a radium needle treatment.

Now, Dr Cutler is a very eminent cancerologist indeed. (Aldous had first met him in April 1954 when he was called in as consultant for Maria. He had seen her case as hopeless, and encouraged the last journey to Europe). Trained at Johns Hopkins and the Curie Institute in Paris, co-author with the late Sir Lenthal Cheatle of a medical classic, Dr Cutler had been for many years the head of the Chicago Tumor Institute before going into private practice in Los Angeles. Aldous wrote about him, "I find that both here and in Europe he is regarded among the greatest living surgeons and radiologists." Dr Cutler nevertheless insisted on a second opinion. Aldous with Laura flew to San Francisco the next morning; here he was examined by the Professors of Radiology and Surgery[2] at the University of California Medical Center. They advised him to take the radium treatment and to take it with Cutler.

Aldous's second decision was to keep the whole thing secret. He did not want to worry people necessarily or unnecessarily, and he wanted to protect himself from the inevitable atmosphere of apprehension and inquiry. *No* one was to know, neither his son, nor his brother, nor his friends, and above all not the press and the professional world. Laura entirely concurred (one should think of the burden this put on her). Thus Aldous's illness became known only to Virginia Pfeiffer and the Kiskaddens, Bill having long acted as Aldous's private medical adviser, and of course to the doctors concerned. On 31st May Aldous went into hospital for six days under the name of Mr Leonard, Matthew Leonard. The treatment was successful—the tumour was knocked out, and Aldous's speech remained perfect. The next ten weeks of convalescence at home were what he called unpleasant. Even so, he was able to take part in a symposium at Tecate, Mexico, as early as the 24th of June. In July he was at work again on his novel.

At this time Betty Wendel's daughter, Jeff Corner, a young and

1 Laura's full account of these events and the nature of Aldous's illness can be found in *This Timeless Moment*.
2 Drs Franz Buscke and Maurice Galante.

happily married woman, lost her husband in a sudden, meaningless accident. Aldous wrote:

What can one say? There are no consolations; there is only the bearing of the unbearable for the sake of the life—your own and the children's—that has to go on and be made the best of.

I never knew Doug well—but I always felt, whenever I met him, a renewal of the liking and respect that my first meeting had inspired. One had a sense when one was with him that there was an intrinsically good human being, decent, fair, kind . . with that blessed capacity for seeing himself with a humorous eye which is a true manifestation of the Christian virtue of humility. And now this dreadful, senseless thing has happened . . . As I said, there are no consolations; but out of my own experience I can tell you certain things which may be of some practical help. It is profoundly important to remember that, over and above the grief and the loneliness and the near-despair, there will be an organic reaction, closely resembling surgical shock. A bereavement such as yours . . . produces a state of psychic and physical shock—a state which may last for weeks or months. For so long as this state of shock persists, the mind-body requires appropriate supportive treatment in the form of adequate rest, a good diet etc. The bereaved person's tendency is to resent this—to feel that it is an ignoble kind of escape from the situation. But neglecting the amputated organism will do nothing to spiritualize the bereavement. On the contrary, it may physiologize it, transform it into a sickness that leaves the sufferer no power to think with love about the past or act constructively in the present . . . God bless you.

Before the end of the summer, the novel had to be laid aside for more pressing homework. In September Aldous left California to take part in a convention on medicine and ethics at Dartmouth College, then flew to Boston from which Matthew drove him in his microbus to Durham, New Hampshire, to receive another honorary degree (Laura, busy with her own book, did not come East), thence he went on to New York, and to Pennsylvania to give a lecture at the University of Pittsburgh. And on the 23rd of September, Aldous alone—his equipment in two Revelation suitcases—boarded a train bound for the most glamorous of his academic appointments, Carnegie Visiting Professor at M.I.T., the Massachusetts Institute of Technology.

## Chapter Eleven

# Cambridge, Massachusetts—Carnegie Professor in Humanities

" AN interesting job in an interesting place . . ." The Massachusetts Institute of Technology is known as one of the great purely scientific universities of America and the world. Less well known perhaps is the fact that it has also made a point of setting up an excellent department of the humanities, and that all students, whether they are going to be mathematicians, scientists or engineers, have to give twenty-five per cent of their time to literature, history and philosophy. This is how Aldous's appointment came about: Professor Patrick Wall, M.D. (now of the University of London), then a professor of biology at M.I.T., talking to Matthew, learned that Aldous would be interested in spending some time in a scientifically and technologically oriented institution. Professor Wall approached John Ely Burchard, then Dean of the School of Humanities and Social Sciences, who took up the suggestion immediately. After a very brief correspondence Aldous agreed to come in the autumn semester of 1960, to give seven public lectures and take part in the Humanities Senior Seminar. He was to be designated Centennial Carnegie Visiting Professor in Humanities (M.I.T. was celebrating its 100th year), and to receive $9000 for a nine weeks' residence. (The funds came from a grant of the Carnegie Corporation.) Aldous accepted this large fee with pleasure, snapped it up, it could be said. If there was one thing he was proud of it was to have been able to earn his living with his pen, and to this his growing lecturing successes now added another dimension, as it were.

The major educational experiment under the Carnegie grant was the Humanities-and-Science, and Humanities-and-Engineering Curriculum, and the director of this was Professor Roy Lamson.[1]

I was delighted to have Aldous at M.I.T., and our faculty, both humanists and scientists, were enthusiastic about the prospect. Dean Burchard asked me to take charge of the arrangements . . .[2]

[1] Roy Lamson, Professor of Literature, Director of Course XXI (Humanities and Science and Engineering) at M.I.T.
[2] Roy Lamson in conversation and a memorandum to S. B.

So Roy Lamson had flown to Topeka in the spring and spent four days at Menninger's with Aldous, whom he observed in action as the main discussant in a conference on the Constructive Uses of Anxiety. For the rest of the time the two men talked, about music, about art, about what Aldous wanted to do at M.I.T.; there was the beginning of a friendship. Aldous decided to make the subject of his lectures *What a Piece of Work Is Man.*

It was Roy and his wife, Peggy, who found Aldous an apartment in Cambridge, three rooms and kitchen on the ground floor of a modern building, 100 Memorial Drive, near the campus; and arranged for an office in the Hayden Library. ("Aldous took one look at the office and the Institute mail on his desk, and never returned to it.")

Aldous arrived. The Lamsons met his train at Back Bay Station in Boston. Roy stepped forward to seize the suitcases, dropped them and nearly dropped himself—the weight was staggering: not only were these expanding cases stuffed with books to breaking point, Aldous had packed his typewriter as well. He liked the apartment.

His first lecture was on 5th October, a Wednesday, at 8 pm (all of them, except one, were on Wednesday night). Beforehand the Lamsons took Aldous to dinner at the Faculty Club. Aldous ate and talked without the slightest sign of performer's nerves, "at precisely 7.40 pm finished a hefty meal", and went with Lamson to the auditorium a quarter of a mile away. They went in by the back door and up the stage lift.

When they came in, the auditorium was filled to the last seat, and so were the aisles. Under the fire regulations, anyone standing had to be asked to leave. Aldous said it would not disturb him to have students sit on the stage with him while he spoke, so two hundred students came up from the aisles. Dean Burchard introduced Aldous. Aldous introduced his lecture. What a piece of impertinence, he said, for "an encyclopaedically ignorant man to come to talk to extremely learned people." Yet really learned people are inhibited by their vast amount of knowledge from straying beyond the boundaries of their own particular province, and it is perhaps the function of the "widely interested literary man to go crawling about in the woodwork between the pigeon holes, and to look in here, and to look in there, and to try to make some kind of coherent picture of the whole elaborate system of compartments which has grown up in our academic worlds.

In this series, I propose to talk . . about our most profound, searching, and difficult problem, the problem of human nature . . .

"Aldous lectured from a small sheaf of notes[1]. Occasionally he would bring the notes very close to his face to read a quotation, but otherwise he seemed to be pouring out his well-planned essay. He was strict in his timing, keeping his lecture to three or four minutes under an hour. Following each lecture he met students, and faculty.

"The lectures were immensely popular. Kresge Auditorium seats 1238; some 200 more sat on the stage. For the other lectures we put loud speakers in the corridor and also in the two rehearsal rooms under the auditorium, so that another 400 to 500 listened there. Attendance at these lectures is even today a record unsurpassed. . . The audience was mostly students—M.I.T., Harvard, Radcliffe, Boston University, Wellesley and the many schools and colleges in the Boston area."

Indeed the influx of these outside listeners was so heavy that they jammed traffic all across the Charles River into Boston, and extra police were called out to cope on Wednesday nights.

"A group of students complained that these outsiders were arriving an hour early and taking up seats. So Aldous offered to give an extra lecture just for the students.

"Once a week, on the Monday following last Wednesday's lecture, Aldous taught a seminar . . Thirty seniors, who had been studying for their degree of B.Sc. and had backgrounds in literature, history, philosophy and music, met Aldous and other members of the faculty for a two to three hours' session.

"At the opening meeting of the seminar on 10th October, in the Humanities lounge of the Hayden Library, the room was filled. Students enrolled in the seminar were given the front rows, and it was clear that we could not exclude the visitors, about fifty in all, faculty and students and some outsiders.

"Aldous often sat for a few minutes, head bowed, without a word. Then gave a short speech on a specific problem based on the general statements of the public lecture before. Then faculty and students pitched in with questions. At the end Aldous would often sum up the discussion or raise a new question and leave it to develop for the next session. The seminar was lively and often profound in that Aldous elicited comment from such people as Gyorgy Kepes,[2] Dr John Spiegel, psychologist from Brandeis, Huston Smith.[3]

"In addition Aldous offered to be at home every Tuesday from 2-5 pm to talk with students. His small apartment was always

---

[1] I am indebted for all quotations from these lectures to Roy Lamson's working copy, a transcription made from the tapes recorded at the lectures.
[2] Painter, Professor of Architecture, Director of the Center for Advanced Visual Studies of M.I.T.
[3] Professor of Philosophy of M.I.T.

jammed. Once I recall when students were in a cross-fire with each other, Aldous slipped out into the pantry-kitchen and made tea . . ."

Aldous's third lecture was introduced by Professor Giorgio de Santillana, who said *inter alia*, ". . I happen to say at times to my students . . 'Gentlemen, you are the men from Mars, you are to get acquainted with this, our planet . . .' I should like, therefore, to pay my special respects to Mr Huxley, who was not only Master to my generation but . . the one who perhaps did most to introduce us to this planet. If I play a little with the time co-ordinate, one name comes to my mind . . it is the name of Plutarch with his moral essays . . Sometime, someone should draw that parallel . . He would find, for instance, that Mr Huxley has it harder as he's caught in the paws of progress while Plutarch is not . . . There is no . . end of the trail problem for Plutarch. All is quiet curiosity and serenity. On the other hand . . Plutarch . . lacks the definiteness that modern science has built into our thought and into our language . . . Of the great exponents of culture . . .

> Mr Huxley is the one who has remained closest through the years to the scientific awareness. This is what gives point and relevance to his criticism, to his doubts, to his mystical conclusions . . .[1]

There was an immense excitement during Aldous's stay at M.I.T. ("It was an intellectual event and a 'worship' . . .")[2] A discovery for Aldous, too, who originally had been such a reluctant and not very effective public speaker, a reader rather of written speeches, when out of a sense of duty he had stood up for the Peace Pledge Union with Gerald Heard. Later he began to get some pleasure out of talking to learned institutions in America; the big change came in the 1950's when to Maria's astonishment he found that he would like to, and could, speak *extempore*. ". . he had made himself", Yehudi Menuhin wrote,[3]

> into an instrument of music—concentrated as he was in the spoken word, his voice was the gentlest melody, ennobled beyond hate, violence and prejudice, yet not without passion, which sang of all that had ever touched his senses as of all the myriad impressions his mind had made its own.
>
> . . . as pure in his maturity and ready to respond like a tuned violin

[1] From Professor de Santillana's introduction to the M.I.T. transcript of the tape recording of the original lecture.
[2] Roy Lamson.
[3] *Mem. Vol.*

to a trained hand . . . this was a man in whom wisdom never destroyed innocence. He was scientist and artist in one—standing for all we most need in a fragmented world where each of us carries a distorting splinter out of some great shattered universal mirror. He made it his mission to restore these fragments and, at least in his presence, men were whole again. To know where each splinter might belong one must have some conception of the whole, and only a mind such as Aldous's, cleansed of personal vanity, noticing and recording everything, and exploiting nothing, could achieve so broad a purpose.

After nearly fifty years of solitary confinement at his desk, M.I.T.—like Santa Barbara and other colleges before—must have been to a high degree rewarding and refreshing. (The fates, which so obstinately had refused him that successful play, at work in their mysterious way.) Even so, Aldous stuck to his sheet anchor, every or nearly every morning he stayed in and worked on the Utopia: *Island*; there was a title now . . On his free afternoons, he prowled about, often on his own. He walked across the long bridge into Boston, on the exiguous footway brushed by traffic; he prowled about the bargain-basement of Filene's department store, where you pay in scrip and the prices tumble week by week in some elaborate mathematical degression; he discovered a health-shop and carried home fruit, cereals and honey; he made his culinary messes of frozen fish and vegetables. Peggy Lamson did a certain amount of unobtrusive looking after him. Both Lamsons were a great asset to Aldous, and he was often in their house on Francis Avenue. The Wednesday night pre-lecture dinners at the Faculty Club became a ritual, Aldous eating through his three courses, finishing his stewed pears to the minute, Roy taking him across the campus, up the stage lift to the stand before the crowd of waiting men and women. Aldous stood as he lectured, "very erect, quietly commanding". The friendship with the Lamsons was also a private friendship, with them he could laugh as well as talk. In Peggy, herself a writer,[1] bright, gay, warm, he found the feminine company he always valued, they got on like a house on fire. They throve on nonsense. Aldous's riddle: The greatest invention of the twentieth century? The aeroplane? No, Scotch tape. They invented a personage who was a resident priest in a rosary factory; they thought of writing a sketch together (they did plunge later on into an actual dramatic project, the stage adaptation of a little known story of Aldous's called "Voices"; a good

[1] Author of *Few Are Chosen: American Women in Political Life Today* and *The Glorious Failure: Black Congressman Robert Brown Elliott and the Reconstruction in South Carolina*, etc.

deal of work ensuing for both). When Peggy got a new Nash car and it wouldn't start, Aldous said, "try this", jiggled a button below the dashboard and it did. His own apartment was kept in order by a weekly cleaning woman. The cleaning woman demanded a vacuum cleaner; Aldous asked Peggy to lend hers. Every Tuesday morning, regardless of the needs of her own household, she drove into Cambridge, parked, and lugged the thing across the campus. Once, vacuum cleaner in arms, she ran across the wife of the President of M.I.T. "Why, Mrs Lamson?" "Taking my vacuum cleaner to Aldous Huxley."

As ever he wanted to see anything that was going and was driven about a good deal by the Lamsons (here again the same tale: when Roy lost his way, it was Aldous who gave directions). Wanting to do all he could, he took on supplementary activities, such as speaking to some of the organizations within the Institute.

In all, he met with twenty groups—scientists, humanists . . . [Roy Lamson] He went to dinner with the chaplains but did not open his mouth except to the people on his right and left, and spent the rest of the—early—evening wrapt in one of his silences. One Monday he went reluctantly (because he had been in the Seminar from 2-5 pm) to talk to our commuters, a group not living in the campus. We promised one hour—no more, but Aldous found the group so responsive that he stayed until midnight, refreshed and vibrant.

Aldous also lectured at Boston University (arranged by Roy's son David Lamson), at Wellesley and at Harvard, and gave radio and TV interviews on WGBH, the educational station, and the most remarkable thing about this very heavy programme was Aldous's unhurried serenity.

The weeks moved on; Aldous was not going to stay the full semester but leave soon after his seventh and last lecture on 16th November, having to flee, because of that bronchial weakness, before the onset of the New England winter. Meanwhile he had visitors. Laura came; Matthew drove over in his microbus; Humphrey Osmond arrived for a three-day visit on Election Day (Kennedy v. Nixon). "I wish," Aldous had written to Matthew, "one cd feel much enthusiasm for Messrs Kennedy and Johnson.

The thought of old Joe Kennedy, with $200 millions amassed . . . on the stockmarket, lurking in the background of the young crusader is very distasteful. But perhaps the man may turn out to be a winner and a good president—quien sabe? And do we need a good president!

To Humphrey, Aldous spoke of his illness. He said the doctor thought that he had a good chance; enjoined Humphrey not to tell any member of his family as they would worry and it would not help him. Then he dismissed the matter and read out a chapter from *Island*.

Aldous saw a good deal of Huston Smith, Professor of Asian Philosophy at M.I.T. Huston Smith had studied Zen in a monastery in Kyoto, looked after refugees on the border of Tibet; he had met Aldous once before, twenty years ago, when as a very young man he had sought him out in California. At the Los Angeles apartment there was only a Negro maid, who told him what wonderful people she was working for and directed him to Llano. There he found Aldous and Maria. Huston Smith talked to me about the quality of the days he spent with them in the desert. Of Maria . . . Of beginning it all by making up a bed with her . . . "It was so unexpected." Now at M.I.T. he accompanied Aldous on some of his out-of-town engagements (with Aldous punctually appearing thirty to forty seconds before the arranged time and asking, "Anything unusually disastrous happened in the world today?"). Four years after, Huston Smith wrote,[1]

> More impressive than the range of the man's mind, however, was its sympathy and interest. Few major intelligences since William James have been as open. Huxley's regard for mysticism was well known by dint of being so nearly notorious. What some overlooked was equal interest in the workaday world . . . To those who, greedy for transcendence, deprecated the mundane, he counselled that "we must make the best of *both* worlds." To their opposites, the positivists, his word was "All right, one world at a time; but not half a world!"
>
> . . . If he lost his [literary] reputation, it was . . because he wasn't content simply to do what he could do well. His competence bored him. So the master of words moved on to what eludes them, remarking over his shoulder that "language is a device for taking the mystery out of reality." . . .
>
> He could [relegate his writing, as it were] because he had so little egoism. A supreme unpretentiousness characterized him to the end. "It's a bit embarrassing," he said, "to have been concerned with the human problem all one's life and find at the end that one has no more to offer by way of advice than 'Try to be a little kinder.' " If, as he had earlier remarked, the central technique for man to learn is "the art of obtaining freedom from the fundamental human disability of egoism," Huxley achieved that freedom.
>
> But this wasn't his supreme achievement, for his personal problem was . . pessimism—"tomorrow, and tomorrow, and tomorrow, creeps in this petty pace from day to day." His final victory, there-

---

[1] "A Tribute", *The Psychedelic Review*, Vol. I, No. 3, 1964.

fore, lay not in emerging selfless but in winning through to equanimity, to evenness of spirit and a generalized good cheer . . .


Aldous's M.I.T. lectures[1] are important. Much of their material was derived from previous sources, themes and expositions recurrent throughout his work[2]—the lectures are important because, in Roy Lamson's words, they *pull together* so much of Aldous's thought. And this is exactly what the lectures do. *Island*, contemporaneous to the lectures, also pulls together Aldous's thought, if perhaps in a more rigid mould. The great point about Aldous's spoken word—in which, I hope even on paper, one can hear his voice—is, I find, that it is looser, lighter, less didactic and a good deal more concise than some of the essays and expository passages in the novels; there is, as there was in his conversation, a kind of open-endedness about it: speaking as he was, assumedly, *inter pares*, he did not have to wrap it up; he was exploring, and so may we go on exploring after him . . .


Shortly before leaving, Aldous was dining in a small French restaurant in Boston with Patrick Wall and some other friends. "People at a nearby table got up.[3] Aldous was handed an anonymous note." (By the time he opened the note, the people had left.)

'Thank you so much for all the pleasure you have given us.'

"Aldous read it; showed it round; then put it in his pocket. His *look*."

This story brings to my mind the words of Aldous's niece Claire.[4] How often had he not thought of himself as deficient in emotion; yet "When he died," she wrote, "he left such grief behind as only a man of great feeling could have evoked."


[1] The titles of the *What a Piece of Work Is Man* lectures are: 1. Ancient Views of Human Nature. 2. The Contemporary Picture. 3. The Individual in Relation to History. 4. Symbols and Immediate Experience. 5. Why Art? 6. Visionary Experience. 7. Human Potentialities.

[2] And indeed in some of his own previous lectures.

[3] As told to S. B. by Professor Wall.

[4] Claire Nicolas White, "Aldous Huxley, A Reminiscence", in *Soundings*, N.Y. State University, 1962.

# PART TWELVE

## Years of Grace: 1960–1963

He could hold his own in the world: even at his most aloof he has always been, as Degas said of the painter Moreau, "A hermit who knows the times of all the trains."

SIR JOHN COLLIER about
Aldous Huxley

Of all man's miseries the bitterest is this, to know so much and to have control over nothing.

(The words which Herodotus put into the mouth of the Persian who talked with Thersander at Thebes.)

# Chapter One

## "An Interesting Challenge"

AFTER Cambridge, Massachusetts, the Hollywood hills, another winter of sun, peace, hard work. "All goes well here . . . except that everybody is too busy, Laura with her disturbed and unhappy people (what a lot there are, my God . . .) I with my book and arrears of correspondence . . . I've been working like mad . . and hope and pray that I may get the damned thing finished by the spring." There was one more nudge about the literary papers that were stacked "somewhere or other" in the house, a note from Aldous's old friend Jake Zeitlin, who had a customer for the MS of *St Mawr* which D. H. Lawrence had given to Maria. Again Aldous consulted his son. "Now what do you think? Wd you like me to hang on to it and bequeath it to you or the children in my will?

> Or shall I sell it and put the cash into the children's fund? I myself incline to the second alternative, as I have no collector's itch and don't feel sentimental about objects and mementos. But if you prefer, I will keep it.

The year ended well. Aldous had been seen by Dr Cutler and given a clean bill of health.

Of the book nearly all was done except the end and a going over some of the earlier chapters. "This matter of death—how badly we handle it! I have a whole chapter illustrating the art of dying, as practised by my hypothetical islanders—plus other passages concerning the fear of death and the training for its acceptance.

> My own experience with Maria convinced me [to Humphrey] that the living can do a great deal to make the passage easier for the dying, to raise the most purely physiological act of human existence to the level of consciousness and perhaps even of spirituality. The last rites of Catholicism are good, but too much preoccupied with morality and the past. The emphasis has to be on the present and the posthumous future, which one must assume—and I think with justification—to be a reality. Eileen told me that, in one of her contacts with what she was convinced was Maria, there was a message for me to the effect that what I had said had helped to float the soul across the chasm . . .

In January Aldous allowed himself a break, a week in Hawaii with Laura. ". . the motive a wish to look at the islands, the excuse . . some lectures" (at Honolulu). They liked the volcanoes and the forests but not the "frightful Hawaiian music" and the tourists. From this jaunt they went on first to a conference on Mind Control at San Francisco, then to Salem, Oregon, because Aldous wanted to have a look at the state mental hospital which was introducing the open ward system pioneered in England by Maxwell Jones. Then back, for another two months, to the grindstone: "All is pretty well here—tho' I am much too busy with this damned book as Laura is with her therapy."

An Aldous Huxley bibliography[1] had been compiled, and sent to him. "I stand appalled at the thought of all I have written over the years. 'What, Mr Gibbon! Nothing but scribble, scribble, scribble' . . .

"Even the bibliography will be thick, damned and square—and it is merely the logarithm of the millions of scribbled words to which it refers."

In the spring, Aldous went again to M.I.T. for a week of their centennial celebrations. He stayed with the Lamsons, took part in a number of panels with distinguished artists, scientists, engineers, and gave an address on Education on the Non-Verbal Level. A day or two with Matthew in New York, and return to California to polish off the book before a long travelling summer —there were plans for London, France, a conference at Copenhagen, Italy with Laura; India in the autumn. By May, *Island* was nearly done, and Dr Cutler had just told Aldous that he was one of his most successful cases.

In the evening of Friday, 12th May, one of those murderous sage-brush fires sprang up in the Hollywood hills. Fanned by a gale the flames spread up the canyon and house after house was set a-blaze. By nine o'clock 3276 Deronda Drive was on fire, before midnight the house and everything in it was gone.

Aldous and Laura's movements on that night can be reconstructed about as follows. At 7.30 pm Aldous was at home and working; Laura went over to Virginia Pfeiffer's house (empty, as Virginia was away) to feed the cat. From there she first saw fire and realized that this house was menaced. She became strangely paralysed and for some valuable time did nothing, but eventually went to fetch Aldous. When Aldous came, he too stood speechless, though he rescued one box of Virginia's papers. Soon after the house began to burn. Television trucks and police cars began

---

[1] *Aldous Huxley: A Bibliography 1916–1959*, by Claire John Eschelbach and Joyce Lee Shober. Foreword by Aldous Huxley, University of California Press, 1961.

arriving though no fire engines. Aldous and Laura managed to get back to their own house—the road beyond already swept by flames—with the help of a stranger and his car. Here they found that the flames had reached the plants on the slope below their terrace; the house itself was still clear. Aldous went inside and upstairs and got out the manuscript of *Island*. When he came out he said to Laura, "Don't you think I should take some suits?" Laura said yes, but herself remained standing, looking. Aldous re-emerged with three suits on hangers, telling her that she too had better take some clothes. This she did, in slow motion, and also picked up her violin, a Guarnieri. An unknown young boy rescued their car. The fire took over. Still no engines. At midnight Aldous and Laura left the scene, drove down the hill and took refuge from sympathy and reporters in a modest hotel on Franklin Avenue.

Laura, in her book, tells of her own remarkable passivity: ". . something unexplainable happened to me. From that moment [of seeing the flames leaping up the canyon] until the end of the evening I behaved in a way totally contrary to my nature. In emergencies I have usually responded with immediate action. When faced with adverse circumstances, I have hardly ever accepted them; almost always I have tried . . applying whatever intuition, determination, logic I could muster. Here . . . what did I do? I stood immobile, fascinated by the wild grace of the flames . . .

Why did I not immediately take the hose and wet the roof and everything around the house?

At Virginia's house the swimming pool was full.

. . Why did I not call for help? Why did I not take clothes and valuables away? I could easily have packed dozens of suitcases with necessary and some irreplacable things. Instead, what did I do? First, I went into the kitchen, still propelled by my initial purpose of opening a can of cat food . . .

And in their own house, "I was looking—and only looking. How beautiful everything was! The flames from the outside were giving to the white walls a soft rosy glow . . .

'At last,' I thought, 'the perfect illumination.'

"I walked from one room to the other, touching the objects I loved . . . There were cases of letters and diaries and notes for future writings . . . It was usually Aldous and I who took the initiative. But in that moment we were stunned. If a friend had been there he could have awakened us to action. Cases and suit-cases and drawers could have been put in the empty driveway, which remained untouched by the fire . . ."

Next morning Aldous and Laura went back up the hill and saw that indeed everything was gone. Poking in the ashes, Aldous found the one thing that remained, the marble bust of Maria, done when she was fourteen years old. He telephoned Mme Nys —the fire had been visible last night both in the sky and on the television screen—and reassured her, "d'une voix forte et calme". He spoke to Matthew in New York; Anita Loos, faithful friend in every crisis, rang up, to her he said, "It was quite an experience, but it does make one feel extraordinarily *clean*."

It was some days before they were able to take in their loss. Not only were Aldous and Laura homeless and, except for the MS, the three suits and the violin, without belongings, objects, house-hold goods, but Aldous had lost his papers, notebooks, old letters, he had lost his books, some four thousand books with his own working references, annotations, markings, "I am now a man without possessions and without a past," he wrote to his son five days later.

> This last I regret as much for you as for myself; for what has gone is a piece of your life and heart as well as of mine. But there is nothing to do except try to start from scratch.

Not easy. "It is odd to be starting from scratch at my age—" he wrote to Robert Hutchins, "with literally nothing in the way of possessions, books, mementoes, letters, diaries. I am evidently intended to learn a little in advance of the final denudation, that you can't take it with you."

Talking to Humphrey later on, he put it even more starkly: "I took it as a sign that the grim reaper was having a good look at me."

*Time* magazine, too, had a word about Aldous's reaction to the disaster.

> Flames licked through dry grasses and gutted twenty-four luxury homes in Hollywood Hills. Destroyed were author Aldous Huxley's two-storey house, his manuscripts and mementoes of a lifetime. While firemen restrained the nearly blind British author from running into the blaze, Huxley wept like a child.[1]

[1] *Time*, 26th May 1961.

This was one of the few occasions on which Aldous picked up the public cudgels.[1]

> Sir,
>     As an old hand at fiction, may I congratulate the write-up artist who penned the account of my actions on the night my house was burned down (May 12).
>     The facts are these. My wife and I started the evening at the house, a little way down the road, of an absent friend. Having rescued a box of her papers and tried in vain to locate the cat, we left this house in flames and were driven back to our own home by a friendly onlooker. Here we picked up a few clothes, my wife's Guarnieri violin, and the MS of the book on which I have been working for the past two years. By the time these had been taken to the car, the house was burning. There was nothing we could do, and all the local fire engines (though not the TV trucks) were somewhere else.
>     So we got into the car and drove away—sadly enough, goodness knows, but (ignoring those conventions of the romantic novelette to which your write-up artist so faithfully adhered) not crying like babies, nor requiring to be restrained from running back into the flames.
>
> Aldous Huxley

Offers of hospitality poured in from the Kiskaddens, the Wendels, the Stravinskys; Aldous decided to hole himself up with Gerald Heard at Santa Monica and finish *Island* (". . 'tho at the moment writing seems difficult"). Laura with Virginia Pfeiffer, of course also homeless, moved into a rented house.

Besides Aldous's library and the fragments of two unfinished novels,[2] there had gone all those collector's items[3] he had failed to sell in time—a first edition of Voltaire's *Candide* which had belonged to Aldous's grandfather T. H. H. who had travelled with it across the world (as had Aldous), first editions of *Du Côte de chez Swann* and *Lady Chatterley's Lover*; signed volumes by T. S. Eliot, Pound, Wells and Gide; forty letters from D. H. Lawrence to Aldous and Maria, letters from Max Beerbohm, Virginia Woolf, Valéry, Elinor Wylie, H. L. Mencken, Wells and Bennett; a large number of MSS of Aldous's works, among them *Antic Hay* and *Point Counter Point*. The most valuable single item, always

---

[1] *Time*, 16th June 1961.

[2] One of them most likely the historical one on Catherine of Siena.

[3] I am indebted for this listing to the kindness of Mr Jacob Zeitlin, who at the time made a valuation for Aldous. It is bound to be rather incomplete as it was based on Aldous's memory of his possessions.

from the bibliophile's point of view, was the MS of D. H. L.'s *St Mawr*. The irreparable loss for Aldous (and for Aldous's biographers) was Maria's pre-war journal and Maria's letters to her sister Suzanne; these were letters written during her last twelve years or so with the expressed purpose of leaving a record of Aldous's life (. . "pour raconter la vie d'Aldous . ."). How did these letters happen to be in the house? Because Aldous, beginning to think about writing his own memoirs, had asked Suzanne for their return. They had arrived from Holland only a short time ago and were still in their original box or boxes.

Worse. "Yes," Aldous wrote to Eileen Garrett, "all the MSS were burned and all my letters from others and in the case of Maria, my letters to her." These were the letters Aldous had written to the girl he was in love with, from London, from Garsington, as a master at Eton, day after day during the years of separation in the First World War, after Maria had been whisked off to Italy by her mother; the letters Maria had re-read and tied up again and taken with her to America when they left the Sanary house in 1937. They are gone; as are the letters of that time to Aldous from Maria. "So there is no more tangible link with the past. It is an interesting challenge and I hope I shall be able to cope with it properly."

## Chapter Two

## London—Summer 1961

ON 15th June (*Island* finished) Aldous arrived in London. Julian and Juliette met him at the airport. Having builders in their house, they took him to a service flat in Kensington.[1] The rooms gave on to a large garden full of trees, and he was delighted by this and the country quiet. Aldous had not been in England since the summer of 1958. It was a few weeks before his sixty-seventh birthday: to his friends he looked thin, lath-thin, and he had gone very grey; he still moved lightly, and he looked elegant, dandified and at the same time of transcendant distinction. Here is how he appeared to someone who had not seen him before, Rosamond Lehmann:[2]

> . . . photographs had not prepared me for his extraordinary, his unique beauty. It was like being all at once in the presence of someone of another and higher planetary order. This may sound extravagant and trite as well; but there was really something angelic, in the strict sense, about his physical appearance: I mean he seemed at first sight a luminous intelligence incarnate.

It was the fifth return to England since they went away in 1937, his fifth return in twenty-four years. Maria once said that if Aldous felt any nostalgia at all for Europe in their early American days, it was not for Italy, not for France, but for English trees, the English countryside. Then that too, she said, dried up. Aldous passed through a period of indifference, the past became encumbrance, indulgence; the first return in 1948—no eagerness about it—was dealt to him by circumstances (involvement with a film; almost identically the pattern that had originally brought him to California). Now that, too, lay behind. He came and went at ease; at home; detached; attached. This year he revisited scenes of his childhood. The remarkable thing is that he was able to do so—that corner of rural Surrey, the country west of Godalming and Milford, where he had spent the fourteen steady years of his happy, his very happy, late-Victorian and Edwardian childhood, with its fields and woods and houses was still recognizable and there: Laleham, the house in the parish of Compton Aldous was

---

[1] At 4 Ennismore Gardens.
[2] In a B.B.C. broadcast, August 1964.

born in; Prior's Field, the school his mother had founded, its land intact and functioning as a school (the portrait of Julia Frances Huxley in the hall, WE LIVE BY ADMIRATION HOPE AND LOVE engraved upon the gate); Hillside, the Huxley boys' preparatory school.

On the Saturday after Aldous's arrival, Julian had to attend a meeting of the governors of Prior's Field and Aldous went with him. While they did their work, Aldous took himself for a long walk. When Julian joined him again, he found him full of joy—remembered haunts, the trees he had seen planted and which were now sixty feet high and looked as if they had been there for three hundred years. One of the oddest changes, he remarked, were the tangles of brambles and wild roses on what were once smooth grassy slopes; rabbits used to eat the young shoots as they came up, and now the rabbits were exterminated. Before going home Aldous asked to be taken to the cemetery, to Compton and the small hill-side graveyard where his and Julian's parents and Trevenen were buried in one grave.

> We were both strangely moved [Julian in his *Memories*] to see that wild meadow saxifrage, one of Mother's favourite flowers, had sprung up on the grassy grave, and were in full bloom; they seemed a spontaneous tribute of the nature that both my parents had so much loved.

Here, Aldous was overcome with grief.

When presently he spent a long weekend with Gervas and his wife, Elspeth, in their house in Wiltshire, Gervas too drove him into Surrey to have a look at what had been their prep school. Hillside, at that point about to be converted, was a shell, yet Aldous was still able to place everything. Out here was the giant-stride . . Here was our cubicle . . Here was the stage (where the two boys and Lewis Gielgud did *The Merchant of Venice*) . . Here was the blackboard . . .

On his first Tuesday in London Aldous, on Dr Cutler's advice, had a consultation with a specialist, Sir Stanford Cade, the surgeon. "He confirmed Cutler's diagnosis, admired the excellent job Cutler did . . ." Aldous wrote to Laura. "So this is all very satisfactory." The same night Aldous went to the theatre to see *The Devils of Loudun* in John Whiting's adaptation which had been playing in the West End since February. (He thought production and performance excellent, and wrote to John Whiting to tell him so. On 27th June, he and Aldous had a talk about *The Devils* on the B.B.C.)

During the first minutes of our meeting, I, too, only saw the greyness and the frailty. When Aldous began to speak animation took over. The year before I had been reporting the *Lady Chatterley* trial and Aldous surprised me by treating the whole business much less solemnly than had our eminent literary and sociological experts in the witness box. He dismissed the four-letter words— "Poor Lawrence, well, I mean, this is simply one of the ways in which a novelist can *not* do it." He delighted me by his whole-hearted rejection of the new French novels of the Robbe-Grillet variety—"unutterably boring. Well, they just bore me stiff . . . I don't think they ever express *anything* . . ." The subject I could not help talking about was the fire, of which Aldous spoke with the detachment we find in the letters. How did he do it, I asked, hoping to learn a way to stoicism, how did you begin again? "Well, I went out," he said, "and bought a toothbrush." Concern about Aldous's appearance waned because of the matter of fact energy he displayed. We had been dining at Rules off the Strand and afterwards walked towards St Paul's; from there we turned west again through Holborn and New Oxford Street (where Aldous commented on the fashion dummies in the windows looking like Jackie Kennedy this year); it was he who decided when to cross a road. At St Giles' Circus the traffic streams were particularly confusing; Aldous firmly stopped my dithering and steered me across. We wandered about Bloomsbury for a while, headed towards Regent's Park—the night was very warm; when we reached my door north of the Marylebone Road it must have been after the best part of a two hours' walk. Only then, with no sense of urgency, did Aldous decide that he might as well go back to Kensington in a cab.

Nor was it that his days were exactly inactive. He had to prepare his speech for the Congress on Applied Psychology in Copenhagen; he gave long interviews; he was not even altogether rid yet, as it turned out, of the book he had just finished. Ian Parsons and Cass Canfield had been corresponding about the length of some of the discursive passages in *Island*. They hesitated about approaching him. In their long publishing association with Aldous, neither had ever dreamt of asking him to change a comma. (As a point of fact, Aldous *had* once been given, and taken, Ian's advice, and cut some of the horror in the torture scenes of the English, though not the American, edition of *The Devils of Loudun*.) Ian decided to talk to Aldous and did so soon after his arrival. Aldous, to his relief, took it with calm professionalism, agreeing that some passages might well be too lengthy. He went through his text again and made some cuts, which must have caused some chopping and changing, as he appears to have had the book retyped. For the rest, he went about seeing people. He looked up Dr Felix Mann, the young acupuncturist with whom he had been in correspondence, "to talk acupuncture and, professionally, to be practised on." Previously he had written:

> I was glad to get your description of yourself. Long acquaintance with your namesake, Thomas, had led me to visualize you as an eccentric German of about 65. It is very gratifying to find that I was mistaken!

To Laura he reported that Dr Mann cures people "who can't be cured by other doctors (mostly chronic cases). The state health service pays him to spend a day each week acupuncturing difficult patients in a public hospital—a good mark in favour of official medicine in England. He felt my pulse, found general health good, but detected a certain weakness in kidneys and liver, which he tonified with needles in the foot and knee . . ."

Aldous had dinner with Dr William Sargant (having read his *Battle for the Mind*) to talk psychotherapy; dinner with his friends at Chatto's, Ian Parsons and Norah Smallwood, who gave a party for him at which he met Iris Murdoch; went to see his old friend Moura Budberg who was living round the corner, and his old friends Harold and Vera Raymond in Kent; saw Huxley grandchildren and cousins at Julian and Juliette's, went to tea with Ethel Sands. And there was Enid Bagnold. They hadn't seen each other for rather more than half a century.

> "I'm Enid Bagnold," I said.[1] "I was at Prior's Field. You were an odious little boy."
> Aldous (leaning about like a serpent) "I'm ODIOUS still!"
> But this time it was said with humour—like an indulgent bogeyman. I told him the little story. [About him, aged seven, snubbing her efforts of conversation at Mrs Huxley's table.]

He saw Rosamond Lehmann.

> . . He let me describe an overwhelming mystical experience. He told me I was very fortunate, said that he himself had never had one, adding with characteristic humility, "Perhaps I don't love enough."
> . . . I know that personally he radiated something that made it impossible to say one liked him—one had to think of him in terms of love.[2]

1 Enid Bagnold in conversation with, and letter to, S. B.
2 Rosamond Lehmann in B.B.C. broadcast.

People every day. Yet so many of Aldous's old friends were away or dead or ill, that he found London rather sad, he wrote to Laura. "Not all the time, however,

> for the colouring is so beautiful when the sun comes out, and the foliage and flowers are so rich that I find myself at moments almost in an LSD state. And I have met some very nice people; so don't let me complain.

It was Laura whom he missed very much—though here, too, he would not complain—and he wrote to her almost every day. (As well as being occupied with patients and her book, Laura was staying on in California to look after Virginia, who had broken her collar-bone.) He had been thinking of her all day, Aldous wrote in one of those letters,[1]

> with a strange kind of intensity—thinking how extraordinary you are in your power and your vulnerability, your capacity for loving and your "noli me tangere" passion for being left alone . . . I would like to feel that I could—would like to feel that I can love you with so much understanding tenderness that I shall always know what to do, or what to refrain from doing in order to help you in your strength and support you in your vulnerability . . .

This letter ends with,

> Be well, my sweetheart, and let us try to be happy and peaceful malgré tout—because of one another.

At Moura Budberg's, Aldous had met Professor Tolstoy (a distant relative of the great Tolstoy), come to London in charge of a Soviet scientific exhibition, who urged him to visit Russia. What about it? Aldous asked Laura. What about their both going for a week or two after Copenhagen?

> . . My own feeling is that we should go to Russia. I have never been anxious to go; but Tolstoy's extreme cordiality and obvious desire to be helpful have changed my feelings, and I think we ought to take the opportunity that is being presented to us. (Maybe this is one of the hints for which I have been waiting!) [Since the onset of his illness, since finishing *Island*, Aldous had been asking himself about the best use he ought to make of his life.]
> . . . Professor Tolstoy . . [would] arrange for us to see whatever we like. I told him that you and I were particularly interested in the

---

[1] Published, not in the collected edition, but in *This Timeless Moment*.

preventive medicine and mental health side of Russian life, and he would undoubtedly be able to get us into hospitals, rest homes, clinics etc. Let me know as soon as possible what you feel about this project . . .

. . . Goodbye, my darling. I don't imagine that either of us will ever be able to do what St Ignatius said he could do. [Father Ignatius's well-known reply when asked what he would do if the Pope dissolved the Society of Jesus and thus swept away his life work, "One quarter of an hour in orison and it would be all the same."] But even if the final All Rightness of the world may never be vouchsafed to us as a permanent experience (only perhaps in flashes), I believe we can do quite a lot—you complementing me, I complementing you—to achieve a relative all rightness for ourselves and a few other people in the midst of the awful all wrongness of what Keats called "the giant misery of the world." Ti voglio bene.

Laura was interested in the Russian visit, and Aldous went to the Soviet Consulate for his visa. "What a mess!

First of all half an hour's wait, because the consul hadn't turned up. When he did turn up, he was single-handed . . so everything took a very long time. Finally I asked for my visa: but it seems that unless one is travelling in one of the Intourist Groups, one has to have an official invitation to go. Of course I *could* get such an invitation from the Writers' Group there—but (a) there is not much time for this ' and (b) I don't want to go officially . . . meanwhile there is the problem of hotels, about which the consul was gloomy. So it really looks as though our Russian trip is off. Do you mind very much? Another year we will make the necessary arrangements 6 months in advance. Last minute plans are unworkable these days. Now I must go and see if we can get rooms at Gstaad.

For meanwhile Laura had given the date of her coming over and they planned to meet in Switzerland where Krishnamurti and the Yehudi Menuhins were going to be.

. . Krishnaji . . came yesterday to see me for a few minutes [Aldous to Laura]—looked well, but also curiously different from what he used to be; for he is now a small bright old man, with a bald head ringed by white hair. But I was very glad to see him . . .

The long recorded interview, often referred to in the course of this narrative as the London interview, took place that summer— two long afternoons, punctuated by tea and sherry, in Aldous's sitting-room with the leafy view in Ennismore Gardens. The range of subjects was very wide; Aldous, as the case might be, responded to John Chandos, his interviewer, side-stepped or expanded. The point of the interview is that it has left us with such a characteristic record not only of Aldous's thought but of Aldous's way of expressing it; more informal still than his lectures, than his radio and television broadcasts—there was no time limit, no audience: he was talking to one man who himself talked a good deal—this record comes as near as anything to the way Aldous talked to his friends. *This was* his conversation. I shall come back to this record once again; here I would like to place a few of Aldous's comments and ideas on one thing and another. Some will sound familiar to all who knew him.

Writers. Writers of our time. Is there anyone, in your opinion, who will survive? who will be read?

Aldous: I don't know. A difficult question. [Pause] For some reason no *one* author has had a great influence over me. I get things out of all reasonably good authors and even out of some bad authors . . But as to naming any one of them who had a great influence on me—I've often been asked this question . . . I don't get as much out of James as some people say they get out of him. I never found him very interesting.

I used to get a lot out of Proust. I re-read some of it the other day and was rather disappointed—I don't know why. I read the last volume, *Le Temps Retrouvé*, it seemed to me curiously remote and—unbelievable and unreal.

And even the first volume . . which I thought was very beautiful in the early days—I didn't get very much out of it . . . It's very strange, because it moved me immensely when it first appeared. I must have another look at it.

Well, I think some of Hemingway's stories are *very* remarkable, his short stories. I haven't read any of the more recent books which I understand are not very good.

Nor have I read any recent Faulkners. I liked some of the early books very much. *Soldier's Pay* and *Light in August* and *Sanctuary*—but I confess I haven't read anything recently.

That subject soon ran dry. "Which do you find the most interesting art products in our time, music, literature, painting?"

I suppose there have been interesting ones in all, haven't there? I find myself out of sympathy with some . . . I personally get very bored with this endless repetition of non-representational expressionism, which goes on and on and on. But the trend towards abstraction was a very useful and valuable one in the earlier phases. I think it's *time we grew out of it*. But most painters don't. Music—

music is *very far* away . . . it seems to me that fully self-conscious and artistic music is far remoter from popular music than Tallis was remote from Greensleeves. It *was* remote from Greensleeves but not *nearly* as remote as Boulez, say, from *My Fair Lady*.

And this doesn't seem to me to be at all a healthy situation—when you have an immense gap between the ordinary taste and the taste of the highly refined and educated. It's a fact; but is it a *desirable* fact? There just is *no communication* . . . These are things which puzzle me extremely: I just have no idea what happens when you get this kind of *gap* between the masses of the people and the high priests of their culture. It's a most unfortunate phenomenon.

### Literature?

Well, there is a slight tendency in the same direction. Extremely obscure poetry. But there, it seems to me, you get a number of good writers who *are* prepared to communicate to more people than the good composers as a rule are prepared to communicate.

### The present trend of literary and historical criticism?

I do think it's inferior, quite definitely. After all, life *is* immensely complex, so why pretend that it isn't. Why not attempt . . . to make some kind of synthesis, some kind of meaningful pattern? . . . I find this new kind of criticism unspeakably *boring*. It seems to me so barren—and this hideous jargon they've invented—I don't know what it's all about—it *bores* me absolutely stiff, this whole thing. It seems so *trivial* . . .

Probably some of this work has to be done—this kind of very elaborate, meticulous linguistic work is probably useful, but re-garded as the be all and end all of criticism it seems to be *absolutely absurd*.

Does anyone want to read him [the modern critic]? *I* don't want to read him . . . perhaps his fellow critics want to read him . . . Do people at large get much out of him? Perhaps they do. *I* don't happen to get much out of him.

. . Literary criticism is not the best way of criticizing life as it is today—there's a pharisaical element in it . . .

At one point they talk about the relation of content to style, the simple against the rich. Aldous says,

. . . I don't really like the bare bold classical style—because it is to my mind hopelessly over-simplified and therefore not true. Life . . . is incredibly complex and very very subtle—therefore I would say that any form of art which is as simplified as, say, the French tragedy of the seventeenth century is intrinsically an inferior art—it may be very elegant and beautiful—but if you can impose order on a much more complex mass of material as Shakespeare was able to do, this seems to me an intrinsically superior form of art . . . A great composition where enormous numbers of elements, both formal and literary in the widest sense, and emotional, are brought together and harmonized . . . is a higher form of art than the simple, elegant, so-called classical form.

A need for new forms?

Take composers of the grand period, like Mozart, or early John Sebastian Bach—they had this immense advantage that they had a tradition which they were quite prepared to exploit to the limit . . . and when you listen to both of them, you have this extraordinary sense of *good faith* in them, I mean they are never trying to produce effects for the sake of effects, they are never trying to produce originality for the sake of originality . . . They are content to work within a medium which they completely accepted and which they developed to the most extraordinary limits . . .

Now we have reached a point where we really don't accept any tradition without question and we run through an immense capital of artistic forms and are continually trying to amass new capital and exploit new forms, and so much of contemporary artistic effort is somehow *spent* in this *desperate* procedure of trying to find wholly novel methods of saying things . . . This is particularly true of music I would say, and also of painting, to some extent of literature—this kind of simple good faith in the expression of simple emotions in what appears to be a simple, but is in effect an extremely subtle mode: this is awfully difficult now. It is inconceivable now for us, you see, to write the kind of melodies, or the kind of contra-puntal arrangements, which Bach and Mozart did . . . It's really unfortunate—an enormous amount of artistic energy has to go into work which for the older composers had already been done for them . . the main structure had been laid down and they were ready to accept this, with minor modifications of course all the time . . In this sense we are curiously badly off in comparison with those people in the past . . .

What *is* the relation of the artist to his time?

The relation between life and art? *I don't know.* It's much less *clear* than some critics maintain that it is—there are other factors: this internal logic of art is of immense importance in the whole history of the development of the arts, and has very little to do with external events. Take Schuetz, for example, his life consisted of continually running away from the Thirty Years' War, he lived in the middle of the most appalling circumstances—but you can see no trace of this in his music at all . . .

. . . I have this curious feeling that this extraordinary roulette wheel of heredity plays such a part in literature. Sometimes you get twenty-seven reds in a row at Monte Carlo, and this may happen in certain periods of history—with an extraordinary series of people turning up, who happen to have a fairly good environment and can do something with it. After all, the advances in literature *depend* on these purely fortuitous arrivals of extraordinary people. I mean, nobody could have conceivably foreseen Shakespeare . . Nothing in Russian literature could have told one that Tolstoy would come along . . .

Presently they discussed the Ideal Society:

Well, I don't know whether any age has done it completely. The Greeks did probably pretty well up to a point. But the Greeks had appalling limitations—their whole view of women was utterly unsatisfactory; they had no adequate kind of marriage, no view of permanent love relationships between the sexes. In that way they were frightfully limited. On the other hand they handled the problem of the irrational very well . . . I don't know enough about older civilizations . . Many of them obviously did it pretty well . . The Chinese did . . But I'm quite sure that we could improve upon it. I don't think that *we* do it very well.

The Church now, the Catholic Church—"How do you see its role in the history of Europe? As an instrument of repression? or of enlightenment?"

. . I'm not an historian, of course . . I should say it did both: it did *preserve* culture and learning, and it did *repress* learning . . . The whole thing is so ambivalent. In some ways it did good, in others it did an enormous amount of harm.

And if the Reformation could have been postponed?

. . . We would have had the rise of scepticism, of Voltaireanism—*les Libertins* rather than Protestantism and a second and even more violent and intense religion than the old Catholic one. The wars of religion might have been avoided. That would have been a good thing. Those wars were *unspeakably* horrible.

Is there a need of organized religion? Historically, it looks like that, said Aldous, then went off on his own:

> I hope it's possible to have an a-septic mysticism. I think certain people can have it; but whether there can be a general atmosphere on the basis of a non-superstitious and non-dogmatic set of beliefs, I've no idea. I profoundly hope so. But at certain times I rather doubt it. I mean, the human mind *is a symbolific instrument*. It exists to manufacture symbols . . to turn immediate experience into symbols for the purpose of managing it in a fairly convenient way. The question is, can we get on with scientific symbols, realist symbols, and then concentrate on the immediate experience? I simply don't know whether this is a possible general attitude towards the world. It's certainly possible in isolated individuals . . . Whether it will ever turn out something that appeals to a great number of people, I have no idea.
>
> . . . This whole problem of dealing with the irrational is surely to find out means by which these irrational drives can be given satisfaction without harming the person who has the drives and without harming his neighbours—it is not beyond the wit of man to devise these methods. This is something William James discussed years ago in his essay "The Moral Equivalent of War." This is an inadequate essay, but it touches on one aspect of an extraordinarily important way of dealing with human beings . . of dealing with the irrational side of man. Which requires satisfaction . . . The most difficult problem of reason is—how can we allow the irrational its proper scope within a general framework of rationality and benevolence?
>
> Empirically all cultures have worked out various methods . . . The Greek method of Maenadism, Bacchic orgies and so on, were all methods of getting rid of these *intolerable tensions* in society in harmless and even beneficient ways . . . Carnivals, saturnalia . . . and I think that one of our troubles is that we haven't got enough of these devices. Christianity became so wildly respectable that it gave up *dancing*. Which was a *grave mistake*, it seems to me.
>
> Muscular actions have great importance. It's very significant that the extremely, quotes, *spiritual* sect of the Quakers *quaked*. Here there was this voluntary quaking movement of the muscles which was an immense release . . . this was an empirical invention of great value . . . And any civilization that seriously takes account of man's nature tends to invent these kind of things; they've been invented again and again by primitive and even by quite advanced people, and we made the awful mistake of dropping the lot of them. The best we can do is Rock and Roll, which is something which the boys and girls had to invent for themselves—but there is no sort of social or religious sanction for this . . whereas in the past there was.

"To be satisfactory, haven't these activities got to be linked with some, let us say, religious authority?"

There is no particular reason why people shouldn't be realistic about them . . We didn't have to say that when the Quakers quaked or the Shakers shook this was necessarily the operation of the Holy Ghost . . They were getting rid of tensions . . . I think we can talk about this in realistic terms without invoking supernatural explanations. But at the same time, what we may call the sort of basic supernaturalism, what we may call the life force, are of value in so far as they permit basic sources of energy and enlightenment to flow freely through an organism which is constantly blocking itself up and obstructing itself by the operation of the conscious ego. There are *ways* of *getting rid* of the *conscious ego*, of *getting out of our own light*. Which is of course what everybody has been talking about since the beginning of time.

And I think we are now in a position to be able to talk about it in more or less naturalistic terms and not necessarily in these supernatural terms . . .

Every now and then the questions would take a personal turn. Literary plans?

I would very much like to find another good biographical or historical episode such as I dealt with in *Grey Eminence* . . and the essay on Maine de Biran . . . For the moment I haven't been able to find something which I could tackle well . . .

"Have you still any interest in writing for the theatre, Mr Huxley?"

Hm, yes, sometime I might write another play . . .

There were of course long passages dealing with immediate sociological problems. These, however, overlap, not textually but in substance, with another interview of that summer, a B.B.C. interview with John Morgan, telecast on 23rd July. Here one saw Aldous, looking fragile, gently attending to each question—the fraction of a pause, hear the flowing answer, the clear voice, often rising to a higher note . . . The programme was introduced by a few bars from the slow movement of Beethoven's A-minor quartet.

John Morgan: Mr Huxley, you've described that passage . . as the greatest music ever written—now why do you think that?
Aldous: Well, I would say that it's the greatest of its kind, though

unfortunately that was such a small snatch of it that we didn't get the full impression of this kind of sublime serenity in the music; and then of course it goes on into a very extraordinary passage where there's the counter-point of two melodies playing against one another, and doing this thing which only music can do, saying two things at the same time, something which, as a writer, I would long to be able to do, but the nature of language is such that one can't do it, one can't say two things at the same time.

J. M.: Would you like to have been a composer?

A.: Well, only if I'd been a prodigious genius—well, I would like to have been a prodigious genius in anything. But unfortunately, I love music but as for understanding what it must be like to be able to think in terms of musical sequences, I just don't know; I mean, I feel in relation to the great composers, as a dog must feel in relation to a human being. That those are creatures of another order altogether.

J. M.: . . . you've derived a very rich experience from a lifetime study of both art and society, would you say . . . more rich from art?

A.: Surely in a sense the two things are different. Art springs from . . . a very deep, what may be called an urge to order . . . an almost instinctive urge in human beings to impose order upon the profusion and chaos of existence . . . The whole problem of society is to find a way of imposing order, without imposing a too rigid order . . .

And from this, by way of *Brave New World*, they came to the menace of a technological take-over.

A.: . . I think when the . . scientific means are developed they just tend to be *used* . . . if you plant the seeds of applied science or technology it proceeds to grow. . . hence the sense which many people have . . . that man is now the victim of his own technology . . . instead of being in control of it.

J. M.: How could he be in control of it?

A.: . . . I think this is perhaps one of the major problems of our time. How do we make use of this thing? After all, this was stated in the gospel . . the Sabbath was made for man and not man for the Sabbath, and in the same way, technology was made for man, not man for technology, but unfortunately [we have] created a world in which man seems to be made for technology . . .

. . in the West we still remember John Stuart Mill, James Mill, Jefferson and so on, we still remember vaguely the precepts of Christianity, and we are a little reluctant . . to allow technology to take over. In the long run we generally succumb. I'm reminded of the line in Byron's "Don Juan" about this lady who vowing she would ne'er consent, consented . . . In the short run we sort of higgle-haggle about it and we are reluctant, but we tend to be pushed by the advancing technology in a certain direction . . . We do have to start thinking how we can get control again of our own inventions. This is a kind of Frankenstein monster problem.

J. M.: . . . You did say that over-population, over-organization were the great problems now?

A.: They're closely related. It's quite obvious that where you have a very rapidly rising population with its extreme pressures on food and production; upon problems of getting enough education, housing and so on, you necessarily must have a higher and higher degree of organization . . . you have to have organization comparable in complexity and tightness to the technology that has to be worked. I think the two things run hand in hand—technology, over-population, over-organization, are three factors which work together and which are all pushing us . . .

J. M.: . . . isn't it always possible, while human beings remain much as they are, that they will find means of over-throwing modern, scientific dictatorship?

A.: Well I would like to think so. But do reflect on this simple fact. For example in the revolution of 1848, when the crowds put up the barricades and resisted the soldiers, the arms on either side . . were about equal—they were just muskets. But now, on one side you may have muskets and on the other side you will have tanks and flame-throwers and, if the air force remains faithful to the regime, you will have aeroplanes dropping bombs and firing machine-guns from above. It is obviously much more difficult now to overthrow by force; the other thing is that the modern government has incomparably more efficient methods first of propaganda and then of information. I mean if you compare Napoleon's Chief of Police, Fouché, with any efficient police force today, it's childish what he could do . . .

Questions about *Island, Antic Hay*, D. H. Lawrence, Mrs Grundy, LSD versus alcoholism, then back full circle to the "major problems of the rest of this century."

A.: . . First of all there is this question are we going to blow ourselves up or not. I think and hope that we shall not. But if we don't then the most urgent problem of the next fifty and I would say a hundred years or more, is the problem of explosive population increase. In this country of course it's not a major problem, but when you go to countries in Central America or in South America, and find increases at the rate of three percent per annum, which doubles the population in twenty-four years, what on earth do you do if you're an under-developed country? Even if you can solve the food problem, which in many cases they probably can, what do you do about the housing problem, about the educational problem, how do you build enough schools, how do you find enough teachers—what do you do about the roads and sewage systems . . . ?

John Morgan asked if nevertheless it were not possible, given the will and abandoning preparation for war, to raise everyone's standard of living?

    A.: I think it is. But the point is that it does look as if quantity were the enemy of quality on this matter. After all, it isn't simply a question of food, it's a question of is it pleasant to live in a town of ten million inhabitants such as Tokyo is? Is it pleasant to live in a place with fourteen hundred people to the square mile such as Barbados is? This seems to me the problem. Is life under such conditions as good as life where, as throughout nature, there is a balance between the birth-rate and the death-rate, where you have a kind of stable population, based on a low birth-rate and a low death-rate, where you can plan ahead . . and where it is possible to organize the good life much better.

    J. M.: Are you hopeful or pessimistic about the rest of the century?

    A.: I think I am both. We have it within our power, I think, *to do extraordinary things* if we want to. The question is do we want to enough? And also do we have enough—it's not merely a question of good will, it's a question of extreme intelligence . . .

## Chapter Three

## Travels—An *Amende Honorable*

ALDOUS left London on the 15th of July to go to Eileen Garrett's for another of her parapsychological conferences at Le Piol in the South of France. (A spacious house, terraces, shade trees, flowering shrubs, a pool.) Eileen found him low in spirit. When she suggested ways of replacing his burned books, he discouraged her; he hadn't got enough time, he said. "You have some time." "Not enough."

The conference started. Psychiatrists, neurologists, French, Italian, Dutch. "Quite interesting group . . .

a Swiss or two, the Englishman Gray Walter [to Laura] . . very bright and well-informed. And of course Eileen in the midst of it—mostly silent, but sometimes describing her experiences very well, and making comments, generally very sensible . . .

On an off day, Eileen took Aldous for a long drive up into the barren country in the mountains above Vence. There he talked to her about D. H. Lawrence.

On the 21st, Jeanne Neveux with Noële came to pick him up. They spent the night in Aix-en-Provence. "I had forgotten how beautiful Aix is—a town with fountains and very sober, noble 17th-century houses. It was a pleasure to see [it] again." Next day they drove up the valley of the Rhône to Vaison-la-Romaine where once more a play of Georges Neveux's was being staged for the Festival. "The countryside is very beautiful—vineyards, orchards, wind-breaks of cypress trees.

But the agriculture is becoming completely mechanized, industrialized, chemically controlled as in America. They have now reached a point at which they can make half a dozen different types of wine out of the same batch of grape juice . . .

At Vaison the lodgings were the same he and Maria had had in 1954. With the Neveuxes he went to Georges' *Voyage de Thésée* in the Roman theatre, and the next night to *Troilus and Cressida*. "Aldous very happy," noted Jeanne. ("If I dared to wish for genius," he once wrote, "I would ask for the grace to write *Troilus* and *The Canterbury Tales*.") In the mornings he waited impatiently for the post. Rina came; proceeded to wash his shirts and generally look after him; he accepted it.

. . Rina, who came to us in 1924, when she was 13, turned up at Vaison to see me. Such a wonderful example of the most civilized and noble kind of peasant of the old school. She is now a woman of 50, married to a younger man (very happily) who has worked his way up to the head of a transport company . . Rina organizes the whole business and at the same time retains all her old qualities of simplicity, kindness, native common sense and goodness. One has a sad feeling that people of this kind are becoming rarer and rarer . . .

On their third day he had a long talk with Jeanne. He spoke about 1954; about the letters that were gone; about his feelings for Laura—the desire he now had to *give* . . . Jeanne offered to let him have her own letters from Maria. He said, We'll see . . . later perhaps . . .

On the 26th Jeanne took him to Orange to catch the early morning train to Geneva. Aldous was absent and remote and did not leave a forwarding address. He never returned to France.

Next day, in a hired car, he met Laura at the airport and they went on to Gstaad. The ten days in Switzerland were good ones. They had rooms in one of those large, old-fashioned hotels, the Palace; the weather was brilliant. "Laura has rejoined me [to Humphrey] and we breathe good air, eat large meals and listen to Krishnamurti . . ." The Menuhins were there.

Yehudi Menuhin and Aldous knew each other for a few years only. They met seldom but there was a kinship. When they were together, says Yehudi's wife, Diana, they were like brothers: "holding hands spiritually."

How sad those unforgettable reunions à quatre, so spread in space— from Gstaad through London to Los Angeles—should have been so confined in time . . .[1]

Krishnamurti was giving some talks at Gstaad; they were, Aldous wrote, "among the most impressive things I ever listened to.

It was like listening to a discourse of the Buddha—such power, such intrinsic authority, such an uncompromising refusal to allow the *homme moyen sensuel* any escapes or surrogates, any *gurus*, saviours, *führers*, churches. "I show you sorrow and the ending of sorrow"—

[1] Yehudi Menuhin, *Mem. Vol.*

and if you don't choose to fulfil the conditions for ending sorrow, be prepared, whatever gurus, churches etc you may believe in, for the indefinite continuance of sorrow.


Aldous and Laura went to Turin on 7th August for a few days with her family, thence on to Copenhagen for the Congress of Applied Psychology. On their return they stopped at Basle and met Dr Albert Hofmann, who had first synthesized lysergic acid. Then back to Italy for some weeks with Laura's sister at Torre del Mare on the Ligurian coast. On 12th September Aldous went again to London, staying with Julian and Juliette; Laura flew back to California. He followed her before the beginning of October, by way of New York and a weekend shared between the Lamsons at Cambridge, Massachusetts, and Colgate University at Hamilton, New York.

In Los Angeles, Virginia Pfeiffer had moved, with splendid courage, into a house quite near her old one. (The drought persisted and there was in fact that autumn another vast fire nearby.) Here, at 6233 Mulholland Highway, she offered hospitality to Aldous—"A simple, white-washed bedroom [Laura writing] overlooking a large expanse of the still wild Hollywood hills."

However, Aldous's travels for that year were by no means over. On 7th November he and Laura flew off to Hong Kong on their way to what he called a headlong trip to India. They attended the Congress celebrating Tagore's centenary at New Delhi; spent a few days at Madras; stopped at Agra, Bombay, and Colombo; continued to Japan. "*India is almost infinitely depressing.*" (Aldous had used identically these words in 1926.) ". . there seems to be no solution to its problems in any way that any of us wd regard as acceptable . . .


. . And of course, so long as the more prosperous countries spend 40% of their revenues on armaments, nothing effective can be done about India and all the other places in the same fix. *Quos Deus vult perdere, prius dementat.*


"He was received, of course, with immense respect . . ." writes Isaiah Berlin,[1] who was a fellow delegate at the Congress. "We—Huxley, the American delegate Mr Louis Untermeyer and I—went to a reception at which six or seven hundred students came to do him homage and collect his autograph. There was dead silence as he stood, distinguished and embarrassed, looking beyond

---

[1] *Mem. Vol.*

their heads. An ironical young man broke the silence with some such words as these:

> After the late Mr Gandhi the Taj Mahal is certainly the most precious possession of the Indian people. Why then, did you, Mr Huxley, in your book *Jesting Pilate*, speak in so disparaging a fashion of it? May I inquire, Sir, if you continue to adhere to this unfavourable view?

"Huxley was amused and faintly put out. He said that perhaps he had spoken a little too harshly about the Taj Mahal, that he had not intended to wound anyone's feelings, that aesthetics was an uncertain field, that tastes were incommensurable, and then he gradually slid from this perilous ground to his central Tolstoyan belief—the unnatural lives that men lead today. But he wondered afterwards whether perhaps he had been unjust, and so we decided to re-visit Agra . . . We . . went together to Fatehpur Sikri, Akbar's dead city. Huxley adored it. He moved with the slow-footed, slightly gliding step of a somnambulist: his grave and urbane charm was moving and very delightful.

". . he described his earlier visit to India in the 'twenties, when he had stayed with one of his Oxford contemporaries, now a member of the Upper House in India, a distinguished man who had welcomed him on this occasion too. He described Jawaharlal Nehru's father, Motilal, who, he said, was a man of exquisite appearance and manners, and sent his shirts to be washed in Paris; he had belonged to the rich and power-loving aristocracy that had sought to use Gandhi for its purposes; but they found that he had outwitted them . . . Huxley described the relations of these distinguished and autocratic Brahmins to Gandhi with a kind of benevolent irony, even-toned, slow, deliberate and exceedingly entertaining . . . He was very simple, very serene, very easy to talk with. The fact that . . his house and all his books had been destroyed by fire seemed hardly to trouble him at all, nor did he by the slightest allusion reveal the fact that he knew that he was suffering from a mortal disease; he complained of his eyesight—his old familiar infirmity . . .

"When he finally saw the Taj Mahal again, he relented; and decided that it was not as unsightly as he had supposed, but on the contrary, but for the minarets—'chimney pots' which he still thought a mistake—it was a creditable building after all. We spent the evening together; . . Monsieur Guéhenno, the French writer, was also there . . Guéhenno, a melancholy, interesting and idealistic man, was not likely—nor did he intend—to raise anyone's spirits; the lights in the hotel were very low owing to some permanent power failure. One might have thought that the whole occasion would be one of extreme, if dignified, gloom and depression. But it was not. Huxley was simple, natural and unselfconscious, what he said was unusual and absolutely authentic. Everything about him was so sincere and so interesting that the occasion was wholly enjoyable, and inspired, at any rate in me, a lasting affection and a degree of respect bordering on veneration."

## Chapter Four

## Mulholland Highway and Professor at Large

ALDOUS and Laura now settled down at Virginia's. Laura's great friend proved a very good friend indeed to Aldous. She and her sister Pauline had belonged to that American *jeunesse dorée* of the Paris twenties, the world of the Gerald Murphys and the Scott Fitzgeralds and of *Tender Is the Night*. The Pfeiffer girls met Ernest Hemingway; in due course Pauline became his second wife. Virginia travelled with them, shared boat and houses. More than mere sister-in-law, she was a fast friend of Ernest's. Their friendship outlasted the eventual divorce from Pauline, went on through the war and into the final bad years. "And now Hemingway's death," Aldous had written to Laura when the news had come last summer. "Where, you ask, is the All Rightness? Certainly not on the level where he lived and killed himself . . .

. . Would it be good for Ginny to remember all the good and the bad of the past times in the light of another LSD or psilocybin experience? It might be.

Ginny, Virginia: a quiet woman; observant, intelligent; of precarious health herself,[1] good with the ill, the depressed; helpful and self-forgetting in a crisis. Aldous liked her. "She has no Bovaristic angle," he would say. Laura thought that he felt more comfortable with her than with any other friend. (Once I was able to draw Virginia out about that pattern of her life, the link, the domestic proximity with those two literary men. Aldous was the best man, she said, she ever knew, getting better and better . . . Ernest: the opposite, he got steadily worse. "And they call him a hero.")

Virginia's house on Mulholland Highway was a light house with a large, light, high-ceilinged and high-windowed living-room downstairs. Deer came from the hills at night; if one kept still one saw the gleam of their eyes in the dark foliage of the bushes. Laura, running in and out, had her own studio on Graciosa Drive a couple of miles down the hill. Virginia's children, Pauline and Juan, were part of the household. Aldous took an interest in their development. Here an ambiguity persisted: he was at ease,

---

[1] She died in 1973.

often tender, with those (and most) children, we just heard how comfortable he was with Virginia, how easy to talk to he appeared to Isaiah Berlin; yet he could still create a field of silence, freeze. One of their local friends, Bernadine Fritz, introduced an admirer to Aldous who complained afterwards that he did not "get through".

I am distressed to hear that I can be so paralyzing to people—[in an unpublished letter to Mrs Fritz of 24th January 1962] a defect attributable to a certain shyness and difficulty in personal communication which it has taken me a lifetime to reduce to its present level and which, I suppose, I will never entirely get rid of.

Aldous slept and worked in his white-washed room with the view. There were two reproductions on the walls, one of Degas's *After the Bath* and Rembrandt's *Polish Rider*. He was correcting the proofs of *Island*, preparing lectures and the *n*th revision of *The Genius and the Goddess* for an English production. Marie Le Put, the Bretonne of North Kings days, still cooked for them. Some days Aldous would ask her to eat with him; they would talk French; he liked the soups she made, knew every herb. Virginia read aloud to him. Laura tried once or twice. "It didn't work," she says. At times he read to *her*. He read to himself, that is he listened to recordings of poetry he had made himself. (This was an old habit.) From the house, he could take a walk he loved, the walk around the Hollywood reservoir. Often Gerald came. Topographically, it was possible to get about from Mulholland without a car— walking down the hill some twenty minutes to the nearest bus stop; a taxi home. Taking things as they came was now a conscious principle with Aldous, Peggy Kiskadden affirms, and he lived up to it. He made no demands, ". . . ate the food set before him." Laura used the same words, "he ate everything he was given." Neither less nor more. This, too, was an old process. Peggy tells of an occasion in Maria's day when he had cleaned his plate of some revolting mess at someone's house. "Aldous, how *could* you?" Maria said as the door shut behind them. "Mortification."

Betty and Aldous had resumed their working luncheons. One day Betty, who has a lot of Boswell in her, asked him, "Aldous, do you pray?" "I always say my prayers—in the simplest possible words, I always begin 'Now I lay me down to sleep,' and my prayers are nearly always answered."

On 22nd January Aldous took psilocybin, monitored by Laura. Her tape recording of what was said during the session can be found in *This Timeless Moment*.

Many people had been offering help in remaking Aldous's

library. Cass Canfield asked him to accept a set of his own works and any book he chose from Harper's trade list. This he did.[1] He also responded to an offer from Mrs Lucille Kahn. Now, in 1947 Aldous had written a commissioned article for *House and Garden* on the subject "If My Library Burned Tonight." (This was republished after the fire.[2]) "If my library burned down . . ." Aldous wrote then, "fortunately for me, it never has.

> . . . To enter the shell of a well-loved room and to find it empty, except for a thick carpet of ashes—the very thought is depressing. But happily books are replaceable—at any rate the kind of books that fill the shelves of my library. For I . . have never been interested in first editions and rare antiquities. It is only about the contents of a book that I care, not its shape, its date or the number of its fly-leaves . . .
>
> In principle I would like to possess all the poetry worth reading in all the languages I have a nodding acquaintance with. But as an emergency measure, in the first few weeks after our hypothetical fire, I shall buy myself only the most indispensable . . .
>
> There will be Shakespeare—because, like the giraffe, there ain't no such animal . . . There will be Chaucer—because of all the great poets, I feel towards him the warmest personal affection . . . There will be Homer . . an absolutely truthful poet, who accepted life as it actually is . . . There will be Dante . . (though, as a human being, he seems to me second only to Milton himself in unpleasantness) . . . There will be Donne . . . There will be Marvell—because his small gift was perfect. There will be Wordsworth . . . There will be Baudelaire . . . Rimbaud . . . Mallarmé—because he was the most perfectly self-conscious of artists, and because his poetry has been, for me, a kind of obsession, ever since, as a boy of twenty, I tried my hand at translating his *Après-Midi d'un Faune*. There will be Yeats . . . There will be Eliot—because his is the most beautifully articulate voice of the generation to which I happen to belong . . .

As for the great novelists. There would have to be Tolstoy in Aldous's new library, and Dostoevski, Dickens, Balzac, a set of Stendhal, Choderlos de Laclos, "the author of that extraordinary book, *Les Liaisons Dangereuses*, and that other romantic analyst, Benjamin Constant. Nor must we forget the eighteenth-century master of narrative—Henry Fielding, whom we must love for his truthfulness . . . akin to that of Chaucer and Homer;" and the Voltaire of *Candide*, and Swift. "As for Smollett—no; my sense

---

[1] The list of the books chosen by Aldous can be found in a note by Professor Grover Smith to Letter 881 in the *Letters*.
[2] In *House and Garden's Weekend Book*, 1969.

of humour is not robust enough to rejoice unreservedly in syphilis and broken legs. And as for Goethe's *Wilhelm Meister*—

> the book, no doubt, is a work of genius, but full of so complacent an egotism that I never want to read it again. Returning again to the nineteenth century, I find myself very well able to support the loss of Scott and Thackeray . . . But I would re-possess myself of quite a lot of Trollope . . .

And what about Flaubert? What about Wells, Conrad, D. H. Lawrence? *Bouvard et Pécuchet*, certainly; but *L'Education Sentimentale*, one of his favourite books, sadly disappointed him on re-reading. Of Wells, only the scientific romances. A set of Conrad in spite of some reservations; D. H. Lawrence, unreservedly.

The essayists. Montaigne and Pascal inevitably. Thomas Traherne, John Dryden, Voltaire, David Hume, Samuel Johnson, Coleridge, Charles Lamb, De Quincey, "Macaulay who writes like a military band and is the best possible reading for a rainy afternoon. And Emerson who writes like an oracle and possesses authentic wisdom." Walter Bagehot, Sainte-Beuve, Matthew Arnold, Ruskin ("whom I must be allowed to read in selections, for he maddeningly mixes nonsense with the humanest social wisdom"). Schopenhauer, "one of the few great Germans who does not display the 'nimiety', or 'too-muchness' "; Heine; More and Irving Babbitt; E. M. Forster and Virginia Woolf.

Biographies, diaries, letters. "I can only name a few at random" —the letters of Keats, the letters of Byron; the note-books of Constant and Stendhal. The autobiographies of Alfieri, and of Lorenzo da Ponte. The Goncourt Journals . . The diaries of Scawen Blunt . . .

And now let us have a look at Aldous's actual requests when the hypothetical fire *had* occurred. He would like, he wrote to Mrs Kahn, "The poets first of all. A compendious Shakespeare and Chaucer. Then Wordsworth, Keats (and the letters as well as the poetry), Browning, Arnold, Hopkins, Yeats, Eliot—and Auden's anthology of English verse, plus the *Oxford Books* of 17th century verse, German verse, Latin and medieval Latin verse.

> Then I'd like, if it isn't asking too much, some of the books on oriental philosophy and religion which I valued. Conze's *Buddhism* and his anthology of Buddhist texts. Suzuki's *Zen Essays* and *Zen Doctrine of No-Mind*, Evan Went's 3 books published by Oxford U. Press, *Tibetan Book of the Dead*, *Milarepa*, and *Great Wisdom* . . Also Zimmer's *Philosophy of India* and *Myths and Symbols of India*. Krishnamurti's *Commentaries on Living*. Benoit's *Supreme Doctrine*.

And from the West, Eckhart—the 1 vol selection by Blakney. William Law—selected by Hobhouse. Wm James, *Varieties of Religious Experience*. Russell's *History of Western Philosophy*.

And if anyone has a spare Dostoievsky or two, a spare *War and Peace* and *Karenina* and short stories of Tolstoy, a spare odd volume of Dickens, I shall be grateful to them.

Aldous had been nominated visiting Ford Research Professor at Berkeley. No functions were attached to the appointment and he hoped to use the salary to finance a reflective travel book about the West Coast, from Canada to Mexico, in the manner of *Beyond the Mexique Bay*. At the intervals of looking at scenery, sewage plants and lunatic asylums, he proposed to give a seminar. He went up to Berkeley for the spring semester of 1962 in early February. Laura drove him there and helped to find a pleasant apartment near the campus. Nothing turned out well. Aldous arrived with a cold in the chest and had to creep into bed, not much good for anything except listening to an educational programme on a portable radio found among the furnishings.

. . And in spite of this stupid little flu [he wrote to Laura], I love you—though it is difficult, when you were here, to manifest anything except a cough and a wheeze. That's one of the worst things about not being well: one's ailments eclipse one's feelings and shut out other people, even those one loves the most.

. . I have just been listening to a broadcast by an American historian on the life of the troops during the Civil War—a record of inconceivable incompetence and inefficiency, resulting in tens of thousands of unnecessary deaths and incalculable amounts of avoidable suffering. So this too is an old story!

Goodbye, my darling. Ti voglio bene.

The cold lingered on and on, then turned into pneumonitis and Aldous had to fly back to Los Angeles for a course of antibiotics. When he was on his feet again, he returned to Berkeley. Nothing much materialized, somehow things had got mismanaged. For instance, the university was to have arranged for him to have the use of a car and student driver; neither appeared. Aldous let it go. Few people seemed to be aware of his presence. Julian turned up (from Reed College) and was shocked to see Aldous fending for himself. "Throwing all the food into a blender and messing it up—not nice. He was lonely, poor boy."[1] Betty Wendel went to Berkeley on 8th March with Frank Hauser of the Oxford Playhouse, the producer-director who was to put on *The*

---

[1] Sir Julian talking to S. B.

*Genius and the Goddess* at Oxford and with luck in London. They began their two-day conference by doing Aldous's washing up. Aldous, who described Hauser as an intelligent, sensitive and very professional man, promised to come to London for the West End opening if there were one. For the rest of the Berkeley semester, Aldous kept coming and going—breathers at Los Angeles, trips with Laura, endless journeyings to give lectures, attend conferences. Laura kept his engagement list.

| | | |
|---|---|---|
| March 14-16th | Santa Barbara | (Conference on Technology at Robert Hutchins's Center for Democratic Studies) |
| March 17-19th | Los Angeles | |
| March 19th-27th | Berkeley | |
| March 27th | Los Angeles | |
| March 29th | Alabama | (University lecture) |
| March 31st | Philadelphia | (Lecture) |
| April 1st | New York | (Luncheon and afternoon with Matthew; lecture at the Poetry Center) |
| April 2nd | Boston | |
| April 4-6th | Hamilton, N.Y. | (Conference on Hypnosis at Colgate University) |
| April 7th | New York | |
| April 8-14th | Berkeley | |
| April 14th | Los Angeles | |
| April 18-22nd | Portland, Oregon | (To meet Julian, who was lecturing there) |

. . Julian seems well—though a bit tired [to Laura]. We drove out yesterday in beautiful weather to the Bonneville Dam. Magnificent country—and the fish making their way up the "fish ladders" at the side of the dam were fascinating.

. . talked with the professor of psychiatry at the Medical Center here—he is working on the problem of recognizing the children who will be specially vulnerable to schizophrenia and devising ways in which they . . may avoid the disease in spite of their inborn tendency. It was most heartening to find that anything so sensible is being thought of and worked at.

This morning we visited the zoo where a female elephant has just given birth to a 220 pound baby . . . The baby, I must say, is very touching—and it is fascinating to see the other female elephants as well as the mother, clustering round, like Aunts and Grannies, with an intense solicitude for the little creature (who anyhow weighs twice as much as you do!).

Tonight Julian speaks . . Now I must get ready for dinner. Goodbye, my darling.

And on a picture postcard a couple of days later:

> Here we are at the end of a most beautiful drive through pastures, wheat fields, rice paddies, olive and orange groves, forests and mountains . . Tomorrow we are to be taken round by a forester. Let's hope it won't be rainy.

The engagement list continued.

| | | |
|---|---|---|
| April 22nd-May 2nd | Berkeley | |
| May 2nd | Los Alamos | (Lecture to the scientists) |
| May 6th | Anaheim, Cal. | (Lecture) |
| May 7-17th | Berkeley | |

And that was the end of what Aldous referred to as his Full Professorship of Nothing-in-Particular.

| | | |
|---|---|---|
| May 17th-21st | Los Angeles | |
| May 21-25th | New York | (Talk at the American Academy) |

Here Aldous read the news of the death of Peggy Kiskadden's former husband, Curtis Bok,[1] whom he had known long ago at Dartington. He wrote to her,

> . . These vital threads that link the present to the past—how many of them have already been broken, and how increasingly often, as one grows older, does one receive the news of yet another break! And the questions keep multiplying. How are we related to what we were? Who are we now and what were we then? And who were the others—in our minds, in their minds, in the mind of omniscience? There are no answers, of course—only the facts of living, changing, remembering and at last dying.

| | | |
|---|---|---|
| May 25th | Philadelphia | |
| May 27th | Los Angeles | |
| May 30th | San Francisco | (For the loan exhibition of Chinese Paintings from 900 A.D.) |

Meanwhile *Island* had been published in March both in England and the U.S.A. Aldous had felt rather discouraged at the proof correcting stage. He found himself wondering, he had written to Humphrey, "if the book is any good, or at least more

---

[1] The American jurist, author and philanthropist.

than spottily good. Heaven knows." Cyril Connolly opened his review in the *Sunday Times*, "This is Mr Huxley's most important novel since *Time Must Have a Stop*." On the whole, the reception was divided; the book was treated as a phantasy, a piece of fiction, science fiction at that. For once Aldous felt not indifferent.

## Chapter Five

## Summer and Autumn 1962

THERE had not been any recurrence of Aldous's original trouble of two years ago. Now, on his return from New York, he suspected that something was wrong with a small gland on the side of his neck. He saw Dr Cutler on the 31st of May who eventually decided to remove the gland, which proved malignant. Aldous took it calmly and wrote to Laura, who happened to be in Italy, in reassuring terms. Cutler had told him that, even at the worst, these kinds of metastases were not really serious. Yet he had a very unpleasant dream; a dream about some nameless, faceless person who was going to kill him and kept leading him from room to room. "So the unconscious evidently got a shock!

. . And meanwhile—perhaps just *because* death seems to have taken a step nearer—everything seems more and more beautiful, the leaves on the trees, the flowers, the sky . . . and my memories of you and all the people I have loved or felt concerned about.

The actual operation (in July) was quite minor; Aldous stayed in hospital for two days only. Again he went in as Mr Matthew Leonard. Afterwards he had a series of cobalt treatments as an out-patient.

Aldous had just been elected a Companion of Literature by the Royal Society of Literature, but was not able to come to London for the presentation as he had intended. (At the beginning of 1962 there were four living Companions of Literature: Winston Churchill, E. M. Forster, John Masefield and Somerset Maugham. The present election added Edmund Blunden, Aldous Huxley and Robert Graves, who declined the honour.)

*The Genius and the Goddess* had opened at the Oxford Playhouse[1] on 23rd April, directed by Frank Hauser, starring Constance Cummings, Paul Massie and George Pravda. It went on to Manchester, Leeds, Streatham Hill and reached the Golder's Green Hippodrome on 28th May. No West End theatre being available at once, the opening at the Comedy Theatre was held over till 28th June. Again there had been cuts and changes, "detrimental and unauthorized", according to Betty Wendel,

[1] Produced by the Meadow Players Ltd, in association with the Arts Council of Great Britain.

who held the fort in England. Aldous's presence was urgently requested. But Aldous of course was ill and did not come. The notices were tepid and the play was taken off after twenty-one nights.

In August, well before the end of the cobalt treatment, Aldous was active—planning to go to the Argentine, to Brussels. With Christopher Isherwood he went to the aviation plant at Los Angeles to have a look at the Apollo moon-shot capsules and the latest missiles they were working on. "The plant executives were full of resounding phrases [Christopher Isherwood[1]] about Man's great mission and destiny in Outer Space. Aldous sat listening, his head slightly bowed, ghost-pale, aloof. He was like a ghost they had raised to speak to them of the future—but they hadn't bargained for what they heard . . ."

> All this concentrated knowledge [Aldous for his part to Humphrey], genius, hard work and devotion, not to mention all those incalculable billions of dollars, poured forth in the service of vast collective paranoias—and meanwhile our three billion mainly hungry people are to become six billions in less than forty years and, like parasites, are threatening to destroy their planetary host and, with their host, themselves.

At the end of August Aldous set out for Belgium on his own. (Laura was too busy trying to meet the deadline of her book; they arranged to meet in the Argentine in October.) The reason for the journey was the meeting of the new World Academy of Arts and Sciences in Brussels, "started by a lot of Nobel Prizemen who would like to see that their science is used in a relatively sane manner." It seems worth trying at least, Aldous thought, "to do something to mitigate the current organized insanity . . ."

He looked up Maria's uncle Baltus; then went on to Holland, to Suzanne and Joep, and Sylvia. How well his other Nicolas niece, Claire, has described these autumnal wanderings[2] "from one member of his own and of Maria's family to the other . . New York, England, France, Belgium, Holland . . He sought them out, braving foul weather and bad trains, contracting bronchitis here, pneumonia there . . ." This was almost literally the course of the present journey—slow hours of cross-country trains to get to Tegelen in the Limbourg province. He looked too gaunt, too worn, for it to be taken as a casual visit. Nothing, of course, was said. Aldous was in an affectionate mood, took pleasure in Suzanne's garden, looked intently at an enormous black-faced

---

1 *Mem. Vol.*
2 Claire Nicolas White, "Aldous Huxley, A Reminiscence".

sunflower that had sprung up outside her kitchen door, went on long walks as they had done in their early days, walks at sunset along the wooded sandhills that form the natural border between Germany and Holland. They drove to Haarlem for a Franz Hals Exhibition. Here the September weather changed, an icy wind sweeping the town: Aldous began to cough in a terrifying manner. They took him to Amsterdam, put him to bed in a warm hotel, called in a doctor who prescribed penicillin. Suzanne and Sylvia kept him company. "Il semblait heureux d'être dorloté." He had started writing *Literature and Science*, and asked Sylvia to read the beginning out to him. These two had long talks, with Sylvia, a story-teller, able to make him laugh. From his bed he telephoned to Laura in California, asked Suzanne to say a word to her as they had never met. The chest cold cleared up after a few days, but he still felt weak and not only cancelled the Argentinian journey but gave up his plans for Paris—perhaps he could not face showing himself to Jeanne—and flew straight to London. There he stayed at Pond Street with his brother, under Juliette's admirable care. He gradually picked up. Nearly every day Juliette had friends to tea for him, never more than two at a time. His cousin Renée Tickell came, as on all his visits. And Jill Greenwood, the cousin who could have been his niece in age, whom he had not been able to take his eyes off when they first met at the Gargoyle night club and who had fallen in love with his portrait at the age of seventeen.

. . He asked me to bring my younger daughter Dinah, which I did . . .[1] He was lying in a chair looking just like an autumn leaf—you know, one of those skeleton leaves, very very gentle and quiet, and very sweet. He talked; and he talked to Dinah, which I thought was nice of him . . .

As ever, he went about his London business—publishers, haberdashers, quacks; saw about getting up a trust fund for Matthew's children; spent a weekend at Gervas's; wandered about with Humphrey Osmond. Humphrey, a Surrey man himself, was spending the summer in Godalming; with him Aldous again re-visited old haunts. Aldous was saddened, even angered, by the fact that there were no more birds in the hedges, "The insecticides have killed them all!" Once, when Julian was with them, Aldous described how as a boy he bicycled down the Devil's Punch Bowl towards Milford at forty miles an hour. Julian was sceptical. "I clocked it," Aldous said. And there used

[1] Gillian (Mrs Anthony) Greenwood, talking to S. B.

to be a sweetshop where they were able to get thirty caramels for a penny. "Very *small* caramels, Aldous," said Julian. "*Thirty* caramels, all the same," said Aldous.

One afternoon as Juliette was driving him, they passed Laleham. "He and I[1] got out of the car, A. leant on the gate silently. I saw a man in the garden, and said this was Aldous Huxley who was born there, and could he see the house, please. The owner said of course, and took us in and showed every room, including the old nursery upstairs, which A. thought very small and not at all as he remembered . . . The people in the house were very nice . . . So we drove back. I felt that Aldous was very happy."

The Huxley brothers met the Menuhins at Claridges. Julian was holding forth on the quality of genes—there was an aristocracy of genes . . . Aldous piped up, "You mean blue genes?" with a very long vowel in the blue.[2]

In late September Aldous was back in California, back in Virginia's house. It was now a year and a half since the fire. Did you not think of remaking a home? I once asked Laura. Yes, there had been plans to re-build—the site on Deronda Drive was still theirs—they had looked for something to rent . . . "He was docile, he would have done what I wanted . . . but the houses we saw—we looked at houses—were so unlike *my* dream . . . my design . . ." For some weeks Aldous worked away on his long essay on literature and science. All the essays on the subject, he wrote to Matthew, "from T. H. Huxley's and Matthew Arnold's in the 1880's (still the best in the field) to . . Trilling's and Oppenheimer's—are too abstract and generalized. I am trying to approach [it] in more concrete terms . . ."

Presently Aldous broke off for a month of lecturing in the Middle West and East. From New York he went to stay with Claire, as he so often did, at St James, the Stanford White estate on Long Island where she lived pastorally with her husband, Bobby, the numerous members of the White family and her own four children (how Aldous had scolded her about their number! Yet he was fond of them, and had much affection for Claire's eldest son, Sebastian, a brilliantly intelligent boy). Matthew, too, since his divorce, had a home-base at St James. Aldous came equipped with rubber overshoes and an English umbrella which opened automatically when one pressed a button. He would join "our

---

[1] Juliette in a letter to S. B.
[2] In the words told by Yehudi Menuhin to S. B. I am afraid there is more than one story about blue jeans; Aldous was too fond of puns to let it go at that. I chose this version as the neatest.

tribal existence [Claire writing] with apparent enjoyment and great adaptability . . ." He shared in the children's games,

> tickled them with a long feather and then would sensuously stroke his own cheek with it. He sat on the sofa and read aloud . . from *The Doors of Perception* while the children listened spell-bound, and one of them drew his portrait.

And how lucky, he would say, to live in the country, "to still be able to go for walks like these". Claire had been reading a life of Thomas More, and told Aldous that his visits reminded her of those of Erasmus, "that other avid traveller, keeping us in touch with the world . . . ." Later he wrote to her,

> It is always a great delight to see you and Bobby and the children . . . Alas for Erasmus! How I shd like to be like him! And how sadly I realize that his sweet reasonableness made him abhorrent to both parties, who went on with their wars and agreed only in denouncing the apostle of good will, intelligence and compromise.

In this same November, Aldous met Judy—Judith Wallet Bordage—Matthew's future wife. There had so far been no mention of a marriage, but Aldous was not born yesterday. Matthew asked him to have dinner with her at her apartment on 54th Street. It was a four floor walk-up and when the bell rang,

> I[1] thought it would surely be Matthew, a feeling that was confirmed by the tread on the stairs and the cough on the floor below. When Aldous rounded the corner I expected to be desperately nervous, but no.

There was a large and cherished tabby, who stole the cheese biscuits while they had their drinks. This helped.

> Matthew got there soon after and we had a splendid meal—you know I have an odd memory for inconsequential things—I remember making Julia Child's escalope de veau . . . and as Matthew told me after, Aldous adored eating well. Matthew was marvellous in helping the talk . . . he knew what to ask him, how to turn the conversation, how to keep the talk going. Finally Aldous left—Matthew put him in a taxi and came back up—it was after 11.30 and I asked whether M thought the evening had gone well . . . Matthew laughed and said that if it hadn't gone well, Aldous would have left at ten . . .

---

[1] Judy, the present Mrs Matthew Huxley, in a letter to S. B.

Next evening Aldous took them both to a Swiss restaurant, and they went on to see *Beyond the Fringe*. "This had opened about a week or two before, I think, and was a raving hit.

> . . we had house seats, something like seventh row centre. That was a heavenly evening—giggly and relaxed—the show, by American standards, erudite—a very Oxonian type show and Aldous rolled in the aisles along with the two of us. I remember suggesting afterwards to A. that he might go back to tell the young actors (Moore, Jonathan Miller . . .) that he had indeed enjoyed it—and A. answered that he didn't know them and it would be presumptuous (although that isn't the word he used) . . . After, we all walked up Sixth Avenue and then to the Plaza where he was staying—it was then the first time I was aware that he saw things very clearly—that he *looked*—seeing people, expressions, things that neither M. nor I saw because certainly we weren't looking—but that was when I realized that his sight was not impaired in the way I had always believed from what I had read.
>
> That evening we all walked arm in arm and—how do I say this?— nothing sexual, but very much the electricity of—maybe benign flirtatiousness is the right way to say it.

(Benign flirtatiousness is a very good way of describing Aldous's rapport with attractive women in his later years.) Next day, a Saturday, Aldous with Matthew, Trev and Tessa had a picnic lunch at Judy's apartment.

> . . . relaxed, lovely—we had a very good Italian delicatessen nearby . . and we had found all kinds of good things. When Matthew told the kids to sit up or not to talk with a full mouth, Aldous nodded approvingly and muttered, "Manners, manners . . ."

Then they went out to St James and spent the night at Claire's. Next morning Aldous had to catch a plane to Texas from La Guardia to give a lecture. Matthew cut it too fine:

> . . . a terrible drive [Judy's comment] . . . Aldous nervous and put out, obviously trying to control his irritation with Matthew. Aldous and I getting out at the proper airline, both of us rushing through the gate—on time. Great enormous hugs . . and off he went . . .

## Chapter Six

## 1963—Winter, Spring, Summer

BACK to Los Angeles, back to work. Before Christmas Aldous had finished his short book, *Literature and Science*, Laura had finished her book, her first one, the Recipes for Living based on her psychotherapeutic methods. The title was to be *You Are Not the Target*. Aldous, who had taken a delighted interest, was doing the preface. Now, what next?

> .. And tomorrow we start a new year [Aldous wrote to Maria Petrie]. Will the few scores of people who decide the world's immediate fate permit it to be a tolerably good year? And will the impersonal forces which determine our long-range destiny permit themselves to be controlled for man's benefit—and shall we even attempt to control them?

Meanwhile, wishes to his friends, wishes for good health, good work and "*malgré tout*, inner peace." And on 8th January Aldous writes to Matthew that he has a project for a "rather long and complicated novel." For the present: journalistic grind, proof-correcting, a working session at Santa Barbara.

It was Aldous's custom to request both his publishers, each January, to send a statement of his past year's earnings to his accountants so that they might work out his income tax. ("Faith, Hope, Charity—these three, and the greatest of all is Income Tax.") In 1962 Aldous's gross income from book royalties came to £6,496 and $26,646 respectively. *Island* had been doing well financially. But, in prosperous years or lean, he still did not really go into his royalty statements. He liked to hear that a particular book had been doing well, or being paid a nice round sum like $1,000 for an article; he enjoyed the size of his lecture fees; but he did not give much thought to his financial landscape as a whole. (He used to write his cheques without filling in the stubs. "My Bank will tell me when I'm overdrawn.") His rough view of the overall position was that he was fairly certain of a largish living as long as he was working, but that subsistence for himself or his dependents on earnings from past books was unpredictable at best. He never "accumulated a fortune" (he helped far too many people) and such savings as he had were accidental. He still had money panics ("We all get them," say his Huxley cousins), Laura would laugh him out of them. (Maria had skimped on herself and worried, but could not learn to manage money; Laura did not believe that there was any need to manage it.)

Matthew and Judy proposed to each other on St Valentine's Day. Aldous was very happy about this indeed—"All seems for the best." To Eileen Garrett he spoke of Judy as being just what Matthew needed—"warm, intelligent and good."

On 9th March Aldous flew to Rome for the F.A.O. conference on their campaign against hunger. In a letter to me, written on the plane, he mentioned again that he was "feeling his way into a kind of novel.

. . I don't yet know what it will really be like and proceed by a process of trial and error, guided by whatever turns up, from paragraph to paragraph.

He expected to be in England in the early summer.

In Rome Aldous had an audience with Pope John, who was then already very ill. On his way home he stopped two days in New York for Matthew's wedding on the 22nd. The day before he spent talking to Humphrey Osmond; at night he dined at Longchamps with the bride and groom. He was remote, and Judy was disconcerted by their not being able to pick up from where they had left off in November.

On the wedding day, Aldous was obviously not well. "He was aged, we thought. Age being somehow acceptable." Matthew had lunch with Aldous and Trev; Tessa helped Judy dress. They met at an apartment on Park Avenue for the ceremony, performed by a judge. Aldous was their witness. "Then crosstown to Central Park West for the reception. A. tired. He sat in a small study off the main room with Cass and Jane Canfield and Anita Loos, apart from the sixty or so standing wedding guests, the cake and the champagne . . ."

Los Angeles. Another of those brief talking trips: to Oregon, Berkeley, Stanford. In April another tumour appeared on Aldous's neck. Cutler told him; Aldous did not seem very alarmed. He brought up a theory they had often discussed: the body's own remarkable capacity to destroy cancer cells. "Cancer isn't always the winner," Aldous said. Perhaps his body was building up its own resistance. "If it isn't, there isn't much we can do about it, is there?" But Dr Cutler was no longer hopeful; he told Laura. Again he insisted on a second opinion. Aldous, Laura with him, flew to New York on 23rd April for a consultation. Laura decided that the time had come when she must tell Matthew. As it happened, a letter from him had arrived that very morning; they read it on the plane and it was such a happy letter that Laura lost heart. She could not bring herself, she wrote, to intrude. They had gone to New York unannounced and returned the same day, having made no attempt to reach Matthew. Perhaps it might have been better for him if she had; perhaps better for her not to have had to go on bearing that silence on her own, private silence, public silence, silence also now to Aldous.

On 1st May Aldous went into the Cedars of Lebanon Hospital for a few days of observation. It should be said that medically everything possible was being done.[1] Throughout, Dr Cutler not only insisted on examinations by eminent colleagues in San Francisco, London, New York, he also corresponded about Aldous's case with such authorities as Dr F. Baclesse of the Institut de Radium, Dr Tailhefer of the Foundation Curie, Professor Guidetti of the University of Turin. Humanly, too, Dr Cutler was the right choice—gentle, kind and highly intelligent, he was very good at that personal doctor-patient relationship that Aldous had feared he would have failed in had *he* become a doctor. He was fond of Max Cutler, and the two men were able to talk to one another profitably.

*You Are Not the Target* was about to be published; Laura was faced with a painful dilemma.

. . I was scheduled to go to New York for a series of public appearances, synchronized with the publication of my book. Never was the duality of life more evident. On one side I was having every satisfaction that a new writer could wish for; on the other . . .
. . I did not want to go away even for a week. Yet my New York appearances had been carefully scheduled. They would acquaint a large audience with my book. If I cancelled my trip, I certainly would have to give a valid reason . . .

She asked Dr Cutler; he advised her to go. Aldous meanwhile carried on as usual, coming down to eight o'clock breakfast with Virginia's children, going back to his room to work, taking his afternoon walk; but Laura thought that he was being inaccessible and silent in a new way. Her book, which was a run-away success, was the one thing that distracted him.

L. is just back from New York [he wrote to Julian on 2nd June] . .

[1] Dr Cutler, with much care and kindness, not only talked to me at length but let me see the actual file on Aldous's case.

and making TV and radio appearances . . her book . . is turning
into a rampaging best seller. A second printing after a week—and
the computers predict a sale of 107,000 by August! . . The publisher
is out of his mind with joy and we are feeling elatedly flabbergasted.
   Otherwise there isn't much to report. I have just finished an essay
on the ambivalence of culture . . .

Aldous had never had a sale of such dimension and commented
on that fact with delight and glee.
   Presently it was decided to resort once more to radiation therapy.
Between 13th June and 2nd July Aldous underwent twenty-five
exposures to radioactive cobalt, an extremely exhausting treatment which left him very low and weak. He had to cancel his
engagements. (He was to have lectured in Munich on behalf of
the British Council on 14th June and addressed the Royal Society
of Literature in London on the 22nd.) During July he regained
some little strength, and seemed preoccupied with his novel.
There was good news too: Matthew's marriage was turning out
extremely well. "He is happier now than he has ever been,"
Aldous wrote to Julian. And Ellen, also, was about to get married
again. So here all was for the best.

   . . and the children are thoroughly enjoying the experience of
having a father and a deputy father whom they like, and a mother
and a deputy mother with whom they get on extremely well.

And Matthew had a new job (on a planning committee at the
National Institute of Mental Health) and was moving to
Washington in September. "He is delighted at the prospect." Nor
had those computers been wrong, *Target* continued a best-seller—
"Laura is very busy signing books and giving interviews."

   At the end of July Aldous was emerging from his low state just
enough to keep his engagement in Stockholm for a meeting of the
World Academy of Arts and Sciences. Laura came with him and
they flew by way of Greenland—twelve hours and eight time
changes—arriving on the 28th. Aldous had never been to Sweden
before and at once took strolls "about this pleasant town with its
mixture of rather solemn and respectably old-fashioned architecture and brand new . ." Humphrey Osmond arrived. Aldous
confessed to him that he had been unsure whether he could come
at all. "Yet he worked zealously to persuade members of the
Academy to study human potential." He succeeded, and was
asked to undertake, with Humphrey, the editing of a volume on

Human Resources for publication by the Academy. Aldous at once "set to and prepared an outline.

> I[1] sat with him while he was completing this in his hotel room. He was engrossed in his task. Watching him I felt that I might never see him again . . . I was uneasy when we parted, but tried to ignore my misgivings. He was to visit me in Princeton during October, which was only two months away . . .

After Stockholm Laura went to Italy, Aldous flew to London. ("It seems best for each of us," she wrote, "to visit our families.") Julian and Juliette met him at Heathrow; they saw at once that something was appallingly wrong. Aldous's colour was ashen and his voice down to half its volume. Yes, he said, he was very tired, having sat up all night drafting an outline for the Academy . . . He would soon recover, he assured them, with a quiet month in England.

> We brought him to Pond Street and settled him down [Julian's *Memories*], but soon saw that the promised improvement was failing to occur. In fact Juliette got so worried that she arranged a consultation with the best specialist at Bart's Hospital and took him there, rather against his will . . . he did not want us to know; indeed, we never had the slightest suspicion . . . He merely told us on returning from Bart's that the doctors had advised a quiet spell, and that his voice would soon be normal . . We were only too anxious to believe him.

"He was spectral, waxen, shockingly changed," Rosamond Lehmann said of him; "speaking only when he was addressed, and then replying with all his customary alertness . . . recovering his spirits once, for a brief time . . discussing the problem of world population . . ."
The Julians took him into Devonshire for a weekend at Dartington, that extraordinarily beautiful place, with its vast expanse of trees and lawns and gardens breathing peace. Leonard and Dorothy Elmhirst gave them a great welcome.

> . . Leonard Elmhirst has done wonderful things at Dartington [Aldous wrote—it was a very long time since he had whisked Matthew away from the school], which is one of the very few places in the world where one can feel an almost unqualified optimism.

They were taken out on Dartmoor, stopped by a small pond to watch a tame seal, "and the sun came out of clouds to sparkle on

---

[1] Humphrey Osmond in *Mem. Vol.*

the disturbed water [Juliette writing]. Aldous was silent as he walked away, then suddenly said: 'How could one describe that sun and water—the ripples catching the bright light . . .' A little further, on that wild moor, I saw high grass bowed by a sharp gust of wind just as a cloud passed over the sun, painting the grass with a shadow which looked as if it were bending the grass. Aldous stopped at once and looked intently until he had seen what I meant. He looked very tired when we returned to the car, but his face had a peaceful expression."

At night they listened to the Music Festival in the Great Hall. One evening it was early English music on the guitar, "the most tedious music possible. Aldous was boiling with rage—why didn't they play Purcell . . . The next evening Nell Gotkowsky, the young violinist, played Beethoven magnificently. After the concert the Elmhirsts took us to the artists' room . . . we made the usual remarks. Just as we were going away, Nell Gotkowsky rushed after us and flung herself on Aldous, saying that she had only just realized WHO he was, and breathlessly poured out her admiration for him . . . Aldous looked down on this brilliant young creature with a glow of pleasure, listened to her words with a sort of detached enchantment."

Later they went to stay at Lawford Hall in Essex, the home of their old family friends, the Nicolses. Robert, the poet, who had loved Aldous so well, was long dead; his brother, Sir Philip, who had been up at Balliol with Aldous, had died the year before. His widow, Phyllis Nichols,[1] wrote:

. . When Aldous came here . . . his physical appearance was "transparent", and his mind detached from all worldly possessions and struggles. His face lit up with a radiance that was all the more striking because it shone out of a body that seemed like a half-discarded shell.

Lady Nichols's younger son had had a breakdown at Oxford and was suffering from insomnia and depression. When Aldous realized this he tried to help him. He talked to the young man and gave him some magnetic passes—a not unstrenuous procedure—to ease his state of anxiety.

. . I [Lady Nichols] asked Aldous what was his overwhelming feeling when in the visionary world of mescalin, and he replied, "Gratitude." This is the feeling I had after this visit in August 1963.

1 Lady Nichols, who died herself in 1971, in a letter to Julian Huxley.

Again, almost daily, Aldous wrote to Laura.

I keep asking myself what I ought to do in the immediate future—in the probably not very long future that is left me. How to be more loving, more aware, more useful ·or (if that isn't possible) more content and accepting. So far the answer hasn't come but perhaps it will—especially if you help me to find it . . .

. . . I am feeling reasonably well—though not very energetic—well enough to do what I have to do, but without the extra power to do what one would like to do in the way of creating something or initiating some new course of action. But one musn't complain. And anyhow, unexpected things may happen—unforeseen changes occur . . .

. . . you must forgive me, my sweetheart, for being so gloomy and burdensome. I haven't yet learned to accept the fact of not feeling very well, of being mentally and physically diminished—to accept and to make the best of it. But I hope to learn. Meanwhile please be patient with me and remember that underneath the gloom and the sense of being lost, I love you very much . . .

. . . here it is unseasonably chilly and rainy—but the country is beautiful and there are wonderful clouds when the sun comes out between the showers—like Constables and Turners. And maybe I have some good ideas for my hypothetical novel!

One day he went to Simpson's in Piccadilly and bought himself a very smart new raincoat. The last country visit with Julian and Juliette was to the Kenneth Clarks at Saltwood Castle.

This mediaeval fortress had been made into a wondrous place . . . from which narrow Gothic windows open on a wide courtyard surrounded by a battlemented wall. At the further end of the courtyard, K. had established his library in a large tower . . . The library was a place of silence—striking in its harmony and beauty, its scholarly atmosphere and the essence of so much that Aldous loved. It made a deep impression on him—as did the house itself, with all its modern and ancient treasures, and the feeling of continuity with its historical past.[1]

Aldous wandered about the rooms and grounds, stooping to smell the scented roses. He was gay at times, Sidney Nolan said who was there, talked of Rimbaud . . . One evening it was Nolan who went up to his room to call him, knocked at the door, " 'Dinner is ready,' Aldous was reading in the twilight through

[1] Sir Julian Huxley, *Memories*, Vol. II.

his hand . . . looked up slowly with a remote smile . . . came back from very very far . . ."

Alas, Aldous did not see Gervas, who himself was ill.

> I was so sorry to have missed you on this visit . . . I do hope you are making satisfactory progress towards complete health. "Growing old gracefully"—it isn't easy when the physiological machine starts to break down . . . One learns the Second Law of Thermodynamics by direct experience.

In the last week of August Aldous left England for Italy. "He never by any hint or murmur [Julian wrote] allowed us to guess his fate. He had made up his mind that it would be simpler just to ignore it . . . to let things come as they would. The last we saw of him was at the airport—he said goodbye, and opened his briefcase to take out some papers . . ."

Aldous joined Laura in Turin after, she wrote, "three long, and for me, anxious weeks." They took trips into the mountains, to Courmayeur, a funicular ride half way up Mont Blanc, up the Val di Susa to Salice d'Oulx:

> where an Alpine village is in process of being transformed into a town of 10 and 15-storey apartment houses . . We've come a long way from the Swiss chalet!

They were back in Los Angeles and Mulholland Highway on 24th August. Aldous counted on a full month of writing before starting for his next lectures in the East. On 4th September he sent his plan for the Human Resources volume to Humphrey, ". . I hope to come East early in October . . and hope to spend a day or two at Princeton discussing the book with you. After which we slip down to Philadelphia . . ."

## Chapter Seven

## *Island* and After . . .

"WE must dream in a pragmatic way." *Island* was not Aldous's testament; he expected to write more, to move on. Nevertheless it is the serious and deliberate expression of his thought on the for him over-riding theme of human happiness and the quality of life. Two-thirds of all sorrow is home-made and, so far as the universe is concerned, unnecessary. What can we do to avoid this sorrow? What can we do to make people more happy, more fulfilled, more loving? *Island* was intended as a not unworkable prescription of a good society in our age and on our planet. The locale is Pala, a hypothetical island between Ceylon and Sumatra which happens to have remained independent because of its rocky coast and lack of a natural harbour. In the 1840s Dr MacPhail, a Scottish surgeon of formidable intellect and character, saved the then Raja's life by operating on him under hypnotic anaesthesia. The doctor remained, became the philosopher-king's friend, and the two men set out to change their society by adopting desirable features from different cultures of the East and West. This work was continued by the descendants of the Scotchman and the ruler for the next three generations. The book opens in the 1960s: we see and hear about the good society through the mediation of a ship-wrecked visitor from England. The island is beautiful and inhabited by a handsome race of human beings. "These things don't have to happen," our Gulliver is told (a highly civilized and very unhappy foreign correspondent). These things being hunger, war, urban squalor regimentation. "They happen only when people are stupid enough to allow them to happen . . . we're not overcrowded, we're not miserable, we're not under a dictatorship . . We chose to behave in a sensible and realistic way."

"How on earth were you able to choose?" Farnaby asked.
"The right people were intelligent at the right moment."[1]

Now, as Aldous used to say, it would be very nice if we were all good and happy and intelligent—but what on earth do you do to *implement* these intentions? How do you set about it? What sort of

[1] *Island*, Chatto & Windus, 1962. All quotations in this chapter, unless otherwise stated, are from *Island*.

upbringing? What sort of social, economic arrangements? What do you do about the problem of power? Of beliefs? And this is what he tried to work out in *Island*.

> "And which are the best answers?"
> "None of them is best without the others."
> "So there's no panacea?"
> "How could there be."

So Aldous has them try to make the best of all the worlds. There is enough to eat. "More than enough. We eat better than any other country in Asia, and there's a surplus for export." Why? "Lenin used to say that electricity plus socialism equals communism. Our equations are rather different. Electricity minus heavy industry plus birth control equals democracy and plenty. Electricity plus heavy industry minus birth control equals misery, totalitarianism and war." The population of Pala (about two million) has been stable for a century—due to a low death rate (advanced medicine and sanitation) *and* a low birth rate: two children per family the usual, three the limit. Agriculture is scientifically developed . . . "in the fifties we built the first super-phosphate factory east of Berlin . ."), the economy is neither capitalist nor socialist.

> ". . None of those blood-sucking usurers that you find all over the Indian countryside. And no commercial banks in your western style. Our borrowing and lending system was modelled on those credit unions that Wilhelm Raiffeisen set up more than a century ago in Germany. Dr Andrew persuaded the Raja to invite one of Raiffeisen's young men to come here and organize a co-operative banking system . . ."

In a word (Aldous does not go into it in detail), they have solved the economic problem. "It wasn't difficult.

> . . Not being over-populated, we have plenty. But although we have plenty, we've managed to resist the temptation that the West has now succumbed to—the temptation to over-consume . . . And finally we don't spend a quarter of the gross national product preparing for World War III or even World War's baby brother, Local War MMMCCXXXIII . . . If war, waste and money-lenders were abolished, you'd collapse. And while you people are over-consuming, the rest of the world sinks more and more deeply into chronic disaster. Ignorance, militarism and breeding, these three—and the greatest of these is breeding. . . . Another ten or fifteen years

of uninhibited breeding, and the whole world, from China to Peru
via Africa and the Middle East will be fairly crawling with Great
Leaders, all dedicated to the suppression of freedom, all armed to the
teeth by Russia or America or, better still, by both at once . . .

Once or twice we get a glimpse of the other, the contemporary,
the "real" world beyond Pala. Again through Farnaby Gulliver,
the special correspondent, who remembers the cocktail party at
the Foreign Office on Rendang, the neighbouring totalitarian
island. "Everybody who was anybody was there.

All the local dignitaries and their wives—uniforms and medals.
Dior and emeralds. All the important foreigners—diplomats galore,
British and American oilmen, six members of the Japanese trade
mission, a lady pharmacologist from Leningrad, two Polish engineers, a German tourist who happened to be a cousin of Krupp
von Bohlen, an enigmatic Armenian representing a very important
financial consortium in Tangiers, and . . the fourteen Czech technicians who had come with last month's shipment of tanks and
cannons and machine guns from Skoda. And these are the people . .
who rule the world . .Ye are the cyanide of the earth . . .
". . . Nice comfortable people just don't have any idea what the
world is like. Not exceptionally, as it was during the War, but all the
time. All the time." And as he spoke he was seeing . . . all the hateful
scenes he had witnessed in the course of those well-paid pilgrimages
to every hell-hole and abattoir revolting enough to qualify as News.
Negroes in South Africa, the man in the San Quentin gas chamber,
mangled bodies in an Algerian farm-house, and everywhere mobs,
everywhere policemen . . paratroopers . . .

In Pala the political arrangements make it as good as impossible
for anyone to dominate on a large scale, while the drive to power
is already curbed on the individual level. "The power problem
has its roots in anatomy and bio-chemistry and temperament."
So has delinquency. Neither are hard to cope with if you start
early enough.

Blood tests, psychological tests, somato-typing . . an EEG . . . And
when they've been spotted, the potentially aggressive or retarded . .
appropriate treatment is started immediately. Within a year
practically all of them are perfectly normal . . . In your part of the
world, delinquency is still left to clergymen, social workers and the
police . . . With what results? . . A year in jail won't cure Peter Pan
of his endocrine disbalance or help the ex-Peter Pan to get rid of its
psychological consequences . . . what you need is early diagnosis and
three pink capsules a day before meals . . .

Palanese medicine, likewise, is mainly preventive.

"Well, there was that group of American doctors [who] came last year [this is a young nurse speaking] . . They wanted to find out why we have such a low rate of neurosis and cardio-vascular trouble. Those doctors! . . they really made . . everybody's hair stand on end in the whole hospital."

"So you think our medicine's pretty primitive?" [asks Farnaby]

"That's the wrong word . . . It's fifty per cent terrific and fifty per cent non-existent. Marvellous antibiotics—but absolutely no methods for increasing resistance, so that antibiotics won't be necessary. Fantastic operations—but when it comes to teaching people the way of going through life without having to be chopped up, absolutely nothing . . . Alpha Plus for patching you up . . but Delta Minus for keeping you healthy . . ."

And what do you do to keep people well? "Chemical answers, psychological answers, answers in terms of what you eat, how you make love, what you see and hear . ." The Palanese, of course, are given early training in the perceptions (non-verbal education), training which allows them to realize the inter-connectedness of things; and their love making is encouraged to begin spontaneously, sensuously, free of guilt . . .

*One must dream in a pragmatic way* . . . An empirical way . . . A major point about *Island* is that Aldous was not indulging in pure phantasy. His epigraph on the title page is a dictum of Aristotle, "In framing an ideal we may assume what we wish, but should avoid impossibilities." Most of the Palanese social arrangements and techniques, from somato-typing to those Bismarckian co-operatives, had been, at the time of writing, thought of here, tried out there, experimented with at some university, laboratory, hospital or school. Take that operation on the Raja under hypnosis which started off the whole thing: this is an almost verbatim description of an operation performed by Dr James Esdaile[1] on 3rd June 1846 in Calcutta. Esdaile, who practised in India in the nineteenth century, was one of the pioneers of hypnotic or mesmeric anaesthesia. He performed some three hundred major operations without anaesthetics and without pain, and this with a staggeringly low mortality rate for the time. "Which shows", as Aldous once wrote to Humphrey, "what can be done by psychological means to minimize shock and increase resistance to infection.

1 See Esdaile's *Mesmerism in India* (1846) and William Neilson's *Mesmerism in Relation to Medical Practice* (1855).

These facts have been known for more than a century. But nobody seems to have drawn the obvious conclusions or done anything about them [Esdaile and his fellow pioneers were attacked and, in some cases, hounded out of the medical profession] . . .

Or take the way the Palanese condition their infants in the novel (Pavlov for a *good* purpose). The mother strokes the baby while she is feeding it, and talks to him; then while it is sucking and being caressed she introduces it to the animal or person— dog, snake, father, stranger—she wants it to love, rubbing its body against theirs and murmuring the word, *good, good*. At first the child will only understand the tone of voice. "Later on, when he learns to speak, he'll get the full meaning. Food plus caress plus contact plus 'good' equals love. And love equals pleasure, love equals satisfaction." And so a conditioned reflex of a most valuable nature will have been built up.

We should certainly not be too proud to learn from people, however primitive they may seem. [Aldous remarked in one of his M.I.T. lectures] Their method seems to be an extraordinary brilliant invention, and heaven knows we have need enough of love in this extremely loveless world we live in.

Palanese schoolchildren start science education at the time of elementary arithmetic. Ecology—"Never give children a chance of imagining that anything exists in isolation.

Make it plain from the very first that all living is relationship. Show them relationships in the woods, in the fields, in the ponds and streams, in the villages, and the country around it. Rub it in.
And . . we always teach the science of relationship in conjunction with the ethics of relationship. Balance, give and take, no excesses— it's the rule in nature and, translated out of fact into morality, it *ought* to be the rule among people . . . children find it very easy to understand an idea when it's presented to them in a parable about animals . . .

And now for a condensation of some essentials Aldous tried to state.

"The point . . is to get people to understand that we're not *completely* at the mercy of our memory and our phantasies. If we're disturbed by what's going on inside our heads, we can do something about it. It's all a question of being shown what to do and then practising—

the way you learn to write or play the flute . . . [to learn] a technique that [will] develop . . into a method of liberation. Not complete liberation, of course . . This technique won't lead you to the discovery of your Buddha Nature: but it may help you to prepare for that discovery—help you by liberating you from the hauntings of your own painful memories, your remorses, your ceaseless anxiety about the future . . ."

And here something which Aldous always emphasized in one way and another:

Public health and social reform are the indispensable preconditions of any kind of general enlightenment.

What chance is there of fulfilment of these pre-conditions?

"One's justified [says the contemporary Dr MacPhail] in feeling extremely pessimistic about the current situation. But despair, radical despair—no, I can't see any justification for that."
"Not even when you read history?"

No, says the doctor, not even when he reads history.

"How do you manage to do that?"
"By remembering what history is—the record of what human beings have been impelled to do by their ignorance and the *enormous bumptiousness that makes them canonize their ignorance as a political or religious dogma*. [My italics.]

And here a passage about our present historical situation. The Palanese do not wish to produce or buy armaments, nor have they the faintest desire to land on the moon. "Only the modest ambition to live as full human beings on this island at this latitude on this planet.

. . If the politicians in the newly independent countries had any sense . . they'd do the same. But they want to throw their weight around; they want to have armies, they want to catch up with the motorized television addicts of America and Europe. You people have no choice—you're irretrievably committed to applied physics and chemistry, with all their dismal consequences, military, political and social. But the under-developed countries aren't committed. They don't *have* to follow your example. They're still free to take the road we've taken . . *the road that leads towards happiness from the inside out* [my italics], *through health, through awareness, through a change in one's attitude towards the world; not towards the mirage of happiness from the outside in, through toys and pills and non-stop distractions. They could still choose our way; but they don't want to, they want to be exactly like you, God help them . . .*

From Mesmerism and bio-chemistry, from Taoism, Tantra, Zen, from the *Bardo Thodol* and Gestalt philosophy, from psychedelics, from the Greeks, the Chinese, the Quakers, from Victorian novelists and Christian saints, from Darwin, Mendel, Myers, William James, John Dewey, Sheldon, Alexander, Bates, from echoes of the E-therapy and Menninger and Laura's improvisations, from Aldous's own experiences, from all of these the Islanders derive their knowledge and their understanding and their practice, their techniques for living, for dealing with the young, the ageing, the well; their techniques for dealing with the pains of the heart, with loss, with *dying*, for coming to terms with the irreducible one third of sorrow. As in *Brave New World* there is no violence on Pala, no crime or cruelty or hunger, no material fears; unlike *Brave New World*, there is full consciousness of the basic *misère de l'homme*, the appalling possibilities, the certainties of unhappiness.

". . . Painless bereavement—no. And of course that's as it should be. It wouldn't be right if you could take away all pain of bereavement; you'd be less than human."

When Dr MacPhail's wife lies dying he, too, helps her through her last hours. Throughout *Island* there can be found traces of the private Aldous, as if he had wished to leave an auto-biographical squiggle here, a tribute there, a summing-up, a joke shared with himself . . . There is a glancing evocation of that very powerful memory of D. H. Lawrence's death at Vence. "Over there in the corner," says the dying woman, "I can see myself there. And she can see my body on the bed." There is a piece of defunct Aldous surfacing through Farnaby, the man from the West. Was he ever interested in power? they ask him. Never, he answers, "One can't have power without committing oneself."

"And for you the horror of being committed outweighs the pleasure of pushing other people round?"

"By a factor of several thousand times."

Defunct. Yet how much heart-searching it had caused the man who wrote *Point Counter Point*, who struggled over *Eyeless in Gaza*, that horror of his younger years of being committed, that desire to remain the spectator with the telescope, remain in the role he regarded as his guilty privilege and his prison. And here his middle-aged view—how quiet, how detached—of having to live in urban England.

Well, you won't like the climate, you won't like the food, you won't like the noises or the smells or the architecture. But you'll almost certainly like the work and you'll probably find that you can like quite a lot of people.

And here Aldous's "favourite worst line of poetry", the oddly unpronounceable

*Who props, thou ask'st, in these bad days my mind?*

which happens to be by his own Uncle Matthew.

There is Maria. "You used to say I was like a flea," the wife in the book says to her husband before she dies. "Here one moment and then, hop! somewhere else, miles away. No wonder you could never educate me!"

"But *you* educated *me* all right," he tells her. "If it hadn't been for you coming in and pulling my hair and making me look at the world and helping me understand it, what would I be today? A pedant in blinkers . . . But luckily I had the sense to ask you to marry me, and luckily you had the folly to say yes and then the wisdom and intelligence to make a good job of me. After thirty-seven years of adult education I'm almost human."

"But I'm still a flea . . ." she says, "And yet I did try. I tried very hard; I don't know if you ever realized it . . I was always on tiptoes, always straining up towards the place where you were doing your work and your thinking and your reading. On tiptoes . . Goodness, how tiring it was! What an endless series of efforts! And all of them quite useless. Because I was just a dumb flea hopping about down here among the people and the flowers and the cats and dogs. Your kind of highbrow world was a place I could never climb up to . . . I never *knew* anything . . . I could only *see*."

Why did Aldous choose—with indeed a good many misgivings —to cast his prescription for the good society in the form of a novel? (A philosophic novel, to be sure.) Because he believed, in spite of contemporary cluckings, that the novel is the most effective literary form. In *War and Peace* we learn more about war and peace than we would from any documentary of comparable talent. Aldous was only too aware that he would never write *War and Peace*, but thought that even fiction on another level was likely to be more persuasive, leave traces on a larger public, than an essay. Up to a point his choice may also have been influenced by the career of *Brave New World*. In fact *Island*, too, was to reach a large public; did it persuade? Aldous thought that it had not, that its propositions, on the whole, were not seriously discussed or looked at in the light of applicability. To a number of his readers Pala with its happiness and kindliness and good sense was immensely moving, made them long for a world in which such happiness was an aim within sight for themselves and their children. To a great many others, and this must be faced, the book was a boring tale of preaching goody-goodies. The attraction of Pala may well lie in the mind of the beholder.

*Island*, of course, is also a religious novel. The islanders are compassionate not by mere Pavlovian training. We cannot love our neighbour as we should, unless we love God as we should—the true end of their existence in this mortal world is the Perennial Philosophy, is contemplation, is religion, but religion held lightly, non-combatively, a religion without specific gravity, as it were: non-revealed, non-dogmatic, non-organized. "Mahayana Buddhism, with a bit of Shivaism on the side," as a Palanese remarks. When Gulliver presses him as to exact beliefs, he is told,

"That's one of the questions the Buddha always refused to answer. Believing in the eternal life never helped anyone to live in eternity. Nor, of course, did dis-believing . . ."

And there, I think, we come to another stumbling block. It is hard enough nowadays to write about religion, and here we have religion which is not only alien to both Christians and Agnostics (though goodness knows that Aldous's readers ought to be familiar with the terminology), uncomfortable to the unregenerate, to *l'homme moyen sensuel*, but at the same time so subtle and elusive that it seems nearly impossible to get it across to anyone who has not already "bought his ticket to Athens". It can and has been got across, of course, at times by music, a landscape, a flash of intuition in the night—Aldous had to do it in cold print. A great deal of cold print at that. This may well have been one of the causes for the resistance and impatience generated by the book.

There is one other thing. The inhabitants of Aldous's pragmatic dream use drugs. In *Brave New World*, it was *soma*, the forerunner of a tranquillizer cum euphoric, which the citizens were conditioned into taking to stifle discontent with their own lot and muffle cosmic questions; *soma,* in fact, was dope; Aldous deplored it. On *Island* the substance is a perfected version of LSD used sacramentally by men and women who desire to get out of their own light and look over the wall. For Aldous—there is no getting around this—the whole thing was tremendously serious and he did believe in the possibility of a widely applicable mind-enlarging drug. He derived this belief from the reports of researchers and clinicians contemporarily using such drugs in cases of alcoholism and neuroses, and primarily from his own experiences. This is how he felt and thought about these in 1959, six years, that is, after he had swallowed his first fraction of a gram of mescalin and was waiting for the results with Humphrey Osmond and Maria.

. . . I have taken mescalin twice and lysergic acid three or four times [he wrote to Father Thomas Merton in January 1959]. My first experience was mainly aesthetic. Later experiences were of another nature and helped me to understand many of the obscure utterances to be found in the writings of the mystics, Christian and Oriental. An unspeakable sense of gratitude for the privilege of being born into this universe. ("Gratitude is heaven itself," says Blake— and I know now exactly what he is talking about.) A transcendence of the ordinary subject-object relationship. A transcendence of the fear of death. A sense of solidarity with the world and its spiritual principle . . . Finally, an understanding, not intellectual, but in some sort total, an understanding with the entire organism, of the affirmation that God is Love. The experiences are transient, of course; but the memory of them, and the inchoate revivals of them which tend to recur spontaneously or during meditation, continue to exercise a profound effect upon one's mind. There seems to be no evidence in the published literature that the drug is habit-forming or that it creates a craving for repetition. There is a feeling . . that the experience is so transcendently important that it is in no circumstances a thing to be entered upon light-heartedly or for enjoyment. (In some respects, it is not enjoyable; for it entails a temporary death of the ego, a going-beyond.) Those who desire to make use of this "gratuitous grace," to co-operate with it, tend to do so, not by repeating the experiment at frequent intervals, but by trying to open themselves up, in a state of alert passivity, to the transcendent "isness", to use Eckhart's phrase, which they have known and, in some sort, *been* . . .

Aldous concluded this long letter, "There is, obviously, a field here for serious and reverent experimentation." A year or so later on, in his lecture on Visionary Experience, he approached the subject in different terms.[1]

> . . . there are other directly chemical methods [for inducing visionary experiences]. There is an enormous history in this field . . . In the past the majority of these substances, these mind-changing, vision-inducing substances, have been dangerous. Opium, of course, is a dangerous substance; even dear old alcohol is a dangerous substance . . . the really startling fact about recent pharmacological developments is that a number of chemical substances had been discovered in recent years which permit . . enormous changes in consciousness . . without inflicting serious damage upon the body . . .
> . . Experiments, of course, have been made by eminent psychologists for a long time. William James, for example, made considerable experiments with nitrous oxide and incidentally was much blamed by some of his colleagues for such a frivolous undertaking and for taking it so seriously. James was defended by Bergson in his *The Two Sources of Morality and Religion*, where he said we must remember that the nitrous oxide was not the cause of Professor James's "remarkable experience," it was the occasion that removed certain obstacles which permitted this other material to come through. The obstacles could have been removed . . by other psycho-physical means, but this particular means did open the door, and the nature of the experience which came through is not affected by the nature of the key which is used to open the door. This is a very interesting passage in Bergson, and I think it is fundamentally true, although there seems to be something rather discreditable and unfair about the possibility of opening the door by a means so simple as psilocybin or LSD-25. There seems to be no reason to doubt that what comes through is of the same nature as what comes through via breathing exercises, or fasting, flagellation . . .

What *comes through*—after swallowing a powder or a pill—is it qualitatively, substantially the same as what comes through after weeks or years of asceticism and the more violent physical austerities? *Ought* it to be the same? As Aldous said, there seems to be something discreditable and unfair about it; indeed to many of us the whole thing is offensive or at least disquieting—it goes against the grain of what is left of our Christian or Puritan tradition. Professor Zaehner[2] stated this notion very simply after his own rather unrevealing experience (*trivial* was his word—"In Huxley's terminology, 'self-transcendence' of a sort did take

---

[1] This is a lecture Aldous delivered on several occasions. I am quoting from the text of Professor Lamson's working copy transcribed from the tapes at M.I.T. where "Visionary Experience" was the 6th Huxley Lecture.

[2] R. C. Zaehner, *Mysticism Sacred and Profane*. Oxford, at the Clarendon Press, 1957.

place, but transcendence into a world of farcical meaninglessness. All things were one in the sense that they were all, at the height of my manic state, equally funny . . ."); the conclusion he then came to was,

> I would not wish to take the drug again, but purely on moral grounds . . . the more the experience fades into the past, the clearer does it seem to me that, in principle, artificial interference with consciousness is, except for valid medical reasons, wrong.

To which argument Aldous had already replied the year before, in *Heaven and Hell*,[1] "But in one way or another, *all* our experiences are chemically conditioned,

> and if we imagine that some of them are purely "spiritual", purely "intellectual", or purely "aesthetic", it is merely because we never troubled to investigate the internal chemical environment . . . Furthermore, it is a matter of historical record that most contemplatives worked systematically to modify their body chemistry, with a view to creating the internal conditions favourable to spiritual insight. When they were not starving themselves into low blood sugar and a vitamin deficiency, or beating themselves into intoxication by histamine, adrenalin and decomposed protein, they were cultivating insomnia and praying for long periods in uncomfortable conditions in order to create the psycho-physical symptoms of stress . . . or, if they were Orientals, they did breathing exercises to accomplish the same purpose. Today we know how to lower the efficiency of the cerebral reducing valve by direct chemical action, and without the risk of inflicting serious damage on the psycho-physical organism. For an aspiring mystic to revert, in the present state of knowledge, to prolonged fasting and violent self-flagellation would be as senseless as it would be for an aspiring cook to behave like Charles Lamb's Chinaman, who burned down the house in order to roast a pig . . .

In 1961, after eight years of psychedelic experiences, Aldous is once more on record. In the London interview he was questioned at some length by John Chandos, to whom the subject appears to have been novel—as indeed it then was to the public at large—and a trifle alien.

"How often have you taken mescalin?"
"I've taken mescalin twice, and LSD about five times, I suppose."[2]
"Is the effect the same on everyone?"

1 Chatto & Windus, 1956.
2 After that point, Aldous appears to have taken a psychedelic drug twice, possibly three times, more. In the chapter "The Door in the Wall" (Part X, 3), I put the total, including mescalin, LSD and psilocybin, as between nine and eleven times; Laura speaks of twelve times in all, and is very likely right.

"It varies. On the whole, no. Statistically about 70% get a good and positive and happy result from it, a certain percentage get no results, and a certain percentage get very unpleasant and hell-like results out of it. They get very frightened."

"And what were yours?"

"Mine were always positive . . ."

"How long does the effect last?"

"Eight hours."

"During this time, do you just sit, or do you move about?"

"You move about if you want to . . You spend a lot of time sitting quietly looking at things—getting some of these strange metaphysical insights into the world . . ."

"Is it a habit-forming drug?"

"No, no, absolutely not . . . Most people I know haven't any special desire to go on taking it. They would like to take it every six months or every year or something of this kind . . ."

"Is it not a condition one wants to be in, or continue to be in?"

"You couldn't be in it all the time . . . The world becomes so extraordinary and so absorbing that you can't cross the street without considerable risk of being run over . . ."

"But if this vision is so valuable, doesn't one want to go on . . .?"

"Well, I would like to take it about once a year. Most people . . who have taken it have no *desire* to sort of fool with it constantly . . . You *take it too seriously* to behave in this way towards it. You don't want to wallow in it."

"Would it be wallowing if it opened up a life . .?"

"Well, you need a good deal of time to digest this, I think . . ."

Much of this has a hollow ring today, twelve years after and more. Aldous, who foresaw so much, did not foresee much of the squalid, catastrophic sequel. *Anything* can be misused, he said, and stuck to his guns—self-improvement and insight are intrinsically valuable, to the individual, to the world as a whole, even if they are, like so much else, chemically induced. One way in which Aldous went wrong, I think, was in failing to take into account that there might be an extremely close relation between the quality of the man who takes the drug and the quality of the experience. Baudelaire, whose own excursions were more prolonged and terrifying, made this extremely important point.[1] (He is speaking of experience under hashish.)

. . . L'ivresse . . ne sera, il est vrai, qu'un immense rêve . . . mais elle gardera toujours la tonalité particulière de l'individu. L'homme a voulu rêver, le rêve gouvernera l'homme; mais ce rêve sera bien le fils de son père . . .

[1] Charles Baudelaire, *Les Paradis Artificiels*, "Le Théater de Séraphin."

[The intoxication, indeed, will simply be an immense dream . . . but it will always keep the pattern, the style, the quality of the individual dreamer. Man wants to dream . . . the dream will take charge; but the dream will be its father's son.]

*Mine were always positive*—the insights, the transcendence, the immense reality or dream that rose in Aldous's consciousness, were they not related, were they not conditional upon who or what *he* was?

To Aldous the dream was good; he wished, believed, that it could be shared. On the mundane level, to researchers, to friends, he counselled caution. ("Always Aldous emphasizes," Laura wrote, "how delicately and respectfully these chemicals should be used; and that they are only one of many means through which it is possible to increase good will among men.") One must not take them without doctor's consent, take them peacefully, deliberately, in the right health and frame of mind, at the right place and time, in friendly surroundings, wise company . . . Under no circumstances must one touch the dubious, adulterated substances peddled by crooks (which is, of course, precisely what the majority of drug-takers nowadays resort to). Aldous deplored the antics of young Timothy Leary, that enthusiast and high priest of the psychedelic cult. (He and Humphrey had first met Leary at Cambridge, Massachusetts, in November 1960, when he was conducting experiments with mind-expanding drugs at Harvard.) Aldous often tried to warn him; had urged him, for instance, without much success, to get his followers to desist from taking green LSD[1], a boot-legged liquid in plastic bottles which was circulating at the time.

. . Yes, what about Tim Leary? [Aldous wrote to Humphrey in December 1962] I spent an evening with him here a few weeks ago—and he talked such nonsense . . that I became quite concerned. Not about his sanity—because he is perfectly sane—but about his prospects in the world; for this nonsense-talking is just another device for annoying people in authority, flouting convention, cocking snooks at the academic world; it is the reaction of a mischievous Irish boy to the headmaster of his school. One of these days the headmaster will lose patience . . . I am very fond of Tim . . but why, oh why, does he *have* to be such an ass? . . .

I must now return to the question, to what extent Aldous can be regarded as a causative factor in the present drug scene? *Was* he a major link? Or an incidental, if much publicized, one? A seducer, a misleader? Or an alibi at second or third-hand? Was

1 Dr Humphrey Osmond in letters to S. B.

he inadequately informed, should he and could he have known more about the potential dangers, physical, genetic, social, of these drugs? Evidence is elusive and the whole matter beclouded by emotion and by hearsay[1]—Aldous acclaimed as an apostle, Aldous deplored as wicked or gullible and woolly-minded; and of course Aldous no longer here to give his answer. I can only say, what I tried to say some two hundred pages earlier about *The Doors of Perception*, that I do not know. There *are* questions. Some, inevitably, quantitative. How many individual people, particularly among the serious, well-intentioned young, pinned their hopes on psychedelics, did actually take drugs in consequence of reading, or listening to Aldous? How many of them came to harm? How far did *their* example cause a further spread? Can one seriously assert that what is called the drug explosion would not be with us today had there been no Aldous Huxley? His public contribution consists of one distinctly highbrow book, *The Doors*,[2] passages of a lecture delivered in academic institutions and two scenes in a novel, *Island*, one of them a not entirely re-assuring description of a trip, the other a long, solemn account of a psychedelic rite. What weight is to be attached to these in the historical context—the waning of authoritative religion, the revulsion from consumers' existence, the perennial human longing to side-step the daily world, the aftermath of the Vietnam war? On the other hand, ought one to take into account the legend of Aldous's mescalin allegiance which may well have been more consequential than his actual words? And what of the future? Is the present messy, tragic footling with drugs a passing side-phenomenon, an *accident de parcours*, on the road to the beneficent pharmacological revolution Aldous liked to predict?

Leaving aside the accumulated mass of controversial material, I feel that I should mention the fragmentary comments by two people very close to Aldous. One is entire, almost casual, dismissal by Krishnamurti.[3]

Well, Aldous used to discuss it with me, but of course the whole thing is meaningless. Why go so far? We all know that human consciousness can be disturbed with stimulus. An alcoholic drink will do that much for you.

The other comes from Maria. Why are they making all this fuss, she is supposed to have said, in effect, to one or two friends when

[1] Such as people, whom he may not even have met, claiming to have been on trips with Aldous.

[2] *Heaven and Hell*, surely, is more of a cadenza on visual and visionary art.

[3] Talking to Chaman Nahal, from *Drugs and the Other Self* by Chaman Nahal. Harper & Row, 1970.

Aldous and Gerald Heard first described their transfigured world of mescalin. "I have known that it *is* like this all along." It has the ring of truth: Maria knew, did have the experience spontaneously (and one can hear her throw off that kind of remark). But I don't think it is the whole truth. I never had a chance to talk to her about it. In Rome, in 1954, *The Doors of Perception* came up for a few seconds (Aldous had dedicated it to her; of his whole *œuvre* only two books bear a dedication, *The Doors* to Maria, *Island* to Laura). Maria said little; what she implied, in her kind of shorthand, was approval, a feeling at peace with the book and all that it meant to Aldous.

*Meant to Aldous* . . . Let us give the last word here to him. Prefaced—irresistible temptation—by Baudelaire.

> . . . C'est une espèce de hantise, mais de hantise intermittente, dont nous devrions tirer, si nous étions sage, la certitude d'une existence meilleure et l'espérance d'y atteindre par l'exercice journalier de notre volonté . . .
>
> . . . C'est pourquoi je préfère considérer cette condition anormale de l'esprit comme une véritable grâce, comme un miroir magique où l'homme est invité à se voir en beau, c'est-à-dire tel qu'il devrait et pourrait être; une espèce d'excitation angélique, un rappel à l'ordre . . .[1]
>
> [. . . It is a kind of obsession, but intermittent . . from which we should extract, if we were wise, the certainty of a better life and the hope of finding it through the daily exercise of our will . . .
>
> [. . . This is why I prefer to regard this anomalous condition of the spirit as a true grace, a magic mirror where man is invited to see himself *en beau*, that is, such as he ought to be and could be . . .]

Baudelaire wrote this more than a century ago, Baudelaire who came to the immense dream by a different road—poetic genius, private despair—but who, too, kept compass with the diamond clarity of his intelligence. Now to Aldous. In the course of the London interview, he had answered questions quietly, patiently; at one point he quickened—

> Different, yes . . . I mean the intensity of the experience is entirely unlike an ordinary experience . . . But on the other hand, it quite obviously resembles spontaneous experiences which certain artists and religious people have unquestionably had . . .
>
> . . It's an immense intensification, a transfiguration of the external world into incredible beauty and significance . . .

---

1 *Les Paradis Artificiels*, "Le Goût de l'infini."

There is a quiet conviction in those words as they are spoken, something very simple, very moving; to get the feeling of this one ought to hear that happy, mellow voice.[1]

> . . . It's also beyond that kind of aesthetic experience—there may be . . a sense of solidarity with the universe, solidarity with other people . . . Understanding of such phrases as you get in the Book of Job, "Yea, though he slay me, yet I will trust in him"—this thing opens the door to these experiences . . Which can be of immense value to people. If they choose to make use of them. If they don't choose, well, this is what the Catholics call Gratuitous Grace: it doesn't guarantee salvation, it isn't sufficient and it isn't necessary for salvation; it can be collaborated with and it can be used in an intelligent way; it can be of immense help to people.
>
> And then there is the sense that *in spite of Everything*—I suppose this is the Ultimate Mystical conviction—in spite of Pain, in spite of Death, in spite of Horror, *the universe* is in some way A l l R i g h t, capital A, capital R . . .

Aldous wrote one more book, *Literature and Science*, begun in 1962, finished in the spring of 1963. It has perhaps been somewhat overlooked—another long essay, a slim volume—taken for the earlier, quite different, *Science, Liberty and Peace*; yet it is probably one of the most revealing of his later books, a re-casting and further distillation of the M.I.T. lectures, the most up-to-date as to his thought, and mood and stand. It is an unsolemn, ultimately optimistic book, good-tempered, easy to read, with a return to the wit and fun and playfulness of the early essays. The primary theme is stated in the three words of the opening sentence, "Snow or Leavis?" Aldous's answer can be inferred from his title, Literature *and* Science, not Literature *versus* Science.

> The world with which literature deals is the world into which human beings are born and live and finally die . . . the world of sufferings and enjoyments, of madness and common sense, of silliness, cunning and wisdom; the world of social pressures and individual impulses, of reason against passion, of instincts and conventions, of shared language and unshareable feeling and sensation; of innate differences and the rules . . the solemn or absurd rituals imposed by the prevailing culture . . .[2]

---

[1] I am delighted to be able to say that we *can* hear it. An admirable condensation of that interview on two gramophone records has been released by Denis Preston, the original instigator. "Personally Speaking."

[2] From *Literature and Science*. Chatto & Windus, 1963 (as all following quotations).

The scientist, as a professional,

> is the inhabitant of a radically different universe—not the world of
> given appearances but the world of inferred fine structures, not the
> experienced world of unique events and diverse qualities, but the
> world of quantified regularities.

The man of letters accepts the uniqueness of events, the diversity
of the world, the radical incomprehensibility of existence,

> . . accepts the challenge which uniqueness, multifariousness and
> mystery fling in his face and . . addresses himself to the paradoxical
> task of rendering the randomness and shapelessness of individual
> experience in highly organized and meaningful works of art.

The medium of these works of art is language—*La poésie s'écrit
avec des mots.* "There exists in every language a rough and ready
vocabulary for the expression of the individual's more private
experiences. Anyone capable of speech can say, 'I'm frightened',
or 'How pretty!' . . . In good literature . . the blunt imprecisions
of conventional language give place to subtler and more penetrating forms of expression. The ambition of the literary artist is to
speak about the ineffable, to communicate in words what words
were never intended to convey . . . [he] must therefore invent or
borrow some kind of uncommon language . . ." And here Aldous,
as he had so often done, invokes once more that potent line of
Mallarmé's, "*Donner un sens plus pur aux mots de la tribu*—that is the
task confronting every serious writer . . ." To purify, to enrich,
the language of the tribe . . . For a few pages Aldous, recalling the
serenities of *Texts and Pretexts*, returns to his old loves.

> . . There is the magic . . of unfamiliarly beautiful syntax and
> sentence construction; the magic of names and words that, for some
> obscure reason, seem intrinsically significant; the magic of well-
> ordered rhythms, of harmonious combinations of consonants and
> vowels. One thinks of such exquisite treasures of syntax as "Not to
> know me argues yourselves unknown," or *Tel qu'en Lui-même enfin
> l'éternité le change.* And at the other extreme of phrase-making one
> recalls the spell-like efficacy of such juxtaposed simplicities as "Cover
> her face: mine eyes dazzle: she died young"; as "I wak'd, she fled,
> and day brought back my night" . . .
> The supreme masters of syntactical magic are Milton and Mallarmé
> . . . *Paradise Lost* is Syntax Regained and completely remade . . . Else-
> where, and in lighter keys, we find such enchantments as "crossing
> the stripling Thames at Bablock Hithe", or "Amyntas now doth with
> Chloris sleep under a sycamore" . . . On a higher level of intrinsic

significance we find such Shakespearean marvels as "defunctive music", "sole Arabian tree", "multitudinous seas incarnadine." And what about Milton's "elephants endors'd with towers"? What about "sleek Panope" and "that two-handed engine at the door"! . . .

Some degree of verbal recklessness is characteristic of good poetry. There are slightly reckless good poets, and there are good poets who, at times, are extremely reckless . . . here is the final stanza of Yeats's *Byzantium.*

> *Astraddle on the dolphin's mire and blood,*
> *Spirit after spirit! The smithies break the flood,*
> *The golden smithies of the Emperor!*
> *Marbles of the dancing floor*
> *Break bitter furies of complexity*
> *Those images that yet*
> *Fresh images beget,*
> *That dolphin-torn, that gong-tormented sea.*

Now for the antithesis. "In the scientist, verbal caution ranks among the highest of virtues. His words must have a one-to-one relationship with some specified class of data or sequence of ideas.

By the rules of the scientific game he is forbidden to say more than one thing at a time, to attach more than one meaning to a given word, to stray outside the bounds of logical discourse . . . Poets and, in general, men of letters are permitted, indeed are commanded, by the rules of *their* game, to do all the things that scientists are not allowed to do . . .

The writer, then, must perform "the tasks for which his talents uniquely qualify him—namely, to render . . his own and other people's more private experiences . . [and] to relate these experiences in some humanly satisfying way to public experiences . . .

. . . Eliot is a great poet because he purified the words of the tribe in novel, beautiful and many-meaninged ways, not because he extended the field of subject-matter available to poetic treatment: he didn't. And this is true of most of his poetical successors. From their writings you would be hard put to it to infer the simple historical fact that they are contemporaries of Einstein and Heisenberg, of computers, electron microscopes and the discovery of the molecular basis of heredity, of Operationalism, Diamat and Emergent Evolution . . .

Whether we like it or not, Aldous postulates, ours is the Age of Science. And the question is, What can a writer do about it? And what, as a literary artist and a citizen, *ought* he to do about it?

.. For the non-specialist, a thorough and detailed knowledge of any branch of science is impossible. It is also unnecessary. All that is necessary .. is a general knowledge of science, a bird's-eye knowledge of what has been achieved in the various fields of scientific enquiry, together with an understanding of the philosophy of science and an appreciation of the ways in which scientific information and scientific modes of thought are relevant to individual experience and the problems of social relationships, to religion and politics, to ethics and a tenable philosophy of life . . .

The sciences of life have need of the artist's intuitions and, conversely, the artist has need of all that these sciences can offer him in the way of new materials on which to exercise his creative powers . . .

. . . Science, it seems hardly necessary to remark, provides no justification for slaughter and oppression. Hand in hand with progressive technology, it merely provides the means for implementing the old insanities in a novel and more effective way . . . To keep drawing attention to this grotesque and increasingly dangerous state of affairs is surely one of the functions, one of the prime duties, of the twentieth-century man of letters.

Aldous tried to convey something also of the tremendous implications of the new material available to the artist. " 'For the first time in history [he is quoting Werner Heisenberg, the physicist] man, on this planet, is discovering that he is alone with himself, without a partner and without an adversary.'

To put it more picturesquely, man is in the process of becoming his own Cataclysm, his own Saviour and own invading horde of Martians. And in the realm of pure science the same discovery— that he is alone with himself—awaits him as he progressively refines his analysis of matter. "Modern science," says Heisenberg, "shows us that we can no longer regard the building blocks of matter, which were considered originally to be the ultimate objective reality, as being 'things in themselves' . . . Knowledge of atoms and their movements 'in themselves', that is to say independent of our observation, is no longer the aim of research; rather we now find ourselves from the very start in the midst of a dialogue between nature and man, a dialogue of which science is only one part, so much so that the conventional division of the world into subject and object, is no longer applicable . . For the science of nature, the subject matter of research is no longer nature in itself, but nature subjected to human questioning, and to this extent man, once again, meets only with himself."

Presently Aldous comes to the point of how very little even the best informed philosophers and writers knew until very recently about man-the-species and man-the-product-of-culture. "The earth was largely unexplored, archaeology had not been invented . . .

Virtually everything we know about ourselves as the resultants of evolution, as the earth's dominant, wildly proliferating and most destructive species, as creators, beneficiaries and victims of culture, as the genius inventors and idiot-dupes of language, has come to us, during the last three or four generations, from paleontologists and ecologists, from systematic historians and . . the social scientists. And from geneticists, neurologists and bio-chemists has come, in great measure during the present century, most of what we now know about human beings as members of the animal kingdom, as living organisms with an inherited anatomy and an inherited chemical and temperamental individuality . . .

Then, "Who are We? What is our destiny? How can the often frightful ways of God be justified?

Before the rise of science, the only answers . . came from the philosopher-poets and poet-philosophers. Thus, in India the enigma of man's individual and collective destiny was unriddled in terms of a theory—implausibly simple and suspiciously moralistic—of reincarnation and *karma*. Present good luck was the reward for past virtue, and if you were suffering now, it was your fault . . .

In the Christian West the riddle was solved (or perhaps it would be truer to say that it was re-stated) in terms of some completely unobservable act of supernatural predestination . . . It was a matter simply of the arbitrariness of omnipotence, of God's good pleasure.

Men's destiny is a matter, among other things, of the observable differences between human individuals. Are these differences inherited or acquired, or inherited *and* acquired? For many centuries it seemed reasonable to debate the problem of Nature versus Nurture in terms of theology and metaphysics. Augustinians fought with Pelagians; Proto-Behaviourists, such as Helvétius, reacted against Jansenist Christianity by maintaining, in the teeth of all probability and on no evidence whatever, that any shepherd boy from the Cevennes could be transformed, by suitable tutoring, into another Isaac Newton or (if the tutor preferred) into a replica of St Francis of Assisi. "Everything," said Rousseau, "is good that comes from the Creator; everything is perverted by the hands of man." The Creator is now out of fashion; but environmental determinism remains the frame of reference within which many social scientists and many men of letters still do their feeling and their thinking. Theirs, surely, is an inexcusable one-sidedness; for the science of genetics has been with us for a long life-time and the unscientific study of innate human differences is as old as literature . . .

*Manners maketh man,* but on the other hand *you can't make a silk purse out of a sow's ear.* The old proverbs flatly contradict one another, but both are correct. Predestined by their heredity, human beings are post-destined by their environment . . .

From individual *karma* we now pass to the enigma of collective destiny. Kipling was probably wrong in asserting that there were lesser breeds without the law. But, along with other observers, he was probably right in thinking that the manifest differences in racial temperaments were more than merely cultural and must be due, at least in part, to hereditary factors.

The ways of God have never been justified, but they can be explained, at least partially, in non-theological terms. Why do these things happen to us? . . a number of fragmentary, but nonetheless useful and even enlightening answers to the riddle of human destiny are now forthcoming. And the same thing is true of the closely related riddle of human nature. Who and what are we? A complete scientific answer is still lacking. We know a great deal, but we do not yet know how to correlate what we know into an explanation . . .

To the twentieth-century man of letters science offers a treasure of newly discovered facts and tentative hypotheses. If he accepts this gift and if, above all, he is sufficiently talented and resourceful to be able to transform the new raw materials into works of literary art, the twentieth-century man of letters will be able to treat the age-old, and perennially relevant theme of human destiny with a depth of understanding, a width of reference, of which, before the rise of science, his predecessors (through no fault of their own, no defect of genius) were incapable.

Thought is crude, matter unimaginably subtle. [This is the final paragraph of Aldous's last book] Words are few and can only be arranged in certain conventionally fixed ways; the counterpoint of unique events is infinitely wide and their succession indefinitely long. That the purified language of science, or even the richer purified language of literature should ever be adequate to the givenness of the world and of our experience is, in the very nature of things, impossible. Cheerfully accepting the fact, let us advance together, men of letters and men of science, further and further into the ever expanding regions of the unknown.

Aldous's own philosophy was dynamic; he never said, This is enough; he never stood still. He asked, Where are we Going? and Where Ought we to be Going? His beliefs were both immensely complex and quite simple, (. . *it's a bit embarrassing to find at the end that one has no more to offer by way of advice than "try to be a little kinder*"). He believed in knowledge, pursued it with the same ardour he had expressed when he went down from Oxford—*I should like to go on for ever learning*, straightforward knowledge (yes, yes, he did more or less read through the whole of the Britannica as anecdote will have it) *and* intuitive knowledge, intangible knowledge, the end of explorative experience.

. . . I do think that the whole idea of the cognitive value of music, and indeed of all art, is probably very important. [He said at M.I.T.[1]] In a certain sense, art is something which imposes forms upon the flux of reality . . but in another sense it is also discovering, not merely forms, but that which lies behind the forms . . this view, after all, is profoundly important in the ideas of Plato—that in beauty we discover something about the nature of the world; that in some way or another, an entirely ineffable and inexplicable way, beauty is built into the fundamental nature of things, and that art is a method of discovering this. Music above all, with its strange capacity for discovering a sort of pure incorporeal, dynamic essence of life, does perhaps provide the most powerful weapon for exploring this aspect of the ultimate nature of the world.

"*What place has the supernatural in your own life?*" (How convenient to be able to resort to John Chandos's questions.)

"Well, I don't know what people mean exactly by the *supernatural*. In practice, I would say that what people call the *natural* in our Western tradition *is in fact* our projection of concepts upon the world . . It is *our picture* of the world with its names and labels . . utilitarian and scientific . . the general day-to-day picture . . . The *super*natural is the world as it comes to us in its mystery . . I mean, anyone who has ever had the experience of seeing the world without any labels and concepts, immediately has the impression of its being supernatural. In a curiously paradoxical way nature as it is in itself—and as much as we can ever know it—*is* supernatural . . . One is sometimes suddenly aware of *this bottomless mystery of existence*—sometimes *one is hit by this thing*. If you choose to call it the supernatural, I mean I don't know what other sense it has . . I mean, I don't believe in mysterious beings going around arranging things . . ."

"*A* mysterious Being going around arranging things?"

"Well, I do think [chuckling] there is a mysterious being . . but whether he arranges things is another question . . . *I just don't know* . . . I mean, one can be a complete agnostic and a complete mystic at the same time."

Chandos, still hoping to pin Aldous down, went on, "I want to

[1] In the 5th Lecture "Why Art?", on 2nd November 1960.

know whether you, yourself, felt you had any direct line . . to an individual upstairs . . ? As professing Catholics do?"

"No, no," Aldous said with utter detachment, faintly amused, "I certainly don't. I mean, what Blake calls 'Nobodaddy Aloft', I have no feelings about." And then again on the rising voice, the violin, "I am entirely on the side of the mystery. I mean, any attempts to explain away the mystery is ridiculous . . . I believe in the *profound and unfathomable mystery of life* . . which has a sort of divine quality about it . . ."

He was also on the side of happiness, as an absolute good, an intrinsic value. *The world is an illusion, but an illusion which we must take seriously.* He would say that people, adults and children could be made happier by decent living conditions, by love received and given . . . he thought that Bertrand Russell was right when he said[1] "Man is an animal and his happiness depends on his physiology more than he likes to think"; and at the same time Aldous's philosophy was governed by another equation—Man cannot be happy unless he is virtuous; man cannot be virtuous without God; God cannot be realized by man without virtue. "Virtue," he said, "is the essential preliminary to the mystical experience." And the mystical experience—enlightenment—is the supreme end of man.

The dialectic might be prolonged; one conclusion seems to impose itself, the conclusion that Aldous was a man who, for himself, had solved the question of how to live, for better and for worse, as a human being in this given world. To many of us he has left much to learn.

[1] In his essay "The Road to Happiness".

## Chapter Eight

## 1963—September, October, November

O N the 6th of September Aldous was getting ready for his lecture tour in the East; on the 13th he cancelled it. There had been a relapse. He spoke of it as a secondary inflammation, an after-effect of radiation. He was feeling pretty low again, he wrote to Humphrey, and would not be able to come and see him in October.

> Alas! But I think the sensible thing is to lie low and try to build up resistance and general health.

Whether he would be able to undertake the job of editing the Human Resources volume remained to be seen. "At present I have my doubts . . ." In a postscript he said, "I send you my news in confidence—so please don't mention it to Ellen or Matthew."

In fact Laura wrote to Matthew on the same day. "This is the letter I have been hoping I would not have to write . ."[1] She told him what had now become evident, that Aldous was a very ill man indeed. ". . He may or may not write you and J. and J. I would prefer that he tell you in his own way and time. But now I feel you must know. *Nobody knows* . . ." What Aldous knew she could not tell. ("Never during the difficult days of his illness," Dr Cutler wrote,[2] "did he question me too closely concerning his own case.")

On 24th September Aldous did write to his son. (A three-page letter, unpublished, in his usual firm hand.) "The trouble began in 1960 . . ." As for the present, the secondary inflammation of a neck gland is "painful and debilitating . . . This state of affairs will doubtless wear off in time . . . so patience is the watch word. Meanwhile please keep this information as private as possible. It's appalling how quickly one's private affairs can get into the tabloids."

The stress of this privacy was mainly borne by Laura.

> . . To all appearances our life was the same . . . friends . . would call up, to make plans to meet. Invitations . . requests for interviews . .

---

[1] The whole of this long letter, and a very detailed account of these and the following ten weeks, can be found in Laura's *This Timeless Moment*.
[2] *Mem. Vol.*

continued as though Aldous were well. My own life had never been so involved with the public as at this time. My book was at its peak of popularity. I had been scheduled for lectures and appearances; I received calls and letters from people in urgent need, who hoped and believed that one or two meetings with the author of a book which had already helped them were essential . . Since spring I had put off seeing people who had been working with me previously. I could not bring myself to cancel their appointments unless I could give them a very solid reason.

But if she had, "Friends and admirers would have pressed around us with their love and encouragement—but also, unwittingly, with their grief . . I was afraid their feelings would affect me and rob me of that strength I was jealously keeping for Aldous . . . I did not want to be distracted by anyone's sadness, even if it were in sympathy with Aldous . . ."

On 29th September Aldous broke his silence to Julian and Juliette. He led on from remarks about the weather, "In my own case meteorology has been compounded by a spell of ill health." He gave a factual outline of the medical history. "Result: I have had to cancel my lecture tour . . ." He supposed it would not be manageable for Julian to take over some of his engagements? "Another handicap is my persistent hoarseness, due to the nerve that supplied the right-hand vocal cord having been knocked out either by an infiltration of the malignancy, or by radiation. I hope this hoarseness may only be temporary, but rather fear that I may carry it to the grave.

What the future holds, one doesn't know. In general these malignancies in the neck and head don't do much metastasizing. Meanwhile I am trying to build up resistance with the combination of a treatment which has proved rather successful at the University of Montreal and the U of Manila—the only institutions where it has been tried out over a period of years . . . When this damned inflammation dies down, which it may be expected to do in a few weeks, I hope to get back to regular work. For the present I am functioning at only a fraction of normal capacity.

During those weeks and into October, Aldous, though very weak, got up every morning, had his meals downstairs, went for walks, did a little work. He was beset by a number of varying discomforts, backache, shortness of breath, exhaustion, but no pain that aspirin could not disperse. Friends came to see him. Gerald of an afternoon.

. . We sat in the garden.[1] His thinness was extreme, his voice tended to tire, but the vivacity of interest . . and concern, the power to entertain showed no abatement. Agilely he had come down the flight of stairs from his bedroom study to sit with us in his garden. When we[2] left he came with us down the steep slope at the foot of which cars had to park . . .

There is a story going round that Aldous and Gerald in days of health had made a pact to discuss their impending death if either of them fell very ill, and that Gerald went to him then in dread of this discussion, and was relieved when Aldous talked to him of everything but death.

Jake Zeitlin came to lunch. "We talked of old friends—we ticked them off, this one and that one . . . We spoke of ourselves as survivors.[3]

We walked silently on Mulholland Highway for a while. He asked if I thought that men would learn to live in peace before it was too late? Before parting I told him a story of meeting his brother Julian in Texas in the 1920's and of our discussing Aldous's irreverent essay on Beethoven in *Vanity Fair*. Julian said, "But Aldous is very young, you know."

*Literature and Science* came out. Aldous had a copy sent to Mrs Hubble, the astronomer's widow—Edwin and Grace, two of Aldous and Maria's closest friends of the first Californian decade. Now he had not seen Grace for some time and her cat, whom Maria used to find uncanny, had died.

. . I think [he wrote to her on 2nd October] Edwin wd have approved of *Literature and Science,* and hope that you will like it.
. . I have been under the weather and have had . . to confine myself to the house and a regimen of not too *dolce far niente*. When things go better I hope we can make the Pasadena trip and drink a cup of tea with you. I shall miss Nicolas.

Aldous had been commissioned by *Show* Magazine to write an article on "Shakespeare and Religion" for the poet's quater-

---

[1] Again from his *Kenyon Review* article of 1965. Gerald Heard was already a very ill man when I began my round of talking to Aldous's California friends in 1968, and I was not able to see him. So I never spoke to Gerald after 1941.
[2] I presume that the *we* refers to Gerald's friend Michael Barry who would have driven him to see Aldous.
[3] Jacob Zeitlin (to the best of my recollection) in an interview with George Wickes of Claremont College.

centenary in 1964, and this was what he was working at. On 3rd
October Betty drove him to the L.A. public library. Aldous moved
from shelf to shelf, knowing exactly what he wanted, where to
find it, pulled out a book, got his reference, put it back, with
swift efficiency. He insisted on going to the post office to mail a
package, would not let Betty do it for him. It was a copy of the
French edition of *Island* which Maria's cousin Marthe, married
to Masurel the French tycoon, had asked him to inscribe for her
husband's birthday. Aldous wrote his dedication in the post
office, laughing when he read it to Betty who had met Masurel
and knew his way of life.

> For Ernest Masurel,
>    A voyage to an island that cannot be arranged by Thomas Cook's.

On 9th October he wrote to Ellen, mainly about recorded
literature; on the 10th he wrote to Jeanne. Lightly. She had
thought of coming over but had given the idea up—"Je le
regrette," he wrote, he would have loved to have seen her. He
thanked her for a cheque she had sent to be put into an emergency
fund for Mère—who, he was sure would preside over all their
funerals, daughters', sons-in-law's, perhaps one or two grandchildren's.[1] He hoped that *The Genius and the Goddess* would be at
last produced in France, and had she noticed that those idiots of
publishers at Plon's had given *Island* the title *L'Isle*, when it ought
to have been *Isle*. "In Italy the book is called *Isola*, in Sweden *Ön*
and in Denmark (miracle of brevity) *Ø*. Tendresses à Noële et à
toi."

Of his own health not one word.

But by that time friends were beginning to know. On 11th
October Laura went to Mme Nys to prepare her for the truth.
That was also the day Aldous did not want to get up for the first
time. In the evening Betty wrote to Jeanne.

> . . Both your mother and Laura have asked me to write to you . . .
> your mother has written you her fears which have been mine too
> for many months—especially since he and Laura returned from
> Europe. I did not tell you, and until this moment have told no one,
> Jeanne dear, because I had no right to, and because I had the
> feeling that telling made *true* what I prayed some miracle might make
> untrue. About a week ago, however, Laura told me a long, heart-
> breaking story . . . and of Aldous's determination to get well, his
> faith that he would recover. He wanted no one to know because he
> was working, and still works for a while nearly every day.

---

[1] Mme Nys died in 1966.

He knows now that I know, from Laura, but we do not speak of it. I see him fairly often and *something* has made it possible for me to talk about all kinds of things—even gossip—and jokes.

It was then that Betty asked him, "Didn't you have a nick-name, Aldous, when you were small?" and that Aldous said, "They called me Ogie. Short for Ogre." He told her about life at Prior's Field, how at bed-time he used to run away and hide in his sister Margaret's room.

. . . At the post office a week ago . . . that was one of the moments I believed in a miracle, but I don't today . . . He looks dreadful, but has had no pain.

Jeanne was still debating whether to come or not—would her arrival be a shock to him? Betty was not sure. "My own answer to such questions—should I phone?—should I go there?—should I do this or that or nothing?—generally comes from wondering what Maria would have wanted me to do.

In the wish to help—with grapes or a book or a risqué story or an offer to go on errands—I haven't been wrong—so far. Maybe your answer will come from asking Maria. If you do come, please write Aldous a flock of lies . . .

On 15th October Aldous wrote to Humphrey at some length. ". . In our hypothetical volume on human resources there will obviously have to be a chapter—by you, no doubt—on the best emotional contexts in which the learning of new ways to use the mind should be placed.

The Indians tried to solve the problem by means of the guru system. But this lends itself to all kinds of psychological and social abuses (you should hear Krishnamurti on the subject of gurus!), and something less dangerous will have to be worked out.
. . I still don't know if I shall be able to undertake the work. At the moment I am so low . . . that I feel I shall never again be good for anything. But I hope and think this state of affairs will pass in due course. ("It will pass"—the only motto appropriate to every human situation, whether good or bad.)

The day before, a Monday, Matthew and Judy had arrived for the inside of a week, a visit disguised as a business trip. Aldous was propped up in bed in his white-washed room, his head in his hand, Matthew sat beside him, *his* head in his hand—the identical gesture (how many times we had seen it). Matthew talked to him about the book he was then writing about his experiences in Peru;[1] Aldous talked to him about his Shakespeare article—it was finished in his head but he didn't have the strength to tap it out on the machine. Matthew suggested that he dictate to him but Aldous, who had never dictated a line, who had always worked alone, thought he could not change his life-long method. There was time and vitality in those five days for Aldous and Matthew to have long talks by themselves. Once or twice Judy sat with him alone.

. . Once he said something about would this end all right? [Judy in a letter to S. B.] And I said it would and we both knew I was lying and I felt terribly ashamed . . .

On their last afternoon Aldous was well enough to get up for tea.

And there we were, he and Laura and Matthew and I sitting around the table in his room and Matthew getting him to talk about Forte and Sanary and people from the early days and Maria and the Fakir who got the lady's foot in his fly at the restaurant table—and when Aldous would tell one story, Matthew would say, but do you remember this—I think this is perhaps the first and only time I heard Matthew call Aldous Pa—and we all giggled. Aldous was the centre of the stage and Matthew the prompter—and I felt this was a father and his son—Laura and I were the spectators, but not shut out—we were able to share what those two men had known, and I thought this must have been what it was like, that household, when they lived in Europe . . . (When they lived in Sanary with Rina, Matthew said, they were settled and had things; from the time they came to America they were always gypsies . . .)

Next day, 19th October, Matthew and Judy left. Sandy Wendel took them to the airport. Betty went to look in on Aldous; they talked about his article. "He was full of enthusiasm, brilliant and funny . . ."

On 21st October Betty wrote to Jeanne again. "Poor sweet Aldous—and poor us—the doctor believes that he cannot live longer than a few months. He has promised Laura that Aldous will have no pain. She is distraught about his illness and in her cheerfulness with Aldous is being extraordinarily brave . . . He stays in bed and works for short periods nearly every day. To discourage him would be wrong. Telling him not to work would be telling him not to live."

On the afternoon of the 25th Betty found Aldous typing in the

---

1 Matthew Huxley, *Farewell to Eden*. Harper & Row, 1965.

garden in his pyjamas. She stayed and made some tea. On the 27th he was taken to the Cedars of Lebanon Hospital for observation. Betty visited him on the 1st and again on the 4th of November—Laura's birthday. She read to him and they discussed making a dramatic version of one of Aldous's early stories, "The Tilotson Banquet"[1] for TV. Christopher Isherwood came on the 5th.

Aldous looked like a withered old man, grey-faced, with dull blank eyes.[2] He spoke in a low, hoarse voice which was hard to understand; I had to sit directly facing him because it hurt him to turn his head. And yet—seeing what I saw and knowing what I knew—I could still almost forget about his condition while we talked, because his mind was functioning so well. I was nervous at first and talked at random. I mentioned Africa, and Aldous said that all the African nations would soon be governed by their armies. I mentioned V. V. Rozanov's *Solitaria*, which I had just been reading. Aldous promptly quoted a passage from it . . "the private life is above everything . . just sitting at home and picking your nose and looking at the sunset" . . .

Laura had told me that Aldous did not realize how sick he was. But now he began to speak about old age, and I couldn't help suspecting that this was a kind of metaphor, a way of referring to his own death. He spoke of it almost with petulance, as a wretched hindrance which prevented you from working. He told me that he did not think he would ever write another novel. "I feel more and more out of touch with people." And he added that when one is old one is absolutely cut off from the outside world. I told him, quite sincerely, that I have the impression that, as I grow older, my character gets worse and worse. This made him laugh a lot—not, I think, because he disbelieved me but because he found the statement somehow reassuring. We parted almost cheerfully . . .

On 6th or 7th November Aldous was taken home again to Virginia's house. Meanwhile, to his relief, Laura had telephoned New York and managed to extend the deadline for the Shakespeare article to 30th November. More than half of the first draft was down on paper, but now Aldous was no longer strong enough to type. He went on in longhand—large letters written with a marking pencil (he never went back to spectacles). There were a few things that still gave him pleasure. He could not listen to much music, but he enjoyed looking at objects if they were very near

---

[1] First published in the *Cornhill* Magazine, January 1921; then in *Mortal Coils*, Chatto & Windus, 1922.
[2] *Mem. Vol.*

and in strong light. Once Laura took Rembrandt's Polish Rider
off the wall and they looked at it together. ("The great confidence
of the man," Aldous said, "is so wonderful, isn't it?") Every day
Peggy Kiskadden came with roses from her garden and Laura
would place one a few inches from his face.

Books remained. Virginia read to him by the hour, day after
day. "It was his . . capacity to *listen*," Laura wrote, "that, more
than anything else, made those last weeks bearable . . even in
great discomfort, he was able to direct his attention to what was
read to him . . ." Small doses of Dilaudid[1] now supplemented the
aspirin. There were two nurses; Cutler and two other doctors
came daily. One can imagine the life of the house ("This illness,
darling—" Aldous said to Laura, "this is the very last thing I
wanted you to have to put up with"). Virginia took it on as a
matter of course, coped with it admirably—with two children
underfoot—coped with the nurses, the Spanish maid, the constant
demands on every household resource, the coming and going of
friends, the telephone, the deliveries. ("Virginia is my greatest
help," Laura wrote to Matthew and the Julians, "particularly
for the unobtrusive and nonchalant way in which she helps.")

Laura had by now alerted Rosalind Rajagopal, who came
regularly from Ojai bringing the oranges grown on her ranch
Aldous had asked for, sitting with him, giving him massage.

On the morning of 10th November, a Sunday, Aldous talked to
Laura about his situation. He had not done so before. Laura was
telling him that he should try to remember what was happening
to him now so that he might use it for his writing. "Yes," he said, "it
is important that I remember because this is such a different
universe . . ."

. . then I said [Laura in a letter to the family of 17th November]
"what do you make of this, what does it signify, your illness . . what
sense does it have . . ?" And he said, "it doesn't seem to make any
sense, it's just a sequence of events and it goes on and on . . . ." But I
kept insisting if he could not find more sense in this seemingly
wasteful disintegration which he is going through, but he said "no,
it's just impossible. I don't know what the answer is . . . ." He was
tired and I said, "before you go to sleep ask one question, maybe
you get an answer." "Well," he said, "there are so many questions."
So I said, find just one question . . . He said, "Well, the most natural
question is that if I get out of this what am I to do with the few
remaining years of my life? Because, as you know, I am living on
borrowed time." "What do you mean by borrowed time?" "Well,
a hundred years ago when this thing happened . . there would have

---

[1] A morphine derivative.

been no way to stop it and I would be dead by now. But now that we have been able to handle it, it means that I have more time to live, that I live on borrowed time, and the point is the best way for me to use this time that I still have." So that was the question with which I left him.

And later in the day I asked him if he had an answer, and he said, "obviously it is that—if I get out of this—those few years will be very important, because this experience that I am going through now will be of the greatest significance." And with that [the subject] was closed for the time being.

Over the next days it became physically impossible for him to write, and at times to speak. His mind was active, and Laura could see that "it was painful for him to keep this effervescence within and muted". Virginia had given them a tape-recorder and this was put by Aldous's bed with the idea that he might use it for making notes. (Laura also recorded what they were saying to one another, as well as some of Aldous's conversations with his doctors.) The unfinished article was weighing on his mind. On 15th November he began working with Laura. With the tape machine going she read to him the part already in typescript, he stopped her for corrections. A friend transcribed the tape. Laura read the transcript back to Aldous; Aldous made a new set of recorded corrections. And so it went on. It is only by listening to this tape that one can realize the painful laboriousness of the process. Aldous was almost completely deprived of physical strength and with hardly enough energy left to breathe; he was not used to dictating, nor was Laura used to being dictated to. His voice, interrupted by coughing, by fatigue, was often near inaudible; Laura appears bewildered by some of the Shakespearian words, misunderstanding, mispronouncing the unfamiliar. The whole thing was a nightmare. Laura carried on with great self-control. What made it harder for her was the actual text, of which she had known nothing—some of the most harrowing lines on death in English literature. Claudio's speech,

> *Ay, but to die, and go we know not where . . .*

Next day they reached the hand-written part, one page and a half, and matters, if conceivable, became worse. Aldous realized that it was almost impossible for him to work; meanwhile Laura was having trouble with his script.

Laura: "Inter". It says here "inter". The first word—I already don't understand. [She is trying hard.]
Aldous: Interpretation?
L.: Is it "interpretation"? "Interpretation of . . ."
A.: What was all this about, darling?

L.: Well, this is the page you wrote . . .

A.: Oh, I see "Shakespeare divided . . .

L.: His . . his . . .

A.: Oh, wait. Wait a minute. "Interpreters of Shakespeare have divided his career. [He goes on quoting his paragraph from memory and comes to] . . history, biography and chronicle fiction." I think it is . . .

L.: "Chronic"?

A.: . . . I don't think it matters, but I can look it up in a place. "The time of the 'depth' " inverted commas "when . . ."

There were pauses between each word. At one point Aldous wanted to see for himself, and was trying to hold both the page and his magnifying glass; Laura was holding the microphone. Somehow they got through another paragraph. "It's the last period, the plays of the last period," he explained to her. Then in an almost inaudible voice, "I am exhausted."

On the morrow, 17th November and another Sunday, Aldous had a better day. He and Laura got to the end of the hand-written passage; after the words "In our religious context," Aldous began composing straight on to the tape.

He asked me to show him how to start and stop the recorder. He did not want me to hold the microphone for him, to have control over the machine gave him a greater feeling of comfort and independence. I stood silently by. He would think for a while, then press a button and speak a phrase, then stop the machine and think.

After two paragraphs he almost smiled. "I begin to see how one could develop a technique to write in this way . . . Yes, I can see how one could do this . . it is different . . quite different . . . One has to think the sentence through . . ."

Aldous used his new learned skill the same day, dictating a business letter about various dramatic rights[1] (he had written to no one since his letter to Humphrey on 15th October). In the afternoon, Gerald came once more. He brought an inscribed copy of his latest book; it was large and heavy, so he quoted George III's brother's remark to Gibbon, " 'What! Another big, fat book!' " Aldous pounced. " 'Another damned, thick *square* book!' "

The same evening he told Laura that something should be done to speed up his recovery. It was true, he said, that he was better, but it was depressing not to have the strength to do what one

[1] To Max Kester of Foster's Agency in London. This letter, according to Professor Grover Smith, remained on tape and was not posted.

wanted to. On Monday 18th he took some interest in his food, worked on the article and dictated a note to Victoria Ocampo.

> Thank you for your good wishes, which I certainly need at this time. I hope we may soon find an auspicious moment for our long delayed meeting and your first acquaintance with Laura.[1]

On the 19th, in the early morning, Aldous returned to the great longing he had always had for the unattainable in art, the bringing together of *all* the multiplicities. What he had stated in the hand theme in *Those Barren Leaves*, what he had tried to achieve with the concert at Tantamount House in *Point Counter Point*—the music and the fiddle *and* the fiddler; the sound, the ear, the mind, the given *and* the experience—"Almost the whole course of life" fused in one simultaneous whole. Now, he told Laura (in an unexpectedly strong, his own, his former, voice) that one could write the greatest book ever written, *if one knew how*, "By bringing it all in!" At the same time? Laura asked. "Somehow . . ." Aldous said, "around a central story with episodes."

"You mean you want to do it like Bach . . .?"
"Well, I mean Bach is music and this is something else."
"Can you do your new novel like that?"
"Well, it would be marvellous if I could."
"Can you apply it to any little thing, even a little short story?"
"No, I wouldn't want to."
. . . . . . . . . . . . . . . .
Laura: ". . . And yet it's different from a polyphonic thing, is it?"
"Well, it has to be virtually analogous to polyphony."
"But you cannot speak all at once."
"Well, no, one can't, after all. It's not like Bach where you can have five parts going on. When you have words, you interrupt the thing . . each part blurs the other."
"That's probably why people write opera . . ."
". . This is what Wagner hoped to do and didn't. Unfortunately, he was an unspeakably vulgar man . . ."

On that day Aldous finished the Shakespeare article except for the last paragraph. He dictated Prospero's speech.

> *Our revels are now ended* . . . . . . . . . . .
> . . . . . . . . . . . . . . . . . . . . . . . . . . . . . .
> . . . . . . . . . . . . . . . . .*We are such stuff*
> *As dreams are made on; and our little life*
> *Is rounded with a sleep.*

[1] This, again according to Professor Smith, was almost certainly Aldous's last letter.

Prospero is here enunciating the doctrine of Maya. The world is an illusion, but is an illusion which we must take seriously, because it is real as far as it goes, and in those aspects of the reality which we are capable of apprehending. Our business is to wake up. We have to find ways in which to detect the whole of the reality in the one illusory part which our self-centred consciousness permits us to see. We must not live thoughtlessly, taking our illusion for the complete reality, but at the same time we must not live too thoughtfully in the sense of trying to escape from the dream state. We must continually be on our watch for ways in which to enlarge our consciousness. We must not attempt to live outside the world, which is given us, but we must somehow learn how to transform it and transfigure it. Too much 'wisdom' is as bad as too little wisdom, and there must be no magic tricks. We must learn to come to reality without the enchanter's wand and his book of the words. One must find a way of being in this world while not being of it. One must find a way of living in time without being completely swallowed up in time.

> *But thought's the slave of life, and life time's fool;*
> *And time, that takes survey of all the world,*
> *Must have a stop.*[1]

The day after Aldous said, "I think we must finish on our subject matter, 'Shakespeare and Religion.' " He dictated the last paragraph to its ending—"How many kinds of Shakespeare."

Laura: You want an exclamation?
Aldous: Mark. Yes.
L.: But there are not many kinds of Shakespeare . .
A.: But darling, that's exactly what we've been talking about . . . and stop the damn thing now.

Next day, Thursday 21st, Aldous had the tape played back to him, "was slightly amused, added a comma." When Dr Cutler came he said again how different the universe of the sick was from that of the well, saying it, Cutler wrote, "in that wonderfully mellow voice . . there was no bitterness in his observations, only dispassionate objectivity . . We talked for a while of the nature of cancer . . a conversation between two scientists . . . Aldous had an incredible fund of medical knowledge . . . Although I was the doctor, it was he who kept up my morale and that of his wife . . ."
That evening Aldous told Laura that they could not go on

---

[1] "Shakespeare and Religion", *Show* Magazine, 1964 (Hartford Publications, Inc., 1964). Republished in *Mem. Vol.*

imposing in this manner on Virginia; Laura tried to laugh him out of it, Aldous insisted: they must do something about it—take an apartment for the time being. He spoke with now unaccustomed energy; but only a few minutes later it became evident to Laura that he was losing ground.

Aldous slept through the night. When Laura saw him again at half past six in the morning of Friday, 22nd November, she felt that something was more wrong than usual, and telegraphed for Matthew. Towards 9 a.m. Aldous became very agitated; Cutler gave him something to ease respiration and he became more comfortable. Rosalind Rajagopal arrived and remained in the house. At 10 Aldous asked for a "big, big piece of paper." Laura brought him a writing tablet. "If I go . . ." he wrote. The pen did not work, Rosalind found a red one. Aldous wrote out instructions for an insurance policy to be transferred to Matthew. Laura promised to do what was necessary and Aldous appeared relieved not to have to take further action. A young man came into the room with a tank of oxygen. "These tanks are heavy," Aldous said; and when Laura looked about her, "there're some dollar bills in my trouser pocket in the cupboard." Peggy Kiskadden came in the course of the morning: Aldous took her hand and said, "Good bye, *dear* Peggy."

He grew weaker. At one point he murmured, "Who is eating out of my bowl?"

Around noon he asked again for the writing tablet.

LSD—Try it
intermuscular
100 mm[1]

Laura left the room to speak to Cutler. She found Virginia, doctors, nurses clustered round the television set in the hall, and was overcome by a sense of nightmarish irreality. She did not know that it was the hour of the Kennedy assassination.

After some hesitation Dr Cutler consented.[2] Aldous had not

---

[1] Aldous's written request for LSD is reproduced in *This Timeless Moment*. Some of the words appear very blurred; "LSD . . . Try it" and "100 mm" are entirely clear.

[2] Dr Cutler told me that he allowed Laura to give the LSD injection because at that stage it could have made no difference whatsoever. He could not say, when asked, whether it had had any effect. He confirmed that Aldous had died very peacefully. Yes, he said, after reflection, "*very* peacefully." This could be construed as meaning "exceptionally" peacefully.

When I reported this conversation to Laura (on the day it had taken place), she was surprised and taken aback that Dr Cutler had not told me that he had in fact observed a marked beneficial effect of the LSD. Her personal account of Aldous's last hours can of course be found in *This Timeless Moment*.

touched a psychedelic for the last two years; Laura was certain that he was deliberately choosing to do what he had written about in *Island*—taking a mind-enlarging drug *in extremis*, and she saw it as a sign of his awareness and acceptance. She gave the injection herself. (And a second one some two hours later.)

Aldous became very quiet. Laura felt that he was interested, relieved, at peace. She stayed by him, holding his hand, speaking to him, telling him to let go, to go with ease, helping him as he had Maria. The good black nurse was in the room, and Rosalind, doctors were gently moving to and fro; all was peaceful. At twenty minutes past five, very quietly, Aldous died.

Matthew, delayed by the countrywide confusions of that frightful weekend, arrived late at night. Next day Aldous was cremated, without a service of any kind. No one was present. On Sunday afternoon, on Matthew's suggestion, they held a private ceremony; family and friends assembled at Mulholland Highway for tea and a commemorative walk. They were Laura and Virginia, Matthew and Judy, Mère, Rose with her son Siggy, Betty and Sanford Wendel, Peggy Kiskadden and Christopher Isherwood. They went for the walk Aldous had gone for every day as long as he was able to stand up, the track along the canyon with the view over the Hollywood hills and the tree-lined reservoir he had called the Lake.

In London, there was a Memorial Service at Friends' House on 17th December 1963. Yehudi Menuhim played the Chaconne by Bach; Julian Huxley, David Cecil, Stephen Spender and Kenneth Clark spoke.

Eight years after, in 1971, Aldous's ashes were removed from an anonymous depository and returned to England and to Surrey. Here, on 27th October, a warm and brilliant day, accompanied by Julian and Juliette, Jeanne, Sophie, Noële, his step-mother Rosalind and his half-brothers David and Andrew, Huxley nephews and cousins and a handful of his friends, Aldous's ashes were buried after a brief committal service in his parents' grave in the hillside cemetery at Compton. The year after, on 10th October 1972, the same service was held for Maria Huxley; her ashes returned to Europe and were put to rest by the side of Aldous.

741

*References*

# Short List of Works Consulted

Bertalanffy, Ludwig von. *Problems of Life*. London: C. A. Watts & Co. Ltd., 1952.

Bibby, Cyril. *T. H. Huxley: Scientist, Humanist and Educator*. London: C. A. Watts & Co. Ltd., 1959.

Bronowski, J. *Science and Human Values* (revised edition). New York: Harper & Row, 1965.

Chen-Chi Chang, Garma. *The Practice of Zen*. New York: Harper & Row, 1970.

Clark, Ronald W. *The Huxleys*. London: William Heinemann Ltd.; New York: McGraw-Hill Inc., 1968.

Davis, Dennis Douglas. "Aldous Huxley's Pacifist Work: Death of a Sceptic". A dissertation, available at the Library of the University of California at Los Angeles and Santa Barbara, and at the Detroit Public Libraries.

———. *Aldous Huxley: A Bibliography, 1965–1971*. To be published.

Eschelbach, Claire John, and Shober, Joyce Lee. *Aldous Huxley: A Bibliography, 1916–1959*, and *A Supplementary Listing, 1914–1964*. Berkeley: University of California Press, 1961 and 1972.

Ford, Hugh, ed. *Nancy Cunard: Brave Poet, Indomitable Rebel*. Philadelphia: Chilton Book Company, 1968.

Frost, Fr. Bede. *The Art of Mental Prayer*. London: P. Allan, 1935; New York: Macmillan, 1949.

Godel, Dr Roger. *Essais sur l'expérience libératrice*. Paris, 1952.

Huxley, Aldous. Complete Works (see page 769).

———. *Collected Poems*. Edited by Donald Watt, with an introduction by Richard Church. London: Chatto & Windus; New York: Harper & Row, 1971.

———. *The Letters of Aldous Huxley*. Edited by Professor Grover Smith. London: Chatto & Windus, 1969; New York: Harper & Row, 1970.

Huxley, Gervas. *Both Hands: An Autobiography*. London: Chatto & Windus, 1970.

Huxley, Sir Julian. *Memories*. 2 volumes. London: Allen & Unwin, 1970 and 1973; New York: Harper & Row, Volume I, 1971.

Huxley, Leonard. *The Life and Letters of T. H. Huxley*. 2 volumes. London: Macmillan, 1900.

Huxley, Laura Archera. *This Timeless Moment: A Personal View of Aldous Huxley*. New York: Farrar, Straus & Giroux, Inc., 1968; London: Chatto & Windus, 1969.

745

James, William. *Varieties of Religious Experience*. London: 1902.

Lawrence, D. H. *Reminiscences and Correspondence*. (Letters to Earl H. and Achsah Brewster, with reminiscences by them.) London: Martin Secker, 1934.

———. *The Letters of D. H. Lawrence*. Edited and with an introduction by Aldous Huxley. London: William Heinemann Ltd; New York: The Viking Press, Inc., 1932.

———. *The Collected Letters of D. H. Lawrence*. 2 volumes, edited by Harry T. Moore. London: William Heinemann Ltd; New York: The Viking Press, Inc., 1962.

Leary, Timothy. *The Politics of Ecstasy*. New York: G. P. Putnam's Sons, 1968.

———. *High Priest*. New York: World Publishing Company, 1968.

Maisel, Edward, ed. *The Resurrection of the Body: The Writings of Frederick Matthias Alexander*. New York: University Books, 1969.

Moore, Harry T. *The Intelligent Heart: The Story of D. H. Lawrence*. London: William Heinemann Ltd.; New York: Farrar, Straus, 1955.

Morrison, Sybil. *I Renounce War: The Story of the Peace Pledge Union*. London: Sheppard Press Ltd., 1962.

Mumford, Lewis. *The Pentagon of Power*. London: Martin Secker and Warburg, 1971.

Nahal, Chaman, ed. *Drugs and the Other Self*. New York: Harper & Row, 1970.

Plumb, J. H., ed. *Studies in Social History: A Tribute to G. M. Trevelyan*. London: Longmans, Green & Co. Ltd., 1955.

Sheldon, Dr William. *The Varieties of Human Physique*. New York: Hafner, 1940.

———. *The Varieties of Human Temperament*. New York: Hafner, 1942.

———. *The Varieties of Delinquent Youth*. New York: Hafner, 1949.

Stravinsky, Igor, and Craft, Robert. *Conversations with Igor Stravinsky*. London: Faber and Faber; New York: Doubleday & Co., 1959.

———. *Memories and Commentaries*. London: Faber and Faber; New York: Doubleday & Co., 1960.

———. *Expositions and Developments*. London: Faber and Faber; New York: Doubleday & Co., 1962.

———. *Dialogues and Diary*. London: Faber and Faber; New York: Doubleday & Co., 1963.

Vittoz, Dr Roger. *Traitement des psychonévroses par la rééducation du controle cérébral*. Paris: J. B. Bailliere, 1907.

Worthington, Marjorie. *The Strange World of Willie Seabrook*. New York: Harcourt, Brace, & World, 1966.

Zaehner, Professor R. C. *Mysticism, Sacred and Profane*. Oxford: Clarendon Press, 1957.

Zamyatin, Evgenii I. *We*. New York: E. P. Dutton & Co., Inc., 1924.

# Acknowledgements

*The author and publishers wish to thank the following for permission to reprint excerpts from copyright material:*

Sir Isaiah Berlin for his contribution to the *Aldous Huxley Memorial Volume*.

Anne Charlton for Robert Nicols's letters to Dr and Mrs Henry Head.

Cyril Connolly and the British Broadcasting Corporation for an interview with Aldous Huxley.

Harcourt Brace Jovanovich, Inc., for *The Strange World of Willie Seabrook* by Marjorie Worthington.

The Harvard University Library for Miss Dorothy Ward's letter to Miss Jewett.

Mrs Laura Huxley, Chatto & Windus Ltd., and Farrar, Straus & Giroux, Inc., for *This Timeless Moment: A Personal View of Aldous Huxley*.

Mrs Laura Huxley, Chatto & Windus Ltd., and Harper & Row, Inc., for the complete works of Aldous Huxley.

The editors of *The Kenyon Review* for Gerald Heard's article "The Poignant Prophet" (Copyright © 1965 Kenyon College).

Professor Roy Lamson and the Massachusetts Institute of Technology for *Ancient Views of Human Nature* and *Modern Views of Human Nature*.

John Lehmann and the British Broadcasting Corporation for an interview with Aldous Huxley.

Longmans, Green & Co. Ltd. for Lord Annan's contribution, entitled "The Intellectual Aristocracy", in *Studies in Social History: A Tribute to G. M. Trevelyan*, edited by J. H. Plumb.

John Morgan and the British Broadcasting Corporation for an interview with Aldous Huxley.

The Peace Pledge Union.

Laurence Pollinger Ltd., William Heinemann Ltd., and the Estate of the late Mrs Frieda Lawrence for *The Collected Letters of D. H. Lawrence*.

Denis Preston and Record Supervision Ltd. for taped interviews with Aldous Huxley from *Speaking Personally*, record number LRS 003–4.

Professor Grover Smith, Harper & Row, Inc., and Chatto & Windus Ltd. for *The Letters of Aldous Huxley*.

Mrs Betty Wendel for recollections of Aldous Huxley.

# *Chronology*

*1914*

| | |
|---|---|
| January/June | Balliol College |
| May | Aldous's paternal grandmother, T. H. Huxley's widow, dies at Eastbourne |
| 4th August | England at war with Germany |
| 23rd August | Death of Aldous's brother Trevenen *aet.* 24 |
| October | Aldous returns to Oxford, lives out of college with the Haldanes at Cherwell Edge |

*1915*

| | |
|---|---|
| January/June | Oxford, Cherwell Edge; competes for the Newdigate with a long Byronic poem; 1st publication of verse in *Oxford Poetry* |
| Summer | Connel Ferry, Scotland; Westbourne Square, London; Prior's Field |
| September | Westbourne Square |
| October/December | Return to Balliol College |
| 5th December | First visit to Garsington |
| December | First meeting with D. H. Lawrence at Hampstead |

*1916*

| | |
|---|---|
| January/June | Balliol College, Oxford |
| January | Aldous rejected by Army as totally unfit |
| February | 1st issue of the *Palatine Review* founded and edited by T. W. Earp and Aldous; 1st publication of "Mole" and other poems |
| June | Acting assistant editor of *Oxford Poetry*. Schools examination; down from Oxford with a first in English and the Stanhope Historical Essay Prize |
| July/August | Temporary schoolmaster at Repton |
| August/September | Garsington; London; Prior's Field |
| September | Publ. *The Burning Wheel* |
| September/December | Aldous lives at Garsington, working on Philip Morrell's farm |

*1917*

| | |
|---|---|
| January/April | Garsington, ibid. |
| April/July | Clerical job at the Air Board. Living with his father and step-mother at 16 Bracknell Gardens, Hampstead |
| July/September | London; Oxford; Garsington |
| 18th September | Aldous takes up post as schoolmaster at Eton. Living at the Old Christopher (to February 1919) |
| December | Publ. *Jonah*. Contributed, in course of year, poems to *Wheels, Oxford Poetry*, the *Nation, Form* |

*1918*

| | |
|---|---|
| January/December | Master at Eton |
| January/February | Working on *Leda* |

| | |
|---|---|
| Easter | Holidays London, Surrey, Garsington |
| Summer | Holidays Garsington, Prior's Field |
| November | Armistice. Working on "The Farcical History of Richard Greenow" |
| Christmas | Garsington |
| *1919* | |
| January/April | Last Half at Eton. Aldous resigns |
| April | Easter Holidays. Aldous goes to Belgium to see Maria Nys at St Trond after two and a quarter years' separation. Meets the Nys and Baltus families. Aldous officially engaged to Maria Nys |
| April | Starts editorial job on the *Athenaeum* under Middleton Murry (till October 1920) |
| June | Furnishes and moves into a flat at 18 Hampstead Hill Gardens N.W.3 (till December 1920) |
| 10th July | Aldous married to Maria Nys at Bellem, Belgium |
| July/December | London. Miscellaneous journalism chiefly for the *Athenaeum* |
| *1920* | |
| January/December | London |
| January | Brief stay with Drieu La Rochelle in Paris |
| February | Publ. *Limbo* |
| 24th March | Death of Mrs Humphry Ward |
| 19th April | Birth of son, Matthew Huxley |
| 20th April | Starts additional job as dramatic critic on the *Westminster Gazette* |
| May | Publ. *Leda*. Takes on third job as assistant Chelsea Book Club (till August) |
| October | Resigns from the *Athenaeum*. Starts job on *House and Garden* |
| December | Aldous and Maria give up the Hampstead flat. Maria and child move to Belgium for the winter |
| *1921* | |
| January/March | Aldous at 26 Regent Square, W.C.1 with Tommy Earp and Russell Green. Maria and Matthew at Brussels and Florence |
| April/May | Aldous and Maria's first stay in Florence. Villa Minucci |
| August | First visit to Rome (one week) |
| May/August | Aldous writes *Crome Yellow* |
| May/September | First stay at Forte dei Marmi (29 Viale Morin) |
| October | Aldous and Maria return to London. New job with Condé Nast (till late |

|  |  |
|---|---|
|  | spring 1923). New flat: 155 Westbourne Terrace, W.2 (till December 1922) |
| November | Publ. *Crome Yellow* |
| *1922* | |
| January/December | London. Office job with Condé Nast |
| May | Publ. *Mortal Coils* |
| June | Paris |
| August/September | Holiday at Forte dei Marmi, Villa Tacchella |
| *1923* | |
| January | New flat: 44 Princess Gardens S.W.7 (till May or June) |
| 8th January | First Three-Year Contract with Chatto & Windus at £500 a year |
| April | Holiday in Florence (2-3 weeks) |
| May | Publ. *On the Margin* |
| May or June | Sudden departure from England to live in Italy |
| Summer | Forte dei Marmi (Villa Fasola?). Writing *Antic Hay* |
| August | *Antic Hay* finished. Move to Florence, Castel a Montici, 15 Via Sta Margherita a Montici (till June 1925) |
| November | Publ. *Antic Hay* |
| *1924* | |
| January/December | Castel a Montici, Florence |
| February | *Little Mexican* finished |
| March | Aldous starts writing *Those Barren Leaves*. Car travels in Italy |
| April | Maria's sister Suzanne marries Joep Nicolas. Joep and Suzanne spend part of their honeymoon with Aldous and Maria in Florence |
| May | Publ. *Little Mexican* |
| June | Publ. *The Discovery*, an adaptation of the play by Sheridan. Car travels in Italy |
| July/August | Forte |
| August | Aldous finishes *Those Barren Leaves* at Ambérieu, Savoie, France |
| September | Paris; London (King's Rd, Chelsea). Motor tour Holland and Belgium |
| October | Paris. Return to Florence (car journey through central and southern France. Starts *Along the Road* |
| November | Motor journey Rome and southern Italy |
| *1925* | |
| January/June | Castel a Montici, Florence |
| January | Publ. *Those Barren Leaves. Along the Road* finished |
| March/April | Tunisia |

| | |
|---|---|
| June | Florence house searched by Fascisti |
| End June | Leave Castel a Montici for good |
| July | London. Aldous makes arrangements for round the world journey |
| August | Belgium. Aldous and Maria leave Matthew at St Trond for 11 months |
| September | Publ. *Along the Road* |
| 15th September | Aldous and Maria sail from Genoa. Travel diary *Jesting Pilate* begun at sea |
| October | Bombay; Srinagar; Kashmir |
| November | Srinagar; Agra; Jaipur; Cawnpore for All India Congress. Encounters Gandhi and Nehru. Lahore |
| December | Lahore; Peshawar; Amritsar |
| *1926* | |
| January | Benares; Lucknow; Delhi; Calcutta |
| February | Aldous and Maria leave India for Burma. Rangoon. Up the Irrawaddy. Bhamo |
| March | Malaya: Penang; Singapore |
| 5th March | Sail for Java. Stops at Batavia; Garoet; Buitenzorg; Miri; Sarawak; Labuan; Kudat; Sandakan |
| March | Change ship at Zamboanga in Southern Philippines to Manila |
| 7th April | At Manila catch liner to San Francisco. Stop Hong Kong |
| April | Few days Japan. Cross Pacific |
| 5th May | Arrive San Francisco. First visit U.S.A. Los Angeles. |
| May | By train to Chicago |
| 17th May | New York for two weeks |
| May | Publ. *Two or Three Graces* |
| June | Sail for England. London. Aldous sits for his portrait to his uncle, the Hon. John Collier. 2nd Agreement with Chatto & Windus |
| July | London |
| August | St Trond. Aldous and Maria move to the mountains for Matthew's health |
| August/December | Cortina d'Ampezzo (Villa Ino Colli) |
| October | Publ. *Jesting Pilate*. Aldous starts writing *Point Counter Point*. Aldous and Maria meet D. H. Lawrence in Florence: Aldous and D. H. L.'s first meeting since the single one in 1915 |
| December | Publ. *Essays New and Old* |
| *1927* | |
| January/February | Cortina d'Ampezzo. Aldous breaks off work on *Point Counter Point* and starts *Proper Studies* |

| | |
|---|---|
| Mid-February | The Huxleys leave Cortina. Brief stay Florence (D. H. L.) |
| March/April/May | London |
| May | Aldous and Maria at St Trond for the death of Maria's grandfather, R. Baltus |
| June/November | Forte dei Marmi (Villa Majetta) |
| June | Rina Rontini, aged 15, enters the Huxley household. Brief visit of D. H. Lawrence. |
| July | *Proper Studies* finished. D. H. L. very ill in Florence: Aldous and Maria go to assist him until Frieda's return from Germany |
| August | Aldous takes up work again on *Point Counter Point* |
| November | Publ. *Proper Studies* |
| December | Christmas at Florence with D. H. L. and Frieda |

*1928*

| | |
|---|---|
| January/February | Les Diablerets, Vaud, Switzerland with Julian and Juliette and their boys; the D. H. L.'s join them |
| March/May | London (Onslow Mews, S.W.7). Getting Matthew off to his 1st school, Frensham Heights, Surrey |
| May | *Point Counter Point* finished |
| June | Paris. Aldous and Maria take a house near Paris, 3, rue du Bac, Suresnes |
| Late June/September | Forte dei Marmi (Villa Il Cannetto) |
| July | *Point Counter Point* selected by the Literary Guild in the U.S.A. |
| October | The Huxleys, Maria's sister Jeanne Moulaert and her daughter, Sophie, move into the house at Suresnes. Maria's grandmother Emérence Baltus dies |
| November | Publ. *Point Counter Point* |

*1929*

| | |
|---|---|
| January/December | Suresnes, Paris |
| January | Aldous's first meeting with Gerald Heard in London at Raymond Mortimer's |
| Late January | Aldous and Maria stay for ten days with D. H. L. and Frieda at Bandol (Hôtel Beau-Rivage) |
| February | Florence |
| March | D. H. L. very ill, stays with the Huxleys at Suresnes. D. H. L. sits for his portrait to Aldous's brother-in-law, Joep Nicolas |
| April | Aldous and Maria's first visit to Spain |
| May | Publ. *Arabia Infelix. Do What You Will* finished. London till mid-June |

754

| | |
|---|---|
| June/September | Aldous and Maria's last summer at Forte dei Marmi (Il Cannetto) |
| June | D. H. L. at Forte |
| July | Aldous takes the cure at Montecatini with Pino Orioli |
| August | A week in the Apuan mountains |
| 15th September | Return to Suresnes |
| October | Publ. *Do What You Will* |
| October/November | Aldous and Maria go on a long motor tour through Spain |
| December | Family Christmas at Suresnes |

*1930*

| | |
|---|---|
| January/April | Suresnes, Paris |
| January | London for production of play adapted from *Point Counter Point*, *This Way to Paradise*, at Daly's Theatre by Campbell Dixon |
| 30th January | *This Way to Paradise* opens (Closes 1st March) |
| February | London; Suresnes; Vence, where D. H. L. has entered the sanatorium Ad Astra |
| 2nd March | Death of D. H. Lawrence at Vence (at the Villa Robermond) |
| March | Bandol. Aldous and Maria buy a house at Sanary |
| April | Aldous and Maria move into Villa Huley, La Gorguette, Sanary-sur-Mer |
| May | Publ. *Brief Candles*. Aldous in London in connection with D. H. L.'s letters |
| September/October | London. Journey with J. W. N. Sullivan to Paris and Berlin. London, Durham and Nottingham with Maria. London |
| October/December | Sanary |
| November | Publ. *Vulgarity in Literature* |

*1931*

| | |
|---|---|
| Mid-January/Mid-March | London (Dalmeny Court, Duke Street, St James's) |
| March | Aldous's first play, *The World of Light*, produced in London at the Royalty Theatre (closes after a brief run) |
| March/Late September | Sanary |
| May | Publ. *The Cicadas* |
| May/August | Aldous writes *Brave New World* |
| September | Publ. *Music at Night* |
| October/December | London (Dalmeny Court, later Rosa Lewis's old Cavendish Hotel in Jermyn Street) |

*1932*

| | |
|---|---|
| January/May | Sanary |

| February | Publ. *Brave New World* |
| May/June | Aldous and Maria dine with the King and Queen of the Belgians in Brussels. Travels in Germany with Raymond Mortimer |
| June/December | Sanary. Aldous writes unpublished play, *Now More Than Ever* (believed to be lost) |
| September | Publ. *The Letters of D. H. Lawrence* edited by Aldous |
| October | Matthew enters Dartington School |
| November | Publ. *Texts and Pretexts* |
| December | London |

*1933*
| January | Sanary |
| January/May | Aldous and Maria travel in the West Indies, Guatemala, Mexico |
| 3rd May | Death of Aldous's father, Leonard Huxley |
| June/December | Sanary. Aldous writes *Beyond the Mexique Bay* |
| November | Aldous and Maria's 3rd Spanish journey |

*1934*
| January/March | Sanary. Aldous working on *Eyeless in Gaza* |
| April | Publ. *Beyond the Mexique Bay*. Car journey in Italy |
| April/September | Sanary |
| June | Aldous briefly in London |
| October/December | London (18 St Albans Place, Regent Street, S.W.1) |
| December | Aldous and Maria take a seven year's lease on a flat in Albany |
| Mid-December | Move into E2 Albany, Piccadilly, W.1 |

*1935*
| January/March | E2 Albany |
| January | Aldous in Paris (journalism), a few days |
| February | Few days Paris again |
| March/October | Sanary. At work on *Eyeless in Gaza* |
| October/December | E2 Albany. Aldous starts taking lessons with F. Matthias Alexander |
| October or November | Aldous joins Dick (The Rev. H. R. L.) Sheppard's Peace Pledge Union |
| 3rd December | Aldous gives his first address on pacifism at Friends' House |

*1936*
| January/March | E2 Albany. Aldous working for Peace Pledge Union with Dick Sheppard and Gerald Heard |
| March | *Eyeless in Gaza* finished |
| April/September | Sanary |

CHRONOLOGY

| | |
|---|---|
| April | Publ. Peace Pamphlet *What Are You Going To Do About It?* |
| June | Publ. *Eyeless in Gaza* |
| September/October | Aldous and Matthew in Belgium and Holland |
| October/November | London (Mount Royal Hotel). Aldous and Maria work for the P.P.U. |
| December | Publ. *The Olive Tree*. Sanary |

*1937*

| | |
|---|---|
| January/February | Sanary. Aldous starts *Ends and Means*. Death of Maria's father, Norbert Nys |
| 19th February | Aldous and Maria leave their Sanary house for good |
| March | London (Mount Royal Hotel) |
| 7th April | Aldous, Maria and Matthew with Gerald Heard and Christopher Wood sail for New York on the s.s. *Normandie* |
| April | Brief stay in New York |
| April/May | Aldous, Maria, Matthew and Gerald Heard on a five weeks' car journey across the United States |
| May/September | The four spend the summer at Frieda Lawrence's Ranch, San Cristobal, Taos, New Mexico. Aldous finishes *Ends and Means* |
| October/November | Colorado; Hollywood |
| November | Publ. *Ends and Means* |
| November/December | Aldous and Gerald Heard lecture on peace throughout the United States. Gerald breaks his arm in Iowa, Aldous carries on |
| December | Maria takes a house on a Hudson Valley estate, Dairy Cottage, Foxhollow Farm, Rhinebeck, N.Y. Aldous and Matthew join her for Christmas |

*1938*

| | |
|---|---|
| January | Rhinebeck, N.Y. Aldous continues lecture tour. Aldous and Maria plan return to Europe |
| February | A scenario by Aldous apparently accepted by a film studio in Hollywood. Aldous and Maria change plans. Drive again across the continent. Stay at Frieda's Ranch. Arrive Hollywood. Take house on North Laurel Avenue. Aldous had severe bronchitis. Weeks in Hospital. |
| March | More or less acute aftermath lasting for over a year. Convalescence. Maria's |

757

|  |  |
|---|---|
| | mother injured by an accident in Mexico City |
| April | Death of Lady Ottoline Morrell |
| April/July | Aldous at work on a long novel (abandoned) |
| July | Move into house on North Linden Drive, Beverly Hills |
| August/September | Aldous works for Metro-Goldwyn-Mayer on a script of *Madame Curie* |
| September/October | House move in mid-Munich crisis to North Crescent Heights Boulevard, Hollywood. Matthew off to University of Colorado |
| October | Aldous decides to write a short phantasy with a Californian locale (*After Many a Summer Dies the Swan*) |
| November | Approximate beginning of Aldous's attempt to improve his sight by the Bates Method. Intensive training with a Bates teacher. Aldous temporarily forbidden to read or write. Some improvement of sight noted by Maria |

*1939*

| | |
|---|---|
| January/February | At North Crescent Heights Boulevard, Hollywood |
| January | Further improvement in Aldous's sight. Allowed to read and write again. |
| February | Working on *After Many a Summer Dies the Swan* |
| April | Aldous and Maria move to a furnished house, 701 Amalfi Drive, Pacific Palisades (until February 1942) |
| May | Maria reports very definite improvement in Aldous's sight. Aldous does all his reading and writing without spectacles |
| June or July | First meeting with Christopher Isherwood |
| 25th July | *After Many a Summer Dies the Swan* finished |
| 26th July | Aldous's 45th birthday |
| July | Aldous describes his Bates training and precisely assesses his present sight in a letter to Julian |
| August | Aldous undertakes an adaptation of *Pride and Prejudice* for Metro-Goldwyn-Mayer |
| 3rd September | England at war with Germany |
| September/December | Aldous and Maria live at 701 Amalfi Drive, Pacific Palisades, California, U.S.A. |
| | Aldous at work at Metro-Goldwyn- |

|  | Mayer on an adaptation of *Pride and Prejudice*. |
| October | Publ. *After Many a Summer Dies the Swan* |
| November | Sophie Moulaert, Aldous and Maria's niece, arrives from Europe. Lives with the Huxleys until 1944 |
| December | Brief visit Gervas Huxley |
|  | Christmas visit Julian Huxley |

*1940*
| January/December | At 701 Amalfi Drive, Pacific Palisades |
| January | Continues work on *Pride and Prejudice* for M.G.M. |
| February | On half-pay at M.G.M. Tinkering with a Utopian novel |
| April/June | Aldous in ill health. Unable to work |
| July | Decides to write a biographical study of Père Joseph, Richelieu's Grey Eminence |
| August/September | Research reading for *Grey Eminence* |
| October | Aldous starts writing *Grey Eminence* |

*1941*
| January/December | At 701 Amalfi Drive, Pacific Palisades |
| May | *Grey Eminence* finished. Aldous's Aunt Ethel Collier, the last of T. H. Huxley's daughters, dies |
| July | Film work at Twentieth Century-Fox |
| October | Publ. *Grey Eminence* |
| November | Aldous starts work on a new novel, *Time Must Have a Stop* |

*1942*
| January/February | At 701 Amalfi Drive, Pacific Palisades |
| February | Aldous and Maria move to Llano del Rio, a house in an oasis in the Mojave Desert |
| March | At work at Twentieth Century-Fox on *Jane Eyre* |
| April | Novel laid aside. Starts writing *The Art of Seeing* |
| July | *The Art of Seeing* finished |
| October | Publ. *The Art of Seeing* |

*1943*
| January/December | Main home base: Llano |
| March | Aldous resumes work on novel |
|  | Matthew in U.S. Army Medical Corps |
| April | Matthew seriously ill in Army hospital |
| June | Matthew invalided out of U.S. Army |

| | |
|---|---|
| July | Aldous stays with Gerald Heard at Trabuco College |
| October | The Huxleys take a *pied-à-terre* in Beverly Hills, at 145 1/2 South Doheny Drive |

*1944*
| | |
|---|---|
| January/December | Llano and Beverly Hills flat |
| February | *Time Must Have a Stop* finished |
| April | Work with Christopher Isherwood on some film scripts |
| May | Starts *The Perennial Philosophy*. Writes article on Dr William Sheldon's Human Typology |
| 26th July | Aldous's fiftieth birthday |
| August | Publ. *Time Must Have a Stop* |
| Autumn | Aldous learns to drive a car |

*1945*
| | |
|---|---|
| January/August | Llano and Beverly Hills |
| March | *The Perennial Philosophy* finished |
| June | Aldous and Maria buy a chalet in the mountains at Wrightwood, California. Matthew becomes a U.S. citizen |
| Spring/Summer | Writing *Science, Liberty and Peace* |
| July/August | At Wrightwood |
| September | Publ. *The Perennial Philosophy* |
| October | Matthew at University of California at Berkeley. (Takes degree in 1947) |
| November/December | Aldous works with Walt Disney on film of *Alice in Wonderland* |

*1946*
| | |
|---|---|
| Winter/Spring | At Llano |
| March | Publ. *Science, Liberty and Peace* |
| Summer | At work on film version of *The Gioconda Smile*. At Wrightwood |
| September | Work on stage version of *The Gioconda Smile* |

*1947*
| | |
|---|---|
| February | Llano given up for good. Definite move to Wrightwood |
| January/March | Continues work of stage version of *Gioconda* |
| March | Work on a novel laid in 14th-century Italy (abandoned). First reference to a post-atomic novel |
| May | At work on and off at Rank on the *Gioconda* film |
| September | Aldous and Maria leave by car for New York. Their first absence from California |

since 1938

| | |
|---|---|
| October/November | New York at 26 West 59th Street. Long weekends at the Joep Nicolases' house at Islip, Long Island |
| November/December | At Doheny Drive, Beverly Hills. Working on *Ape and Essence* |
| December | At Wrightwood |

*1948*

| | |
|---|---|
| January/December | At Wrightwood and Beverly Hills |
| February | Publ. (U.S.) play *Mortal Coils* (Title later changed back to *The Gioconda Smile*) Release of *Gioconda* film under title *A Woman's Vengeance*. *Ape and Essence* finished |
| 3rd June | *The Gioconda Smile* opens at the New Theatre in London (a 9 months run) |
| 10th June | New York, St Regis Hotel |
| 24th June | Aldous and Maria sail on s.s. *Queen Mary* Their first post-war return to Europe |
| 29th June | Arrival at Cherbourg and Paris |
| 29th June/8th July | Paris at 82 rue Bonaparte VIme staying with Georges and Jeanne Neveux |
| 9th July/2nd August | Siena at Palazzo Ravizza. Work on film of "The Rest Cure" |
| 2nd August/28th August | Rome at Hôtel de la Ville |
| 30th August/ 18th September | Sanary at Villa La Rustique |
| 20th September/ 2nd October | Paris at 67 Bld Lannes XVIme at Mimi Gielgud's flat |
| 2nd October/Mid-October | London at Claridges. Interview with Cyril Connolly |
| October | Return by sea to U.S.A. |
| October/November | New York. Aldous has a new severe attack of bronchitis |
| November/December | At Palm Desert (Sun & Sage Apartments) on doctor's orders. Work on stage version of *Ape and Essence* |

*1949*

| | |
|---|---|
| January/February | Palm Desert |
| February | *Le Sourire de la Gioconde* (in collaboration with Georges Neveux) opens in Paris |
| February/May | At Beverly Hills. Collecting material for biographical study of Maine de Biran |
| May | Aldous and Maria buy a house in Los Angeles at 740 North Kings Road |
| May/September | At Wrightwood |
| October | *Themes and Variations* finished. Move to 740 North Kings Road |
| December | Matthew engaged to Ellen Hovde |

*1950*

| | |
|---|---|
| January/March | At North Kings Road |
| April | New York at Hotel Warwick. Matthew marries Ellen Hovde |
| | Publ. *Themes and Variations* |
| 9th May | Aldous and Maria sail for France on s.s. *Queen Mary* |
| May/Mid-June | Paris. Hotel Paris-Dinard |
| June | Rome, Hotel Flora, Siena, Palazzo Ravizza |
| July | Paris, Hotel Paris-Dinard |
| 11th July | Aldous goes to London for two weeks. Stays with Julian and Juliette at 31 Pond Street, NW3 |
| August | Aldous and Maria at Sanary. Villa La Rustique |
| 1st September/ 11th September | Juillac, Corrèze, Maison de Joyet with Georges, Jeanne, Noële Neveux |
| 11th September/ 22nd September | Paris at Mimi Gielgud's |
| 22nd September | Sail for New York |
| September/October | New York. Last weeks of rehearsal of *The Gioconda Smile* |
| 3rd October | *Gioconda* opens on Broadway, Lyceum Theatre (5 weeks' run) Aldous and Maria return to Los Angeles by car. Visit Frieda Lawrence *en route* |
| November/December | North Kings. Aldous begins work on *The Devils of Loudun* |

*1951*

| | |
|---|---|
| January/December | At North Kings, Los Angeles. Work on *The Devils of Loudun* |
| March/April | Influenza affecting Aldous's eyes |
| July/August | Aldous has a severe attack of iritis |
| 20th October | Birth of Matthew's son, Mark Trevenen |

*1952*

| | |
|---|---|
| January/December | North Kings, Los Angeles |
| January | Maria seriously ill |
| | *The Devils of Loudun* finished |
| October | Publ. *The Devils of Loudun* |

*1953*

| | |
|---|---|
| January/December | North Kings, Los Angeles |
| | Aldous at work on miscellaneous essays, articles, film projects |
| February | Death of Lewis Gielgud |
| May | Aldous's first mescalin experiment with Dr Humphrey Osmond |
| June | Car journey through the U.S. North-western states and national parks |

| June/July | Writing *The Doors of Perception* |
| 28th September | Edwin Hubble dies |
| October | Birth of Matthew's daughter, Tessa |

*1954*
| January/December | North Kings, Los Angeles |
| February | Publication *The Doors of Perception* |
| March | New York. Aldous starts *The Genius and the Goddess* |
| 7th April | Aldous and Maria sail for Cherbourg on the s.s. *Queen Elizabeth* |
| 12th–19th April | Paris, Hôtel Pont Royal |
| 19th April/3rd May | St Paul-de-Vence for Eileen Garrett's symposium on Philosophy and Parapsychology |
| May | Ismailia; Cairo; Jerusalem; Beirut; Cyprus |
| June | Athens; Rome |
| 19th June/4th July | Paris |
| July | Dieulefit, Drôme and Vaison-la-Romaine with the Neveuxes |
| August | Aldous in London with the Julian Huxleys. Maria in Paris |
| 21st August | Aldous and Maria sail for New York on the s.s. *Mauritania* |
| September | New York |
| 7th September | Return to Los Angeles |
| October | Aldous lectures at Washington, D.C., Duke University and University of N. Carolina. *The Genius and the Goddess* finished. Visit from Julian |
| November | Visit from Humphrey Osmond. Aldous starts play script of *The Genius and the Goddess* and work on miscellaneous essays |

*1955*
| January/April | At North Kings, Los Angeles |
| January/December | Work on dramatisation of *The G & G*, miscellaneous essays and articles |
| 12th February | Maria Huxley dies |
| April/May | Aldous drives to New York with Rose de Haulleville |
| May/June | New York at 1035 Park Avenue |
| June | Publ. *The Genius and the Goddess* (the novel) |
| July/August | Aldous stays with Matthew and his family at Guilford, Connecticut. Finishes *Heaven and Hell* |

| | |
|---|---|
| September | Aldous returns to North Kings, Los Angeles |
| September/December | At North Kings |

*1956*
| | |
|---|---|
| January/July | At North Kings, Los Angeles |
| February | Publ. *Heaven and Hell* |
| 19th March | Aldous is married to Laura Archera at Yuma, Arizona |
| July | Aldous and Laura move to a house on 3276 Deronda Drive, Los Angeles |
| 11th August | Death of Frieda Lawrence |
| Summer | Aldous starts *Island* |
| September | A visit from Julian and Juliette |
| October | Publ. *Adonis and the Alphabet* (U.S. title *Tomorrow and Tomorrow and Tomorrow*) |

*1957*
| | |
|---|---|
| January/July | At Deronda Drive, Los Angeles |
| July/November | New York, Hotel Shoreham, working on the stage production of *The Genius and the Goddess* |
| November/December | Deronda Drive, L.A. Starts writing *Brave New World Revisited* |
| 10th December | *The Genius and the Goddess* opens on Broadway. The play closes after five nights |

*1958*
| | |
|---|---|
| January/July | Deronda Drive, L.A. |
| Spring | *Brave New World Revisited* finished. Aldous returns to his Utopian novel *Island* |
| July/August | Aldous and Laura in Peru and Brazil |
| September | Aldous and Laura in Italy |
| October | Aldous in London, at Julian's house in Hampstead. Publ. *Brave New World Revisited* |
| October | Aldous and Laura in Paris. Later Venice |
| November | Aldous lectures at Turin, Milan, Rome and Naples |
| December | Return to Deronda Drive, L.A. |

*1959*
| | |
|---|---|
| January/December | At Deronda Drive, L.A. Work on and off on *Island* |
| February/May | Aldous's first semester as visiting professor at the University of California at Santa Barbara. Delivers a course of lectures on The Human Situation |

| | |
|---|---|
| May | Award of Merit for the Novel by the American Academy of Arts and Letters, New York |
| September/December | Second semester at Santa Barbara |

*1960*

| | |
|---|---|
| January/December | At Deronda Drive, L.A. Matthew and Ellen's marriage is dissolved |
| March/April | Aldous visiting professor at the Menninger Foundation, Topeka, Kansas |
| April/May | Aldous lectures at Berkeley, Idaho State University, University of Arizona |
| May | Diagnosis of serious illness |
| June/July | Radiation treatment and apparent good recovery |
| September | Takes part in a Conference on Medical ethics at Dartmouth College; Boston. Receives Honorary Degree at University of New Hampshire. New York. Lectures at University of Pittsburgh |
| 23rd September | Aldous takes up Carnegie visiting professorship at the Massachusetts Institute of Technology |
| September/November | At M.I.T., Cambridge, Mass. Gives course of lectures and seminar, *What a Piece of Work Is Man* |
| December | Deronda Drive, L.A. |

*1961*

| | |
|---|---|
| January/May | Deronda Drive, L.A. |
| January | Aldous and Laura in Hawaii |
| February | Aldous takes part in conference on Mind Control at San Francisco |
| April | Cambridge, Mass. Aldous speaks at M.I.T. centennial celebration |
| 12th May | The house on Deronda Drive is destroyed by fire with its contents. Aldous loses his library and all his papers |
| June | Aldous finishes *Island* |
| June/July | Aldous in London at 4 Ennismore Gardens, Kensington. Gives important interviews |
| July | At St Paul-de-Vence. Takes part in Eileen Garrett's annual conference on Parapsychology |
| August | Laura joins Aldous in Europe. Stay at Gstaad in Switzerland seeing Krishnamurti and the Yehudi Menuhins. |

|  | Copenhagen for conference on Applied Psychology |
|---|---|
| September | Return to Los Angeles. At Virginia Pfeiffer's house, 6233 Mulholland Highway |
| November | Aldous and Laura fly to India for the Tagore Centenary celebration at New Delhi. Aldous revisits the Taj Mahal. Brief stay in Japan |
| December | Return to Los Angeles |

*1962*

| January/December | At Virginia Pfeiffer's house on Mulholland Highway, L.A. |
|---|---|
| February/May | Aldous Visiting Professor at the University of California at Berkeley |
| March | Publ. *Island.* Aldous takes part in conference on Technology in the Modern World at Santa Barbara |
|  | Lectures: Alabama, Philadelphia |
| April | Conference on Hypnosis at Colgate University, Hamilton, N.Y. |
|  | Stays at Boston and New York |
|  | Aldous meets Julian at Portland, Oregon |
| May | Aldous lectures to the scientists at Los Alamos |
|  | Lecture at Anaheim, California |
|  | New York. Talk at the American Academy of Arts and Letters |
| June | First recurrence of Aldous's illness |
|  | Aldous elected Companion of Literature by the Royal Society of Literature. |
|  | *The Genius and the Goddess* performed at Oxford, Manchester, Leeds and at the Comedy in London |
| July | Minor operation followed by cobalt treatment |
|  | Aldous makes a slow recovery |
| August/September | Aldous flies to Brussels for the meeting of the World Academy of Arts and Sciences |
|  | Stay with Joep and Suzanne Nicolas in Holland |
| September | London at Julian and Juliette's |
| October | Los Angeles. Working on *Literature and Science* |
| November | A month of lecturing in the Middle West and East. Stay in New York |

*1963*

| January/November | At Virginia Pfeiffer's, Mulholland Highway, L.A. |
|---|---|

| | |
|---|---|
| January | Aldous "ruminating a long and complicated novel" |
| March | Aldous flies to Rome for a conference of F.A.O. (United Nations Food and Agricultural Organisation.) Audience with Pope John XXIII |
| | New York for Matthew's marriage to Judith Wallet Bordage |
| March/April | Aldous lectures at Oregon, Berkeley, Stanford |
| April/May | Aldous has another relapse |
| May | Few days in hospital for observation |
| June/July | Radiation treatments. Followed by very slow recovery of strength |
| August | Aldous and Laura fly to Stockholm for a meeting of the World Academy of Arts and Sciences |
| | Aldous accepts to edit a volume on Human Resources (with Dr Humphrey Osmond) for the Academy |
| | London. Aldous stays with Julian and Juliette |
| | Visits to Dartington, to Lawford Hall (the home of his late friends, the Nicholses), to Kenneth Clark's Saltwood Castle |
| | Aldous joins Laura in Italy |
| 24th August | Aldous returns to Los Angeles |
| September | Publ. *Literature and Science* |
| October/November | Aldous writes "Shakespeare and Religion" |
| 22nd November | Aldous dies (in the house on Mulholland Highway, Los Angeles). There is cremation by undertaker with no funeral service |
| 17th December | A Memorial Service is held in London at Friends' House. Yehudi Menuhin plays Bach's Chaconne. Julian Huxley, David Cecil, Stephen Spender and Kenneth Clark speak |
| *1971*<br>27th October | Aldous Huxley's ashes returned to England and buried in his parents' grave at Compton, Surrey |
| *1972*<br>10th October | Maria Huxley's ashes are returned to England and buried by the side of Aldous |

# Chronological List of Works
# by Aldous Huxley

*Dates are the year of first publication*

[1] His first book to be published in the United States by Harper & Brothers (later Harper & Row), which remained his U.S. publisher thereafter.

[2] First published in the United States; all other books were first published in England.

# Index

iii

Sybille Bedford was born in Charlottenburg and educated privately in England, Italy, and France. Her first book, *The Sudden View* (now reprinted as *A Visit to Don Otavio*), a description of travels in Mexico, was followed by her best-known novel, *A Legacy*, upon whose publication Evelyn Waugh wrote, "We gratefully salute a new artist." Two other internationally praised novels followed: *A Favorite of the Gods* and *A Compass Error*. In addition to her biography of Aldous Huxley, Mrs. Bedford has written *The Trial of Dr. Adams, The Faces of Justice*, and the autobiographical *Jigsaw: An Unsentimental Education*. She lives in London and is at work on a memoir.

James B. Simpson, ed., *Veil and Cowl*
Tess Slesinger, *On Being Told That Her Second Husband Has Taken His First Lover, and Other Stories*
Red Smith, *Red Smith on Baseball*
Donald Thomas, *Swinburne*
B. Traven, *The Bridge in the Jungle*
B. Traven, *The Carreta*
B. Traven, *The Cotton-Pickers*
B. Traven, *General from the Jungle*
B. Traven, *Government*
B. Traven, *March to the Montería*
B. Traven, *The Night Visitor and Other Stories*
B. Traven, *The Rebellion of the Hanged*
B. Traven, *Trozas*
Anthony Trollope, *Trollope the Traveller*
Ivan Turgenev, *Literary Reminiscences*
Rex Warner, *The Aerodrome*
Rebecca West, *A Train of Powder*
Thomas Wolfe, *The Hills Beyond*
Wilhelm Worringer, *Abstraction and Empathy*
The Shakespeare Handbooks by Alistair McCallum
    *Hamlet*
    *King Lear*
    *Macbeth*
    *Romeo and Juliet*

## Theatre and Drama

Linda Apperson, *Stage Managing and Theatre Etiquette*
Robert Brustein, *Cultural Calisthenics*
Robert Brustein, *Dumbocracy in America*
Robert Brustein, *Reimagining American Theatre*
Robert Brustein, *The Siege of the Arts*
Robert Brustein, *The Theatre of Revolt*
Stephen Citron, *The Musical from the Inside Out*
Irina and Igor Levin, *Working on the Play and the Role*
Keith Newlin, ed., *American Plays of the New Woman*
Louis Rosen, *The South Side*
Bernard Sahlins, *Days and Nights at The Second City*
David Wood, with Janet Grant, *Theatre for Children*
Plays for Performance:
    Aristophanes, *Lysistrata*
    Pierre Augustin de Beaumarchais, *The Barber of Seville*
    Pierre Augustin de Beaumarchais, *The Marriage of Figaro*
    Georg Büchner, *Woyzeck*
    Anton Chekhov, *The Cherry Orchard*
    Anton Chekhov, *Ivanov*
    Anton Chekhov, *The Seagull*
    Anton Chekhov, *Uncle Vanya*
    Euripides, *The Bacchae*
    Euripides, *Iphigenia in Aulis*
    Euripides, *Iphigenia Among the Taurians*

Euripides, *Medea*
Euripides, *The Trojan Women*
Georges Feydeau, *Paradise Hotel*
Henrik Ibsen, *A Doll's House*
Henrik Ibsen, *Ghosts*
Henrik Ibsen, *Hedda Gabler*
Henrik Ibsen, *The Master Builder*
Henrik Ibsen, *When We Dead Awaken*
Henrik Ibsen, *The Wild Duck*
Heinrich von Kleist, *The Prince of Homburg*
Christopher Marlowe, *Doctor Faustus*
Molière, *The Bourgeois Gentleman*
*The Mysteries: Creation*
*The Mysteries: The Passion*
Luigi Pirandello, *Enrico IV*
Luigi Pirandello, *Six Characters in Search of an Author*
Budd Schulberg, with Stan Silverman, *On the Waterfront* (the play)
Sophocles, *Antigone*
Sophocles, *Electra*
Sophocles, *Oedipus at Colonus*
Sophocles, *Oedipus the King*
August Strindberg, *The Father*
August Strindberg, *Miss Julie*
The Shakespeare Handbooks by Alistair McCallum
    *Hamlet*
    *King Lear*
    *Macbeth*
    *Romeo and Juliet*


**Philosophy**
Philosophers in 90 Minutes by Paul Strathern
    *Thomas Aquinas in 90 Minutes*
    *Aristotle in 90 Minutes*
    *St. Augustine in 90 Minutes*
    *Berkeley in 90 Minutes*
    *Confucius in 90 Minutes*
    *Derrida in 90 Minutes*
    *Descartes in 90 Minutes*
    *Dewey in 90 Minutes*
    *Foucault in 90 Minutes*
    *Hegel in 90 Minutes*
    *Heidegger in 90 Minutes*
    *Hume in 90 Minutes*
    *Kant in 90 Minutes*
    *Kierkegaard in 90 Minutes*
    *Leibniz in 90 Minutes*
    *Locke in 90 Minutes*
    *Machiavelli in 90 Minutes*
    *Marx in 90 Minutes*
    *J. S. Mill in 90 Minutes*
    *Nietzsche in 90 Minutes*

Leonard W. Levy, *The Palladium of Justice*
Heather Mac Donald, *The Burden of Bad Ideas*
Myron Magnet, ed., *The Millennial City*
Myron Magnet, ed., *Modern Sex*
Seymour J. Mandelbaum, *Boss Tweed's New York*
Thomas J. McCormick, *China Market*
John Harmon McElroy, *American Beliefs*
Wendy McElroy, ed., *Liberty for Women*
Gerald W. McFarland, *A Scattered People*
Walter Millis, *The Martial Spirit*
Nicolaus Mills, ed., *Culture in an Age of Money*
Nicolaus Mills, *Like a Holy Crusade*
Roderick Nash, *The Nervous Generation*
Keith Newlin, ed., *American Plays of the New Woman*
William L. O'Neill, ed., *Echoes of Revolt: The Masses, 1911–1917*
Gilbert Osofsky, *Harlem: The Making of a Ghetto*
Edward Pessen, *Losing Our Souls*
Glenn Porter and Harold C. Livesay, *Merchants and Manufacturers*
John Prados, *The Hidden History of the Vietnam War*
John Prados, *Presidents' Secret Wars*
Patrick Renshaw, *The Wobblies*
Edward Reynolds, *Stand the Storm*
Louis Rosen, *The South Side*
Richard Schickel, *The Disney Version*
Richard Schickel, *Intimate Strangers*
Richard Schickel, *Matinee Idylls*
Richard Schickel, *The Men Who Made the Movies*
Edward A. Shils, *The Torment of Secrecy*
Robert Shogan, *Bad News*
Geoffrey S. Smith, *To Save a Nation*
John David Smith, *Black Judas*
Robert W. Snyder, *The Voice of the City*
Bernard Sternsher, ed., *Hitting Home: The Great Depression in Town and Country*
Bernard Sternsher, ed., *Hope Restored: How the New Deal Worked in Town and Country*
Bernard Sternsher and Judith Sealander, eds., *Women of Valor*
Athan Theoharis, *From the Secret Files of J. Edgar Hoover*
Nicholas von Hoffman, *We Are the People Our Parents Warned Us Against*
Norman Ware, *The Industrial Worker, 1840–1860*
Robert Weisbrot, *Maximum Danger*
Mark J. White, ed., *The Kennedys and Cuba*
Tom Wicker, *JFK and LBJ: The Influence of Personality upon Politics*
Robert H. Wiebe, *Businessmen and Reform*
T. Harry Williams, *McClellan, Sherman and Grant*
Miles Wolff, *Lunch at the 5 & 10*
Randall B. Woods and Howard Jones, *Dawning of the Cold War*
American Ways Series:
John A. Andrew III, *Lyndon Johnson and the Great Society*
Roger Daniels, *Not Like Us*
J. Matthew Gallman, *The North Fights the Civil War: The Home Front*
Lewis L. Gould, *1968: The Election That Changed America*
John Earl Haynes, *Red Scare or Red Menace?*